Using Microsoft Word 5.5

IBM® Version

2nd Edition

Bryan Pfaffenberger

CORPORATION

LEADING COMPUTER KNOWLEDGE

Using Microsoft Word 5.5
IBM Version
2nd Edition

Copyright© 1990 by Que® Corporation

Library of Congress Catalog No.: 90-62950

ISBN 0-88022-642-0

93 92 91   4 3

Interpretation of the printing code: the rightmost double-digit number is the year of the book's printing; the rightmost single-digit number, the number of the book's printing. For example, a printing code of 90-1 shows that the first printing of the book occurred in 1990.

This book is based on Microsoft Word Versions 5.5 and 5.0.

DEDICATION

To the memory of John Longley, writer and Word user.

Publisher

Lloyd J. Short

Acquisitions Editor

Karen A. Bluestein

Project Manager

Paul Boger

Production Editor

Gregory Robertson

Editors

Jo Anna W. Arnott
Fran Blauw
Sharon Boller
H. Leigh Davis
Lori A. Lyons
Heidi Weas Muller
Susan Shaw

Technical Editors

Walter R. Bruce III
Dean Samuels
Toni Thompson

Editorial Assistant

Patricia J. Brooks

Indexer

Hilary Adams

Book Design and Production

Lisa Naddy
Jeff Baker
Sarah Leatherman
Cindy L. Phipps
Howard Peirce
Lisa A. Wilson

*Composed in Garamond and Macmillan Mono
by Que Corporation.*

ABOUT THE AUTHOR

Bryan Pfaffenberger

A specialist in explaining computer technology to computer users, Bryan Pfaffenberger, Ph.D., teaches in the School of Engineering and Applied Science at the University of Virginia, where he is Associate Professor of Humanities. He is the author of more than 20 books, including *Que's Computer User's Dictionary* and *Using Microsoft Word 4: Macintosh Version*, both published by Que Corporation, and *Microcomputer Applications in Qualitative Research*, published by Sage. Dr. Pfaffenberger's interests include the social history and sociology of technology, international studies, and the anthropology of science and engineering. He lives in Charlottesville, Virginia.

CONTENTS AT A GLANCE

Part V   Word 5.5's Style Sheets and Macros

TABLE OF CONTENTS

II   Extending Your Knowledge of Word

3   Word 5.5 Writing and Editing Strategies 93

4   Word 5.5 Formatting Strategies: Characters and Paragraphs 129

5   Word 5.5 Formatting Strategies: Page Formatting 185

III   Word 5.5's Features and Applications

8   Finding and Managing Documents 261

IV Desktop Publishing with Microsoft Word

19   Page Layout II: Multiple-Column Text and Newsletters 575

V   Word 5.5's Style Sheets and Macros

20   Style Sheet Formatting 595

ACKNOWLEDGMENTS

I'm gratified that *Using Microsoft Word 5* has been received well enough to merit a second edition, and I thank the many people who have found its comprehensive coverage useful. The book's aim has always been to provide a clear, logical path from Word basics to Word mastery, and every word has been written with the assumption that anyone can reach the heights of this powerful program.

This edition covers Word's exciting new user interface and, what's more, the many features that have made the program simpler and easier to use. To do full justice to the many well-conceived changes in Word 5.5, nothing less than a complete revision of the book was required. Even if you've used Word before, you will find many new approaches here—approaches that take full advantage of Word 5.5's new on-screen personality. This edition also features expanded coverage of intermediate and advanced Word features, such as desktop publishing, style sheets, and macros. You'll also find Quick Reviews at the end of each chapter, which summarize the procedures you've learned in that chapter. Keep *Using Microsoft Word 5.5: IBM Version*, 2nd Edition, next to your computer! You'll find the Quick Reviews very helpful when you need to "brush up" on procedures you've already learned.

I'd like to thank the many readers who wrote me with suggestions for this edition, as well as the many production people who brought this book to you. In particular, thanks are due to Que's world-class editorial team, including Paul Boger, Greg Robertson, Jo Anna Arnott, Fran Blauw, Sharon Boller, Leigh Davis, Lori Lyons, Heidi Weas Muller, and Susan Shaw. Karen Bluestein suggested the Quick Review concept. Very special thanks go to the technical editors for this book—Dean Samuels, Toni Thompson, and Walter Bruce—for a superb technical review of the manuscript. Most of all, my warm thanks to Lloyd Short, a publishing professional in the very best sense of the term.

TRADEMARK
ACKNOWLEDGMENTS

Que Corporation has made every effort to supply trademark information about company names, products, and services mentioned in this book. Trademarks indicated below were derived from various sources. Que Corporation cannot attest to the accuracy of this information.

Diagram-Master is a trademark of Decision Resources.

Harvard Graphics is a trademark of Software Publishing Corporation.

Hercules Graphics Card is a trademark of Hercules Computer Technology.

Hewlett-Packard is a registered trademark of Hewlett-Packard Co.

IBM is a registered trademark and DisplayWrite and PS/2 are trademarks of International Business Machines Corporation.

Lotus, Symphony, and 1-2-3 are registered trademarks of Lotus Development Corporation.

Macintosh is a registered trademark of Apple Computer Corporation.

Microsoft is a registered trademark of Microsoft Corporation.

MultiMate and dBASE are registered trademarks of Ashton-Tate Corporation.

PageMaker is a registered trademark of Aldus Corporation.

PC Paintbrush is a registered trademark of ZSoft Corporation.

PostScript is a registered trademark of Adobe Systems Incorporated.

SideKick and Quattro are registered trademarks of Borland International.

SuperCalc is a registered trademark of Computer Associates International, Inc.

Ventura Publisher is a registered trademark of Ventura Software, Inc.

VP-Planner is a registered trademark of Paperback Software, Inc.

WordPerfect is a registered trademark of WordPerfect Corporation.

CONVENTIONS USED IN THIS BOOK

T he conventions used in this book have been established to help you learn to use the program quickly and easily.

1. When you are to select a command sequence, the letters you press are in bold type ("Select **F**ile **S**ave.")

2. Buttons (indicated by < > on-screen) don't have the angle brackets around them in the text. Instead, they are in normal type. Most of these buttons have a single letter you can press to issue the command; these letters appear in bold, with the remainder of the command in initial caps (**P**rinter Setup).

   The OK and Cancel buttons are referred to as such and do not have bold letters ("Click the OK button").

3. Dialog box names are in initial caps (the Mark Revisions dialog box).

4. Keyboard shortcuts are indicated in the margins by the keystrokes involved (Alt-F4).

5. Icons are placed in the margins to indicate features new in Word 5.5 and to highlight mouse procedures.

6. Cautions that you need to note are placed in boxes with a drop shadow.

7. Power user tips have a gray screen over them.

Introduction

Microsoft Word split in two when Microsoft released Windows 3. For those users fortunate enough to own high-powered 386 computers with vast amounts of RAM, there is Word for Windows, which displays fonts and font sizes on-screen (and closely resembles the Macintosh version of Microsoft Word). Word for Windows is good news for anyone with a top-of-the-line PS/2 or 386. But Microsoft has not forgotten the rest of us, who continue to plug away on such antiques as 640K 286 machines, good old 8088s, or even 386 machines *sans* Windows. In Version 5.5, Microsoft Word finally has a user interface that does justice to the program's inherent excellence.

Is this a significant event? You bet. I've been writing books on Microsoft Word since Version 1.0, and, for the first time, I can say that this program is suitable for novice users. Word's new user interface, with its pull-down menus and dialog boxes, makes the program much easier to learn and use. (A user interface is the part of the program that handles communication with the user, such as presenting menus and accepting commands. Even Word's strongest supporters had difficulty appreciating the user interface of previous versions.) Apart from the appealing appearance and clear logic of the new interface, Microsoft has simplified Word, clearing away a welter of needlessly complex procedures without sacrificing the program's legendary power.

Experienced Word users also have cause for celebration. Word 5.5's new user interface is right in line with emerging industry standards; for example, you press F1 for help, Alt to display the pull-down menus, and Ins to toggle the Overtype mode on or off. With these changes, using Word no longer requires you to employ peculiar keyboarding and windowing techniques; they're in line with the procedures you use in PC Tools Deluxe (Version 6), dBASE IV, and other well-conceived PC applications. With PC Tools and Word, you can set up an inexpensive 8088 or 286 as a very convincing alternative to the Macintosh.

Why a Book on Word 5.5?

Microsoft Word 5.5 comes with an outstanding manual and an even better computer-based training program (Learning Word). So why a book about Word 5.5?

Word's documentation, good as it is, suffers from the drawback of all computer program documentation—its purpose is to survey every Word feature, even the ones that people seldom use. Even if you are experienced with word processing programs, unwrapping all those thick manuals filled with page after page of computer commands is a daunting experience. And aside from a few tutorials, the manuals are encyclopedic—they strive to tell you *everything* about a feature. Exhaustive feature coverage is the manual's job, but the effect is dismaying. You get a great deal of information thrown at you all at once.

Word's documentation, moreover, leaves little room for telling you what you want to know most: "How do I put all this information to work on daily writing tasks?" As a Word 5.5 user, you want to produce documents, such as business forms, business reports, newsletters, form letters, legal briefs, alphabetized price lists, and others. But Word's documentation often doesn't make the connection between the detailed information it presents and the specific challenges of producing specific documents. In other words, the manuals show you how to do something, but they often fail to explain just what it is you are doing—and why.

Using Microsoft Word 5.5: IBM Version, 2nd Edition, is intended to remedy these deficiencies in the following three ways:

- First, this book seeks to describe Word 5.5 in the way the best corporate training programs explain subjects: by introducing information in small, manageable units and building knowledge one step at a time. Menu techniques for accomplishing a task always are introduced first, because these techniques help you develop knowledge of the program's command structure. (If a keyboard shortcut is available, it's mentioned right after the menu technique and is highlighted by a special icon in the margin.)

- Second, the book focuses on specific applications, such as creating lists, tables, newsletters, footnotes, and indexes. Throughout the book, the goal is to clarify the concepts that underlie the application of Word 5.5 and to teach you the specific skills you need in order to use the program effectively.

- Third, this book develops an approach to Word gained from long experience in using and teaching others how to use the program. When you see the power user tips (see "Conventions Used in

This Book"), you learn how Word's power users approach daily writing, editing, formatting, and printing tasks. (A *power user* is a professional or business user who depends on the program for high performance on the job and has attained knowledge of the program far beyond the average level.)

Using Microsoft Word 5.5: IBM Version, 2nd Edition, isn't concerned so much with providing an encyclopedic reference as it is with teaching you how to apply this amazing program to the professional, technical, and managerial work you do every day. You can find plenty of detailed information for reference purposes, however, because almost all of Word's functions and commands receive treatment in the book.

This book's ultimate objective is to lead you beyond the basics. The key to high-productivity word processing lies in Word's intermediate and advanced features, such as style sheets and macros. Even if you have never used a computer before, this book shows you how to make these features work for you.

Preparing for High-Productivity Word Processing

Do you really need to learn Word's intermediate and advanced features? If you are planning to use the program to write simple memos and letters, the answer is "No." But chances are you wouldn't have purchased this book if you wanted to use Word in such a simple way. And as the following examples suggest, Word's intermediate and advanced features can help you perform professional, technical, and managerial tasks much more effectively. Here's a sketch of what users are doing with Word 5.5:

- A legal secretary must make absolutely sure that he uses the latest version of standard clauses for wills, leases, and other legal documents. He therefore creates and names standard clauses using Word's bookmarks, which are like named ranges in a spreadsheet. Now when he types a will, he inserts the bookmark with the Insert Bookmark command, and Word uses the text contained in the bookmark.

- A novelist uses Word's on-line thesaurus, an impressive compilation of 220,000 English synonyms, to find just the right word to express a mood or to describe a scene. This method is far faster (and much more convenient) than consulting a printed thesaurus, and because she uses the electronic version frequently, her writing has acquired a new vividness.

- A professional grant proposal writer uses Word's outlining feature to sketch the structure of a proposal before writing it. After the first draft is written, he switches to the outline view to rearrange the proposal's structure in seconds, just by moving headings on the outline.

- An attorney uses Word to generate a table of legal authorities cited in the briefs she writes. The whole process is automatic and takes only two minutes.

- The chairperson of a small community organization uses Word's multiple-column and laser-printing features to produce a simple, but handsome newsletter. He also uses Word's list-sorting feature to maintain a database of newsletter subscribers and the program's merge-printing features to print mailing labels. With these features, he can put out a new issue of the newsletter—including printing the mailing labels—in one afternoon.

- A departmental supervisor uses Word's macro and form-creation features to fill out more than a dozen forms she must complete each month. The macro, a list of instructions that tells Word how to follow a procedure automatically, prompts her for specific information needed to complete the form. After she provides the information, Word performs the necessary calculations automatically and prints the form precisely the way management wants.

- A free-lance computer programmer uses Word to produce handsomely printed documentation for her programs. After structuring the document with Word's outlining feature, she gives Word commands that generate a table of contents. She uses other commands to generate a list of figures, a list of tables, and an automatically compiled index. The whole table-generating and indexing operation takes only a few minutes.

- A high school English teacher uses Word's glossaries—storage places for commonly used (boilerplate) text—to store extensive comments on common writing problems, such as dangling modifiers and comma splices. His students prepare their essays on disk and he reads them on-screen (with a printed copy on hand). When he encounters an error, he enters the relevant boilerplate into the student's paper with one keystroke, adding personalized comments as needed. Students therefore receive extensive, high-quality comments on their writing, and the teacher has more time to interact with the students.

- A business manager uses Word to write reports that automatically incorporate Lotus 1-2-3 spreadsheets and graphs. The text floats around the tables and graphs, which are seamlessly integrated with the report and beautifully printed—complete with informative captions.

Even if you have never used Word, or if you have used Word only for basic word processing, you can learn to take advantage of these and other high-productivity techniques. This book isn't just about Word 5.5; it's also about helping you learn the program well enough to put these techniques within your grasp.

What You Need To Run Microsoft Word 5.5

Microsoft's goal in creating Word 5.5 was to give this powerful, full-featured program the user interface the program has always deserved and to create a program that would run on virtually any IBM or IBM-compatible personal computer, ranging all the way from yesterday's PC and XT to today's high-powered 386s and PS/2s.

At the minimum, however, you need 384K of free random-access memory (RAM) when you start Word. RAM is your computer's internal memory, which stores programs and data so that they are accessible for processing. (You can use the CHKDSK program on your DOS disk to find out how much RAM is available.) Because DOS consumes some RAM, you need at least 512K of RAM in your computer to be on the safe side. Having 640K is better, because more room then is available for memory-intensive operations like sorting and searching.

Although you can run Word 5.5 on a dual-floppy system, this book assumes that a standard system configuration includes a hard disk.

You can use Word with nearly any video adapter and monitor designed for IBM-format computing, including (but not limited to) the Color Graphics Adapter (CGA), the Monochrome Adapter, Hercules Graphics Card, the Hercules Graphics Card Plus, the Genius adapter and full-page monitor, the IBM Enhanced Graphics Adapter (EGA) and Video Graphics Array (VGA) adapters and monitors, and the Hewlett-Packard Vectra adapter and monitor. EGA and VGA color monitors bring out Word at its best.

Word takes full advantage of a Microsoft or Microsoft-compatible mouse, and although the mouse is optional, you should try it. People who use a mouse say that they would never go back to editing with the keyboard alone. But rest assured: You can use just the keyboard without sacrificing any of the program's functions or versatility.

Even if you are new to word processing, you already should know a few computer fundamentals, and this book assumes that you have this knowledge. You should know how to turn on the power and obtain the DOS prompt, which is an on-screen letter (such as A or C) followed by a greater-than symbol (>). You should know how to format disks, switch from one drive to another, display a directory of a disk's contents, copy files from one disk to another, and erase unwanted files. If you have a hard disk, you should know how to create directories and how to switch from one directory to another.

If you don't know how to accomplish these tasks, take some time now to learn them. Read your computer's manual and, above all, get help from someone who has experience using an IBM PC or a compatible computer. *MS-DOS User's Guide*, Special Edition, and *Using DOS* (both published by Que Corporation), are excellent guides for anyone who uses DOS, whether at the novice or advanced level. The better you understand these basic computer tasks, the less chance you have of destroying your work accidentally. And here's a tip: get a copy of PC Tools Deluxe (Version 6), which replaces the usual DOS file-management functions and provides a full set of backup, disk compression, and other system utilities. What's more, PC Tools' user interface adheres to the same, de facto standard that inspired Word 5.5. The two programs go together—and work together—as if they were designed to do so.

How This Book Is Organized—and How To Use It

If you already have installed Word 5.5, begin with the section called "Creating a Document Directory" in the Appendix, "Installing Word 5.5." This book assumes that you have created a document directory for your Word documents and that you will start Word from this directory. If all this sounds technical, don't worry—you find complete instructions in the Appendix and Chapter 1. And if you haven't installed Word, the Appendix shows you how to use Word's installation program, SETUP, the correct way.

Most chapters of this book introduce Word knowledge using tutorials and step-by-step procedures that guide you keystroke-by-keystroke toward mastery of Word. Try out the step-by-step tutorials at your computer. You learn skills that will prove invaluable to you.

Each chapter concludes with a Quick Review of all the procedures the chapter introduced. So keep *Using Microsoft Word 5.5: IBM Version*, 2nd Edition, next to your computer after you read the book. The Quick Reviews will prove to be invaluable in reminding you how to accomplish tasks you already have learned. And if you are familiar with earlier versions of Word, you can skim the chapters and go straight to the Quick Reviews to see how the new user interface handles tasks you already have learned.

Mastering the Basics

If you are new to Word, begin with Part I. And even if you have some previous experience with Word, Part I still is worth skimming. Although the material is introductory and elementary, you learn how power users approach day-to-day tasks with Word.

You should read (or skim) the chapters in order. They introduce key terms, techniques, and strategies in a sequence designed to teach Word skills and concepts. And in each chapter, the Quick Review summarizes the procedures introduced in the chapter.

Part I, "Word 5.5 Fundamentals," assumes that you have no previous knowledge of Word or any other word processing program. Part I doesn't try to be encyclopedic, throwing every nuance and feature of Word at you all at once. Instead, these chapters concentrate on fundamental Word skills and concepts—the ones you should grasp very well if you want to use the program efficiently and productively. Almost all the material discussed in Part I is discussed again in more detail in subsequent parts of the book. For example, you learn the basic procedure for setting tabs in Chapter 2, but the lesson concerns flush left tabs only. You learn how to set other kinds of tabs in Chapter 11, "Creating Tables and Lists with Tabs, Sort, and Math."

Chapter 1, "Getting Started with Word 5.5," introduces the information you need in order to use Word 5.5, including starting the program, understanding the Word 5.5 keyboard and the screen display, using command menus, moving the cursor and scrolling, and managing files.

Chapter 2, "Your First Word 5.5 Document—Quickly!," walks you through the creation, formatting, editing, and printing of a business letter. You learn important fundamentals of Word, such as how to center text, change paragraph alignment, delete and insert text, perform block moves, split and join paragraphs, and print your work. You also learn how to edit and format your text as you are writing with Word. This chapter doesn't attempt to cover all the details of the subject it covers. You find more complete coverage in Chapters 3, 4, and 5, which expand on the material introduced in Chapter 2.

Extending Your Knowledge of Word 5.5

Part II, "Extending Your Knowledge of Word," broadens your knowledge of Word 5.5, drawing on the knowledge you gained in Part I. The Part II chapters discuss topics that should interest every Word user: editing, formatting, checking spelling, and printing. As with the chapters in Part I, you should read these chapters in order.

Chapter 3, "Word 5.5 Writing and Editing Strategies," expands your knowledge of the editing concepts introduced in Chapter 2. You learn how to open files you already have created; when to use the overtype mode; how to move around in a large document; and how to select, copy, delete, and move text. In addition, you learn how to use Word's powerful search-and-replace features and how to make the best use of the Undo command.

Chapter 4, "Word 5.5 Formatting Strategies: Characters and Paragraphs," expands your knowledge of the formatting concepts introduced in Chapter 2. You learn how to understand and use Word's measurement options, how to attach emphasis (such as boldface or italic) to characters, and how to format paragraphs (using formats such as double line spacing, right margin justification, and hanging indents). In addition, you learn how to format paragraphs side-by-side and how to use Word's search-and-replace command to replace character or paragraph styles throughout a document.

Chapter 5, "Word 5.5 Formatting Strategies: Page Formatting," shows you how to alter Word's default page formatting settings. You learn how to set margins and page sizes, add page numbers and line numbers, and create running heads (short versions of a document's title that appear at the top or bottom of each page). You also learn how to divide your document into sections, each with its own distinctive page format.

Chapter 6, "Using the Thesaurus, Checking Spelling, and Controlling Hyphenation," introduces Word's excellent thesaurus, which opens a 220,000-word synonym dictionary right on your screen. After you highlight the word you want, Word inserts the word in your text. This chapter also shows you how to use the much-improved Word 5.5 spelling checker and how to hyphenate your document automatically so that words are broken correctly at the ends of lines.

Chapter 7, "Printing Your Work," shows you how to print your work attractively and correctly. You learn how to preview page breaks and formatting before you print and how to use Word 5.5's large variety of print options, which give you precise control over the printing process. You learn how to print a single page of a document or a range of pages, multiple copies, drafts, and document summary sheets.

Using Advanced Techniques and Applications

Part III, "Word 5.5's Features and Applications," builds on the knowledge you have acquired in Parts I and II. This part of the book focuses on advanced techniques and applications, such as using windows, creating running heads, using annotations, creating newsletters, outlining, using glossaries, linking documents with spreadsheets, and creating form letters.

You need not read every chapter in Part III, and you need not read them in order. Each chapter addresses a single topic, which is explored in depth. Most readers, however, can profit from reading Chapter 8, "Finding and Managing Documents"; Chapter 9, "Customizing Word and Using Windows"; and Chapter 10, "Organizing Your Document with Outlining", which present advanced Word features everyone can use. Choose from the remaining chapters according to the nature of the work you plan to do with Word.

Chapter 8, "Finding and Managing Documents," builds on the knowledge you already have about the basics of saving and loading documents. You learn how to save all active documents in one step, how to save documents as ASCII files, and how to manage disk space and memory. If you are using a hard disk, you learn how to take advantage of Word's remarkable document-retrieval feature, which enables you to search an entire hard disk for documents based on matching key words, authors' names, dates of creation, and other criteria. The chapter also explains how to automate file backup and archiving procedures.

Chapter 9, "Customizing Word and Using Windows," shows you how to shape Word's screen and keyboard to your needs. You learn how to hide the command menu and the window border, how to display the ruler, show line breaks as they will appear when printed, and reveal special characters. The chapter shows how, as you explore Word's windows, you can open new windows on the same or different documents, change window size and zoom windows, and remove windows from the screen. You see how easily you can copy and move text from one window to another.

Chapter 10, "Organizing Your Document with Outlining," covers one of Word's best features—its powerful and flexible outline mode. You can use outlining to organize your thoughts before writing, as you would any outlining utility. But what makes Word's outline mode so powerful is its seamless integration with your document. As you learn in this chapter, you can create an outline so that the outline's headings correspond to section titles in your document. This feature demonstrates Word 5.5's power: Simply by rearranging the headings in your outline, you can restructure your document completely. This editing technique is by far the most powerful.

Chapter 11, "Creating Tables and Lists with Tabs, Sort, and Math," is the first chapter to focus specifically on advanced formatting techniques. You learn how to gain full control over Word's tab features, and you apply this knowledge to the creation and formatting of tables and lists. You also learn how to sort data alphabetically or numerically and how to use Word's math features to add up columns of data (and perform more sophisticated operations).

Chapter 12, "Using Glossaries and Bookmarks," thoroughly explores Word's glossaries, which are storage places for commonly used passages of text called "boilerplate." You learn how to create and insert boilerplate passages and how to save, load, and manage glossary files. This chapter also introduces bookmarks, which you use to assign names to units of text. You can use bookmarks to move around your document quickly, to create automatic cross-references, and to retrieve boilerplate text.

Chapter 13, "Creating Indexes and Tables of Contents," shows you how to use Word so that the program generates an index, a table of contents, and (if you want) additional tables when you print your document. If your job responsibilities include the writing of reports, proposals, or documentation, you will find this chapter invaluable.

Chapter 14, "The Legal and Scholarly Word," introduces the use of Word for attorneys and scholars. You learn how to create, edit, and print attractive footnotes or endnotes. You also learn how to use Word's advanced features to generate a bibliography of works you have cited and how to use one of the macros supplied with Word to generate a table of legal authorities. Don't think for a minute that Word is inferior to any other program in this area!

Chapter 15, "Enhancing Group Productivity: Using Annotations and Redlining," covers the use of Word in collaborative writing situations. You learn how to retrieve standardized, authoritative versions of text automatically, how to insert comments in a draft, and how to propose and approve editorial changes.

Chapter 16, "Creating Form Letters," is for anyone who must send the same letter to many people. Word's form-letter and mailing-list features are extremely flexible and powerful. You can even create a letter that includes special text for just those people who meet the criteria you specify.

Applying Word to Desktop Publishing

Part IV, "Desktop Publishing with Microsoft Word," shows you how Version 5.5 features can make short work of many business and professional applications in desktop publishing, such as creating business forms, departmental newsletters, and illustrated reports.

Chapter 17, "Creating Forms and Illustrations," introduces the Word features that help you design, print, and even fill out business forms. If you have ever paid a printer to design and print a business form, this chapter can save you money as well as time.

Chapter 18, "Page Layout I: Adding Graphics and Anchoring Paragraphs," fully explores Version 5.5's graphics features. You learn how to incorporate graphics into Word documents and "anchor" their position so that text flows around the graphics.

Chapter 19, "Page Layout II: Multiple-Column Text and Newsletters," is for anyone who currently is producing a newsletter—or thinking of starting one. You learn how to use new Word 5.5 features that display multiple columns of text on-screen even while you are editing, and how to show precisely the way columns, running heads, and all other formatting features will appear when printed. You also learn how you can mix single- and multiple-column text on one page.

Customizing the Program with Style Sheets and Macros

Part V, "Word 5.5's Style Sheets and Macros," shows you how to customize and automate Word so that the program works precisely the way you want.

The material in Part V is advanced, but these chapters are important. In them you find the road to professional productivity. If you want Word to jump through hoops for you, you need to learn to use style sheets and macros and work them into everything you do with Word. Even if you have never programmed your telephone to dial numbers automatically, these chapters can teach you to write highly effective style sheets and macros immediately. You learn quickly because the chapters are keyed to, and draw on, skills and concepts that you have developed by reading Part II and selected chapters of Part III.

Chapter 20, "Style Sheet Formatting," introduces one of Word's most powerful—and least understood—features. In this chapter, you learn how to customize Word's keyboard so that with a single keystroke you can enter precisely the formats you want. You learn how to create a style sheet, which is a list of your own formatting instructions linked to an Alt-key formatting command. You also learn how you can set up Word to take full advantage of your printer's fonts, making a special font such as Helvetica the default font for all your documents. Style sheets may seem like an advanced feature, but after reading this chapter, you will undoubtedly agree that everyone should use them. You will be amazed at how easily you can create and use style sheets.

Chapter 21, "Creating and Using Word 5.5 Macros," shows you how to automate Word operations with macros—lists of instructions that tell Word to perform a complex series of actions automatically. With Word's elegant and powerful macro programming language, you can write macros that enter text and give commands just as if someone were typing them at the keyboard. Using the language's looping and conditional branch statements, you can write macros that perform such operations over and over, or perform them only if a condition is met. Word's macro programming language is a real jewel—it is simple and easy to learn, yet powerful enough for professional applications.

The Appendix shows you how to install Word.

Conventions Used in This Book

To assist you in learning Microsoft Word, this book uses icons in the margins and special text formatting. These visual cues are your key to special features of this book.

- *Keyboard shortcut icon.* This icon alerts you to keyboard shortcuts you can substitute for menu command techniques. Look for the key combination in the margin (Ctrl-F7, for example). To facilitate learning, the menu technique always is presented first and then the keyboard shortcut—if one is available. Try the keyboard shortcuts. You probably will find that some or most of them deserve to be part of your everyday working repertoire of Word techniques.

- *Mouse icon.* This icon calls your attention to mouse techniques you can substitute for the keyboard methods described in the text. If you are using a mouse, you will find these icons helpful. If you are not using a mouse, you can skip over the sections highlighted by these icons.

- *Power user tips.* These tips highlight techniques or approaches that power users of Microsoft Word have developed through experience. Power user tips are separated from regular text by shading. These tips show you the road to Word mastery.

- *Word 5.5 icon.* This icon highlights information of special interest to readers who have used previous versions of Word.

- *Cautions.* This material is set off in a box with a drop shadow and the word ***Caution*** preceding the text. These sections warn you of problems people frequently encounter when they are learning Word, and they chart a course around those problems.

You will notice some special typefaces in this book. They provide more clues to the learning process.

- Material that you type is either set off on a line by itself or printed in italic. For example, if you see the instruction, "Type *demo.doc* in the File Name area," you type the italicized material exactly as it appears.

- When menu and command names are mentioned (for example: **F**ile **S**ave), the letters that you can type to select the menu or command are boldfaced. Whether you type uppercase or lowercase letters doesn't matter. To choose the **F**ile **S**ave command, for example, you hold down the Alt key and then type *FS* or *fs*. As you learn in Chapter 1, you also can choose commands with the mouse or by pressing the arrow keys and Enter. For more information on choosing commands, see Chapter 1.

- The messages Word displays on-screen are printed in a special typeface. If you try to save a file with a name DOS doesn't permit, for example, you see the message, `File name or path is not valid.`

A Note from the Author

Word processing with Word 5.5 is computer-assisted writing at its best, and I hope this book helps you realize Word's promise—and your own promise. Anyone who can turn on the computer can journey to the far reaches of Word mastery! Just remember to take Word one step at a time, without trying to learn everything at once. Part I of this book strips away the complexities of the program and gets down to the fundamentals—without throwing all of Word's complexity at you before you are ready. In Part II, you extend and broaden your knowledge of Word, and by Part III, you are well on your way to mastery of this outstanding program.

Part I

Word 5.5
Fundamentals

Includes

Getting Started with Word 5.5

Your First Word 5.5 Document—Quickly!

Getting Started with Word 5.5

B efore you begin using Word 5.5, you need to learn some fundamentals, such as how to start the program, navigate the menus and dialog boxes, get on-screen help, save your work, and quit the program.

If you master these fundamentals now, you will save time and frustration later as you learn more advanced skills and concepts. Even if you are an experienced user of other word processing programs, at least skim this chapter. You will learn how to do the following:

- Start Word at the beginning of a writing or editing session
- Understand the features of the Word 5.5 screen
- Learn how Word assigns special keys such as Ins, Del, Ctrl, and Alt
- Choose commands from drop-down menus and dialog boxes
- Move the cursor and scroll the screen
- Get help
- Save your work
- Quit Word

Note: This chapter assumes you have installed Word 5.5 following the instructions in the Appendix. In these instructions, you learn how to create a directory called C:\WORD\DOCS for your Word documents, and you also choose an option that permits you to start Word from any directory. *The Lessons in this chapter assume you have installed the program in this way*. If you haven't installed Word yet, turn to the Appendix now before proceeding.

Starting and Exiting Word

When you start Word, the program creates a new, blank document, which is assigned a temporary name (DOCUMENT1). In this section, you learn how to start Word and quit the program.

To start Word and create a new, unnamed document, follow these steps:

1. **Important**: Activate the Word document directory.

   If your document directory is called C:\WORD\DOCS, type *cd c:\word\docs* and press Enter.

2. Type *word* and press Enter.

Whether you type uppercase or lowercase letters, or a combination of both, doesn't matter.

The Word 5.5 document display screen appears (see fig. 1.1). In the next section of this chapter, you explore the screen's features.

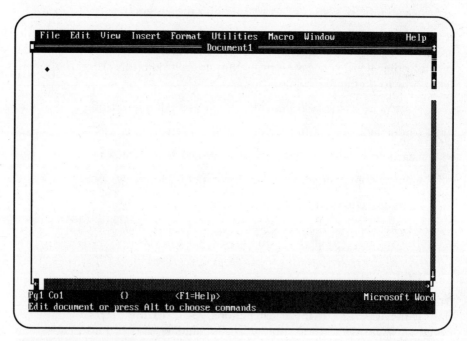

Fig. 1.1. The Word display screen.

Note: If you see the message Bad command or file name, you may have misspelled Word or switched to the wrong directory. If you are in the correct directory and you spelled the Word program name correctly, however, you may need to run SETUP again. For more information on running SETUP correctly, see the Appendix.

If you see the message `Insufficient memory to run Word` when you try to start Word, you don't have enough free memory in your computer's random access memory (RAM) to run Word. You need 384K of free RAM to run Word 5.5—RAM that isn't occupied with other programs, such as DOS or terminate-and-stay-resident (TSR) programs. DOS and other system programs can consume as much as 70K, so to be on the safe side, you should have about 100K more RAM than Word requires. If your computer doesn't have enough RAM to run Word, you must add additional RAM before you can start the program.

If your computer is equipped with sufficient RAM to run Word, but the program still doesn't start, you may need to deactivate the terminate-and-stay resident (TSR) programs you are using (such as SideKick or PC Tools Deluxe). Most of these programs have commands that remove them from memory. Check the program's documentation.

To quit Word 5.5, follow these steps:

1. Press Alt to activate the menu bar.

   File is highlighted on the menu bar.

2. Press Enter to pull down the File menu.

3. Use the down-arrow key to highlight the Exit Word option.

4. Press Enter to quit Word.

To exit Word without using the menus, press Alt-F4.

Alt-F4

If you have used previous versions of Word, this chapter already has demonstrated how much Word's user interface has changed. The following is an overview of some of the changes you have encountered so far:

- The Esc key has lost its former function of displaying the command menu. To display the menus, you press Alt. You learn other (and better) ways to display the menus in later lessons.

- Command names have changed. The new name for the old Quit command is **File Exit**.

- Function key assignments have changed. For example, the Alt-F4 (**File Exit**) shortcut you just learned doesn't exist in previous versions of Word. If you just cannot give up the Version 5.0 function keys, however, there is a way you can activate them in Word 5.5. You learn more about this option, and other ways you can customize Word 5.5, in Chapter 9.

Exploring the Word Screen

Word 5.5's display screen (see fig. 1.1) includes the following features:

- *Menu Bar.* Along the top of the screen are the names of the drop-down menus. When you press Alt, Word activates the menu bar and highlights the *accelerator keys*. (In line with industry standards, you also can press F10 to highlight the accelerator keys.) Accelerator keys are the boldfaced letters you can press to choose an option immediately, without having to use the arrow keys to highlight the option first. (On certain monitors, the accelerator keys may be underlined or displayed in reverse video).

- *Document Window.* You view and edit documents within a document window. Each window can be sized and moved, and you can display up to nine documents on-screen at the same time. When you start Word, the program creates a new, unnamed document. After you add text to this document, you save the document to disk. You can close this document and open a new, blank document with the New command in the File menu. You learn more about windows and using multiple documents in Chapter 9.

- *Text Area.* You create and edit text in the text area. In a new, blank document (like the one on-screen), you see nothing but the blinking cursor, which shows you where your text appears when you start typing, and the end mark (a diamond), which shows you where your document ends. (When you create text, Word moves the end mark down to make room for your work.)

- *Status Bar.* This line displays information about the cursor's location, the contents of a temporary storage area called the Scrap, and the status of Word's many toggle keys. You learn more about the Scrap and the toggle keys later in this chapter. For a list of key status indicator symbols and what they mean, see the Quick Review section at the end of this chapter.

- *Message Bar.* This line displays information about the command you are using. When Word is carrying out an operation you request, such as saving or printing, the message bar tells you what Word is doing.

The Word 5.5 Keyboard

Like most programs, Word 5.5 makes use of the special keys on the IBM Personal Computer's keyboard, such as Ctrl, Ins, Del, Alt, Num Lock, and others. Just where these keys are located depends on which PC or compatible you are using. Figure 1.2 shows the keyboard layout used on early IBM Personal Computers and compatibles. Figure 1.3 shows the keyboard layout used with earlier Personal Computer AT and AT-compatible computers, and Figure 1.4 shows the latest layout for ATs.

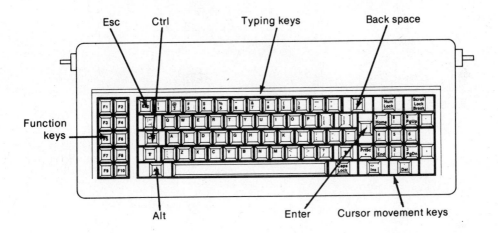

Fig. 1.2. The keyboard layout for early IBM Personal Computers and compatibles.

Many of Word 5.5's keyboard assignments have changed from Version 5.0. Here's a quick summary: The Del key no longer sends the selection to the Scrap—you press Shift-Del instead. The Ins key now is used (in line with industry standards) to toggle between the insert and overtype modes. To insert the Scrap's contents, you press Shift-Ins. Esc no longer is used to access command menus—you press Alt instead. And because Alt is used to display menus, the Ctrl key is used instead of Alt for the speed-key formatting commands. The function key assignments also have major changes. These changes are discussed as they arise.

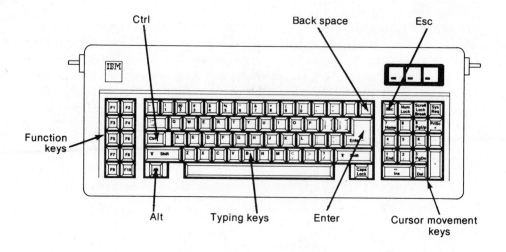

Fig. 1.3. *The keyboard layout used with earlier Personal Computer ATs and compatibles.*

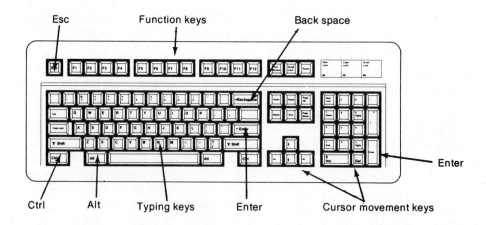

Fig. 1.4. *The latest keyboard design.*

Most keys function differently in Word's two modes—the *edit mode* and the *command mode*. In the edit mode, the cursor is within an active document window and you see the message `Edit document or press Alt to choose commands` on the message bar. In the command mode, the menu bar is highlighted and you are choosing a command.

In the edit mode, you press Enter when you want to start a new paragraph. You don't have to press Enter at the end of every line. In fact, you should insert a paragraph mark by pressing Enter only when you come to the end of a paragraph. Word, like all personal computer word processing programs, includes a feature called *word wrapping*, in which words "wrap" down to the next line if they extend over the right margin.

Num Lock, Scroll Lock, and Caps Lock are irritants if you press them accidentally. Num Lock changes the numeric keypad so that the arrow and other cursor-control keys enter numbers rather than move the cursor. If you press the down-arrow key and get the number 2 entered in your document, you must have inadvertently pressed Num Lock. Similarly, Scroll Lock changes the function of the arrow keys so that they scroll the document as well as move the cursor. The effect can be disconcerting if you press the key accidentally. And if everything you type appears in capital letters, you probably pressed Caps Lock. Fortunately, Word tells you whether you have touched these keys; the codes `NL`, `SL`, or `CL` appear on the status line. To cancel one of these modes, just press the appropriate key again.

Alt-Backspace

The Del key *permanently* deletes the character on which the cursor is positioned. You can hold down the key to send into oblivion all the text to the right of the cursor (until you release the key). You can recover text deleted with the Del key by choosing the **Edit Undo** command, but you must do so immediately after the deletion, before performing any additional editing or command actions. Pressing Alt-Backspace is the same as choosing **Edit Undo**.

The Backspace key deletes the character to the left of the cursor. If you hold down the Backspace key, the cursor races back over the text you have typed, erasing it. (You can recover text deleted with this method if you use the **Edit Undo** command immediately after the deletion occurs.)

The Ins key toggles Word between the insert mode and the overtype mode. In the insert mode, the text you type moves existing type right and down. In the overtype mode, the text you type replaces existing text. The insert mode is Word's default mode. If you press Ins to toggle the overtype mode on, you see the message `OT` on the status line.

Use the Space bar only to enter a blank space between words or numbers. Do not use the Space bar to move the cursor! To control cursor movement, use the arrow keys instead. Also, avoid using the Space bar to align text in columns. Even if you succeed in aligning the text on-screen, Word may not print the text correctly.

In the edit mode, the Tab key is useful for aligning text in columns on-screen. In the command mode, you use Tab to move from one area to another in dialog boxes. For more information on using tabs, see Chapter 11.

> *Caution:* Do not use the Tab key to indent paragraphs. A much better method is to set up a paragraph format that includes an automatic first-line indent. You then can eliminate or change the indent throughout your entire document with just one command. For more information on paragraph formatting, see Chapter 4.

To use Ctrl or Alt, hold down the key while you press another key. (Throughout this book, a hyphenated key combination indicates that you should hold down the first key while you press the second. For example, Ctrl-F8 means that you hold down the Ctrl key and press F8; Alt-F means that you hold down the Alt key and press F.) Word 5.5, in line with industry standards, employs the Alt key to access the drop-down menus. When you are in the command mode, you use Alt in combination with boldfaced letter keys, called *accelerator keys*, to choose options from menus and dialog boxes. You learn more about choosing commands later in this chapter. The Ctrl key is used extensively to provide formatting shortcuts called *speed keys*.

Word does not depend on function keys quite as much as WordPerfect and other programs do, thanks to Word's excellent system of on-screen menus and dialog boxes. You can carry out most commands by choosing them from menus. Even so, function keys provide useful shortcuts for menu procedures that are time-consuming and tedious to carry out regularly, such as choosing Save from the File menu. Instead, you can use the Alt-Shift-F2 keyboard shortcut to save your work. And the function keys provide your only avenue to some Word functions, such as toggling the Extend Selection mode on and off. Rather than throwing these important function keys at you all at once, this book introduces the function keys as you need to learn them.

If you have used previous versions of Word, keep in mind that Del now deletes text permanently. Word doesn't store text temporarily in the Scrap. If you press Del to erase a block of text and then discover you want the text back, you cannot retrieve the text from the Scrap because the text was not sent there. You can, however, choose Edit Undo, but you must do so immediately. If you perform another command or action, the text will be lost completely.

Choosing Commands and Navigating Dialog Boxes with the Keyboard

You already have learned that you can press the Alt key to activate the menu bar. After activating the menus in this way, you can use the right- and left-arrow keys to highlight the menu you want, press Enter to drop the menu down, and press the down-arrow key to choose an option (such as File Exit). But that is a lot of fussing with the keyboard. Using the method introduced in the following tutorial is much easier. You also learn how to navigate Word 5.5's dialog boxes. You can use the Character dialog box to change the point size and turn boldface character emphasis on.

Note: Even if you plan to use the mouse, you still should try this technique. Some keyboard techniques are faster and more convenient than their mouse counterparts. Even those users who are most devoted to the mouse still use some keyboard commands occasionally. Learn both techniques now, then you can choose between them as you please.

To choose commands from menus and dialog boxes, follow these steps:

1. Press the Alt key to activate the menu bar.

   You do not have to hold the Alt key down. After you press Alt, the menu bar is highlighted (see fig. 1.5).

Fig. 1.5. Menu bar with highlighted menu names.

2. Press T to choose the Format drop-down menu.

   The Format drop-down menu appears (see fig. 1.6). All the options on this menu end in ellipses. The ellipses tell you that Word displays a *dialog box* when you choose one of these options. A dialog box is an on-screen window in which you choose or type information Word needs to carry out the command.

3. Press C to choose the Character option.

   The Character dialog box appears (see fig. 1.7), which contains many options for modifying the appearance of individual characters in your document. You learn more about character formatting in subsequent chapters. For now, you explore the characters of Word 5.5's dialog boxes.

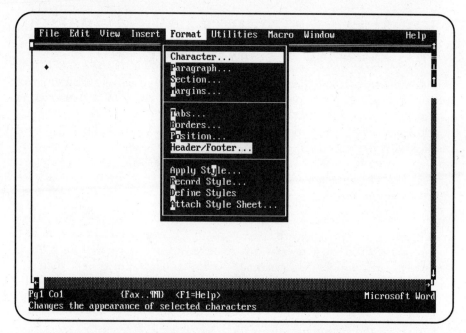

Fig. 1.6. *The Format drop-down menu.*

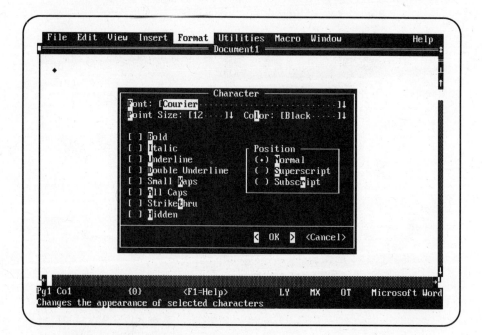

Fig. 1.7. *The Character dialog box.*

The Character dialog box is divided into several areas. At the top of the box are three *drop-down list boxes*, from which you can choose **F**ont, **P**oint Size, and **C**olor options. In a drop-down list box, you don't see the whole list until you select the area and give the command (Alt-down arrow) that displays the list.

4. Press Tab to select the **P**oint Size area.

   If you go too far, press Shift-Tab to select the preceding area. The term *point* refers to a standard printer's measurement of the height of printed characters. Word's default point size is 12 points (Pica). Depending on your printer's capabilities, you may have other choices, such as the smaller 10 point (Elite) or larger sizes (such as 14 or 18 points), which are useful for headings or titles.

5. Press Alt-down arrow to display the list of **P**oint Size choices.

   The list you see depends on your printer's capabilities. You may have only one or two options.

6. Use the down-arrow key to highlight one of the **P**oint Size options.

7. Press Alt-down arrow to confirm your **P**oint Size choice and close the drop-down list.

   Don't press Enter, or Word closes the whole dialog box and accepts your choices up to this point.

   In the next step, you move to the *check box* area. In a check box area, you can choose one or more options.

8. To choose the **B**old check box, press Alt-B (hold down the Alt key and type *b*).

   You see an X beside the **B**old option, indicating that you have selected this option.

9. Press the down-arrow key to move down the list of check boxes. Try turning one of them on and off by pressing the Space bar.

   In the next step, you move to the *option button* area. In an option button area, you can choose one option only.

10. To choose the **S**uperscript option, press Alt-S.

    You see a dot beside the **S**uperscript option, indicating that you have selected this option.

11. Cancel superscripting by pressing Alt-N.

    The dot returns to the Normal option.

In the next step, you move to the final area of the screen, the command button area at the bottom. You press Enter to choose OK to execute the command (with the options you have chosen) or Esc to choose Cancel. If you choose Cancel, Word ignores the choices you made in the dialog box.

12. Press Tab until you have highlighted the OK command button.

13. Press Enter to confirm your choices in the menu.

Esc
Enter

If you finish your business near the top of a dialog box, you need not tab all the way down to the bottom just to choose OK or Cancel. You can choose OK immediately just by pressing Enter anywhere in the dialog box, just as you can choose Cancel immediately by pressing Esc.

Note that the OK command button doesn't have an accelerator key—but its brackets are highlighted, meaning that Word will carry out this button's action if you press Enter.

> *Tip:* As you have just learned, you can press accelerator keys to choose menus, options within menus, and even options within dialog boxes. If you memorize the accelerator key sequence, you need not wait for Word to display the menus—just type the key sequence as quickly as you want. If you press Alt-TCP, for example, Word displays the Character dialog box with the **P**oint Size area activated.

Note: In the rest of this book, it's assumed you have learned how to choose commands from menus and dialog boxes. Instead of saying "Hold down the Alt key, press U to display the Utilities menu, and press W to choose the Word Count option," you see instructions such as "Choose Utilities **W**ord Count (Alt-UW)." Remember, to choose such a command, all you do is press Alt and the accelerator keys (Alt-UW).

Choosing Commands and Navigating Dialog Boxes with the Mouse

If your computer is equipped with a Microsoft or Microsoft-compatible mouse, and if you chose the Setup option that installed the mouse software (see the Appendix), you can take advantage of Word's well-implemented mouse features. Many mouse techniques are faster or more flexible than their keyboard counterparts. In this tutorial, you repeat the same steps you learned in the preceding section, but you use the mouse instead of the keyboard.

If your system isn't equipped with a mouse, skip this tutorial.

1. Move the mouse pointer to Format on the menu bar and click the left mouse button.

   You see the Format drop-down menu.

2. Move the pointer to Character and click the left mouse button.

   You see the Character dialog box.

3. Move the pointer to the Point Size box (within the brackets) and click the left mouse button.

   You have selected the Point Size box. If you click the words "Point Size," Word doesn't select the box. You must place the pointer within the brackets before clicking.

4. Move the pointer to the down arrow and click the left mouse button to display the list.

   The Point Size list box appears (see fig. 1.8). This list box includes *scroll arrows*, which you can click to scroll the list up or down one item at a time, as well as a *drag box*. To use the drag box, you move the pointer to the box, hold down the left button, and drag the box up or down. As you drag, Word scrolls the list.

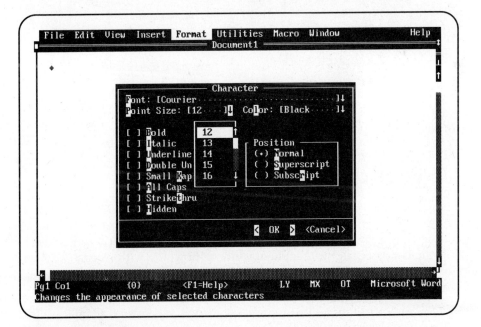

Fig. 1.8. The Point Size list box.

5. Click the up or down arrows (or drag the drag box) until the option you want is visible in the window.

   If your printer has only one or just a few point size options, you may not be able to scroll the list box.

6. Move the pointer to the desired option and click the left mouse button to choose the option.

   Word places the option you have chosen in the **Point Size** box.

7. Choose **Italic** by moving the pointer to the **Italic** check box and clicking the left mouse button.

8. Choose **Subscript** by moving the pointer to the **Subscript** option button and clicking the left mouse button.

9. Cancel subscript formatting by moving the pointer to the **Normal** option button and clicking the left mouse button.

10. Move the pointer to the OK command button and click the left mouse button to execute the command.

Tip: To choose an option from a menu or dialog box and execute the command simultaneously, move the pointer to the option and double-click the left mouse button. (To double-click means to click the button twice in rapid succession.) Double-clicking an option is the same as choosing the option and then choosing OK.

Note: In the rest of this book, it's assumed you have learned how to choose commands from menus and dialog boxes. Instead of saying "Move the pointer to Utilities and click the left mouse button, and then move the pointer to the **Word Count** option and click the left mouse button again," you see the instruction, "Choose Utilities Word Count."

Moving the Cursor and Scrolling

When you begin a new document, you have ample reason to move the cursor around the screen: you can move the cursor back over text you already have created, for example, to correct an error or add a phrase. You can create a document larger than the document window, however, with Word 5.5. When you do, you must *scroll* as well as move the cursor. To scroll means to bring other portions of your document into view in the document window.

Word 5.5 comes equipped with a variety of keys and mouse techniques for moving the cursor on-screen and scrolling up and down in your document. (If you create lines longer than the line lengths Word can display in a normal document window, you also can scroll left and right.) You don't need to learn all these techniques to use Word effectively, but you should try them all now. Choose the ones that seem easy to use and remember.

If you learned how to move the cursor and scroll in previous versions, note the following changes: you press Ctrl-Home to move to the beginning of the document and Ctrl-End to move to the bottom of the document. Ctrl-PgUp now moves the cursor to the top of the window and Ctrl-PgDn moves the cursor to the bottom of the window. Other keyboard assignments do not differ.

All readers, even those who plan to use the mouse, should try the keyboard techniques for cursor-movement and scrolling. Mouse users may discover some keyboard techniques that are faster or more convenient than their mouse counterparts.

Note: You cannot move the cursor past the end mark. If you try these cursor-movement and scrolling techniques in a blank document, Word beeps to signal an error. To create some room to move around and experiment, type a couple of paragraphs. You abandon these paragraphs at the end of this chapter.

Keyboard Techniques for Moving the Cursor and Scrolling

The keys for cursor movement and scrolling, which are listed in table 1.1, are simple, well organized, and convenient to use. Try all of them, especially the Home and End keys, which you will use often. Ctrl-Home and Ctrl-End also come in handy for jumping immediately to the beginning or end of a document.

Note: If you hold down certain keys (those marked in the table with an asterisk), they repeat their action. For example, if you hold down the down-arrow key, Word moves the cursor to the bottom of the screen. If you have more text to display, Word scrolls the screen to bring the text into view and continues moving the cursor down, line by line.

Scrolling with the Scroll Lock Key

Holding down the up- or down-arrow keys causes the screen to scroll when you reach the top or bottom borders. But the screen doesn't scroll until you touch the borders. When you press Scroll Lock to toggle the Scroll Lock (SL) mode on, some of the cursor-movement keys change their function so that they scroll all the time. These keys are listed in table 1.2. The other cursor-movement keys work the way they do when the Scroll Lock mode is off.

Table 1.1
Keys for Moving the Cursor

Key	Moves cursor
Up arrow*	Up one line
Down arrow*	Down one line
Left arrow*	Left one column
Right arrow*	Right one column
Home	To beginning of line
End	To end of line
PgUp*	Up one screen
PgDn*	Down one screen
Ctrl-PgUp	To top of screen
Ctrl-PgDn	To bottom of screen
Ctrl-right arrow*	To next word
Ctrl-left arrow*	To previous word
Ctrl-up arrow*	To previous paragraph
Ctrl-down arrow*	To next paragraph
Ctrl-Home	To beginning of document
Ctrl-End	To end of document

*Key repeats action when held down

To scroll with the Scroll Lock key, press the Scroll Lock key until you see the code SL on the status line.

To resume normal scrolling, press the Scroll Lock key until you see the code SL on the status line.

Note: If you haven't created a line longer than Word's screen, the left and right arrows don't work when Word is in the Scroll Lock mode (with the SL code displayed on the key status indicator). To get the left- and right-arrow keys to work again, press Scroll Lock to toggle off the Scroll Lock mode.

Table 1.2
Scrolling the Screen (with Scroll Lock On)

To scroll	Press
Up one line	Up arrow
Down one line	Down arrow
Left (1/3 screen)	Left arrow
Right (1/3 screen)	Right arrow

Mouse Techniques for Moving
the Cursor and Scrolling

Moving the cursor with the mouse is simple. You move the pointer to the place
you want the cursor positioned and click the left mouse button. The mouse
techniques for moving the cursor and scrolling take advantage of the window
features shown in figure 1.9. In subsequent chapters, you learn about other
mouse-related window features that are used for such purposes as sizing
windows, splitting the screen into two panes, and displaying the ruler.

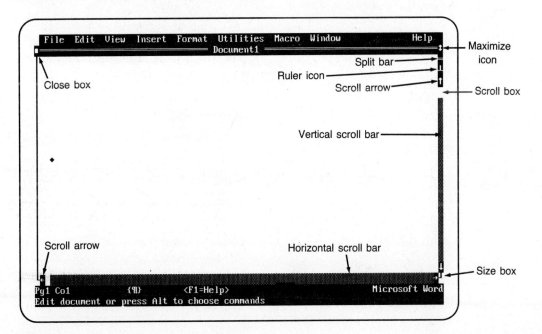

Fig. 1.9. Window features for mouse users.

The Word 5.5 document window includes the following features, which are designed for mouse actions:

- *Scroll Bar.* Every document window has a vertical and a horizontal scroll bar. If the line length you choose fits within the window, you cannot scroll horizontally.

- *Scroll Box.* This dark rectangle in the scroll bar shows the cursor's location within the document. In the vertical scroll bar, the cursor is at the beginning of the document if the scroll box is at the top of the bar. If the box is in the middle of the bar, the cursor is about halfway through the document. (The page number indicator on the status line gives you more accurate information about the cursor's location.)

- *Scroll Arrows.* Each scroll bar has two scroll arrows, which you can click to move the cursor in the direction indicated.

Table 1.3 lists the mouse scrolling techniques. The horizontal techniques work only if the window is too narrow to display the longest line of text in your document.

Table 1.3
Mouse Scrolling Techniques

To scroll	Click the left button on
Up or down one line	Up or down scroll arrow
Up or down continuously down the button	Up or down scroll arrow, and hold
Up or down one screen	Scroll bar background, above or below the scroll box
Up or down more than one screen	Scroll box, and drag up or down
Left or right one column	Left or right scroll arrow
Left or right continuously down the button	Left or right scroll arrow, and hold
Left or right one-third screen	Scroll bar background, left or right of the scroll box
Left or right more than one screen	Scroll box, and drag up or down

Getting On-Screen Help

Like other excellent programs, Word's on-screen Help provides information about the program. What distinguishes Word's Help feature from similar utilities in other programs, however, is its breadth of coverage. Most Help features convey only a little information about the command you have chosen and what the command does. In Word 5.5's help feature, you can obtain descriptions of commands. You also can find procedural information (how-to instructions, given step by step), conceptual information (definitions of key terms, the way Word defines them), keyboard maps, mouse hints, and even a section on Word 5.5 for Word 5.0 users.

The Two Ways To Get Help

You obtain Help in two different ways. To obtain context-sensitive Help, you press F1 to display a screen of information about the command or feature that currently is highlighted. To view the Help Index, which provides access to the keyboard maps, Word 5.5 upgrade information, definitions, and procedures, you choose the **Help** command. The following tutorials explain how.

To obtain context-sensitive Help at any time, follow these steps:

1. Using the keyboard or mouse techniques you have just learned, display the Character dialog box. (Hint: Use Alt-TC or click Forma**t** and choose the **C**haracter option.)

2. Press F1.

   The Help screen for the Character dialog box appears (see fig. 1.10).

3. Press PgDn or choose the Page **D**n command button to display the next page.

   Note that the Page **U**p button is grayed. The gray color means the option isn't available now and you cannot choose it.

   To choose the Page **D**n button, which isn't grayed, you can click the button or press Alt-D.

4. When you finish reading about the Character dialog box, choose OK by clicking the button or pressing Enter.

   The screen redisplays the Character dialog box.

File   Edit   View   Insert   Format   Utilities   Macro   Window   Help
══════════════════════════ Document1 ══════════════════════════
─────────────────── Help ───────────────────

CHARACTER DIALOG BOX   (Screen 1 of 2)

Font
    Type or select from the list the font you want.
    Font is the design of the text alphabet.

Point Size
    Type or select from the list the point size you
    want. Point size is the size of text. There are
    72 points per inch.

Color
    Type or select from the list the color you
    want your text to appear.

    <Page Up>   <Page Dn>   ⟨ OK ⟩

Pg1 Co1   {}   <F1=Help>   Microsoft Word
Changes the appearance of selected characters

Fig. 1.10. Help screen for the Character dialog box.

To display a screen of procedural information, follow these steps:

1. Choose **Help**.

   The **Help** drop-down menu appears (see fig. 1.11).

2. Choose **Index**.

   The **Help Index** screen appears (see fig. 1.12).

3. Choose the Procedures command button.

   The command buttons in Help don't have accelerator keys, so
   you cannot choose them by pressing Alt and an accelerator key.
   But you can select one of them by pressing the option's first
   letter. Alternatively, use Tab or the arrow key to select an option.
   When you select an option, Word highlights the brackets.

   You see an alphabetical list of procedures, such as aligning
   paragraphs, bold, center, and many more.

4. Choose **Aligning Paragraphs**.

   You see a screen of instructions about aligning paragraphs with
   keyboard shortcuts.

5. Choose Exit to return to your document.

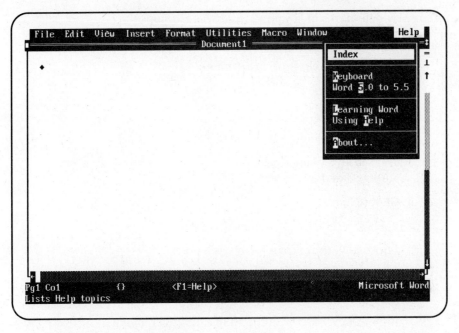

Fig. 1.11. *The Help drop-down menu.*

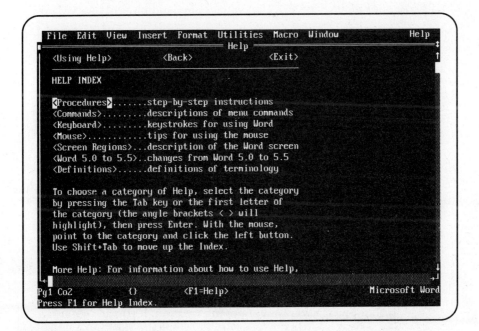

Fig. 1.12. *The Help Index screen.*

To display definitions of key terms, follow these steps:

1. Choose **Help**.

   You see the Help drop-down menu.

2. Choose Index.

   You see the Help Index screen.

3. Choose the Definitions command button.

   You see an alphabetical list of terms, such as annotation, array, autosave, and many more.

4. Choose Active.

   You see a screen that defines this term.

5. Choose OK to return to your document.

To view help screens about the keyboard, follow these steps:

1. Choose **Help**.

2. Choose Keyboard from the **Help** drop-down menu.

   You see the Keyboard help menu.

3. Choose the Moving in a Document command button.

   You see a list of the cursor-movement and scrolling keys you learned in this chapter. You can display this list at any time to refresh your memory.

4. Choose Exit to quit Help.

More Help Resources

In addition to the Help procedures you already have learned, you can view Help screens about the following subjects. To view these screens, display the **Help Index** menu and choose the appropriate option. (You can choose the Word **5**.0 to 5.5 option directly from the **Help** menu.)

- *Mouse Techniques.* Displays a menu of Help screens about using the mouse. Included are editing, scrolling, selecting, using commands, using tabs, using the Ruler, and using windows.

- *Screen Regions.* Displays a map of the Word screen. You click the region about which you want more information. If you are not using the mouse, you can use the arrow keys to highlight the region and press Enter.

- *Word 5.0 to 5.5*. Displays a menu of Help screens about Word 5.5 for Word 5.0 users. Included are command, option, keyboard, mouse action, and terminology changes.

- *Commands*. Displays the same Help screens you see in context-sensitive Help, except you choose them from a list organized by menu name.

Navigating in Help

The various Help screens aren't isolated entities. When you are in Help, you can move around as you please. Choose Index to display the Help Index at any time. Choose Back to display the screen you just viewed. If you are in a Help screen that permits you to scroll down, the Index, Back, and Exit buttons may scroll out of view. To view and use the buttons again, press Ctrl-Home.

Controlling the Display

Word 5.5 is designed to take full advantage of your computer's video capabilities. With today's high-resolution graphics monitors, you may be able to choose from among as many as six different display modes. These modes fall into two categories: text modes and graphics modes.

In the text modes, Word relies on your computer's built-in set of 254 standard characters. Because your computer does not need to construct these characters each time they are displayed, the program runs more quickly in this mode. An additional advantage of the text mode is that, with some monitors, you can choose modes that display up to 50 lines of text per screen (as opposed to the standard, 24-line display). However, Word does not display character emphases on-screen in this mode (such as italic, superscript, underlining, small capitals, strike-through formatting, and double underlining). If you are using a monochrome monitor, distinguishing some of these character formats on-screen is difficult. Underlining and italic, for example, appear with underlining on monochrome monitors. If you are using a color monitor, however, the various character formats appear in distinctive colors.

In the graphics mode, Word displays character emphases the way the characters will appear when printed. If you are creating a document that uses both underlining and italic, seeing these formats on-screen the way they will print can be helpful. Word 5.5 cannot display fonts and font sizes, however, except in Print Preview (File menu), which displays a graphic simulation of your font size choices and all of your other formatting choices.

In previous versions of Word, mouse users found good reason to prefer the graphics mode. In graphics mode, the mouse changed shape fluently on-screen, revealing when (and where) one could use the mouse to perform such actions as selecting lines, sizing windows, and turning on the Ruler. In text mode, these shape changes were obscured, so mouse users were better off with the graphics mode. In Word 5.5, most of the graphics mode shape changes are gone, replaced by just two shapes: a left arrow (the normal pointer) and a right arrow (the pointer when positioned in the selection bar). The change is equally visible in the text mode. In monochrome, the pointer dims when it touches the selection bar, while in color, you see a distinctive color change. Therefore, mouse users no longer have any reason to prefer the graphics mode.

The chief drawback of the graphics mode is its sluggish performance. This is not a problem on computers with reasonably fast clock speeds (such as 16 MHz) and 80286 or 80386 microprocessors. However, if you are using a slower computer—or worse, an 8088-based machine—the graphics mode may operate too sluggishly.

> *Tip:* If you have a high-resolution color display (an Enhanced Graphics Adapter [EGA] or Video Graphics Array [VGA]), choose the text mode. Word operates at maximum speed, and you soon will learn the distinctive colors that Word assigns to character emphases such as underlining (yellow), italic (cyan), and boldface (bright white).

To change the video display mode, follow these steps:

1. Choose View Preferences (Alt-VE).

   (A reminder: If you are using the keyboard, press Alt to highlight the menu bar, and then press View to drop down the View menu. Press E to choose the Preferences option. If you are using the mouse, click View on the menu bar and Preferences on the View menu.)

   The Preferences dialog box appears (see fig. 1.13).

2. Pull down the Display Mode list box.

   (A reminder: If you are using the keyboard, press Alt-D to highlight the Display Mode list box and then press Alt-down arrow to pull down the list. If you are using the mouse, click the drag-down arrow to the right of the Display Mode list box.)

3. Choose one of the text or graphics modes.

4. Choose OK.

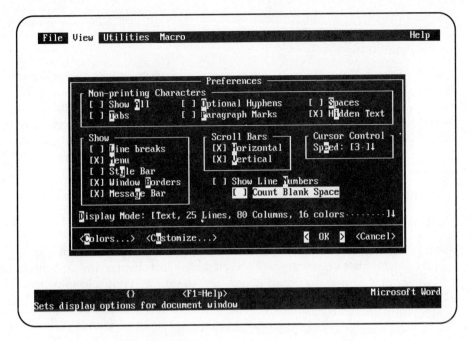

Fig. 1.13. *The Preferences dialog box.*

Tip: You can customize Word 5.5's screen display in many ways besides choosing between the graphics and text modes. You can hide the menu bar so that the bar comes on-screen only when you press F10 or Alt. You can remove the window borders, the scroll bars (vertical, horizontal, or both), and even the message bar. If you have a color monitor, you can paint the screen with the colors you prefer. All these and other customization choices are explained in Chapter 9.

Saving Your Work

Computer word processing can save you time and extend your reach as a writer, but it's a risky business. Just about every computer user loses work sooner or later because of a sudden interruption in power. Because your Word document is stored in your computer's random-access memory (RAM) until you deliberately save the file to disk, all your unsaved work is lost if the power fails. RAM needs flowing electricity to retain data.

You can avoid catastrophic data losses by saving your work to disk frequently. Don't start a new document and work for hours without saving. Instead, save your work frequently, and continue working. You can use Word's Autosave option, which saves your work automatically at an interval you specify (such as every 10 minutes).

Note: By default, Word assumes that you want to save your documents to the directory from which you start Word. If you start Word from the Word document directory, as this book strongly recommends, the document directory becomes the default directory to which Word saves your files. You do not need to specify any path information to save files to this directory, so long as the directory is the one from which you started Word. For more information on setting up your disk the correct way, see the Appendix.

Saving a New, Unnamed Document

For the tutorial in this section, you save a document with a sentence or two of text. If you have kept a document on-screen during this chapter, the document probably contains enough "experimental" text to suffice. If not, add some text.

Alt-F2 To save a new, unnamed document, follow these steps:

1. Choose **F**ile Save **A**s (Alt-FA). Alternatively, use the Alt-F2 keyboard shortcut.

   The Save As dialog box appears (see fig. 1.14). The cursor is positioned in the File **N**ame text box. The DOS path that is indicated just above the **D**irectories area should be that of your default document directory (such as C:\WORD\DOCS).

2. In the File **N**ame text box, type the file name *test*.

   The file name must conform to DOS conventions (eight characters maximum, and you cannot use most punctuation marks).

   If you omit the period and the extension, Word supplies the default Word extension, DOC, so that your file is named TEST.DOC.

   > *Tip:* Always allow Word to supply the default extension, DOC. As you learn in subsequent chapters, Word is set up to list documents automatically if they have this extension. File retrieval operations are much more convenient if you stick to the default extension.

3. Choose OK.

   When you choose OK, you accept Word's default choice (Word format) in the Format list box. This choice retains all the formatting

Chapter 1: Getting Started with Word 5.5 **43**

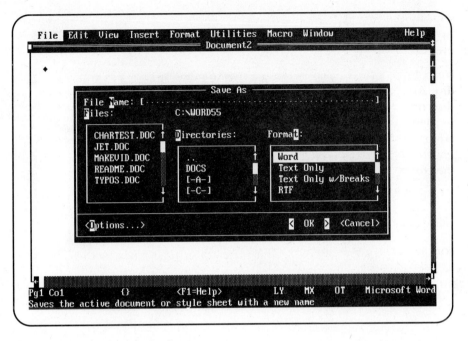

Fig. 1.14. The Save As dialog box.

you have done. You choose other options only if you want to give your work to people using other programs or to send your work via telecommunications services.

If you see the message File name or path is not valid, make sure that you have adhered to DOS conventions in assigning the file name. Use a maximum of eight letters and/or numbers, with no spaces or punctuation marks.

The Summary dialog box appears (see fig. 1.15).

> **Tip:** If you want, you can skip the Summary dialog box by pressing Esc. However, it's best if you fill out the dialog box. If you do, retrieving documents using Word's superb File Management capabilities, which are discussed in Chapter 8, is much easier.

4. Type the document's title in the Title text box.

5. Type the document's author in the Author text box.

   If only one author's Word documents are to be stored on this computer, you can skip this step.

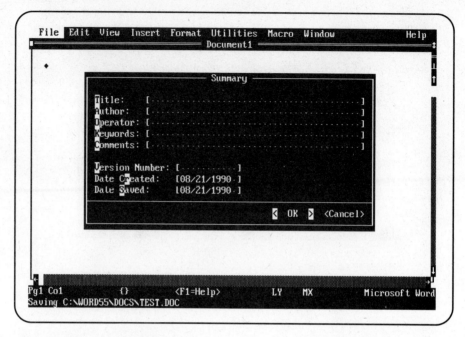

Fig. 1.15. The Summary dialog box.

6. Type two or three key words or phrases in the **Keywords** area.

    Categorize the document with words such as "Jennings contract," "quarterly report," and so on.

7. Type comments, if you want, in the **Comments** text box.

    Use this area for notes to yourself, such as "Needs revision."

8. Choose OK.

Saving a Document Again

When you save a new document for the first time, Word writes to disk the version that was in memory when you chose the Save **As** command. After you save the document, it remains on-screen. If you perform any additional editing or formatting, or if you add text, you must save these changes.

Alt-Shift-F2 To save a document again, choose File **S**ave (Alt-FS). Alternatively, use the Alt-Shift-F2 keyboard shortcut.

Word saves the document using the file name you choose and the document remains on-screen. If you haven't saved the document, Word displays the Save As dialog box.

Storing Changes Automatically

Autosave is an important Word feature that can save you a great deal of grief. This command saves your work automatically at an interval you specify, such as every 5 or 10 minutes. When the Autosave operation occurs, your work is interrupted momentarily, which is better than losing several hours of work due to a power failure.

To turn on Autosave, follow these steps:

1. Choose Utilities Customize (Alt-UU).

   The Customize dialog box appears (see fig. 1.16).

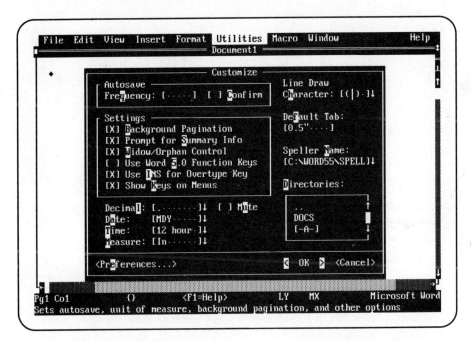

Fig. 1.16. The Customize dialog box.

2. In the Frequency box, type the interval (in minutes) that you want Autosave to save your document to disk.

   Ten minutes is a good choice, although if you are working with exceptionally important material, five is better.

3. Choose OK.

Note: Word "remembers" all the choices you make in the Customize dialog box by saving them to a file called MW.INI. Word consults this file every time you start the program. If by some chance you erase this file, however, Word reverts to the program's default settings. Be careful not to erase the MW.INI file.

If the power fails while you are using Autosave, relax. You can restore all your changes up to the point that Autosave last saved them to disk. When the power comes back on and you re-start Word, you see an on-screen alert box informing you that autosave backup files exist. To recover them, choose **Yes**. Your document returns to the screen.

> *Caution:* Using Autosave is not the same as saving your work with **Save** or Save **As**. Autosave merely is a backup procedure to be used in case of a computer crash or power failure. Even if you are using Autosave, you still must save your work by saving your files to disk.

Closing the Document

As you have just learned, a document remains on-screen after you have saved it. If you are planning to exit Word, this is not a problem—the work is saved, so you can proceed directly to the Exit Word command in the File menu. If you want to continue working with a different document, however, you may want to close the document. To close the document means to remove its document window from the screen.

To close a document, choose **File Close** (Alt-FC). Alternatively, click the close box in the upper left corner of the window.

If you haven't saved the changes you made, you see an alert box. Choose **Yes** to save the changes, **No** to abandon them, or Cancel to leave the document on-screen and continue editing.

You can quit Word by choosing the Exit Word command from the **File** menu.

Quitting Word

Like other well-designed programs, Word 5.5 warns you if you are about to quit the program without saving work. When you choose Exit Word from the **File** menu, the program checks each open document to see whether you have saved all your changes. If you haven't, you see an alert box asking you whether you want to save the changes you made to the document. To save the changes, choose **Yes**. To abandon your changes, choose **No**. If more than one document is open with unsaved changes, you see additional alert boxes. The program returns to DOS only after you have dealt with all your unsaved work.

Caution: Do not quit Word simply by turning the power off while Word still is on-screen. You must choose the Exit Word command and return to DOS before you switch off the power. When you choose the Exit Word command, Word closes the many temporary files the program created and also saves your configuration choices to a special configuration file (MW.INI). If you turn off the power without quitting Word, the temporary files (with the extension TMP) clutter up your disk and, if you made any configuration choices, these choices are lost.

Chapter Summary

This chapter prepared you to begin using Microsoft Word 5.5 by showing you how to start Word, understand the screen display, choose commands from drop-down menus and dialog boxes, and move the cursor and scroll the screen. You also learned how to get on-screen Help, save your work, and close documents and exit Word in an orderly fashion. These are the fundamentals of effective, day-to-day writing with Microsoft Word 5.5.

Now that you are familiar with these fundamentals, you are ready to begin composing, editing, formatting, and printing a document. Chapter 2 shows you how to create your first Word document—a business letter that, as you will see, needs quite a bit of revision before the letter is printed.

Note: The Word knowledge you have learned in this chapter is summed up concisely in the Quick Review that follows. Material introduced in tutorials is honed down to the basics and stated in the simplest possible language. The Quick Review contains all you need in order to remember the specifics about a procedure you already have learned. (The procedures are listed alphabetically.)

Quick Review

Accelerator Keys

To choose commands from drop-down menus or options within dialog boxes, hold down the Alt key and press the accelerator key (the boldfaced letter).

Autosave

To turn on Autosave and specify an interval:

1. Choose Utilities Customize (Alt-UU).

2. Type the interval (in minutes).

3. Choose OK.

Closing a Document

Choose File Close (Alt-FC). Alternatively, click the close box in the upper left corner of the window.

Commands

To choose commands with the keyboard:

1. Press Alt to highlight the menu bar.

2. Press the menu name's accelerator key (the boldfaced letter).

3. Press Alt and an accelerator key to choose an item from the drop-down menu.

4. If you see a dialog box, press Alt and the accelerator key of the area you want to change. Make the change. If the cursor is within a list of option buttons or check boxes, you can use the arrow keys to move to a button and press the Space bar to turn one on or off.

5. Repeat step 4 until you have made all the changes.

6. Press Enter to choose OK and confirm your changes. Alternatively, press Esc or choose Cancel. Word ignores your changes.

To choose commands with the mouse:

1. Click the menu name on the menu bar.

2. Click an option on the drop-down menu.

3. If you see a dialog box, activate the area you want to change by clicking within the box, and then make the change.

4. Repeat step 3 until you have made all the changes.

5. Click OK to confirm your changes or click Cancel to abandon them.

Cursor-Movement Keys

Key	Moves cursor
Up arrow*	Up one line
Down arrow*	Down one line
Left arrow*	Left one column
Right arrow*	Right one column
Home	To beginning of line
End	To end of line
PgUp*	Up one screen
PgDn*	Down one screen
Ctrl-PgUp	To top of screen
Ctrl-PgDn	To bottom of screen
Ctrl-right arrow*	To next word
Ctrl-left arrow*	To previous word
Ctrl-up arrow*	To previous paragraph
Ctrl-down arrow*	To next paragraph
Ctrl-Home	To beginning of document
Ctrl-End	To end of document

*Key repeats action when held down

Dialog Boxes

To move from one area to another within a dialog box, press Tab. To move in the opposite direction, press Shift-Tab. Alternatively, activate an area by holding down the Alt key and pressing the accelerator key.

To display a drop-down list box, activate the area, hold down the Alt key, and press the down-arrow key. If you are using a mouse, click the down-arrow symbol next to the list box.

To close a drop-down list box without changing the current setting, press Alt-down arrow again. If you are using a mouse, click the down-arrow symbol next to the list box again.

To select a check box item, press Alt and the box's accelerator key. If you are using the mouse, click the box.

To select an option button, press Alt and the button's accelerator key. If you are using the mouse, click the button.

To select a command button, press Tab to highlight the button and then press Enter. Alternatively, press Enter to choose OK immediately or press Esc to choose Cancel immediately. If you are using the mouse, click the button.

Exiting Word

Choose File Exit Word (Alt-FX). Alternatively, use the Alt-F4 keyboard shortcut.

Help

To obtain context-sensitive Help at any time:

1. Highlight the command name or dialog box area for which you want help.

2. Press F1.

3. Press PgDn or choose the Page **Dn** command button to display the next page, if one is available.

4. Choose OK.

To obtain an on-screen list of instructions for common Word procedures:

1. Choose **Help Index** (Alt-HI).

2. Choose the Procedure command button.

3. Choose the procedure you want from the alphabetical list. If necessary, use PgUp, PgDn, or scroll with the mouse to see additional pages of the Procedure Index.

4. Choose Exit to return to your document.

To display definitions of key terms:

1. Choose **Help Index** (Alt-HI).

2. Choose the Definitions command button.

3. Choose the term you want from the alphabetical list. If necessary, use PgUp, PgDn, or scroll with the mouse to see additional pages of the Procedure Index.

4. Choose OK to return to your document.

To view help screens about the keyboard:

1. Choose **Help Index** (Alt-HI).

2. Choose the Mouse command button.

3. Choose a topic from the Mouse menu.

4. Choose Exit to return to your document.

To view help screens about display screen regions:

1. Choose **Help Index** (Alt-HI).

2. Choose the Screen Regions command button.

3. Point to the region of the screen you want to explore and click the left button. Alternatively, use the arrow keys to place the cursor in the region and press Enter.

4. Click OK to return to the screen region display.

5. Repeat steps 5 and 6 for additional screen regions, if you want.

6. Choose Exit to return to your document.

To view help screens about learning Word 5.5 for Word 5.0 users:

1. Choose **Help Word 5.0 to 5.5** (Alt-H5).

2. Choose a topic from the Word 5.0 to 5.5 menu.

3. Choose Exit to return to your document.

Key Status Indicator Codes

Code	Key or Command	Explanation
CL	Caps Lock	Enters all letters as uppercase
CS	Ctrl-Shift-F8	Column select mode
EX	F8	Extend selection mode
OT	Ins	Overtype mode
LD	Utilities Line Draw	Draw lines
LY	View Layout	Display page layout
MR	Ctrl-F9	Record a macro
MX	Ctrl-F10	Maximize (zoom) the window
NL	Num Lock	Keypad enters numbers
RM	Utilities Revision Marks	Mark revisions
SL	Scroll Lock	Arrow keys scroll screen
ST	Macro Run (Step)	Run macro line by line

Menu Bar

To activate the menu bar with the keyboard, press F10 or Alt. To activate the menu bar with the mouse, click the name of the menu you want to display.

Overtype Mode

Press Ins to toggle between the Insert mode (default) and the Overtype mode. When you choose Overtype, you see the code OT on the status bar.

Saving Your Work

To save a new, unnamed document:

1. Choose File Save As (Alt-FA). Alternatively, use the Alt-F2 keyboard shortcut.

2. In the File Name text box, type a file name. Omit the period and the extension so that Word supplies the default extension, DOC.

3. Choose OK.

4. In the Summary dialog box, type the document's title in the **Title** text box.

5. Type the document's author in the **Author** text box.

6. Type two or three key words or phrases in the **Keywords** area.

7. Type comments, if you want, in the **Comments** text box.

8. Choose OK.

To save a document again:

Choose File Save (Alt-FS). Alternatively, use the Alt-Shift-F2 keyboard shortcut.

Scrolling with the Keyboard (Scroll Lock On)

To scroll	*Press*
Up one line	Up arrow
Down one line	Down arrow
Left (1/3 screen)	Left arrow
Right (1/3 screen)	Right arrow

Scrolling with the Mouse

To scroll	*Click the left button on*
Up or down one line	Up or down scroll arrow
Up or down continuously	Up or down scroll arrow, and hold down the button
Up or down one screen below the scroll box	Scroll bar background, above or
Up or down more than one screen	Scroll box, and drag up or down
Left or right one column	Left or right scroll arrow
Left or right continuously	Left or right scroll arrow, and hold down the button

To scroll	*Click the left button on*
Left or right 1/3 screen	Scroll bar background, left or right of the scroll box
Left or right more	Scroll box, and drag up or down than one screen

Starting Word

To start Word and create a new, unnamed document:

1. Activate the Word document directory.

2. Type *word* and press Enter.

Video Display Modes

To change the video display mode:

1. Choose View Preferences (Alt-VE).

2. Pull down the **Display Mode** list box.

3. Choose one of the text or graphics modes.

4. Choose OK.

Your First Word 5.5 Document—Quickly!

Word is well known as one of the most powerful word processing programs available for any computer, but the program is quite easy to use at an elementary level. You can start producing letters, memos, and brief reports immediately. In this chapter, you learn how to use Word in a straight-forward, simple way. Specifically, you create, format, edit, save, and print a simple document (a business letter).

If you are just getting started with word processing, this chapter helps by explaining and illustrating fundamental word processing concepts as well as the basics of using Word 5.5. Word processing enables you to keep revising your work until it meets the highest professional standards. You will understand why almost everyone who has tried word processing cannot imagine going back to a typewriter.

Even if you already have some familiarity with Word, this chapter may be well worth skimming. The material is elementary, but presents an approach to Word that has been developed by experts through long experience with the program. Take note, particularly, of the power user tips and cautions. Another reason for skimming this chapter is that the chapters in Part II develop and extend the topics covered here. All those chapters show how to go beyond the fundamentals and take full advantage of Word 5.5's remarkable features.

This chapter introduces important Word procedures, but doesn't try to be encyclopedic. For example, you learn how to set a flush-left tab, but for simplicity's sake, nothing is said about setting flush-right, centered, or decimal tabs. Tabs are covered in more detail in Chapter 11. Similarly, Chapters 3, 4, and 5 extend and broaden the editing and formatting knowledge this chapter introduces.

In this chapter, you learn how to do the following:

- Create a new Word 5.5 document and enter text, correcting errors as you type

- Center and boldface text—and, along the way, learn important concepts about how Word handles text formatting

- Insert the current date automatically, using one of Word's built-in glossaries

- Join and split paragraphs the way Word experts do

- Select and delete text

- Insert new text into existing text

- Move text from one location to another with the keyboard or the mouse

- Set up a special tab format for typing a complimentary close

- Check your document's spelling

- Preview your letter's appearance on-screen to see how it will look on the page

- Print your document

Remember, this chapter draws on the Word 5.5 knowledge introduced in Chapter 1. In particular, you should know how to start Word, understand the basic features of the Word screen, choose commands from drop-down menus and dialog boxes, move the cursor and scroll, save your work, and exit Word in an orderly fashion. If you cannot remember everything, don't worry. This chapter reminds you how to accomplish these actions.

Note: Be sure to set the system time and date correctly when you start your computer. Word needs this information to help you accomplish one of the tutorials in this chapter. If you are using a 286 or 386 computer, the computer probably contains clock-calendar circuitry that sets the time and date correctly when you turn on your computer. If you are using a PC or an XT, however, you may need to set the system time and date manually by using the DOS DATE and TIME commands.

Creating and Formatting a Letter

Every time you send a first-class letter, you put yourself and your organization on the line. You have the opportunity to create either a favorable or a negative impression of your company. For this reason, preparing letters with a fine word processing program like Word 5.5 is a good idea. Using a word processor enables you to experiment with the wording until you get it exactly right.

This entire chapter is a single tutorial that walks you through a "real world" writing experience. You start with a poorly written letter and alter the letter to meet the professional standards of today's business environment.

Suppose that you are the director of a small training firm that specializes in training corporate employees in security techniques. You frequently use videos to illustrate potential security problems. Last week, you spent a day training some employees at Atlantic Electronic Enterprises, Inc. Everything went fine, except that the video projection device's bulb blew during the final moments of the presentation. You had a backup, however, and soon were back in action. A week later, you receive a letter from Mr. Nelson T. Jones, your contact at the firm, thanking you for the presentation but complaining—rather unfairly and gruffly—about the equipment breakdown. The ball's in your court now; you must answer the letter.

Typing and Centering the Return Address

Begin this tutorial by typing the return address as follows:

1. Start Word with a new, unnamed document.

    If you already have been working with Word and have a document on-screen, choose **New** command from the **File** menu.

    The New dialog box appears.

2. In the New dialog box, make sure that the Document button is turned on and then choose OK.

3. Choose Forma**t** **P**aragraph (Alt-TP).

    (A reminder: If you are using the keyboard, press Alt to activate the menu bar. Next, press T to drop down the Format menu and press P to choose the **P**aragraph option. If you are using the mouse, click Forma**t** on the menu bar and **P**aragraph on the Format menu.)

    The Paragraph dialog box appears (see fig. 2.1). You explore this dialog box in detail in Chapter 4.

4. Choose the **C**enter option button in the Alignment field.

    (A reminder: If you are using the keyboard, press Alt-C to choose the **C**enter button. If you are using the mouse, click the **C**enter button.)

5. Choose OK.

(A reminder: If you are using the keyboard, press Enter to choose OK. If you are using the mouse, click OK.

The cursor jumps to the middle of the screen.

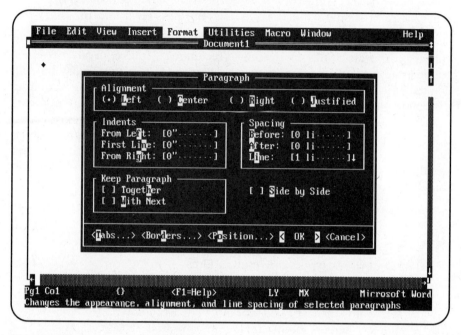

Fig. 2.1. The Paragraph dialog box.

Ctrl-C

Note: As noted in Chapter 1, using the menus just to choose one option from a dialog box can be tedious. Many keystrokes are required just to choose the Center option button. That's why most Word users prefer to use the keyboard shortcuts if they are choosing just one formatting option. Pressing Ctrl-C is the same as choosing Center from the Paragraph dialog box.

The dialog boxes are best used when you want to choose more than one option at a time. In this chapter, you use the menu technique the first time you use a dialog box. After all, part of this chapter's goal is to introduce you to these dialog boxes, so it's worth the few extra keystrokes. However, you use the keyboard shortcuts subsequently.

6. Now type the return address as follows, pressing Enter at the end of each line. If you make a mistake, use the Backspace key to rub out the error.

Albemarle Valley Associates
Business Security Training and Development
13987 Oakfair Parkway
Suite 128
Charlottesville, VA 22987
(804) 111-9000

When you press Enter, Word copies the centered format to the next line automatically. In fact, the format remains in effect until you deliberately cancel it by choosing another alignment option in the Paragraph dialog box.

7. When you finish typing the telephone number, press Enter.

8. Press Ctrl-L (left alignment).   **Ctrl-L**

This key is the keyboard shortcut for the Left option button in the Paragraph dialog box (see fig. 2.1).

The cursor jumps back to the left margin.

Your document should look like figure 2.2. Welcome to what-you-see-is-what-you-get word processing!

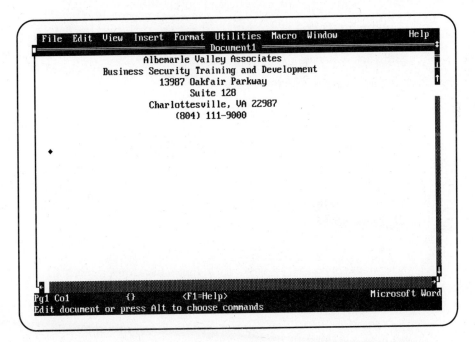

Fig. 2.2. Letter with centered return address.

9. Choose **F**ile Save **A**s (Alt-FA) and save your document using the file name LETTER1. Let Word supply the automatic extension (DOC).

Selecting and Boldfacing the Firm's Name

Now boldface the firm's name (Albemarle Valley Associates). To attach a character emphasis to text you already have typed, you need to *select* the text so that the text is highlighted on-screen. Selecting the text is your way of telling Word which text you want affected by a formatting command. The text you highlight is called the *selection*.

Selection is an important Word technique, and you can perform selection using the keyboard or the mouse. If you are using the mouse, skim the keyboard section and skip to "Selecting Text with the Mouse," later in this section.

Selecting Text with the Keyboard

To boldface the firm's name using the keyboard, follow these steps:

1. Place the cursor on the first character of the firm's name.

   (A reminder: Press Ctrl-PgUp to position the cursor on the first character in the window, which happens to be the first character of the firm's name.)

2. Press F8 (Extend Selection).

   You see the code EX on the status bar (see fig. 2.3).

   Users of previous versions of Word should note that the F6 key no longer extends the selection. You press F8 instead, and the key works differently—as you learn quickly. The more times you press F8, the more you select.

3. Press F8 twice more to expand the selection to the end of the line (see fig. 2.3).

4. Choose Format **C**haracter (Alt-TC).

   (A reminder: Press Alt to activate the menu bar. Next, press T to drop down the Format menu and press C to choose the Character option.)

   The Character dialog box appears (see fig. 2.4). You explore this dialog box in detail in Chapter 4.

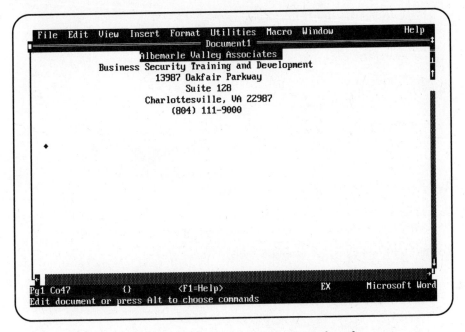

Fig. 2.3. The EX *code, indicating that Word is in the Extend mode.*

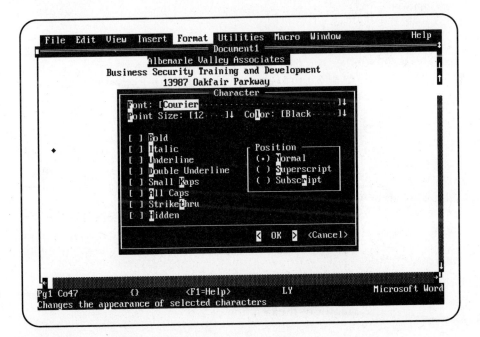

Fig. 2.4. The Character dialog box.

5. Choose the **Bold** check box.

(A reminder: Press Alt-B to choose the **Bold** check box. If you are using the mouse, click the **Bold** box.)

6. Choose OK.

(A reminder: Press Enter to choose OK.)

The firm's name appears in boldface. Word cancels the Extend Selection mode and the EX code disappears from the status bar.

Selecting Text with the Mouse

Mouse users can draw from a variety of useful techniques to select text. In the following steps, you learn the first technique, which is called *dragging*.

To select a line of text by dragging, follow these steps:

1. Point to the first character of the document.

2. Hold down the left button and drag the pointer to the end of the line.

Word extends the selection.

3. So that you can try the next (alternate) technique, click anywhere in the window to cancel the selection.

The dragging technique is an effective way of selecting text, but you must visually assess whether you have come to the end of the line. Dragging is fine, if you have an eye for detail and some patience. If you are selecting a fixed unit of text, such as a word, line, sentence, or paragraph, however, Word can determine where the unit of text ends. In the following steps, you use the *selection bar* technique to highlight the line.

The selection bar is a column that runs down the left side of the screen, just inside the left window border. You cannot see the selection bar—it's just a blank vertical column on-screen. When you move the mouse pointer into the selection bar, however, the pointer changes. In graphics mode, the left-facing arrow becomes a right-facing arrow when it touches the selection bar. In monochrome text mode, the pointer dims. And in color text mode, the pointer changes color. The tone or color change tells you that the mouse is ready to select fixed units of text.

To select a line of text using the selection bar, follow these steps:

1. Move the pointer to the first line of text on-screen, Albemarle Valley Associates.

2. Move the pointer slowly to the left side of the window, directly aligned with the first line of text, until you see the pointer's tone or color change.

3. Click the left mouse button.

   Word selects the entire line.

The extend selection techniques are quick and useful. You learn additional techniques in Chapter 3.

Formatting the Word Way

The tutorials you have completed so far have introduced two fundamental distinctions: paragraph versus character formatting, and formatting-as-you-type versus formatting later. Take a break from the letter to consider these important distinctions.

Paragraph versus Character Formatting

Basic to Word is a distinction between paragraph formatting and character formatting. Paragraph formats, which affect all the text in a paragraph, include the following:

- The alignment of text (whether the text is positioned flush left, centered, flush right, or justified on both margins)

- Indentation from the right or left margin and on the paragraph's first line

- Line spacing, such as single- or double-spacing

- Blank lines before and after the paragraph

Word defines a paragraph as all the text you type until you press Enter. This definition is not semantic and has nothing to do with the paragraphs with which you are familiar, which are units of meaning. On the contrary, Word defines paragraphs as the text between two Enter keystrokes. A Word paragraph can be just one line (such as the company's name in the letter you are writing), a heading, or an ordinary text paragraph.

Character formats include emphasis (such as boldface, italic, and underlining); position (subscript, superscript, or normal); and font (type style, such as Pica, Elite, or Helvetica). Character formats can affect any unit of text, from one character to an entire document. After you choose a special character format and start typing, Word continues to use that format until you cancel it by pressing Alt-Space bar.

Formatting As You Type versus Formatting Later

You can format characters (with emphases such as boldface) and paragraphs (with formats such as centering) in the following two ways:

- *As you type.* With this technique, you "program" the cursor to "lay down" a format as you enter the text. You used this method when you typed your letter's return address. After you chose the Center alignment option in the Paragraph dialog box, Word continued to center your paragraphs until you pressed Ctrl-L (left alignment). Whether you choose a character or a paragraph format, the format remains in effect until you cancel it or choose a conflicting format.

- *Later.* With this technique, you type your text first, as you did with the firm's name in the letter. Later, you select or highlight the text and choose a formatting command. The format applies only to the text you have selected. After you selected the first line of the letter, the **Bold** check box in the Character dialog box affected the selection only.

Which approach is best depends on you. Some writers find concentrating on the content of their writing easier if they format later. Others find composing easier when they see their text formatted on-screen, just the way the text will appear when printed.

Both types of formatting, formatting as you type and formatting later, are explored in Chapters 4 and 5.

Inserting the Date Automatically

You can type the date manually, if you prefer, but Word can enter the date for you. The date will be wrong, however, if your computer doesn't set the date automatically and you don't use the DOS DATE command. If the system date is correct, follow these steps:

1. Use the down-arrow key or the mouse to move the cursor to the end-of-file mark. Press Enter two or three times to leave some blank space under the return address.

2. Choose **Edit Glossary** (Alt-EO).

The Glossary dialog box appears (see fig. 2.5).

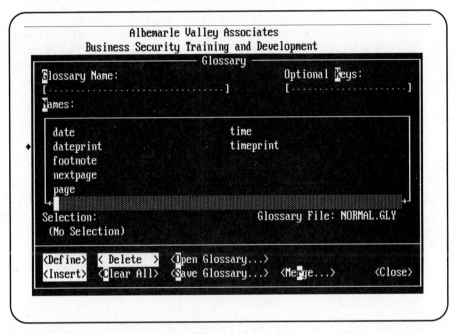

Fig. 2.5. The Glossary dialog box.

3. Press Tab twice or Alt-N to activate the **Names** list box and then choose the date option. If you are using the mouse, click date.

You see the contents of the date glossary below the Names list box. You should see today's date.

4. Choose the **Insert** button.

To choose this command button with the keyboard, press Alt-I. To choose this command with the mouse, click the button.

Word inserts today's date in your document.

You have just used one of Word's built-in glossaries, which are discussed thoroughly in Chapter 12. A *glossary* is a storage place for holding a certain type of information that you can insert into your document as you please. The date glossary is an example of a *built-in* glossary, a glossary that is predefined and assigned to a specific function (such as entering the current date or time). When you choose the date glossary, Word inserts today's date in your document at the cursor's location.

Word 5.5's glossaries now are accessed by the aptly named Glossary option, rather than the old Insert and Delete commands. Chapter 12 explains the extensive changes in detail.

As you can see from this example, the menu technique requires so many keystrokes that you may as well type the date yourself. The keyboard shortcut, however, is much faster. This shortcut illustrates why learning at least some of the shortcut techniques can be worth your while. The following two steps show you how to insert a built-in glossary using the keyboard shortcut:

F3

1. Position the cursor at the end of the date you just entered and press Backspace to erase the entire date.

2. Type *date*.

3. Press F3.

   Word inserts the date glossary automatically and erases the word date.

Previous Word users may be wondering if anything works the old way. F3 does.

4. Press F3. The glossary name disappears, and in its place, the current date appears.

Typing the Text of the Letter

You now are ready to type the correspondent's address, the salutation, and the body of the letter, as shown in figure 2.6.

Note: This letter breaks many rules of good business writing. The errors are intentional. You will improve this business letter later.

To continue the business letter, follow these steps:

1. Position the cursor at the end of the date you just entered and press Enter twice to create a blank line.

2. Type the following inside address, pressing Enter at the end of each line. If you make a mistake, use the Backspace and Del keys to correct errors. Press Enter twice to create a blank line after the inside address.

   Nelson T. Jones
   Engineering Department
   Atlantic Electronic Enterprises, Inc.
   5878 Sycamore Drive
   Beltway, VA 22787

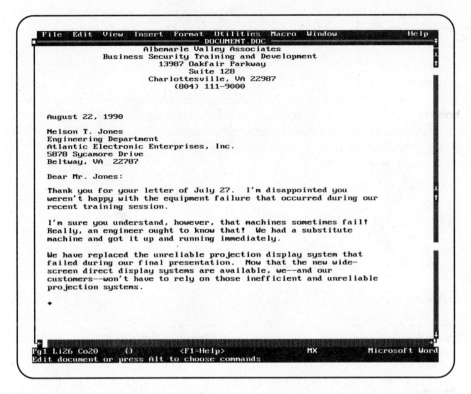

```
  File  Edit  View  Insert  Format  Utilities  Macro  Window              Help
                          ═══ DOCUMENT.DOC ══════════════════════════
                       Albemarle Valley Associates
                 Business Security Training and Development
                           13987 Oakfair Parkway
                               Suite 128
                       Charlottesville, VA 22987
                           (804) 111-9000


          August 22, 1990

          Nelson T. Jones
          Engineering Department
          Atlantic Electronic Enterprises, Inc.
          5878 Sycamore Drive
          Beltway, VA  22787

          Dear Mr. Jones:

          Thank you for your letter of July 27.  I'm disappointed you
          weren't happy with the equipment failure that occurred during our
          recent training session.

          I'm sure you understand, however, that machines sometimes fail!
          Really, an engineer ought to know that!  We had a substitute
          machine and got it up and running immediately.

          We have replaced the unreliable projection display system that
          failed during our final presentation.  Now that the new wide-
          screen direct display systems are available, we--and our
          customers--won't have to rely on those inefficient and unreliable
          projection systems.


             ◆



  Pg1 Li26 Co20      {}          <F1=Help>              MX        Microsoft Word
  Edit document or press Alt to choose commands
```

Fig. 2.6. *A first draft of a business letter.*

3. Type the following salutation and press Enter twice to create a blank line.

    Dear Mr. Jones:

4. Now type the first paragraph as follows. Don't press Enter at the end of a line; let Word "wrap" the text to the next line down. Use Backspace and Del to correct errors as you type. When you reach the end of the paragraph, press Enter twice.

    Thank you for your letter of July 27. I'm disappointed you weren't happy with the equipment failure that occurred during our recent training session.

5. Now type the second paragraph and press Enter twice when you come to the end.

    I'm sure you understand, however, that machines sometimes fail! Really, an engineer ought to know that! We had a substitute machine and got it up and running immediately.

This really is a terrible letter. You can see why the letter will need revision.

6. Now type the third paragraph and press Enter twice when you come to the end of it.

We have replaced the unreliable projection display system that failed during our final presentation. Now that the new wide-screen direct display systems are available, we—and our customers—won't have to rely on those inefficient and unreliable projection systems.

Joining Paragraphs

This letter obviously needs revision. The letter is hasty, angry, and accusatory. To begin, you decide to join the first two paragraphs.

To join paragraphs efficiently, displaying the hidden *paragraph marks* is helpful. Paragraph marks are special symbols that Word inserts in your document to show where you have pressed the Enter key. After you display the paragraph marks, joining paragraphs is a simple matter. You just delete the mark, and the paragraphs separated by the mark are joined.

To display paragraph marks, follow these steps:

1. Choose **View Preferences** (Alt-VE).

The Preferences dialog box appears (see fig. 2.7).

2. In the Non-printing Characters field, choose **Paragraph Marks**.

3. Choose OK.

Now you see paragraph marks everywhere you pressed Enter (see fig. 2.8).

4. Select the two marks that divide the first and second paragraphs.

To select the marks with the keyboard, place the cursor on the first mark and press F8 (Extend Selection). Next, press the down-arrow key. To select the marks with a mouse, place the pointer on the first mark and drag down slightly until the highlight covers the second mark.

5. Press Del to erase the two paragraph marks.

The two paragraphs are joined.

6. Press the Space bar twice to separate the two sentences where the paragraphs were joined (see fig. 2.9).

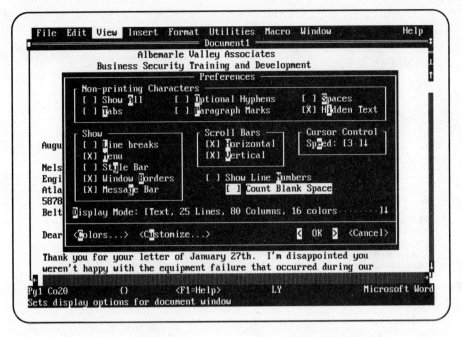

Fig. 2.7. The Preferences dialog box.

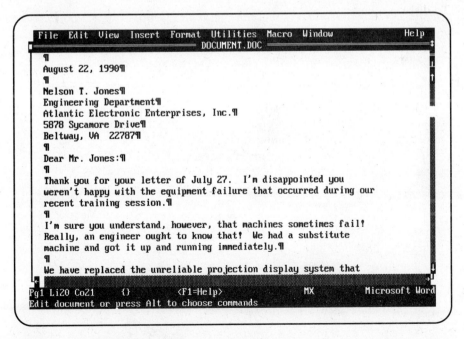

Fig. 2.8. Displaying paragraph marks to see where you have pressed Enter.

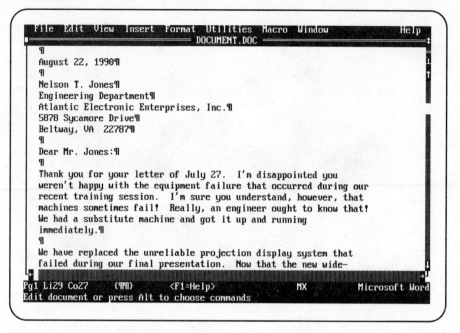

Fig. 2.9. After joining the first and second paragraphs.

Some users find on-screen paragraph marks distracting. But as you can see, rejoining paragraphs is easy when the paragraph marks are displayed. If the marks are invisible, joining and splitting paragraphs is like groping in the dark. For editing purposes, you need to see precisely where you have pressed Enter.

Caution: If you are editing without displaying paragraph marks, you easily can delete a mark by accident. If you delete a mark, the next paragraph "collapses" into the first one. See the next section, "Splitting Paragraphs," to learn how to restore the second paragraph.

Splitting Paragraphs

You will have many occasions to split paragraphs. For example, a real paragraph should be unified and should express and develop a single idea. If you have more than one idea in a paragraph, you should split the paragraph into two paragraphs. To practice the technique for splitting a paragraph, follow these steps:

1. Use the mouse or the arrow keys to position the cursor on the character at which you want the split to occur. Because you are just experimenting, position the cursor at the beginning of any sentence in one of the letter's paragraphs. (You will rejoin the split paragraphs in a moment.)

2. Press Enter.

As you can see, Word breaks the paragraph into two parts. Press Enter again to leave a blank line between the two paragraphs, if you prefer.

To rejoin the paragraphs you split, simply select the new paragraph marks Word has inserted and press the Del key.

Deleting and Undeleting a Paragraph

As you inspect your letter after joining the two paragraphs, you decide that the entire first paragraph must go. The paragraph is too negative and violates the first principle of professional business communication: focus on the customer, not your own feelings and preoccupations.

> *Tip:* When you are deleting a large amount of text, you probably should delete the text to the Scrap. The Scrap is a temporary storage place for deleted text. The text stays there until you delete more text to the Scrap or exit Word. If you change your mind about the deletion, you can restore the Scrap text anywhere in your document.
>
> The fact that the Scrap retains text until you overwrite it (or quit Word) gives the Scrap an advantage over the Edit Undo command, which you also can use to restore text you have deleted. (You also can press Alt-Backspace to choose Undo.) To use Undo successfully, however, you must use Undo *immediately*—Undo always undoes your most recent action, so if you perform additional editing or command actions after the deletion, you cannot get the text back. If you delete text to the Scrap, you can perform *any* editing or command action (save cutting to the Scrap again) without losing the text permanently.

To delete the paragraph to the Scrap, follow these steps:

1. Place the cursor anywhere in the first paragraph.

Alt-F10
2. Select the paragraph.

    If you are using the keyboard, press Alt-F10. If you are using the mouse, move the pointer to the selection bar adjacent to the paragraph and click the *right* mouse button.

    The whole paragraph is selected (see fig. 2.10).

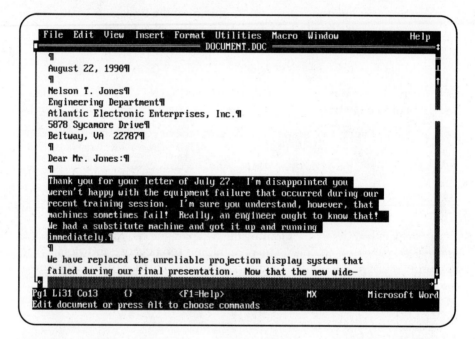

Fig. 2.10. Selecting a paragraph.

Shift-Del
3. Choose Edit Cut (Alt-ET) or use the Shift-Del keyboard shortcut to delete the selection.

    The paragraph is cut to the Scrap. To show you what's in the Scrap, the Scrap indicator on the status bar shows the beginning and ending characters of the deletion within the curly braces (see fig. 2.11).

4. Press Del to delete the extra paragraph mark.

    Note that pressing Del does not affect the Scrap.

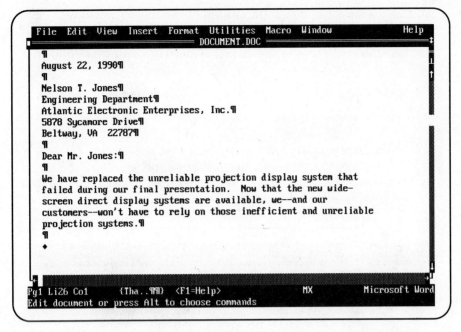

Fig. 2.11. Scrap's contents shown within curly braces on the status bar.

Users of previous Word versions should note that the Del key no longer cuts text to the Scrap. Del now cuts text permanently. You must press Shift-Del to route text to the Scrap.

Why did Microsoft make this change? For one reason, wiping out the text you are moving is very easy in previous versions. You delete the text to be moved to the Scrap and scroll to the place you want to paste the text. Say you get distracted by performing some minor edit, such as deleting an extra paragraph mark, and you press Del to perform the edit. Poof! The text you are moving is wiped out. In short, block moves are much less dangerous now that Del doesn't route deletions to the Scrap.

Inserting Additional Text

While looking over the remaining text of the letter, you realize that you goofed when you deleted the whole first paragraph. Nothing is wrong with the sentence "Thank you for your letter of July 27." You can bring the whole paragraph back from the scrap, but retyping the sentence is almost as easy. Follow these instructions to insert the new sentence at the beginning of the letter:

1. Check the status line. If the key indicator says OT, press Ins to cancel the Overtype mode.

2. Use the arrow keys or the mouse to place the cursor on the second paragraph mark below the salutation.

3. Type a new first paragraph, as shown highlighted in figure 2.12.

   Thank you for your letter of July 27. Mr. Jones, it was a pleasure meeting you and your staff! Won't you consider firming up your plans for training your staff in the security techniques we detailed in our presentation? If you will give me a call or drop me a note, I'll have a proposal ready for you right away.

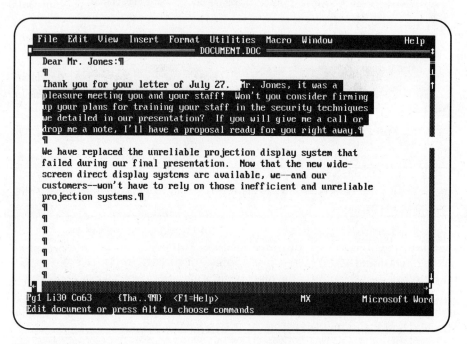

Fig. 2.12. Inserting text.

Note that existing text moves right and down automatically. This feature is called *automatic reformatting* and—like word wrapping—is one of the reasons computers make writing a pleasure.

Moving Text

This letter is looking better, but as you read over what you have inserted, you realize that some of this material belongs at the end of the letter, not the beginning. A good business letter closes with a call for action, but yours begins with one. You therefore decide to do a block move.

A *block move*, as the name suggests, involves moving a block of text from one part of a document to another. Doing block moves with Word is exceptionally easy.

If you are using the keyboard, you begin by selecting the text you want to move. (You can select any amount of text, from a single character to dozens of pages.) You then cut the text to the Scrap using the Edit Cut command (or the Shift-Del shortcut), move the cursor to the new location, and use the Edit Paste command (or the Shift-Ins shortcut). These steps are explained in the section entitled, "Performing a Block Move with the Keyboard."

If you are using a mouse, you use a special mouse technique that's really worth learning. Mouse users should skip to the section entitled, "Performing a Block Move with the Mouse."

Performing a Block Move with the Keyboard

Try this technique if you are using the keyboard. If you are using a mouse, skip to the next section.

1. Place the cursor on the M in Mr. Jones in the first paragraph.

2. Press F8 (Extend Selection).

   You see the EX code in the status bar.

3. Press Ctrl-Down arrow to select all the remaining text in the paragraph.

   The cursor-movement commands really come in handy. If Ctrl-Down arrow is new to you, re-read the section on cursor-movement keys in Chapter 1. You may have missed other useful keys.

   Your selection should duplicate the one in figure 2.12.

4. Choose Edit Cut (Alt-ET) or use the Shift-Del keyboard shortcut.

   Word cuts the text to the Scrap.

5. Move the cursor to the end mark (the diamond at the end of your document).

Shift-Ins   6. Choose **Edit Paste** (Alt-EP) or use the Shift-Ins keyboard shortcut.

Word pastes the Scrap text at the cursor's location, and your document now should look like the one in figure 2.13. (You may need to enter a blank line here and there, however.) Welcome to computer-assisted writing!

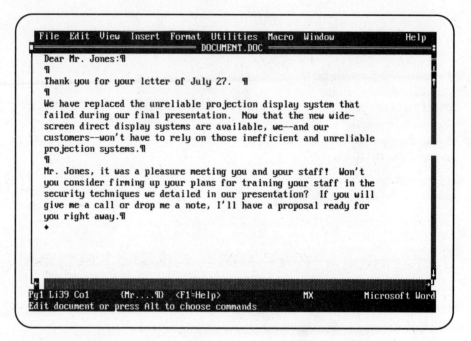

```
 File  Edit  View  Insert  Format  Utilities  Macro  Window          Help
═══════════════════════════════ DOCUMENT.DOC ══════════════════════════════
Dear Mr. Jones:¶
¶
Thank you for your letter of July 27.   ¶
¶
We have replaced the unreliable projection display system that
failed during our final presentation.  Now that the new wide-
screen direct display systems are available, we--and our
customers--won't have to rely on those inefficient and unreliable
projection systems.¶
¶
Mr. Jones, it was a pleasure meeting you and your staff!  Won't
you consider firming up your plans for training your staff in the
security techniques we detailed in our presentation?  If you will
give me a call or drop me a note, I'll have a proposal ready for
you right away.¶
◆



Pg1 Li39 Co1      {Mr....¶}  <F1=Help>            MX        Microsoft Word
Edit document or press Alt to choose commands
```

Fig. 2.13. The letter after the block move.

Users of previous Word versions should note that the Ins key no longer inserts text from the Scrap. Ins now toggles the Overtype mode on and off. You must press Shift-Ins to insert text from the Scrap.

Performing a Block Move with the Mouse

Mouse users can use an even easier and speedier technique to move text. To move text with a mouse, follow these steps:

1. Place the pointer on the M in Mr. Jones in the first paragraph.

2. Drag down until you have selected the whole paragraph, including the paragraph mark at the end.

Your selection should duplicate the one in figure 2.13.

3. Release the mouse button.

   The selection remains on-screen.

4. Move the pointer to the end mark (the diamond at the end of your document).

5. Hold down the Ctrl key and click the *right* mouse button.

   Word moves the selection to the pointer's location, and your document now should look like the one in figure 2.13. (You may need to enter or remove a blank line here and there, however.)

Setting Custom Tabs

Now you need to add the complimentary close, which is indented 3.5 inches from the left margin. To indent the close, you can use Word's built-in tab stops, which are placed every half inch across the screen. To introduce the Word techniques for setting custom tab stops, however, this tutorial shows you how to set a custom flush-left tab stop at the 3.5-inch mark. After you set this tab stop, you press Tab once to move the cursor 3.5 inches across the screen.

Creating the Custom Tab Format with the Keyboard

Read this section if you are using the keyboard. If you are using a mouse, skip to the next section.

1. Position the cursor on the end mark. If necessary, press Enter to leave a blank line beneath the last paragraph.

2. Choose **View Ruler** (Alt-VR) to display the Ruler (see fig. 2.14).

3. Activate the Ruler by pressing Shift-Ctrl-F10.

   The cursor moves to the Ruler.

4. Use the right-arrow key to move the cursor to the 3.5-inch mark on the Ruler.

5. Type *l* to select a flush-left tab stop at the cursor's location.

   An L appears on the Ruler.

6. Press Enter to confirm the custom tab stop.

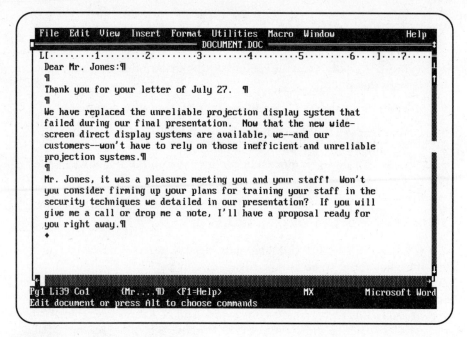

Fig. 2.14. Displaying the Ruler.

Note: The tab stop you have created affects only the currently selected paragraph. If you select more than one paragraph, the tab applies to all the paragraphs you select. Because you selected only one paragraph, the tab applies only to the paragraph in which the cursor was positioned when you pressed Shift-Ctrl-F10.

When you set a custom tab, Word cancels all the default tab stops to the left of the custom tab. In this paragraph, therefore, the cursor jumps to the 3.5-inch mark when you press Tab.

Creating the Custom Tab Format with the Mouse

If you are using a mouse, read this section. If you are using the keyboard, skip to the section entitled, "Typing the Complimentary Close."

1. Display the Ruler by clicking the Ruler icon in the right window border.

   The Ruler icon is an upside-down "T" positioned just above the upward-facing scroll arrow.

2. Check to make sure that the letter L is showing on the left side of the Ruler. If the L isn't showing, click the letter on the left side of the ruler until you see the L.

3. Point to the 3.5-inch mark on the Ruler and click the left mouse button.

Typing the Complimentary Close

Now that you have set a flush-left tab stop at 3.5 inches, typing the complimentary close is easy.

1. With the cursor positioned on the last line, the line that contains the 3.5-inch tab stop, press Tab.

   The cursor jumps to the 3.5-inch mark.

2. Type *Sincerely,* and press Enter four times.

   Note that Word copies the tab stops every time you press Enter. Tab formats are a paragraph format. When you press Enter, Word always carries the current paragraph format to the new paragraph.

3. Press Tab and type *Diane B. Smith, Director*. Press Enter.

4. Press Tab and type *Corporate Training*.

   Your letter now should look like the one in figure 2.15.

Checking Spelling

Correct spelling is essential in business correspondence. Just as you wouldn't show up at a job interview in jeans, you shouldn't send a letter that contains misspellings, and for exactly the same reasons.

Word 5.5's spelling checker, Spelling, represents a major improvement over the balky, slow, and confusing spelling checkers that afflicted previous versions of Word. In this tutorial, you learn how to perform a quick spell-check with this much-improved spelling checker, but without exploring all its capabilities. You learn more about Spelling in Chapter 6.

To use Word's spelling checker, follow these steps:

1. Press Ctrl-Home to position the cursor at the beginning of your document. Be sure that only one character is selected, not a word.

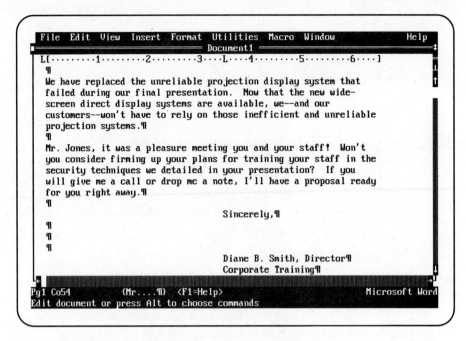

```
    File  Edit  View  Insert  Format  Utilities  Macro  Window              Help
    ══════════════════════════════ Document1 ══════════════════════════
    L[········1·········2·········3···L····4·········5·········6····]
    ¶
    We have replaced the unreliable projection display system that
    failed during our final presentation.  Now that the new wide-
    screen direct display systems are available, we--and our
    customers--won't have to rely on those inefficient and unreliable
    projection systems.¶
    ¶
    Mr. Jones, it was a pleasure meeting you and your staff!  Won't
    you consider firming up your plans for training your staff in the
    security techniques we detailed in your presentation?  If you
    will give me a call or drop me a note, I'll have a proposal ready
    for you right away.¶
    ¶
                              Sincerely,¶
    ¶
    ¶
    ¶
                              Diane B. Smith, Director¶
                              Corporate Training¶

  Pg1 Co54        {Mr....¶}  <F1=Help>                        Microsoft Word
  Edit document or press Alt to choose commands
```

Fig. 2.15. Letter with complimentary close added.

If you start **Spelling** with a word selected, **Spelling** checks the spelling of that one word and then quits.

F7

2. Choose Utilities **Spelling** (Alt-US) or use the F7 keyboard short-cut.

   Spelling starts by splitting the screen, leaving your document in the top window. The **Spelling** dialog box appears in the bottom half of the screen (see fig. 2.16).

   When **Spelling** encounters a word that's not in its dictionary (see fig. 2.16), it highlights the word in the document window and echoes the word in the **Not Found** field. The first word not found is `Albemarle`, which is spelled correctly.

3. Choose **Ignore** if you spelled the word correctly. If not, press Alt-R to activate the **Replace With** field and type the correction. (When you start typing, **Spelling**'s proposed correction, which is highlighted in the **Replace With** text box, disappears.) After you type the correct spelling, choose **Change**.

4. Repeat step 3 until you have ignored or corrected all the words that **Spelling** flags.

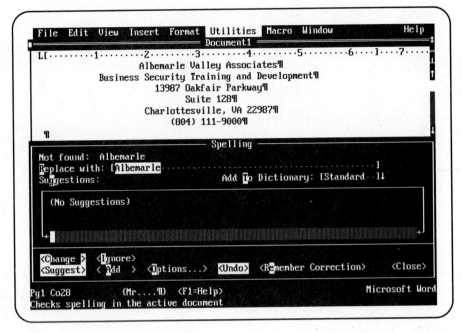

Fig. 2.16. *The Spelling dialog box.*

Spelling flags additional correctly spelled words, such as "Oakfair," "Charlottesville," and "Inc." Spelling also may flag words that you misspelled or mistyped. If so, correct them.

> ***Tip:*** Spelling flags many correctly spelled proper nouns, such as "Albemarle," "Oakfair," and "Charlottesville." When you spell-check your own letters and memos, you should add these words to Spelling's dictionary so that Spell doesn't flag them in the future. You learn how to add words to the dictionary in Chapter 6.

Previewing Your Letter before Printing

Your letter looks pretty good on-screen, but how will it look when printed? After all, you cannot see the whole page, including the margins, in the document window. Will the letter be balanced on the page? You can find out by using the File Print Preview command.

Ctrl-F9 To preview your letter on-screen, follow these steps:

1. Choose File Print Preview (Alt-FV) or use the Ctrl-F9 keyboard shortcut.

2. When the preview screen appears, as shown in figure 2.17, note how the text is laid out relative to the entire page.

   The letter is placed a little high on the page.

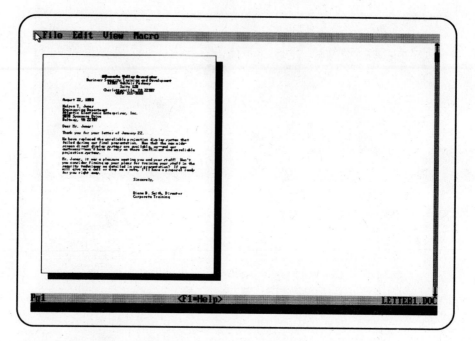

Fig. 2.17. Using Print Preview.

3. Choose File Exit Preview or press Esc to return to your document.

4. Place the cursor just below the return address (but above the date), and press Enter three or four times.

5. Choose File Print Preview (Alt-FV) or use the Ctrl-F9 keyboard shortcut.

   Now the letter is balanced on the page (see fig. 2.18).

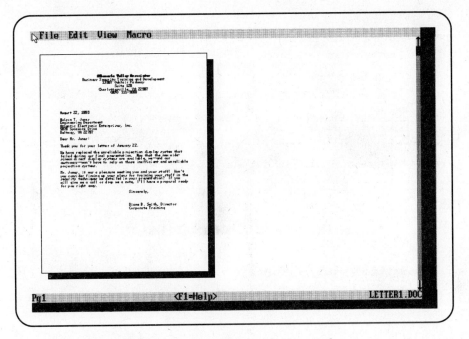

Fig. 2.18. Previewing the letter after balancing the text on the page.

Printing Your Letter

If Print Preview shows that your document is well balanced on the page, you are ready to print. You have revised the letter successfully and even checked your spelling.

Assuming that you have installed your printer with the SETUP program (see the Appendix), you can print directly from Print Preview.

1. Make sure that your printer is turned on and selected (ready to receive instructions) and that the cable is connected securely between your computer and the printer.

2. Choose **File Print** (Alt-FP) or use the Shift-F9 keyboard shortcut.　　　　　**Shift-F9**

   The Print dialog box appears (see fig. 2.19).

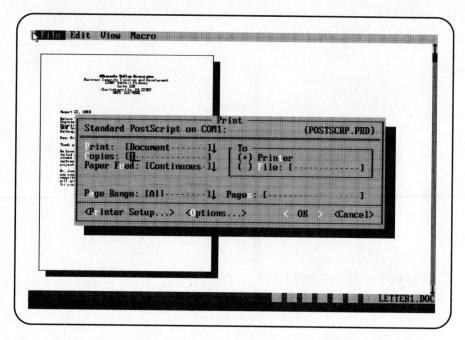

Fig. 2.19. *The Print dialog box.*

3. Choose OK to start printing.

   You accept all the default Print dialog box settings. You learn more about these settings, and the Print dialog box, in Chapter 7.

4. When printing is complete, choose **File Exit Preview** (or press Esc).

5. Choose **File Save** to save your letter.

6. Choose **File Exit Word** to return to DOS.

Users of previous Word versions should note that the Shift-F9 (Print) keyboard assignment is new; the previous key was Ctrl-F8.

Chapter Summary

In this chapter, you learned the basics of how to write, format, edit, and print a simple business letter. The next three chapters explore editing and formatting in detail, showing you many more command options and techniques. You will find complete lists of Word's text editing and formatting commands and their keyboard shortcuts. For now, however, congratulations on finishing this tutorial. You have learned a great deal about Word, and you have had an opportunity to explore this wonderful program's personality.

Quick Review

Block Move (Keyboard)

To move a block of text when using the keyboard:

1. Select the text.

2. Choose **Edit Cut** (Alt-ET) or use the Shift-Del keyboard shortcut.

3. Move the cursor to the place you want the text to appear.

4. Choose **Edit Paste** (Alt-EP) or use the Shift-Ins keyboard shortcut.

Block Move (Mouse)

To use a block of text when using a mouse:

1. Select the text.

2. Move the pointer to the place you want the text to appear.

3. Hold down the Ctrl key and click the right mouse button.

Boldface

To boldface text as you type:

1. Choose Format **Character** (Alt-TC) and choose the **B**old check box.

2. Choose OK to confirm your choice. Alternatively, use the Ctrl-B keyboard shortcut.

To boldface text you already have typed:

1. Select the text.

2. Choose Format **Character** (Alt-TC) and choose the **B**old check box.

3. Choose OK to confirm your choice. Alternatively, use the Ctrl-B keyboard shortcut.

Centered Alignment

To center text as you type:

1. Choose Format **P**aragraph (Alt-TP) and choose the **C**enter option button in the Alignment field.

2. Confirm your choice by choosing OK. Alternatively, use the Ctrl-C keyboard shortcut

To center text you already have typed:

1. Select the text.

2. Choose Format **P**aragraph (Alt-TP) and choose the **C**enter option button in the Alignment field.

3. Confirm your choice by choosing OK. Alternatively, use the Ctrl-C keyboard shortcut.

Custom Tab Stops (Keyboard)

To set custom tabs when using the keyboard:

1. Display the Ruler.

2. Activate the Ruler by pressing Shift-Ctrl-F10.

3. Press the right-arrow key to move the cursor to the location of the new tab stop.

4. Type *l* to select a flush-left tab stop at the cursor's location.

5. Repeat steps 3 and 4 to set additional tabs.

6. Press Enter to confirm the tabs and return to your document.

Custom Tab Stops (Mouse)

To set custom tabs when using a mouse:

1. Display the Ruler.

2. Check to make sure that the letter on the left side of the Ruler is L. If it isn't, click the letter until you see L.

3. Point to the place you want the tab stop to appear and click the left mouse button.

4. Repeat steps 2 and 3 to set additional flush left tabs.

Date

To insert the current date in a document:

1. Place the cursor where you want the date to appear.

2. Choose **Edit Glossary (Alt-EO)** and choose date in the **Names** list box. Next, choose **Insert.** Alternatively, type *date* directly in your document and press F3.

Deleting Text

To delete text:

1. Select the text.

2. Choose **Edit Cut (Alt-ET)** or use the Shift-Del keyboard shortcut.

Flush-Left Alignment

To align text flush left as you type:

1. Choose Format **Paragraph (Alt-TP)** and choose the **Left** option button in the **Alignment** field.

2. Confirm your choice by choosing OK. Alternatively, use the Ctrl-L keyboard shortcut

To align flush-left text you already have typed:

1. Select the text.

2. Choose Format **Paragraph (Alt-TP)** and choose the **Left** option button in the **Alignment** field.

3. Confirm your choice by choosing OK. Alternatively, use the Ctrl-L keyboard shortcut.

Joining Paragraphs

To join paragraphs:

1. Display the paragraph marks, if they're not already displayed.

2. Highlight the paragraph mark or marks that divide the two paragraphs.

3. Press Del.

Paragraph Marks

To display paragraph marks:

1. Choose View Preferences (Alt-VE).

2. In the Non-Printing Characters field, choose **Paragraph Marks**.

3. Choose OK.

Print Preview

To preview a document's appearance before printing:

1. Choose **File Print Preview** (Alt-FV) or use the Ctrl-F9 keyboard shortcut.

2. Choose **File Exit Preview** or press Esc to return to your document.

Printing

To print a document:

1. Choose **File Print** (Alt-FP).

2. Choose OK.

Ruler

To display the Ruler:

Choose View **Ruler** (Alt-VR) or click the Ruler icon (the upside-down "T") on the right window border.

Selecting Text

To select text using the F8 (Extend Selection) key:

1. Place the cursor on the first character to be selected.

2. Press F8 (Extend Selection).

3. Use the cursor-movement keys to expand the highlight until it covers all the text you want to select.

To select text with the mouse by dragging:

1. Position the pointer on the first character of the text you want to select.

2. Press the left mouse button and hold it down.

3. Move the mouse so that the highlight expands.

4. When the highlight covers all the text you want to select, release the button.

To select a line of text using the selection bar:

1. Move the pointer to the selection bar (the vertical column between the left edge of the text and the left window border) until the pointer changes tone or color.

2. Click the left mouse button.

To select a paragraph of text using the selection bar:

1. Move the pointer to the selection bar (the vertical column between the left edge of the text and the left window border) until the pointer changes tone or color.

2. Click the right mouse button.

Spelling

To check the spelling of the words in a document:

1. Press Ctrl-Home to position the cursor at the beginning of your document. Be sure that only one character is selected, not a word.

2. Choose Utilities Spelling (Alt-US) or use the F7 keyboard shortcut.

3. When Spelling flags a word, choose **Ignore** if you spelled the word correctly. If not, press Alt-R to activate the **Replace With** field and type the correction. After you type the correct spelling, choose **Change**.

4. Repeat step 3 until you have ignored or corrected all the words that Spelling flags.

Splitting Paragraphs

To split paragraphs:

1. Place the cursor where you want the paragraph split to occur.

2. Press Enter once or twice.

Part II

Extending Your Knowledge of Word

Includes

Word 5.5 Writing and Editing Strategies

Word 5.5 Formatting Strategies: Characters and Paragraphs

Word 5.5 Formatting Strategies: Page Formatting

Using the Thesaurus, Checking Spelling, and Controlling Hyphenation

Printing Your Work

Word 5.5 Writing and Editing Strategies

One of the joys of word processing is the ease with which you can create text. You can type away, and the computer handles line breaks automatically. When you are ready to revise your work, you find Word is infinitely adaptable—you can insert, delete, copy, and move as you please. You needn't send anything out the door until your text looks and reads as if it were created by a professional.

You already have learned much of what you need to know in order to create and edit your text with Word. You have learned how to enter text and how to correct errors with Backspace and Delete as you type. In Chapter 2, you learned how to harness Word's powerful tools for revision. This chapter expands your knowledge of Word writing and editing techniques. In this chapter, you learn how to do the following:

- Retrieve files you have created and saved to disk

- Create a new document using the **File New** command

- Use the full range of Word options (such as nonbreaking spaces and optional hyphens) as you create text

- Use the Overtype mode for quick editing

- Use the full range of options for selecting and deleting text

- Explore the many alternative ways you can copy and move text in your document

- Search your document for text you specify, or automatically replace one text string with another throughout your document

- Move around in a large document without paging through the document manually

You needn't memorize everything in this chapter in order to learn Word effectively. Word gives you many options for accomplishing basic editing tasks, so you can choose the methods that suit you best. For this reason, you should try all the techniques in this chapter, striving all the while to develop a "short list" of the techniques you prefer.

Retrieving Documents

You already have learned how to create new documents. In this section, you learn how to retrieve existing documents, which you then can expand, edit, or print as you want.

Starting Word and Opening a Document at the Same Time

In Chapter 1, you learned how to start Word and create a new, unnamed document. In this section, you learn how to start Word and display an existing, named document at the same time.

1. At the DOS prompt, activate the Word document directory.

   If your Word document directory is named C:\WORD\DOCS, for example, you type *cd c:\word\docs* and press Enter.

2. Type *word* followed by a space and the file name of the document you want to open. You can omit the period and the extension, as long as you allow Word to save the file with the default extension, DOC.

   To start Word and open the file LETTER1.DOC, for example, you type *word letter1*.

3. Press Enter.

Word starts and displays the document you named.

Retrieving Documents after Starting Word

After you start Word, use the **File Open** command to move documents from disk to Word's memory. Retrieving documents from the default directory, the one from which you started Word, is simple. You also can retrieve documents from other directories.

Users of previous Word versions should note that Version 5.5's new **File Open** command conveniently arranges in one dialog box all that was offered by the Transfer Load command in Version 5.0, including the many functions of the Transfer Load command that were accessible only by pressing F1 after choosing the command. In addition, the command no longer is destructive. Previously, if you chose Transfer Load without having saved your work and you failed to respond to Word's warning message, you could load the new document into the current window and wipe out your work. The **File Open** command creates a new window for the document you are opening, so destroying your work through the innocent act of loading another file is impossible.

Retrieving a Document from the Default Directory

The directory from which you start Word becomes the default directory for file storage and retrieval. If you start Word from C:\WORD\DOCS, for example, Word uses that directory to store and retrieve files (unless you specifically instruct the program to do otherwise).

To open an existing document with the File Open command, follow these steps:

1. Choose **File Open** (Alt-FO) or use the Alt-Ctrl-F2 keyboard shortcut.   **Alt-Ctrl-F2**

   The Open dialog box appears (see fig. 3.1).

   In the **File Name** field, you see the mask (*.DOC) that Word is using to search for your files. Files that conform to the mask are displayed in the Files list box.

2. Choose your document in the Files list box.

   (A reminder: If you are using the keyboard, press Alt-F to select the Files list box, and then use the arrow keys to highlight the file. If you are using a mouse, click the name of the file.)

   If you don't see your document in the Files list box, turn to the next section, "Retrieving a Document from Another Directory." Alternatively, type the document's path name and file name in the File Name field. To load the file REPORT4.DOC in the directory C:\REPORTS, for example, you type *c:\reports\report4* (you can omit the period and extension).

3. Choose OK.

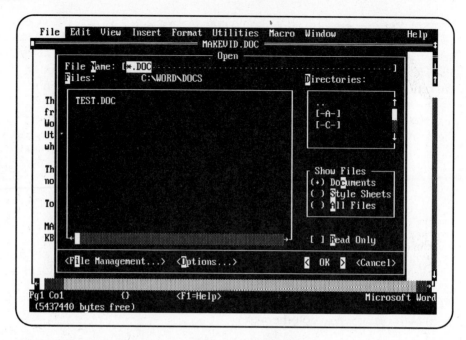

Fig. 3.1. *The Open dialog box.*

Retrieving a Document from Another Directory

If you don't see your document when you use the **File Open** dialog box, you probably saved your document to a directory other than the Word document directory. To use the **File Open** command to retrieve such a file, follow these steps:

1. Choose **File Open** (Alt-FO) or use the Alt-Ctrl-F2 keyboard shortcut.

   The Open dialog box appears (see fig. 3.1).

2. Activate the **Directories** list box.

   The **Directories** list box shows your disk's directories, relative to the position of the default directory (the one from which you started Word). The two dots (..) indicate the default directory's *parent directory*, the directory that is directly above the default directory in the tree structure. The directory name or names you may see below the two dots list the default directory's *subdirectories*, the directories that are nested within the default directory. (If you don't see any directory names, then this directory doesn't have any subdirectories.) You also see two or more *drive names*, such as [A] and [C]. You also may see [B] if your system is equipped with a second floppy drive.

3. Activate a new directory by choosing one of the directory names in the **Directories** list box. (To see a list of directories, you may need to choose the parent directory symbol—two dots—to move up one level in the disk's tree structure.) Look for your file in the **Files** list box.

4. Repeat step 3 until you find your file.

5. Choose OK.

If Word Cannot Find Your Document

If you try to open a document and see the message `File does not exist. Create now?`, choose Cancel and don't panic. Getting this message doesn't necessarily mean that your document has disappeared. The message simply may mean that one of the following situations has occurred:

- *The file isn't in the current drive or directory.* See the preceding section entitled "Retrieving a Document From Another Directory."

- *You saved the file with an extension other than DOC.* Activate the File **Name** text box, use the Backspace key to erase DOC, and type the correct extension.

- *The document is on some other disk.* To open a file on a floppy drive, activate the **Directories** field and choose [A] or [B].

If these techniques don't help you locate the file, you still may be able to locate the file by using the **File File Management** command, which is capable of searching your entire hard disk for a file that contains characters or summary information you specify. For more information on **File File Management**, see Chapter 8.

Defining the Word Document Directory

As you already have learned, you save time and trouble by starting Word from the document directory. If you forget to start Word from this directory, however, opening and saving documents becomes a hassle. You must use the **Directories** box to look for your document.

Tip: An excellent way around this problem is to define the default Word document directory in the Open and Save dialog boxes. Word "remembers" your choice, and your choice will be in effect the next time you use the program. After you define the default directory, the directory you are in when you start Word doesn't matter—the program will use this directory as the default directory for storage and retrieval purposes.

To define a default directory for your Word documents, follow these steps:

1. Choose **File Open** (Alt-FO) or use the Alt-Ctrl-F2 keyboard shortcut.

2. Choose **Options**.

   The File Options dialog box appears (see fig. 3.2).

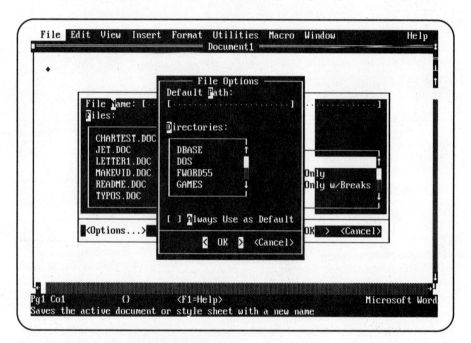

Fig. 3.2. The File Options dialog box.

3. Activate the **Directories** list box.

4. Choose the Word document directory in the **Directories** list box.

   If you don't see the Word document directory, choose the Word directory and press Enter. When the Word document directory appears (DOCS), press Enter.

You see the Word document directory (C:\WORD\DOCS) in the Default **Path** text box.

5. Choose the **Always Use as Default** check box.

6. Choose OK.

7. Choose Cancel to close the Open dialog box.

Note: The choice you make in the File Options dialog box also affects how Word stores your files when you choose the File **Save** and File Save **As** commands. Note also that the File Option dialog box accessed through these two commands is one and the same.

This solution isn't appropriate when you use more than one document directory. For example, many users like to create directories for different kinds of documents (they put letters in one and reports in another, for instance). Two or more users who share a computer, moreover, may prefer to store documents in directories bearing their names. Word's summary sheets, however, make these additional directories unnecessary. As you will learn in Chapter 8, you can use File Management to display a list of all the documents by a given author, or conforming to a specified keyword (such as "letter" or "report"), and then retrieve the document from the list.

Creating a New Document within Word

In Chapter 1, you learned how to start Word and create a new, unnamed document. In Chapter 2, you learned how to close a document after you have saved your work. In this section, you learn how to create a new, blank document within Word.

To create a new document, follow these steps:

1. Choose File **New**.

   The New dialog box appears (see fig. 3.3).

2. Choose OK.

Word creates the new document and places it in a new window.

In previous versions of Word, creating a new document was risky because you had to save and clear the window first. In Version 5.5, Word creates a new window for the new document. If one or more windows already are open, they move to the background. You can activate these windows and save them later. For more information on Version 5.5's convenient windowing features, see Chapter 9.

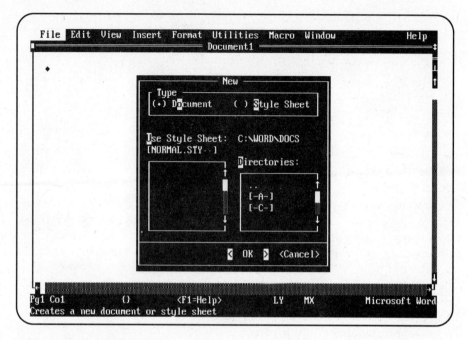

Fig. 3.3. The New dialog box.

Note: You can open up to nine documents simultaneously. If more than one document is open at once, you can activate the document you want by using the Window menu. The box at the bottom of the Window menu shows the names of all the documents that are currently open, even if you cannot see more than one of the documents on-screen. To activate a hidden document, choose its name in the Window menu. You learn more about working with two or more documents in Chapter 9.

More about Creating Text with Word

In Chapters 1 and 2, you learned the basics of creating a new document with Word. This section presents additional information about creating text with Word. You may find some of this material helpful to you for specific writing purposes.

Using Nonbreaking Spaces

Occasionally, you may want to prevent Word from separating two words (such as a first and last name) or breaking a mathematical formula when the program prints your document. (The line breaks you see on-screen aren't necessarily the ones Word uses when you print.) To prevent Word from separating two words, connect them with a nonbreaking space.

To enter a nonbreaking space, follow these steps:

1. Type the first word.

2. Press Ctrl-Shift-Space bar.

3. Type the second word.

Rather than create a line break between the words linked by a nonbreaking space, Word moves both words to the next line if necessary.

Using Nonbreaking Hyphens

If you are typing two words or numbers separated by a hyphen, as in "E. E. Evans-Pritchard," you may want to prevent Word from placing a line break at the hyphen. Rather than type an ordinary hyphen, use a nonbreaking hyphen.

To enter a nonbreaking hyphen, follow these steps:

1. Type the first word.

2. Press Ctrl-Shift-Hyphen

3. Type the second word.

Word will not create a line break between the words linked by a nonbreaking hyphen; instead, the program moves both words down to the next line.

Word offers additional hyphenation options, including a powerful automatic hyphenation utility. For more information on hyphenation, see Chapter 6.

Using Optional Hyphens

A lengthy word can cause Word to insert large, unsightly spaces between the words of a line as the program attempts to even the right margin. The narrower the line length, the likelier that a lengthy word will cause this problem.

To solve this problem, you can use automatic hyphenation, as explained in Chapter 6. Word's automatic hyphenation utility, however, works only for words contained in its hyphenation dictionary, which isn't as large as the spelling dictionary. Lengthy words that are specific to a special area of professional or technical expertise are not likely to be found in the hyphenation dictionary Even if you run the Utilities Hyphenate command, therefore, your document still may contain unsightly gaps caused by lengthy words.

You can avoid this problem by inserting *optional hyphens* in such words when you type them. An optional hyphen is a special hyphen that doesn't appear unless Word needs the hyphen to even the margin.

To enter an optional hyphen, hold down the Ctrl key and type a hyphen.

Using Foreign and Technical Characters

The IBM Personal Computer was designed for a world market, so its built-in set of 254 characters includes most of the special symbols needed for work in European languages as well as English. In addition, the character set includes Greek and other characters commonly used in technical and scientific writing, as well as graphics characters.

To enter these characters, you need to know the character's code (a code of two or three numbers). You can find the code number of a given character by opening the document called CHARTEST.DOC, which is in Word's directory.

To enter a special character, follow these steps:

1. Press the Num Lock key to activate the numeric keypad.

    You see the code NL on the status bar.

2. Hold down the Alt key and type the two- or three-letter code.

Word enters the character after you finish typing the code and release the Alt key.

> *Tip:* Don't try to type graphics characters manually to create lines and boxes—Word's Line Draw mode does this for you. You just use the arrow keys, and Word takes care of drawing lines, making corners, and joining other lines. You learn how to use the Line Draw mode in Chapter 17.

> *Caution:* Your printer may not be able to print all the characters you see in CHARTEST.DOC, even though you can see them on the screen. To find out which characters will print, display CHARTEST.DOC and choose the **File Print** command.

Using Line Numbers

If you are planning to perform legal or technical editing, displaying line numbers on the status line may be helpful. Word counts lines per page, starting from the top, and excluding page numbers and headers. You choose whether you want Word to count blank spaces as lines, or to count only lines containing text.

To turn on line numbers, follow these steps:

1. Choose View Preferences (Alt-VE).

2. Choose the Show Line Numbers check box.

3. If you want, choose the Count Blank Space check box.

4. Choose OK.

You see the line number indicator between the page number and column number indicators on the status bar (see fig. 3.4).

```
Pg1 Li1 Co1        {}          <F1=Help>                    Microsoft Word
Edit document or press Alt to choose commands
```

Fig. 3.4. Status bar with line number displayed.

Caution: If you are working with a slow computer, think twice about turning on line numbers. With line numbers turned on, Word must recalculate the current line number position every time you move the cursor. That can take time on 8088s and slow 286 computers. If Word performs sluggishly after you turn line numbers on, turn line numbers off by repeating the procedure you used to turn them on.

Starting a New Line without Breaking the Paragraph

As you type with Word, the program "wraps" text down to the next line if the text goes beyond the right margin. You don't press Enter until you want to start a new paragraph. Sometimes, however, you may want to break the line before the text reaches the right margin—for example, when you are typing a table, a poem, or a return address. You can break the line in the following two ways:

- Press Enter. Word starts a new paragraph.

- Use the Newline command (Shift-Enter). The Newline command breaks the line *without* starting a new paragraph. All the lines you type with the Newline command remain a single paragraph, so far as Word is concerned, for editing or formatting purposes.

  Why use the Newline command? The answer lies in Word's mechanical definition of the word "paragraph." You don't normally think of a poem or a return address as a paragraph, but if you break the lines with the Newline command, Word regards them as a paragraph. You then can use any editing or formatting command applicable to entire paragraphs to affect all the lines immediately. You can select the entire poem or the entire return address, for example, by placing the cursor anywhere within the body of text and pressing Alt-F10.

  You will find many uses for the Newline command in this book. Subsequent chapters alert you to situations where the Newline command is especially helpful.

Starting a New Page

Word paginates your document automatically, starting a new page when you run out of room on the current page. Sometimes, however, you may want to start a new page before you run out of room—at the end of a chapter of a business report, for example. In such cases, you can start a new page manually.

To force Word to start a new page, do the following:

1. Place the cursor where you want Word to start a new page.

2. Choose Insert **B**reak (Alt-IB).

   You see the Break dialog box, and the **P**age button is selected.

3. Choose OK.

   You can press Ctrl-Enter in place of steps 2 and 3.

A manual page break looks like a row of dots without spaces. A manual page break differs from an automatic page break, in which the dots are separated by spaces. (Fig. 3.5 compares the two types of page breaks.) Another way to tell the difference between automatic and manual page breaks is that you cannot select or position the cursor on an automatic page break, but you can select a manual page break. You can delete a manual page break if you decide that you don't need it.

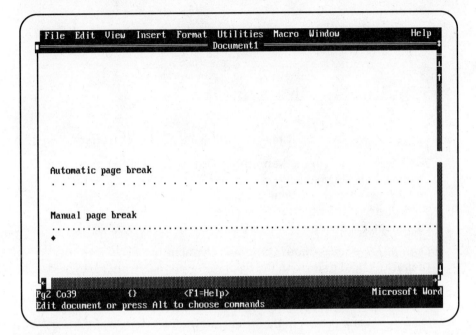

Fig. 3.5. Automatic and manual page breaks.

To remove a manual page break, do the following:

1. Place the cursor anywhere on the manual page break.

2. Press Del.

Caution: Use manual page breaks sparingly, particularly if you plan to subject your document to moderate or heavy editing. As you delete and insert text above the forced page break, the manual break may become unnecessary. As a general rule, you should insert manual page breaks only when you have finished editing your document and are ready to print.

Tip: Don't use manual page breaks to keep headings from appearing by themselves at the bottom of a page. A far better method is to format headings by choosing the With Next check box in the Keep Paragraph field of the Paragraph dialog box. For more information on ways to format headings, see the section "Controlling Page Breaks," in Chapter 5.

Displaying Hidden Characters

In Chapter 2, you used the View Preferences command to display paragraph marks. If you want, you can display the following hidden characters as well:

- *Tabs.* Choose **Tabs** in the Nonprinting Characters field to turn on the display of tab characters. Every time you press the Tab key, Word enters a tab character in your document. If you turn on the display of these characters (a right arrow), you can edit more easily. To delete a tab indent, for example, you just delete the tab character.

- *Optional Hyphens.* Choose Optional Hyphens in the Nonprinting Characters field to turn on the display of optional hyphens, even if Word doesn't need them to even the margin. The optional hyphens appear as if they were ordinary hyphens.

- *Spaces.* Choose **Spaces** in the Nonprinting Characters field to turn on the display of space marks (a small dot positioned above the line to distinguish space marks from periods). Nonbreaking spaces are blank, so you can distinguish them from ordinary spaces.

- *Hidden Text.* Choose Hidden Text in the Nonprinting Characters field to turn off the display of text formatted with the **Hidden** check box. By default, hidden text is displayed.

- *Paragraph Marks and Newline Characters.* Choose **Paragraph Marks** in the Nonprinting Characters field to turn on the display of Newline characters (right arrows) as well as paragraph marks.

- *All.* Choose Show **All** in the Nonprinting Characters field to turn on the display of all hidden characters.

Tip: Experienced Word users like to display paragraph marks and tabs while editing. Deleting paragraphs and indents is easier, and deleting a paragraph or tab character by accident is less likely. Unless you must control spacing very carefully, however, you should avoid displaying spaces. Telling the difference between the space character and a period is difficult.

Selecting Text for Editing and Formatting

Selecting text is a basic Word skill. You select text to perform editing operations (such as copying, deleting, or moving) as well as for formatting purposes (such as centering or boldfacing).

Word gives you many keyboard and mouse options for selecting text. You can select words, sentences, paragraphs, and even the whole document. In most cases, these units of text correspond to the way they are used in everyday language. But you need to realize that Word defines units of text in a "mechanical" way. Table 3.1 explains the rules Word follows to distinguish between such units as "words" and "characters."

Table 3.1
How Word Defines Units of Text

Text unit	Includes
Character	Anything you can type at the keyboard, as well as the paragraph and Newline marks Word inserts in your document
Word	Any group of characters that is set off by spaces, tabs, hyphens, or punctuation (can even be a group of characters like *MXPTX11995*); includes trailing spaces but not punctuation
Line	All the characters on a single line
Sentence	Any group of characters that is surrounded by sentence-ending punctuation (periods, question marks, exclamation marks) or by a paragraph or Newline mark (can even be a jumbled group of characters such as *Mrpph alkjd 331.*); includes trailing punctuation and spaces
Paragraph	Any group of characters that ends with a paragraph mark (can even be a one-word heading); includes the trailing paragraph mark
Column	A vertical line of characters on the screen; (if you use the screen borders, you can display 75 columns of text on the screen; if you hide the borders by using the Options command, you can display 77)
Document	All the characters in a document except footnotes, running heads, and page numbers

Pay special attention to what is included with each unit in Word's definitions. When you select a word and delete it, Word also deletes the space that follows the word. When you select a sentence and delete it, Word deletes the punctuation and spaces that immediately follow the sentence. When you select a paragraph and delete it, Word also deletes the paragraph mark, eliminating the blank line that would have remained on the screen after the paragraph was deleted.

(Note in table 3.1 that Word can select columns, or vertical rectangles of text, on-screen. This technique is extremely handy for rearranging columns of data in tables but seldom used for other purposes. For this reason, selecting columns is discussed in Chapter 11.)

Whether you are using the keyboard or a mouse, you can select fixed or variable amounts of text. Selecting a fixed amount of text means that you select one of the text units that Word knows how to identify, such as a word, a sentence, a line, or a paragraph (see table 3.1). When you select a variable unit of text, as you did in Chapter 2 by using F8 (Extend Selection) or the dragging technique, you select just the amount of text you want—such as part of a word, part of a sentence, or part of a paragraph. You also can use this technique to expand the highlight to include additional text after you select a fixed amount.

As you can see in table 3.1, Word defines a word to include trailing spaces, a sentence to include trailing punctuation and spaces, and a paragraph to include the trailing paragraph mark. When you are deleting or moving text, therefore, always use commands that select these fixed units. That way, you don't have any extraneous spaces, punctuation, or lines left after you perform the editing operation.

Selecting Fixed Units of Text with the Keyboard

As you learned in Chapter 2, you can use the F8 (Extend Selection) key in two ways. You can use the key to select variable amounts of text. But you also can use F8 to select fixed amounts of text, such as the line `Albemarle Valley Associates` at the top of the business letter you created.

To select fixed amounts of text with the F8 (Extend Selection) key, follow these steps:

1. Press F8.

   You see the code `EX` in the status line.

2. Press F8 again until you have selected the amount of text you want.

The second time you press F8, you select the current word. The third time, the current sentence. The fourth time, the current paragraph. The fifth time, the whole document.

If you select more text than you wanted with F8, press Shift-F8 to "shrink" the selection back down (in the sequence document, paragraph, sentence, word, character).

3. Press Esc to exit the Extend Selection mode.

    Word leaves the highlight on the screen.

You also can press certain function keys to select fixed units of text, which are listed in table 3.2.

Table 3.2
Selecting Fixed Units of Text with the Keyboard

To select	Press this key
Current word	Alt-F6
Current sentence	Alt-F8
Current paragraph	Alt-F10
Whole document	Ctrl-5 (on the numeric keypad)

Tip: Users of previous versions of Word should note the new functions of the F8 (Extend Selection) key, which formerly was F6. Now you can press Extend Selection more than once, and as you do, select fixed amounts of text. This function has rendered obsolete many of the former version's function key assignments for text selection. These assignments have changed completely, and only three fixed-unit selection keys remain on the function key pad (Alt-F6, Alt-F8, Alt-F10).

Selecting Fixed Units of Text with the Mouse

Mouse users also can select fixed units of text. Try some of the techniques listed in table 3.3. You are sure to find several of them useful.

Mouse users of previous Word versions should note that every one of the mouse techniques in table 3.3 departs from the Version 5.0 techniques. The Version 5.5 techniques now are more in line with Macintosh standards (Macintosh mice have only one button!), but you have to relearn them.

Table 3.3
Selecting Fixed Units of Text with the Mouse

To select	Point to	Mouse action
Word	Word	Double-click the left button.
Line	Selection bar	Place the pointer in the selection bar and click the left button.
Sentence	Sentence	Place the pointer in the sentence, hold down the Ctrl key, and click the left button.
Paragraph	Selection bar	Place the pointer in the selection bar and double-click the left button.
Document	Selection bar	Place the pointer in the selection bar, hold down Ctrl, and click the left button.

When you are selecting a paragraph for formatting (not editing), you needn't highlight the whole paragraph. Just position the cursor anywhere within the paragraph and use the Format **P**aragraph command. For more information on paragraph formatting, see Chapter 4.

Selecting Variable Amounts of Text with the Keyboard

In Chapter 2, you learned how to use the F8 (Extend) key to select variable amounts of text. The following is a quick review of how to extend the selection with the F8 (Extend) key:

1. Place the cursor where you want the highlight to begin.

2. Press F8 (Extend Selection).

   The code EX appears in the status bar.

3. Press any cursor-movement key to expand the highlight. If you go too far, use the cursor-movement keys to shrink the highlight back to its proper size.

4. When you finish expanding the highlight, press Esc to exit the Extend Selection mode. Alternatively, choose a Format command.

You also can select variable amounts of text by using the Shift key. Follow these steps to select variable amounts of text:

1. Hold down the Shift key and press any key that moves the cursor.

   As long as you hold down the Shift key, the highlight is "anchored" at the cursor's original location, and you can expand the highlight as needed.

2. When you finish expanding the highlight, release the Shift key.

The highlight remains on-screen. To cancel the highlight, touch one of the cursor-movement keys.

Selecting Variable Amounts of Text with the Mouse

In Chapter 2, you learned how to use the dragging technique to select variable amounts of text. This section contains more information and a variation of this technique that uses the Shift key.

To select variable amounts of text with a mouse, follow these steps:

1. Position the pointer on the first character of the text you want to select.

2. Press a mouse button and hold it down.

   If you hold down the left button, Word expands the selection character by character.

   If you hold down the right button, the selection expands word by word.

   If you hold down both buttons, the selection expands sentence by sentence.

3. Move the mouse so that the highlight expands.

4. When the highlight covers all the text you want to select, release the button.

You can select variable amounts of text easily this way. If you drag to the top or bottom window borders, Word scrolls the screen and continues to expand the highlight.

To select variable amounts of text with the mouse and the Shift key, do the following:

1. Position the pointer at the beginning of the text you want to select.

2. Click the left mouse button to place the cursor at this location.

3. Move the mouse pointer to the place you want the selection to end.

4. Hold down the Shift key and press the left mouse button.

Deleting Text

You can delete text in the following ways with Word 5.5:

- *Backspace.* Press this key to rub out the character to the left of the cursor. Hold down the key to continue rubbing out the characters left of the cursor. To recover text deleted this way, you must choose Edit Undo immediately after performing the deletion (and before you perform any other action).

- *Del.* Press this key to rub out the character on which the cursor is positioned. Hold down the key to delete characters to the right of the cursor. To recover text deleted this way, you must choose Edit Undo immediately after performing the deletion (and before you perform any other action).

- *Shift-Del.* Press this key combination to delete the selection to the Scrap, where the text can be recovered later in the operating session (provided no additional text has been cut to the Scrap).

- *Edit Cut command (Alt-ET).* Same as pressing Shift-Del.

> **Caution:** Users of previous Word versions should note that the Del and Shift-Del keys have exchanged functions. Del is now destructive: it doesn't route the deletion to the Scrap. Shift-Del does route the selection to the Scrap. Because you probably will use Del to cut most text, bear in mind that you cannot recover these deletions unless you choose Undo immediately. If you think you may want to recover the cut text, use Shift-Del.

You also can cut text to glossaries, where the text can be stored for use in a subsequent operating session. For more information on glossaries, see Chapter 12.

Using the Overtype Mode

Most word processing programs have two text-creation modes, an Insert mode and an Overtype mode. In the Insert mode, which is Word's default mode, the text you type pushes existing text to the right and down. In the Overtype mode, which you can access by pressing Ins, the text you type replaces existing text.

Some people are content to write in the Insert mode at all times, but you may want to experiment with the Overtype mode. Overtype can be useful when you are doing extensive rewriting. Writing experts know that wiping out a bad paragraph and rewriting the paragraph from scratch usually is better than just adding clarifying words here and there.

Note: The Backspace key does not work in the Overtype mode the way it does in the Insert mode. The Backspace key doesn't delete text left of the cursor. To restore the Backspace key to full functionality, press Ins until the OT code disappears from the status line.

Moving and Copying Text

As you learned in Chapter 2, moving text with Word is easy, whether you are using the keyboard or the mouse. Using variants of the same techniques, you also can copy text from one location in your document to another.

When you are moving or copying text from one part of a document to another, or from one document to a second document, try using two windows. You can display both locations (the source and destination) at the same time so that you can keep track of what you are doing more easily. Because you don't have to scroll or load a second document while the text you cut or copied is in the Scrap, you have less chance of using a command that wipes out that text.

Moving Text: A Review

Keyboard and mouse techniques for performing block moves were discussed in Chapter 2, but you may want to scan the following quick review.

To perform a block move with the keyboard, do the following:

1. Select the text.

2. Choose **Edit Cut** (Alt-ET) or use the Shift-Del keyboard shortcut.

3. Move the cursor to the place you want the text to appear.

4. Choose **Edit Paste** (Alt-EP) or use the Shift-Ins keyboard shortcut.

To perform a block move with the mouse, do the following:

1. Select the text.

2. Move the pointer to the place you want the text to appear.

3. Hold down the Ctrl key and click the right mouse button.

Copying Text

You can use the keyboard or the mouse to copy text you typed previously. You also can use the F4 (Repeat) key to repeat text you just typed.

Ctrl-Ins   To copy text with the keyboard, do the following:

1. Select the text.

2. Choose Edit Copy (Alt-EC) or use the Ctrl-Ins keyboard shortcut.

3. Move the cursor to the place you want the text to appear.

4. Choose Edit **Paste** (Alt-EP) or use the Shift-Ins keyboard shortcut.

To copy text with the mouse, do the following:

1. Select the text you want to copy.

2. Move the pointer to the place you want the text to appear.

3. Hold down the Ctrl and Shift keys and click the right button.

Repeating the Last Text You Typed

The Edit Repeat command key has its own special memory. This memory stores all the keys you have pressed since the last time you moved the cursor to enter new text or issued a command. You can use Edit Repeat to copy text throughout your document. When you choose Edit Repeat, Word enters at the cursor's location whatever is stored in Edit Repeat's memory.

To copy text with Edit Repeat, follow these steps:

F4   1. Press Esc twice to clear Edit Repeat's memory.

2. Type the text you want to copy.

3. Move the cursor to a new location and choose Edit Repeat (Alt-ER). Alternatively, use the F4 keyboard shortcut.

   The text you typed appears at the new location.

4. To repeat the text again, move the cursor to another new location and choose Edit Repeat.

You can continue to move the cursor to new locations and choose **Edit Repeat** to repeat the text throughout your document.

Note: If you press Enter, type more text, or give a command, you clear F4's memory.

Mouse users of previous versions should note that the mouse commands for transposing text have been eliminated.

Searching for Text

When you create a document that's several pages long, searching the document on-screen for a certain passage is tedious—and tiresome for the eyes. Fortunately, Word can search for you. Using the Search command, you can specify search text—a series of up to 254 characters that you want Word to find. Word then goes through your document at high speed, trying to find an exact match for the search text in your document. Whenever you think, "I know I discussed such-and-such somewhere, but where?" use the Search command. Put that expensive computer to work.

Note: You can search your entire document or just the selected text. If you select text before choosing **Edit Search**, Word searches only the text you selected. If you want to search your whole document, make sure that only one character is selected before launching the search.

Doing a Simple Search

A simple search doesn't employ options, such as the **Whole Word** and **Match Upper/Lowercase** options in the Search dialog box. A simple search searches down, toward the end of your document. You learn more about search options in "Customizing the Search," later in this section.

To perform a simple search, follow these steps:

1. Press Ctrl-Home to position the cursor on the first character of the document.

   The search will begin from the cursor's location.

2. Choose **Edit Search** (Alt-ES).

   The Search dialog box appears (see fig. 3.6). The default options initiate a search in the **Down** direction (from the cursor to the end of the document).

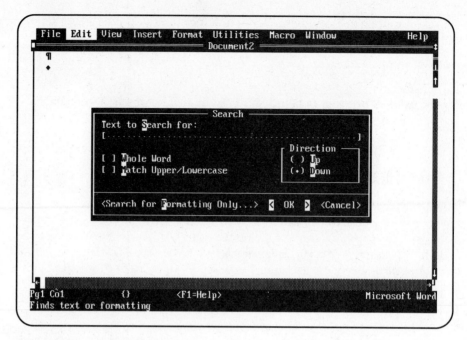

Fig. 3.6. The Search dialog box.

3. Type the search text in the Text to Search For field.

   You can type up to 254 characters, including spaces and punctuation marks.

4. Choose OK.

Word searches for the search text. If Word finds a match for the text string you entered, the program scrolls the screen to the first match and highlights it. If Word finds a match for your search text, and you want to look for additional places in your document that contain the text, choose Edit Search again or press Shift-F4.

If the search didn't commence from the beginning of the document, you see the message Reached end of document. Continue searching at beginning?. Choose Yes to continue the search or No to abandon the search.

If Word cannot find the search text, you see the message Search text not found. Choose OK.

To speed up the search, keep the search string short, but not so short that Word finds unwanted matches. If you want to search for *all-inclusive*, for example, type the whole word. If you use just the first few letters, *all*, Word will find *alley*, *alligator*, and *all-important*, and anything else beginning with *all*.

Customizing the Search

You can tailor your search using the Match Upper/Lowercase and Whole Word check boxes in the Search dialog box. For example, you can customize a search so that Word matches *HIMALAYAS*, but not *Himalayas*. This search, a *case-sensitive* search, tries to match the exact case pattern (lower- and uppercase) of the text you enter. You also can customize a search so that Word matches *cat*, but not *catatonic*, *catastrophe*, or *Magnificat in C Major*. This search, a *whole-word* search, matches the search string only if the "match" is surrounded by spaces or punctuation.

To perform a case-sensitive search, do the following:

1. Press Ctrl-Home to position the cursor on the first character of the document.

2. Choose Edit Search (Alt-ES).

3. Type the search text in the Text to Search For field.

4. Choose the Match Upper/Lowercase check box.

5. Choose OK.

To perform a whole-word search, do the following:

1. Press Ctrl-Home to position the cursor on the first character of the document.

2. Choose Edit Search (Alt-ES).

3. Type the search text in the Text to Search For field.

4. Choose the Whole Word check box.

5. Choose OK.

Replacing Text

Like Edit Search, the Edit Replace command finds text that matches the search text you specify. But Edit Replace has one crucial difference: it deletes the text that matches the search string and replaces that text with other text you specify.

You can replace text with or without confirmation. If you search with confirmation, Word displays each substitution it proposes to make and asks for your approval before making the substitution. If you search without confirmation, Word performs the substitutions automatically, throughout your document, without showing them to you or asking your approval.

> ***Caution:*** Avoid searching without confirmation. Word may make substitutions you didn't anticipate. Suppose that you want to remove the word "very" throughout your document. Word then proceeds to remove the characters "very" from the words "every" and "everything," leaving "e" and "ething" in their place. (You could have forestalled this accident by choosing the **W**hole Word check box, but you still should avoid replace operations without confirmation.)

Note: You can search your whole document, or just the selected text. If you select text before choosing **E**dit **R**eplace, Word performs the replacements only within the text you selected. If you want to replace text throughout your document, make sure that only one character is selected before launching the search.

To replace text, follow these steps:

1. Press Ctrl-Home to position the cursor at the beginning of the document.

2. Choose the **E**dit **R**eplace (Alt-EE) command.

   The Replace dialog box appears (see fig. 3.7).

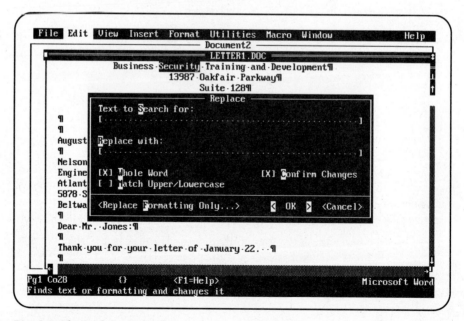

Fig. 3.7. *The Replace dialog box.*

3. In the **Text to Search For** field, type the search text.

   You can type up to 254 characters.

4. In the **Replace With** field, type the text you want to substitute for the search text.

   Again, you can type up to 254 characters.

5. Choose the **Whole Word** check box option.

6. If you want, choose the **Match Upper/Lowercase** check box.

7. Make sure that the **Confirm Changes** check box is checked.

8. Choose OK.

   If Word finds a match, a second Replace dialog box appears (see fig. 3.8).

9. Choose **Yes** to make the replacement, **No** to skip this selection and continue searching, or Cancel to return to your document.

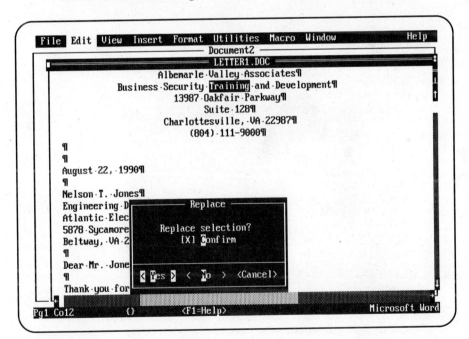

Fig. 3.8. The second Replace dialog box.

Moving Around in a Lengthy Document

As you create and edit text, Word actively paginates your document, inserting automatic page breaks where needed, and adjusting them as necessary. (If you don't see page breaks, choose Utilities Customize (Alt-UU) and make sure that the Background Pagination check box is checked.) You can jump directly to a page number you specify by using the Edit Goto command.

F5   To jump to a specific page, follow these steps:

1. Choose Edit Goto (Alt-EG) or use the F5 keyboard shortcut.

   The Go To dialog box appears (see fig. 3.9). Note that the Page option button is selected.

2. Type the page number in the Go To field.

3. Choose OK.

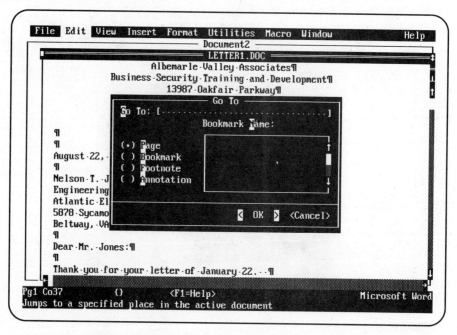

Fig. 3.9. The Go To dialog box.

Chapter Summary

This chapter rounded out your knowledge of Word writing and editing techniques. You learned how to accomplish many fundamental editing tasks, such as retrieving files; using nonbreaking spaces and hyphens; selecting, deleting, inserting, copying, and transposing text; searching for and replacing text; and moving around in a lengthy document.

To complete your editing skills, however, be sure to read Chapters 9, 10, and 12. Multiple-window, outlining, and glossary techniques aid your revision efforts in ways that are unimaginable without computer experience—and without Word.

Quick Review

Block Move (Keyboard)

To move a block of text when using the keyboard:

1. Select the text.

2. Choose **Edit Cut** (Alt-ET) or use the Shift-Del keyboard shortcut.

3. Move the cursor to the place you want the text to appear.

4. Choose **Edit Paste** (Alt-EP) or use the Shift-Ins keyboard shortcut.

Block Move (Mouse)

To move a block of text when using a mouse:

1. Select the text.

2. Move the pointer to the place you want the text to appear.

3. Hold down the Ctrl key and click the right mouse button.

Copying Text (Mouse)

To copy text when using a mouse:

1. Select the text you want to copy.

2. Move the pointer to the place you want the text to appear.

3. Hold down the Ctrl and Shift keys and click the right button.

Copying Text (Edit Repeat)

To copy text by using **Edit Repeat**:

1. Press Esc twice to clear **Edit Repeat**'s memory.

2. Type the text you want to copy.

3. Move the cursor to a new location and choose **Edit Repeat** (Alt-ER). Alternatively, use the F4 keyboard shortcut.

4. To repeat the text again, move the cursor to another new location and choose **Edit Repeat** again.

Copying Text (Keyboard)

To copy text when using the keyboard:

1. Select the text.

2. Choose **Edit Copy** (Alt-EC) or use the Ctrl-Ins keyboard shortcut.

3. Move the cursor to the place you want the text to appear.

4. Choose **Edit Paste** (Alt-EP) or use the Shift-Ins keyboard shortcut.

Default Document Directory

To choose the default document directory:

1. Choose **File Open** (Alt-FO) or use the Alt-Ctrl-F2 keyboard shortcut.

2. Choose **Options**.

3. Activate the **Directories** list box.

4. Choose the Word document directory in the **Directories** list box.

5. Choose the **Always Use as Default** check box.

6. Choose OK.

7. Choose Cancel to close the Open dialog box.

Deleting Text

To delete text permanently:

- Press Backspace to delete the character left of the cursor.
- Press Del to delete the character on which the cursor is positioned.

To delete text to the Scrap:

1. Choose **Edit Cut** (Alt-ET) or press Shift-Del.

Foreign and Technical Characters

To enter foreign and technical characters:

1. Press the Num Lock key to activate the numeric keypad.

   You see the code NL on the status bar.

2. Hold down the Alt key and type the two- or three-letter code.

   Word enters the character after you finish typing the code and release the Alt key.

Go To a Page

To go to a particular page:

1. Choose **Edit Goto** (Alt-EG) or use the F5 keyboard shortcut.
2. Type the page number in the **Go** To field.
3. Choose OK.

Line Numbers

To display numbers on the status line:

1. Choose **View Preferences** (Alt-VE).
2. Choose the Show Line **Numbers** check box.
3. If you want, choose the Count Blank Space check box.
4. Choose OK.

Manual Page Break

To insert a manual page break:

1. Place the cursor where you want Word to start a new page.
2. Press Ctrl-Shift-Enter.

New Document

To start a new document:

1. Choose File New.
2. Choose OK.

Newline Command

To insert a Newline command, press Ctrl-Enter.

Nonbreaking Hyphens

To insert nonbreaking hyphens:

1. Type the first word.
2. Press Ctrl-Shift-Hyphen
3. Type the second word.

Nonbreaking Spaces

To insert nonbreaking spaces:

1. Type the first word.
2. Press Ctrl-Shift-Space bar.
3. Type the second word.

Optional Hyphens

To insert optional hyphens, hold down the Ctrl key and type a hyphen.

Removing a Manual Page Break

To remove a manual page break:

1. Place the cursor anywhere on the manual page break.

2. Press Del.

Replacing Text

To replace text:

1. Press Ctrl-Home to position the cursor at the beginning of the document.

2. Choose the **E**dit **R**eplace (Alt-EE) command.

3. In the Text to **S**earch For field, type the search text.

4. In the **R**eplace With field, type the text you want to substitute for the search text.

5. Choose the **W**hole Word option.

6. If you want, choose the **M**atch Upper/Lowercase check box.

7. Make sure that the **C**onfirm Changes check box is checked.

8. Choose OK.

9. Choose **Y**es to make the replacement, **N**o to skip this selection and continue searching, or Cancel to return to your document.

Retrieving a Document from Another Directory

To retrieve a document from another directory:

1. Choose **F**ile **O**pen (Alt-FO) or use the Alt-Ctrl-F2 keyboard shortcut.

2. Activate the **D**irectories list box.

3. Activate a new directory by choosing one of the directory names in the **D**irectories list box. Look for your file in the File list box.

   Choose the parent directory symbol (two dots), if necessary, to move to a higher level on the tree.

4. Repeat step 3 until you find your file.

5. Choose OK.

Retrieving Documents after Starting Word

To retrieve a document after starting Word:

1. Choose File **Open** (Alt-FO) or use the Alt-Ctrl-F2 keyboard shortcut.

2. Choose your document in the **Files** list box.

3. Choose OK.

Searching for Text

To perform a simple search:

1. Press Ctrl-Home to position the cursor on the first character of the document.

2. Choose **Edit Search** (Alt-ES).

3. Type the search text in the **Search For** field.

4. Choose OK.

To perform a case-sensitive search:

1. Press Ctrl-Home to position the cursor on the first character of the document.

2. Choose **Edit Search** (Alt-ES).

3. Type the search text in the **Search For** field.

4. Choose the **Match Upper/Lowercase** check box.

5. Choose OK.

To perform a whole-word search:

1. Press Ctrl-Home to position the cursor on the first character of the document.

2. Choose **Edit Search** (Alt-ES).

3. Type the search text in the **Search For** field.

4. Choose the **Whole Word** check box.

5. Choose OK.

Selecting Fixed Units of Text with the F8 (Extend Selection) Key

To select text with the F8 key:

1. Press F8.

2. Press F8 again until you have selected the amount of text you want.

   The second time you press F8, you select the current word. The third time, the current sentence. The fourth time, the current paragraph. The fifth time, the whole document.

   If you select more text than you wanted with F8, press Shift-F8 to "shrink" the selection back down (in the sequence document, paragraph, sentence, word, character).

3. Press Esc to exit the Extend Selection mode.

Selecting Fixed Units of Text with the Mouse

To select	Point to	Mouse action
Word	Word	Double-click the left button.
Line	Selection bar	Click the left button.
Sentence	Sentence	Hold down the Ctrl key and click the left button.
Paragraph	Selection bar	Double-click the left button.
Document	Selection bar	Hold down Ctrl and click the left button.

Selecting Variable Amounts of Text with the F8 (Extend Selection) Key

To select text using the F8 (Extend Selection) key:

1. Place the cursor on the first character to be selected.

2. Press F8 (Extend Selection).

3. Use the cursor-movement keys to expand the highlight until it covers all the text you want to select.

Selecting Variable Amounts of Text with the Mouse

To select text with a mouse:

1. Position the pointer on the first character of the text you want to select.

2. Press a button and hold it down.

   If you hold down the left button, Word expands the selection character by character.

   If you hold down the right button, the selection expands word by word.

   If you hold down both buttons, the selection expands sentence by sentence.

3. Move the mouse so that the highlight expands.

4. When the highlight covers all the text you want to select, release the button.

Selecting Variable Amounts of Text with the Shift Key

To select text with the Shift key:

1. Hold down the Shift key and press any key that moves the cursor.

2. When you finish expanding the highlight, release the Shift key.

Starting Word and Opening an Existing Document

To start Word and open an existing document:

1. At the DOS prompt, activate the Word document directory.

2. Type *word* followed by a space and the file name of the document you want to open.

3. Press Enter.

4

Word 5.5 Formatting Strategies: Characters and Paragraphs

I n Chapter 2, you learned the basics of formatting with Word, including centering text, attaching boldface character emphasis, joining and splitting paragraphs, and adding custom tab stops. You learned the difference between character and paragraph formatting, and you learned that you can format in two ways—as you type and after you type. Chapter 3 added to this knowledge by showing you more ways to select fixed and variable units of text, a step that's necessary to format characters after you type.

This chapter broadens your knowledge of character and paragraph formatting with Word 5.5. You learn how to do the following:

- Use Word's default character and paragraph formatting settings— the settings the program applies if you issue no formatting commands

- Use the many measurement options available with this precision program

- Use character emphasis (such as boldface or italic), employ your printer's special fonts and font sizes, and add hidden comments to your document

- Control paragraph alignment (including right-margin justification), paragraph indentation, and line spacing

- Copy character and paragraph formats quickly and easily from one part of your document to another

- Search for character and paragraph formats so that you can locate quickly a given format in your document

- Replace character and paragraph formats so that Word substitutes one format (such as boldface) for another (such as underline) throughout your document

Before reading this chapter and trying out the new formatting techniques with your computer, be sure that you have installed your printer as described in the Appendix.

In addition, before you begin, choose View Preferences and choose the Paragraph Marks check box. Making the paragraph marks visible helps you avoid formatting errors. When you choose this option, Word saves your preference and displays paragraph marks even when you start the program in a new editing session.

The following character and paragraph formats are covered elsewhere in this book:

- To format a paragraph so that Word does not break pages within or after the paragraph, see Chapter 5.

- To set new default character styles for page numbers, line numbers, and footnote reference marks, and to set new default paragraph styles for footnotes, running heads, and headings, see Chapter 20.

- To create lines and boxes with the Format Borders command, see Chapter 17.

- To create side-by-side paragraphs with the Format Paragraph command, see Chapter 19.

Examining Word's Default Formats

Every word processing program comes with certain default formatting settings. The program uses these settings unless you give commands to the contrary. Word's default character and paragraph formats are listed in table 4.1. (For a list of the default page style formats, see table 5.1 in the following chapter.) When you create or print a document that has more than one page, the default formats ensure that your document prints with well-proportioned margins, page breaks, and—thanks to wordwrap—an attractively aligned right margin.

Table 4.1
Word's Default Character and Paragraph Formats

Format	Setting
Emphasis	None
Font	Printer's standard (such as Pica or Courier)
Line height	12 points (6 lines to an inch)
Measurement	Inches
Paragraphs	Single-spaced, flush-left alignment
Tabs	Every 0.5 inch
Type size	12-point height, 10 characters per inch (10 pitch)

As explained in this chapter, you can alter any of these formats in a document. After you change a format, Word saves your changes with the document so that the changes are available the next time you edit. Every time you create a new blank document, however, all the default formats listed in table 4.1 are in effect.

You can create new default formatting settings in a number of ways. For example, you can change the default tab stops by choosing Utilities Customize and entering a new measurement in the Default Tab text box. As you learn in Chapter 5, you can set new default margins by using the Format Section Margins dialog box. The best way to set new defaults, however, is to create a custom style sheet and make the style sheet the new default for the program. If you want Word to come on-screen at the start of every editing session with precisely the font, font size, margins, and other choices you want, be sure to read Chapter 21. Choosing your own defaults is the best of many good reasons for using style sheets regularly.

Knowing Your Measurement Options

As indicated in table 4.1, by default Word measures horizontally in inches (including fractions of an inch). For the most part, the program measures vertically in 12-point lines (6 lines to an inch). You can see these measurements in the command fields of the Paragraph dialog box (see fig. 4.1). When you type numbers in these fields to change default formats, Word assumes that you are using these measurements. In figure 4.1, for example, the From Left, First Line, and From Right text boxes receive and display measurements in inches ("), and the Before, After, and Line text boxes receive and display measurements in lines (li). To specify these measurements when you type them in a text box, you type " or *in* for inches, and *li* for lines.

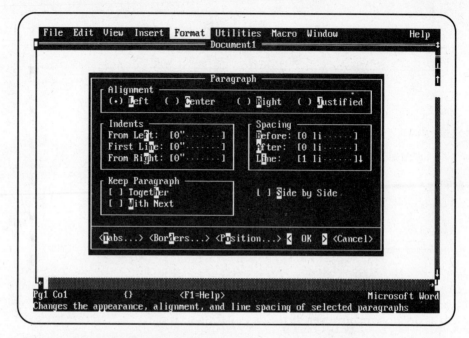

Fig. 4.1. The Paragraph dialog box.

Word responds to measurements entered not only in inches and lines, but also in printer's points, metric units, and fixed-font character positions.

Changing the Default Measurement Format

If you are accustomed to metric measurements, prefer to think in terms of spaces for indents, or want to use printer's picas or points for precision formatting, you probably want to change the default measurement format. To change the default measurement format, follow these steps:

1. Choose Utilities Customize (Alt-UU).

   You see the Customize dialog box.

2. Drop down the Measure list box (see fig. 4.2).

   A reminder: To drop down the list box with the keyboard, activate the Measure field by pressing Alt-M. Next, press Alt-down arrow to drop down the list. If you are using a mouse, click the down arrow next to the Measure list box.

3. Scroll the list box until you see the option you want.

   See table 4.2 for a list of the measurement options.

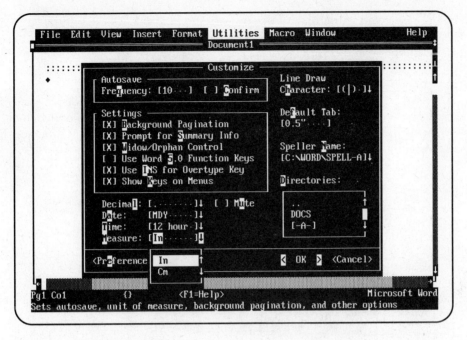

Fig. 4.2. The Measure list box.

Table 4.2
Measurement Options

Abbreviation	Measurement Format
In or "	inches (default)
Cm	centimeters
P10	character positions in Pica fixed-width font (10 characters per inch)
P12	character positions in Elite fixed-width font (12 characters per inch)
Pt	printer's points (72 per inch)

4. Choose the measurement option.

A reminder: To choose the selected measurement option with the keyboard, press Alt-down arrow or press Enter to choose the option and close the Customize dialog box. To choose the selected measurement option with the mouse, click the option with the left button (or double-click the option to choose the option and close the dialog box).

5. Choose OK.

After you change the **M**easure list box and choose OK, Word displays all measurements in the format you selected. If you choose printer's points, for example, both vertical and horizontal formats are measured in points (see fig. 4.3).

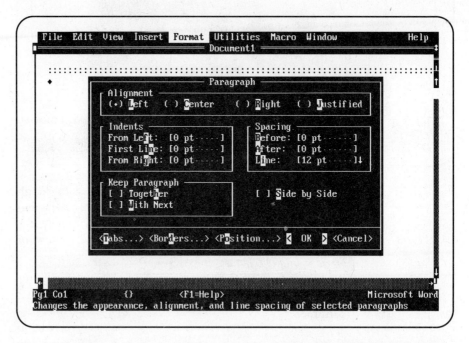

Fig. 4.3. Paragraph dialog box with measurements shown in printer's points (pt).

After you change the default, Word saves your change so that it's available the next time you use the program. To change back to the original settings, choose the In option in the **M**easure list box.

Overriding the Default Measurement Format

Whether you are using Word's default measurement format or a new format you have chosen from the Options menu, you can override the default for a specific measurement by typing a number and one of the measurement codes from table 4.2. To specify a line height in printer's points rather than lines, for example, you can type *14 pt* in any text box that accepts line measurements.

> *Caution:* If you omit the measurement code, Word uses the default measurement format. Therefore, if you are using the default settings (lines and inches) and you type *14* in the Line Spacing text box of the Paragraph dialog box, Word leaves 14 blank lines between each printed line. To enter a line spacing of 14 points, you must type *14 pt*.

Formatting Characters

When you format characters, you attach character emphasis (such as boldface or italic), change the character's position (normal, superscript, or subscript), or assign the character's type style (font, point size, and—if your computer system is capable of color printing—print color).

Word gives you a full storehouse of emphasis options, including strikethrough text (useful for showing clauses that have been struck out of legal contracts) and small caps (text that prints in small-sized capital letters). You also can hide text so that the text doesn't appear on-screen or on the printout (unless you want it to).

If you are using the graphics video display mode, you can see all these character emphases on-screen. In text mode, color monitors display emphases and point size choices in distinctive colors. You cannot see your font choices on-screen, though. A new Word 5.5 feature called the Ribbon makes it much easier to keep track of your font choices as you work.

You can format characters in two ways: as you type or after you type. And you can choose character formats in three ways: with the Character dialog box, with keyboard shortcuts, or with the Ribbon, which is described in detail later in the chapter.

The basic unit of character formatting is the character. You can assign a format to a single character or to as many characters as you like, including all the characters in your document. By default, Word formats characters with "plain vanilla" settings: for most printers, that means a 12-point typescript without emphasis. You can change this default by choosing one or more character formats, and you can change character formats as often as you please within your document.

> *Caution:* Your printer may not be able to print all these character emphases and positions. Before formatting a document, create a test document and use all the formats so that you can see which formats print and which ones don't. Consult your printer manual for more information on the printer's capabilities.

What You See On-Screen

As you can see in figure 4.4, Word can display all the emphasis options (as well as superscript and subscript) on-screen, provided that your computer can display graphics and you are using Word in graphics mode. With most monochrome monitors, much of the formatting becomes invisible (or indistinguishable from other emphases) in monochrome text mode (see fig. 4.5).

With color monitors, however, the formats take on distinctive colors and are easier to see. An additional benefit of color monitors is that distinctive colors are assigned to your font size choices. As you learn in Chapter 9, you can choose from two default color sets, and the colors assigned to the character formats and font sizes have some variations (see table 4.3).

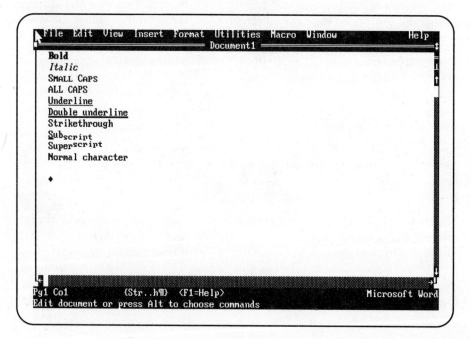

Fig. 4.4. Screen display of character emphasis and position in graphics mode.

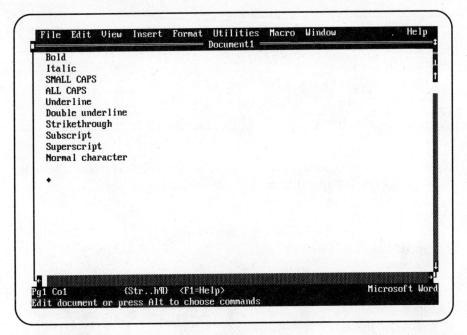

Fig. 4.5. *Screen display of character emphasis and position in text mode.*

Table 4.3
Colors Assigned to Character Formats

Format	Color Set 1	Color Set 2
Bold	Bright white	White
Italic	Light blue	Light blue
Small Caps	Pink	Pink
All Caps	Pink	Pink
Underline	Yellow	Orange
Double Underline	Yellow	Orange
Strikethrough	Orange	Red
Subscript	Pink	Pink
Superscript	Pink	Pink
Font (8.5 points or smaller)	Light green	Light green
Font (9.0 to 10 points)	White	White

continues

Table 4.3—*continued*

Format	Color Set 1	Color Set 2
Font (10.5 to 12 points)	White	White
Font (12.5 to 14 points)	Pink	Pink
Font (larger than 14 points)	Orange	Red

If you have a color monitor, you can assign the colors you like to each character emphasis font size so that the character formats are more easily distinguished. For more information, see Chapter 9.

> ***Tip:*** If you are not sure which formats are in effect for text you already have typed, place the cursor on a character within this text. Next, choose the Format Character command (Alt-TC). The Character dialog box appears, showing the current format choices. Alternatively, turn on the Ribbon to see an on-screen display of your current font, point size, and emphasis choices. For more information on the Ribbon, see "Using the Ribbon" later in this chapter.

Formatting Characters as You Type

When you format characters as you type, you begin by choosing a formatting command. Word "programs" the cursor to "lay down" a format as you type. The format remains in effect until you perform one of the following actions:

- You choose Format Character and change the setting in the Character dialog box

- You use the keyboard shortcut to toggle off the format that's in effect

- You press Ctrl-Space bar to cancel all nondefault character formats (including font, point size, color, emphasis, and position)

- You restore the default format on the Ribbon

- You press Ctrl-Z to cancel position and emphasis formats, but without canceling font, point size, and color choices

Formatting Characters after You Type

When you format after you type, you begin by selecting the text. You then choose a formatting command. The format applies only to the text you select.

To format character emphasis after you type, follow these steps:

1. Select the text.

2. Choose Format Character (Alt-TC) and choose a character format. Alternatively, use one of the keyboard shortcuts or choose a font, point size, or emphasis from one of the Ribbon drop-down list boxes.

To cancel character formatting in text you already have typed, do the following:

1. Select the text.

2. Press Ctrl-Z to cancel all your position and emphasis choices, without cancelling your font, point size, and color choices. Alternatively, press Ctrl-Space bar to cancel all your character formatting choices, including font, point size, and color choices.

About the Character Dialog Box

When you choose Format Character (Alt-TC), the Character dialog box appears (see fig. 4.6). You can choose the following formats in this dialog box:

- **Font.** This drop-down list box displays all the fonts available for the printer you installed when you ran SETUP (as explained in the Appendix). Every printer has a default font, which is the font that Word uses unless you specifically instruct Word otherwise. For most laser printers, for example, the default font is Courier.

- **Point Size.** This drop-down list box displays all the point sizes your printer is capable of producing for the font you selected in the Font list box. Again, what you see in this box depends on which printer you have installed. With most printers, the default point size is 12 (Pica).

- **Color.** If you have a printer with color capabilities, this list box shows your color choices. These are the colors when printed; you don't see the colors on-screen. The default color is black.

- **Emphases,** such as **Bold** or **Italic.** You can choose as many of these check boxes as you like. For example, you can format a word with bold, small caps, and underline. In practice, however, you should restrict yourself to a single emphasis at a time. All emphases are turned off by default.

- Position. These option buttons adjust characters upward (**Super-script**) or downward (**Subscript**) from the base line. The default position is Normal (not superscripted or subscripted).

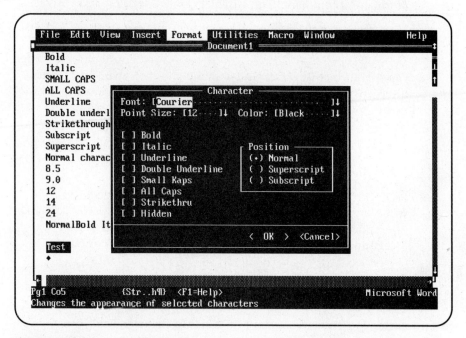

Fig. 4.6. *The Character dialog box.*

Tip: One major advantage of using style sheets is that you can create your own standard or default font, which applies to all the documents to which you attach the style sheet. This capability should be of great interest to owners of laser printers with multiple-font capabilities. You can create a style sheet called REPORT, for example, that prints in Times Roman, and another style sheet called LETTER that prints in Helvetica. For more information on style sheets, see Chapter 20.

Using Keyboard Shortcuts for Character Formatting

Word 5.5's drop-down menus and dialog boxes make choosing commands easy. But using keyboard shortcuts often is faster. Table 4.4 lists the Word 5.5 keyboard shortcuts for character emphasis.

The keyboard shortcuts are *toggle* commands. The first time you press the key, you turn a selection's format on. The second time you press the key, you turn the selection's format off.

Character-formatting keyboard shortcuts have changed in several ways. First, you press Ctrl, not Alt, to access the character-formatting keyboard shortcuts. Second, some key assignments have changed: you press Ctrl-= (equal), not Ctrl-hyphen, to subscript characters; and you press Ctrl-H, not Ctrl-E, to hide text. Third, strikethrough formatting no longer has a keyboard shortcut. Fourth, these keys now function as toggle keys: you press the same key to turn the format on and off. (It's not necessary to press Alt-Space bar to cancel a format.) If you want to cancel more than one format at a time, a new command (Ctrl-Z) cancels emphasis and position choices without also canceling your font and font size choices.

Table 4.4
Keyboard Shortcuts for Character Formatting

Format	Shortcut
Bold	Ctrl-B
Double underline	Ctrl-D
Hidden	Ctrl-H
Italic	Ctrl-I
Small caps	Ctrl-K
Subscript	Ctrl- =
Superscript	Ctrl- + (or Ctrl-Shift- =)
Underline	Ctrl-U
Cancel formats	Ctrl-Space bar
Cancel formats without changing the current font and point size	Ctrl-Z

Tip: If you plan to use fonts and point sizes other than your printer's defaults, use Ctrl-Z rather than Ctrl-Space bar to cancel character formats. Ctrl-Space bar cancels all character formats, including font and point size choices. If you press Ctrl-Space bar, Word reverts to the default printer font and point size. Ctrl-Z cancels emphasis and position without changing the font and point size.

Using the Ribbon for Character Formatting

Compared to Word for Windows, one of Word's drawbacks is that you cannot see your font and point size choices on-screen. If you like to use all your printer's fonts and sizes, you sometimes feel as if you are writing in the dark—you cannot see your fonts and sizes until the document is printed. If something goes wrong with the formatting, you have to print all over again.

Word 5.5 cannot display fonts and point sizes on-screen (although you can see a simulation of point sizes in Print Preview). This version of the program, however, offers an intelligent alternative—the Ribbon. The Ribbon is a bar displayed above the window border (see fig. 4.7), which shows the current style (Normal, if you are using the default style sheet), font, point size, and emphasis (bold, italic, underline). The Ribbon is useful not only for viewing current character formats, because you also can use the Ribbon to change the formats.

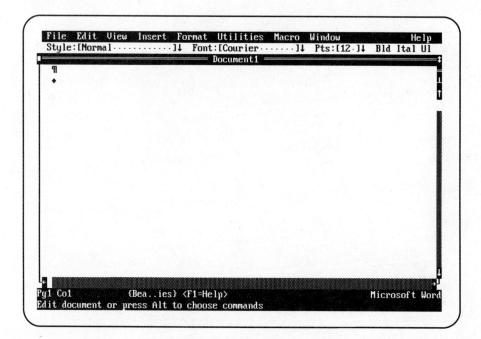

Fig. 4.7. The Ribbon.

To display the Ribbon, choose View Ribbon (Alt-VB). If you have a mouse, point to the ruler icon (the upside-down T on the right window border) and click the *right* button.

The Ribbon contains the following fields:

- *Style.* This drop-down list box is most useful after you learn to create your own style sheets. Style gives you an easy way to see the styles you create and to choose them for formatting purposes. For more information on styles, see Chapter 20.

- *Font.* From this drop-down list box, you can choose any of your printer's fonts. What's on the list depends on your printer's capabilities. If your printer can print many fonts, you see many options on the list.

- *Pts.* This drop-down list box displays the point sizes your printer can print for the font that is selected currently in the Font list box.

- *Emphases* (Bld, Ital, Ul). If you have a mouse, you can click these words to choose or cancel these three emphases. You can format fonts and point sizes with the keyboard and the mouse. You need a mouse to choose emphasis on the Ribbon.

To choose fonts from the Ribbon, follow these steps:

1. Choose **View Ribbon** to activate the Ribbon, if it's not visible.

2. Press Ctrl-F, then press Alt-down arrow to activate the Font field and pull down the list box (see fig. 4.8). Alternatively, click the Font field's down arrow.

3. Choose a font from the drop-down list box.

To choose point sizes from the Ribbon, follow these steps: **Ctrl-P**

1. Choose **View Ribbon** to activate the Ribbon, if it's not visible.

2. Press Ctrl-P, then press Alt-down arrow to activate the Pts field and pull down the list box. Alternatively, click the Pts field's down arrow.

3. Choose a point size from the drop-down list box.

To choose bold, italic, or underline with the mouse, do the following:

1. Choose **View Ribbon** to activate the Ribbon, if it's not visible.

2. Click Bld (Bold), Ital (Italic), or Ul (Underline).

Tip: If you use multiple fonts and point sizes, and especially if you use style sheets (or plan to use them), display the Ribbon and become accustomed to using it. The Ribbon is a major convenience and can help you avoid costly printing mistakes.

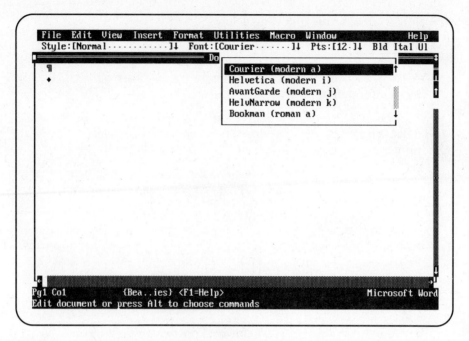

Fig. 4.8. *Font list box in the Ribbon.*

More about Character Emphasis

You can choose as many emphases as you like, but avoid overusing them. A good rule of thumb is to choose just one emphasis (bold or italic, for example) for your document, and use it sparingly.

To format character emphases as you type, do the following:

1. Place the cursor where you want to start typing.

2. Select Format Character (Alt-TC) and choose a character format. Alternatively, use one of the keyboard shortcuts. If you have a mouse, click Bld, Ital, or Ul on the Ribbon.

3. Type the text.

4. When you finish typing the text you want formatted this way, choose Format Character (Alt-TC) and restore the default format. You also can cancel the format by using the same keyboard shortcut again or clicking the same format on the Ribbon (to turn off bold, for example, press Ctrl-B again or click Bld on the Ribbon again).

Do not cancel character formatting by using Ctrl-Space bar if you have chosen a font or point size other than the default, unless you specifically want to cancel these formats and revert to the printer's default font and point size.

To format fonts, point sizes, or colors as you type, follow these steps:

1. Place the cursor where you want to start typing.

2. Choose Format Character (Alt-TC), choose an option from the Font, Point Size, or Color list boxes, and select OK. Alternatively, choose a font or point size from the Ribbon.

3. Type the text.

4. To cancel the font, point size, or color (and all other character formats), press Ctrl-Space bar. To cancel just the font, point size, or color, and leave other character formats in effect, choose Format Character and restore the default in the list box. Alternatively, restore the default font or point size option on the Ribbon.

If You Choose More than One Point Size

Although Microsoft Word 5.5 doesn't display fonts and point sizes on-screen in the normal editing modes, you still can take full advantage of your printer's multiple font and multiple point size capabilities. You may run into two problems, however, if you choose more than one point size for the characters in your document—adjusting line spacing and visualizing line breaks.

Adjusting Line Spacing

By default, Word uses 12-point line spacing. Whether you choose an 8-point font or a 48-point font, Word *still* uses 12-point line spacing—which, obviously, can lead to problems (see fig. 4.9).

You can solve this line spacing problem. For any paragraph containing a nondefault point size (a point size other than 12 points, for most printers), you must select the paragraph and use the Format Paragraph command's Line option. You learn more about paragraph formatting later in this chapter. For now, you can use auto line spacing to adjust automatically to the largest point size you have chosen.

To choose auto line spacing, follow these steps:

1. Select the paragraph that contains a nondefault point size.

2. Choose Format Paragraph.

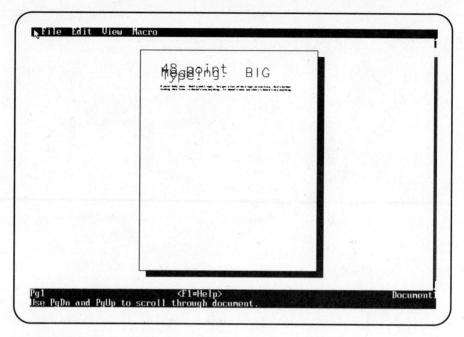

Fig. 4.9. Print Preview of document with line spacing problems.

3. Drop down the Line list box in the Spacing field.

4. Choose the Auto option.

5. Select OK.

Visualizing Line Breaks

Word 5.5 doesn't display your fonts and point sizes on-screen. In figure 4.10, all text is shown in a 12-point monospace font. Visualizing where line breaks will occur is difficult. The 48-point heading looks exactly like the 8-point body text on-screen. Obviously, the line breaks aren't accurate. In 48-point type, you can fit only two or three words on a line. In 8-point type, you can fit as many as two dozen words on a line.

You can solve this problem in the following two ways:

- Choose View Layout (Alt-VL) so that the LY code appears on the status bar. Word shows the line breaks as they will appear when printed. *Note:* The program runs more slowly in View Layout mode.

- Turn View Layout off but choose Line Breaks in the Preferences dialog box (View Preferences). Word runs more quickly, and you see line breaks where they will occur when printed.

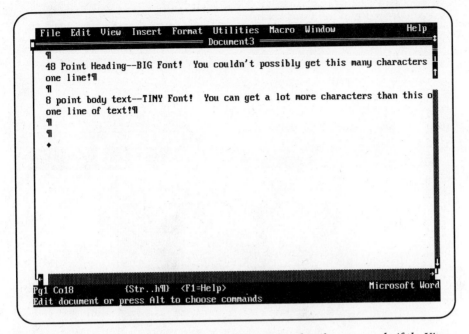

Fig. 4.10. Monospace screen font doesn't display line breaks accurately if the View Layout mode is switched off.

Changing the Font for the Whole Document

You may prefer to print in a font other than your printer's default. The default font for most laser printers, for example, is the fixed-width "typewriter" font, Courier. If you have purchased a cartridge to print in a more handsome font, such as Helvetica or Times Roman, you may want to print all or most of your documents in this alternative font.

In previous versions of Word, assigning a font to your whole document was risky if you planned to format after assigning the font. If you pressed Ctrl-Space bar to cancel character formatting, Word canceled the font you chose and reverted to the default printer font. But you wouldn't have known that until you printed your document. With Word 5.5's new Ctrl-Z command, you can cancel character formatting without losing your font, point size, and color choices. Always use Ctrl-Z instead of Ctrl-Space bar.

To choose a nondefault font for your entire document, follow these steps:

1. Press Ctrl-5 (on the numeric keypad) to select your entire document.

2. Choose Format Character (Alt-TC).

3. Drop down the Font list box.

   You see a list of the font choices available for your printer (see fig. 4.11).

4. Choose a font.

5. Select OK.

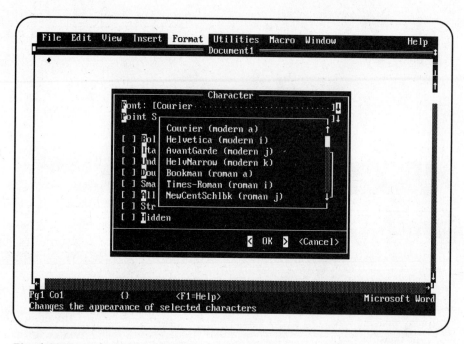

Fig. 4.11. Font choices for PostScript laser printers.

Changing Case

After typing text, you may decide to change its case (for example, from lowercase to uppercase). You can change the case of a selection in the following two ways:

- Choose the All Caps check box in the Character dialog box. If you change case this way, the capital letters are a character format (such as boldfacing or italic). You can cancel the capitalization by selecting the text and pressing Ctrl-Z. If you choose the Text Only or Text Only with Line Breaks options when you save your document, the capitalization will be lost.

- Press Shift-F3 to cycle selected text through three modes: all lower-case, all caps, and initial caps. If you change case this way, the case of the letters is stored as if you typed the letters that way at the keyboard. You cannot cancel the case pattern as you would cancel a character format, and Word doesn't abandon the case pattern if you choose the Text Only or Text Only with Line Breaks options when you save your document.

Shift-F3

Users of Word 5.0, alert! The function key that formerly toggled case, Ctrl-F4, now closes the current window. Word asks you for confirmation before abandoning your changes, so be sure to choose No or Cancel if you choose this command accidentally.

Using Hidden Text

Hidden text has many uses in Word 5.5. Hidden text is used most frequently to embed comments in a document. As you will learn in several of the chapters in Part III, you also can use hidden text to accomplish tasks such as marking words for later inclusion in an index or table of contents. Because you will have many occasions to use hidden text, learning how to create, display, hide, and print hidden text passages is well worth your while.

Creating Hidden Text

To create hidden text, you format the text as if it were a character format. You can create hidden text as you type. You also can format ordinary text as hidden text after you have typed the text.

The keyboard shortcut for hidden text has been changed to the more mnemonic Ctrl-H (it was formerly Alt-E).

To create hidden text as you type, follow these steps:

1. If you see the LY code on the status line, choose View Layout to turn the View Layout mode off.

   You cannot see hidden text in the View Layout mode, and because you are creating the text as you format, you must be able to see what you are doing.

2. Choose View Preferences and see whether the Hidden Text check box contains an X. If it doesn't, choose Hidden Text.

3. Select OK.

4. Choose Format Character (Alt-TC) and choose the **Hidden** check box so that you place an X in the check box. Next, choose OK. Alternatively, use the Ctrl-H keyboard shortcut.

5. Type the text to be hidden.

6. Choose Format Character (Alt-TC) and choose the **Hidden** check box again to remove the X. Next, choose OK. Alternatively, use the Ctrl-H keyboard shortcut again.

To create hidden text after you type, follow these steps:

1. Select the text.

2. Choose **View** Preferences and check to see whether the Hidden Text check box contains an X. If it doesn't, choose Hidden Text.

3. Choose OK.

Hiding the Text on the Screen

When you create hidden text, you can hide the text so that it isn't visible in your document. After you hide the text, you have the option of displaying a symbol (an arrow that points two ways) to show where hidden text is located, or hiding the text completely.

To hide the text and display a symbol where the hidden text is located, do the following:

1. Choose **View** Preferences (Alt-VE).

2. Turn on **Paragraph Marks**, if necessary, by choosing the check box. You should see an X in the box.

3. Turn off Hidden Text, if necessary, by choosing the check box. The check box should be blank (no X).

4. Choose OK.

To hide text completely, follow these steps:

1. Choose **View** Preferences (Alt-VE).

2. Turn off **Paragraph Marks**, if necessary, by choosing the check box. The check box should be blank (no X).

3. Turn off Hidden Text, if necessary, by choosing the check box. The check box should be blank (no X).

4. Choose OK.

Note: In the View Layout mode, you cannot display hidden text even if an X is in the Hidden Text check box (Paragraph dialog box). To view hidden text, choose View Layout (Alt-VL) to toggle the View Layout mode off.

For information on printing hidden text, see Chapter 7.

Solving Problems with Unwanted Character Formatting

Many new Word users find that boldface, underlining, and other character emphases pop up where they aren't needed. To understand why, you need to realize that the paragraph mark is a character like any other in that the paragraph mark can receive character formatting. When you press Enter, Word creates a new paragraph mark with the same formatting. If you later position the cursor on this new paragraph mark and start typing, your text will have the paragraph mark's formatting—which is the same as the text you have been typing.

This concept is easier to grasp if you take the following quick tutorial. Be sure to try the tutorial—it reveals a peculiarity of Word that most users learn only through frustrating experience.

To understand why you sometimes see unwanted character formatting, try these steps:

1. In a new, blank Word document, choose the **View Preferences** command and make sure that the **Paragraph Marks** option is checked.

2. Press Enter twice and press the up-arrow key so that the cursor is positioned on a paragraph mark. Type a word.

3. Use a variable text selection technique to select the word and the paragraph mark.

4. Press Ctrl-B to boldface the selection. Note that the paragraph mark also appears in boldface!

5. Place the cursor on the paragraph mark and press Enter several times. All the new paragraph marks display in boldface.

6. Place the cursor on any of the new paragraph marks and start typing. The text appears in boldface.

Now you know another reason why displaying paragraph marks as you work is so important. If you don't, you may format a paragraph mark without realizing it and get unwanted character formatting.

To cancel character formatting in a paragraph mark, do the following:

1. Position the cursor on the mark.

2. Press Ctrl-Z.

Formatting Paragraphs

When you choose a paragraph format from the Paragraph dialog box, you choose paragraph *alignment* (flush left, centered, flush right, and full justification), *indents* (from the left margin, from the right margin, first line only, and hanging indentations), and *spacing* (blank lines before the paragraph, blank lines after the paragraph, and line spacing within the paragraph). Figure 4.12 shows Word's paragraph formats. All these formatting choices show on-screen.

You can format paragraphs in two ways: as you type or after you type. To choose paragraph formats, use the Paragraph dialog box, keyboard shortcuts, or the Ruler (if you have a mouse).

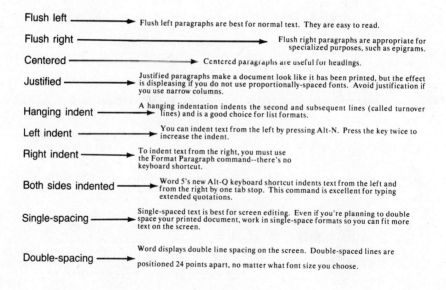

Flush left — Flush left paragraphs are best for normal text. They are easy to read.

Flush right — Flush right paragraphs are appropriate for specialized purposes, such as epigrams.

Centered — Centered paragraphs are useful for headings.

Justified — Justified paragraphs make a document look like it has been printed, but the effect is displeasing if you do not use proportionally-spaced fonts. Avoid justification if you use narrow columns.

Hanging indent — A hanging indentation indents the second and subsequent lines (called turnover lines) and is a good choice for list formats.

Left indent — You can indent text from the left by pressing Alt-N. Press the key twice to increase the indent.

Right indent — To indent text from the right, you must use the Format Paragraph command--there's no keyboard shortcut.

Both sides indented — Word 5's new Alt-Q keyboard shortcut indents text from the left and from the right by one tab stop. This command is excellent for typing extended quotations.

Single-spacing — Single-spaced text is best for screen editing. Even if you're planning to double space your printed document, work in single-space formats so you can fit more text on the screen.

Double-spacing — Word displays double line spacing on the screen. Double-spaced lines are positioned 24 points apart, no matter what font size you choose.

Fig. 4.12. Word's paragraph formats.

The basic unit of paragraph formatting is the paragraph. You cannot assign any of these formats to a unit smaller than a paragraph. If that seems unduly constraining, however, remember that a Word paragraph is simply any number of characters between two paragraph marks. You can create paragraphs that contain only one character, if you want. You can change this default by choosing one or more paragraph formats, and you can change paragraph formats as often as you please within your document.

By default, Word formats paragraphs with a "plain vanilla" paragraph format: single line spacing, no indents, no blank lines before or after.

Formatting Paragraphs as You Type

When you format paragraphs as you type, you begin by choosing a formatting command. Word "programs" the cursor to "lay down" a format as you type. The format remains in effect until you perform one of the following actions:

- You choose Format Paragraph and change the setting in the Paragraph dialog box.

- You use an alignment key that conflicts with the format; if you are typing centered paragraphs, for example, pressing Ctrl-L (flush-left alignment) cancels centering.

- You press Ctrl-X to cancel all nondefault paragraph formats.

- If the format is an indent format, you restore the default indent on the Ruler.

To format paragraphs as you type, do the following:

1. Place the cursor where you want to start typing.

2. Choose Format Paragraph (Alt-TP) and choose a paragraph format. Alternatively, use one of the keyboard shortcuts. If you have a mouse, you can set indents on the Ruler.

3. Type the text.

4. When you finish typing the text you want formatted, choose Format Paragraph (Alt-TP) and restore the default format. You also can cancel the format by using the same keyboard shortcut again. If you choose an indent, you can cancel the format by moving the indent symbols on the Ruler.

If you like to format as you type, begin your document by setting up a standard paragraph format. For example, choose justification, an automatic first-line indent, double line spacing, and one blank line before each paragraph. Type the first paragraph. When you press Enter, Word copies these formats to the next paragraph.

Formatting Paragraphs after You Type

When you format paragraphs after you type, you begin by selecting the text. You then choose a formatting command. The format applies only to the text you select.

Tip: You do not need to highlight the whole paragraph if you are selecting just one paragraph. Placing the cursor within the paragraph is sufficient to select it for paragraph formatting purposes.

To format paragraphs after you type, do the following:

1. Select the paragraphs.

2. Choose Format Paragraph (Alt-TP) and choose a paragraph format. Alternatively, use one of the keyboard shortcuts, or, if you are choosing an indent, drag one of the indent symbols on the Ruler.

About the Paragraph Dialog Box

When you choose Format Paragraph (Alt-TP), the Paragraph dialog box appears (see fig. 4.13).

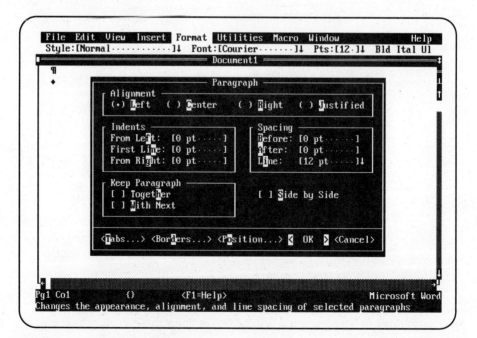

Fig. 4.13. The Paragraph dialog box.

You can choose the following formats in this dialog box:

- *Alignment* (**L**eft, **C**enter, **R**ight, **J**ustified). These choices affect the way Word aligns your paragraphs within the margin. If you choose **L**eft, Word aligns the left margin but leaves the right ragged. If you choose **C**enter, Word centers all the lines. If you choose **R**ight, Word aligns the right margin but leaves the left ragged. If you choose **J**ustified, Word aligns both margins, producing the effect you see in many books and magazines. These choices are option buttons, which means you can choose just one of them. The default alignment is Left. Keyboard shortcuts are available for these options.

- *Indents* (From **L**eft, **F**irst Line, From **R**ight). These choices affect the way Word indents your paragraphs from the margin. If you choose From Left and type a measurement, Word indents all the lines of the paragraph from the left margin by the amount of space you specify. (If you type *.25 in* in the From Left text box, for example, Word indents all the lines of the paragraph one-fourth inch from the left margin.) If you choose First Line, Word indents the first line only (a useful choice for text paragraphs). If you choose From Right, Word indents all the lines of the paragraph from the right margin. You also can indent text using the stepped paragraph shortcut (Ctrl-N and Ctrl-M) keys . For more information on these keys, see "Special Paragraph Formatting Techniques" later in this chapter.

- *Spacing* (**B**efore, **A**fter, **L**ine). These choices affect the way Word spaces lines. If you choose **B**efore, Word inserts one or more blank lines before the paragraph. If you choose **A**fter, Word inserts one or more blank lines after the paragraph. You use Line to control line spacing in your document (type *1 li* for single spacing, *2 li* for double spacing, and so on). Keyboard shortcuts are available for adding a blank line before a paragraph and for choosing single or double line spacing.

- *Side by Side*. Choose this check box to align the selected paragraphs (up to 32 of them) side-by-side on a page, in a special double-column format.

- *Keep Paragraph*. These useful options control page breaks. Choose To**g**ether to prevent Word from inserting a page break within the lines of the paragraph. If a page break is necessary, Word moves the whole paragraph to the next page. Choose **W**ith Next to prevent Word from inserting a page break between this paragraph and the next one. You can use this check box to prevent page breaks below headings, a common formatting flaw.

- *Command Buttons*. At the bottom of the Paragraph dialog box are the Tabs..., Borders..., and Position... command buttons, which (as the ellipses indicate) display additional dialog boxes. In these dialog boxes, you can choose additional paragraph formats, including custom tab stops, lines and borders, and absolutely positioned text and graphics. These options are discussed in Chapters 11, 17, and 18.

Using Keyboard Shortcuts for Paragraph Formatting

You can choose paragraph formatting options from the Paragraph dialog box. Using keyboard shortcuts is often faster, however, particularly if you want to choose only one option. Table 4.5 lists the Word 5.5 keyboard shortcuts for paragraph formatting.

Table 4.5
Keyboard Shortcuts for Paragraph Formatting

Format	Shortcut
Alignment:	
Justified	Ctrl-J
Flush-left	Ctrl-L
Flush-right	Ctrl-R
Centered	Ctrl-C
Indentation:	
Increase left indent	Ctrl-N
Decrease left indent	Ctrl-M
Hanging indent	Ctrl-T
Indent left and right	Ctrl-Q
Line Spacing and Blank Lines:	
Blank line before paragraph	Ctrl-O (letter, not zero)
Double line spacing	Ctrl-2
Single line spacing	Ctrl-1

Like the character-formatting shortcuts, paragraph formatting commands have changed from previous Word versions. The following changes are extensive:

- You press Ctrl, not Alt, to access the character-formatting keyboard shortcuts.

- Word no longer has a key for automatic first line indent.

- The normal paragraph command is now Ctrl-X, not Ctrl-P.

- You press Ctrl-A, not Alt-X, to access the default keyboard shortcuts if you are using a style sheet.

- Word has a new single line spacing command (Ctrl-1).

If you usually pressed Alt-P to restore default paragraph formats in previous versions of Word, be aware that you have better ways to accomplish this objective in Word 5.5. The paragraph alignment keyboard shortcuts (Ctrl-L, Ctrl-C, Ctrl-R, and Ctrl-J) function like the option buttons in the Paragraph dialog box: only one option can be in effect at a time, so you can change the alignment just by pressing the key you want. (Ctrl-L, for example, cancels centered alignment and restores flush-left alignment.) You can press Ctrl-1 to restore single line spacing.

If you prefer, you can press Ctrl-X to restore all default paragraph formats, but bear in mind that this command cancels all your paragraph formatting choices, including blank lines before and after a paragraph and line spacing. If you are using a style sheet, you press Ctrl-A to access the default keyboard shortcuts.

> *Caution:* Don't try to change the margins by setting new paragraph indents. With Word, left and right margins—and line length, which is determined by margin settings—are *page formats*, not paragraph formats. A page format runs through an entire document or a section of a document. For more information on margins and line length, see Chapter 5.

Paragraph Formatting with the Ruler

The ruler contains symbols that help you understand the formatting settings for the selected paragraph (the one in which the cursor is positioned). These symbols and their meanings ar as follows:

Symbol	Meaning
|	First-line indent (or hanging indent's first line)
[	Left indent from margin
]	Right indent from margin

You should know one more important point about the ruler. The ruler always shows the indents of the currently selected paragraph. As you move the cursor from one paragraph to another that has different indents, you see the ruler change.

The ruler also shows the custom tab stops you have chosen for a paragraph. For more information on tabs, see Chapter 11.

Using the Ruler for Setting Indents

If you have a mouse, you can take advantage of a very convenient Ruler technique for setting left, right, and first-line indents.

To display the Ruler, choose **View Ruler** (Alt-VR).

The Ruler appears on-screen (see fig. 4.14). The Ruler displays the current line length (in inches, unless you changed the default measurement format), the current left and right indents (the brackets), and custom tabs (if you set any).

To hide the Ruler, choose **View Ruler** (Alt-VR) until the dot next to the **Ruler** option disappears.

Note: The brackets on the Ruler do not show the current margin settings, they show the current paragraph indents from the margin. This distinction is important. When you set margins, you set them for the entire document (or the current section, if you divide your document into sections as explained in the next chapter). When you set paragraph indents, you alter the margins temporarily. The indents you set apply only to the paragraph or paragraphs that you select before you change the indents.

To indent the paragraphs from the left or right, do the following:

1. Place the cursor within the paragraph you want to format, or select two or more paragraphs.

2. If the Ruler isn't displayed, choose **View Ruler** (Alt-VR) or click the Ruler icon (the upside-down T in the right window border) with the left mouse button.

3. Place the pointer on the left or right indent symbol.

   The left indent symbol is a left bracket ([), and the right indent symbol is a right bracket (]).

4. Hold down the right button and drag the bracket left or right.

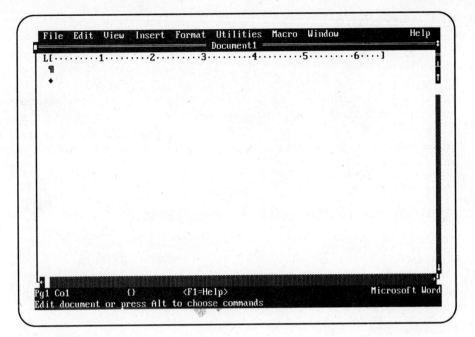

Fig. 4.14. The Ruler.

Caution: You do not need to indent paragraphs to create a left margin, because a 1-inch left margin already is included in Word's default margin settings. If you indent all your text 1 inch on the screen, you get a 2-inch left margin on your printout.

To set a first-line indent with the Ruler, do the following:

1. Place the cursor within the paragraph you want to format, or select two or more paragraphs.

2. If the Ruler isn't displayed, choose View **R**uler (Alt-VR) or click the Ruler icon (the upside-down ⊤ in the right window border) with the left mouse button.

3. Place the pointer on the left indent symbol.

4. Hold down the right button and drag the bracket right about one inch so you can see the first line indent symbol (|).

5. Drag the first line indent symbol to its new location.

6. Drag the left indent bracket back to its original position.

Line Spacing Techniques

With Word, line spacing—whether you are choosing double line spacing or just adding blank lines before or after a paragraph—is a *paragraph* format. If you format as you type, the line spacing options you choose remain in effect as you type, until you cancel the options. If you format after you type, the line spacing options you choose apply only to the selected paragraph or paragraphs. For this reason, you can change line spacing or blank line options as many times as you like in a document. You can, for example, double-space your body text while single-spacing footnotes.

Double-Spacing Your Document

If you want to print your document double-spaced, you can attach the format as you type, or format later. In either case, you see the double line spacing on-screen. Formatting later may be preferable if you plan to edit your document heavily. With single spacing, you can see more lines of text in the document window.

To double-space your text as you type, follow these steps:

Ctrl-2
1. Choose Format **P**aragraph (Alt-TP) and type *2 li* in the Line text box. Alternatively, use the Ctrl-2 keyboard shortcut.

2. Type the text.

To double-space your text after you type, do the following:

1. Select the text.

2. Choose Format **P**aragraph (Alt-TP) and type *2 li* in the Line text box. Alternatively, use the Ctrl-2 keyboard shortcut.

Note: When you choose double line spacing, Word always starts the paragraph by adding a blank line automatically. In other words, the blank line comes at the beginning of the paragraph, not at the end. Keep this point in mind if you add additional blank lines before or after the paragraph.

To restore single line spacing as you type, follow these steps:

1. Press Enter to start a new paragraph.

Ctrl-1
2. Choose Format **P**aragraph (Alt-TP) and type *1 li* in the Line text box. Alternatively, use the Ctrl-1 keyboard shortcut.

To restore single-line spacing after you type, follow these steps:

1. Select the paragraphs.

2. Choose Format **P**aragraph (Alt-TP) and type *1 li* in the Line text box. Alternatively, use the Ctrl-1 keyboard shortcut.

Caution: With Word, line spacing and point size are independent. In other words, if you choose a 14-point font with the Format dialog box, Word still uses the default single line spacing. Because an inch contains 72 points (6 lines), each line is 12 points in height. For this reason, the lines will look as if they are jammed together too closely. Similarly, if you use a tiny font (6 or 8 points), Word still uses 12-point lines, and the lines will look double- or triple-spaced, even if you intended single line spacing.

When you use a large or small font, therefore, you should adjust the Line text box in the Format dialog box accordingly. You may have to experiment to get the spacing right, but begin by typing the font's size in the line spacing field. If you are using a 14-point font, for example, select all the text you formatted with that font, choose Format **P**aragraph, and type *14 pt* in the Line text box. Alternatively, use the drop-down list in the Line text box and choose the Auto option. This option adjusts line spacing to fit the largest font you used in the line.

Adding Blank Lines before and after a Paragraph

Because blank lines are paragraph formats, you can set up a format that includes the precise number of blank lines before or after a paragraph. These lines are entered automatically; you need not press Enter.

If you are typing single-spaced body text, as in a letter or business report, you may want to open up the space between the paragraphs with a blank line. You also may want to add blank lines to headings.

Caution: Do not get into the habit of creating blank lines in your document by pressing Enter. Although you can do so in many cases without harmful results, you find later that this method forecloses some advanced options for you, such as automatic list sorting and the prevention of widowed headings. If you want blank lines between paragraphs, always create them by setting up a paragraph format that includes blank lines in the Spacing text boxes of the Paragraph dialog box.

To enter a blank line before each paragraph as you type, follow these steps:

Ctrl-O
1. Choose Format Paragraph (Alt-TP) and type *1 li* in the **B**efore text box. Alternatively, press Ctrl-O (the letter, not zero).

2. Type the text.

3. To cancel the blank line, press Enter to start a new paragraph. Choose Format Paragraph (Alt-TP) and type *0 li* in the **B**efore text box.

To enter a blank line before each paragraph after you type, follow these steps:

1. Select the paragraphs.

2. Choose Format Paragraph (Alt-TP) and type *1 li* in the **B**efore text box. Alternatively, press Ctrl-O (the letter, not zero).

To enter blank lines before and after a paragraph, follow these steps:

1. Select the paragraph.

2. Choose Format Paragraph (Alt-TP).

3. Type the number of blank lines before the paragraph in the **B**efore text box.

4. Type the number of blank lines after the paragraph in the **A**fter text box.

5. Choose OK.

Being Careful with Paragraph Marks

Think of a paragraph's ending paragraph mark as the place where Word stores the paragraph formats you chose for that paragraph. When you delete the paragraph mark, therefore, the paragraph loses all its formatting.

This fact comes into play in two situations—one intentional, and one accidental. If you are joining two paragraphs, as you learned to do in Chapter 2, you delete the first paragraph's paragraph mark; that's the only way you can join the two paragraphs. But if you are editing without displaying the paragraph marks, you may delete a mark accidentally.

In both cases, the result is the same: the two paragraphs join, and the first paragraph takes the formatting of the second. Why? Remember that a paragraph gets its formatting from the information stored in the paragraph mark at the end of the paragraph. Therefore, in the joined paragraph, the paragraph mark that determines the format is the only mark left—the mark at the end of what used to be the second paragraph.

If the two paragraphs are formatted exactly the same way, joining them accidentally has no adverse consequences, and you can press Enter to restore the break. If the paragraphs are formatted differently, however, joining them can give you an unwanted surprise: you lose the formatting of the first paragraph, and all the text takes on the formatting of the second paragraph. (That's because only the second paragraph's mark is left intact!) To restore the deletion, choose Edit Undo (Alt-EU) or use the Alt-Backspace keyboard shortcut.

Special Formatting Techniques

Word's paragraph formatting commands enable you to create the following special formats, which have many uses in business and professional writing:

- *Stepped Paragraphs* employ indents to show the logical relationship between one paragraph and the next.

- *Hanging Indents* are useful for items in a lengthy list, such as bibliographic references, product names, or employee names. The first line is flush to the left margin, while the second and subsequent lines are indented.

- *Headings* can be formatted so that Word inserts the correct number of blank lines before and after a heading, and prevents page breaks between the heading and the following text.

Creating Stepped Paragraphs

You can create stepped paragraphs by using the Paragraph dialog box, but the easiest way is to use the Ctrl-N and Ctrl-M keyboard shortcuts.

Ctrl-N

The Ctrl-N keyboard shortcut indents the left margin of a paragraph by the default tab width. If you press Ctrl-N twice, you indent the paragraph by two tab widths. If you press Ctrl-N three times, you indent three tab widths, and so on. If you indent a paragraph with Ctrl-N, you can "unindent" the paragraph by pressing Ctrl-M. Ctrl-M reduces the left indent by one tab width. You can use Ctrl-N and Ctrl-M to create stepped paragraphs, as shown in figure 4.15.

Ctrl-M

To indent a paragraph from the left margin, follow these steps:

1. Place the cursor in the paragraph you want to indent.

2. Press Ctrl-N to indent the paragraph one tab stop.

   Press Ctrl-N again to indent the paragraph two tab stops, and so on.

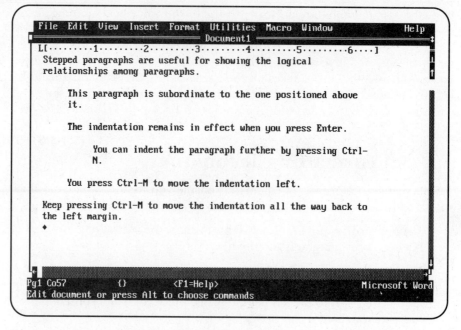

Fig. 4.15. Stepped paragraphs.

To decrease the indentation of a stepped paragraph, follow these steps:

1. Place the cursor in the indented paragraph.

2. Press Ctrl-M.

To cancel an indentation, do the following:

> Press Ctrl-M until the text is flush to the left margin, or press Ctrl-X to cancel all nondefault paragraph formats.

Creating Hanging Indents

Ctrl-T Like stepped paragraphs, hanging indents, shown in figure 4.16, are best created with a keyboard shortcut (Ctrl-T). When you press Ctrl-T, Word formats the first line of the paragraph flush to the left margin. Subsequent lines, called turnover lines, are indented one tab stop (0.5 inch, unless you set a custom tab or change the default tabs). If you press Ctrl-T again in the same paragraph, Word adds another tab stop to the indent.

To create a hanging indent, do the following:

1. Place the cursor in the paragraph you want to format with a hanging indent.

2. Press Ctrl-T to indent the paragraph one tab stop.

   Press Ctrl-T again to indent the paragraph two tab stops, and so on.

To cancel a hanging indentation, press Ctrl-X to cancel all nondefault paragraph formats.

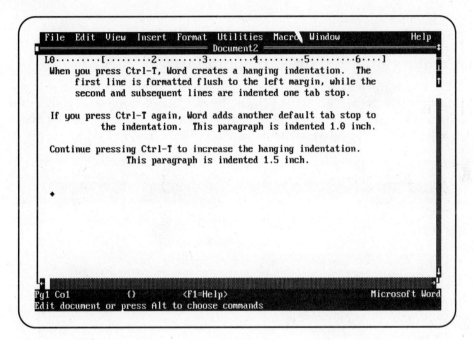

Fig. 4.16. *Hanging indents.*

Formatting Headings

If you are creating a business report, a scholarly article, a price list, or some other document with headings, beware of the heading positioned at the bottom of the page and with no text under it. This formatting flaw is very common and is difficult to avoid. Murphy's Law, it seems, dictates that Word will insert a page break right after a heading. To avoid this flaw, you can format the heading with the Keep Paragraph With Next check box in the Paragraph dialog box. If you choose this option, Word keeps the heading with the next paragraph—true even if you add blank lines beneath the heading.

To prevent Word from breaking a page beneath a heading, follow these steps:

1. Type the heading.

2. Place the cursor in the heading's paragraph.

3. Choose Format **P**aragraph (Alt-TP).

4. Add blank lines below the heading by typing the number of blank lines in the **A**fter text box in the Spacing field.

   To add two blank lines below the heading, type *2 li*.

5. Choose the **W**ith Next option in the Keep Paragraph field.

6. Choose OK.

Creating Bulleted or Numbered Lists

After you learn how to create a hanging indent, formatting a bulleted or numbered list is easy (see fig. 4.17). On the first line of every hanging-indent paragraph, enter a number, a hyphen, or a bullet (try Alt-248 or Alt-254) and then press Tab. The tab stop should line up with the turnover lines.

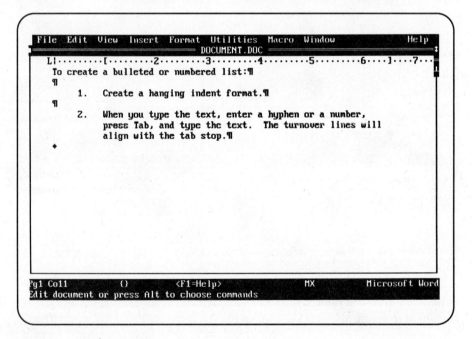

Fig. 4.17. A numbered list.

Repeating and Copying Character and Paragraph Formats

Whether you format as you type or format later, you will want to know how to repeat your last formatting command and how to copy character or paragraph formats from one selection to another. This section explains how to repeat your last character or paragraph format command and provides an undocumented—but nifty—technique for copying formats from other parts of a document.

Repeating a Format

When you format after you type, you must select the text you want to format. Because the text you select must be a contiguous unit on-screen, however, you may have to give the command several times if the text to be formatted is separated by text with different formats.

Suppose that you want to emphasize headings with boldface, and you have 27 headings in your document. You cannot select all the headings at the same time because body text that shouldn't be printed in boldface type is between the headings. Do you have to give the bold command 27 times? No, thanks to Word's **Repeat** command. This command repeats your last action. If the last action was a formatting choice, Word repeats the format. You can use this command to repeat a format throughout your document.

Note: This technique works only for the last formatting command you chose, so you cannot repeat multiple formats. If you want to assign multiple formatting choices here and there in a document, see the next section, "Copying Formats."

To repeat a format, follow these steps:

1. Select the first instance of the text you want to format.

2. Choose the character or paragraph formatting command.

3. Move the cursor to the next occurrence of the text you want to format the same way.

4. Choose **Edit R**epeat (Alt-ER) or use the F4 keyboard shortcut.   **F4**

Copying Formats

Mouse users can take advantage of a convenient command that copies character or paragraph formatting choices from already-formatted characters or paragraphs.

To copy a character format with the mouse, do the following:

1. Select the characters to be formatted.

2. Point to a word that contains the character formats you want to copy.

3. Hold down the Ctrl and Shift keys and then click the left mouse button.

To copy a paragraph format, follow these steps:

1. Select the paragraph or paragraphs you want to change.
   Note: You may just click the mouse in a single paragraph.

2. Point to the selection bar (left of the paragraph that has the format you want to copy).

3. Hold down the Ctrl and Shift keys and click the left button.

Searching for Character and Paragraph Formats

After formatting a long document, you may want to find a place where you used a specific character or paragraph format. You can search for a format with the Edit Search command.

To search for a character format or formats, use the following procedure:

1. To search your entire document, press Ctrl-Home to position the cursor at the beginning of the document.

2. Choose **Edit Search**.

3. In the Search dialog box, choose Search for **Formatting Only**.

   The Search for Formatting dialog box appears (see fig. 4.18).

4. Choose **Character** or **Paragraph**.

   If you choose **Character**, the Search for Character dialog box appears (see fig. 4.19), which looks like the Character dialog box. If you choose **Paragraph**, the Search for Paragraph dialog box appears (see fig. 4.20), which looks like the Paragraph dialog box.

5. Choose the format or formats for which you want to search.

   Choose the options in the dialog box. To search for a centered paragraph for which you have chosen the **With Next** option, for example, choose **Center** and **With Next**.

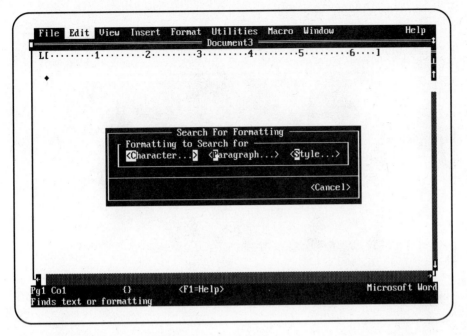

Fig. 4.18. *The Search for Formatting dialog box.*

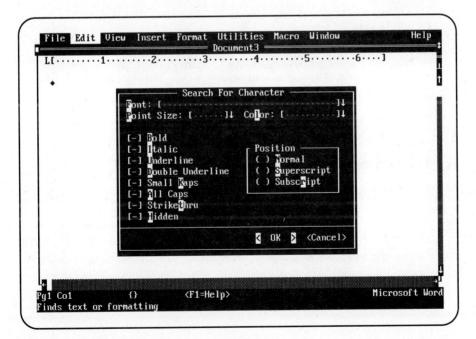

Fig. 4.19. *The Search for Character dialog box.*

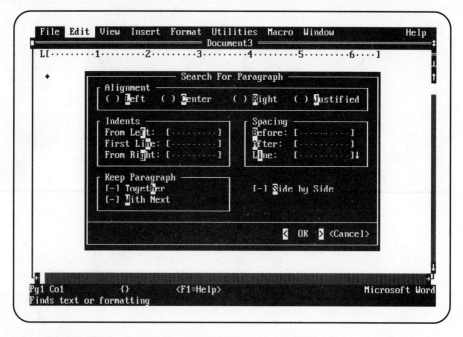

Fig. 4.20. The Search for Paragraph dialog box.

6. Select OK.

   If Word finds the format, the program highlights the text to which you have attached these formats. If Word cannot find the format, you see an alert box with the message Search format not found. Choose OK to close the alert box.

7. To repeat the search, press Shift-F4.

Replacing Character and Paragraph Formats

This feature is terrific for productivity. Suppose that you have just finished formatting a lengthy manuscript, and you used italic type extensively. Now you find out that the style guidelines you are working with don't permit italic, and you must use underlining instead. Must you scroll through your document and reformat every instance of italic manually? Not with Word. You can replace formats throughout your document automatically.

To replace formats throughout your document, do the following:

1. Press Ctrl-Home to position the cursor at the beginning of your document.

2. Choose **E**dit **R**eplace (Alt-EE).

3. In the Replace dialog box, choose Replace **F**ormatting Only.

   You see the Replace Formatting dialog box.

4. Choose **C**haracter or **P**aragraph.

   If you choose **C**haracter, you see the Replace Character Formatting dialog box, which looks like the Character dialog box. If you choose **P**aragraph, you see the Replace Paragraph Formatting dialog box, which looks like the Paragraph dialog box.

5. Choose the format or formats that you want Word to remove from your document.

   Choose the options in the dialog box. To search for bold character formatting, for example, click the **B**old check box.

6. Choose **R**eplace With.

   You see the Replace With Character Formatting dialog box or the Replace With Paragraph Formatting dialog box.

7. Choose the format or formats that you want Word to place in your document.

   To substitute italic for bold, for example, choose the **I**talic check box.

8. Choose OK. If Word finds the format, you see a Replace dialog box that asks you to confirm the selection. To confirm the replacement, choose **Y**es. To skip this instance of the format, choose **N**o. To make the changes throughout your document without confirmation, remove the X from the **C**onfirm check box.

Note: Performing this search-and-replace operation on formats is much less risky than on text. Replacing formats without confirmation is less risky than replacing text. Make sure that you want to change every occurrence of the format before you choose this option.

Why You Should Learn Style Sheet Formatting

Unfortunately, most Word users never bother with style sheets. Style sheet formatting isn't difficult to learn, and the payoffs are huge. And anyway, you're already using one: Word's default style sheet, NORMAL.STY. NORMAL.STY contains the definitions for all those formatting keyboard shortcuts you have learned in this chapter—the shortcuts you enter with the Ctrl key. *What makes style sheet formatting so useful is that it gives you a way to redefine the keyboard shortcuts.*

The keyboard shortcut formats defined in NORMAL.STY are appropriate for many uses, but you probably want to change at least some of them. You may, for instance, want to have a key combination that would, in one keystroke, create a paragraph with all these formats:

Automatic 0.5-inch first-line indent

Double line spacing

Justified right margin

10-point Helvetica font

You can do exactly that with a style sheet. After creating a style sheet and defining a keyboard shortcut with these formats, you can enter all of them with just one stroke of the shortcut keystroke. Obviously, your efforts in learning style sheet formatting will be repaid handsomely!

Before reading Chapter 20, "Style Sheet Formatting," you should read the next chapter, which explains page formatting. After you complete the next chapter, you will have all the knowledge you need to tackle style sheet formatting.

Chapter Summary

Word's default formats include an 8 1/2-by-11-inch page size, top and bottom margins of 1 inch, left and right margins of 1 inch, tabs every 0.5 inch, single line spacing, flush-left alignment, and (with most printers) a "plain vanilla" Pica type style and size. Even if you do no formatting at all, your text still will print on separate pages with neat margins (but without page numbers). If you format your document, Word saves your formatting instructions with the document, so they're available the next time you load the document.

This chapter introduced you to character and paragraph formatting. You learned how to use different units of measurement; control character emphasis and position; use your printer's fonts; use hidden text; control paragraph alignment, indentation, and line spacing; copy character and paragraph formats; and search for and replace character and paragraph formats. The next chapter explores Word 5.5 formatting even further by introducing you to page formatting.

Quick Review

Alignment

To center a paragraph:

1. Choose Format **P**aragraph (Alt-TP).

2. Choose the **C**enter option button.

    Alternatively, use the Ctrl-C keyboard shortcut.

To format a paragraph flush-right:

1. Choose Format **P**aragraph (Alt-TP).

2. Choose the **R**ight option button.

    Alternatively, use the Ctrl-R keyboard shortcut.

To justify a paragraph:

1. Choose Format **P**aragraph (Alt-TP).

2. Choose the **J**ustified option button.

    Alternatively, use the Ctrl-J keyboard shortcut.

To restore flush-left formatting:

1. Choose Format **P**aragraph (Alt-TP).

2. Choose the **L**eft option button.

    Alternatively, use the Ctrl-L keyboard shortcut.

Auto Line Spacing

To adjust line height automatically to the largest point size you have chosen:

1. Select the paragraph that contains a nondefault point size.

2. Choose Forma**t** **P**aragraph.

3. Drop down the Line list box in the Spacing field.

4. Choose the Auto option.

5. Choose OK.

Blank Lines

To enter a blank line before each paragraph as you type:

1. Choose Forma**t** **P**aragraph (Alt-TP) and type *1 li* in the **B**efore text box. Alternatively, press Ctrl-O (the letter O, not zero).

2. Type the text.

3. To cancel the blank line, press Enter to start a new paragraph. Choose Forma**t** **P**aragraph (Alt-TP) and type *0 li* in the **B**efore text box.

To enter a blank line before each paragraph after you type:

1. Select the paragraphs.

2. Choose Forma**t** **P**aragraph (Alt-TP) and type *1 li* in the **B**efore text box. Alternatively, press Ctrl-O (the letter O, not zero).

Canceling Character Formats

To cancel a character format, do one of the following:

- Choose Forma**t** **C**haracter (Alt-TC) and turn off the format in the dialog box.

- Press the keyboard shortcut again to toggle the format off.

- Press Ctrl-Z to cancel position and emphasis choices, without canceling font, point size, or color choices.

- Press Ctrl-Space bar to cancel all your character formatting choices, including font, point size, and color choices.

Canceling Paragraph Formatting

To cancel paragraph formatting, do one of the following:

- Choose Forma**t** **P**aragraph (Alt-TP) and change the setting in the Paragraph dialog box.

- Use a different alignment keyboard shortcut (to cancel alignment formats only).

- Press Ctrl-X to cancel *all* nondefault paragraph formats.

- Restore the default indent format on the Ruler.

Changing Case

To format text in uppercase letters:

1. Choose the **All Caps** check box in the Character dialog box.

2. Choose OK.

To cycle a selection through three case options:

Press Shift-F3 until you see the option you want.

Changing the Default Measurement Format

To change the default measurement format for all the documents you create:

1. Choose **Utilities Customize** (Alt-UU).

2. Drop down the **Measure** list box.

3. Scroll the list box until you see the option you want.

4. Choose the measurement option.

5. Choose OK.

To override the default measurement format temporarily:

In the Character or Paragraph dialog boxes, type a measurement using one of the measurement codes (in, cm, p10, p12, or pt).

Character Emphasis

To choose a character emphasis as you type or for the current selection:

Choose Format **Character** (Alt-TC) and choose the emphasis options you want. Alternatively, use a character emphasis keyboard shortcut.

To choose boldface emphasis:

Choose **Bold** in the Format Character dialog box. Alternatively, press Ctrl-B or click Bold in the Ribbon.

To choose italic emphasis:

Choose **Italic** in the Format Character dialog box. Alternatively, press Ctrl-I or click Ital in the Ribbon.

To choose underline:

Choose **Underline** in the Format Character dialog box. Alternatively, press Ctrl-U or click Ul in the Ribbon.

Character Formatting after You Type

To format characters after you type:

1. Select the text.

2. Choose Format Character (Alt-TC) and choose a character format. Alternatively, use one of the keyboard shortcuts or choose a font, point size, or emphasis from one of the Ribbon drop-down list boxes.

Character Formatting as You Type

To format characters as you type:

1. Choose Format Character (Alt-TC) and choose the formats you want from the Character dialog box. Alternatively, use one of the keyboard shortcuts.

2. Type the text.

3. To cancel the format and return to normal text, press Ctrl-Z to cancel your position or emphasis choices. Press Ctrl-Space bar to cancel all character formatting choices, including font, point size, and color. To cancel just one format, press the keyboard shortcut to toggle the format off.

Character Formatting Keyboard Shortcuts

Format	*Shortcut*
Bold	Ctrl-B
Double underline	Ctrl-D
Hidden	Ctrl-H
Italic	Ctrl-I
Small caps	Ctrl-K
Subscript	Ctrl- =
Superscript	Ctrl- + (or Ctrl-Shift- =)
Underline	Ctrl-U
Cancel formats	Ctrl-Space bar
Cancel formats without changing the current font and point size	Ctrl-Z

Copying a Format

To copy a format with a mouse:

1. Select the characters to be formatted.

2. Point to a character or paragraph that already has the format you want.

3. Hold down the Ctrl and Shift keys and click the left mouse button.

Fonts

To change the font as you type or for the current selection:

1. Choose Format Character (Alt-TC).

2. Drop down the Font list box.

3. Choose the font.

4. Choose OK.

To choose a nondefault font for your entire document:

1. Press Ctrl-5 (on the numeric keypad) to select your entire document.

2. Choose Format Character (Alt-TC).

3. Drop down the Font list box.

    You see a list of the font choices available for your printer.

4. Choose a font.

5. Choose OK.

Hanging Indents

To create a hanging indent:

1. Place the cursor in the paragraph you want to format with a hanging indentation.

2. Press Ctrl-T to indent the paragraph one tab stop.

    Press Ctrl-T again to indent the paragraph two tab stops, and so on.

Hidden Text

To create hidden text as you type:

1. If you see the LY code on the status line, choose View **L**ayout to turn the View Layout mode off.

2. Choose **V**iew **P**references and check to see whether the Hidden Text check box contains an X. If it doesn't, choose Hidden Text.

3. Choose OK.

4. Choose Format **C**haracter (Alt-TC) and choose the Hidden check box so that you place an X in the check box. Choose OK. Alternatively, use the Ctrl-H keyboard shortcut.

5. Type the text to be hidden.

6. Choose Format **C**haracter (Alt-TC) and choose the Hidden check box again to remove the X when you are finished typing hidden text. Choose OK. Alternatively, use the Ctrl-H keyboard shortcut again.

To create hidden text after you type:

1. Select the text.

2. Choose **V**iew **P**references and check to see whether the Hidden Text check box contains an X. If it doesn't, choose Hidden Text.

3. Choose OK.

Indenting Text

To indent text with the keyboard:

Choose Format **P**aragraph (Alt-TP) and choose the indent you want in the From Left, First Line, or From Right text boxes. Alternatively, use the Ctrl-N (indent one tab stop), Ctrl-T (hanging indent), or Ctrl-O (indent left and right) keyboard shortcuts.

To indent text with the mouse:

1. Place the cursor within the paragraph you want to format, or select two or more paragraphs.

2. If the Ruler isn't displayed, choose **V**iew **R**uler (Alt-VR) or click the Ruler icon (the upside-down T in the right window border) with the left mouse button.

3. Place the pointer on the left or right indent symbol.

   The left indent symbol is a left bracket ([), and the right indent symbol is a right bracket (]).

4. Hold down the right mouse button and drag the bracket left or right.

To set a first-line indent with the mouse:

1. Place the cursor within the paragraph you want to format, or select two or more paragraphs.

2. If the Ruler isn't displayed, choose **View Ruler** (Alt-VR) or click the Ruler icon (the upside-down ⊤ in the right window border) with the left mouse button.

3. Place the pointer on the left indent symbol.

4. Hold down the right mouse button and drag the bracket right about one inch so that you can see the first line indent symbol (|).

5. Drag the first line indent symbol to its new location.

6. Drag the left indent bracket back to its original position.

Keeping Text with the Next Paragraph

To prevent Word from breaking a page beneath a paragraph:

1. Place the cursor in the paragraph.

2. Choose **Format Paragraph** (Alt-TP).

3. Choose the **With Next** option in the Keep Paragraph area.

4. Choose OK.

Line Spacing

To double-space your text as you type:

1. Choose **Format Paragraph** (Alt-TP) and type *2 li* in the Line text box. Alternatively, use the Ctrl-2 keyboard shortcut.

2. Type the text.

To double-space your text after you type:

1. Select the text.

2. Choose Format **Paragraph** (Alt-TP) and type *2 li* in the Line text box. Alternatively, use the Ctrl-2 keyboard shortcut.

To restore single line spacing as you type:

1. Press Enter to start a new paragraph.

2. Choose Format **Paragraph** (Alt-TP) and type *1 li* in the Line text box. Alternatively, use the Ctrl-1 keyboard shortcut.

To restore single line spacing after you type:

1. Select the paragraphs.

2. Choose Format **Paragraph** (Alt-TP) and type *1 li* in the Line text box. Alternatively, use the Ctrl-1 keyboard shortcut.

Paragraph Formatting after You Type

To format paragraphs after you type:

1. Select the paragraphs.

2. Choose Format **Paragraph** (Alt-TP) and choose a paragraph format. Alternatively, use one of the keyboard shortcuts or, if you're choosing an indent, drag one of the indent symbols on the Ruler.

Paragraph Formatting as You Type

To format paragraphs as you type:

1. Place the cursor where you want to start typing.

2. Choose Format **Paragraph** (Alt-TP) and choose a paragraph format. Alternatively, use one of the keyboard shortcuts. If you have a mouse, you can set indents on the Ruler.

3. Type the text.

4. When you finish typing the text you want formatted this way, choose Format **Paragraph** (Alt-TP) and restore the default format. You also can cancel the format by using the same keyboard shortcut again. If you chose an indent, you can cancel the format by moving the indent symbols on the Ruler.

Paragraph Formatting Keyboard Shortcuts

Format	*Shortcut*
Alignment:	
Justified	Ctrl-J
Flush-left	Ctrl-L
Flush-right	Ctrl-R
Centered	Ctrl-C
Indentation:	
Increase left indent	Ctrl-N
Decrease left indent	Ctrl-M
Hanging indent	Ctrl-T
Indent left and right	Ctrl-Q
Line Spacing and Blank Lines:	
Blank line before paragraph	Ctrl-O (the letter O, not zero)
Double line spacing	Ctrl-2
Single line spacing	Ctrl-1

Point Size

To change the point size as you type or for the current selection:

1. Choose Format Character (Alt-TC).

2. Drop down the **P**oint Size list box or type the point size in the box.

3. Choose the point size you want.

4. Choose OK.

Repeating a Format

To repeat a single format:

1. Select the first instance of the text you want to format.

2. Choose the character or paragraph formatting command.

3. Move the cursor to the next instance of the text you want to format the same way.

4. Choose **Edit R**epeat (Alt-ER) or use the F4 keyboard shortcut.

Replacing Formats

To replace formats throughout your entire document:

1. Press Ctrl-Home to position the cursor at the beginning of the document.

2. Choose **Edit R**eplace (Alt-EE).

3. In the Replace dialog box, choose Replace **F**ormatting Only.

4. Choose **C**haracter or **P**aragraph.

5. Choose the format or formats that you want Word to remove from your document.

6. Choose **R**eplace With.

7. Choose the format or formats that you want Word to place in your document.

8. Click X to change Replace Selection to Replace All, and then click Y.

Ribbon

To display the Ribbon:

Choose **V**iew **R**ibbon (Alt-VB). If you have a mouse, point to the ruler icon (the upside-down ⊤ on the right window border) and click the *right* button.

To choose fonts from the Ribbon:

1. Choose **V**iew **Ri**bbon to activate the Ribbon, if it's not visible.

2. Press Ctrl-F and Alt-down arrow to activate the Font field and pull down the list box. Alternatively, click the Font field's down arrow.

3. Choose a font from the drop-down list box.

To choose point sizes from the Ribbon:

1. Choose **V**iew **Ri**bbon to activate the Ribbon, if it's not currently visible.

2. Press Ctrl-P and Alt-down arrow to activate the Pts field and pull down the list box. Alternatively, click the Pts field's down arrow.

3. Choose a point size from the drop-down list box, or type in a point size.

To choose bold, italic, or underline with the mouse:

1. Choose **View Ribbon** to activate the Ribbon, if it's not visible.

2. Click Bld (**Bold**), Ital (*Italic*), or Ul (Underline).

Ruler

To display the Ruler:

Choose **View Ruler** (Alt-VR).

Searching for Formats

To search your entire document:

1. Press Ctrl-Home to position the cursor at the beginning of the document.

2. Choose **Edit Search**.

3. In the Search dialog box, choose Search for **Formatting** Only.

4. Choose **Character** or **Paragraph**.

5. Choose the format or formats for which you want to search.

6. Choose OK.

7. To repeat the search, press Shift-F4.

Stepped Paragraphs

To indent a paragraph from the left margin:

1. Place the cursor in the paragraph you want to indent.

2. Press Ctrl-N to indent the paragraph one tab stop.

Press Ctrl-N again to indent the paragraph two tab stops, and so on.

To decrease the indentation of a stepped paragraph:

1. Place the cursor in the indented paragraph.

2. Press Ctrl-M.

To cancel an indentation:

Press Ctrl-M until the text is flush to the left margin, or press Ctrl-X to cancel all nondefault paragraph formats.

Subscript

To position text slightly below the line:

Choose Format Character (Alt-TC) and choose the Subscript option button. Alternatively, use the Ctrl- = keyboard shortcut.

Superscript

To position text slightly above the line:

Choose Format Character (Alt-TC) and choose the Superscript option button. Alternatively, use the Ctrl- + (or Ctrl-Shift- =) keyboard shortcut.

Word 5.5 Formatting Strategies: Page Formatting

As you already have learned, Word distinguishes between character formatting and paragraph formatting, the subjects of the preceding chapter. Character formats affect emphasis, position, font style, and font size, in units of text ranging from one character to an entire document. Paragraph formats affect alignment, indentation, and line spacing for one or more paragraphs.

This chapter focuses on the third level of formatting, page formatting. With Word, page formats include margins, page size, page numbers, and running heads. (Running heads are short versions of a document's title that print at the top or bottom of every page.) You can set page formats for your entire document, or, if you prefer, you can break your document into two or more sections, each with its own distinctive page formats.

With Word, you can create a single but complex document, such as a business report, that has distinct sections (such as chapters and appendixes), each with its own running heads, margins, page-number styles, and page-number sequence. Most of the time, however, you will create documents with just one page format running throughout the document, so this chapter is primarily about document-wide page formatting.

In this chapter, you learn how to do the following:

- Work with Word's default page style formats, the ones the program uses unless you give your own page format commands

- Change Word's default page size and margins, and set new defaults for every document you create

- Add page numbers to your document and print them precisely the way you want

- Add headers and footers to your document, including page numbers, if you want

- Break up your document into two or more sections, each with its own distinctive pattern of page styles

Some page formats, such as footnotes and multiple-column formatting, are discussed elsewhere in this book. For information on footnotes, see Chapter 14, "The Legal and Scholarly Word"; for multiple-column formatting, see Chapter 19, "Page Layout II: Multiple-Column Text and Newsletters." Line numbers, used most frequently in legal documents, are also discussed in Chapter 14. Also, see Chapter 18, "Page Layout I: Adding Graphics and Anchoring Paragraphs," for a discussion of page design with figures and illustrations.

Getting To Know Word's Default Page Styles

Word's default settings for page styles define the way your document will print unless you give commands to the contrary. Table 5.1 lists these default settings.

In previous versions of Word, the left and right margins were set to 1.25 inches by default. The new defaults are 1.0 inch left and right.

Table 5.1
Word's Default Page Styles

Style	Default setting
Margin: bottom	1.0"
Margin: left	1.0"
Margin: right	1.0"
Margin: top	1.0"
Page length	11"
Page number position	0.5" from top or bottom of page, 7.25" from left
Page number style	Arabic (1, 2, 3, and so on)
Start page number at	1
Page numbers	No (off)
Page width	8.5"
Running head position	0.5" from top or bottom of page

Note that Word doesn't print page numbers automatically. You must deliberately turn on page numbering for each document you create, using the Insert Page Numbers command. Remember, though, that some of the documents you create will be one-page letters, and you don't want a page number on a single-page letter. As you will learn in this chapter, turning on page numbers for longer documents, such as reports and proposals, is easy.

Page Style Commands

The options that control page styles in Word 5.5 are found in the following dialog boxes:

- **Margins Dialog Box** (Format Margins [Alt-TM]). You choose this command to change the default page size and margins for the document you're creating. The choices you make in this dialog box affect your entire document (unless you deliberately divide it into sections). You also can use this dialog box to set new defaults for all your Word documents.

- **Page Numbers Dialog Box** (Insert Page Numbers [ALT-IU]). You can choose this command to print page numbers on the pages of your document, but most Word 5.5 users will be better off adding page numbers to headers and footers. If you add page numbers using this dialog box, the page numbers always appear on the first page of your document, an infraction of the rules in most style handbooks.

- **Header/Footer Dialog Box** (Format Header/Footer [ALT-TH]). You choose this command to mark paragraphs of text so that they print as headers or footers, which are short versions of a document's title (or other information) that is printed within the top (headers) or bottom (footers) margins of each page. You can include page numbers within headers or footers. You also can suppress the printing of headers or footers on a document's first page. If you're planning to photocopy your document on both sides of the page and bind it, you can create different headers or footers for the odd and even pages.

- **Section Dialog Box** (Format Section [Alt-TS]). You choose this command to create multiple-column layouts, turn on automatic line numbering, and control footnote placement. These options are discussed in Chapter 14, "The Legal and Scholarly Word."

Users of previous versions of Word should note that most page style formats have migrated out of the Section dialog box, formerly called the Division menu, and the confusing word "division" has been replaced by more sensible "section." You can make choices from the Margins and Header/Footer dialog boxes without ever thinking about sections and section formatting; the page style formats you choose apply to the whole document. And that's an excellent change, because most Word users don't divide their documents into two or more sections.

If you like to divide your documents into sections, however, don't be concerned: it's still possible to insert division marks (now called *section marks*) into your document, and you can format each section with a distinctive page style. All the old division functionality is there, in short, but with none of the confusion.

Watch out for one major change: you don't press Ctrl-Enter any more to enter a section break. Ctrl-Enter creates a manual page break in Word 5.5. To enter a section break, you choose **Insert Break** and choose the Section option button. After inserting the section mark, the Margin, Page Numbers, and Header/Footer dialog boxes affect the section in which the cursor is positioned.

About the Section Mark

After you make a choice in the Margins, Page Numbers, or Section dialog boxes, Word inserts a section mark in your document (see fig. 5.1). This mark, a double row of dots across the screen, appears at the end of your document, just above the end-of-file mark. You see the section mark no matter which option you choose in the Preferences dialog box.

Caution: You need to remember two important facts about the section mark. First, the formats you choose affect the text *above* the mark, not below it. After the section mark appears, then, be sure to type above it, not below it.

Second, the section mark is like a paragraph mark: it "stores" the page formats you choose. If you delete the mark, you lose the page style formats you have chosen. If you accidentally delete the section mark while editing at the end of your document, choose the **Edit Undo** command to restore the mark.

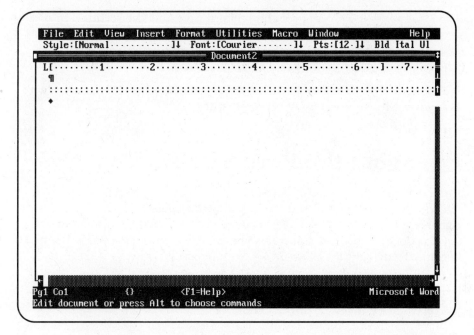

```
 File  Edit  View  Insert  Format  Utilities  Macro  Window           Help
 Style:[Normal··········]↓  Font:[Courier·······]↓  Pts:[12·]↓  Bld Ital Ul
                           Document2
L[·········1······2········3·······4·······5······6···]··7···
 ¶
 ::::::::::::::::::::::::::::::::::::::::::::::::::::::::::::::::::::::::::::
 ◆




















Pg1 Co1              {}          <F1=Help>                    Microsoft Word
Edit document or press Alt to choose commands
```

Fig. 5.1. Section mark.

Remember: In previous versions of Word, you pressed Ctrl-Enter to insert a
section mark (called division mark in all previous versions of the program). But
Ctrl-Enter is now used to insert a manual page break. The only way to insert a
section mark in Word 5.5 is to use the **Insert Break** command.

Word 5.5

Creating a Document with More than One Page Format

Sometimes you may want to create a document with more than one page
format. Suppose that you are writing a report that has three chapters and an
appendix, each with its own header text. You want to print the chapters' body
text with 1.25" margins left and right, and the appendix with 1.0" margins.

To employ more than one page format in a document, you divide your
document using the **Insert Break** command. After you use this command, Word
inserts a section mark in your document. You can format each section with the
headers and margins (and other page formats) you want.

The documents you create probably will not have multiple sections. In these documents, the choices you make in the page formatting dialog boxes automatically apply to the entire document, as long as the section mark is positioned where it belongs—at the very end of the document.

For more information on using more than one section, see "Documents with More than One Section," elsewhere in this chapter.

Changing the Page Size and Margins

If you're using Word outside North America, you may want to change the page size to suit local standards. And you may want to change Word's default left and right margins. You can make the change temporarily, so that it affects only the current document, or, if you want, you can save your choices so that they become the defaults for all the new documents you create.

Changing the Page Size

Word can print on nearly any size of standard paper, including common European sizes such as A4. You can change the page size for the active document. If you want, you can save new defaults so that all your Word documents will print on the page size you chose.

To change the page size for the active document, do the following:

1. Choose Format Margins (Alt-TM).

   You see the Section Margins dialog box (see fig. 5.2). The cursor is positioned in the Width text box, and the default setting (8.5 inches) is selected. Because the default setting is selected, you need not delete it to make a change. When you start typing, Word deletes the selection automatically.

2. Type the new page width.

   If you're using Word's default measurement format, type the measurement in inches, using the abbreviation *in* or the inch symbol ("). For information on changing the measurement format, see Chapter 4, "Word 5.5 Formatting Strategies: Characters and Paragraphs."

3. Choose the Height text box.

   A reminder: To choose this text box, press Alt-H, press Tab, or place the pointer on the text box and click the left mouse button.

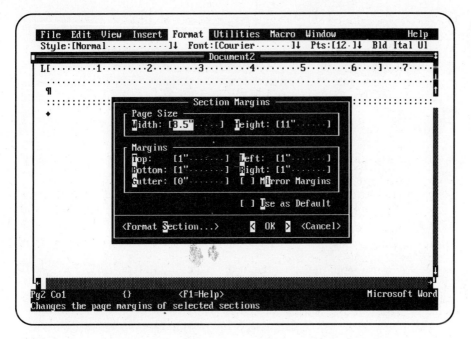

Fig. 5.2. *The Section Margins dialog box.*

4. Type the new page height.

5. Choose OK.

    A reminder: To choose OK, press Enter or move the pointer to the command button and click the left mouse button.

To change the page size defaults for all your Word documents, do the following:

1. Choose Format Margins (Alt-TM) and type a new page width and height.

2. Choose Use as Default.

3. Select OK.

Setting Margins

Margins are the white space at the top, bottom, left, and right of the printed page. By default, Word uses margins of 1 inch on all four sides. You can change the margins for the active document, or, if you want, you can save new defaults so that all your Word documents have the margins you choose.

Caution: Remember to distinguish margins from the paragraph indents you can create with the Format **P**aragraph command. A left or right paragraph indent adds to the existing margin. For example, if you choose a left indent of 1 inch in the Paragraph dialog box, Word starts printing the paragraph 2 inches from the left edge of the page.

To change the margins, follow these steps:

1. Choose Forma**t** **M**argins (Alt-TM).

   You see the Section Margins dialog box (see fig. 5.2).

2. Choose **T**op, and type the new top margin measurement in the text box.

   Measure from the top edge of the page. If you type *1.25"*, for instance, Word will print the text 1.25 inches from the top edge of the page.

3. Choose **L**eft, and type the new left margin measurement in the text box.

   Measure from the left edge of the page.

4. Choose **B**ottom, and type the new bottom margin measurement in the text box.

   Measure from the bottom edge of the page.

5. Choose **R**ight, and type the new right margin measurement in the text box.

   Measure from the right edge of the page.

6. Choose OK.

You can quickly change the default margins for all your Word documents by following these steps:

1. Choose Forma**t** **M**argins (Alt-TM), and type the margin measurements that you want for all your Word documents.

2. Choose **U**se as Default.

3. Select OK.

Adding Gutters

A gutter is the extra white space that is added to the inside margin, the one that's next to the binding. If you're binding a document that you plan to print or photocopy on one side of the page only, you don't need a gutter; you just add extra width to the left margin, which is the inside margin for documents printed on one side of the page only.

If you're planning to bind a document printed on both sides of the page, gutters become useful. When you type a gutter measurement in the **Gutter** text box (Section Margins dialog box), Word assumes that you will photocopy the document on both sides of the page. Because of this assumption, Word adds the measurement to the inside margin, that is, to the right side of even-numbered pages and to the left side of odd-numbered pages.

To add a gutter to your document, do the following:

1. Choose Format Margins (Alt-TM).

    You see the Section Margins dialog box (see fig. 5.2).

2. Type the gutter width (such as *0.5"*) in the **Gutter** text box.

3. Select OK.

Using Mirror Margins

Word gives you another way to leave extra room for binding documents printed on both sides of the page besides creating a gutter. If you choose **Mirror Margins** in the Section Margins dialog box, Word prints the margins you choose on the odd pages only. On the even pages, it reverses the choices you have made in the **Left** and **Right** text boxes. If you choose a left margin of 1.5 inches and a right margin of 1 inch, for example, Word prints these margins on the odd-numbered pages. On the even-numbered pages, it prints a left margin of 1 inch and a right margin of 1.5 inches. The effect is exactly the same as choosing a 0.5-inch gutter.

Adding Page Numbers

Like most word processing programs, Word doesn't automatically print page numbers on your documents. You must turn on page numbering manually, and for each document you create.

You can add page numbers in two ways: by choosing the From **T**op or From **B**ottom option in the Page Numbers dialog box, or by adding page numbers to a header or footer.

Note: The second method of adding page numbers is best—include them in a header or footer. If you add page numbers using the Page Numbers dialog box, the page numbers always start printing on the document's first page, which is contrary to most style guidelines (you wouldn't want a "1" on the first page of a two-page letter). You cannot add additional text, such as *Page* or chapter numbers, and you cannot format the page number characters (unless you modify the page number style in the NORMAL.STY style sheet).

To add page numbers with the Page Numbers dialog box, follow these steps:

1. Choose **Insert Page Numbers** (Alt-IU).

   You see the Page Numbers dialog box (see fig. 5.3).

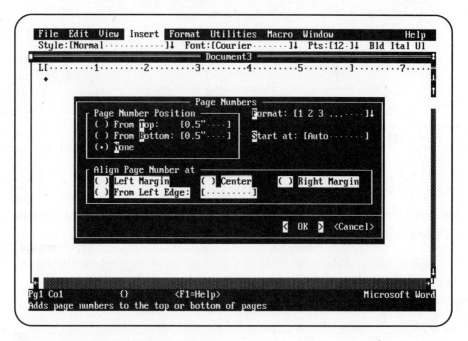

Fig. 5.3. The Page Numbers dialog box.

2. Turn page numbers on by choosing From **T**op (for page numbers at the top of the page) or From **B**ottom (for page numbers at the bottom of the page).

3. To change the vertical placement of the page number from the top or bottom, enter a new measurement in the text box next to From **T**op or From **B**ottom.

4. By default, Word prints the page number 7.25 inches from the left edge of the page. To change the horizontal alignment of the page number, choose an option in the Align Page Number At area.

   You can align the page number at the Left margin, Center, or Right Margin. You also can specify a different measurement from the left edge of the page. (The default measurement is 7.25 inches.) To change this measurement, choose the From Left Edge option and type a measurement in the text box next to this option.

5. If you want, choose a new page number format from the Format drop-down list box.

6. To start page numbering with a number other than 1, type the number in the Start At text box.

   The default option, Auto, starts the page numbers at 1 (if there is only one section in your document).

7. Choose OK.

Creating Headers and Footers

Headers (also called *running heads*) include text or page numbers that are printed within the top margin of your document's pages. Footers appear within the bottom margin. You can print headers or footers on every page of your document, or you can print a given header or footer on just the odd pages and use a different one for the even pages. You also can suppress the printing of headers or footers on the first page.

Because you can suppress the printing of headers or footers on the first page, most Word 5.5 users should turn on page number printing by creating a header or footer. (The header or footer need not contain any text besides the page number.) To add page numbers at the top of the page, you create a header. To add page numbers at the bottom of the page, you create a footer. Another advantage of this technique is that you can format the page numbers easily.

Headers and footers frequently include text that identifies the document. If you're writing a letter that's several pages long, you may want to indicate your correspondent's name. In an essay or report, you may want to place the author's name in a header. Headers and footers also are used in multiple section documents to indicate chapter titles.

You create a header or footer by typing one or more paragraphs and selecting them. You then choose Format Header/Footer. This command marks the paragraph or paragraphs so that they will print as headers or footers. Unless you choose View Layout, you see the header or footer text in your document. To alert you that this text is header or footer text, Word places a caret (^) in the selection bar next to the text. After you have used the Format Header/Footer command to mark header or footer text, you can edit this text or make additions to it, and your changes affect the header or footer when you print your document.

By default, Word prints headers and footers on odd and even pages, but suppresses them on the first page of your document. Header or footer text is aligned at the left margin, and the text is printed 0.5 inches from the top or bottom edge of the page. You can change these defaults.

To add a header or footer to your document, follow these steps:

1. Place the cursor at the beginning of the section in which you want the header or footer to appear.

   If your document has only one section, press Ctrl-Home to position the cursor at the beginning of your document and press Enter.

2. Type the header or footer text and format the text as you please.

   You can center the text or position it with tabs. You can type more than one paragraph of header or footer text, if you want.

3. Make sure that the header or footer text is separated from the rest of your document's text by a paragraph break. If it isn't, position the cursor at the end of the last line of the header or footer and press Enter.

4. Select the header or footer paragraphs.

5. If you see the code LY at the bottom of the screen, choose View Layout to turn off the layout view.

   You cannot add headers or footers in the View Layout mode.

6. Choose Format Header/Footer (Alt-TH).

   You see the Header/Footer dialog box (see fig. 5.4).

7. In the Format As area, choose the Header or Footer option button.

8. Choose OK.

After you select OK, Word places a caret in the selection bar next to the paragraph or paragraphs you have formatted as header or footer text (see fig. 5.5).

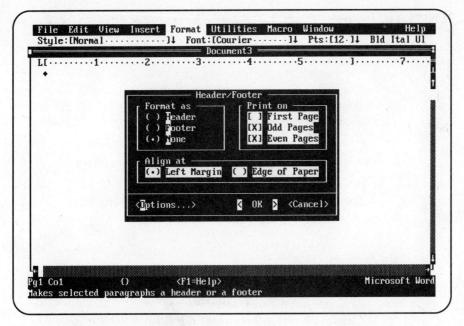

Fig. 5.4. The Header/Footer dialog box.

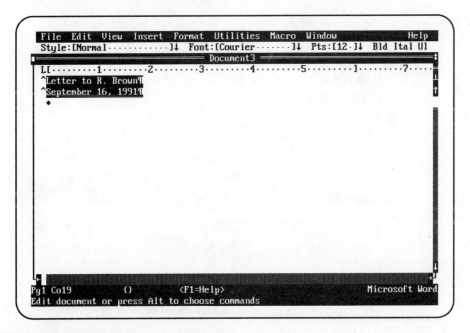

Fig. 5.5. Paragraphs formatted as a header.

Adding Page Numbers to Your Document Using Headers or Footers

As you already have learned, printing page numbers within a header or footer is best. This section tells you how to create a header or footer that contains nothing but the page number. The page numbers print on all the pages except page 1 of your document. Follow this procedure to create page number only headers or footers:

1. Place the cursor at the beginning of the section in which you want the header or footer to appear.

   If your document has only one section, press Ctrl-Home to position the cursor at the beginning of your document, and press Enter.

2. Type *page*.

3. Press F3.

   Word places parentheses around the word "page." The parentheses indicate that Word will not print the word "page." Instead, Word substitutes the correct page number when the document is printed.

4. If you want to format the page numbers, select page and use the Format Character or Format **Paragraph** command.

5. Make sure that the header or footer text is separated from the rest of your document's text by a paragraph break. If it isn't, position the cursor at the end of the last line of the header or footer and press Enter.

6. Select the header or footer paragraphs.

7. If you see the code LY at the bottom of the screen, choose **View Layout** to turn off the layout view.

   You cannot add headers or footers in the View Layout mode.

8. Choose Format **Header/Footer** (Alt-TH).

9. In the Format As area, choose the **Header** or **Footer** option.

10. Select OK.

If you already have used the Header/Footer dialog box to mark a paragraph as header or footer text, you can add the page numbers easily.

To add page numbers to an existing header or footer, follow these steps:

1. Within the header or footer text, place the cursor where you want the page number to appear.

2. Type *page*.

3. Press F3.

If you want, you can add a little text to the page numbers, so that the page numbers print in one of the following ways:

Page 29
-29-
Chapter 1-9
III-27

To print page numbers in one of these ways, add the text to the (page) symbol Word inserted when you pressed F3. The preceding examples would appear on your screen as follows:

```
Page (page)
-(page)-
Chapter 1-(page)
III-(page)
```

When Word prints the document, the program removes (page) and inserts the correct page number.

You can use a Word feature called *bookmarks* to include page numbers in the "Page 1 of 9" format. During printing, Word automatically inserts the total number of pages in your document. You will learn more about bookmarks in Chapter 12, "Using Glossaries and Bookmarks."

Follow these steps to add page numbers in the "Page X of Total" format:

1. Press Ctrl-End to move the cursor to the end of your document.

2. Select the last word in your document.

3. Choose **Insert Bookmark (Alt-IM)**.

4. Type *lastpage* in the **Bookmark** Name text box.

5. Select OK.

6. Press Ctrl-Home to move the cursor to the top of your document.

7. Type *Page page* and press F3.

   Word surrounds the second word with parentheses.

8. On the same line, type a space and then type *of page:lastpage*.

9. Press F3.

    On-screen, you should see

    ```
    Page (page) of (page:lastpage)
    ```

10. Press Enter to separate this text from the rest of your document.

11. Select the header or footer text and choose Format Header/ Footer (Alt-TH) to mark the text as header or footer text.

    You don't see the page numbers until you print your document or choose File Print Preview. *Note:* If the document is only one page, you will not see the header unless you have selected Print on First Page in the Format Header/Footer dialog box.

Choosing a Page Number Format for Page Numbers in Headers or Footers

When you add page numbers to headers or footers using the (page) symbol, you still can choose the page number format (Arabic, Roman, and so on) and the starting number. To choose the format of the page numbers, follow these steps:

1. Place the cursor within the section containing the (page) symbol you want to affect.

    If your document has only one section, make sure to place the cursor anywhere above the section mark at the end of the document, if there is one.

2. Choose Insert Page Numbers (Alt-IU).

    You see the Page Numbers dialog box. Leave the Page Number Position setting at None.

3. Choose a page number format from the Format drop-down list box.

    You can choose the format from Arabic (1, 2, 3), small letters (a, b, c), capital letters (A, B, C), small Roman numerals (i, ii, iii), or large Roman numerals (I, II, III).

4. Choose OK.

Choosing a Starting Page Number for Page Numbers in Headers or Footers

When you add page numbers to headers or footers using the (page) symbol, you haven't given up the ability to specify the starting page number. To start page numbers at a number other than 1, follow these steps:

1. Place the cursor within the section containing the (page) symbol you want to affect.

   If your document has only one section, make sure to place the cursor anywhere above the section mark at the end of the document, if there is one.

2. Choose **Insert Page Numbers** (Alt-IU).

   You see the Page Numbers dialog box. Leave the Page Number Position setting at **None**.

3. Type the number in the **Start** At text box.

4. Choose OK.

Choosing Options for Headers and Footers

By default, Word prints running heads on both odd and even pages but not on the first page. Headers are printed a half inch from the top of the page, and footers are printed a half inch from the bottom. The headers and footers are printed flush with the margins indicated in the Format **S**ection dialog box. You can alter these default settings to create more interesting and complex running heads for your documents.

Using Different Running Heads for Odd and Even Pages

If you're planning to duplicate your document on both sides of the page, consider creating different running heads for the odd (right) and even (left) pages. The following tutorial shows you how to create an attractive pattern of headers for such a document. Each header includes a short version of the document's title and a page number. On the odd-numbered pages, the title and page number are printed flush to the right margin. On the even-numbered pages, the order of the title and page number are reversed: the page number appears first, and it is printed flush to the left margin. In this way, the page numbers are always on the outside. Headers and footers of this type are common in commercially published books and magazines.

The following procedure describes how to create headers or footers for two-sided documents:

1. Place the cursor at the beginning of the section in which you want the header or footer to appear.

   If your document has only one section, press Ctrl-Home to position the cursor at the beginning of your document, and press Enter.

2. Type the text for the odd pages' header or footer, and press Tab.

3. Type *page* and press F3.

4. Press Ctrl-R to align this paragraph flush right.

5. Press Enter to start a new paragraph.

6. Type *page* and press F3.

7. Press Tab.

8. Type the text for the even pages' header or footer.

9. Press Enter to separate this text from the rest of your document.

10. Select the *first* header or footer paragraph.

11. If you see the code LY at the bottom of the screen, choose View Layout to toggle the layout view off.

12. Choose Format Header/Footer (Alt-TH).

13. In the Format As area, choose the **Header** or **Footer** option button.

14. Choose **Even** pages so that the X disappears from the check box.

    Only the **Odd** Pages options should remain checked.

15. Choose OK.

16. Select the *second* header or footer paragraph.

17. Choose Format Header/Footer (Alt-TH).

18. In the Format As area, choose the **Header** or **Footer** option button.

19. Choose **Odd** Pages so that the X disappears from the check box.

    Only the Even Pages options should remain checked.

20. Choose OK.

Your headers or footers should look like the ones in figure 5.6.

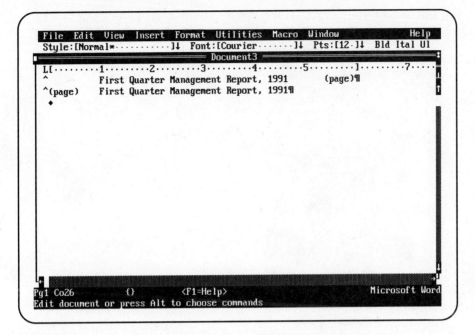

Fig. 5.6. Odd and even page headers for document printed on both sides of the page.

Understanding Header and Footer Codes

If you create more than one kind of header or footer, as suggested in the preceding tutorial, you may want to display running head codes. These codes tell you how you have formatted the header or footer. The header and footer codes are listed in table 5.2.

To display header and footer codes, do the following:

1. Choose **V**iew **P**references (Alt-VE).

2. Choose Style **B**ar in the Show area so that an X appears next to the option.

3. Choose OK.

   Word moves your text over two columns to make room for the style bar, which contains header/footer codes (see fig. 5.7).

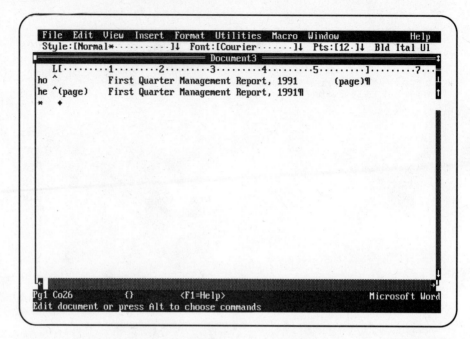

Fig. 5.7. Header/footer codes in the style bar.

Table 5.2
Header/Footer Codes in the Style Bar

Code	Meaning
h	Top (header), odd and even pages
hf	Top (header), first page only
he	Top (header), even pages only
ho	Top (header), odd pages only
f	Bottom (footer), odd and even pages
ff	Bottom (footer), first page only
fe	Bottom (footer), even pages only
fo	Bottom (footer), odd pages only

Changing the Running Head's Vertical Position

As mentioned earlier, by default Word prints header text a half inch from the top of the page and footer text a half inch from the bottom. You can change this vertical position of the running head text by typing new measurements in the running-head position From Top and From Bottom command fields of the Format Header/Footer Options command.

When should you change the vertical position? If you're happy with Word's default top and bottom margins of 1 inch, you have no reason to change them: your running heads will print right in the middle of the top and bottom margins. If you reduce or expand the top or bottom margin, however, you should change the running-head position From Top or From Bottom setting to reposition the running head text in the middle of the margin.

To reposition the header or footer text vertically, follow these steps:

1. Select the header or footer.

2. Choose Format Header/Footer (Alt-TH).

3. Choose Options.

   You see the Header/Footer Options dialog box (see fig. 5.8).

4. Type a new vertical position in the Header Position from Top or Footer Position from Bottom text boxes.

5. Choose OK.

Deleting a Header or Footer

If you want to remove a running head from your document, position the cursor on the running head, select all the header or footer text (including the paragraph mark), and press Del.

Starting a New Version of a Header on a Page Number You Specify

Sometimes you may want to change the text of a header or footer in your document. For example, suppose that you want one version of a header to appear on pages 2 through 10 and another version to appear on pages 11 through 20. To tell Word to stop printing the first version and start printing the second, follow these steps:

1. Place the cursor just above the break of the page where you want the change to occur.

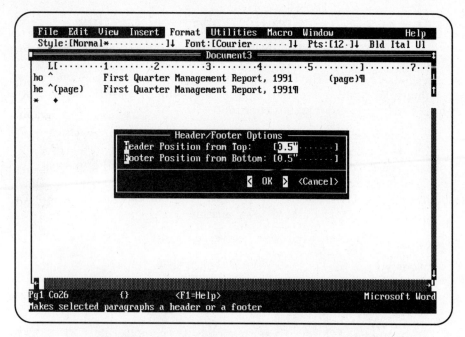

Fig. 5.8. The Header/Footer Options dialog box.

For example, if you want the new header or footer text to start printing on page 11, place the cursor at the bottom of page 10.

2. Type the new text.

3. Choose Format Header (Alt-TH).

4. Choose exactly the same options in the Header/Footer dialog box that you used for the first version of the header. For example, if the first version was a header that appears on odd and even pages, make sure that these options are selected.

5. Choose OK.

Using Two or More Sections in a Document

So far, this chapter has covered page styles as if they applied to an entire document. And normally they do. If you want to create a document with more than one page format, however, you can insert a section break in your document.

Inserting a Section Break

When you choose a page style command, such as Format Margins, Word automatically inserts a section mark (a double row of dots across the screen) at the end of your document, just above the end mark. As you already have learned, this mark "stores" the page style formats of all the text above it, just as the paragraph mark stores the paragraph formats of all the text in the paragraph.

If you want to switch page styles within your document, you must insert a section mark where you want the new page style format to begin. These formats include column layout (single- or multiple-column), footnote placement (same page or end of section), line numbers, margins, footnote numbering sequence, page number position, page number format (Arabic, Roman, and so forth), and header/footer position from the top or bottom of the page.

To divide your document into two sections, follow these directions:

1. Position the cursor where you want the new page style format to begin.

2. Choose **Insert Break** (Alt-IB).

   You see the Break dialog box (see fig. 5.9).

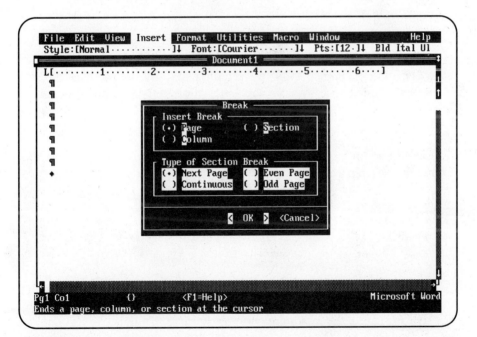

Fig. 5.9. *The Break dialog box.*

3. Choose the **S**ection option.

   After choosing this option, the Type of Section Break options become available.

4. Choose the type of section break you want.

   Choose **N**ext Page if you want Word to start the section on the next page in the pagination sequence. Choose **E**ven Page to start the section on the next even-numbered page, skipping a page if necessary. Choose **O**dd Page to start the section on the next odd-numbered page, skipping a page if necessary. Choose Continuous to begin the new section without a page break.

   If you're creating a technical report, business report, or proposal, and if you're planning to reproduce this document on both sides of the page, choose **O**dd Page to start chapters on the right (odd-numbered) side of the binding.

5. Choose OK.

   Word places a section mark (a double row of dots across the screen) at the cursor's location. (Be careful not to delete the section mark, for it "stores" the page style formats you have chosen for the section above the mark.)

   Now your document is divided into two sections. Section 1 is above the mark, and Section 2 is below the mark.

6. Position the cursor *above* the section mark. Choose the page style formats you want for the first section in the document.

7. Position the cursor *below* the section mark. Choose the page style formats you want for the second section in the document.

You can add additional section breaks, if you want. Word doesn't limit the number of section breaks you can place in your document.

> *Tip:* You can tell which section you're in just by looking at the status bar. After Word inserts a section mark in your document, a section indicator appears between the page and column indicators. When the cursor is in Section 2, for example, you see S 2 on the section indicator in the status bar.

Note: When you insert a section break above an existing section break in your document, the new section (the one *above* the mark) automatically takes on the page style formats of the existing section. To format the new section, you must move the cursor above the section mark and choose the page style formats you want.

Changing the Page Break Style after Inserting a Section Mark

As you noticed in the above tutorial, you choose the page break style when you use the **Insert Break** command. But what happens if you made the wrong choice? You can change the section break choice by using the Section dialog box:

1. Place the cursor within the section.

2. Choose Forma**t** **S**ection (Alt-TS).

   You see the Section dialog box (see fig. 5.10).

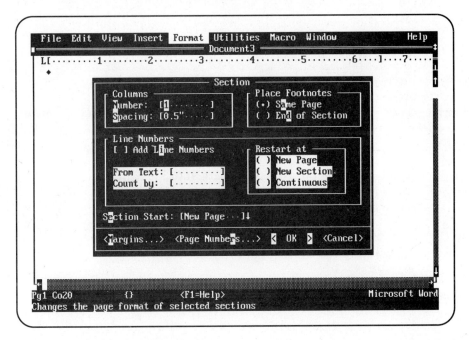

Fig. 5.10. *The Section dialog box.*

3. Choose a page break style from the Section Start drop-down list box.

   Choose **N**ew Page if you want Word to start the section on the next page in the pagination sequence. Choose **E**ven Page to start the section on the next even-numbered page, skipping a page if necessary. Choose **O**dd Page to start the section on the next odd-numbered page, skipping a page if necessary. Choose Continuous to begin the new section without a page break. Choose Column if you have chosen a multiple-column format and want to start the section with a column break.

4. Choose OK.

> ***Tip:*** If you're using a mouse, you can display the Section dialog box quickly by double-clicking the section mark.

As you can see from figure 5.10, the Section dialog box contains options for footnote placement, line numbers, and columns. You learn more about these options in Chapter 14, "The Legal and Scholarly Word."

Deleting a Section Mark

If you change your mind about dividing your document into sections, you can delete any section mark you insert. After you delete the section mark, the text in the section you deleted takes on the page style formats of the section *below* the deleted mark.

To delete a section mark, follow these steps:

1. Place the cursor on the section mark. If you're using a mouse, you can select the section mark by moving the pointer next to the mark in the selection bar and clicking the left mouse button.

   The whole mark is highlighted.

2. Press Del.

If you change your mind about deleting the mark, choose Edit Undo (Alt-EU) immediately, or use the Alt-Backspace shortcut.

Why Create a Document with More than One Section?

Many users are confused by Word's section formatting capabilities. Just remember that page style formats apply to your whole document, *unless* you choose to divide your document into two or more sections by using Insert Break. To understand why a Word user might want to create two or more sections, it's useful to understand the history of programs such as Word.

Word processing programs originally were created for two purposes. The first purpose was to emulate the functions of office typewriters without introducing too much new material, and these programs were given to clerical workers.

Examples of this approach are MultiMate and DisplayWrite. These programs have not done very well in the marketplace because they don't really take advantage of the computer's capabilities.

The second purpose was to aid programmers in the creation and printing of program documentation, complete with automatically generated tables of contents, indexes, and automatically numbered footnotes. The programs created for the latter purpose, such as the fabled mainframe program EMACS, are very powerful and take full advantage of the computer's capabilities. They are the ancestors of programs such as Microsoft Word and WordPerfect.

Now that you know a little about Word's ancestry, you can probably guess why Word includes commands that divide a document into sections. These commands are very useful for creating technical reports, documentation, or other in-house documents that will be reproduced directly from the program's printouts. To create a technical report, for example, you could create a document with the following sections:

- **Title Page** (Section 1). No page numbers printed

- **Front Matter** (Section 2). Section starts on odd page; header containing (page) symbol; no page numbers printed on first page; small Roman numeral page numbers on subsequent pages

- **Chapter 1** (Section 3). Section starts on odd page; header containing (page) symbol and short version of chapter's title; no header on first page; page number and title alternate position on odd and even pages; Arabic page numbers; footnotes are grouped and printed at the end of the section

- **Chapter 2** (Section 4). Section starts on odd page; header containing (page) symbol and short version of chapter's title; no header on first page; page number and title alternate position on odd and even pages; Arabic page numbers; footnotes are grouped and printed at the end of the section

- **Technical Appendix** (Section 5). Section starts on odd page; header containing (page) symbol and short version of the appendix's title; no header on first page; page number and title alternate position on odd and even pages; uppercase letters for page numbers

You learn more about grouping footnotes by section in Chapter 14, "The Legal and Scholarly Word."

Is it really a good idea to create a single, lengthy document with several sections, as this example suggests? If you're planning to reproduce the document directly from Word's printouts, it probably is a good idea, for the following reasons:

- You can use Word's outlining features to compile a table of contents automatically.

- You can mark words to be indexed, and Word compiles an alphabetized index with correct page numbers.

- Using *bookmarks*, you can create cross-references to material elsewhere in the manuscript, and Word automatically supplies the correct page numbers.

In summary, if you write in-house proposals, technical reports, business reports, or other documents that are photocopied directly from Word printouts, you are well advised to divide your document into sections.

Before you place an entire book-length manuscript in a single, large file, however, bear in mind that doing so entails some risk. The longer the manuscript, the slower Word runs, and Word's performance can become irritatingly slow on 8088-based computers. And should something happen to the file, you could suffer a catastrophic work loss. If you do place a lengthy manuscript in a single, large file, you should back up your work frequently.

Previewing Page Formatting

After choosing page formats, use **File Print Preview** (Alt-FV) to display your document's pages one or two at a time, showing you aspects of page style formatting that you don't normally see. These aspects include several page style formats discussed in this chapter, such as margins, running heads, and page numbers.

Crtl-F9   To preview page formatting, do the following:

1. Position the cursor on the page you want to display.

   You can change the page within Print Preview, if you want.

2. Choose **File Print Preview** (Alt-FV) or use the Ctrl-F9 keyboard shortcut.

   You see the Print Preview screen.

3. Press PgDn or PgUp to page through your document. To move quickly to a page number you specify, choose **Edit Go To** (Alt-EG) or use the F5 keyboard shortcut. Type the page number and choose OK.

4. To display more than one page at a time, choose **2**-page or **Facing** pages from the **View** menu.

5. To exit Print Preview and return to your document, choose **File Exit Preview** (Alt-FX) or press Esc.

Chapter Summary

In this chapter, you took another step toward understanding the full capabilities of Word's formatting features. You learned that Word's page style formats include margins, headers/footers, and page numbers. When you choose these formats, they apply automatically to your entire document. But if you break your document into sections, you can create sections within your document that have distinctive page formats. This capability is very useful for creating business or technical reports that will be duplicated directly from Word printouts.

Although you can turn on page numbers by using the **Insert Page Numbers** command, it's best to add page numbers to headers or footers by using the (page) symbol. If you turn on the printing of page numbers this way, you can suppress the page number on page 1.

If you frequently find yourself choosing the page style formats you want for new documents, you should consider modifying Word's default style sheet, NORMAL.STY, which automatically applies to all new documents. For more information on style sheets, see Chapter 20, "Style Sheet Formatting."

The next chapter helps you perfect your documents with Word's Thesaurus and with Spelling, the spell-checking program.

Quick Review

Gutters

To add a gutter to your document:

1. Choose **Format Margins** (Alt-TM).

   You see the Section Margins dialog box (fig. 5.2).

2. Type the gutter width (such as *0.5"*) in the **Gutter** text box.

3. Choose OK.

Headers and Footers

To add a header or footer to your document:

1. Place the cursor at the beginning of the section in which you want the header or footer to appear.

2. Type the header or footer text and format the text as you please.

3. Make sure that the header or footer text is separated from the rest of your document's text by a paragraph break. If it isn't, position the cursor at the end of the last line of the header or footer and press Enter.

4. Select the header or footer paragraphs.

5. If you see the code LY at the bottom of the screen, choose **View Layout** to toggle the layout view off.

6. Choose Format **Header/Footer** (Alt-TH).

7. In the Format As area, choose the **Header** or **Footer** option.

8. In the Print On area, choose First **Page** to turn on headers or footers on page 1. You also may remove the X from **Odd** Pages or **Even** Pages if you want to suppress the header or footer on these pages.

9. Choose OK.

To add page numbers to an existing header or footer:

1. Within the header or footer text, place the cursor where you want the page number to appear.

2. Type *page*.

3. Press F3.

To create headers or footers for two-sided documents:

1. Place the cursor at the beginning of the section in which you want the header or footer to appear.

2. Type the text for the odd pages' header or footer. Add page numbers and formatting.

3. Press Enter.

4. Type the text for the even pages' header or footer. Add page numbers and formatting.

5. Select the *first* header or footer paragraph (the one to be printed on odd pages).

6. If you see the code LY at the bottom of the screen, choose View Layout to toggle the layout view off.

7. Choose Format **Header/Footer** (Alt-TH).

8. In the Format As area, choose the **Header** or **Footer** option.

9. Choose **Even** pages so that the X disappears from the check box. Only the **Odd Pages** options should remain checked.

10. Choose OK.

11. Select the *second* header or footer paragraph.

12. Choose Format **Header/Footer** (Alt-TH).

13. In the Format As area, choose the **Header** or **Footer** option.

14. Choose **Odd Pages** so that the X disappears from the check box. Only the **Even Pages** options should remain checked.

15. Choose OK.

To display header and footer codes:

1. Choose **View Preferences** (Alt-VE).

2. Choose **Style Bar** in the Show area so that an X appears next to the option.

3. Choose OK.

To reposition the header or footer text vertically:

1. Select the header or footer.

2. Choose Format **Header/Footer** (Alt-TH).

3. Choose **Options**.

   You see the Header/Footer Options dialog box (see fig. 5.8).

4. Type a new vertical position in the **Header Position from Top** or **Footer Position from Bottom** text boxes.

5. Choose OK.

To delete a header or footer:

1. Select the header or footer paragraph, including its paragraph mark.

2. Press Del.

To continue a header or footer with new text:

1. Place the cursor just above the page break of the page where you want the change to occur.

2. Type the new text.

3. Choose Format Header (Alt-TH).

4. Choose exactly the same options in the Header/Footer dialog box that you used for the first version of the header.

5. Choose OK.

Margins

To change the margins:

1. Choose Format Margins (Alt-TM).

2. Choose **Top** and type the new top margin measurement in the text box.

3. Choose **Left** and type the new left margin measurement in the text box.

4. Choose **Bottom** and type the new bottom margin measurement in the text box.

5. Choose **Right** and type the new right margin measurement in the text box.

6. Choose OK.

To change the page size defaults for all your Word documents:

1. Choose Format Margins (Alt-TM) and type the margin measurements that you want for all your Word documents.

2. Choose Use as Default.

3. Choose OK.

Mirror Margins

To reverse the left and right margins on even pages:

1. Choose Format Margins (Alt-TM).

2. Choose Mirror Margins so that you see an X in the check box.

3. Choose OK.

Page Numbers

To add page numbers with the Page Numbers dialog box:

1. Choose Insert Page Numbers (Alt-IU).

2. Turn page numbers on by choosing From Top (for page numbers at the top of the page) or From Bottom (for page numbers at the bottom of the page).

3. To change the vertical placement of the page number from the top or bottom, enter a new measurement in the text box next to From Top or From Bottom.

4. To change the horizontal alignment of the page number, choose an option in the Align Page Number At area.

5. If you want, choose a new page number format from the Format drop-down list box.

6. To start page numbering with a number other than 1, type the number in the Start At text box.

    The default option, Auto, starts the page numbers at 1 (if your document has only one section).

7. Choose OK.

To create a header or footer that contains page numbers only:

1. Place the cursor at the beginning of the section in which you want the header or footer to appear.

2. Type *page*.

3. Press F3.

4. If you want to format the page numbers, select (page) and use the Format Character or Format Paragraph command.

5. Make sure that the header or footer text is separated from the rest of your document's text by a paragraph break. If it isn't, position the cursor at the end of the last line of the header or footer and press Enter.

6. Select the header or footer paragraphs.

7. If you see the code LY at the bottom of the screen, choose **View Layout** to toggle the layout view off.

8. Choose Format **Header/Footer** (Alt-TH).

9. In the Format As area, choose the **Header** or **Footer** option.

10. Choose OK.

To add page numbers in the "Page X of Total" format:

1. Press Ctrl-End to move the cursor to the end of your document.

2. Select the last word in your document.

3. Choose **Insert Bookmark** (Alt-IM).

4. Type *lastpage* in the **Bookmark Name** text box.

5. Choose OK.

6. Press Ctrl-Home to move the cursor to the top of your document.

7. Type *Page page* and press F3.

8. On the same line, type a space and then type *of page:lastpage*.

9. Press F3.

10. Press Enter to separate this text from the rest of your document.

11. Select the header or footer text, and choose Format **Header/Footer** (Alt-TH) to mark the text as header or footer text.

To control the page number format for page numbers entered in headers or footers:

1. Place the cursor within the section containing the (page) symbol you want to affect.

2. Choose **Insert Page Numbers** (Alt-IU).

3. Choose a page number format from the **Format** drop-down list box.

4. Choose OK.

To start page numbers at a number other than 1 for page numbers entered in headers or footers:

1. Place the cursor within the section containing the (page) symbol you want to affect.

2. Choose **Insert Page Numbers** (Alt-IU).

3. Type the number in the **Start At** text box.

4. Choose OK.

Page Size

To change the page size for the active document:

1. Choose **Format Margins** (Alt-TM).

2. Type the new page width.

3. Choose the **Height** text box.

4. Type the new page height.

5. Choose OK.

To change the page size defaults for all your Word documents:

1. Choose **Format Margins** (Alt-TM) and type a new page width and height.

2. Choose **Use as Default**.

3. Choose OK.

Print Preview

To preview page formatting:

1. Position the cursor on the page you want to display.

2. Choose **File Print Preview** (Alt-FV) or use the Ctrl-F9 keyboard shortcut.

3. Press PgDn or PgUp to page through your document. To move quickly to a page number you specify, choose **Edit Go To** (Alt-EG) or use the F5 keyboard shortcut. Type the page number and choose OK.

4. To display more than one page at a time, choose 2-page or Facing pages from the View menu.

5. To exit Print Preview and return to your document, choose File Exit Preview (Alt-FX) or press Esc.

Sections

To divide your document into two sections:

1. Position the cursor where you want the new page style format to begin.

2. Choose Insert Break (Alt-IB).

3. Choose the Section option button.

4. Choose the type of section break you want.

5. Choose OK.

6. Position the cursor *above* the section mark. Choose the page style formats you want for the first section in the document.

7. Position the cursor *below* the section mark. Choose the page style formats you want for the second section in the document.

To change the page break style after inserting a section mark:

1. Place the cursor within the section.

2. Choose Format Section (Alt-TS).

3. Choose a page break style from the Section Start drop-down list box.

4. Choose OK.

To delete a section mark:

1. Place the cursor on the section mark. Alternatively, click next to the selection bar.

2. Press Del.

6

Using the Thesaurus, Checking Spelling, and Controlling Hyphenation

Choosing the right word, spelling words correctly, and hyphenating words correctly present challenges for any writer. Word offers a superb on-line thesaurus, a first-rate spelling checker, and an automatic hyphenation utility to assist you with these tasks.

This chapter covers these utilities in detail. In this chapter, you learn how to do the following:

- Use Thesaurus to find the right word—or explore the many shades of meaning for a word

- Check your document's spelling and add correctly spelled words to the dictionary

- Modify the way Spelling works to suit your writing practices and needs

- Create and use your own user and document dictionaries

- Hyphenate your document automatically

Finding the Right Word: Thesaurus

A wonderful aid for creative writers, Thesaurus enriches your writing by supplying synonyms for words that you highlight in your document. Because Thesaurus is organized by 15,000 root words, it's rare (uncommon, extraordinary, exceptional) to use Thesaurus and find no synonyms for the word you highlight. When you see a synonym list, you will be impressed by the range and depth; after all, 220,000 words are stored in this thesaurus, most of them cross-referenced in dozens or even hundreds of ways. A root word stands at the center of an array of related words. *Service*, for example, is related to *army*, *aid*, *tableware*, and *ceremony*. Remember, though, that familiar words are almost always clearer and more meaningful than exotic words.

Thesaurus also is useful for more practical purposes. When you're writing a business letter, for example, being as clear as you can is important—often, being clear means finding the simplest word. If you write "Please send the parcel in an expeditious fashion," think twice: that sentence doesn't motivate action, it puts people to sleep! A little work with Thesaurus persuades you to say, "Please send the parcel quickly."

Use Thesaurus, too, to make sure that you grasp the full meaning of a word—particularly its connotations. Suppose that you write a letter with the following sentence: "Thank you for your trenchant criticism of our presentation. We need to hear from our customers to improve our services!" "Trenchant," as you quickly discover with Thesaurus, isn't the right word: its synonyms include "caustic," "cutting," "vulgar," and "obscene." Obviously, "trenchant" isn't the best word to describe friendly constructive criticism; or more to the point, even if the criticism was caustic, your job in a business letter of this sort is to redefine the situation so that the unfriendly criticism is interpreted as friendly and constructive. It's better to say "Thank you for your helpful criticism."

There's still no substitute for a dictionary, but a good thesaurus—like Word's—can deepen your grasp of a word's meaning in ways that no dictionary can. If you use an unfamiliar word with a meaning and range of connotations that aren't completely clear to you, use Thesaurus to make sure that you're not alluding to connotations you don't want.

Looking Up Synonyms

If you're not sure that you have chosen the right word to express a concept, or if you have used a word too much and you need a synonym to break the monotony, use the thesaurus.

Shift-F7 To look up a word in Thesaurus, perform the following steps:

1. Highlight the word you want to look up.

   You also can place the cursor right after the word.

2. Choose Utilities Thesaurus (Alt-UT). Alternatively, use the Shift-F7 keyboard shortcut.

   The Thesaurus dialog box appears, which has two list boxes: a **D**efinitions window and a **S**ynonyms window (see fig. 6.1).

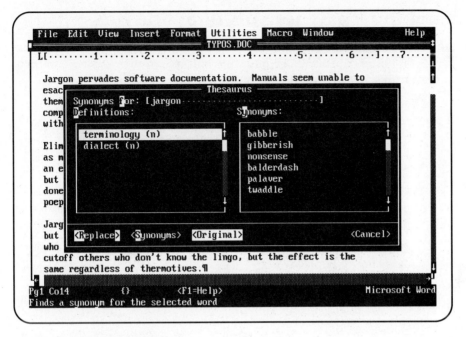

Fig. 6.1. The Thesaurus dialog box.

Why the two windows? Many words have more than one sense. The word "jargon," for example, has two senses—"terminology" and "dialect." The synonyms for the two senses differ. A synonym for "jargon" in the sense of terminology is "twaddle," but a synonym for "jargon" in the sense of dialect is "lingo."

If Word cannot find the word you want to look up, a dialog box with the message Not Found: Choose another word appears. You see a dialog box with 24 words that are close in spelling. To choose one of these words, highlight the word and choose the **Synonyms** command button.

3. If you see two or more words in the **Definitions** list box, choose the sense of the word you want.

   The **Synonyms** list box lists the synonyms available for the sense you chose in the **Definitions** list box.

4. If you see a synonym you want to use instead of the word in your document, highlight the word in the **Synonyms** list box and choose **R**eplace. If you don't find a word you want, choose Cancel.

Looking Up Synonyms of Synonyms

When the Thesaurus window is open, you can look up synonyms of any of the words displayed. You also can type a word and see synonyms of it. Be warned, however; this feature is addictive. When you use it, you set off on a voyage through the interconnections of the English language.

To see synonyms of words in a Thesaurus list, do the following:

1. Highlight a word in the **D**efinitions or **S**ynonyms list box.

2. Choose **S**ynonyms.

   The word you highlighted now appears in the Synonyms **f**or text box, and you see new word lists in the **D**efinitions and **S**ynonyms list boxes.

3. To place one of the words in your document, highlight the word and choose **R**eplace.

Another way to display additional synonym lists is to type a word in the Synonyms **f**or text box. Use this option when you don't see useful synonyms on-screen.

To look up synonyms for a word you don't see in the Thesaurus window, do the following:

1. Type the word in the Synonyms **f**or text box.

2. Choose **S**ynonyms.

3. To place one of the words in your document, highlight the word and choose **R**eplace.

Checking Spelling

Word 5.5's spelling checker leaves nothing to be desired: it has a huge dictionary, and it can detect nonstandard capitalization and repeated words as well as misspellings. The program automatically looks up suggestions for correcting the misspelling, and if you want, it will remember a correction you find yourself making frequently. If you frequently misspell "their" by typing "thier," for example, Word "remembers" this correction and makes it automatically in subsequent spelling sessions. And what's more, the spelling checker now is very easy and convenient to use, thanks to Word 5.5's dialog boxes.

As you use the spelling checker, bear in mind that (like any computer spelling checker) this utility doesn't really proofread your document for errors. It simply matches the words in your document to the words contained in its built-in dictionaries. For this reason, the spelling checker will flag many words that are correctly spelled. These words include plural or possessive forms of some words, terms in highly specialized fields, and many proper nouns. To prevent the spelling checker from flagging these words in the future, you can add these correctly-spelled words to the Spelling dictionary.

Remember, too, that using the spelling checker is no substitute for you doing a final proofreading of your document. The spelling checker cannot detect errors resulting from using a correctly-spelled word in the wrong place (for example, "They're VCR is better than our VCR.").

Spell-Checking Basics

In this section, you learn how to check a document's spelling by using the basic spelling commands. Subsequent sections explore other features of Microsoft Word, such as spelling options and user dictionaries.

Note: On your disk, you will find a Word document called TYPOS.DOC, which SETUP installed in Word's directory. Open this document to serve as a "guinea pig" for experimentation with the spelling checker.

Caution: Word checks your whole document unless you select text before choosing Utilities Spelling. (You can use this feature to check a word or paragraph without going through your entire document.) If you choose Utilities Spelling without being aware that you have left some text selected on-screen, however, you may think that the spelling checker has checked your whole document when it actually checked only the selection. To avoid this situation, press Ctrl-Home before choosing Utilities Spelling. Ctrl-Home cancels any selection that is in effect and places the cursor on the first character of your document.

To check the spelling of a document, perform the following steps:

1. Press Ctrl-Home to start the spelling checker from the beginning of your document.

   Spell checking begins at the cursor's location.

2. Choose Utilities Spelling (Alt-US). Alternatively, use the F7 keyboard shortcut.

You see the messages Loading dictionaries and Checking dictionaries on the message bar. If Word cannot find any misspellings, you see the message No incorrect words found. If Word finds a word it cannot match with the words in its dictionaries, you see the Spelling dialog box (see fig. 6.2).

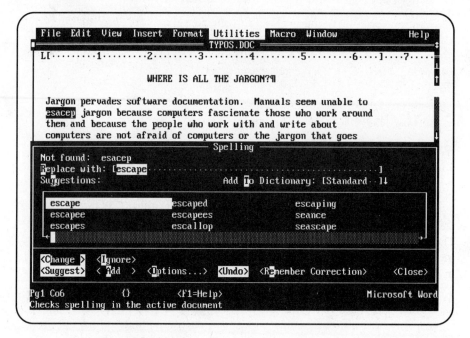

Fig. 6.2. The Spelling dialog box.

In the Spelling dialog box, Word places the discrepant word in the Not Found area. Word lists several possible corrections in the Suggestions list box.

3. You now have several options:

- If the word is spelled correctly, choose **Ignore** to continue. Note that **Ignore** is the highlighted command button; to select it, press Enter.

- If the word is not spelled correctly, activate the Suggestions list box and use the arrow keys to explore the suggestions. If you see the correct spelling, highlight the word and choose **Change**. Mouse users can double-click on the correctly spelled word.

- If you don't see the correct spelling in the Suggestions list box, type the correct spelling in the **Replace With** text box. Choose **Change** or press Enter. If you choose **Change** or press Enter, you are asked to confirm when the word is not in the dictionary.

- If the error is one you make frequently, move the highlight in the Suggestions list box to display the correct spelling in the **Replace With** text box. Alternatively, type the correct spelling in the **Replace With** text box, and then choose **Remember Correction**.

4. After choosing **Change** or **Ignore**, you can choose **Undo** if you decide you made the wrong choice.

   Word displays your last correction again.

5. Repeat steps 3 and 4 until Word reaches the end of the document. Alternatively, choose Cancel or press Esc to stop the spelling checker before it reaches the end (you will not lose the corrections you already made).

The Spelling window disappears, and you see a message in the message bar informing you how many words were checked, how many corrections were made, and how many words were ignored.

Note: You can abandon all the spelling corrections you made by choosing Edit Undo (Alt-EU) immediately after the spelling checker finishes.

Checking the Spelling of a Selection

If you select text before choosing Utilities Spelling, Word checks the spelling of the selected text—not the entire document. You can check the spelling of a word, for example, by highlighting the word and choosing Utilities Spelling. If the word is spelled correctly, you see the message `No incorrect words found`. If the selection contains words that the spelling checker cannot match with its dictionaries, you see the Spelling dialog box.

About Word's Dictionaries

Spelling's main dictionary contains more than 100,000 words, but that is far shy of the estimated half million words used in the English language. Missing from Spelling's dictionary are many proper nouns and technical terms. The dictionary contains many common names of places (including Charlottesville, Washington, and Virginia, for example, but not Crozet or Uppsala) and common personal names (Smith, Jones, Sue, Tom, and Ed, for example, but not Suzanne or Javier). In addition, the spelling checker's dictionary—although copious—doesn't contain technical terms related to professional or scientific specialties.

If you write business letters using many proper nouns, or scientific articles using many technical terms, you may want to add correctly spelled words to one of Word's three supplemental dictionaries. After you add these words to the dictionary, the spelling checker will not flag them as potential errors, and the program checks spelling much more quickly.

When you add words, you can add them to any of the following three supplemental dictionaries:

- *Standard dictionary:* Spell always uses the words in this supplemental dictionary when it checks your spelling. Add words to this dictionary if they're likely to appear in many or most of the documents you create. Examples include your name, your street, your city (if it's not already in Spelling's main dictionary), and names of coworkers.

  Note: The standard dictionary isn't the same as the spelling checker's main dictionary, which is contained in a special, nondocument file (SPELL-AM.LEX). The words you add to the standard dictionary go into a file called UPDAT-AM.CMP. This file is an ordinary document file. If you accidentally add an incorrectly spelled word to the standard dictionary, therefore, you can undo the damage simply by editing UPDAT-AM.CMP.

- *Document dictionary:* This supplemental dictionary is stored with the document containing the spelling that you're checking. The spelling checker consults this dictionary only when you recheck this particular document. Choose the document dictionary to store correctly spelled words that you're not likely to use in any other document.

- *User dictionary:* In addition to checking SPELL-AM.CMP and the standard dictionary (UPDAT-AM.CMP), the spelling checker also checks the user dictionary. By default, this dictionary file name is SPECIALS.CMP. Adding words to the default user dictionary isn't much different from adding words to the standard dictionary, because the spelling checker checks the default user dictionary every time you use the program. You can create a new user dictionary, however, and give it a distinctive name. If you do, the spelling checker does not use the new user dictionary unless you specifically tell it to do so by naming the dictionary in the Add to Dictionary list box of the Spelling dialog box. Use a distinctively named user dictionary to store words that you use for certain documents (but not for others). If more than one person uses Word on your system, you should create user dictionaries for each user. You learn how to create user dictionaries in the next section.

> ***Caution:*** You are not limited to the number of words you can add to these dictionaries. Because the dictionaries are stored in ordinary document formats, however, lengthy word lists slow down the spelling checker. (Spelling's own dictionary, SPELL-AM.LEX, is stored in a special file format for superfast retrieval.)

Adding Words to the Dictionaries

To sum up your dictionary options, most users are best off adding correctly spelled words to the standard dictionary. Use the document dictionary only when you're working with a document that has highly specialized terminology. There's really no reason to add words to the default user dictionary if only one person uses the computer; add words to the standard dictionary instead. If more than one person uses Word, or if you write in two or more completely separate fields or areas, create and name user dictionaries.

You specify the dictionary to which you want to add words in the Spelling dialog box's Add To Dictionary list box. The default option in this list box is the standard dictionary. After you change the option in this list box, it remains in effect until you change it again, even if you shut off and restart your computer.

To add correctly spelled words to the standard dictionary, do the following:

1. When the spelling checker flags a correctly-spelled word, make sure that the Add To dictionary list box contains the Standard option. If it doesn't, choose Standard from the Add To Dictionary list box.

2. Choose **Add**.

To create a document dictionary and add words to it, perform the following steps:

1. When Spelling flags a correctly-spelled word, choose Add To Dictionary and select Document from the drop-down list box.

    Word automatically creates the document dictionary, if one doesn't already exist.

2. Choose **Add**.

To create a user dictionary and add words to it, follow these steps:

1. When Spelling flags a correctly-spelled word, choose Add **To** Dictionary.

2. Choose **O**ptions.

   The Spelling Options dialog box appears (see fig. 6.3).

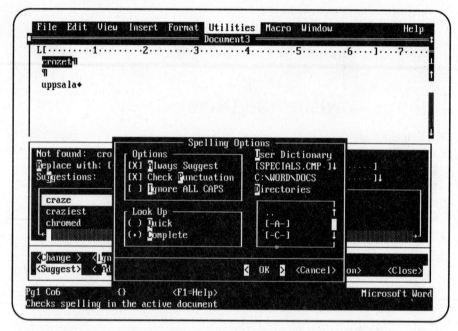

Fig. 6.3. The Spelling Options dialog box.

3. Choose the **U**ser Dictionary list box.

4. Type a DOS file name for the user dictionary in the **U**ser Dictionary list box. Skip the period and extension; Word supplies the required extension (CMP).

5. Choose OK.

   You see an alert box with the message

   ```
   Dictionary does not exist. Create dictionary?
   ```

6. Choose OK.

   The Spelling dialog box appears.

7. Choose the Add To Dictionary list box and choose the User option from the drop-down list.

8. Choose Add.

After you switch dictionaries in the Add To Dictionary list box, remember that Word saves your choice and it becomes the new default. To add words to a dictionary other than the one you last chose, you must choose Add To Dictionary and select the correct dictionary from the list box.

Spelling Options

In the previous section, you learned how to use the Options command button to display the Spelling Options dialog box. In this section, you learn how you can modify Spelling's performance by using this dialog box.

Table 6.1 gives you an overview of the spelling options that haven't been discussed already.

Table 6.1
Using Spelling Options

Option	Effect
Always Suggest Spelling (On)	Displays a list of suggestions in the Suggestions list box. You can turn this option off to speed up Spelling's performance, but you do not see the list of suggested spellings unless you choose the Suggest command button.
Check Punctuation (On)	Tells the spelling checker to look for misplaced punctuation. You can turn this option off to make the spelling checker run more quickly. You may want to do so if you're checking the spelling of a document with many oddly-punctuated technical terms.
Ignore ALL CAPS	Spelling checks the spelling of words typed in capital letters, such as NATO and NASA. If you turn this option on by placing an X in the check box, Word skips these words. If your document contains many words in all caps, such as programming language commands, you may want to select this option to speed up spell-checking.

continues

Table 6.1—*continued*

Option	Effect
Look Up (Complete)	When it tries to present suggestions, the spelling checker does not assume that the first two characters of the unknown word are correct, or in the right order. As a result, the list of suggested words is very comprehensive and includes words that do not begin with the same letter as the unknown word. If you choose Quick, Spelling assumes the first two characters are correct. The spelling checker runs more quickly, but the suggested word list may not contain the correct spelling.

Tip: If your computer is slow, turn off the **Always Suggest** option. The spelling checker runs much more quickly, and you still can see suggestions by choosing the **Suggest** command button in the Spelling dialog box.

Hyphenating Your Document

If you plan to create multiple-column text (see Chapter 19), you will find that narrow columns produce unsightly effects—especially if you justify the right margins (see fig. 6.4). The only way to correct this problem is to hyphenate your document. Hyphenating your text would be tedious if you had to do it manually. Word's **Utilities Hyphenate** command, however, can do the job for you automatically.

When Word hyphenates your document, the program inserts *optional hyphens*. These hyphens do not appear in your document's printout unless Word needs them to even out a line. If you want, you can confirm each hyphen's placement before Word makes the insertion. You also can choose an option that prevents Word from inserting hyphens in capitalized words. The rationale for this option is that most style handbooks forbid the hyphenation of proper nouns, such as personal and place names.

To hyphenate your document, follow these steps:

1. Press Ctrl-Home to place the cursor at the beginning of your document.

2. Choose **Utilities Hyphenate** (Alt-UH).

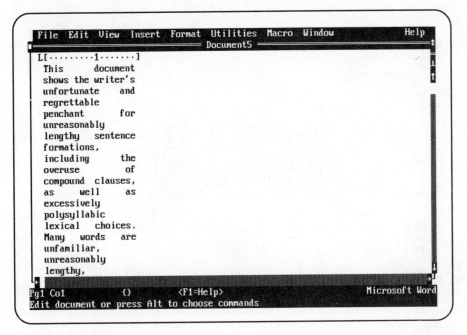

Fig. 6.4. A document that needs hyphenation to make the right margin even.

You see the Hyphenate dialog box (see fig. 6.5). This dialog box contains two check boxes, Confirm and Hyphenate Caps, both of which are toggled on. With these options, Word confirms each hyphen placement, and the program attempts to place hyphens in capitalized words.

3. Choose OK from the Hyphenate dialog box.

   Word searches for words contained in its hyphenation dictionary. If it finds a match, you see a Hyphenate dialog box such as the one in figure 6.6.

4. Word shows you all the places where the word can be hyphenated. The hyphen Word proposes to use is highlighted. You can use the arrow keys to position the cursor where you would rather place the hyphen if you don't like Word's choice. After you highlight the hyphen you want Word to use, choose Yes to confirm the option.

   If you want, you can turn off hyphenation or the hyphenation of capitalized words. Choose Confirm or Hyphenate Caps.

5. Repeat step 4 until Word finishes hyphenating your document.

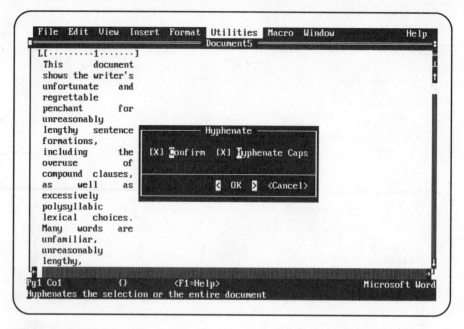

Fig. 6.5. *The Hyphenate dialog box.*

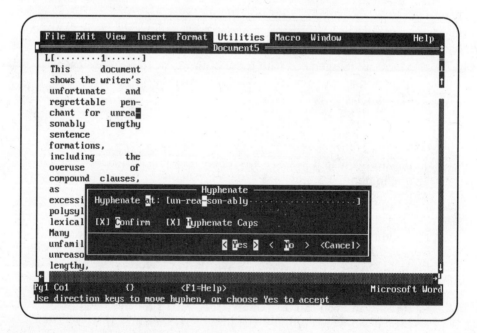

Fig. 6.6. *Confirming hyphen placement.*

When Hyphenation finishes its work, the message bar reports the number of words that have been hyphenated.

You still may need to use manual hyphenation techniques after running the hyphenation utility. Word's hyphenation dictionary is much smaller than its spelling dictionary, and **Hyphenate** skips any word that isn't in its dictionary (even if the word legitimately could be hyphenated).

Chapter Summary

Word 5.5's Thesaurus, Spelling, and Hyphenate features provide useful tools for choosing the right word, spelling correctly, and inserting optional hyphens throughout your document.

Use Thesaurus at every opportunity; it's useful for practical applications as well as for creative writing. Use it to make sure that you grasp all the connotations of words with which you're not completely familiar.

Spell checking is a necessity for business and professional writing, and Word Version 5.5's **Spelling** command is truly a pleasure to use. Be sure to save proper nouns to the standard dictionary, and don't forget to use the **Remember Correction** button when you run across an error you make frequently.

Word's **Hyphenate** command inserts optional hyphens throughout your document, but because the command's hyphenation dictionary is small, you may have to hyphenate some words manually to even out the right margin.

Quick Review

Hyphenation

To hyphenate your document:

1. Press Ctrl-Home to place the cursor at the beginning of your document.

2. Choose Utilities **Hyphenate** (Alt-UH).

3. Choose OK.

4. To confirm the hyphen placement, choose Yes. Word shows you all of the places where the word can be hyphenated. The hyphen Word proposes to use is highlighted. You can use the arrow keys

to reposition the highlight. After you highlight the hyphen you want Word to use, choose **Yes** to confirm the option.

5. Repeat step 4 until Word finishes hyphenating your document.

Spelling

To start spell-checking your entire document:

1. Press Ctrl-Home to start the spelling checker from the beginning of your document.

2. Choose Utilities Spelling (Alt-US). Alternatively, use the F7 keyboard shortcut.

To check the spelling of a word or selection:

1. Select the text.

2. Choose Utilities Spelling (Alt-US) or use the F7 keyboard shortcut.

To choose options for words that the spelling checker cannot find in its dictionaries:

- If the word is correctly spelled, choose **Ignore** to continue or **Add** to add the word to the dictionary currently selected in the Add **To** Dictionary list box.

- If the word is not spelled correctly, activate the Suggestions list box and use the arrow keys to view the suggestions. If you see the correct spelling, highlight the word and choose **Change** or double-click the correct word with the left mouse button.

- If you don't see the correct spelling in the Suggestions list box, type the correct spelling in the **Replace With** text box. Choose **Change**.

- If the error is one you make frequently, move the highlight in the Suggestions list box to display the correct spelling in the **Replace With** text box. Alternatively, type the correct spelling in the **Replace With** text box. Choose Remember Correction.

To start spell-checking of a word or selection only:

1. Select the text.

2. Choose Utilities Spelling (Alt-US) or use the F7 keyboard shortcut.

To cancel and redo the last spelling action, choose **Undo** from the Spelling dialog box.

To cancel all the changes that the spelling checker made, choose Edit Undo (Alt-EU) immediately after Spelling finishes.

Spelling Dictionaries

To add correctly spelled words to the standard dictionary:

1. When Spelling flags a correctly-spelled word, make sure that the Add **To** dictionary list box contains the Standard option. If it doesn't, choose Standard from the Add **To** Dictionary list box.

2. Choose **Add**.

To create a document dictionary and add words to it:

1. When Spelling flags a correctly-spelled word, choose Add **To** Dictionary and select Document from the drop-down list box.

2. Choose **Add**.

To create a user's dictionary and add words to it:

1. When Spelling flags a correctly-spelled word, choose Add **To** Dictionary.

2. Choose **Options**.

3. In the Spelling Options dialog box, choose User Dictionary.

4. Type a DOS file name for the user dictionary in the **User** dictionary list box.

5. Choose OK.

6. When the alert box appears, choose OK to confirm the creation of the user dictionary.

7. In the Spelling dialog box, choose Add **To** Dictionary and choose the User option from the drop-down list.

8. Choose **Add** to add a word to the new user dictionary.

Spelling Options

To turn off automatic retrieval of suggested spellings:

1. From the Spelling dialog box, choose **Options**.

2. Choose **Always Suggest** so that the X disappears from the check box.

3. Choose OK.

To turn off automatic detection of punctuation errors:

1. In the Spelling dialog box, choose **Options**.

2. Choose Check **P**unctuation so that the X disappears from the check box.

3. Choose OK.

To ignore words typed in capital letters:

1. In the Spelling dialog box, choose **Options**.

2. Choose **I**gnore ALL CAPS.

3. Choose OK.

To assume that the first two characters of a word are spelled correctly and speed up the retrieval of suggested words:

1. From the Spelling dialog box, choose **Options**.

2. Choose **Q**uick.

3. Choose OK.

Thesaurus

To look up a word in Thesaurus:

1. Highlight the word you want to look up.

2. Choose Utilities **T**hesaurus (Alt-UT). Alternatively, use the Shift-F7 keyboard shortcut.

3. Choose the sense of the word in the **D**efinitions list box.

4. Highlight the synonym you want and choose **R**eplace. If you don't find a word you want, choose Cancel.

To see synonyms of words in a Thesaurus list:

1. Highlight a word in the **D**efinitions or **S**ynonyms list box.

2. Choose **S**ynonyms.

3. To place one of the words in your document, highlight the word, and choose **R**eplace. Alternatively, repeat step 2, choose **O**riginal to display the synonym list of the first word you looked up, or select Cancel to return to your document.

To look up synonyms for a word you don't see in the Thesaurus window:

1. Type the word in the Synonyms for text box.

2. Choose **S**ynonyms.

3. To place one of the words in your document, highlight the word and choose **R**eplace. Alternatively, look up additional synonyms of synonyms, choose **O**riginal to display the synonym list of the first word you looked up, or select Cancel to return to your document.

7

Printing Your Work

Word 5.5's printing features are flexible and easy to use. In most cases, printing your work is as simple as choosing the File Print command. Word prints the document displayed in the active window on-screen. If you prefer, you can preview your document's formatting and page breaks before printing.

This chapter assumes that you have installed your printer by using the SETUP program and that your printer is connected to your computer and working properly with DOS and other programs (for information on the SETUP program, see the Appendix).

In this chapter, you learn to do the following:

- Preview document formatting and page breaks

- Set up your printer with the Printer Setup dialog box

- Choose print options to print more than one copy, choose draft printing, print document summaries, print hidden text, choose graphics resolution, and print selected pages of your document

- Initiate the printing operation and deal with common printing problems

- Use other printing strategies, such as printing directly and printing to a file

- Get the most out of your laser printer

- Solve common printer problems

Note: Before you print with Word, you should run SETUP so that Word copies the correct printer files to your disk. Because these printer files are in compressed form on the original Word disks, you cannot load the printer files from these disks directly to Word; you must run SETUP, which includes a

from these disks directly to Word; you must run SETUP, which includes a decompression program.

If you change your printer after installing Word, run SETUP again and select a new printer file. For information, see the Appendix.

Getting Ready To Print: Previewing Formatting and Page Breaks

You do not have to preview your document's formatting and page breaks before printing, but you can save money if you do—particularly if you own a laser printer. Toner cartridges are expensive! Why print a 35-page document, only to find that you haven't used Format Header/Footer on your header text, or that a bad page break is on page 3? The next sections explain how you can preview the formatting and page breaks of your document before you print it.

Previewing Formatting with Print Preview

If you have used any format you cannot see very well on-screen, such as page numbers or headers, you should use File Print Preview to make sure that you have handled these formats correctly (see Chapter 5 for more information).

This checklist of common formatting problems gives you an idea of what to look for when you use Print Preview:

- Do the headers or footers appear in the top or bottom margin? If not, you probably forgot to use Format Header/Footer to mark the header or footer paragraphs so that Word prints them as headers and footers.

- Are there no page numbers, even though you wanted them? If you tried to turn on page numbers with the Insert Page Numbers dialog box, you may have forgotten to choose the From Top or From Bottom option, which turn on page number printing.

- Do paragraphs appear appropriately spaced? If you are printing a single-spaced document, you may find that the document looks more attractive if a blank line appears between paragraphs. To insert a blank line, return to your document, select all the text paragraphs, and press Ctrl-O.

- If you're printing a letter, does it look balanced on the page? A letter should be positioned vertically on the page so that the text's center point is slightly above the center of the page. If the text is too high, return to your document, position the cursor under the letterhead, and press Enter several times. Make the margins wider (1 1/2 inches left and right) if the letter is brief; make the margins narrower (1 inch) if the letter is lengthy.

- Did you use character emphasis consistently? Have you switched from italic to underline? To make your emphasis consistent, return to your document and choose **Edit Replace**. Choose the Replace Formatting Only button to remove the inconsistent formats. (See Chapter 4 for more information on replacing formats in your document.)

- If you use a nonstandard point size, are there sections of your document where Word has inserted the normal point size against your wishes? Remember that pressing Ctrl-Space bar cancels all special character formatting, including fonts and font sizes. If you write a document with the Helvetica 10 font, and then press Ctrl-Space bar, Word returns to Courier 12.(You cannot see font changes in Print Preview, unfortunately, but you can see point size changes.) Return to your document, select the inappropriately formatted text, and use **Format Character**. (For more information on character formatting, see Chapter 4.)

- Does a heading appear at the bottom of a page? If so, return to your document, select the heading, and choose the **With Next** option in the Paragraph dialog box. (Make sure that the blank lines under the heading are entered with measurements in the After text box of the Paragraph dialog box, not with Enter keystrokes.) (For more information on paragraph formatting, see Chapter 4.)

Previewing Page Breaks

As you probably have learned, it's easy to produce a document with unattractive page breaks. If you add text on the third page of a document, for example, you may not realize that the insertion pushed your text down and produced an unsightly page break on the tenth page.

You can preview page breaks by using Print Preview, but the recommended way is to do so with the **Utilities Repaginate Now** command. This command provides you with an opportunity to preview and confirm the exact location of each page break in your document.

To preview and confirm all the page breaks in your document, follow these steps:

1. Choose Utilities Repaginate Now (Alt-UP).

   The Repaginate Now dialog box appears (see fig. 7.1).

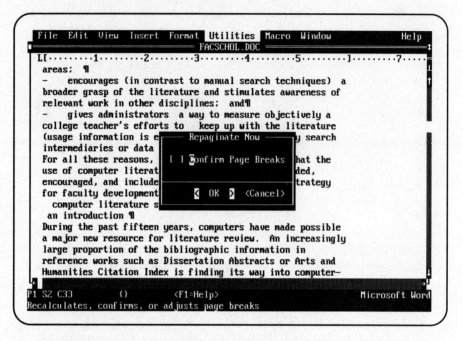

Fig. 7.1. The Repaginate Now dialog box.

2. Choose the Confirm Page Breaks option.

3. Choose OK.

   If Word encounters a page break you entered manually, you see the message

   ```
   Press Enter to confirm or the delete key to
   remove page break.
   ```

   If Word encounters a page break that Word entered as it pagi-nated your document, you see the message

   ```
   Press Enter to confirm page break or use
   direction keys to reposition.
   ```

4. Press Enter to confirm the page break. Alternatively, press Del to remove a manual page break or press the up-arrow key to reposition an automatic page break, and then press Enter.

5. Repeat step 4 until you confirm all the page breaks in your document.

Checking Your Printer's Settings

When you ran the SETUP program (see the Appendix), Word recorded your printer setup choices in the Printer Setup dialog box (see fig. 7.2). Before you print for the first time, and especially if your printer doesn't work properly with Word, you should check these settings to make sure that they are correct.

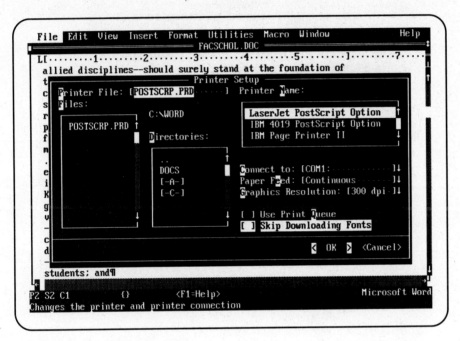

Fig. 7.2. The Printer Setup dialog box.

To check your printer's settings in the Printer Setup dialog box, follow these steps:

1. Choose **File Printer** Setup (Alt-FR).

   The Printer Setup dialog box appears.

2. Check the following information to make sure that it is correct:

   - *Printer File.* Does this text box contain the name of the correct printer file for your printer? If not, choose the correct printer file from the Files list box. If you don't see the correct printer file in this list box, run SETUP again, following the directions in the Appendix.

- *Printer Name.* Is your printer model highlighted in this list box? If not, highlight it. Many printer files contain information for more than one make or model of printer.

- *Connect To.* Does this drop-down list box contain the name of the port to which your printer is connected? Your computer probably has two ports—a serial port (COM1) and a parallel port (LPT1), and it may have several serial and parallel ports. Your printer cannot work unless you select the correct port in this list box. If you didn't name the port correctly when you installed Word with SETUP, you can change the port here. Highlight the correct port in the Connect To list box.

- *Paper Feed.* Does this drop-down list box contain the correct *default* paper feed option for your printer? (The choice you make here appears in the Print dialog box as the default choice for your printer. You can change the setting in the Print dialog box temporarily, if you want.) Depending on your printer's capabilities, you can choose from continuous feed, manual feed, envelope feed, and other options (such as multiple paper bins or mixed feed).

3. When all the information is correct, choose OK. If you don't need to make any changes, choose Cancel.

Choosing Printing Options

You choose printing options in two ways:

- Choose commonly selected options, such as number of copies, paper feed, and page range, in the Print dialog box.

- Choose less frequently used options, such as including summary information or changing graphics resolution, by choosing Options in the Print dialog box.

Looking at Print Options in the Print Dialog Box

If you choose File Print or use the Shift-F9 keyboard shortcut, you see the Print dialog box (see fig. 7.3). At the top of this dialog box, you see the printer file, printer name, and port options currently chosen in the Printer Setup dialog box.

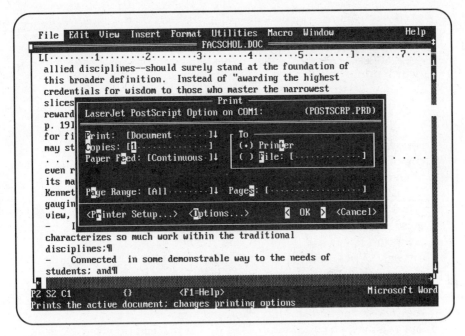

Fig. *7.3 The Print dialog box.*

The following list shows you the printing options you can choose in the Print dialog box:

- *Print.* Choose Summary Info to print the document summary without the document (see Chapter 8). Choose Glossary to print the current contents of Word's glossaries (see Chapter 12). Choose Style Sheet to print the current style sheet (see Chapter 20). Choose Direct Text to send the characters you type directly to the printer (see "Printing Directly from the Keyboard," later in this chapter). The default setting is Document.

- *Copies.* Type the number of copies you want to print in this text box. The default setting is 1.

- *Paper Feed.* Choose Continuous if your printer has a cut-sheet or tractor-feed mechanism. Choose Manual if you want Word to stop and wait for confirmation before printing the next page. Choose Bin 1, Bin 2, or Bin 3 to choose the bin from which you want your printer to draw paper. Choose Mixed to draw the first page from Bin 1 and all other pages from Bin 2. (These options apply only to printers with more than one paper bin.) Choose Envelopes if your printer has a special envelope-feed mechanism and you want to print an envelope. The default setting depends on the choice you made in the Printer Setup dialog box.

- *Page Range.* Drop down this list box to choose the Pages option (which prints only the pages you specify in the Pages text box) or the Selection option (which prints only the text you select on-screen). The default setting is All.

- *Pages.* In this text box, you can type the number of a single page you want to print, or a series of individual pages separated by commas (*1,2,8,14*). You also can type a page range using a hyphen or colon (*8:14* and *8-14*; both tell Word to print pages 8 through 14, inclusive). You can type the number of a page in a section (*14s2* prints the fourteenth page of section 2). You can combine any of these page expressions to print precisely the pages you want (*1, 2, 5-9* prints pages 1, 2, 5, 6, 7, 8, and 9, while *8s2-15s2* prints pages 8 through 15 of section 2). When you type a page number or expression in this text box, Word automatically selects the Pages option in the Page Range list box. The default setting is Blank.

- *To.* Choose File and specify a file name to print your document to a file. You may want to print to a file so that you can print the document later from DOS or transfer the file to another application program. Saving the file as an ASCII text file, however, is better. For more information, see Chapter 8. The default is Printer.

Looking at Print Options in the Print Options Dialog Box

At the bottom of the Print dialog box you find the Options command button. If you choose this button, you see the Print Options dialog box, which enables you to select further printing options (see fig. 7.4).

The printing options available from the Print Options dialog box are as follows:

- *Options.* Choose Draft to print your document without microspace justification or graphics. If your printer is capable of printing on both sides of the page, choose Duplex to turn on two-sided printing. This area has no default setting.

- *Include.* Choose Summary Info to print the summary sheet with the document. This option differs from the Summary Info option in the Print list box of the Print dialog box, which prints *only* the summary sheet, but not the document. Choose Hidden Text to print text formatted as hidden text. This area has no default setting.

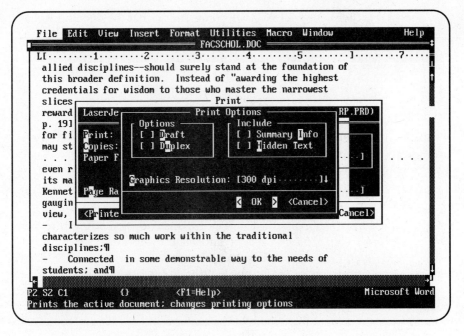

File   Edit   View   Insert   Format   Utilities   Macro   Window   Help
══════════════════════════════ FACSCHOL.DOC ══════════════════════════════
L[········1·········2·········3·········4·········5··········]········7·····
allied disciplines--should surely stand at the foundation of
this broader definition. Instead of "awarding the highest
credentials for wisdom to those who master the narrowest
slices ┌─────────────────────── Print ───────────────────────
reward │ LaserJe┌──────────── Print Options ────────────┐ RP.PRD)
p. 19] │   │ ┌─ Options ──────┐ ┌─ Include ───────┐ │
for fi │ Print: │ │ [ ] Draft   │ │ [ ] Summary Info│ │
may st │ Copies:│ │ [ ] Duplex   │ │ [ ] Hidden Text │ │
. . . │ Paper F│ └────────────────┘ └─────────────────┘ │·]
even r │   │   │
its ma │   │ Graphics Resolution: [300 dpi········]↓ │
Kennet │ Page Ra│   │·]
gaugin │   │   ◄ OK ► <Cancel>   │
view, │ <Printe│   │ancel>
-   I └──
characterizes so much work within the traditional
disciplines;¶
-     Connected   in some demonstrable way to the needs of
students; and¶
P2 S2 C1   {}   <F1=Help>   Microsoft Word
Prints the active document: changes printing options

Fig. 7.4. The Print Options dialog box.

- *Graphics Resolution.* If more than one option is shown, choose a
  lower resolution for quick printing and the highest resolution for
  the final draft. The default setting depends on what you choose in
  the Printer Setup dialog box.

Printing Your Document

Printing your document with Word is easy after you install your printer properly
and choose the printing options you want.

To print your document, follow these steps:

1. Choose **File Print**. Alternatively, use the Shift-F9 keyboard shortcut.

   The Print dialog box appears.

2. Choose OK to start printing.

You can use more complicated printing strategies, if you want. You can print
in the background while you continue to write and edit. You also can chain

documents together with the INCLUDE command so that the documents have continuous pagination. You can even print directly from the keyboard.

These approaches to printing are described in the following sections.

Using Queued Printing

If you choose Use Print Queue in the Printer Setup dialog box, your document prints in the background, enabling you to write and edit as the printer works. You probably will find, however, that your computer slows down considerably.

After you choose the Use Print Queue option, the File Print command works differently. After you choose this command, Word sends the information needed to print your document to a disk file instead of sending it to your printer. Because your disk can accept information more quickly than your printer, this operation is concluded much sooner than printing. Control returns to you, and you can continue editing, open another document, or create a new document. In the meantime, Word waits for moments when you're not doing anything, and during those moments, it sends information to the printer. In this way, printing occurs in the background while you continue to write and edit. With this technique, your computer isn't tied up while your printer churns through a lengthy document.

To print in the background while you continue to write and edit with Word, follow these steps:

1. Choose File Printer Setup (Alt-FR).

   The Printer Setup dialog box appears.

2. Choose Use Print Queue.

   You see an X in the check box.

3. Choose OK.

4. Open the first document you want to print.

5. Choose File Print. Alternatively, use the Shift-F9 shortcut.

6. Repeat steps 4 and 5 for additional documents.

While queued printing is occurring, you may need to interrupt the printing so that you can have complete control over Word, restart the printing from the beginning of the file (if a problem occurred at the printer), or cancel queued printing. To interrupt queued printing, use File Print Queue.

To pause, continue, restart, or cancel queued printing, do the following:

1. Choose **F**ile Print **Q**ueue.

   The Print Queue dialog box appears.

2. Choose **P**ause to interrupt printing temporarily, **C**ontinue to continue printing after you pause, **R**estart File to start printing from page 1, or **S**top Queue to cancel queued printing.

3. Choose OK.

Chaining Documents for Continuous Printing and Pagination

In Chapter 5, you learned how to create a multisection document. The advantage of creating a document with several sections is that you can use advanced Word commands to compile an index and table of contents automatically. The disadvantage—and it's a severe one on 8088-based systems—is that Word runs sluggishly when you try to create a huge document (more than 250 pages).

As an alternative to a lengthy multisection document, you can chain several documents together by using INCLUDE commands. Word keeps the documents in separate files and joins them (with continuous pagination) only at the time of printing. Because you can break the document down into small files, you will find it easy to work with. Word cannot compile an index and table of contents, however, if you chain documents together by using the INCLUDE command.

You can place an INCLUDE command in any document you create. The command tells Word to insert the file you name at the command's location. To chain documents together, you can place several INCLUDE commands at the end of the first section of the document. An even better way to link documents, however, is to create a new document that includes all the INCLUDE commands you need.

To create an INCLUDE command, follow these steps:

1. Place the cursor where you want the INCLUDE instruction to occur.

2. Press Ctrl-left bracket ([).

   Word inserts a left chevron.

3. Type *include*, followed by a space.

4. Type the file name of the document you want to include.

You don't need to type the period and the extension. Word assumes that you're including a Word document with the default extension DOC.

5. Press Ctrl-right bracket (]) to end the INCLUDE command.

Word inserts a right chevron.

To print documents you chained together by using the INCLUDE command, follow these steps:

1. Use the **File Open** command to load the document containing the first INCLUDE instruction.

If you created a new document that contains all the INCLUDE instructions, load this document.

2. Choose **File Print Merge**.

The Print Merge dialog box appears.

3. Choose **Print**.

Note: If you try this procedure and see the INCLUDE instruction in your document instead of the file it was supposed to include, check to make sure that you entered the chevrons correctly (you cannot just type them in; you must use Ctrl-[and Ctrl-]). Also, you must print by using the **File Print Merge** command. If you choose **File Print**, the INCLUDE instructions will not work.

Printing Directly from the Keyboard

If you have ever felt the need to turn your sophisticated, expensive computer system into a glorified typewriter, here's good news: you can send up to one line of text (50 characters) at a time directly to the printer. This technique isn't very useful for filling out forms, unless you're willing to spend hours trying to position the paper correctly; it's useful only for adding a brief note to a page.

To print directly from the keyboard, follow these steps:

1. Choose **File Print**. Alternatively, use the Shift-F9 keyboard shortcut.

2. Choose Direct Text in the **Print** drop-down list box.

3. Choose OK.

The Print Direct Text dialog box appears (see fig. 7.5).

4. Type the text.

5. Choose **Print** Text.

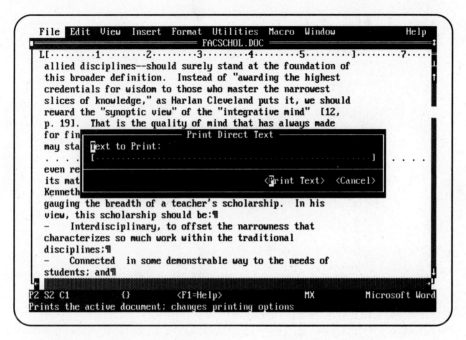

File   Edit   View   Insert   Format   Utilities   Macro   Window   Help
═══════════════════════════════ FACSCHOL.DOC ═══════════════════════════════
L[········1·········2·········3·········4·········5·········]·········7····

allied disciplines--should surely stand at the foundation of
this broader definition. Instead of "awarding the highest
credentials for wisdom to those who master the narrowest
slices of knowledge," as Harlan Cleveland puts it, we should
reward the "synoptic view" of the "integrative mind" [12,
p. 19]. That is the quality of mind that has always made
for fin┌───────────── Print Direct Text ──────────────┐
may sta│ Text to Print: │
· · · ·│ [···] │ · · · ·
even re│   │
its mat│   <Print Text> <Cancel>   │
Kenneth└───┘
gauging the breadth of a teacher's scholarship. In his
view, this scholarship should be:¶
-    Interdisciplinary, to offset the narrowness that
characterizes so much work within the traditional
disciplines;¶
-    Connected in some demonstrable way to the needs of
students; and¶

P2 S2 C1   {}   <F1=Help>   MX   Microsoft Word
Prints the active document; changes printing options

Fig. 7.5. The Print Direct Text dialog box.

Chapter Summary

To make sure that your document has been formatted and paginated properly before printing, use File Print Preview and Utilities Repaginate Now. Check headers/footers, page numbers, paragraph spacing, page balancing, character emphasis, point sizes, and headings in Print Preview. Preview and confirm page breaks by using Utilities Repaginate Now. Check the Printer Setup dialog box to make sure that Word is properly configured for your printer. If you want, choose printing options from the Print or Print Options dialog boxes.

This chapter ends the discussion of the fundamentals of Word 5.5. In Part III of this book, "Word 5.5's Features and Applications," you learn how to use many of the features that have helped seal Word's reputation as one of the top programs on the market. Don't be afraid to read this section if you're a newcomer to personal computing! Anyone can learn how to use Word's file-management, windowing, and outlining features; you will find that these features are indispensable after you try them.

Quick Review

Chain Printing

To create an INCLUDE command:

1. Place the cursor where you want the INCLUDE instruction to occur.

2. Press Ctrl-[to enter a left chevron.

3. Type *include*, followed by a space.

4. Type the file name of the document you want to include.

5. Press Ctrl-] to enter a right chevron.

To print documents you chained together by using the INCLUDE command:

1. Use the **File Open** command to load the document containing the INCLUDE instruction.

2. Choose File Print **Merge**.

3. Choose **Print**.

Checking the Printer Setup

To check your printer's settings in the Printer Setup dialog box:

1. Choose File **Printer** Setup (Alt-FR).

2. Check the information to make sure that it is correct.

3. When all the information is correct, choose OK. If you don't need to make any changes, choose Cancel.

Previewing Page Breaks before Printing

To preview and confirm all the page breaks in your document:

1. Choose Utilities Re**p**aginate Now (Alt-UP).

2. Choose the **C**onfirm Page Breaks option.

3. Choose OK.

4. Press Enter to confirm the page break. Alternatively, press Del to remove a manual page break or press the up-arrow key to reposition an automatic page break.

5. Repeat step 4 until you confirm all the page breaks in your document.

Printing Options

To print more than one copy:

1. Choose **File Print**. Alternatively, use the Shift-F9 keyboard shortcut.

2. Type the number of copies you want to print in the **Copies** text box.

3. Choose OK to start printing.

To change the paper feed method temporarily:

1. Choose **File Print**. Alternatively, use the Shift-F9 keyboard shortcut.

2. Choose the paper feed method you want from the Paper Feed list box.

3. Choose OK to start printing.

To set a new default paper feed method:

1. Choose **File Printer** Setup.

2. Choose a paper feed method from the Paper Feed drop-down list box.

3. Choose OK.

To print selected pages from the document:

1. Choose **File Print**. Alternatively, use the Shift-F9 keyboard short-cut.

2. Type the page numbers separated by commas, the page range separated by a hyphen or colon, or a combination of numbers and ranges in the **Pages** text box.

3. Choose OK to start printing.

To print a draft of your document quickly (without microspace justification or graphics):

1. Choose **File Print**. Alternatively, use the Shift-F9 keyboard shortcut.

2. Choose **Options**.

3. Choose **Draft**.

4. Choose OK to start printing.

To change the graphics resolution temporarily:

1. Choose File **P**rint. Alternatively, use the Shift-F9 keyboard shortcut.

2. Choose **O**ptions.

3. Choose one of the resolution options from the Graphics Resolution drop-down list box.

4. Choose OK to start printing.

To set a new default graphics resolution:

1. Choose File P**r**inter Setup.

2. Choose a graphics resolution option in the Graphics Resolution list box.

3. Choose OK.

To print text directly from the keyboard:

1. Choose File **P**rint. Alternatively, use the Shift-F9 keyboard shortcut.

2. Choose Direct Text in the **P**rint drop-down list box.

3. Choose OK.

   The Print Direct Text dialog box appears.

4. Type the text.

5. Choose **P**rint Text.

Printing Your Document

To print your document:

1. Choose File **P**rint. Alternatively, use the Shift-F9 keyboard shortcut.

2. Change any default printer options you want.

3. Choose OK.

Queued Printing

To print in the background while you continue to write and edit with Word:

1. Choose File P**r**inter Setup (Alt-FR).

2. Choose Use Print **Q**ueue.

3. Choose OK.

4. Open the first document you want to print.

5. Choose **File Print**. Alternatively, use the Shift-F9 shortcut.

6. Repeat steps 4 and 5 for additional documents.

To pause, continue, restart, or cancel queued printing, follow these steps:

1. Choose **File Print Queue** (Alt-FQ).

    The Print Queue dialog box appears.

2. Choose **Pause** to interrupt printing temporarily, **Continue** to continue printing after you pause, **Restart File** to start printing from page 1, or **Stop** Queue to cancel queued printing.

3. Choose OK.

Part III

Word 5.5's Features and Applications

Includes

Finding and Managing Documents

Customizing Word and Using Windows

Organizing Your Document with Outlining

Creating Tables and Lists with Tabs, Sort, and Math

Using Glossaries and Bookmarks

Creating Indexes and Tables of Contents

The Legal and Scholarly Word

Enhancing Group Productivity: Using Annotations and Redlining

Creating Form Letters

259

Chapter 8

Finding and Managing Documents

A good word processing program makes it easy to create and save documents—so easy, in fact, that you will be amazed at how fast you can fill up a 40M hard disk with dozens or even hundreds of document files. What began as a pleasure—the ease of using a high-quality word processing system—turns into a nightmare. Someone has to cope with organizing the files, with their cryptic names (11XMRPH.DOC) and unidentifiable origins. The problem is compounded when more than one person uses a single computer. No sooner do you erase an apparently useless file than someone comes charging angrily into the office, saying, "You've just wiped out the only copy of a $50,000 contract!" (If this happens to you, incidentally, the retort of choice is, "Our procedures call for disk and print-based backup at the end of every session.") But it's far better to avoid the whole problem by using Word intelligently.

A professional word processing program doesn't just help you create documents; it also helps you find and manage the documents you create. When you know the file name and location of a document, the easiest and fastest way to load a document is with the Open command on the File menu. Using Open, you can navigate your disk manually to find a file. If you're not sure where a document is or what its file name is, File Management—again on the File menu—gives you powerful tools to search the contents of an entire hard disk to track down an elusive file. File Management navigates your disk automatically, searching at high speed for files that meet criteria you specify. The criteria can include any information in the document's summary sheet, or even in the document's text. What's more, File Management provides easy-to-use tools for performing essential file maintenance tasks, such as backing up your work to floppy disks and deleting unwanted files.

The following is a brief overview of what you can do with this **File Management** feature:

- You can search for documents using any of the fields in the document summary sheet, such as title, author, date of creation, date of revision, version number, or keywords. Using this technique, you can track down the first version of the document titled "Letter to J.P. Jones," written on November 19.

- You can retrieve all the documents that meet specific criteria. You can ask, in effect, "Show me all the documents on the whole disk that were written by JONES in 1989," and the list appears in seconds.

- You can search for documents containing specific text anywhere in the files themselves. You can ask, in effect, "Show me any document mentioning the McAndrews contract," and the list appears on the screen.

In this chapter, you find a comprehensive approach to file and disk management, covering the following:

- Loading documents with the **File Open** command, including the use of path statements and wild cards

- Using the **File Save** command, including filling out summary sheets and saving documents in ASCII format

- Searching for documents with **File Management**

- Using **File Management**'s disk management capabilities to the fullest extent

- Gaining access to DOS while working with Word

An introduction to the **Save** command is presented in Chapter 2, "Your First Word 5.5 Document—Quickly!" For an introduction to the **Open** command, see Chapter 3, "Word 5.5 Writing and Editing Strategies."

Note: This chapter presupposes a basic working knowledge of hard disk organization with DOS. You should know what directories are and how to create, change, and delete directories.

About the File Menu

The File menu (see fig. 8.1) has many file-management options. Table 8.1 gives an overview of these options. Each is discussed in detail in this chapter.

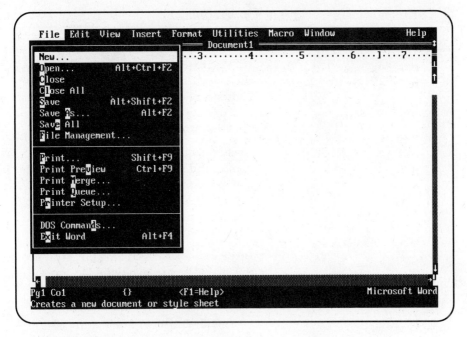

Fig. 8.1. The File Menu.

Table 8.1
File Management Options on the File Menu

Option	Shortcut	Description
New...		Displays the New dialog box. You can open a new, unnamed document or style sheet with this dialog box, and you also can use it to attach an existing style sheet to a new document. (For more information on style sheets, see Chapter 20, "Style Sheet Formatting.")
Open	Alt-Ctrl-F2	Displays the Open dialog box. Using this dialog box, you can specify the name of the file you want to open. If you're not sure of the name, the dialog box displays a list of all the files with Word's default extension (.DOC) that it finds in the default document directory. You can display files with other extensions (or

continues

Table 8.1—continued

Option	Shortcut	Description
		with no extensions), if you want. Using the **D**irectories list box, you can view the contents of other directories and drives. You use the Open dialog box to search for files manually.
Save	Alt-Shift-F2	Saves a document you have previously named and saved. If you haven't named and saved the document, you see the Save As dialog box, which gives you an opportunity to name the file and tell Word where you want the file stored.
Save **As**	Alt-F2	Displays the Save As dialog box. You use this dialog box to name the file and to tell Word where to store the file. You also can choose among four file formats, including ASCII characters only.
Sav**e** All		Saves all open documents. If you haven't named and saved a document, you see the Save As dialog box, which gives you an opportunity to name the file and tell Word where you want the file stored.
File Management		Displays the File Management dialog box. You can use this dialog box to search an entire hard disk for an elusive file, and you also can use it in place of DOS for routine file-management tasks, such as backing up your work and deleting unnecessary files.
DOS Commands		Displays the DOS Command dialog box, in which you can type a DOS command to perform such actions as formatting a data disk or running the MODE command.

More about Creating Documents

When you choose File New, you see the New dialog box (see fig. 8.2). Thus far, you have been pressing Enter to confirm the default settings in the New dialog box: Word creates a document file and attaches to it the default style sheet, NORMAL.STY. You learn more about style sheets in Chapter 20, "Style Sheet Formatting." As you will learn, style sheets are special Word files that contain your own specifications for formatting defaults and keyboard shortcuts.

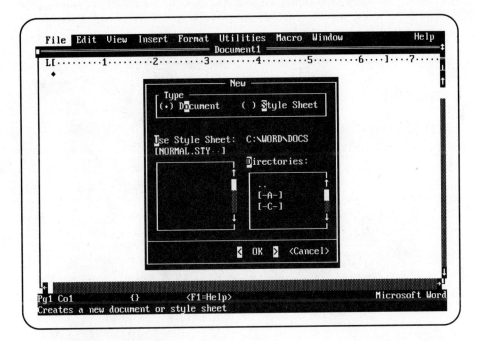

Fig. 8.2. *The New dialog box.*

At this point in your acquisition of Word skills, you use the New command to create new documents with the default formats, so when you see the New dialog box, you just choose OK. In Chapter 20, you learn how to use the New dialog box to create new style sheet files, and how to set up a new document with the custom style sheets you create. The Directories list is provided to help you locate these style sheets if they're not in the default directory.

Opening Files in Other Directories and Drives

In Chapter 3, you learned to use the Open dialog box (see fig. 8.3) to load documents you previously created and saved. If you started Word from the document directory, as this book advises, that directory is automatically the default directory for storing and retrieving documents. To make sure that Word always treats this directory as the default directory, you also learned how to type the default directory's path name in the File Options dialog box. Now Word automatically checks the default document directory for files containing the extension DOC (Word's default extension), and the program lists these files in the Open dialog box's Files list.

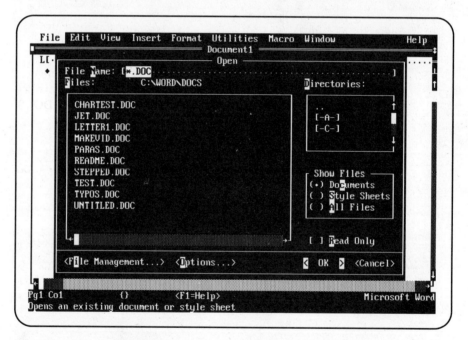

Fig. 8.3. *The Open dialog box.*

In this section, you learn to open a document that is not in the default drive or directory. Using this technique, you can open a Word file that is in a directory other than the default document directory, and you also can open a Word file that is on a floppy disk.

A document that's not in Word's directory can be opened in two ways. You can type its full path name in the File Name text box. If you don't like typing path names, or if you're not sure of the file's name, you can use the **Directories** list to list another drive's or directory's DOC files. By using wild cards in the File Name list box, you can control how Word lists files in the **Files** list box.

Typing a Path name in the File Name Text Box

A path statement tells DOS how to find a file. If you know how to type a path name, you can open a document in another drive or directory quickly: just type the full path statement and file name in the File **Name** text box. This method is fast, but you must know how to type path names and you must know the exact name of the file.

In case you have forgotten about them, here's a quick review of path names. To indicate a disk drive, type the drive's letter followed by a colon (for example, *c:* or *a:*). To indicate a directory, type a backslash followed by the directory's name (for example, *docs* or *letters*). To add a file name to the path statement, type a backslash before the file name. For example, the following path statement tells DOS, in effect, "The file called REPORT88.DOC is in the DOCS directory on drive C":

    C:\DOCS\REPORT88.DOC

To load the file REPORT89.DOC on the disk in drive A, you type *a:\report89.doc* in the File **Name** area.

Using the Directories List Box

If you don't like to type path names, or if you're not sure of the document's name, use the **Directories** list box to open files on a drive or directory other than the default. To use the **Directories** list box to open files, follow these steps:

1. Choose **File Open** or use the Alt-Ctrl-F2 keyboard shortcut.

   You see the Open dialog box.

2. Activate the **Directories** list box.

   A reminder: To activate an area in a dialog box, press Alt and the boldfaced key (here, Alt-D). Alternatively, press Tab until the cursor is in the list box, or click one of the options in the list box with the left mouse button.

3. To move out of the default document directory, choose the parent directory symbol (two dots).

   A reminder: To choose an option in a list box, highlight the option with the arrow keys and press Enter. Alternatively, double-click the option.

   This instruction assumes you have followed the instructions in the Appendix and created a subdirectory within Word's directory (such as C:\WORD\DOCS).

   Word moves the cursor to the File Name text box.

4. Activate the **Directories** list box again, and scroll the list box to display the name of the directory in which the file is stored.

   Press the down- and up-arrow keys to scroll the list, or click the arrow keys on the list's scroll bar.

5. Choose the name of the directory in which the file is stored.

   In the Files window, Word displays the DOC files in this directory.

6. Activate the **Files** list and select the file you want to open.

7. Choose OK or double-click on the file name.

To open a file in a drive other than the default, use this procedure:

1. Choose **File Open** or use the Alt-Ctrl-F2 keyboard shortcut.

2. Activate the **Directories** list box.

3. Choose the drive name (such as [-A-] or [-B-]) if you want to access a different drive.

4. Activate the **Files** list and select the file you want to open.

5. Choose OK or double-click on the file name.

Using Wild Cards To Limit the Display of Files

If you have created many Word files, the list of files in the Files list box may become too lengthy to be useful. If so, you can limit the display of files by typing a combination of text and wild cards in the File Name text box. The expression you type in the File Name text box serves as a mask for the list of files in the Files list box. By default, Word uses the expression *.DOC, which displays any file in the directory that has Word's standard extension (DOC). The valid DOS wild cards are listed in table 8.2.

Table 8.2
Using DOS Wild Cards with Word

Wild Card	Function
?	Matches any single character or number
*	Matches any single or multiple characters

The following examples show how to use these wild cards to limit the display of files:

- *REPORT8?.DOC.* Matches REPORT87.DOC, REPORT88.DOC, REPORT89.DOC, and so on

- **89.DOC.* Matches REPORT89.DOC, PROPSL89.DOC, and so on

- *LETTER??.*.* Matches LETTER10.DOC, LETTER10.BAK, LETTER11.DOC, LETTER11.BAK, and so on

- **.TXT.* Matches any file with the extension TXT

Opening Documents Created by Other Word Processing Programs

Like Word, most of the popular word processing programs on the market employ their own, proprietary files formats to handle formatting. Unfortunately, that means Word cannot read the files created by other programs, such as WordStar or WordPerfect—that is, not without displaying lots of happy faces and other "garbage" characters. To be fully usable by Word, another program's file should be saved as ASCII text (no formatting codes at all) or Rich Text Format (RTF). (RTF is a format coding standard that was developed by Microsoft and IBM to enable the transfer of files to different models of computers without the loss of formatting.)

Word can open an ASCII file without difficulty, but as you will quickly learn, it's difficult to edit ASCII files because there's a paragraph mark at the end of every line. Word needs paragraph marks only at the end of paragraphs. To transform the text into a document you can edit with Word, you must delete the unneeded marks. You can delete these marks easily by using the Replace command. You must do some of the work manually, but the rest is automatic.

To delete these unneeded paragraph marks, follow these steps:

1. Type three asterisks (***) at the end of every paragraph.

   The word "paragraph" here refers to the unit of text as humans recognize it, not as Word does.

2. Press Ctrl-Home to position the cursor at the beginning of the document.

3. Choose **E**dit **R**eplace (Alt-EE).

4. Type ^*p* (a caret followed by the letter "p") in the Text to **S**earch For list box.

5. Activate the **R**eplace With text box and press the Space bar.

6. Choose the **C**onfirm Changes check box so that the X disappears.

7. Choose OK.

8. Choose **E**dit **R**eplace (Alt-EE) again.

9. Type *** in the Text for **S**earch For list box.

10. Type ^*p* in the **R**eplace With text box.

11. Choose the **C**onfirm Changes check box so that the X disappears.

12. Choose OK.

More about Saving Your Work

As you learned in Chapter 2, you should fill out the summary sheet that appears when you use Save **A**s (or Save for the first time) if you want to make the most of the **F**ile Management command. In this section, you learn more about the summary sheet, as well as other facets of storing your work. You learn about the BAK files Word creates, how to save your work to an ASCII file, and how to save all your open files with one command.

Filling Out Summary Sheets

The first time you save a document with **F**ile **S**ave, Word displays a blank summary sheet. Following are some tips for filling it out.

Text Box Name	Length	Description
Title	40	Use this text box to type a short version of the document's title, with the most significant words first. (Word displays only the first two or three words of the title when you view lists with File Management.) If your document is titled "Report to the Directors on the Advisability of Investing in OK Products, Inc.," type *OK Products Report to*

Text Box Name	Length	Description
		Directors in the title text box. *Note:* The document title in the summary sheet has nothing to do with the document's DOS file name. By typing a title in the summary sheet, you do not change the DOS file name.
Author	40	You don't need to fill out this text box unless your computer is used by more than one person. If it is, be sure to fill out this text box for every document that you (and all other users) create. Be consistent: Always use one spelling and one form of your name. Don't type *Dr. Margaret Smith* for one document and *Maggie* for the next.
Version Number	10	If you want to keep track of the versions of a document you save, type a number (or any identifying text up to 10 characters in length) in this text box. *Note:* Word does not update version numbers automatically.
Operator	40	Use this text box only if you're typing someone else's document. Type your name in this text box.
Creation Date	8	Word fills in this text box automatically. If you forgot to set the system time and date, however, Word fills in these text boxes with the date of the beginning of the world (so far as MS-DOS is concerned): early in the morning of January 1, 1980. You can edit these text boxes to set the correct date and time.
Revision Date	8	Word fills in and updates this text box automatically.
Keywords	80	Use this text box to enter a few short, descriptive words that identify your document's contents. Use descriptors, or keywords that classify your document (such as letter, contract, report, memo), and identifiers, or keywords that identify its specific content (such as Jones, Acme Manufacturing, or National Science Foundation). *Note:* File Management cannot search for words you used in the Title box, so be sure to echo these words in the Keywords box.

Text Box Name	Length	Description
Comments	220	Use this text box to add any text that might help you identify the contents of a document (for example, "Contains the text of a proposal to the National Science Foundation for a study of professional ethics in artificial intelligence").

If you don't want to fill out the summary sheet, just press Enter when it appears. But think twice before doing so. Months from now, will you be able to tell what's in a file just by looking at that cryptic, eight-character DOS file name?

Tip: If you didn't fill out a summary sheet when you saved a document, you can add the missing information by using the Summary command button in the File Management dialog box. For more information on this command, see "Updating the Summary Sheet" later in this chapter.

About the BAK Files Word Creates

As you already have learned, Word creates an automatic backup file (with the extension BAK) when you resave your document. (No backup file is created the first time you save.) This backup file, however, does not contain the current version of your document, the one saved in the DOC file. Rather, the backup file contains the previous version of the file.

Caution: The BAK file Word creates is very useful if you want to abandon the changes made since the last time you saved a document. It's important to bear in mind, however, that the BAK file isn't a true backup file. To make a backup of the *current* version of your document, you must employ a backup procedure such as the one discussed later in this chapter.

Saving Documents in ASCII File Format

A pure ASCII file has no formatting or printer commands, and each line ends with a carriage return (displayed as a paragraph mark with Word). If you want to give your file to someone using another program, or if you want to upload your file through electronic mail links, save it as an ASCII file:

1. Choose File Save As (Alt-FA) or use the Alt-F2 keyboard shortcut.

2. When the Save As dialog box appears, type a file name for the document in the File Name text box.

   Many personal computers users employ the extension TXT to indicate that a file contains ASCII text.

3. Choose the Text Only or Text Only w/Breaks options from the Format list box.

   The Text Only option saves your document without formatting. Carriage returns (paragraph marks) are inserted only at the end of each paragraph. Choose this option if you want to exchange your file with someone who is using another word processing program, such as WordPerfect.

   The Text Only w/Breaks option also saves your document without formatting, but it places a carriage return (paragraph mark) at the end of each line. Choose this option if you are creating a file to send via an electronic mail system.

4. Choose OK.

Saving All Open Files

If you work with more than one document at a time, as you will learn to do in Chapter 9, "Customizing Word and Using Windows," you can save all your changes at once by using the Save All command.

Tip: If you create glossaries and style sheets for your Word documents, Save All is useful even if you're saving a single file. The command automatically saves the current glossary and all open style sheets as well as documents. For more information on glossaries, see Chapter 12, "Using Glossaries and Bookmarks." For more information on style sheets, see Chapter 20, "Style Sheet Formatting."

Retrieving Documents with File Management

If you're reasonably sure that you know the name of a document, what's in it, and where it's located, use the Open dialog box to find and load the file. But if you have any doubt about a document's name, contents, or location, or if you want to see a list of all the files conforming to specific criteria, use the File Management command to retrieve files instead.

Like the Open command, the File Management command initially displays a list of all the documents in the default document directory, but that's just the beginning. By specifying more than one search path, you can set up File Management so that Word automatically searches for documents in two, three, or more directories and displays all the files simultaneously. If you like to store your documents in subdirectories divided by topic, such as c:\WORD\REPORTS and C:\WORD\LETTERS, this feature will prove very useful to you.

File Management does far more than merely display lists of files in two or more directories. By using the Search command button in File Management, you can tell Word to search these directories for documents that meet criteria you specify. And these criteria can include any information you stored in the documents' summary sheets, such as Author, Keywords, Date Saved, or Date Created (or a combination of these). You can even search for documents that contain text you specify.

File Management is very useful for retrieving files, as well as for managing them. Using File Management, you can copy one or more files to another drive or directory—and, if you want, you can delete the original copies. This procedure is useful for backing up files you no longer use to a floppy disk for archival purposes. You also can use File Management to rid your disk of unwanted files. File Management is much easier to use than DOS for these copying, moving, and deleting operations.

Starting File Management

You can start File Management within any Word document, and you also can start it when no document is displayed on the screen. Think of File Management as a utility you can use at any time within Word. When you finish your File Management tasks, you return to writing and editing Word documents.

To start File Management, choose File File Management (Alt-FF). You see the File Management window (fig. 8.4).

To quit File Management, choose the Close command button. You return to your document.

About the File Management Dialog Box

The File Management dialog box contains three areas. At the top of the dialog box you see information about the assumptions File Management is using to display the files. The files are sorted by directory, the file names are displayed in the Short view (file name only), and File Management will search the C:\WORD\DOCS directory for files to display. You change this information by choosing the Search and Options command buttons at the bottom of the screen.

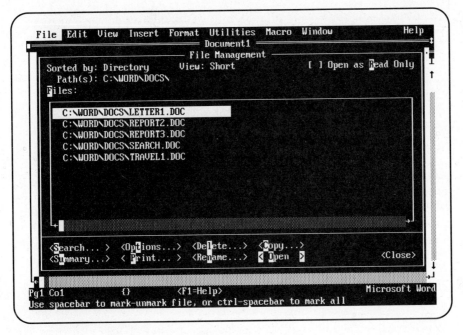

Fig. 8.4. The File Management window.

In the middle of the dialog box you see the **Files** list box, which displays all the files that meet the criteria specified in the Search dialog box (which is accessed through the **S**earch command button).

At the bottom of the File Management dialog box, you see nine command buttons. The following is an overview of these command buttons (listed in the order they're discussed in this chapter):

- **S**earch. Choosing this option displays the Search dialog box. You use this dialog box to specify search criteria for file retrieval. For example, you can search for all the files by an author, or all the files created between March 15, 1990, and June 1, 1990.

- **O**pen. Selecting **O**pen retrieves the selected file and opens a document window to display it.

- Options. Selecting this option provides options for sorting the file display, for viewing file names, and for updating the list after copy or rename operations.

- **S**ummary. Choose **S**ummary to display the summary sheet for the file highlighted in the **Files** list box. This command button displays the summary sheet whether or not you filled out the sheet the first time you saved the file. You can edit or complete the sheet.

- Copy. Using the Copy command copies the selected file or files to a drive or directory you specify. If you want, you can delete the files after they're copied.

- Rename. You can rename the selected file as though you were doing so from DOS by using this command.

- Delete. Delete the selected file or files with this command.

- Print. Display the Print dialog box, from which you can initiate printing of one or more files, by choosing the **Print** command.

As you can see, you can accomplish many tasks with File Management. You can retrieve files by using a variety of search criteria, and after you have identified the file you want, you can open it immediately. You can display files sorted by author, date of creation, size, or directory location. You can view just the DOS file names, or, if you prefer, you can choose a display that also includes the summary sheet information. You can copy, move, rename, and delete files, using techniques that are much easier than the ones DOS provides. You can even print one or more files directly from File Management.

Specifying the Search Paths

If you started Word from the Word document directory, as this book recommends, the document directory is listed in the **Search Paths** text box. To this directory you should add the path names of any directory that might contain Word files. Having added these path names, Word automatically displays any Word files it finds in the directories you have listed.

Note: You may not enter more than 128 characters in the Search Paths text box.

To change the default search paths, do the following:

1. Choose File File Management (Alt-FF).

   You see the File Management dialog box.

2. Choose Search.

   You see the Search dialog box (see fig. 8.5). As you can see, this dialog box contains text boxes corresponding to those of a document summary sheet. Your interest here, however, lies in the Search Paths text box and the Directories list box.

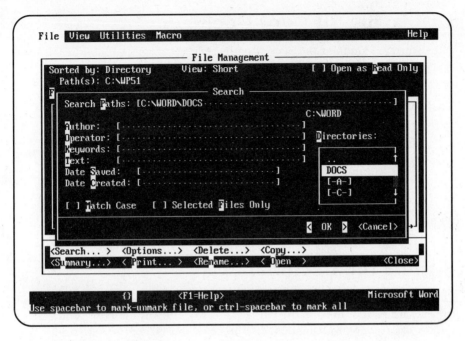

Fig. 8.5. *The Search dialog box.*

3. Activate the **Directories** list box, and use the arrow keys to highlight a directory that contains Word documents.

   To move up one level in the directory tree, highlight the parent directory symbol (two dots) and press Enter.

4. Press the comma key or click on the directory name that appears right above the **Directions** list box.

   Word adds the directory to the Search **Paths** text box.

5. Repeat steps 3 and 4 until you have added all the directories that might contain Word documents.

   The maximum number of characters in a DOS path statement is 128, including punctuation. You cannot exceed this limit.

6. Choose OK.

   The search paths you have chosen appear in the Path(s) area in the File Management dialog box.

Word saves your choice in the Search **Paths** text box until you change it again. Your choice will remain in effect the next time you use your computer.

Displaying All Word Documents

After you have defined the search paths, File Management is already set to display all the Word documents (that is, all the files with the extension DOC) in the directories you have named.

To display all Word documents, do the following:

1. Choose **File File Management** (Alt-FF).

2. Choose **Search.**

   You see the Search dialog box of the File Management command.

3. Leaving all the text and check boxes blank, except Search **Paths,** choose OK.

Sorting the Document List

File Management provides several options for sorting documents displayed in the Files list box. By default, the Files list box sorts files by directory, and if there is more than one Word document in a directory, it lists them alphabetically. You also can display files sorted by author, by operator, by date saved, by date created, or by size (in characters).

To choose a sort option, follow these steps:

1. Choose Options.

   You see the Options dialog box (see fig. 8.6).

2. In the area titled Sort Files By, choose one of the option buttons.

3. Choose OK.

Changing the View

By default, File Management displays the Short version of file names in the Files list box. In the Short version, you see the DOS file name only. You can choose options, however, that display more information (at the expense of showing fewer files in the list box at a time). The Long version (see fig. 8.7) displays the DOS file names, the document's author, and the first 21 characters of the document's title. (This information is drawn from the document's summary sheet.) The Full version reduces the size of the list box, and displays the summary sheet of the file on which the highlight bar is positioned (see fig. 8.8).

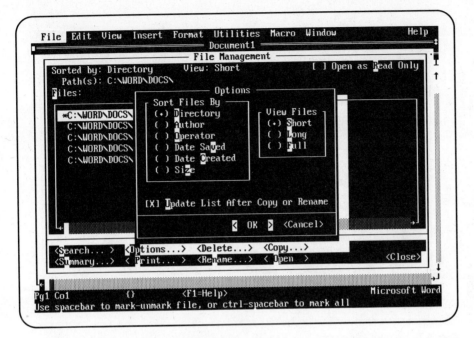

Fig. 8.6. *Options dialog box (File Management).*

To change the view, do the following:

1. Choose Options.

2. In the area titled View Files, choose Short, Long, or Full.

3. Choose OK.

Updating the Summary Sheet

If you haven't filled out summary sheets, or if you haven't filled them out systematically, you have handicapped File Management. To be sure, you can display all Word files, even if you didn't fill out a single summary sheet. But you cannot take advantage of the excellent search features discussed in the next section, "Refining the Search." As you will learn, it's possible to reduce the scope of the search so that the Files list displays only the documents that conform to criteria you specify. For example, you can tell Word to display only the files created by A.R. Jones after September 21, 1990, but you can do so only if you have filled out the summary sheets completely and accurately.

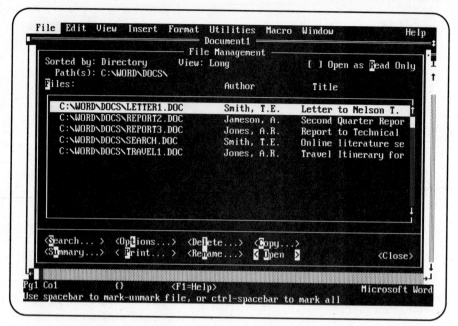

Fig. 8.7. The Long view of files.

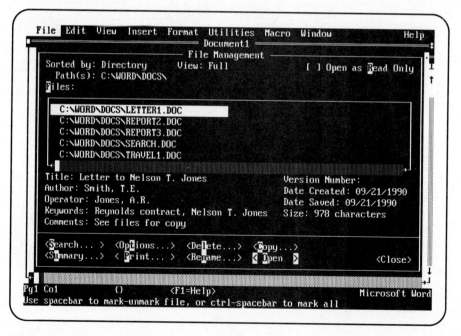

Fig. 8.8. The Full view of files.

In File Management, you can update summary sheets if you left out some information. You also can fill them out for the first time if you skipped the summary sheet when you saved the file for the first time.

To update a summary sheet for a document, follow these steps:

1. In the Files window, place the highlight bar on the file that contains the summary sheet you want to update.

2. Choose Summary.

   You see the Summary dialog box (see fig. 8.9), which closely resembles the one you see when you save a document for the first time.

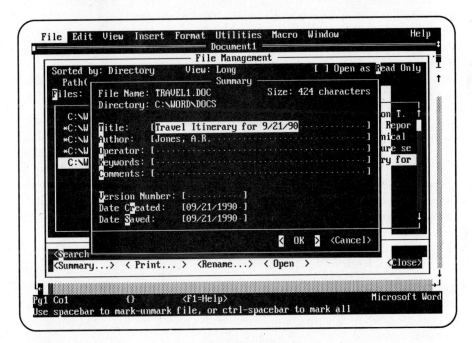

Fig. 8.9. The Summary dialog box (File Management).

3. Update the summary sheet.

4. Choose OK.

Refining the Search

After you have created many files, you may want to reduce the number of files that appear in the File Management dialog box so that Word displays only the files that meet the criteria you specify. For example, you may want to display just the files you created between March 15 and June 15, 1990; just the files that contain the text "recommendation letter" in the Keywords text box of their summary sheets; or just the files that include the characters "Spencer T. James Foundation" somewhere in the actual text of the document. To do so, you use the Search command button in the File Management dialog box. This button displays the Search dialog box (see fig. 8.5).

The Search dialog box includes many of the text boxes you fill out in summary sheets, such as Author, Operator, Keywords, Date Saved, and Date Created. When you type something into these text boxes, Word limits the search to just those documents that match the text you have typed. For example, if you type *Jane Arrowsmith* into the Author text box, File Management retrieves only those files whose summary sheets contain the characters "Jane Arrowsmith." Only those files are displayed in the File Management dialog box's file list.

If you have ever worked with a database management program, you will recognize this search technique, called *query by example*. To retrieve data using query-by-example techniques, you type the search criteria in a special, blank version of the data form (the form used to store data). When you fill in two areas of the form, the program retrieves only those records that match *both* of the items you typed. For this reason, a query-by-example search is highly restrictive. The more you type, the fewer data records you retrieve. (In computer terminology, typing text in two or more areas is the same as writing a search question using the AND operator.) When you fill out the form, you formulate a *query* (a set of criteria for retrieving documents) by providing *examples*.

Word's Search dialog box works the same way. If you type *Jane Arrowsmith* in the Author field and *9/21/90* in the Date Created field, File Management will display only the documents Jane Arrowsmith created on 9/21/90 (assuming, that is, that she filled out the summary sheet).

Within the text boxes, you can take advantage of many special features:

- **Logical Operators.** In any text box, you can formulate expressions using the following logical operators: OR (symbolized by a comma), AND (symbolized by an ampersand [&] or a space), NOT (symbolized by a tilde [~]), LESS THAN (<), and GREATER THAN (>). Word evaluates any expression containing logical operators by reading the NOT operator first, followed by the AND operator and the OR operator. You can change the order of evaluation by enclosing an expression in parentheses. Word always considers the expression in parentheses before considering the others. You learn more about logical operators in the following section.

- **Wild cards.** You can use the DOS wild cards (* and ?) in any text box (except Date Created or Date Saved) to broaden the search.

- **Searching for Document Text.** If you type up to 80 characters of text in the Text box, Word searches the actual text of all the documents retrieved by the query. You can use this option, for example, to search for all the files that mention "NSF Contract" or all the files that mention "Edward Smith." Be careful. Because this command searches the entire text of the document, it is very slow and may require several minutes to complete its work on an entire disk full of Word files.

- **Matching Case.** If you choose the Match Case check box so that an X appears in the box, Word takes the pattern of upper- and lower-case letters into account when it performs the search.

- **Searching the Selected Files Only.** If you choose the Selected Files Only check box so that an X appears in the check box, Word searches only the files you have marked in the File Management dialog box. To mark a file in the Files list box, you highlight the file and press the Space bar. Word places an asterisk by the file to indicate that it has been selected. You can select one or more files.

Using Logical Operators

You use logical operators within a text box to refine the search. The following table shows some of the ways these operators can be used.

Operator	Field	Result
Smith, Jones	Author	Retrieves documents written by Smith, and also retrieves documents written by Jones
Smith~Jones	Author	Retrieves documents written by Smith, but not those written by Jones
Smith&Jones	Author	Retrieves documents only if they were jointly written by Smith and Jones
>9/21/90	Date Created	Retrieves documents created after 9/21/90
<9/21/90	Date Created	Retrieves documents created before 9/21/90
>9/15/90&<9/21/90	Date Created	Retrieves documents created between 9/15/90 and 9/21/90

Performing the Search

When you perform a search that narrows the list of documents displayed, Word tries to find files that match the examples you have typed.

To reduce the number of files displayed in the **F**iles list, follow these steps:

1. In the File Management dialog box, choose **S**earch.

   You see the Search dialog box.

2. Type the search criteria in one of the text boxes.

   If you're typing a date in the Date **C**reated or Date **S**aved fields, be sure to use the date format you chose in the **D**ate field of the Customize dialog box. (To display the Customize dialog box, choose Utilities **C**ustomize [Alt-UU]). If you chose the DMY format, you must type a date in the format 21/9/90 or 21-9-90 (not 9/21/90 or 9-21-90).

   Use logical operators if you want, but remember that Word treats spaces as AND operators. If you type an OR operator (a comma), be sure not to leave a space before or after it.

3. Repeat step 2 for other text boxes, if you want.

   Bear in mind that every time you add characters to an additional text box, you narrow the search; Word retrieves files only if they match all the criteria you have listed.

4. Choose **M**atch Case to match the exact pattern of upper- and lowercase letters, if you want.

5. Choose OK.

If Word cannot find any files that meet the criteria you specify, the **F**iles list will be blank. Try the search again, but with less restrictive criteria this time. Make sure that you have spelled the search text correctly.

After you have successfully narrowed the search, Word displays only those files that match the search criteria you have specified. If the file you want isn't among those listed, it's possible that you neglected to fill out the summary sheet. Remember, Word doesn't "know" that Jane Arrowsmith created the document LETTER19.DOC. It merely "knows" that the document's summary sheet contains the text "Jane Arrowsmith" in the Author field. Note, too, that if you spelled "Jane Arrowsmith" incorrectly, either in the Search dialog box or in the summary sheet, Word won't display the file. You must have an exact match before Word will display the file.

> *Tip:* If you have just performed a search and Word doesn't display a file that ought to have been retrieved, check the document's summary sheet to make sure that you typed the information correctly. You learn how to check the summary sheet in the section titled "Checking the Summary Sheet," elsewhere in this chapter.

Restoring the Display of All Word Files

After performing a search that reduces the number of files displayed in the Files list box, Word retains the search criteria you typed in the Search dialog box. These criteria remain in effect even if you close the dialog box and return to your document. Only if you exit Word or deliberately change the search criteria does File Management return to the default display of all Word files.

If you have just narrowed a search but want to display all files again, you must return to the Search dialog box and remove the criteria you have typed.

To delete these criteria, follow these steps:

1. Choose Search.

2. Delete all the text in the Search dialog box's text boxes.

3. Choose OK.

Opening Documents

When you have successfully displayed the document you want to open, you can open it immediately. Alternatively, you can print the document without opening it.

To open a document, do the following:

1. In the File Management dialog box, place the highlight bar on the document's file name in the Files window.

2. Choose Open.

If you have a mouse, you can open a file quickly by pointing to the file you want to open and double-clicking the left button.

Printing Documents in File Management

When you choose the **Print** command in the File menu, you print the document in the active window on screen. Unless you use the print queueing techniques discussed in Chapter 7, "Printing Your Work," you can print only one document at a time.

You can use File Management to set up a print queue. To print selected documents, use the following steps:

1. In the Files window, place the highlight bar on the file name of the first document you want to print.

2. Press the Space bar to select the file.

   You see an asterisk in the selection bar, indicating that the file has been selected.

3. Repeat steps 1 and 2 until you have selected all the files you want to print.

4. Choose **Print**.

   You see the Print dialog box, the same one you see if you open a document and choose **Print** from the File menu.

5. Choose OK to start printing.

Managing Documents with File Management

You already have learned how to retrieve files with **File Management**. Using this command, you can retrieve Word files from one or more directories, and you can refine the search to display just the files that conform to criteria you specify. After you have displayed these files, you can open one of them by highlighting the file and choosing the **Open** button.

But **File Management** is also useful for the file operations you usually do with DOS, such as copying, moving, deleting, and renaming files. Chances are that you already have learned to perform these file operations with DOS. So why bother doing them with **File Management**? Here are some very good reasons:

- With DOS, the only way you can perform copying or moving operations on more than one file is to use wild cards. But it's easy to make mistakes with wild cards, leading to unanticipated results—

even loss of data. With File Management, you simply select all files you want to copy, move, or delete. Word then performs the operation you choose on all the selected files, one by one.

- When you use DOS to copy many files at a time to a floppy disk, you may run out of room on the destination disk. But DOS doesn't tell you which files remain uncopied. With File Management, you can see which files have been copied, and which ones haven't, should you run out of room on the destination disk.

- Unlike DOS, File Management warns you before you overwrite a file on the destination drive or directory that has the same file name as the one you're copying. This warning may help you avoid erasing an important backup version of a document.

- With DOS, it's a tedious job to move a set of files to an archive disk. First you must copy the files, then you must erase them. Unless you can perform these operations with wild cards, you must copy the files and delete them one by one. With File Management, you can move files—copy them to an archive disk, then delete them on the source disk—as easily as you copy them. You also can move more than one file at a time: simply select the files you want to move, and Word does the rest automatically.

In short, File Management is much more convenient (and much less risky) than DOS for performing file operations such as copying, moving, and deleting files. You should take advantage of File Management to perform the following maintenance operations on your Word files: backing up your work to an archival disk, moving unused files to an archival disk, and deleting unwanted files. You also can use File Management to rename files.

Note: If you regularly perform backup operations with a backup program such as PC Tools Deluxe, you need not use File Management to make backup copies of your work. With most backup programs, you can choose options that will back up any files on your hard disk that you have changed or created since the last backup was performed. These programs are convenient and provide an excellent margin of safety against data loss, should your hard disk develop a serious malfunction.

Backing Up Your Work to an Archival Disk

Computers enable writers to work more productively, but computer use carries with it the risk of catastrophic data loss. Without backup copies of your work, your Word documents are at risk: you might erase one of them accidentally, or your hard disk might fail, taking all your Word documents with it. A prudent computer user performs regular backup operations. An excellent way to back up your work for safekeeping is to copy your new or altered Word files to a floppy disk—or better, to *two* floppy disks, which should be kept in separate locations. The rationale for two backup copies goes like this: water, in the form of spilled coffee, rain coming in open windows, or just condensation from excess humidity, is second only to dust and dirt as the leading cause of floppy disk failure.

To back up your Word files to a floppy disk, follow these steps:

1. Choose **File File Management** (Alt-FF).

2. Select the files you want to back up.

   You can select the files in the **Files** list box: place the highlight on the files and press the Space bar to mark the file. If you prefer, you can perform a **Search** operation to limit the display to just the files you want to move. After performing the Search, press Ctrl-Space bar to select all the displayed files.

3. Choose Copy.

   You see the Copy dialog box (see fig. 8.10).

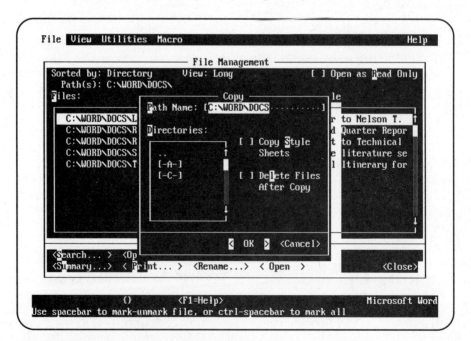

Fig. 8.10. *The Copy dialog box (File Management).*

4. Use the **Directories** window to choose the drive or directory to which you want to copy the files.

   To copy to a floppy disk, choose [-A-] or, if you have a second floppy drive, you may also choose [-B-].

5. Check to make sure that there is no X in the Delete Files After Copy check box. If you see an X, choose the check box so that the X disappears.

   If you have created style sheets for the document, choose the Copy Style Sheets check box so that you see an X.

6. Choose OK.

If Word finds a file on the destination disk with the same file name as a file you're copying, you see an alert box. To overwrite the file, choose OK. To cancel the copying operation, choose Cancel.

Moving Documents

You can easily clutter up your hard disk with hundreds of files of letters, memos, and other ephemeral documents. Rather than deleting them, you should move them to one or more floppy disks for archival purposes. When you move a file, copy it to the destination disk and then delete the source file.

To move files to a floppy disk, follow this procedure:

1. Choose File File Management (Alt-FF).

2. Select the files you want to move.

   You can select the files in the **Files** list box: place the highlight on the files, and press the Space bar to mark the file. If you prefer, you can perform a **Search** operation to limit the display to just the files you want to move. After performing the Search, press Ctrl-Space bar to select all the displayed files.

3. Choose Copy.

   You see the Copy dialog box (see fig. 8.10).

4. Choose the Delete Files After Copy check box so that you see an X.

5. Use the **Directories** window to choose the drive or directory to which you want to move the files.

   To move files to a floppy disk, choose [-A-] or, if you have a second floppy drive, you may also choose [-B-].

6. Choose OK.

If Word finds a file on the destination disk with the same file name as a file you're copying, you see an alert box. To overwrite the file, choose OK. To cancel the copying operation, choose Cancel.

Deleting Files

If you have created files that you're sure you want to abandon completely, you can delete them using the same, easy File Management techniques.

To delete files completely, do the following:

1. Choose File File Management (Alt-FF).

2. Select the files you want to delete.

   You can select the files in the Files list box: place the highlight on the files and press the Space bar. If you prefer, you can perform a Search operation to limit the display to just the files you want to delete. After performing the Search, press Ctrl-Space bar to select all the displayed files.

3. Choose Delete.

   You see an alert box asking you whether you want to delete the marked files.

4. Choose OK to delete the files, or Cancel to cancel the delete operation.

Renaming Files

Renaming files with DOS isn't easy: you must write a complicated expression. In contrast, renaming files with File Management is so simple and straightforward that you will feel free to rename your files as you please.

To rename a file, do the following:

1. Choose File File Management (Alt-FF).

2. Place the highlight bar on the file you want to rename.

3. Choose Rename.

   You see the Rename dialog box (see fig. 8.11).

4. Type the new file name.

   Word automatically deletes the name it proposes (*.DOC).

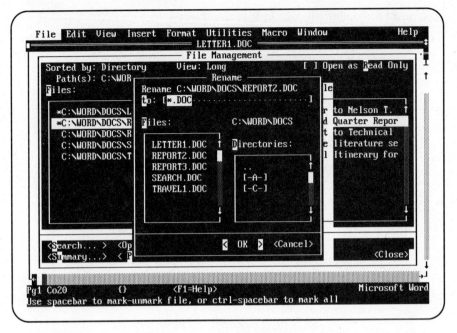

Fig. 8.11. *The Rename dialog box.*

5. Choose OK.

    You see the renamed file in the Files list box.

Using DOS in Word

Anytime you work with Word, you can leave Word temporarily, return to DOS, use DOS commands or other programs, and return to Word. The key to using DOS in Word is the **DOS Commands** option in the File menu.

Why would you want to access DOS from within Word? Suppose that you're archiving files to a floppy disk, but run out of formatted disks. You need to run the DOS FORMAT program. You can exit Word and run FORMAT, but it's much more convenient to run this DOS utility from within Microsoft Word.

You can use DOS commands in two ways. First, you can type a specific DOS command within the Word dialog box that appears when you choose **File DOS Commands**. Second, you can leave Word entirely and return to the DOS prompt, where you can type one more DOS command as you please. To return to Word, you type *exit* and Word reappears on screen.

To type a DOS command within Word, follow these steps:

1. Choose **File Save** (Alt-FS) to save your document (or **File Save All** [Alt-FE] if you are working with more than one document).

2. Choose **File DOS Commands** (Alt-FD).

   You see the DOS Commands dialog box (see fig. 8.12). The word COMMAND is highlighted.

3. Type the DOS command.

   When you start typing, Word erases the selection.

4. Choose OK.

5. When the command is finished executing, press any key to return to Word.

To exit Word temporarily and return to the DOS prompt, do the following:

1. Choose **File Save** (Alt-FS) to save your document (or **File Save** All [Alt-FE] if you are working with more than one document).

2. Choose **File DOS Commands** (Alt-FD).

   You see the DOS Commands dialog box (see fig. 8.12). The word COMMAND is highlighted.

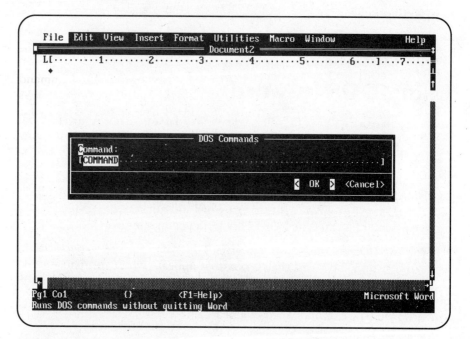

Fig. 8.12. The DOS Commands dialog box.

3. Choose OK.

   You see the DOS prompt.

4. Enter DOS commands.

5. When you are finished using DOS, type *exit* and press Enter to return to Word.

Chapter Summary

If you're reasonably sure that you know the name and location of a file you're trying to retrieve, use the **O**pen command. Don't forget that this command has the capability to load documents not on the default drive or directory, although you must use the **D**irectories list box to navigate your disk manually.

If you're working with dozens or hundreds of Word files, make yourself acquainted with **File Management**, which can automatically display all the Word files in all the directories in which you place Word documents. Be sure to name these directories in the **Search** dialog box of **File Management**.

You can use the **Search** dialog box to search these directories to find just the file you're looking for—provided, that is, that you have been filling out summary sheets. If you haven't filled them out consistently, you can update any document's summary sheet by using the **S**ummary option.

Make regular use of **File Management** to back up your work and clean up Word directories. Designed for use with Word documents, **File Management** performs these functions safely and effectively. If you need DOS while working with Word, use the **D**OS Commands option on the File menu. Keep this command in mind if you run out of space on a disk and you don't have any formatted disks at hand. You can use **D**OS Commands to format a disk without losing your document.

Quick Review

ASCII Files

To delete unnecessary paragraph marks from an ASCII text file:

1. Type three asterisks (***) at the end of every paragraph.

2. Press Ctrl-Home to position the cursor at the beginning of the document.

3. Choose Edit Replace (Alt-EE).

4. Type ^*p* (a caret followed by the letter "p") in the Text to Search For list box.

5. Activate the Replace With text box and press the Space bar.

6. Choose the Confirm Changes check box so that the X disappears.

7. Choose OK.

8. Choose Edit Replace (Alt-EE) again.

9. Type *** in the Text to Search For list box.

10. Type ^*p* (a caret followed by the letter "p") in the Replace With text box.

11. Choose the Confirm Changes check box so that the X disappears.

12. Choose OK.

To save your document as an ASCII file:

1. Choose File Save As (Alt-FA) or use the Alt-F2 keyboard shortcut.

2. When the Save As dialog box appears, type a file name for the document in the File Name text box.

3. Choose the Text Only or Text Only w/Breaks options from the Format list box.

4. Choose OK.

DOS Commands

To type a DOS command within Word:

1. Choose File Save (Alt-FS) to save your document (or File Save All [Alt-FE] if you are working with more than one document).

2. Choose File DOS Commands (Alt-FD).

3. Type the DOS command.

4. Choose OK.

5. When the command is finished executing, press any key to return to Word.

To exit Word temporarily and return to the DOS prompt:

1. Choose File Save (Alt-FS) to save your document (or File Save All [Alt-FE] if you are working with more than one document).

2. Choose File **DOS Commands** (Alt-FD).

3. Choose OK.

   If you see the word COMMAND in theCommand area, select OK. Otherwise, type *command* and choose OK. (Word keeps the last command you use in the Command area.)

4. Enter DOS commands.

5. When you are finished using DOS, type *exit* and press Enter to return to Word.

File Management: Changing the Default Search Path

To change the default search paths:

1. Choose File **File Management** (Alt-FF).

2. Choose **Search**.

3. Activate the Directories list box, and use the arrow keys to highlight a directory that contains Word documents.

4. Press the comma key.

5. Repeat steps 3 and 4 until you have added all the directories that might contain Word documents.

6. Choose OK.

File Management: Controlling the Display of Files

To choose a sort option:

1. Choose Options.

2. In the area titled Sort Files By, choose one of the option buttons.

3. Choose OK.

To change the view:

1. Choose Options.

2. In the area titled View Files, choose **Short**, **Long**, or **Full**.

3. Choose OK.

File Management: Copying Files to a Floppy Disk

To back up your Word files to a floppy disk:

1. Select the files you want to back up.

2. Choose Copy.

3. Use the **Directories** window to choose the drive or directory to which you want to copy the files.

4. Check to make sure that there is no X in the Delete Files After Copy check box. If you see an X, remove it.

5. If you want to copy the document's style sheet, choose Copy Style Sheets.

6. Choose OK.

File Management: Deleting Files

To delete files:

1. Select the files you want to delete.

2. Choose Delete.

3. Choose OK to delete the files, or select Cancel to cancel the delete operation.

File Management: Moving Files

To move files to a floppy disk:

1. Select the files you want to move.

2. Choose Copy.

3. Choose the Delete Files After Copy check box so that you see an X.

4. Use the **Directories** window to choose the drive or directory to which you want to move the files.

5. Choose OK.

File Management: Opening a File

To open a document:

1. Place the highlight bar on the document's file name in the **Files** window.

2. Choose **Open** or double-click on the file name.

File Management: Printing Files

To print documents:

1. In the **Files** window, place the highlight bar on the file name of the first document you want to print.

2. Press the Space bar to select the file.

3. Repeat steps 1 and 2 until you have selected all the files you want to print.

4. Choose **Print**.

5. Choose OK to start printing.

File Management: Refining the Search

To reduce the number of files displayed in the **Files** list:

1. In the File Management dialog box, choose **Search**.

2. Type the search criteria in one of the text boxes.

3. Repeat step 2 for other text boxes, if you want.

4. Choose **Match Case** to match the exact pattern of upper- and lowercase letters, if you want.

5. Choose OK.

To restore the display of all Word files:

1. Choose **Search**.

2. Delete all the text in the Search dialog box's text boxes, except Search **Paths**.

3. Choose OK.

File Management: Renaming Files

To rename a file:

1. Choose **File File Management (Alt-FF)**.

2. Place the highlight bar on the file you want to rename.

3. Choose **Rename**.

4. Type the new file name.

5. Choose OK.

File Management: Selecting Files

To select a file:

1. Place the highlight bar on the file.

2. Press the Space bar.

To select all the files in the **Files** list box:

Press Ctrl-Space bar.

File Management: Starting and Quitting

To start File Management:

Choose **File File Management (Alt-FF)**.

To quit File Management:

Choose the Close command button.

Opening a File in a Nondefault Directory or Drive

To open a file in a directory other than the default:

1. Choose **File Open** or use the Alt-Ctrl-F2 keyboard shortcut.

2. Activate the **Directories** list box.

3. To move out of the default document directory, choose the parent directory symbol (two dots).

4. Activate the **Directories** list box again, and scroll the list box to display the name of the directory in which the file is stored.

5. Choose the name of the directory in which the file is stored.

6. Activate the **Files** list and select the file you want to open.

7. Choose OK or double-click on the file name.

To open a file in a drive other than the default:

1. Choose **File Open** or use the Alt-Ctrl-F2 keyboard shortcut.

2. Activate the **Directories** list box.

3. Choose the drive name (such as [-A-] or [-B-]) if you want to access a different drive.

4. Activate the **Files** list and select the file you want to open.

5. Choose OK.

Summary Sheets

To update a summary sheet for a document:

1. Choose **File File Management (Alt-FF)**.

2. In the **Files** window, place the highlight bar on the file that contains the summary sheet you want to update.

3. Choose **Summary**.

4. Update summary sheet.

5. Choose OK.

Chapter

9

Customizing Word and Using Windows

A fter you master the basics of a word processing program, you can make the program look and behave on-screen the way you want on the screen. Word makes the screen customization process easy.

As you already have learned, Word enables you to open up to nine documents simultaneously. With more than one document open, you easily can copy and move text from one document to another. Word places each opened document in its own window, which you can size and move to suit your needs.

This chapter covers screen customization and windows in detail. In this chapter you learn the following:

- How to create new default settings for Word's many display options so that these settings are available every time you start Word

- How to reduce the screen's complexity by hiding the menu bar, the window borders, and the message bar

- How users of color monitors can customize their screens to display font sizes and other character emphases in distinctive colors

- How to open, size, zoom, and close windows, and how to use multiple windows for high-speed text editing

Users of previous versions of Word will find many improvements in the way Word 5.5 handles screen options and windows. Options are divided logically between the Preferences and Customize dialog boxes. The Preferences dialog box controls how Word appears on the screen, while the Customize dialog box controls the way Word runs. The options you choose affect the display in all the windows you open.

If you're used to Word 5's keyboard and don't want to learn new keyboard assignments, the Customize dialog box (Utilities Customize) offers help: you can choose options that restore the Word 5.0 function keys, and you can restore the Ins key's old function of inserting the Scrap's contents.

Customizing the Screen

Word 5.5 presents a well-designed document display screen, and what's more, you can hide or display every feature individually. If you're using a color system, you can paint every element of the screen, and you can assign distinctive colors to character emphases and point sizes.

Ribbon, Ruler, and Status Bar

You can hide or display the Ribbon, Ruler, and Status Bar by toggling these options off or on on the View menu. To toggle an option is to use the same command to turn the option on or off. The first time you use the **R**uler command, for example, you turn on the Ruler display. The second time you use the command, you turn the Ruler display off. When the option is toggled on, you see a dot next to the option's name in the View menu.

To toggle the display of the Ribbon:

> Choose **V**iew Ri**bb**on (Alt-VB).

To toggle the display of the Ruler:

> Choose **V**iew **R**uler (Alt-VR). Or, click the Ruler icon (an upside-down T) on the top of the right scroll bar.

To toggle the display of the Status Bar:

> Choose **V**iew **S**tatus Bar (Alt-VS).

You learned about the Ribbon and Ruler in Chapter 4, "Word 5.5 Formatting Strategies: Characters and Paragraphs." For more information on setting tabs with the Ruler, see Chapter 11, "Creating Tables and Lists with Tabs, Sort, and Math."

Display Options in the Preferences Dialog Box

The Preferences dialog box (see fig. 9.1) contains many options for customizing Word's screen. These options are grouped in the following areas of the dialog box:

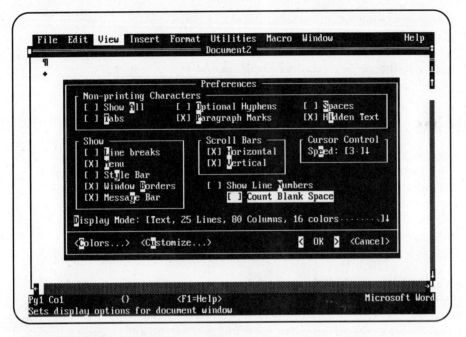

Fig. 9.1. The Preferences dialog box screen.

- **Non-printing Characters**. This option enables you to display paragraph marks, tabs, optional hyphens, spaces, and hidden text on-screen, which makes editing tasks easier. Word shows hidden text by default. The other non-printing characters must be toggled on if you want them to appear on-screen.

- **Show**. Toggle these options on or off to control the display of the following screen features: menu, window borders, message bar, line breaks, and style bar. By default, Word displays the menu, window borders, and message bar, but the printer's line breaks and the style bar must be toggled on if you want to see them on-screen.

- **Scroll Bars**. This option enables you to hide or display the horizontal and vertical scroll bars. If you don't use a mouse, you may want to hide both scroll bars. If you use a mouse but rarely create documents with line lengths wider than Word's screen, you may want to hide the horizontal menu bar. By default, Word displays both scroll bars.

- **Cursor Control**. By choosing a number from one to nine, you can control the speed of the cursor on-screen. If the cursor zips around the screen too fast, choose a lower number. If the cursor moves sluggishly, choose a higher one. The default number is three.

- **Show Line Numbers**. You choose this option to turn on the line counter on the status bar. After choosing this option, Word activates the Count Blank Space option, which gives you the option of including or not including blank lines in the line count. After you toggle on Show Line Numbers, Word inserts the line indicator (abbreviated Li) between the Pg (page) and Co (column) indicators. By default, line numbers are toggled off and blank spaces aren't counted.

- **Display Mode**. You use this option to choose the display modes that are available for your video card and monitor. Depending on your system's capabilities, you may be able to choose from several text modes and one or more graphic modes (in which you see italics, small caps, and other emphases on-screen). By default, Word displays the display mode you chose when you ran SETUP.

Displaying a Clean Screen

Some writers prefer not to see distracting elements on-screen. With Word you can hide every screen feature. You see nothing on-screen but the cursor, the end mark, and your text. You can display the menu by pressing Alt, but when you're finished choosing options, the menu disappears. A clean screen means you see more text on the screen. If your computer is equipped with a high-resolution monitor, it may be able to display up to 50 lines of text on one screen Figure 9.2 shows a clean screen with 25 lines of text.

> *Caution:* When you hide the window borders and scroll bars, you disable the mouse features that require the borders or bars. You must use the menus to perform actions such as closing, moving, and sizing windows, as well as turning on the Ruler and scrolling the screen.

To display a clean screen:

1. If the Ruler or Ribbon is displayed, choose **View Ruler** (Alt-VR) or **View Ribbon** (Alt-VB) to toggle off these features.

2. Choose **View Status Bar** (Alt-VS) to toggle off the display of the status bar.

3. Choose **View Preferences** (Alt-VE).

   You see the View Preferences dialog box.

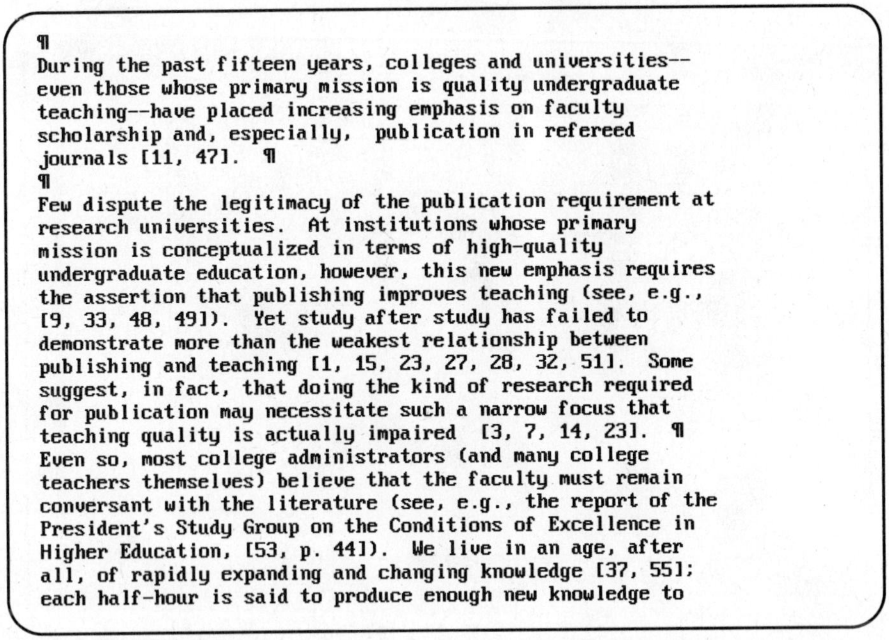

```
¶
During the past fifteen years, colleges and universities--
even those whose primary mission is quality undergraduate
teaching--have placed increasing emphasis on faculty
scholarship and, especially,  publication in refereed
journals [11, 47].  ¶
¶
Few dispute the legitimacy of the publication requirement at
research universities.  At institutions whose primary
mission is conceptualized in terms of high-quality
undergraduate education, however, this new emphasis requires
the assertion that publishing improves teaching (see, e.g.,
[9, 33, 48, 49]).  Yet study after study has failed to
demonstrate more than the weakest relationship between
publishing and teaching [1, 15, 23, 27, 28, 32, 51].  Some
suggest, in fact, that doing the kind of research required
for publication may necessitate such a narrow focus that
teaching quality is actually impaired  [3, 7, 14, 23].  ¶
Even so, most college administrators (and many college
teachers themselves) believe that the faculty must remain
conversant with the literature (see, e.g., the report of the
President's Study Group on the Conditions of Excellence in
Higher Education, [53, p. 44]).  We live in an age, after
all, of rapidly expanding and changing knowledge [37, 55];
each half-hour is said to produce enough new knowledge to
```

Fig. 9.2. Clean Screen display of 50 lines of text (VGA monitor).

4. Choose **Menu**, **Window Borders**, and **Message Bar** until the X disappears from the corresponding check boxes.

5. Choose OK.

Choosing Settings

The Customize dialog box shown in figure 9.3 contains many options that control the way Word operates. You've already learned to use the Autosave option, and you have learned how to choose a default measurement option. The Settings area contains the following options:

- **Background Pagination**. By default, Word inserts page breaks as you enter and edit text. Choose this option to toggle off background pagination.

- **Prompt for Summary Info**. By default, Word displays a summary sheet when you save your document for the first time or save it with a new name using the Save As command. Toggle this option off if you don't want to fill out summary sheets.

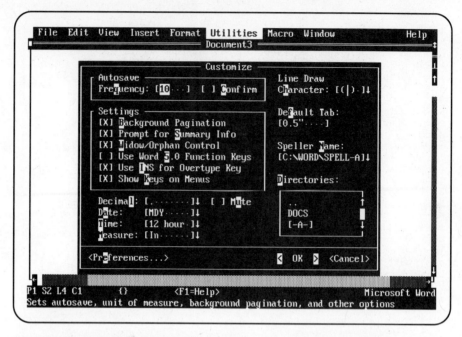

Fig. 9.3. The Customize dialog box.

- **Widow/Orphan Control**. By default, Word suppresses widows (a starting line of a paragraph left alone at the bottom of a page) and orphans (a closing line of a paragraph left alone at the top of a page). When this option is on, Word may not print exactly the same number of lines of text on each page: widows will be moved to the next page, and an additional line will be moved to the next page to give an orphan company. For technical and desktop publishing applications, you may want to turn off this option so you can predict with precision how many lines will print on a given page.

- **Use Word 5.0 Function Keys**. This option enables Word 5.0 users to use the function keys they have learned already. If you're new to Word, or if you're willing to relearn Word, leave the option the way it's set by default, which is off.

- **Use Ins for Overtype Key**. In previous versions of Word, the Ins key inserted the Scrap's contents at the cursor's location. The new Ins key assignment is in line with industry standards: the key toggles between the insert and overtype mode. This option functions by default. You can toggle off this option if you prefer the way the Ins key worked in previous Word versions, but you will have to press Alt-F5 to toggle overtype mode on.

- **Show Keys on Menus**. If a keyboard shortcut exists, Word displays the shortcut next to the options on the drop-down menus. If you don't use the shortcuts and find the keys distracting, you can hide them by choosing this option.

The Customize dialog box also contains the following less frequently used options:

- **Line Draw**. Use this drop-down box to choose the character Word employs in the program's Line Draw mode. You learn more about the Line Draw mode, and what these choices mean, in Chapter 17, "Creating Forms and Illustrations."

- **Default Tab**. Use this text box to change the default tab stops, which are the ones Word enters automatically across the screen. By default, Word places tabs every one-half inch across the screen. You can change the default tab width by typing a new measurement in this box.

  Note: Type the measurement in the measurement format that's currently chosen in the **Measure** list box.

- **Speller Name**. This box is used only if you have ordered one of Microsoft's custom spelling dictionaries. To use a custom dictionary, type its name here.

- **Decimal**. If you prefer, you can display a comma instead of a period to represent the decimal point. Word uses the comma instead of the period when it performs calculations. For information on how Word handles math and decimals, see Chapter 11, "Creating Tables and Lists with Tabs, Sort, and Math."

- **Date**. Word can display the dates it automatically inserts in two formats, MDY (month-day-year) or DMY (day-month-year). The default format is MDY.

  Note: When you type dates in the Search dialog box of the **File Management** command, you must use the date format you choose here.

- **Time**. Word can display the time it automatically inserts in two formats, 12-hour and 24-hour.

- **Mute**. If you don't like Word's beep, you can disable the beep by choosing the **Mute** check box.

Choosing Colors

When you install Word using SETUP, you tell the program which video card and monitor you're using. If you're using a color monitor, SETUP chooses a default color set. You can choose an alternate color set, or, if you want to be creative, you can paint each element of the screen individually. Table 9.1 lists all the features to which you can assign colors individually.

Table 9.1
What You Can Color

Screen Features

Accelerator keys (boldfaced keys on menus)

Dialog box background

Dialog box border (active dialog box)

Dialog box border (inactive dialog box)

Menu background

Message bar background

Ribbon background

Ruler background

Scroll bars

Status bar background

Window background

Window border (active window)

Window border (inactive window)

Window title bar

Text

Bold text

Bold and italic text

Bold and underline text

Dialog box text

Double underline text

Font smaller than 8.5 points

Font between 9.0 and 10 points

Font between 10.5 and 12 points (normal character)

Font between 12.5 and 14 points

Font greater than 14 points

Hidden text

Italic text

Italic and underline text

Menu text

Message bar text

Ribbon text

Ruler text

Small caps text

Status bar text

Strikethrough text

Subscript text

Superscript text

Underline text

Uppercase text

To choose an alternate color set, follow these steps:

1. Choose **View Preferences** (Alt-VE).

2. Choose **Colors** (Alt-C).

   The Colors dialog box, shown in figure 9.4, appears.

3. Choose **Color Set** (Alt-S).

4. Drop down the list box.

   Note: To drop down the list box, press the down-arrow key or click the arrow to the right of the box.

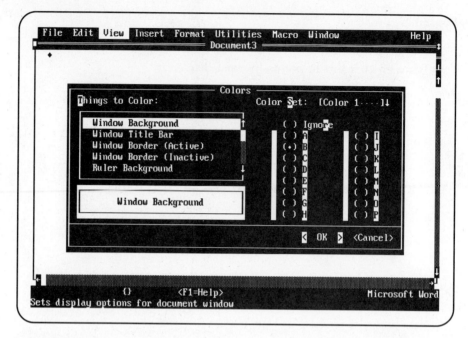

Fig. 9.4. The Colors dialog box lists document features that can be colored.

The options you see depend on your monitor. If you have a VGA monitor, for example, you see three color sets, a monochrome option (four shades of grey), and an LCD option (black and white only). Color 1 is the default, conservative color scheme, with soothing blues and greens. Color 2 is a bit jazzier, showing accelerator keys (the boldfaced keys you press to choose a menu option) in bright red. Color 3 is a monochrome color set designed for monochrome EGA and VGA monitors, which are capable of displaying shades of grey. Choose the Monochrome color set if you want black and white only, and the LCD color set if you're using a portable computer. If you choose the LCD color set, you see a square cursor on the screen. The square cursor is easier to see on a portable computer's display.

5. Choose a Color Set option.

6. Close the list box.

7. Choose OK.

If you're not happy with the colors available in Word's built-in color sets, you can color each screen element independently.

To color individual screen elements, follow these steps:

1. Choose **View** **Preferences** (Alt-VE).

2. Choose **Colors** (Alt-C).

   The Colors dialog box appears (fig. 9.4).

3. Choose what you want to color in the **Things to Color** list box.

   The area just below this list box shows the current color options for the selected screen features.

4. Press the letter or click the left mouse button next to the color you want.

5. Repeat steps 3 and 4 until you have chosen all the colors you want.

6. Choose OK.

> *Tip:* If you work with more than one point size, use the Colors dialog box to find out which colors have been assigned to the various point sizes. Modify these colors so that you can see and understand your point size choices on the screen.

If you're not happy with the results of your coloring efforts, you can restore the default screen colors after making custom color choices.

To restore the default colors, follow these steps:

1. Choose **View** **Preferences** (Alt-VE).

2. Choose **Colors** (Alt-C).

3. Choose **Color** **Set** (Alt-S).

   The Color **Set** box is blank, indicating that you previously chose custom colors.

4. Drop down the list box.

5. Choose a Color Set option.

6. Close the list box.

7. Choose OK.

Using Word 5.5's Windows

A window is a frame through which you view a document. Think of the document window as if it were suspended just above the text, showing you about one-third of a page at a time. When you scroll your document, you move it up or down past the stationary window.

By default, Word displays a single window; you can open up to nine windows at a time. In addition, you can split any window into two panes, in which you can view two different parts of the same document.

The following list gives you a brief overview of the ways you can use windows and panes:

- Using panes, you can look at two parts of a single document, each in its own window. You can scroll one pane while leaving the other pane stationary. After you become comfortable with this feature, you will find it extremely useful when you copy or move text from one part of a document to another.

- As you will learn in Chapter 10, you can look at your document in two ways: as an ordinary document, with all the text visible, or as an outline, with just the headings visible. With panes, you can view your document in both modes at the same time. Looking at both views helps you keep your document organized.

- You can work with up to nine different documents at a time with Word, each in its own window. This feature makes it exceptionally easy to copy or move text from one document to another.

In previous versions of Word, the program's windows were tiled; when you opened a new window, the other windows shrank to make room. You could zoom a window to full size, but in the normal view you were stuck with a window that filled half the screen or less. In Word 5.5, the windows overlap. As shown in figure 9.5, the active window is in the foreground, while two inactive windows are shown in the background. Clicking the background window's border brings this window immediately to the foreground. Clicking the Maximize icon expands the window so that it fills the screen (see fig. 9.6). Clicking the Maximize icon again reduces the window, making the borders of inactive windows visible. In this way, you can quickly move from one window to another. As you learn in the following subsections, there are menu equivalents for all these mouse techniques.

Note: You can display a special pane that shows footnotes and annotations. This window is discussed in Chapter 14, "The Legal and Scholarly Word."

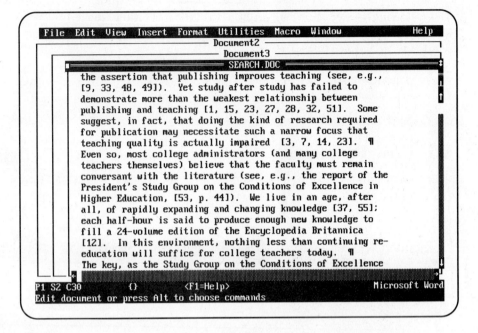

Fig. 9.5. Three documents open at the same time (not maximized).

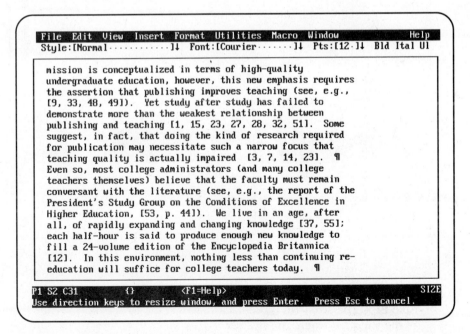

Fig. 9.6. A maximized window.

The following subsections explain how to open a window, make a window active, size a window, move text between windows, zoom windows, and close windows.

> **Tip:** One of several good reasons for using the mouse is the ease with which you can split, zoom, size, and close windows. You can accomplish all these tasks with the keyboard, but the mouse makes it easier and faster.

Window Features

As shown in figure 9.7, Word 5.5's windows have several features on which you can use your mouse to maximize, size, move, and close windows.

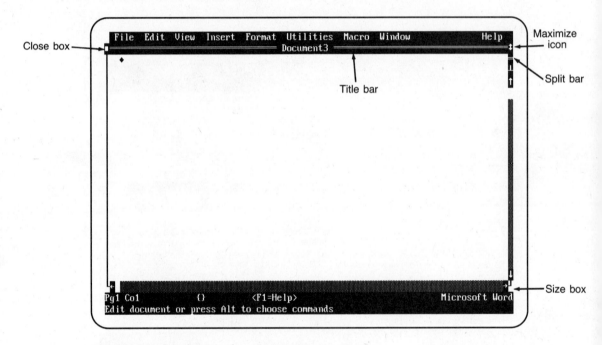

Fig. 9.7. Window features for mouse users.

- **Maximize Icon**. The maximize icon is the vertical arrow at the top of the right scroll bar that points up and down. You click this icon to zoom a window to full size, and to reduce an active window to reveal other windows hidden beneath the active window.

- **Size Box**. The size icon is the backward L in the lower right corner of the window, where the two scroll bars meet. You drag this icon to size windows.

- **Title Bar**. The title bar is the double line on the top border of the window. You drag the title bar to move a window. You also can drag the left window border.

- **Split Bar**. The split bar is the equal sign beneath the maximize icon. You drag this bar down to split a document into two panes.

- **Close Box**. The close box symbol is the square in the upper left corner of the window. Click this square to close the window. If you haven't saved your work, Word prompts you to do so.

Working with More than One Document

When you have a document on-screen, you may decide you want to look at some text in another document. To do so, you open the second document and Word places this document in its own window, without disturbing the first document. The second window, the one you just opened, is now the active window—the one in which the cursor is positioned. After you have read the text you want to see, you can switch back to the first document three different ways: by using the menus, keyboard shortcuts, or a mouse.

To switch between two or more windows on-screen using the menus, follow these steps:

1. Choose Window (Alt-W).

   The Window menu will appear. The bottom third of the menu lists all the open windows.

2. Choose the name or type the number of the document to which you want to switch.

To switch between windows using the keyboard shortcuts, do the following: **Ctrl-F6, Shift-Ctrl-F6**

   Press Ctrl-F6 to activate the next window in the sequence (windows are listed in the Window menu), or press Shift-Ctrl-F6 to activate the previous window.

To switch among windows using the mouse, do the following:

   If you can see the border of an inactive window that you want to activate, click the border with the left mouse button.

Copying or Moving Text Between Two Documents

One of the best reasons for opening more than one document at a time is the ease with which you can copy or move text from one document to another. To accomplish these maneuvers, do the following:

1. Open the first document, the one to which you want to copy or move text.

2. Open the second document, the one from which you want to copy or move text.

3. Find the text, highlight it, and use the **Edit C**opy or **Edit C**ut commands.

4. Choose the first document's name from the **Window** menu.

5. Move the cursor to the place you want the text to appear.

6. Choose **Edit P**aste.

If you cut text from the first document, Word asks whether you want to save the changes you have made when you close the document.

Maximizing Windows

If a window doesn't take up the whole screen, you can increase the window to full size by choosing the **Window Maximize** command, or its keyboard or mouse equivalents. When you maximize a window, the message M X appears on the status bar. If other windows are open, the maximized window hides them, but these other windows remain open behind the maximized window. You can activate a hidden window by choosing its name from the **Windows** menu.

Ctrl-F10   To maximize a window using the menu and keyboard technique, choose **Windows Maximize (Alt-WM)** or choose the Ctrl-F10 keyboard shortcut.

 To maximize a window using the mouse, click the maximize icon.

Sizing Windows

You can change the size of a window by using the keyboard or the mouse.

To size a window with the keyboard, do the following: **Ctrl-F8**

1. Choose **Window Size** (Alt-WS) or choose the Ctrl-F8 keyboard
   shortcut.

   As shown in figure 9.8, Word places an enlarged border around
   the document.

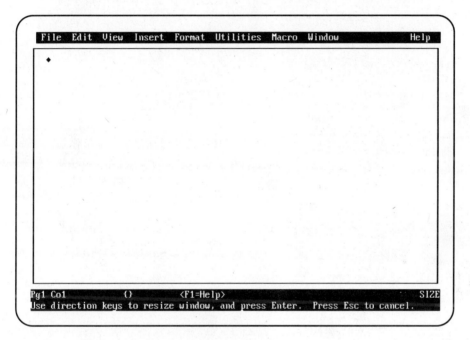

```
 File  Edit  View  Insert  Format  Utilities  Macro  Window          Help

 ♦




















Pg1 Co1           {}          <F1=Help>                        SIZE
Use direction keys to resize window, and press Enter.  Press Esc to cancel.
```

Fig. 9.8. A window ready to be sized.

2. Use the arrow keys to resize the window. Press the left or right
   arrows to change the width. Press the up or down arrows to
   change the height.

3. Press Enter when you are satisfied with the window's size.

   Alternatively, press Esc to restore the window to its size when
   you chose the **Window Size** command.

To size a window with the mouse, follow these steps:

1. Position the pointer on the size icon in the lower-right corner of the window.

2. Drag the size icon until you are satisfied with the window's size.

3. Release the mouse button.

After you have sized a window, Word remembers the size you chose. If you maximize the window so that it fills the screen and then choose the Maximize command to shrink the window, Word reduces the window to the size you chose.

Moving Windows

You can move windows with the keyboard or the mouse.

Alt-WM   To move a window with the keyboard, do the following:

1. Place the cursor in the window you want to move.

2. Choose Windows Move (Alt-WM) or use the Ctrl-F7 keyboard shortcut.

   An enlarged border appears around the document.

3. Use the arrow keys to move the window to its new location.

4. When you are satisfied with the window's location, press Enter.

 Use the following steps to move a window with a mouse:

1. Move the pointer to the title bar.

2. Click and drag the window to its new location.

Displaying Two Different Documents at the Same Time

You may want to view two documents at the same time. If you're working on a proposal, for instance, you can display the client's guidelines in one window while you work on the proposal in another window. Now that you have learned how to size and move windows, you can display two different documents at the same time by using the following steps:

1. Open the first document.

2. Size the document so that it fills only the top half of the screen.

3. Move the document to the bottom half of the screen.

4. Open the second document.

5. Size this document so that it fills only the top half of the screen.

   The first document will be visible beneath the second one.

Displaying Two Parts of the Same Document

When you're moving text within a document, or comparing two sections of a document, it's convenient to see two parts of the document on-screen. You can display two different parts of a document in two ways. You can open an additional window on the same document, or you can split a window into two panes, which you can scroll independently. The second technique is easier because you don't have to size and move the windows. To open an additional window on the same document, use these steps:

1. Place the cursor in the document for which you want to open a new window.

2. Choose **Window New Window** (Alt-WN).

   As shown in figure 9.9, Word changes the name of the original document window by adding a colon and the number one to the window name. In addition, Word opens a new window on the document, numbered two.

3. Size or move the windows so you can see both of them at once, if desired.

When two windows are open on the same document, the changes you make in one window affect the text in the other. In this sense, both windows are active.

You can split a window into two panes with the keyboard or the mouse.

To divide a window into two panes with the keyboard, do the following:

1. Choose **Window Split** (Alt-WT).

   The split bar at the top of the window appears.

2. Use the down-arrow key to move the split bar down the window.

3. Press Enter when you are satisfied with the split's location. To abandon the split, press Esc.

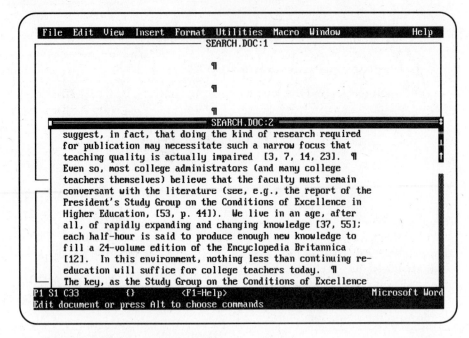

Fig. 9.9. A new window on a document.

To remove the split with the keyboard, use these steps:

1. Choose **Window Split** (Alt-WT).

2. Use the up-arrow key to move the split bar up to the top of the window.

3. Press Enter.

Do the following to divide a window into two panes with the mouse:

1. Place the pointer on the split bar icon.

2. Drag the split bar icon down the scroll bar.

3. Press Enter when you are satisfied with the split's location.

To remove the split with the mouse, use these procedures:

1. Place the pointer on the split bar icon.

2. Drag the split bar to the top of scroll bar, and release the button.

After your document is divided into panes (see fig. 9.10), you can scroll each pane independently so that you can work on one part of a document while viewing another part.

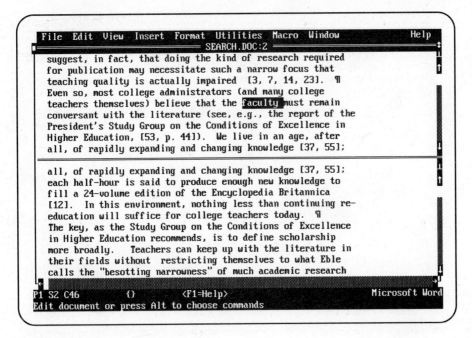

Fig. 9.10. A window with two panes.

After you divide a window into two panes, you can easily move the cursor from one pane to the next. Press F6 to move the cursor to the next pane, and Shift-F6 to move the cursor to the previous pane.

**F6,
Shift-F6**

Arranging all Open Windows

If you are working with several documents at once, you may want to see a portion of all of them briefly to remind yourself of their contents. The **Arrange All** command displays all open windows in a tiled mode, as shown in figure 9.11, with none of the windows overlapping.

Chapter Summary

You can customize Word 5.5's screen, operating settings, and color choices so that the program looks and functions exactly the way you want. You can silence its beep, speed up or slow down its cursor, produce a clean screen effect, and paint each window feature with all the colors available in your monitor's standard palette.

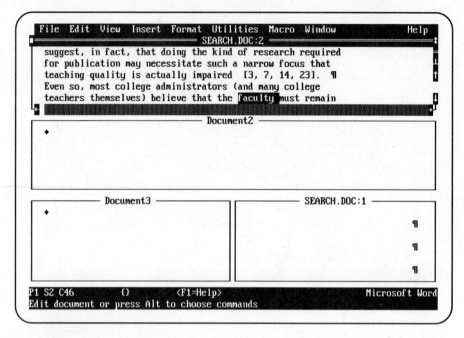

Fig. 9.11. *Windows in a tiled mode.*

Word 5.5's windows overlap each other, unlike the tiled windows of previous versions. This feature makes the windows easier to understand and use. You can move quickly from one document to another, each in its own window, for such operations as copying and moving text. You can size and move windows as needed, and you can split a window into two panes.

As you learn in the next chapter, you can set up windows so that you can see a dynamically updated outline of your document's overall structure in one window while you write in the other! Windows aren't just a special little-used feature of Word; for anyone who wants to write productively and well with the computer, windows are part of the repertoire of basic techniques.

Quick Review

Clean Screen

To display a clean screen:

1. If the Ruler or Ribbon is displayed, choose View **R**uler (Alt-VR) or View Ri**b**bon (Alt-VB) to toggle these features off.

2. Choose **View** **S**tatus Bar (Alt-VS) to toggle off the display of the status bar.

3. Choose **View** **P**references (Alt-VE).

4. Choose **M**enu (Alt-M), Window **B**orders (Alt-B), and Messa**g**e Bar (Alt-G) until the X disappears from these check boxes.

5. Choose OK.

Colors

To choose an alternate color set:

1. Choose **View** **P**references (Alt-VE).

2. Choose **C**olors (Alt-C).

3. Choose Color **S**et (Alt-S).

4. Drop down the list box.

5. Choose a color set option.

6. Choose OK.

To color individual screen elements:

1. Choose **View** **P**references (Alt-VE).

2. Choose **C**olors (Alt-C).

3. Choose what you want to color in the **T**hings to Color list box.

4. Press the letter next to the color you want or click the color.

5. Repeat steps 3 and 4 until you have chosen all the colors you want.

6. Choose OK.

To restore the default colors:

1. Choose **View** **P**references (Alt-VE).

2. Choose **C**olors (Alt-C).

3. Choose Color **S**et (Alt-S).

   The Color **S**et box will be blank, indicating that you previously chose custom colors.

4. Drop down the list box.

5. Choose a color set option.

6. Choose OK.

European Customization Options

To enable commas as decimal points:

1. Choose Utilities Customize (Alt-UU).

2. Choose Decimal (Alt-L).

3. Drop down the list box.

4. Choose the comma (,).

5. Choose OK.

To display dates in day-month-year format:

1. Choose Utilities Customize (Alt-UU).

2. Choose Date (Alt-D).

3. Drop down the list box.

4. Choose DMY.

5. Choose OK.

To display times in 24-hour format:

1. Choose Utilities Customize (Alt-UU).

2. Choose Time (Alt-T).

3. Drop down the list box.

4. Choose 24 hour.

5. Choose OK.

Screen Customization Options

To toggle background pagination on and off:

1. Choose Utilities Customize (Alt-UU).

2. Choose Background Pagination (Alt-B).

3. Choose OK.

To toggle on and off the display of summary sheets when you save a document for the first time:

1. Choose Utilities Customize (Alt-UU).

2. Choose Prompt for Summary Info (Alt-S).

3. Choose OK.

To toggle widow and orphan control on and off:

1. Choose Utilities Customize (Alt-UU).

2. Choose Widow/Orphan Control (Alt-W).

3. Choose OK.

To toggle the display of keyboard shortcuts on menus on and off:

1. Choose Utilities Customize (Alt-UU).

2. Choose Show Keys on Menus (Alt-K).

3. Choose OK.

Settings

To choose a line draw character:

1. Choose Utilities Customize (Alt-UU).

2. Choose Line Draw Character (Alt-H).

3. Drop down the list box.

4. Choose Single, Double, or Hyphen Bar.

5. Choose OK.

To choose a new default tab setting for all Word documents:

1. Choose Utilities Customize (Alt-UU).

2. Choose Default Tab (Alt-F).

3. Type a new measurement in the text box. Be sure to use the measurement format currently displayed in the Measure list box.

4. Choose OK.

To silence Word's beep:

1. Choose Utilities Customize (Alt-UU).

2. Choose Mute (Alt-U).

3. Press Enter to choose OK.

Using Word 5.0 Keys

To toggle the Word 5.0 function keys on and off:

1. Choose Utilities Customize (Alt-UU).

2. Choose Use Word **5**.0 Function Keys (Alt-5).

3. Choose OK.

To toggle the Word Ins key assignment on and off:

1. Choose Utilities Customize (Alt-UU).

2. Choose Use **INS** for Overtype key (Alt-I).

3. Choose OK.

To toggle background pagination on and off:

1. Choose Utilities Customize (Alt-UU).

2. Choose **Background** Pagination (Alt-B).

3. Choose OK.

Windows

To switch between two or more windows on-screen using the menus:

1. Choose **Window** (Alt-W).

2. Choose the name of the document to which you want to switch.

To copy or move text between two documents:

1. Open the first document, the one to which you want to copy or move text.

2. Open the second document, the one from which you want to copy or move text.

3. Find the text, highlight it, and use the **Edit Copy** or **Edit Cut** commands.

4. Choose the first document's name from the **Window** menu.

5. Move the cursor to the place you want the text to appear.

6. Choose **Edit Paste**.

To maximize a window using the menu and keyboard technique:

Choose **Windows Maximize** (Alt-WM) or choose the Ctrl-F10 keyboard shortcut.

To maximize a window (mouse technique):

Click the maximize icon (the arrow pointing both ways at the top of the right scroll bar).

To size a window with the keyboard:

1. Choose **Window Size** (Alt-WS) or select the Ctrl-F8 keyboard shortcut.

2. Use the arrow keys to resize the window. Press the left or right arrow to change the width. Press the up or down arrow to change the height.

3. Press Enter when you are satisfied with the window's size. Alternatively, press Esc to restore the window to its original or previous size.

To size a window with the mouse:

1. Position the pointer on the size icon in the lower-right corner of the window.

2. Drag the size icon until you are satisfied with the window's size.

3. Release the mouse button.

To move a window with the keyboard:

1. Place the cursor in the window you want to move.

2. Choose **Windows Move** (Alt-WM) or use the Ctrl-F7 keyboard shortcut.

3. Use the arrow keys to move the window to its new location.

4. Press Enter when you are satisfied with the window's location. To cancel the move, press Esc.

To move a window with the mouse:

1. Move the pointer to the title bar.

2. Click and drag the window to its new location.

To display two different documents at the same time:

1. Open the first document.

2. Size the first document's window so that it fills only the top half of the screen.

3. Move the window to the bottom half of the screen.

4. Open the second document.

5. Size the second document's window so that it fills only the top half of the screen.

To open an additional window on the same document:

1. Place the cursor in the document for which you want to open a new window.

2. Choose **Window New Window** (Alt-WN).

3. Size or move the windows so you can see both at once, if desired.

To divide a window into two panes with the keyboard:

1. Choose **Window Split** (Alt-WT).

2. Use the down-arrow key to move the split bar down the window.

3. Press Enter when you are satisfied with the split's location. To abandon the split, press Esc.

To move the cursor from one pane to the other pane:

Press F6.

To remove the split with the keyboard:

1. Choose **Window Split** (Alt-WT).

2. Use the up-arrow key to move the split bar to the top of the window.

3. Press Enter.

To divide a window into two panes with the mouse:

1. Place the pointer on the split bar icon.

2. Drag the split bar icon down the scroll bar.

3. Press Enter when you are satisfied with the split's location.

To move the cursor to another pane with the mouse:

Click the mouse anywhere in the pane you want to activate.

To remove the split with the mouse:

1. Place the pointer on the split bar icon.

2. Drag the split bar to the top of scroll bar, and release the button.

Chapter 10

Organizing Your Document with Outlining

Word processing doesn't automatically improve writing. Because the display window provides only a limited view of the document, writers sometimes find it difficult to retain a grasp of the overall structure of a document. The problem is worsened with the penalties imposed by scrolling, which moves text only one-third of a page at a time. What's more, putting a document through a major reorganization is tedious and difficult. As you move big blocks of text around, you can lose sight of how the changes relate to the overall plan. All too often, the result is that lengthy documents created on computers show signs of poor organization. And that's too bad—especially because writing teachers consider the quality of a document's organization to be the single most important factor in good writing.

Microsoft Word solves this problem by offering an outline mode, a remarkable feature that, for anyone who writes documents longer than letters, should make Word the program of choice in personal computer word processing. Word's outlining mode differs from an outline created on paper or with a separate outlining program. The outline is not separate from the document it outlines: the outline is part of the document, another way of looking at the document you're writing. In one view, you see the document's body text, the text that appears when you print. In the outlining view, you see the same document as an outline (with the body text hidden so that you see the document's overall structure). The headings and subheadings in the outline correspond to headings and subheadings in the document. When you shift to outline mode, the body text "collapses," or disappears, leaving the patterns of headings and subheadings you have created. At a keystroke, you can remind yourself how you have organized a lengthy and complex report, chapter, or essay.

And that's not all. When you rearrange headings or subheadings in the outline mode, Word actually restructures your document. Word moves the body text as well as the headings. What this means, in short, is that you can put a document through a major reorganization in just a few keystrokes. If you think the section titled, "The Meaning of Scouting," should come before, "The Founder of Scouting: Baden-Powell," simply rearrange the headings on the outline, and Presto! Word moves the body text too. That's power editing! When you discover Word's editing and outlining capabilities, you may never be satisfied with another word processing program.

In this chapter, you find complete approaches to creating and editing outlines and to restructuring complex documents. This chapter covers all the basic commands, of course, but it also does something more: this chapter shows you how to apply this wonderful outlining feature to the creation, organization, and editing of lengthy, complex documents. Specifically, this chapter covers the following:

- Creating an outline by typing headings and assigning heading levels

- Viewing your outline's structure by collapsing and expanding headings and body text

- Editing and restructuring your outline in the outline-organize mode

- Numbering an outline automatically

- Printing your outline

- Outlining an existing document so that you can see its structure in the outline mode

Users of previous versions of Word, note: Word 5.0 outlining functions and keyboard shortcuts have survived intact in Word 5.5. Exceptions: you activate the outline view by choosing View Outline (Alt-VO), and the keys that formerly required you to press Alt are now assigned to the Ctrl key. If you learned outlining skills in Word 5.0, you will have little difficulty using outlining in Word 5.5. Mouse users, beware: all special mouse techniques for outlining have been disabled. However, you still can use the mouse in outline view to carry out normal editing and selection functions, as you would in document view.

Note: In this chapter, K+, K−, and K* refer, respectively, to the plus, minus, and asterisk keys on the numeric keypad. Pressing the keyboard keys does not produce the same results. When a command uses a number (Alt-9 and Alt-0 for example), you must use the numbers on the top row of the main keyboard.

Creating an Outline

Outlines can be created before you write your document, while you write it, or even after you write it. This section covers the creation of an outline in a blank document window. For information on outlining while or after you write text, see "Outlining an Existing Document," later in this chapter. When you create an outline with Word, you work in the program's *outline-edit* mode. In this mode, you can type, correct, indent, and change the level of outline headings. (You will learn later about another outline mode, the *outline-organize* mode.)

To shift to the outline-edit mode and enter a Level 1 heading, follow these steps: **Shift-F2**

1. Open a new document (Alt-FN).

2. Choose **View Outline** (Alt-VO) or use the Shift-F2 keyboard shortcut.

    Look at the left side of the status bar. The page and column number indicator has changed to read Level 1. This message tells you that the text you type is entered as a first-level heading.

3. Type the title of the document you want to create, such as *Marketing Department Quarterly Report: Winter, 1991.* If you make a mistake, use the Backspace or Del key to correct your mistake and retype the heading. Press Enter.

In this chapter, you see how a proposal writer would develop a business proposal using Word 5.5's outlining tools. In figure 10.1, the title, "Proposal to Certified Industrial Management, Inc.," becomes a Level 1 heading in outline-edit mode. You will see how this outline develops in the pages to come.

Note: Use the Shift-F2 keyboard shortcut to toggle back and forth between document and outline mode.

Note: When you choose the outline mode only, the active window is affected. If other windows are open, they remain in the document mode unless you deliberately toggle the outline mode on for those windows.

Assigning Heading Levels

Every outline uses subheadings, or indented headings. If Level 1 is used for the document's title, Level 2 corresponds to major section titles.

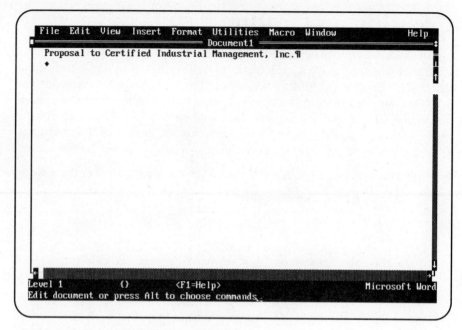

Fig. 10.1. Level 1 heading (document title).

To create a subheading, follow these steps:

1. Place the cursor at the end of the Level 1 heading and press Enter to start a new line.

2. Press Ctrl-0 (on the keyboard, not the keypad) to indicate that you want to type a subheading.

   The cursor jumps one default tab stop to the right. The status line displays Level 2.

3. Type the subheading. In figure 10.2, you see the Level 2 subheading "Executive Summary."

To continue typing Level 2 headings, just press Enter. When you press Enter in outline-edit mode, Word starts a new heading or subheading at the same level. In figure 10.3, you see that a second Level 2 subheading, titled "Introduction," has been added.

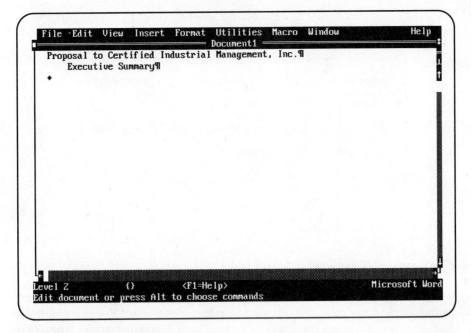

Fig. 10.2. Adding a Level 2 subheading.

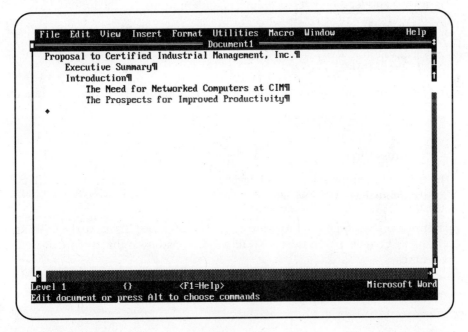

Fig. 10.3. Inserting a Level 3 subheading.

To insert Level 3 subheadings between the existing Level 2 subheadings, follow this procedure:

1. Position the cursor at the end of the last Level 2 subheading.

    In figure 10.3, the last Level 2 subheading is "Introduction."

2. Press Enter to create a blank line.

3. Press Ctrl-0 to indicate that you want to type a subheading.

    The status line displays Level 3.

4. Type the Level 3 subheading.

5. Press Enter to type any additional Level 3 subheadings (see fig. 10.3).

Changing a Subheading's Level

If you change your mind about a heading's level, you can move it left (reduce its indentation) or move it right (increase its indentation). For example, you might decide to change the Level 3 subheading, "The Prospects for Improved Productivity," to Level 2 (see fig. 10.3).

To move a subheading left (to reduce its indentation), do the following:

1. Position the cursor anywhere within the heading you want to move.

2. Press Ctrl-9.

To move a subheading right (to increase its indentation), do the following:

1. Position the cursor anywhere within the heading you want to move.

2. Press Ctrl-0.

The Ctrl-9 key combination (to move a heading left and raise its level) and the Ctrl-0 combination (to move a heading right and lower its level) are difficult to remember, but there is a trick: if you think of these keys as the left and right parentheses keys, their functions are easier to remember. To move the heading left, press Ctrl-left parentheses. To move the heading right, press Ctrl-right parentheses.

Collapsing and Expanding Headings

After you fill out your outline with headings and subheadings on several levels, your outline may be large enough to exceed the size of the screen (see fig. 10.4). If you cannot see the outline's overall structure, the outline mode's usefulness is lessened. For this reason, you can collapse subheadings—that is, hide them so that they are temporarily out of view. You can expand or reveal them later.

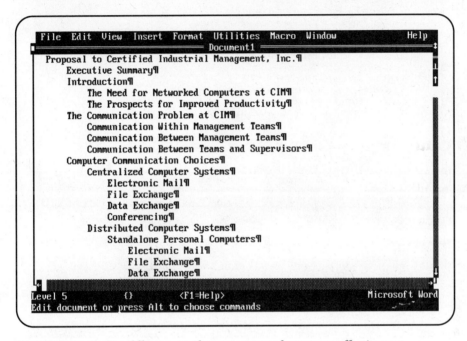

```
 File   Edit   View   Insert   Format   Utilities   Macro   Window              Help
                           ═══════ Document1 ═══════
 Proposal to Certified Industrial Management, Inc.¶
     Executive Summary¶
     Introduction¶
         The Need for Networked Computers at CIM¶
         The Prospects for Improved Productivity¶
     The Communication Problem at CIM¶
         Communication Within Management Teams¶
         Communication Between Management Teams¶
         Communication Between Teams and Supervisors¶
     Computer Communication Choices¶
         Centralized Computer Systems¶
             Electronic Mail¶
             File Exchange¶
             Data Exchange¶
             Conferencing¶
         Distributed Computer Systems¶
             Standalone Personal Computers¶
                 Electronic Mail¶
                 File Exchange¶
                 Data Exchange¶
 Level 5              {}             <F1=Help>              Microsoft Word
 Edit document or press Alt to choose commands
```

Fig. 10.4. An outline filling more than one screen loses some effectiveness.

Collapsing Headings

You can collapse all the subheadings that fall under a single heading. Alternatively, you can collapse all the subheadings down to a level that you specify. After you collapse subheadings, a plus sign (+) appears in the status bar next to the corresponding heading to remind you that subheadings are hidden.

To collapse the subheadings under a heading, follow these steps:

1. Place the cursor on the heading above the subheadings you want to collapse.

2. Press K– (press the minus key on the keypad).

The subheadings disappear from view, and a plus sign appears in the status bar (see fig. 10.5).

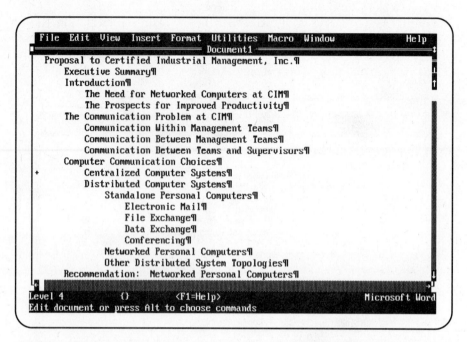

Fig. 10.5. *The plus sign in the status bar indicates collapsed subheadings.*

Note: If you use a laptop computer without a numeric keypad, press Ctrl-8 instead of K–.

To collapse all the subheadings down to a level you specify, hold down the Shift and Alt keys, and press a number corresponding to the last level you want to display. To display only the Level 1 headings, press 1. To display Level 1 and Level 2 headings, press 2, and so on.

Expanding Headings

You can expand the collapsed subheadings one level below a heading, or you can expand all the subheadings beneath a heading.

To expand the collapsed subheadings one level below a heading, follow this procedure:

1. Select the heading below which you want to expand the subheadings one level.

2. Press K+.

To expand all the subheadings under a heading, follow these steps:

1. Select the heading below which you want to expand all the subheadings.

2. Press K*.

Note: If you use a laptop computer without a numeric keypad, you can press the PrtSc key instead of K*.

To expand all the headings and subheadings to a level that you specify, hold down the Shift and Alt keys and press a number corresponding to the last level you want to display. To display only the Level 1 headings, press 1. To display Level 1 and Level 2 headings, press 2, and so on.

Adding and Managing Body Text

When you finish roughing out your outline, you add body text, which is the ordinary text of your document. To add body text to the outline, shift to the document mode, format the titles and headings as you want them to appear in your final document, and type the text under each heading. To view your document's structure, return to the outline mode, collapse the body text, and adjust the outline as you want.

The following sections explain how to do each step of this procedure.

Formatting the Headings

When you choose View Outline (Alt-VO) again (or when you press Shift-F2 again) to return to document mode, the indentations created in outline mode disappear (see fig. 10.6). But don't worry! They're not lost. Just choose View Outline (Alt-VO) or press Shift-F2 again to return to the outline-edit mode, and the indentations return.

At this point, because you want to format the headings, return to document mode. Add character formatting as you want, and use the Paragraph dialog box to add blank lines, indentations, and other paragraph formats (see fig. 10.7).

Note: When you return to the outline-edit mode, you will notice that Word does not show the alignments you chose for your headings. For example, if you chose a centered alignment for your Level 1 headings, those headings will appear flush to the left margin when you switch to outline-edit mode. Don't be concerned about this apparent loss of formatting. In outline-edit mode, you need to see the indentations from the left margin so that you can tell how your outline is organized logically. That's why Word suppresses your alignment choices in outline-edit mode. When you return to the document view, you see your alignment choices again, just as you assigned them.

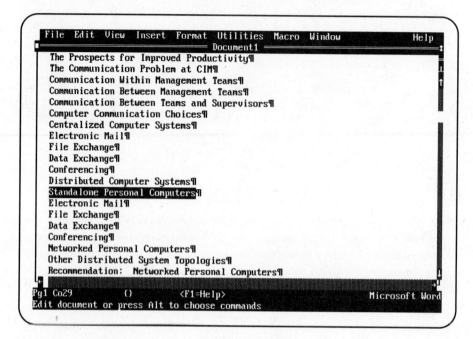

Fig. 10.6. The appearance of the outline in document mode.

Caution: Don't add blank lines or indentations to headings by pressing Enter or Tab. If you do, your outline is more difficult to work with—extraneous "empty" headings and indents appear where they don't belong. If you want indentations and blank lines, use the Format Paragraph command to add these characteristics to the headings.

Adding Body Text

To add body text to your document, follow these steps:

1. If your document is displayed in outline-edit mode, choose **View Outline** (Alt-VO) or press Shift-F2 to switch to the normal document view.

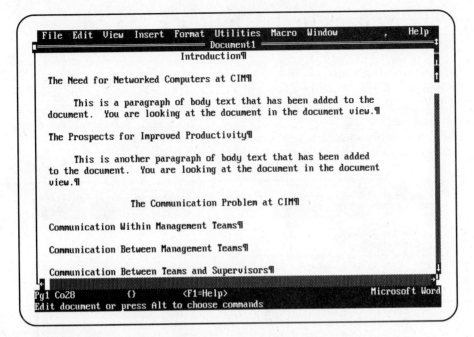

```
 File  Edit  View  Insert  Format  Utilities  Macro  Window        ,    Help
═════════════════════════════ Document1 ═══════════════════════════
                        Introduction¶

The Need for Networked Computers at CIM¶

        This is a paragraph of body text that has been added to the
document.  You are looking at the document in the document view.¶

The Prospects for Improved Productivity¶

        This is another paragraph of body text that has been added
to the document.  You are looking at the document in the document
view.¶

            The Communication Problem at CIM¶

Communication Within Management Teams¶

Communication Between Management Teams¶

Communication Between Teams and Supervisors¶
───────────────────────────────────────────────────────────────
Pg1 Co28          {}            <F1=Help>              Microsoft Word
Edit document or press Alt to choose commands
```

Fig. 10.7. *Formatting the headings.*

2. Place the cursor at the end of the heading to which you want to
   add body text and press Enter.

3. Press Ctrl-X to cancel all the paragraph formats you chose for the
   heading.

   You have to press Ctrl-X because Word carries the heading
   formats down to the next line when you press Enter. If you don't
   press Ctrl-X, Word continues to use the paragraph formatting you
   chose for the headings and the outline level you chose as well.
   Without pressing Ctrl-X, the text you type will appear in the
   outline-edit mode as a heading, not as body text.

4. Press Ctrl-Space bar or Ctrl-Z to cancel the character formatting
   (if any) that you chose for the heading.

5. Add desired paragraph and character formats, and then type the
   text.

Important: Don't forget to press Ctrl-X when you start a paragraph of body
text. If you forget, Word will treat the body text paragraph as if it were an outline
heading!

Shifting Back to the Outline-Edit Mode and Collapsing Body Text

After you add body text to the headings, press Shift-F2 to return to the outline mode. When you do, you find that the body text you added is visible (see fig. 10.8). Each body text paragraph is marked with a capital T in the style bar. To see only the outline, you need to collapse the body text. You can collapse the body text under a single heading, or, to make your job easier, you can collapse all body text in one command.

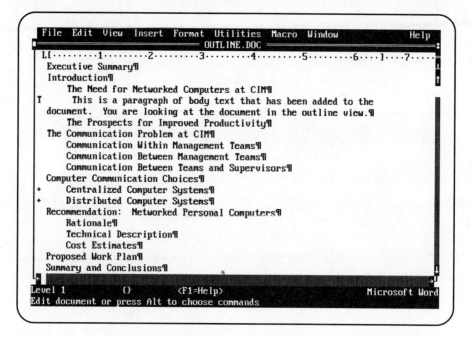

Fig. 10.8. The appearance of the outline in outline-edit mode after adding body text.

To collapse the body text under a single heading, follow this procedure:

1. Select the heading for which you want to collapse the body text.

2. Press Shift-keypad–.

   A lowercase t appears in the style bar to warn you that body text is hidden under the heading (see fig. 10.9).

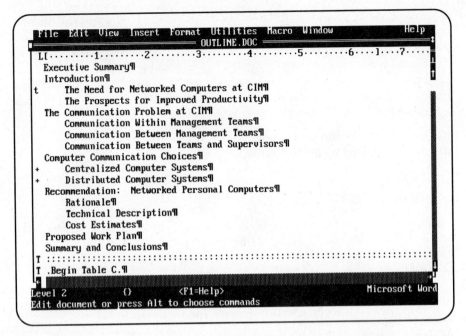

Fig. 10.9. Outline with some body text hidden (lowercase t in style bar).

You can expand the body text under a single heading by using Shift-keypad+, but you probably will do so rarely. Body text is more of a nuisance than an asset in outline-edit mode. You always can see body text by pressing Shift-F2 to return to the document mode.

Note: If you use a laptop computer without a numeric keypad, you can press Shift-Ctrl-8 instead of Shift-keypad–. You can press Shift-Ctrl-7 instead of Shift-keypad+.

To collapse all body text at once while you are in the outline mode, follow these steps:

1. Press Ctrl-keypad 5 to select the whole outline.

    Word automatically shifts to the outline-organize mode when you press Ctrl-keypad 5.

2. Press Shift-keypad–.

3. Press Shift-F5 to exit the outline-organize mode and return to the outline-edit mode.

You learn more about the outline-organize mode later in this chapter. For now, be sure that you exit the outline-organize mode after hiding all the body text.

As you toggle back and forth between document and outline, you quickly realize that it would be nice if you could select a mode that hides body text automatically. (Microsoft, how about making this change for Version 6?) Currently, every time you add body text in the document mode, the new text appears in the outline after you toggle Shift-F2. To see the structure of the outline, you must hide the body text by pressing Ctrl-keypad 5 and Shift-keypad–. Table 10.1 lists outlining keys and commands.

In Chapter 21, "Creating and Using Word 5.5 Macros," you learn how to record macros. Try recording the following keystrokes:

Ctrl-keypad 5

Shift-keypad –

Save the macro with the name Hide_Body_Text. If you want, you can assign the macro to a Ctrl key. See Chapter 21 for more information.

Table 10.1
Keys and Commands for Outlining

Key(s)	Effect
Shift-F2	Toggle between document view and outline view
Ctrl-keyboard 0	Lower the selected heading's level
Ctrl-keyboard 9	Raise the selected heading's level
K– or Ctrl-keyboard 7	Collapse subheadings and body text below selected heading
K+ or Ctrl-keyboard 8	Expand subheadings (not body text) below selected heading
Shift-K+ or Shift-Ctrl-keyboard 7	Expand body text below selected heading
Shift-K– or Shift-Ctrl-keyboard 8	Collapse body text below selected heading
Ctrl-X	Turn heading into text
Ctrl-9	Turn text into heading

Key(s)	Effect
K* or PrtSc	Expand all headings below the selected heading
Shift-Alt-number (1, 2, 3, etc.)	Display headings to the specified level
Shift-F5	Toggle between outline-edit and outline-organize mode

You can display a document in outline mode in one window while displaying the document mode in another. Try zooming the windows to full size. You then can move from document to outline and back, just by pressing F1! For more information on using windows, see Chapter 9, "Customizing Word and Using Windows."

Using Outlining To Move around in a Lengthy Document

Toggling between the document mode and the outline mode, as you have learned, is a wonderful way to keep your document's overall structure in mind as you write. This capability can be useful for another reason as well. In a lengthy document, it can be tedious to scroll using PgUp or PgDn, and if you don't know on which page a section starts, the Jump Page command isn't much help either. But you can scroll with great precision using the outline mode.

To scroll through a lengthy document using the outline mode, follow these steps:

1. Press Shift-F2 to enter the outline mode.

2. Hide the body text so that you can see the outline's structure by pressing Ctrl-keypad 5 and then Shift-keypad–.

3. Place the cursor on the heading to which you want to scroll.

4. Press Shift-F2 again to return to the document mode.

    The cursor is positioned on the heading you chose.

Restructuring an Outline

As you already have learned, you can edit the text within a heading in the outline-edit mode. To restructure your outline by moving headings around, however, shift to the outline-organize mode by pressing Shift-F5. After you press Shift-F5, the word ORGANIZE appears on the status line. When in outline-organize mode, you will find that the cursor keys change their functions (see table 10.2 for a list of the cursor keys and their new functions). The smallest unit of text you can select in the outline-organize mode is an entire heading (with its paragraph mark).

Note: Shift-F5 has no effect in document mode. To use the outline-organize mode, press Shift-F2 to switch to the outline-edit mode, and then press Shift-F5. To leave the outline-edit mode, press Shift-F5 again. To return to your document, press Shift-F2 again.

The following sections explain how to restructure an outline by moving and deleting headings.

Table 10.2
The Keyboard in Outline-Organize Mode

Key	Effect
Up arrow	Selects preceding heading at current level (skips headings at lower levels)
Down arrow	Selects next heading at current level (skips headings at lower levels)
Left arrow	Selects the next heading up, regardless of level
Right arrow	Selects next heading down, regardless of level
Home	Selects nearest heading at next higher level above the selected heading
End	Selects last heading at next lower level below the selected heading
F8	Selects the current heading and all subheadings and/or body text below it
F8-down arrow	Selects the current heading and following headings at the same level

Restructuring Your Document by Moving Headings

You can restructure your entire document by moving headings in outline mode. When you select a heading and choose Edit Cut (Alt-ET) to cut it to the Scrap, Word deletes more than the headings you see in outline mode. The program also deletes the subheadings and body text under the heading. To move the whole package (heading, subheadings, and text) to a new location, simply position the cursor where you want the heading to appear and press Shift-Ins. Presto! You have just restructured your whole document.

As just suggested, you can use any of the standard text copying and moving techniques to restructure your outline and body text in outline-organize mode. You even can use speed-key shortcuts and the super-fast mouse copying and moving techniques described in Chapter 3, "Word 5.5 Writing and Editing Strategies."

Deleting Headings

If you want to remove a heading and everything under it, select the heading in the outline-organize mode and press Shift-Del. If you delete the wrong heading, use Undo immediately (Alt-Backspace).

> *Caution:* The editing capabilities in the outline mode are very powerful. If you are not careful, you can delete body text you want to save. Before deleting a heading in the outline mode, remember that Word deletes not only the heading, but also all the subheadings and body text under the heading. If you want to remove just the heading (but not the subheadings or body text stored under it), delete the heading's text in the document mode, not in the outline mode.

Outlining an Existing Document

You can use all the techniques discussed in this chapter even if you didn't start your document with an outline. If you want to use these techniques, follow this procedure:

1. Open the document. If the document lacks a title and headings, add them.

2. Press Shift-F2 if you need to toggle on the outline-edit mode.

   Remember, if your current active window is in outline mode, any document you open comes up in outline mode.

3. Place the cursor in the first heading.

4. Press Ctrl-keypad 9 to define the heading as a Level 1 outline heading.

5. Move the cursor to the next heading. Press Ctrl-keypad 9. Press Ctrl-0 if you want to lower the heading's levels. As you define subsequent headings, you may continue to press Ctrl-0 to lower the heading still further. If you lower the heading too many levels, press Ctrl-keypad 9 to raise the level.

6. Repeat steps 4 and 5 until you define all the document headings as outline headings.

7. Hide the body text by pressing Ctrl-keypad 5 and Shift-keypad –.

8. To exit the outline-edit mode and return to the outline mode, press Shift-F5. To return to your document, press Shift-F2.

Now your document is outlined! You can use the outline as a guide to the structure of your document while editing and writing, or you can restructure large text units by restructuring the outline.

Numbering an Outline Automatically

Word has the capability to number your outline automatically, using the outline numbering scheme suggested in *The Chicago Manual of Style* (University of Chicago Press). If you want Word to number your outline automatically, follow these steps:

1. In the outline-edit mode, press Ctrl-Home to select the first heading in the outline.

2. Choose Utilities Renumber.

   You see the Renumber dialog box (see fig. 10.10).

3. Choose All and make sure there's an X in the Restart Sequence check box.

4. Choose OK.

Numbers appear in the outline (as shown in fig. 10.11) as well as in the document (as shown in fig. 10.12).

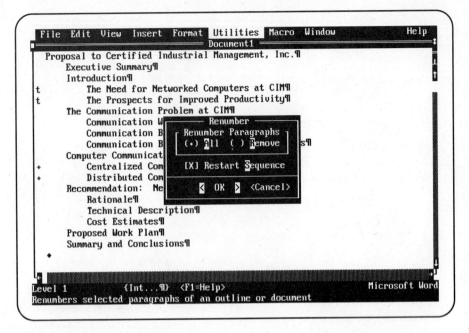

Fig. 10.10. *The Renumber dialog box.*

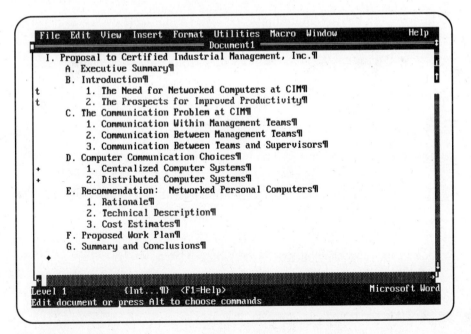

Fig. 10.11. *An automatically numbered outline (outline mode).*

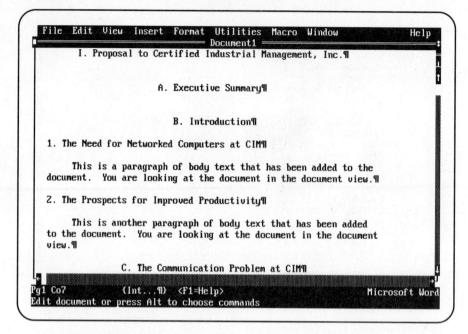

Fig. 10.12. An automatically numbered document (document mode).

To remove automatic numbering from your outline and document, follow these steps:

1. In outline mode, select the first character of the first heading.

2. Choose Utilities **R**enumber (Alt-UR).

3. Choose **R**emove.

4. Choose OK.

Word removes all the numbers it added and also removes the first number you typed.

Printing Your Outline

You can print your outline without printing body text. To print only the outline, do the following:

1. Press Shift-F2 to enter the outline mode.

2. Hide the body text (if any is showing) by pressing Ctrl-keypad 5 and Shift-keypad –.

3. Collapse subheadings to a level you specify by holding down the Shift and Alt keys and pressing a number corresponding to the lowest outline level you want to display.

4. Choose File **P**rint (Shift-F9).

Chapter Summary

Word's outlining capabilities are outstanding in the world of personal computing software. They are so unusual, in fact, that many users probably don't have the slightest idea how to use them! For most people, writing an outline brings back memories of autocratic grade-school teachers, rigid outlines printed out laboriously on lined paper, and other horrors. With Word, however, outlining isn't just a good idea for getting organized before writing; outlining is also a way of intelligently adapting to the computer as a writing medium, a medium that narrows the overall view of your document's structure. What's more, Word's outlining mode is a way to move around in a large document, and even to restructure large text domains at a keystroke. If you frequently write lengthy or complex documents, such as business reports, journal articles, or funding proposals, make Word's outlining features part of your daily repertoire of Word 5 techniques.

Quick Review

Body Text

To convert a heading to body text:

> Press Ctrl-X.

To collapse the body text under a single heading:

1. Select the heading for which you want to collapse the body text.

2. Press Shift-keypad–.

To collapse all body text at once:

1. Press Ctrl-keypad 5 to select the whole outline.

2. Press Shift-keypad–.

3. Press Shift-F5 to exit the outline-organize mode and return to the outline-edit mode.

Collapsing Headings in Outline-Edit Mode

To collapse the subheadings under a heading:

1. Place the cursor on the heading above the subheadings you want to collapse.

2. Press K–.

To collapse all the subheadings down to a level you specify:

Hold down the Shift and Alt keys and press a number corresponding to the last level you want to display.

To display only the Level 1 headings, press 1. To display Level 1 and Level 2 headings, press 2, and so on.

Expanding Headings

To expand the collapsed subheadings one level below a heading:

1. Select the heading below which you want to expand the subheadings one level.

2. Press K+.

To expand all the subheadings under a heading:

1. Select the heading below which you want to expand all the subheadings.

2. Press K*.

To expand all the headings and subheadings to a level you specify:

Hold down the Shift and Alt keys and press a number corresponding to the last level you want to display.

To display only the Level 1 headings, press 1. To display Level 1 and Level 2 headings, press 2, and so on.

Numbering an Outline

To number outline headings automatically:

1. In the outline-edit mode, select the first character in the outline.

2. Choose **Utilities Renumber**.

3. Choose **All** and make sure there's an X in the Restart **Sequence** check box.

4. Choose OK.

To remove the numbers Word entered:

1. In outline mode, select the first character of the first heading.

2. Choose **Utilities Renumber**.

3. Choose **Remove**.

4. Choose OK.

Outline Modes

To shift to the outline-edit mode:

Choose **View Outline** (Alt-VO) or use the Shift-F2 keyboard shortcut.

To return to your document:

Choose **View Outline** (Alt-VO) or use the Shift-F2 keyboard shortcut.

To move to the outline-organize mode:

1. If necessary, choose **View Outline** (Alt-VO) or use the Shift-F2 keyboard shortcut to enter the outline-edit mode.

2. Press Shift-F5.

Outlining an Existing Document

1. Open the document. If the document lacks a title and headings, add them.

2. Press Shift-F2 to toggle on the outline-edit mode.

3. Place the cursor in the first heading.

4. Press Ctrl-keyboard 9 to define the heading as an outline heading. Word defines the first heading as a Level 1 heading.

5. Move the cursor to the next heading. Press Ctrl-keyboard 9. Press Ctrl-0 to lower the heading's level if necessary. As you define subsequent headings, you can press Ctrl-0 to further lower the heading. If you lower a heading too many levels, press Ctrl-9 to raise the level.

6. Repeat steps 4 and 5 until you define all the document headings as outline headings.

7. Hide the body text by pressing Ctrl-keypad 5 and Shift-keypad –.

8. Exit the outline-edit mode by pressing Shift-F2.

Printing an Outline

1. Press Shift-F2 to enter the outline mode.

2. Hide the body text (if any is showing) by pressing Ctrl-keypad 5 and Shift-keypad –.

3. Collapse subheadings to a level you specify by holding down the Shift and Alt keys and pressing a number corresponding to the lowest outline level you want to display.

4. Choose **File Print**.

Scrolling through a Lengthy Document in the Outline-Edit Mode

1. Press Shift-F2 to enter the outline mode.

2. Hide the body text so that you can see the outline's structure by pressing Ctrl-keypad 5 and then Shift-keypad –.

3. Place the cursor on the heading to which you want to scroll.

4. Press Shift-F2 again to return to the document mode.

Selecting Headings in Outline-Organize Mode

Key	Effect
Up arrow	Selects preceding heading at current level (skips headings at lower levels)
Down arrow	Selects next heading at current level (skips headings at lower levels)
Left arrow	Selects the next heading up, regardless of level
Right arrow	Selects next heading down, regardless of level
Home	Selects nearest heading at next higher level above the selected heading
End	Selects last heading at next lower level below the selected heading
F8	Selects the current heading and all subheadings and/or body text below it
F8-down arrow	Selects the current heading and following headings at the same level

Typing Headings in Outline-Edit Mode

To type a heading at the current level:

Type the heading. If you press Enter, you can type an additional heading at the same level.

To lower the heading one level:

Press Ctrl-0.

To raise the heading one level:

Press Ctrl-9.

Chapter 11

Creating Tables and Lists with Tabs, Sort, and Math

C ommon features of most business documents, especially reports and proposals, are tables (such as a table of expenses for a quarter) and lists (such as a bibliography). With Word, creating and formatting tables and lists are easy tasks because Word's text entry, editing, and formatting capabilities, which you are already familiar with, make typing tables and lists a snap. With Version 5.5 of Word, creating tables and lists is even easier than with previous versions; when you change tabs with the Format Tab Set command, Word repositions the aligned text right on the screen, before you carry out the command. You can get your table just right before pressing Enter. If you have a mouse, you can skip the Format Tab Set command completely and just click the tabs you want right on the ruler.

If you frequently prepare documents with more than one or two tables, you're in for a very special treat when you use Word 5.5. Just imagine how much time you can save when Word 5.5 does the following tasks automatically:

- Numbers all the tables in your report and renumbers them if you restructure your text

- Fills in the page and table numbers of tables cross-referenced in the text and corrects the numbers if you rearrange the tables

- Adds precisely drawn horizontal and vertical rules (straight lines) so that your tables appear as if they were professionally typeset

- Adds a column of numbers and performs other arithmetic operations right on the screen

- Sorts columns or lists of numerical or alphabetical data in descending or ascending order

- Imports spreadsheets from Lotus 1-2-3, Microsoft Excel, or Multiplan directly into your Word documents so that the spreadsheet appears as a table

These features aren't only for advanced users of Word; they're for anyone who prepares tables and lists regularly in everyday writing situations. This chapter surveys these useful Word 5.5 features, beginning with a survey of Word 5.5's easy-to-use commands for setting, moving, and deleting custom tab stops. The next section presents a table tutorial that opens the door to Word's powerhouse of table-related features. If you want to create high-quality tables and improve your table-crunching productivity, don't skip this tutorial. Also covered in this chapter are Word 5.5's math and list-sorting features.

 Setting tabs in previous versions of Word wasn't easy, so experienced Word users will be glad to know that the procedures have been greatly simplified in Word 5.5. Keyboard users do not need to use the Tabs dialog box at all, in fact, unless they want to set tabs with precise measurements. You can set tabs easily and quickly with the Ruler, whether or not you're using the mouse.

Changing the Default Tab Width

When you open a new document with Word, the document's tab stops conform to the measurement entered in the Default Tab text box in the Customize dialog box. The preset measurement in this field is 0.5". With this setting, tab stops appear every half inch across the screen.

To set new default tabs for an entire document:

1. Choose Utilities Customize (Alt-UU).

2. Select Default Tab.

3. Type the new default tab width.

   Be sure to use the measurement format that's indicated in the **Measure** text box.

4. Choose OK.

About Custom Tabs

Every word processing program handles tabs in its own, unique way. With Word, it's important to understand that the custom tabs you set are paragraph formats. Much of what you already have learned about paragraph formatting applies to tabs:

- You can format tabs as you type—Word moves the tabs you have chosen to the next paragraph you create after you press Enter and start typing.

- You also can format tabs after you type, but you must select the paragraphs. The tabs you choose affect only the selected paragraphs.

- You can set custom tabs for the whole document by selecting the entire document first (press Ctrl-Keypad 5).

Remember that a paragraph in Word is all the text between two paragraph marks. A paragraph can be a single line or can refer to dozens of lines. Because custom tabs are paragraph formats, you can create a document with many different tab configurations, each assigned to a particular paragraph.

When you set a tab, you can specify its alignment and leader as well as its position. *Alignment* refers to the way Word lines up the text at the tab. The default alignment is flush left, but you can choose flush right, centered, or decimal alignment (numbers are lined up at the decimal point). You also can choose vertical alignment, which enters a vertical line at the tab stop. If you add vertical alignment tabs to a paragraph, all the lines of the paragraph will display a vertical line that runs together to form a rule. You learn more about using the vertical tab in Chapter 17, "Creating Forms and Illustrations."

A *leader* is a row of characters that Word enters automatically to take up the space before the tab stop. Word sets no default leader, but you can choose dots, dashes, or underscore leaders. If you choose dots, Word enters a row of dots automatically. Figure 11.1 shows the custom tab options.

When you use custom tabs, display the Ruler and choose the Preferences option that displays the tab keystrokes you enter. The Ruler makes it a cinch to set tabs, and displaying the tab keystrokes greatly facilitates editing after you have entered tabs.

To display the tab keystrokes, follow these steps:

1. If the Ruler isn't displayed, choose View **Ruler** (Alt-VR) or click the Ruler icon (the upside-down ⊤) at the top of the right scroll bar.

2. If you don't see tab marks on the screen (right arrows) even after you press the Tab key, choose View **Preferences** (Alt-VE) and choose the **Tabs** option.

When you set a custom tab, Word cancels the default tab stops to the left of the first custom tab (but not to the right). For example, suppose that you set a flush left tab at 3.0". Word deletes all the tab stops to the left of the 3.0" tab (that is, between 0 and 3 inches), but retains the default tabs at 3.5", 4.0", 4.5", and so

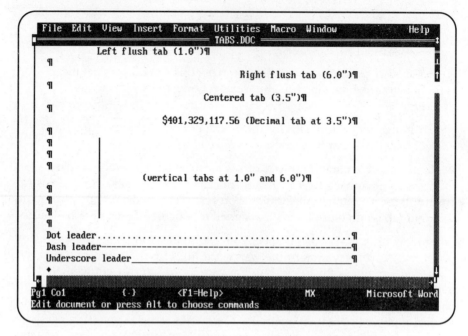

Fig. 11.1. Word's tab stops and leaders.

on. Word deletes the tabs left because, if you set a tab, you probably want the cursor to move to the tab stop without interruption. You can always set custom tabs to the left of a custom tab stop, if you want.

Note: It's a good idea to display the nonprinting tab characters, but keep in mind that you don't see leaders when the tab characters are displayed (see fig. 11.2). If you create a leader and don't see it on the screen, choose View Preferences and choose Tabs to turn off the display of the nonprinting tab characters. You will see the leader characters when you return to the screen.

Caution: Remember to avoid aligning text with spaces. If you use spaces to align text, Word may not print the text aligned properly—even if the text looks fine on-screen. Always use tabs to align text in columns on the screen.

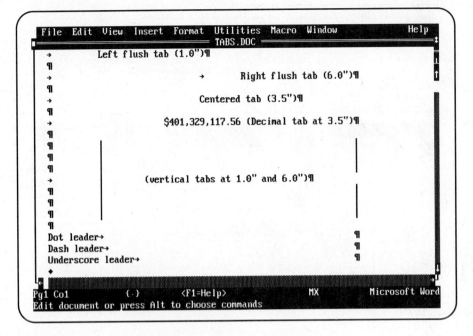

Fig. 11.2. Leaders disappear when tab marks are displayed.

Setting Custom Tabs

Display the Ruler (choose View **R**uler, or Alt-VR), if you haven't done so already. With the Ruler, you can set tabs with the keyboard or the mouse.

To set a custom tab with the keyboard, follow these steps:

1. Select the paragraph or paragraphs to which you want to apply the custom tabs.

   Shift-Ctrl-F10

2. Press Shift-Ctrl-F10 to place the cursor on the Ruler.

   The cursor is positioned at the left indent bracket.

3. Press the right- and left-arrow keys to move the cursor to where you want the tab stop to appear. You also can press PgDn to move the cursor 1 inch to the right, and PgUp to move the cursor 1 inch to the left.

   If you or someone else previously set custom tabs, move the cursor over them. This procedure doesn't cancel previously chosen custom tabs.

4. Press the first letter of the tab alignment you want (**L**eft, **C**entered, **R**ight, **D**ecimal, **V**ertical).

   The letter you press appears on the ruler (see fig. 11.3), indicating where you have set the tab and which alignment you have chosen.

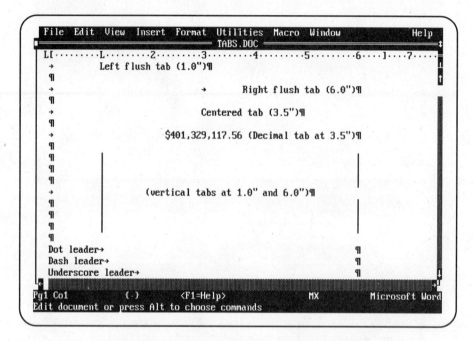

Fig. 11.3. The letter you press for tab alignment appears on the ruler.

5. If you want to add a leader to the tab stop, press the key corresponding to the leader you want to enter (a period, a hyphen, or an underscore character). Skip this step if you don't want a leader.

6. To set additional tabs, repeat steps 3, 4, and 5.

7. To return to your document, press Enter.

If you have a mouse, it's even easier to set tabs; just follow these steps:

1. With the ruler displayed, select the paragraph or paragraphs to which the tab stops are to apply.

2. If you want an alignment other than flush left, click the capital letter next to the left indent marker ([ ) on the ruler until it displays the alignment code you want.

In figure 11.3, for example, the capital letter at the left edge of the ruler is L, indicating that Word will enter a flush left code. If you click this letter, you see the letter C (centered tab). As you continue clicking, you see two letters for right and decimal tabs, and a vertical line for vertical tabs. If you go past the code you want, keep clicking. The code will come into view again, in cyclical fashion.

3. To select a leader character, click the space left of the L on the ruler line until the leader you want appears. To select a dot leader, click the period. To select a hyphen leader, select the hyphen. To select an underscore leader, select the underscore. If you don't want a leader, skip this step.

4. To set the tab, click the ruler where you want the tab stop.

5. To set additional tabs, repeat steps 2 through 4.

Moving Custom Tabs

After you have set custom tabs and typed some text, you may find that the aligned text doesn't please your eye. If so, you can easily move custom tabs by following these steps:

1. Select the paragraph or paragraphs that contain the tab or tabs you want to move.

2. Press Shift-Ctrl-F10 to activate the Ruler.

3. Press the down-arrow key to move to the next tab stop right, and press the up-arrow key to move to the next tab stop left.

4. When you have highlighted the tab you want to move, press Ctrl-right arrow to move the tab right, or Ctrl-left arrow to move the tab left.

5. To move other tabs, repeat steps 3 and 4.

6. Press Enter to return to your document.

You can use a mouse to move custom tabs even more easily. Position the cursor in the paragraph containing the tab stop you want to move. With the ruler displayed, point to the tab stop code you want to move, click the right button, and drag the tab to its new position.

Deleting Custom Tabs

If you find that you want to delete some or all of the custom tabs you have chosen, it's easy to do so. You can use keyboard or mouse techniques to delete one or more custom tabs. If you want to delete all the custom tabs you have chosen for the selected paragraphs, you use the Tabs dialog box.

To delete custom tabs with the keyboard, follow these steps:

1. Select the paragraph or paragraphs containing the custom tab that you want to delete.

2. Press Shift-Ctrl-F10 to place the cursor on the Ruler.

3. Press the down-arrow key to move to the next tab stop right, and press the up-arrow key to move to the next tab stop left.

4. When you have highlighted the tab you want to delete, press Del to delete this tab, or press Ctrl-Del to delete this tab and all other tab stops that appear to the right of this tab on the Ruler.

5. Repeat steps 3 and 4 to delete additional tabs, if desired.

6. Press Enter to return to your document.

To delete custom tabs with the mouse, do the following:

1. Select the paragraphs containing the custom tab that you want to delete.

2. On the Ruler, point to the tab stop letter you want to delete.

3. Drag the letter below the Ruler and release the button.

4. Repeat steps 3 and 4 to delete additional tabs, if desired.

To help you remember the special keys used when creating, moving, and deleting tabs with the keyboard, see table 11.1.

Creating and Editing Tables

Now that you have surveyed the essentials of creating, moving, and deleting tabs, it's time to tackle tables. Running through this section is an extended tutorial to guide you through many seemingly advanced Word commands, most of which you haven't used before. As you surely will agree, however, it's easy to use these powerful features. After you see what they can do for you, you probably will make them part of your everyday working routine with Word.

Table 11.1
Special Keys When Setting Custom Tabs

Key	Effect with format tab set
Shift-Ctrl-F10	Place cursor on Ruler
Down arrow	Select next tab stop right
Up arrow	Select next tab stop left
Right arrow	Move highlight right on ruler
Left arrow	Move highlight left on ruler
PgUp	Move highlight 1 inch left on ruler
PgDn	Move highlight 1 inch right on ruler
Del	Delete custom tab stop
Ctrl-Del	Delete custom tab stop and all custom tab stops to right of cursor

Caution: If you're using a proportionally spaced font, be sure to use tabs, not spaces, to align text. On the screen, Word displays all fonts as if they were monospace, with each character taking up the same amount of space. That's true even for proportionally spaced fonts, in which the letter "m" is much wider than the letter "l." If you align text with spaces, proportionally spaced type will look misaligned when you print your document. Use tabs instead of spaces. When you use tabs to align text, Word prints the text properly aligned, even if you use proportionally spaced text.

Creating the Table Header

The table header contains the table number, the title, the column headings, and the stub (the heading for the left column). In the following tutorial, you create a simple ruled table with two column headings.

Numbering the Table Automatically

To have Word number your tables automatically, enter a series code name instead of the table number when you type the table's header. When you print your document, Word counts all the series code names and replaces them with numbers. For example, the first series code name will be numbered "1," the second "2," and so on.

The reason for using a series code name is that if you create a document with more than one table, Word will renumber the tables automatically if you change the order in which they appear. That's a real benefit, especially if your document will contain many tables and you edit it heavily. Automatic table renumbering also means one less chore when it's time to proofread your work.

A series code name can contain up to 31 characters, including hyphens, periods, and underscore characters, but the series code name must begin and end with a letter or number.

To type a table number line that Word will number automatically, follow these steps:

1. Press Ctrl-C to create a centered paragraph format.

2. Type *Table* and press the Space bar.

3. Type *tablenumber:* (don't forget the colon). Figure 11.4 shows how your document should look.

4. With the cursor positioned just after the colon, press F3, the Glossary function key. Word places parentheses around the series code name that you just typed (see fig. 11.5).

This tutorial has just one table, but in a real document, you might have many more. Creating the table title this way ensures that Word will number each table automatically and correctly.

When you print your document, Word removes the series code name and inserts a number. If this table is the first table in your document, it is called "Table 1."

Typing the Table Title and Entering a Double Ruled Line

Now add the table's title and a double-ruled line under it by working through the following instructions.

Note: If you don't see tab and paragraph marks on-screen, choose View Preference (Alt-VE) and choose those options.

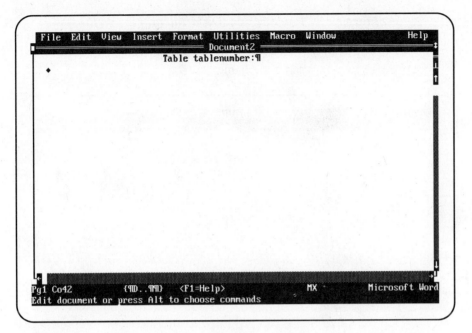

Fig. 11.4. Typing the series code name.

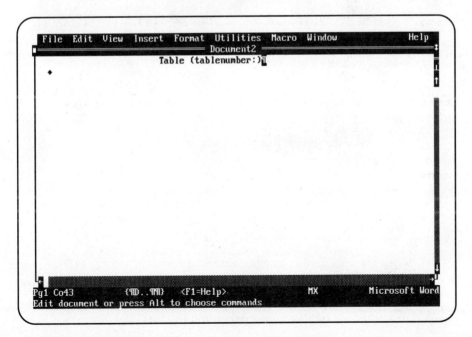

Fig 11.5. Parentheses around the code name after pressing F3.

1. Press Enter twice. Type the title (*Departmental Expenditures*). Press Enter again and type the subtitle. The lines are centered because Word continues the centered format you chose when you entered the series code name (see fig. 11.6).

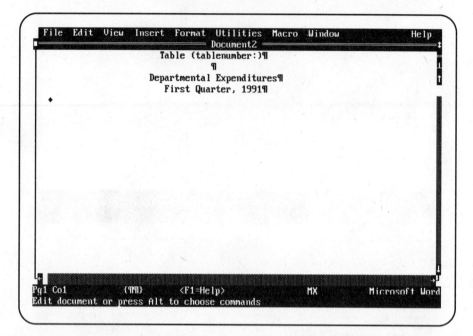

```
 File   Edit   View   Insert   Format   Utilities   Macro   Window          Help
────────────────────────────── Document2 ──────────────────────────────
                          Table (tablenumber:)¶
                                    ¶
                         Departmental Expenditures¶
                           First Quarter, 1991¶
        ◆



















Pg1 Co1            {¶M}         <F1=Help>              MX        Microsoft Word
Edit document or press Alt to choose commands
```

Fig. 11.6. Typing the table's title.

2. Press Enter to create a blank line, and choose Format **B**orders (Alt-TB).

   You see the Paragraph Borders dialog box.

3. Choose the **L**ines option button.

   Word activates the check boxes beneath **L**ines.

4. Choose **B**ottom and **D**ouble for Line style.

5. Choose OK.

   Word enters a double line between the margins (see fig. 11.7).

You learn more about the Paragraph Borders dialog box in Chapter 17, "Creating Forms and Illustrations." For now, remember that lines (such as the one you just entered) and boxes are paragraph formats, like tabs.

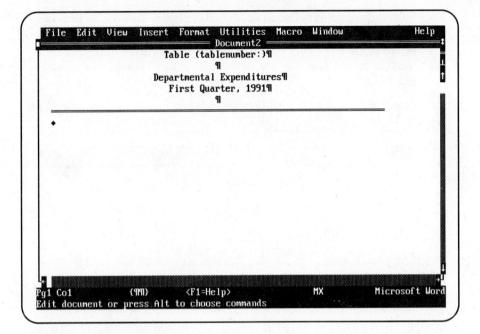

Fig. 11.7. Adding a double line.

Adding Column and Stub Headings

A column heading, positioned above the columns of data, describes the data to be listed in the table. The stub heading describes the categories or items listed and is positioned flush left (and usually one or two lines below the column headings).

Use the following instructions to create simple column headings for a table:

1. Select the end mark under the double-ruled line. Display the Ruler, if it isn't displayed.

   To display the Ruler, choose **View Ruler** (Alt-VR) or click the Ruler icon.

2. Set custom tabs, with centered alignment, for the columns in your table. In this tutorial, you type a table with two columns of data, so set centered tabs at 3.0" and 4.5". Set a vertical tab at 3.75" to separate the two column headings.

3. Type the stub head and column headings.

   To type the stub head and column headings shown in figure 11.8, type *Items*, press Tab, and then type *Marketing*. Press Tab and type *Graphics*.

4. With the cursor positioned on the last line you typed, use the Paragraph Borders dialog box again to enter a single-width line below the stub head. Choose Format Borders (Alt-TB) to display the dialog box. Choose Normal line style, and choose Lines and Bottom to place the line beneath the stub head. Choose OK.

Word creates a single-ruled line under the stub head, as shown in figure 11.8.

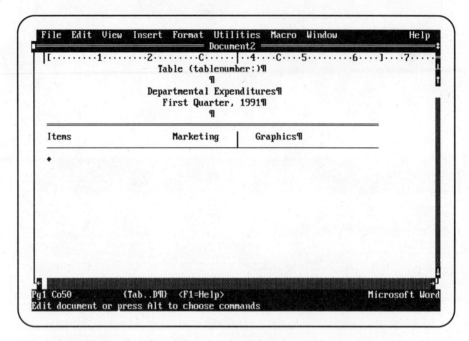

Fig. 11.8. Table head with stub head, column heads, and lines.

Getting Fancy: Using Decked Heads and Vertical Lines

A decked head is a header that spans two or more column headers, as shown in figure 11.9. Use the following instructions to modify the existing table so that it has a decked head:

1. Position the cursor on the paragraph mark above the double line border beneath the table title. If you don't see the paragraph marker on-screen, choose View Preferences (Alt-VE) and choose Paragraph Marks.

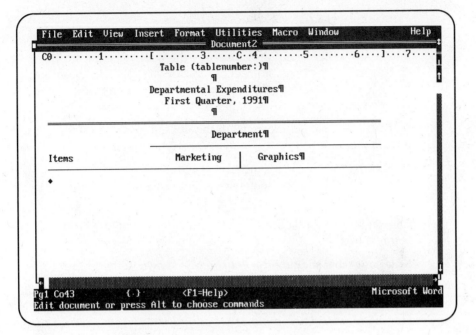

```
  File   Edit   View   Insert   Format   Utilities   Macro   Window              Help
                                  Document2
 C0·········1········[········3······C··4·······5·········6····]····7·····
                          Table (tablenumber:)¶
                                     ¶
                      Departmental Expenditures¶
                         First Quarter, 1991¶
                                     ¶

                              Department¶


   Items                  Marketing    │   Graphics¶

   ◆



Pg1 Co43           {·}          <F1=Help>                    Microsoft Word
Edit document or press Alt to choose commands
```

Fig. 11.9. Table with decked head.

2. Press Enter.

   Note that Word copies the double line border. As mentioned earlier, the lines and boxes you enter with the Paragraph Borders dialog box are paragraph formats. When you press Enter, Word copies the lines—and all other paragraph formats you have chosen—to the next paragraph.

3. Press Ctrl-X to cancel the borders.

4. Determine the center point of the columns.

   If you have columns centered at 3.0" and 4.5", for example, the center point between them is 3.75".

5. Set a centered tab for the decked head at the center point.

   To set the tab with a precise measurement, choose Format Tabs (Alt-TT) and type the measurement (3.75") in the Tab Position list box. Next, choose OK.

6. Press Tab to move to the tab stop you have just set.

7. Type the decked head (*Department*).

8. Use the Paragraph Borders dialog box to enter a Normal Bottom line beneath the paragraph containing the word Department. To display the dialog box, choose Format **B**orders (Alt-TB). Choose Normal and Lines, then choose the Bottom check box, and choose OK.

   Word enters a single line beneath the decked head Department, but it's too long.

9. To shorten the line, place the cursor within the word Department. (This placement selects the paragraph that contains the border format.)

10. Choose Format **P**aragraph (Alt-TP) and enter 2.0" in the From Left text box.

    Now your table should look like the one shown in figure 11.9.

With a little experimentation, you can create more complex headings with boxed heads (column headers enclosed fully in boxes). You may find Word's line-drawing mode helpful to complete the boxes. For more information on the line-drawing mode, see Chapter 17, "Creating Forms and Illustrations."

Creating the Table Body

Now that you have created the table header, it's time to create the table body, the part of the table containing the columns of data. Use the following steps to duplicate the table shown in figure 11.10.

1. Position the cursor on the document's end mark that is positioned below the last line.

2. Set a flush-left tab at 0.2" to indent text in the left column (as shown in fig. 11.10).

3. Set decimal tabs at precisely the same places (3.0" and 4.5") you entered centered tabs in the heading.

4. Set a vertical tab at precisely the same place (3.75") you entered a vertical tab below the decked head.

5. Type the items and the expenditures as shown in figure 11.10. Do not use the space bar to align text; press Tab one time between each item. Press Enter at the end of each line.

   Note that you can tab right over the vertical line.

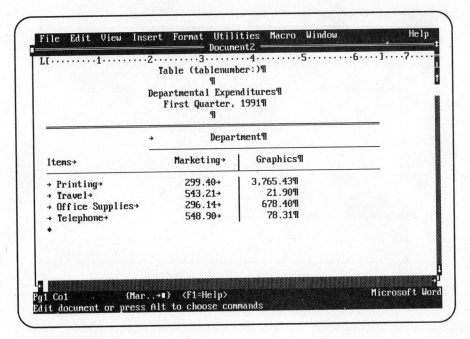

Fig. 11.10. Table with table body added.

6. When you come to the end of the table, use the Paragraph
   Borders dialog box to create a normal line beneath the paragraph.

As you can see, it's easy to create very handsome tables with Word 5.5.

Adjusting the Column's Position

If you didn't align the columns to your satisfaction, no problem. As you might
be able to see in figure 11.10, the figures under Graphics aren't very well
centered under the column header. You simply select all the lines of the table
that contain the errant tab stop, and move the tab stop.

To change the alignment of the Graphics column, do the following:

1. Select the lines that contain the table's body text (see fig. 11.11).

2. Move the decimal tab at 3.0" one-tenth of an inch (one dot on the
   Ruler) to the right.

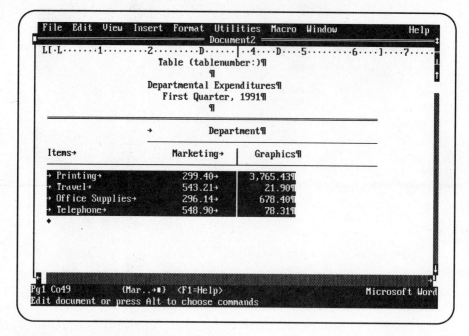

Fig. 11.11. *Selecting the table's body text.*

Note: To move a custom tab stop with the keyboard, press Ctrl-Shift-F10 to place the cursor on the ruler. Move the cursor to the tab stop. Hold down the Ctrl key and press the left- or right-arrow key to move the tab stop, and press Enter when done.

To move a custom tab stop with the mouse, place the pointer on the tab stop then drag the stop left or right.

The alignment now looks better (see fig. 11.12).

Editing Tables with Column Selection

Suppose that you just created the table described in the preceding sections, but your boss says, "This won't do. Graphics comes before Marketing alphabetically—and besides, my favorite protege is in charge of the Graphics Department. So put those expenditures in the left column." With some programs, it might be wiser to delete most of the table and type it over. But Word's column-select mode lets you select columns of data and move them laterally, just as you cut and paste with paragraphs of text.

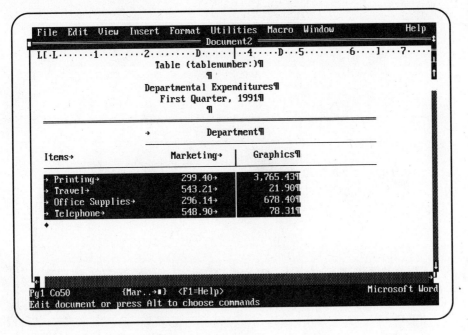

Fig. 11.12. Table after adjusting second column's tab stop.

Tip: To move columns accurately, choose **View Preferences** and turn on the display of tab marks.

To reverse the position of columns in a two-column table, follow these steps:

1. Select the character at the upper left corner of the column you want to move. For this example, begin with the column on the left (Marketing). Place the cursor on the M in Marketing.

2. Press Ctrl-Shift-F8 to turn on the column-select mode.

    You see the CS code in the status bar, telling you that Word is in the column-select mode.

3. Extend the selection to the right and down to encompass the column (see fig. 11.13). Be sure to include all the tab stops that come after the text in the column.

4. Choose **Edit Cut** (Alt-ET) or press Shift Del to cut the column to the scrap. The right column shifts to the left to fill up the blank space left when you cut the column (see fig. 11.14).

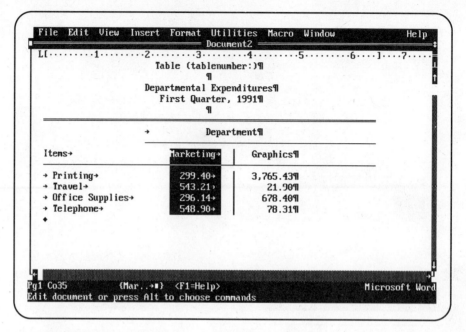

Fig. 11.13. Selecting the column.

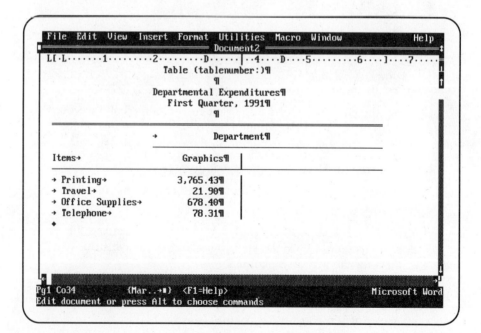

Fig. 11.14. Column cut to the scrap and right column shifts left.

5. Each line of data in the new left column will need a tab character before the paragraph mark so that Word can "receive" a column insertion properly. Use the Preferences dialog box to display tabs and paragraph marks, if necessary.

   To add tab characters to the end of each line, place the cursor at the end of each line and press Tab. After entering all the tab characters, your document should look like the one in figure 11.15.

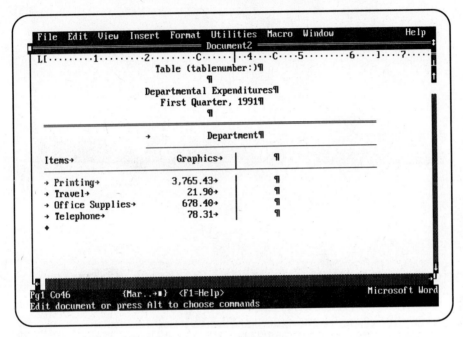

Fig. 11.15. Adding tab marks to the second column.

6. Select the paragraph mark where you want the column to be inserted. In this example, you choose the paragraph mark where the column header *Marketing* will go.

7. Choose Edit Paste (Alt-EP) or press Shift-Ins to insert the column at the cursor's location (see fig 11.16).

You can vary the techniques you just learned to perform other editing operations on columns. After selecting a column using the column-select mode, for instance, you can delete the column by pressing Del, or copy the column (by choosing **Edit Copy** or pressing Ctrl-Ins, moving the cursor to a new location, and choosing **Edit Paste**).

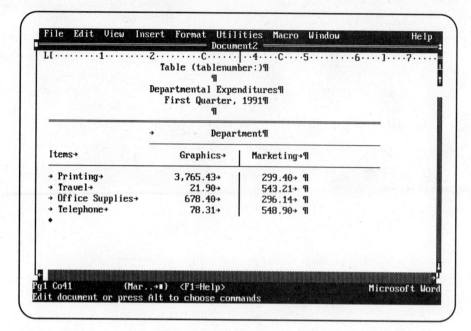

Fig. 11.16. *Restructured table with columns switched.*

Performing Calculations on Tabular Data: Using Math

Word isn't a spreadsheet program, but you can perform simple arithmetic operations right on the screen. With Word's column-select mode, you can add columns of numbers in a few keystrokes.

To add up the numbers in a table's columns, follow these steps:

1. Select the upper right corner of the column of data you want to add.

2. Press Ctrl-Shift-F8 to turn on the column-select mode.

3. Expand the selection to the right and down to encompass just the numbers in the column (see fig. 11.17).

4. Press F2. Word adds the data and enters the sum in the Scrap.

   You also see the result on the message line (fig. 11.18).

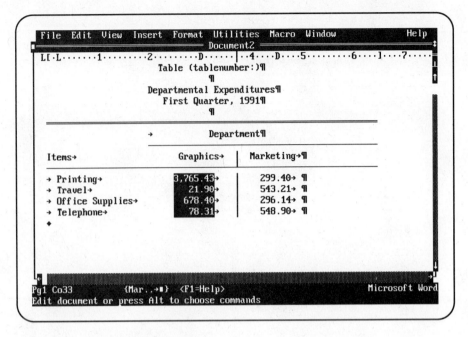

Fig. 11.17. Selecting the numbers.

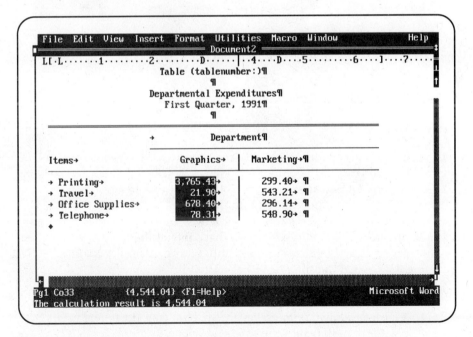

Fig. 11.18. Result of calculation appears in Scraps and on message line.

5. Press Ctrl-Shift-F8 to turn off column-select mode.

6. To insert the sum into your text, place the cursor where you want the sum to appear and press Shift-Ins (see fig. 11.19).

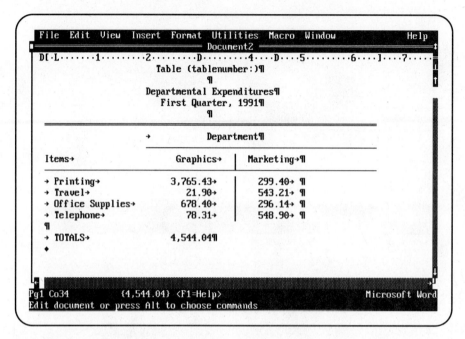

File Edit View Insert Format Utilities Macro Window   Help
══════════════════════ Document2 ══════════════════════
D[·L········1·········2·········D········4···D····5·········6····]····7·····

Table (tablenumber:)¶
¶
Departmental Expenditures¶
First Quarter, 1991¶
¶

→   Department¶

Items→   Graphics→ │ Marketing→¶

→ Printing→   3,765.43→ │ 299.40→ ¶
→ Travel→   21.90→ │ 543.21→ ¶
→ Office Supplies→   678.40→ │ 296.14→ ¶
→ Telephone→   78.31→ │ 548.90→ ¶
¶
→ TOTALS→   4,544.04¶
◆

Pg1 Co34   {4,544.04} <F1=Help>   Microsoft Word
Edit document or press Alt to choose commands

Fig. 11.19. Inserting the sum beneath the column.

More about Math

There's no need to run for a calculator when you're working with Word. As you just learned, you can add a column of numbers by selecting them and pressing F2. You can use the F2 (calculate) key in other ways also. In most cases, you can perform a simple computation right on the screen, such as 4,564 times 11.65 percent. ("What's 11.65 percent of 4,564? Why, 531.706, of course.") You even can add numbers by selecting a sentence that contains them (such as "Included in the survey were 11,983 volunteers and 12,891 salaried personnel") and pressing F2. You get the sum—24,874—instantly.

To use the calculate key, follow these steps:

1. Type an arithmetic expression anywhere in your document using one of the arithmetic symbols, called operators, listed in table 11.2.

2. Select the expression.

3. Choose Utilities Calculate or use the F2 keyboard shortcut. Word calculates the expression and the answer appears in the Scrap.

4. Press Shift-Insert. Word replaces the selected expression with the result in the Scrap.

Table 11.2
Word's Arithmetic Operators

Operator	Arithmetic Function	Example
+ (or no operator)	Addition	8 + 5 or 8 5
– (or parentheses)	Subtraction	8 – 5 or 8(5)
×	Multiplication	8 × 5
/	Division	8 / 5
%	Percent	10%

Keep the order of evaluation in mind if you create complex expressions. Normally, Word evaluates percentages first, followed by multiplication and division operations, and finally addition and subtraction operations. You can alter the order of evaluation using parentheses. If you place an expression in parentheses, Word evaluates the expression in parentheses first. Without parentheses, $2 \times 2 + 4 = 8$, but with parentheses, $2 \times (2 + 4) = 12$.

Importing Spreadsheet Data

If Word's math capabilities aren't sufficient for your number-crunching purposes, prepare your tables in a Lotus 1-2-3, Multiplan, or Excel spreadsheet. Next, use the Insert File command to import the spreadsheet into your Word document. After you import the table, you can format it, using any of the techniques discussed in this chapter.

This technique is extremely useful for two reasons. First, if you commonly use a spreadsheet program to prepare and manipulate tables of data, this method saves you the trouble of retyping the spreadsheet (or importing it after saving it as an ASCII file). Second, and most important, Word makes a record of the table's origin after you import the spreadsheet. With just one command, you can update the link so that your table contains the latest information in your spreadsheet. In this way, you can keep the authoritative version of a spreadsheet table in your Word document. After you import the table into your Word document, you can update the Word table easily after you make changes to the spreadsheet table.

Importing a Table from a Spreadsheet Program

Before you try importing a Lotus or Excel spreadsheet, bear in mind that Word imports a *range* of cells; you must specify a cell range to import a table from a spreadsheet. Word can import named ranges, or ranges of cells to which you apply a name (such as PROFITS or EXPENSES). Typing a name is much easier than typing a range of cells. When you create your spreadsheet, therefore, be sure to name the ranges that you want to import into your Word document.

Hint: Identify all the cells that you want to appear in your Word table and create a range called TABLE.

To import a spreadsheet as a table, perform these steps:

1. Place the cursor where you want the table to appear.

2. Choose Insert File (Alt-IF).

   You see the File dialog box (fig. 11.20).

3. In the File Name text box, type the name of the spreadsheet file you want to insert. If you're not sure of the name, use the Directories list box to activate the directory in which you keep the spreadsheet, and use the Files list box to choose the correct file name.

4. In the Range list box, type the name of the range, if you're importing a named range. Alternatively, type the range of cells you want to import, using the range expression format your program requires. (For Excel or Multiplan, you type a range expression using the format R1C10:R3C15. For Lotus 1-2-3, you type a range expression using the format A1.C9.) You also may choose the All option, but keep in mind that Word can import only 32K of data at a time.

5. Choose Link so that you will be able to update the table automatically if you later make changes to the spread-sheet.

6. Choose OK.

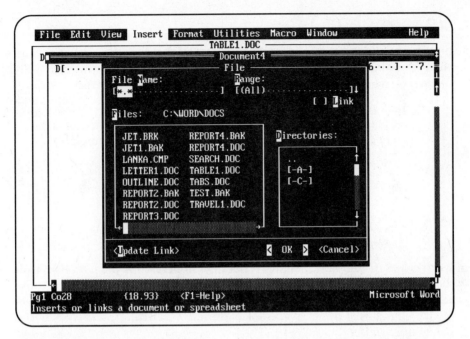

Fig. 11.20. *The File dialog box.*

If the desired spreadsheet isn't in the default directory, use path information other than the file name.

After the table appears, it may not be formatted attractively. During the import, though, Word ends each line with a newline (down arrow) character and places a tab keystroke between each column. For this reason, the entire table is a single paragraph. To align the table more attractively, just place the cursor anywhere in the table and set new tabs.

> **Caution:** Word places codes before and after the table. These codes are formatted as hidden text and tell Word where the spreadsheet came from. Don't delete them. If you do, Word cannot update the spreadsheet. To avoid deleting the codes accidentally, place an X in the Hidden Text field of the View Preferences dialog box..

Updating the Table

If you make changes to your spreadsheet after importing it to Word, and if you chose the Link option when you imported the spreadsheet, you can easily update the table in your Word document by following these steps:

1. Select the table to be updated by double-clicking the selection bar beside the table. If you want to update all the tables in your document at one time, press Ctrl-K5 to select the entire document.

2. Choose Insert File (Alt-IF).

3. Choose Update Link without changing anything on the dialog box.

4. Word highlights the table and displays a dialog box asking you to confirm the update of the table. Choose **Yes** to update the table.

Word erases the old imported table, but does not erase the paragraph mark at the end of the table. For this reason, Word does not lose the tab formatting assigned to the table. Word then imports the new spreadsheet. The new version of the spreadsheet appears and takes the tab formatting preserved by the paragraph mark.

This is a great feature and, as long as you know the range you want to import, it's easy to use.

Sorting Lists and Tables

Word's Utilities Sort command is your ticket to sorting lists in alphabetical or numerical order. But note that this command has its limitations—it's a memory hog. If you try to sort a lengthy list, the insufficient memory message appears. Try saving your document before Sort; if that doesn't work, consider adding expanded memory to your system.

In general, Utilities Sort performs its operations on paragraphs of text. A paragraph in Word, as you know, can be as short as a single line, or as long as several pages. The key point is that paragraphs are units for sorting, as far as Word is concerned. Word sorts each paragraph according to the first few characters in it. If a paragraph starts with "Zelda's zebras were known by a variety of affectionate names," it is likely to wind up last in an alphabetical sort.

You can sort alphabetically or numerically. In an alphabetical sort, Work sorts paragraphs in ascending order (A,B,C) or, if you prefer, descending (Z,Y,X) order. In a numerical sort, Word sorts paragraphs in ascending order (1,2,3) or, if you prefer, in descending order (3,2,1). By default, Word sorts in ascending alphabetical order. Word keeps all the text of a paragraph together when it sorts. When you create a list, therefore, keep the items you want sorted in their own separate paragraphs.

To sort a list, do the following:

1. Create the list in figure 11.21. Type each unit of data as a separate paragraph.

2. Select the list and choose **Utilities Sort** (Alt-UO).

   You see the Sort dialog box (fig. 11.22).

3. Choose the options you want in the Sort dialog box. By default, Word sorts alphanumeric data in ascending order and ignores case.

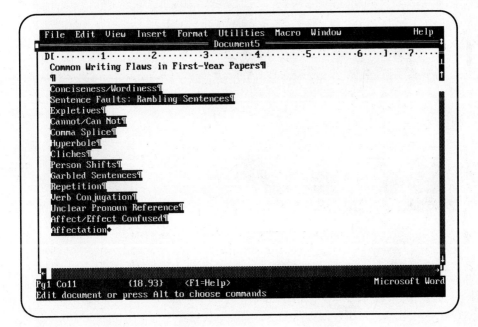

Fig. 11.21. Typing the list to be sorted.

   To sort alphabetically, choose **Alphanumeric**. To sort numerically, choose **Numeric**. To sort in ascending order (A, B, C or 1, 2, 3), choose **Ascending**. To sort in descending order (C, B, A or 3, 2, 1), choose **Descending**. To take case into account as you sort, choose **Case Sensitive**. In a case-sensitive sort, uppercase letters come before lowercase ones.

4. Choose OK.

The sorted text appears highlighted (see fig. 11.23).

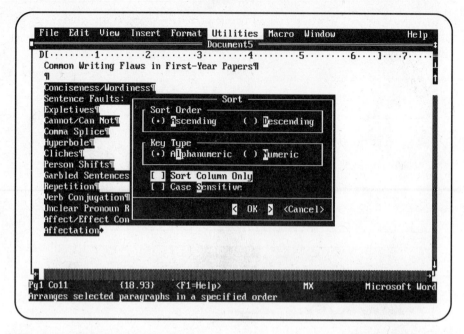

Fig. 11.22. *The Sort dialog box.*

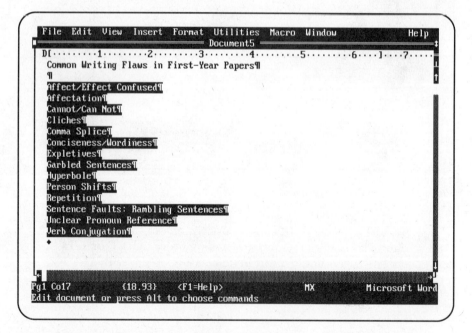

Fig. 11.23. *Highlighted text after sorting.*

Important: If the sort produces erroneous results, use the Edit Undo command immediately. Undo cannot undo the sort if you use another command or add more text after sorting.

More About Sorting

If you plan to use Sort frequently, note the following about how the command works:

- Paragraphs beginning with punctuation marks come before all others, so check to make sure that a paragraph you want to sort doesn't contain extraneous punctuation.

- Sort ignores capitalization unless you choose the Case Sensitive option in the Sort dialog box. If you do select this option, uppercase letters come before lowercase letters.

- Sort ignores diacritical marks such as accents, umlauts, etc., equating such characters with their ASCII equivalents.

Sorting Columns of Data in a Table

You can use Sort to sort the data in a table, even one that has many columns. What is more, you can identify any single column (not just the leftmost one) to serve as the *sort key*, the column that Sort uses as a guide for placing the data in numerical or alphabetical order. The key to this kind of sort is to use the column-select mode to tell Sort which column to use as a guide for sorting the data.

For example, in the departmental expenditures table you created in this chapter, you could sort the data by the Graphics Department expenditures. When Word sorts data that you have selected in the column-select mode, it keeps the lines of data together; it just sorts them according to the column you have highlighted (and not the first few characters in the paragraph).

It's useful to sort data in a table whenever it makes sense to organize the data in some way. If you list items in the left column under the stub, you can sort them alphabetically. You can sort the data numerically, too. You can sort the table in descending numerical order, for example, so that the largest figures are at the top of the column.

Note: Each line must end with a newline character (Shift-Enter) or a paragraph mark.

Perform the following steps to sort a table:

1. Place the cursor in the upper left corner of the column you want to use as the sort key and press Ctrl-Shift-F8.

   Word is in the column-select mode, and you see the C S code in the status bar.

2. Select the column that will serve as the sort key. In figure 11.24, the expenditures of the Graphics Department are highlighted.

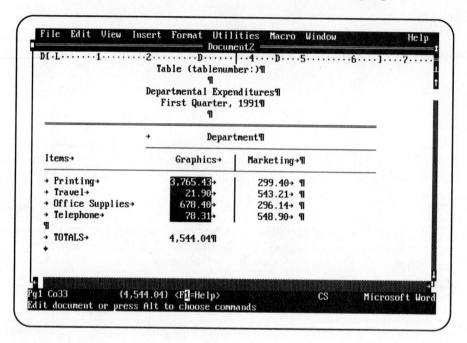

Fig. 11.24. Selecting the data to serve as the sort key.

3. Choose Utilities Sort (Alt-UO) and choose the sorting options you want.

   For this example, **Ascending** and **Numeric** were chosen.

4. Choose OK.

Word performs the sort, keeping all the lines together (see fig. 11.25). The Graphics Department expenditures are sorted in ascending numerical order.

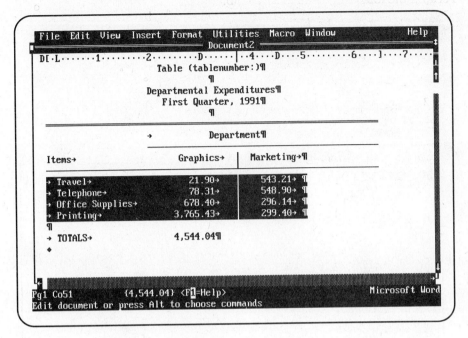

Fig. 11.25. Table with Graphics Department data sorted numerically.

Chapter Summary

In this chapter you learned how Word 5.5 makes it easy to create great-looking tables and lists. Version 5.5's much-improved features for setting and moving tabs make it a snap to set and alter custom tab stops for any paragraph in your document. Whether you're using the keyboard or the mouse, you can easily set tabs on the Ruler.

You also learned how you can type arithmetic expressions on the screen and get answers right away. Word's Utilities Sort command sorts paragraphs alphabetically or numerically and can sort in ascending (A, B, C or 1, 2, 3) or descending (C, B, A or 3, 2, 1) order.

The next chapter tells you how to use two of Word's versatile features: glossaries and bookmarks. They are especially useful for boilerplate text.

Quick Review

Borders

To add a single or double line beneath a heading:

1. Choose Format **B**order (Alt-TB).

2. Choose **N**ormal line style for a single line, or **D**ouble for a double line.

3. Choose **L**ines.

4. Choose **B**ottom.

5. Choose OK.

To cancel a border (and all other paragraph formats):

1. Place the cursor in the paragraph containing the border you want to cancel.

2. Press Ctrl-X.

To cancel a border without canceling other paragraph formats:

1. Place the cursor in the paragraph containing the border you want to cancel.

2. Select Forma**t** **B**orders (Alt-TB),

3. Choose **N**one.

4. Choose OK.

To shorten a border so that it doesn't span all the space between the margins:

1. Place the cursor in the paragraph containing the border you want to shorten.

2. Choose Format **P**aragraph (Alt-TP).

3. Type an indent in the From **L**eft and/or the From **R**ight text boxes.

4. Choose OK.

Default Tabs

To set new default tabs for an entire document:

1. Choose Utilities **C**ustomize (Alt-UU).

2. Choose Default Tab.

3. Type the new default tab width.

4. Choose OK.

Deleting Custom Tab Stops

To delete custom tabs with the keyboard:

1. Select the paragraph or paragraphs containing the custom tab that you want to delete.

2. Press Shift-Ctrl-F10 to place the cursor on the Ruler.

3. Press the down-arrow key to move to the next tab stop right, and press the up-arrow key to move to the next tab stop left.

4. When you have highlighted the tab you want to delete, press Del to delete this tab, or press Ctrl-Del to delete this tab and all the tab stops that appear to the right of this tab on the Ruler.

5. Repeat steps 3 and 4 to delete additional tabs, if desired.

6. Press Enter to return to your document.

To delete custom tabs with the mouse:

1. Select the paragraph or paragraphs containing the custom tab you want to delete.

2. On the Ruler, point to the tab stop letter you want to delete.

3. Drag the letter below the Ruler and release the button.

4. Repeat steps 3 and 4 to delete additional tabs, if desired.

To reverse the position of columns in a two-column table:

1. Select the character at the upper left corner of the column you want to move.

2. Press Ctrl-Shift-F8 to turn on the column-select mode.

3. Extend the selection to the right and down to encompass the column (see fig. 11.13). Be sure to include all the tab stops that come after the text in the column.

4. Choose **Edit Cut** (Alt-ET) or press Shift-Del to cut the column to the Scrap.

5. Make sure that each line of data in the new left column ends with a tab character before the paragraph mark.

6. Select the paragraph mark where you want the column to be inserted.

7. Choose Edit **Paste** (Alt-EP) or press Shift-Ins to insert the column at the cursor's location (see fig 11.17).

Editing Tables

To move a column left or right:

1. Select all the lines you want to move.

2. Move the tab stop that aligns the column.

Importing Lotus or Excel Spreadsheets as Tables

To import a spreadsheet as a table:

1. Place the cursor where you want the table to appear.

2. Choose Insert **File** (Alt-IF).

3. In the File Name text box, type the name of the spread-sheet file you want to insert.

4. In the Range list box, type the name of the range, if you're importing a named range. Alternatively, type the range of cells you want to import, using the range expression format your program requires.

5. Choose Link so that you will be able to update the table automatically if you later make changes to the spreadsheet.

6. Choose OK.

To update the table if you later make changes to the spreadsheet:

1. Select the table to be updated. If you want to update all the tables in your document at one time, press Ctrl-K5 to select the entire document.

2. Choose Insert **File** (Alt-IF).

3. Choose Update Link without changing anything on the dialog box.

4. Word highlights the table and displays a dialog box asking you to confirm the update of the table. Choose **Yes** to update the table.

Math

To add up the numbers in a table's columns:

1. Select the upper right corner of the column of data you want to add.

2. Press Ctrl-Shift-F8 to turn on the column-select mode.

3. Expand the selection to the right and down to encompass just the numbers in the column.

4. Press F2.

5. Press Ctrl-Shift-F8 to turn off column select mode.

6. Place the cursor where you want the sum to appear and press Shift-Ins.

To calculate a math expression:

1. Type an arithmetic expression anywhere in your document.

2. Select the expression.

3. Choose Utilities Calculate or use the F2 keyboard shortcut.

4. Place the cursor where you want to insert the result.

5. Press Shift-Insert.

Moving Custom Tab Stops

To move custom tab stops with the keyboard:

1. Select the paragraph or paragraphs that contain the tab or tabs you want to move.

2. Press Shift-Ctrl-F10 to activate the Ruler.

3. Press the down-arrow key to move to the next tab stop right, and press the up-arrow key to move to the next tab stop left.

4. When you have highlighted the tab you want to move, press Ctrl-right arrow to move the tab right, or Ctrl-left arrow to move the tab left.

5. To move other tabs, repeat steps 3 and 4.

6. Press Enter to return to your document.

To move a tab with the mouse:

1. Select the paragraph or paragraphs that contain the tab or tabs you want to move.

2. Move the pointer to the tab stop on the Ruler.

3. Hold down the left mouse button and drag the tab stop letter to its new location.

4. Release the mouse button.

5. Repeat steps 3 and 4 to move additional tab stops, if desired.

Series Code Names

To type a series code name that Word will number automatically:

1. Type the code (up to 31 characters) followed by a colon.

2. With the cursor positioned just after the colon, press F3.

Setting Custom Tab Stops

To set a custom tab with the keyboard:

1. Select the paragraph or paragraphs to which you would like to apply the custom tabs.

2. Press Shift-Ctrl-F10 to place the cursor on the Ruler.

3. Press the right- and left-arrow keys to move the cursor where you want the tab stop to appear. You can also press PgDn to move the cursor 1 inch to the right, and PgUp to move the cursor 1 inch to the left.

4. Press the first letter of the tab alignment you want (**Left**, **Centered**, **Right**, **Decimal**, **Vertical**).

5. If you want to add a leader to the tab stop, press the key corresponding to the leader you want to enter (a period, a hyphen, or an underscore character). Skip this step if you don't want a leader.

6. To set more tabs, repeat steps 3, 4, and 5.

7. To return to your document, press Enter.

To set custom tabs with the mouse:

1. With the ruler displayed, select the paragraph or paragraphs to which the tab stops are to apply.

2. If you want an alignment other than flush left, click the ∟ next to the left indent marker on the ruler until it displays the alignment code you want.

3. To select a leader character, click the space left of the ∟ on the ruler line until the leader you want appears. If you don't want a leader, skip this step.

4. To set the tab, click the ruler where you want the tab stop.

5. To set additional tabs, repeat steps 2 through 4.

To set custom tabs with precise measurements:

1. Select the paragraph or paragraphs containing the tab you want to set.

2. Choose Format **Tabs** (Alt-TT).

3. Type the measurement in the **Tab Position** text box.

4. Choose the **Alignment**.

5. Choose the **Leader**, if any.

6. Choose OK.

Sort

To sort a list:

1. Create the list. Type each unit of data as a separate paragraph.

2. Select the list and choose **Utilities Sort** (Alt-UO).

3. Choose the options you want in the Sort dialog box.

4. Choose OK.

To sort a table:

1. Place the cursor in the upper left corner of the column you want to use as the sort key and press Ctrl-Shift-F8.

2. Select the column that will serve as the sort key.

3. Choose **Utilities Sort** (Alt-UO) and choose the sorting options you want.

4. Choose OK.

Chapter

12

Using Glossaries and Bookmarks

The big productivity benefits of word processing aren't automatic; you must understand enough about a program like Word 5.5 to put its productivity-enhancing features to work. If you ever find yourself typing the same passage of text over and over, read on, because you're about to learn how you can store dozens of passages of repeatedly used text, called boilerplate, and recall each of them with a few keystrokes.

The keys to this time-saving feature are Word's glossaries, which are named storage spaces for text, and a feature called bookmarks, which are named sections of text in a document. To retrieve text from a glossary, you simply type the document name and press F3. To retrieve text from another Word document that contains bookmarks, you use the Insert File command. Either way, the boilerplate text you have stored is just a few keystrokes away.

Whether you will find uses for boilerplate depends on the kind of writing you're planning to do. Just ask yourself whether you frequently find yourself typing the same text over and over. Following is a brief list of some examples of repeatedly used text:

- A memo header that includes a lengthy distribution list

- Your return address

- The addresses of people with whom you frequently correspond

- Standard responses to letters of inquiry or complaint

- Frequently used text with complex formatting

- Commonly used forms

- Bibliographic citations you use repeatedly

In short, if you type something repeatedly, it's a candidate for storage and retrieval in a glossary. Use your imagination. An English teacher has created glossaries for grading papers on disk. If he runs across a dangling phrase in a student's paper, he inserts an entry called DANGLE, which explains why the construction is wrong and shows how to repair it.

Even if you don't think you will ever use a glossary or bookmark, the material in this chapter is essential reading. As you will learn in Chapter 21, "Creating and Using Word 5.5 Macros," knowledge of Word's glossaries is a prerequisite for creating, storing, and retrieving Word 5.5 macros. Word stores and retrieves macros the same way it stores and retrieves glossary entries: you use the same commands, and you face the same challenges of glossary file management.

In this chapter, you learn to do the following:

- Create a glossary entry and store it so that you can retrieve it with the Insert command or the F3 key

- Assign a glossary entry to a keyboard shortcut for even faster retrieval

- Edit and erase glossary entries

- Create and manage new glossary files to store and retrieve related glossary entries

- Use glossaries to store text safely while editing

- Mark text as a bookmark

- Move around in a lengthy document by using bookmarks

- Import bookmark text by using document-linking commands

- Create in-text cross-references that Word will number automatically

Creating and Managing a Glossary Entry

Word's glossaries are very much like the Scrap, except that there is more than one glossary, and each has a name. It's exceptionally easy to create, retrieve, edit, and delete glossary entries, as you will see in this section, which outlines the basic procedures.

Users of previous versions of Word will be pleased with the simplified approach to creating and inserting glossaries. No longer are there Insert and Delete commands and arcane procedures to display lists of glossaries you have already created; instead, you use a well-designed Glossary dialog box that automatically lists the available glossary entries. If you have any remaining doubts about Microsoft's wisdom in going to the new user interface, the improvements in the Glossary area will put them to rest.

Creating a Glossary Entry

When you create a glossary entry, you select the text to store, name the entry, optionally choose a Ctrl-key combination to enter the glossary, and save the glossary entry.

Caution: Word doesn't object if you assign a Ctrl-key combination that's already used as a keyboard shortcut. For instance, Ctrl-C centers text. But if you choose Ctrl-C for a glossary, Word overrides the default keyboard shortcut. To avoid this problem, use Shift-Ctrl instead of Ctrl for your key combinations.

To create a glossary entry, follow these steps:

1. Type the text you want the entry to contain. You can include character and paragraph formatting. For example, try creating a glossary entry that contains your name and return address. Use boldface and centering.

2. Select the text.

   If you want the paragraph's formatting to be part of the entry, be sure to select the paragraph mark at the end of the paragraph. If you added section formats, also select the section mark. To switch on paragraph marks, choose **Paragraph Marks** in the Non-printing Characters area of the Preferences dialog box. To display the Preferences dialog box, choose **View Preferences** (Alt-VE).

3. Choose **Edit Glossary** (Alt-EO).

   You see the Glossary dialog box (fig. 12.1). This dialog box echoes the text you have selected in its Selection area.

4. In the Glossary Name text box, type a glossary name.

   To store your return address, use the name Return_address. Glossary names must be one word and cannot exceed 31 characters. You can use underscores, periods, and hyphens, although a

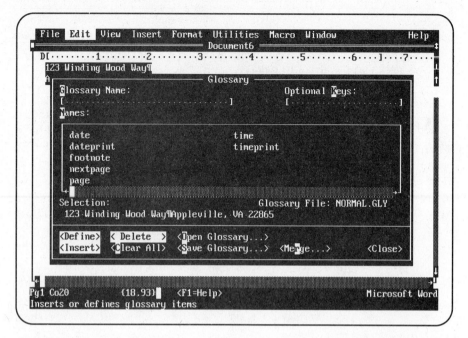

Fig. 12.1. The Glossary dialog box.

glossary entry's name cannot begin or end with these characters. You cannot use other punctuation or spaces.

5. In the Optional **K**eys area, press the keys you want to use to enter the glossary entry at the cursor's location. Always use a Shift-Ctrl key combination instead of Ctrl so you don't inactivate any of Word's default formatting keys.

   To assign a return address to a key combination, for example, press Shift-Ctrl-R.

6. Choose **D**efine.

Caution: If you see the an alert box with the message "Replace glossary entry," you have tried to use a name that has already been used for another entry. Choose Cancel, and choose another name.

Saving a Glossary Entry

The glossaries you create and define during a Word session are stored in Word's memory. If you want to use these glossary entries in the next editing session, you must save them.

You can create more than one glossary file. A glossary file is a disk file (with the special extension .GLY) that contains nothing but glossary entries and related information. By default, Word uses the default glossary file called NORMAL.GLY. But if you prefer, you can save your glossary entries in a different file.

To store your glossary entries, save them in NORMAL.GLY, unless you create a huge number of glossaries and need to divide them so you can retrieve them easily. That way they're always available. You needn't do anything special to retrieve them; they're displayed in the **Names** list box every time you use the Edit **Gl**ossary command.

To save the current glossaries to NORMAL.GLY, do the following:

1. Choose **E**dit **Gl**ossary (Alt-EO).

2. Choose **S**ave Glossary.

    You see the Save Glossary dialog box (fig. 12.2). Word proposes the name NORMAL.GLY in the File **N**ame text box.

3. Choose OK.

You learn more about saving and retrieving glossary files elsewhere in this chapter. For now, keep in mind that you must save your glossary entries as well as defining them in the Glossary dialog box.

Retrieving a Glossary Entry

After you have defined a glossary entry, you can retrieve it in three different ways. If you know the name, you can type it and press F3. If you're not sure of the name, you can choose it from the **Names** area of the Glossary dialog box. And if you assigned the glossary to a key, you can just press the key.

To retrieve a glossary entry when you know its name, do the following:

1. Type the glossary name in your document.

2. Press F3.

    Word erases the glossary entry name and, in its place, inserts the glossary entry's text.

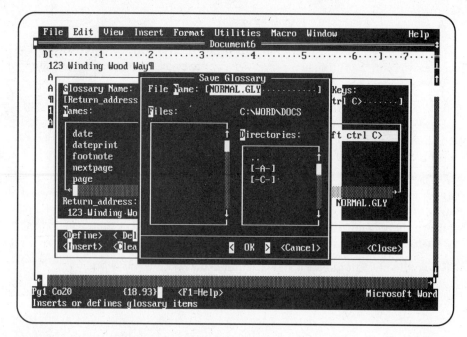

Fig. 12.2. The Save Glossary dialog box.

Follow these steps to retrieve a glossary entry from the Glossary dialog box:

1. Choose Edit Glossary (Alt-EO).

   You see the Glossary dialog box.

2. Choose the Names area and highlight the glossary name.

3. Choose Insert.

   Word inserts the glossary entry at the cursor's location.

To retrieve a glossary entry using the keyboard shortcut you chose, just press the keyboard shortcut keys.

Editing a Glossary Entry

If you have created a glossary entry that contains an error, such as a spelling mistake, you can fix it easily by following these steps:

1. Insert the entry using one of the techniques just presented.

2. Edit the text to correct the errors.

3. Select all the text you want stored in the glossary after you have corrected the errors.

4. Choose **E**dit Glossary (Alt-EO).

5. Highlight the glossary entry's name in the **N**ames list box.

6. Choose **D**efine.

    You see an alert box warning you that the glossary already exists.

7. Choose OK to replace the glossary entry.

If you would like to add a keyboard shortcut to an often-used glossary entry, follow these steps:

1. Insert the entry using one of the techniques just presented.

2. Select the text.

3. Choose **E**dit Glossary (Alt-EO).

4. Highlight the glossary entry's name in the **N**ames list box.

5. Choose the Optional **K**eys area.

6. Press the key combination you want to use.

7. Choose **D**efine.

    You see an alert box warning you that the glossary already exists.

8. Choose OK to replace the glossary entry.

You can use the above procedure if you have chosen a keyboard shortcut that cancels a key combination Word already uses. When you choose a new key combination, Word restores the original function of the key you chose previously.

Deleting a Glossary Entry

If a glossary entry is no longer needed, you can delete it. And it's a good idea to do so. The more glossary names you see in the **N**ames list box, the harder it is to choose the name you want.

Note: You cannot delete the entries called page, date, time, footnote, nextpage, dateprint, and timeprint. These entries are permanent. Their functions are discussed later in the section titled "Using the Supplied Glossary Entries."

> ***Caution***: Deleting glossary entries is one of the few procedures in Word that does not involve a confirmation alert box. Be sure you have highlighted the correct glossary name before you choose Delete.

To delete a glossary entry, follow these steps:

1. Choose **Edit Glossary** (Alt-EO).

   You see the Glossary dialog box.

2. Highlight the glossary entry's name in the Names list box.

3. Choose **Delete**.

4. Choose **Close** to return to your document.

Deleting More Than One Glossary Entry at a Time

Sometimes during a session you create several entries for temporary purposes. If you don't want to save any of the entries, you can delete all the glossaries you have created in the current session. (Word doesn't delete the built-in glossaries, about which more will be said elsewhere in this chapter.)

There are two ways to abandon the glossary entries you create in a session. The first, and easiest, is just skipping the procedure in which you save the entries. When you quit Word, you see an alert box asking you whether you want to save the changes to NORMAL.GLY, the default glossary file. Just choose **No**.

The second way to abandon glossary entries is to choose the Clear All command button at the bottom of the Glossary dialog box. This command button clears all the glossary entries you have chosen in this and previous operating sessions, but doesn't remove the built-in glossary entries (such as date, dateprint, footnote, etc.). However, this command doesn't affect the glossary file on disk unless you choose the Save Glossary command. If you choose Clear All and then Save Glossary, you permanently wipe out all the glossary entries you have chosen and restore the glossary file to the state it was in when you first started Word 5.5.

Managing Glossary Files

When you start Word, the program loads the default glossary, a file called NORMAL.GLY. This file isn't like a DOC file, which contains a document. NORMAL.GLY is a special file for storing and retrieving glossary entries on disk. As you learn in this section, you can save your glossary entries in glossary files so that they are available the next time you use Word. You can even create your own glossary files to contain special-purpose glossary entries.

Saving Glossary Files

You have already learned that you must save your glossary entries to disk if you want to use them in future operating sessions. Most users will be best off saving their entries to NORMAL.GLY, the glossary file that Word automatically uses when you start the program.

If the entries you have created are for special-purpose writing tasks, you can save them to a glossary file other than NORMAL.GLY. Follow these steps:

1. Choose **E**dit Glossary (Alt-EO).

2. Choose **S**ave Glossary.

    You see the Save Glossary dialog box.

3. Type a file name for the glossary file.

    The file name must conform to DOS rules (no more than eight letters or numbers). Omit the period and extension; Word supplies the period and the GLY extension automatically.

    Be sure to use a file name that will remind you of the file's contents.

4. Choose OK.

If you plan to create many glossaries for boilerplating with each having several paragraphs to several pages of text, store and retrieve the boilerplate text with bookmarks. Using bookmarks, you can store boilerplate text in an ordinary Word file. For this reason, bookmark text is much easier to edit than glossary text. See the section called "Boilerplate Applications with Bookmarks," later in this chapter, for details.

Loading Glossary Files

You can load a glossary file you have created so that it completely replaces the one that's already in memory.

To load a glossary file other than NORMAL.GLY, do the following:

1. Choose **Edit Glossary** (Alt-EO).

2. Choose **Open Glossary**.

    You see the Open Glossary dialog box (fig. 12.3).

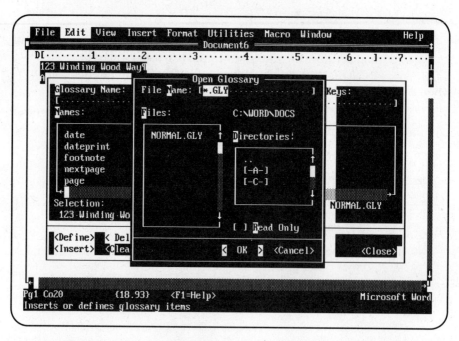

Fig. 12.3. The Open Glossary dialog box.

3. If you see the glossary file name in the Files list box, highlight the name. If not, use the Directories list box to find the file in another directory.

4. Choose **OK**.

Merging Glossary Files

If you want to combine a custom glossary file with another, you can use the Merge command button in the Glossary dialog box. Follow these steps too merge a glossary file:

1. Choose **E**dit Glossary (Alt-EO).

2. Choose **O**pen Glossary and open the first glossary file.

3. Choose Me**r**ge.

    You see the Merge Glossary dialog box, which looks just like the Open Glossary dialog box.

4. If you see the glossary file name in the **F**iles list box, highlight the name. If not, use the **D**irectories list box to find the file in another directory.

5. Choose OK.

    Word merges the two glossaries, but for the current operating session only. You must save the combined glossaries if you want them to be merged in future operating sessions.

6. If you want to save the merged glossaries, choose **S**ave Glossary.

Printing Glossaries

To print the contents of the glossary file now in memory, use the Print dialog box. Follow these steps:

1. Choose **F**ile **P**rint (Alt-FP). Alternatively, use the Shift-F9 keyboard shortcut.

2. Drop down the **P**rint list box.

3. Choose Glossary.

4. Close the Print list box.

5. Choose OK.

Using the Supplied Glossary Entries

As you have already learned, NORMAL.GLY—and even the special-purpose glossary files you create—contains seven supplied glossary entries, which you cannot erase. These entries are useful for certain purposes. In Chapter 5, for instance, you learned how to insert the (page) symbol in headers or footers by typing *page* and pressing F3. You didn't know it at the time, but you were using one of Word's built-in or supplied glossary entries. These supplied glossary entries play a variety of useful roles in Word documents.

After you insert one of these supplied glossary entries into your text, the glossary entry appears in your document surrounded by parentheses, like it does with (page). Those parentheses tell you that the word is a glossary entry, not ordinary text. As you will see, if you move the cursor over the glossary entry, Word treats the whole entry as if it were a single character. You can delete the entry, if you want; just press Backspace or Del to rub it out.

Briefly, the supplied glossary entries are as follows:

- **date.** Word prints the current DOS system date at the entry's location. Word uses the date format you have selected in the date format field of the Options menu.

- **dateprint.** At the time of printing, Word prints the DOS system date at the entry's location. Word uses the date format you have selected in the date format field of the Options menu.

- **footnote.** This entry is used only when you have inadvertently deleted a footnote reference mark. For more information on this entry, see Chapter 14, "The Legal and Scholarly Word."

- **nextpage.** This entry prints the next page number at the entry's location. This entry is very useful for forward references such as "See Figure 4, on page (nextpage)."

- **page.** When you insert this entry into your document, Word prints the current page number at the entry's location.

- **time.** Word prints the current DOS system time at the entry's location. Word uses the time format you have selected in the time format field of the Options menu.

- **timeprint.** At the time of printing, Word prints the DOS system time at the entry's location. Word uses the time format you have selected in the time format field of the Options menu.

Of all these entries, the most useful are page and dateprint. The chief uses of page are in headers and footers, as you have already learned.

Provided your computer has clock-calendar circuitry and a good battery, you can enter the current time and date at any time following these steps:

1. Place the cursor where you want the time or date to appear.

2. Type *time* or *date*.

3. Press F3.

   Word enters the current system time or date at the cursor's location.

If you would rather your document contained the time or date when the document is actually printed, use the timeprint or dateprint glossaries, as follows:

1. Place the cursor where you want the time or date to appear when your document is printed.

2. Type *timeprint* or *dateprint*.

3. Press F3.

   Word surrounds the glossary name with parentheses. You don't see the time or date until your document is printed.

About Bookmarks

A bookmark is simply a named unit of text. If you have ever used a spreadsheet, you will notice a bookmark's similarity to a named range of cells. With spreadsheets, after you have named the range, you can refer to it by its name rather than type the cell references. A bookmark is much the same. After you have named the unit of text, you can refer to it by name. After you have created bookmarks, you can use them in three ways:

- You can jump immediately to any bookmark in your document using the **Edit Go To** command. This feature is useful for moving around in lengthy documents. You can jump immediately to the section of your document that contains the text you mark, such as "Reynolds contract" or "Cooling System Specifications."

- You can cross-reference bookmarks so that, when Word prints your document, the program automatically fills in the correct page number on which the bookmark appears. Instead of typing "See p. 9 for more information," you type the sentence with a bookmark reference instead of the page number. When you print your document, Word removes the bookmark reference and prints the correct page number—and that's true no matter how much you edit or even restructure your document.

- You can import bookmarks from other Word documents using the **Insert File** command. Using this technique, you can create lengthy glossary entries that do not take up room in Word's memory or clutter the Glossary dialog box.

A bookmark has two components:

- **Bookmark text.** When you create a bookmark, you select the text you want to mark. This text can be as short as one character, but in most cases, you select a word, a phrase, a paragraph, or even a passage that's one or more pages in length. When Word marks the text, the first and last characters of the selection become the bookmark's "anchors." For any operation involving bookmarks, the anchors show where the bookmark text begins and ends.

- **Bookmark name.** You assign a name to the bookmark text with **Insert Bookmark**. After you have named the text, you can move to it using **Edit Go To**, and you can also use the name to generate an automatic cross-reference.

Unlike glossary entries, which are stored in a special, separate file or files, bookmarks are stored with the document in which you create them. The bookmarks for one document aren't available when you're editing a second document, unless you deliberately access them using **Insert File**.

Using Bookmarks

This section discusses techniques for creating and canceling bookmark designations, moving around in a complex document using bookmarks, and applying bookmarks to boilerplate applications. Chapter 14 discusses cross-referencing with bookmarks.

Marking Text as a Bookmark

Here are two good reasons for marking text as a bookmark: you can jump to the bookmark immediately, without having to scroll through your document manually or use the Search command; and you can create automatic cross-references. If you plan to use the bookmark for cross-references, be sure to select all the text that pertains to the subject. For instance, if you wanted to cross-reference a section in a proposal called "Cooling System Specifications," you would select the entire section that's pertinent to this subject.

To mark text as a bookmark, follow these steps: **Ctrl-Shift-F5**

1. Select the text you want to include in the bookmark.

   You cannot select text using Word's column-select mode. If you try, you see an alert box when you choose **Insert Bookmark**.

2. Choose **Insert Bookmark** (Alt-EM) or use the Ctrl-Shift-F5 keyboard shortcut.

   You see the Insert Bookmark dialog box (fig. 12.4).

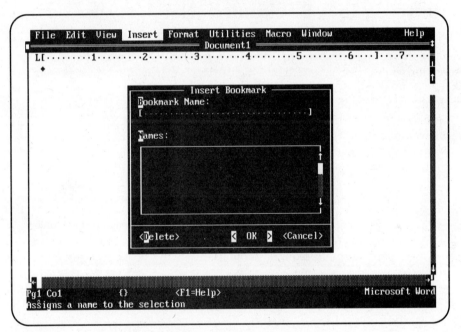

Fig. 12.4. The Insert Bookmark dialog box.

3. Type the bookmark name in the **Bookmark Name** text box.

   Every bookmark's name must be unique and must be one word. You can use up to 31 letters or numbers, and within the word you can use underscore characters, periods, and hyphens. Do not use colons, semicolons, or spaces.

4. Choose OK.

How Editing Affects Bookmarks

A bookmark's anchors are non-printing characters that you cannot see. For this reason, it's quite possible that you will delete one of them while editing the passage. However, Word copes with such deletions automatically. If you delete the first anchor accidentally, Word automatically assigns the anchor to the first character of the remaining bookmark text.

When you copy bookmark text within a document, Word copies the text, but not the bookmark. However, if you move the entire block of bookmark text to the new location, the anchors go with it.

Jumping to a Bookmark

One advantage of creating bookmarks is that you can use them to navigate in a lengthy, complex document. If you have ever thought, "I wish I could find that section where I discuss the climatological effects of irrigation," then bookmarks may prove useful. When you have finished typing an important section that you think you will come back to for further editing, format it as bookmark text. Be sure to give it a distinctive name. Remember, you can use up to 31 characters when you assign a name to a bookmark. Use underscore characters to separate words, as in "climate_and_irrigation."

Follow these steps to jump to a bookmark:

1. Choose Edit Go To or use the F5 keyboard shortcut.

   You see the Go To menu (fig. 12.5). The names of the bookmarks you have created for this document, and this document only, are visible in the Bookmark Name list box.

2. Choose Bookmark.

3. Choose the name of the bookmark in the Bookmark Name list box.

4. Choose OK.

   Word scrolls to the bookmark and highlights all the text between the anchors.

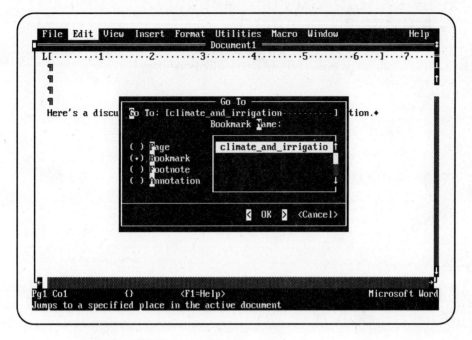

Fig. 12.5. *The Go To menu.*

Moving Bookmark Text to a New Location

To move bookmark text so that the anchors go with it, you must be sure to select the anchors as well as the text. The following procedure ensures that the anchors will be selected:

1. Use **Edit G**o To to jump to the bookmark text.

   The bookmark text is selected, and so are the anchors.

2. Use any selection technique to expand the highlight, if desired, but don't contract it.

3. Choose **Edit C**ut or press Shift-Del to cut the selection to the Scrap.

4. Move the cursor to the place you want the selection to appear.

5. Choose **Edit P**aste or press Shift-Ins to paste the selection at the cursor's location.

Removing a Bookmark

If a bookmark is no longer needed and there are many bookmarks visible in the Bookmark Name list box, you can delete the bookmark without deleting the text.

1. Use **Edit Go** To to jump to the bookmark.

   Edit Go To highlights all the text between the anchors.

2. Choose Insert Bookmark (Alt-IM).

3. Highlight the name of the bookmark in the Bookmark Name list box.

4. Choose **Delete**.

5. Choose OK.

Changing the Text Assigned to a Bookmark Name

Suppose you made an error when you assigned a name to bookmark text, such as not selecting all the relevant text or selecting the wrong text. You can easily change the text to which the name was assigned. Follow these steps:

1. Select the text.

2. Choose Insert Bookmark (Alt-IM).

3. In the **Bookmark Names** list box, choose the name of the bookmark.

4. Choose OK.

   You see an alert box with the message, `Replace bookmark?`

5. Choose OK.

Creating Cross-References

A cross-reference is an in-text reference to another part of the same document, as in "See the discussion of artichokes on page 16." With Word, you can create cross-references so that the program supplies the correct page number automatically. You can also cross-reference an item in a series or a footnote. In all three cases, you can rearrange your document as much as you like without affecting the cross-references. They will all be numbered correctly when the time comes to print your document.

This section discusses the procedure you follow to cross-reference text and items in a series. For a discussion of cross-referencing footnotes, see Chapter 14, "The Legal and Scholarly Word."

Cross-Referencing Text on a Different Page

To cross-reference text on a different page in your document, you create a bookmark. Then you move the cursor to the place you want the cross-reference to appear, and you insert a code name (*page:*) and the name of the bookmark.

Follow these steps to cross-reference text:

1. Select all the text you want to cross-reference, and use **Insert Bookmark** to define it as a bookmark.

2. Move the cursor to the place you want the text to appear.

3. Type the text of the cross-reference, such as "For a discussion of project methodology, see page" followed by a space.

4. Immediately following the cross-reference text, type the code name *page:* (don't forget the colon), followed by the bookmark name. Don't type a space after the colon.

5. Press F3.

   Word encloses the code name and bookmark name in parentheses. This text won't print. In its place will appear the number of the page on which the bookmark text appears.

Cross-Referencing an Item in a Series

In Chapter 11, "Creating Tables and Lists with Tabs, Sort, and Math," you learned how to create a *series code name* so that Word automatically numbers the tables in your document. If you have created series code names to number tables, figures, or other components of your document, you can cross-reference these items.

To create the series code name, follow these steps:

1. Position the cursor where you want the automatic number to appear.

   For example, place the cursor at the top of a table or beneath a figure.

2. Type the text, such as *Table* or *Figure*, that will precede the number Word automatically supplies. Leave a space after the text.

3. Type a series code name, such as *table:* or *figure:* (don't forget the colon).

   You can use up to 31 characters, but the series code name must be one word. Underscore characters are permitted, as are periods and hyphens.

4. Press F3 to define the series code name.

5. Repeat steps 1 through 4 for each additional item (such as additional tables or figures) that you want Word to number automatically.

After you have created the series code name, you can cross-reference an individual item, and Word will automatically print the item's number. First, you attach a bookmark to the series code item so that it can be cross-referenced. Then you place a code in your text where you want the cross-reference to appear.

To mark the series item for cross-referencing, do the following:

1. Place the cursor on the character preceding the series code name.

2. Choose **Insert Bookmark** (Alt-IM), or use the Shift-Ctrl-F5 keyboard shortcut.

3. In the **Bookmark Name** text box, type a name for the bookmark that describes the contents of this specific item.

   For instance, to cross-reference a table containing data on the second quarter of 1991, type *2nd_quarter_91*.

4. Choose OK.

Follow these steps to cross-reference the series item:

1. Position the cursor where you want the series item's number to appear.

For example, position the cursor after "Figure" in the following sentence:

> For *a graphic summary of the company's second-quarter performance, see Figure*

2. Type the series code name, a colon, and the bookmark name, without any spaces.

   For example, suppose the series code name is *figure*, and the bookmark name is *2nd_quarter_91.* You would type *figure:2nd_quarter_91*

3. Press F3.

   Word surrounds the expression in parentheses.

When you print your document, you will see a reference to the series number, as in the following example: "For a graphic summary of the company's second-quarter performance, see Figure 21."

Boilerplate Applications with Bookmarks

As already discussed, bookmarks can be used like glossary entries. You can store bookmark text in a special Word file that contains boilerplate text, and any time you like, you can insert the bookmark text into a document you're writing. The advantage of this technique over using glossaries is that the text is stored on disk, not in Word's memory. What's more, it's easier to edit text on disk than to edit glossaries. If you plan to make extensive use of boilerplate applications, you should store boilerplate text as bookmarks rather than as glossaries.

As you will see, storing boilerplate text in bookmarks has another advantage as well: Word maintains an active connection between the bookmark and the copy of its text that you enter into your document. The significance of this is best grasped by comparing bookmarks to glossaries.

When you import text from a glossary into your document, Word simply copies the glossary text into your document, and that's the end of the connection. The copied text becomes part of the document you're creating. But what happens if you discover that the glossary contains an error? You may have copied it several times. You will have to search for all the copies and correct them manually.

When you import text from a bookmark into your document by using Insert File, however, Word keeps a record of the bookmark's source. If you change the bookmark text, you can update the text you have imported by using a simple command. In fact, you can update all the bookmarks in your document with just one command. This way, you can make sure that all the boilerplate in your document is up-to-the-minute correct before you print the document. This feature is of great value, for example, for businesses whose reputation and legal liability may depend on using a single authoritative version of a critical passage of text.

Creating the Boilerplate Text

Your first step is to create a Word document that contains the boilerplate passages:

1. Open a new Word document and type the boilerplate passages.

2. Type a title for the first boilerplate passage.

3. After the title, and on the same line, type *date* and press F3 to enter today's date.

   It's essential to indicate when the passage was last updated.

4. Press Enter and type the boilerplate passage. When you are finished, press Enter again to separate the boilerplate passage from the text you will place beneath it.

5. Select the first boilerplate passage (but not the title or date).

6. Choose Insert Bookmark (Alt-IM) and assign a bookmark name to the passage.

7. Repeat steps 2 through 6 until you have typed and named all the boilerplate passages.

8. Save the document.

This is the document you will maintain in an authoritative state.

Importing Bookmarks

After you have created a document with authoritative, dated, and up-to-the-minute correct boilerplate passages, you can import one or more of these passages into any document you create. Follow these steps:

1. Place the cursor where you want the imported text to appear.

2. Choose **Insert File** (Alt-IF).

   You see the File dialog box (fig. 12.6).

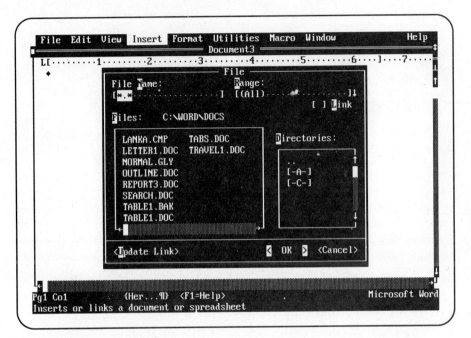

```
 File  Edit  View  Insert  Format  Utilities  Macro  Window              Help
                            Document3
 L[········1········2········3········4········5········6····]····7····
 ◆
                            ── File ──
        File Name:              Range:
        [*.*············] [(All)··········]↓
                                    [ ] Link

        Files:    C:\WORD\DOCS

        LANKA.CMP    TABS.DOC         Directories:
        LETTER1.DOC  TRAVEL1.DOC
        NORMAL.GLY                    ..
        OUTLINE.DOC                   [-A-]
        REPORT3.DOC                   [-C-]
        SEARCH.DOC
        TABLE1.BAK
        TABLE1.DOC

        <Update Link>          ◄ OK ►  <Cancel>


 Pg1 Co1        {Her...¶}  <F1=Help>              Microsoft Word
 Inserts or links a document or spreadsheet
```

Fig. 12.6. The File dialog box.

3. Use the **Files** list box to highlight the name of the boilerplate document, the one containing the boilerplate passages.

   If you don't see the file name, use the **Directories** list box to look for the file in other directories.

4. Drop down the **Range** list box.

   You see a list of the bookmarks you created in the boilerplate document.

5. Choose **Link** to establish an active link between the two documents.

   When you choose this option, you can update the inserted text automatically should you make changes in the boilerplate document.

6. Choose **OK**.

After you use the **Insert File** command, Word inserts the bookmark text at the cursor's location. Above the text, Word inserts a coded line formatted as hidden text.

> *Caution*: Do not remove the line of hidden text. Because it's formatted as hidden text, it will not print. But Word needs this information to tell where the bookmark came from. If you delete the code, Word will not be able to update the bookmark.

Updating a Document's Bookmarks

After you have imported bookmark text into a document using the Link option, you can take advantage of a terrific feature: Word will update all the bookmark passages automatically. Suppose you have recently made a few small, but important, changes to your boilerplate document, the one that contains authoritative passages of text. You want to make sure the proposal you're writing contains the most recent versions of the boilerplate text you have inserted. The steps that follow explain the procedure:

1. Select the bookmark you want to update. Alternatively, select the whole file by pressing Ctrl-K5.

2. Choose **Insert File** (Alt-IF).

   You see the File dialog box.

3. Choose **Update Link**.

   You see an alert box asking you whether you want to update the link.

4. Choose **Yes**. If you selected the whole document, you may see this alert box again. Continue choosing **Yes** until you have updated all the boilerplate passages in the document.

Chapter Summary

Creating and retrieving glossary entries is easy. You have no reason to retype text again and again when Word can do it for you. Examine your day-to-day working habits. If you find yourself typing the same text repeatedly in many or most editing sessions, save it to Word's default glossary, NORMAL.GLY. For text for special-purpose writing applications, create a new glossary file to hold the boilerplate entries. And don't forget that glossaries are useful for purposes other than boilerplate. Explore the supplied glossary entries and use them. If you're moving large chunks of text around, consider using glossaries instead of the Scrap.

If you use numerous or lengthy boilerplate passages, or if it's important to maintain a single, authoritative version of each boilerplate passage, create a file containing boilerplate passages marked as bookmarks. Import the bookmarks using the Library Link Document command. Like glossaries, bookmarks can be used in other ways as well.

You can use bookmarks to move around in a lengthy, complex document. In Chapter 14, you will learn how to use bookmarks for cross-referencing purposes.

Quick Review

Boilerplate Documents

To create a boilerplate file:

1. Open a new Word document and type the boilerplate passages.

2. Type a title for the first boilerplate passage.

3. After the title, on the same line, type *date* and press F3 to enter today's date.

4. Press Enter and type the boilerplate passage. When you are finished, press Enter again to separate the boilerplate passage from the text you will place beneath it.

5. Select the first boilerplate passage.

6. Choose **Insert Bookmark** (Alt-IM) and assign a bookmark name to the passage.

7. Repeat steps 2 through 6 until you have typed and named all the boilerplate passages.

8. Save the document.

To import bookmark text from another document:

1. Place the cursor where you want the imported text to appear.

2. Choose **Insert File** (Alt-IF).

3. Use the **Files** list box to highlight the name of the boilerplate document, the one containing the boilerplate passages.

4. Drop down the **Range** list box.

5. Choose **Link** to establish an active link between the two documents.

6. Choose **OK**.

To update the bookmarks you have imported into a document:

1. Select the bookmark you want to update. Alternatively, select the whole file by pressing Ctrl-K5.

2. Choose **Insert File** (Alt-IF).

3. Choose **Update Link**.

4. Choose **Yes**. If you selected the whole document, you may see this alert box again. Continue choosing **Yes** until you have updated all the boilerplate passages in the document.

Bookmarks

To mark text as a bookmark:

1. Select the text you want to include in the bookmark.

2. Choose **Insert Bookmark** (Alt-IM) or use the Ctrl-Shift-F5 keyboard shortcut.

3. Type the bookmark name in the **Bookmark Name** text box.

4. Choose **OK**.

To jump to a bookmark:

1. Choose **Edit Go To** or use the F5 keyboard shortcut.

2. Choose **Bookmark**.

3. Choose the name of the bookmark in the Bookmark **Name** list box.

4. Choose **OK**.

To move bookmark text:

1. Use **Edit Go To** to jump to the bookmark text.

2. Use any selection technique to expand the highlight, if desired, but don't contract it.

3. Choose **Edit Cut** or press Shift-Del to cut the selection to the Scrap.

4. Move the cursor to the place you want the selection to appear.

5. Choose **Edit Paste** or press Shift-Ins to paste the selection at the cursor's location.

To delete a bookmark:

1. Use **Edit Go** To to jump to the bookmark.

   Edit Go To highlights all the text between the anchors.

2. Choose **Insert Bookmark** (Alt-IM).

3. Highlight the name of the bookmark in the **Bookmark Name** list box.

4. Choose **Delete**.

5. Choose OK.

To change the text assigned to a bookmark name:

1. Select the text.

2. Choose **Insert Bookmark** (Alt-IM).

3. In the **Bookmark Names** list box, choose the name of the bookmark.

4. Choose OK.

5. Choose OK.

Cross-References

To cross-reference text:

1. Select the text you want to cross-reference, and use **Insert Bookmark** to define it as a bookmark.

2. Move the cursor to the place you want the text to appear.

3. Type the text of the cross-reference, such as "For a discussion of project methodology, see page" followed by a space.

4. Immediately following the cross-reference text, type the code name *page:* (don't forget the colon), followed by the bookmark name. Don't type a space after the colon.

5. Press F3.

To mark a series item for cross-referencing:

1. Place the cursor on the character preceding the series code name.

2. Choose **Insert Bookmark** (Alt-IM), or use the Shift-Ctrl-F5 keyboard shortcut.

3. In the **Bookmark Name** text box, type a name for the bookmark that describes the contents of this specific item.

4. Choose OK.

To cross-reference the series item:

1. Position the cursor where you want the series item's number to appear.

2. Type the series code name, a colon, and the bookmark name, without any spaces.

3. Press F3.

Glossary Entries

To create a glossary entry:

1. Type the text you want the entry to contain. You can include character and paragraph formatting.

2. Select the text.

3. Choose **Edit Glossary** (Alt-EO).

4. In the **Glossary Name** text box, type a glossary name (31 characters maximum).

5. In the **Optional Keys** area, press the keys you want to use to enter the glossary entry at the cursor's location. Always use a Shift-Ctrl key combination instead of Ctrl so you don't inactivate any of Word's default formatting keys.

To retrieve a glossary entry when you know its name:

1. Type the glossary name in your document.

2. Press F3.

To retrieve a glossary entry from the Glossary dialog box:

1. Choose **Edit Glossary** (Alt-EO).

   You see the Glossary dialog box.

2. Choose the **Names** area and highlight the glossary name.

3. Choose Insert.

To retrieve a glossary entry using the keyboard shortcut you chose:

Press the keyboard shortcut keys.

To edit a glossary entry:

1. Insert the entry using one of the techniques just presented.

2. Edit the text.

3. Select the text.

4. Choose **Edit Glossary** (Alt-EO).

5. Highlight the glossary entry's name in the **Names** list box.

6. Choose **Define**.

7. Choose OK to replace the glossary entry.

To add a keyboard shortcut to an often-used glossary entry:

1. Insert the entry using one of the techniques just presented.

2. Select the text.

3. Choose **Edit Glossary** (Alt-EO).

4. Highlight the glossary entry's name in the **Names** list box.

5. Choose the Optional **Keys** area.

6. Press the key combination you want to use.

7. Choose **Define**.

8. Choose OK to replace the glossary entry.

To delete a glossary entry:

1. Choose **Edit Glossary** (Alt-EO).

2. Highlight the glossary entry's name in the **Names** list box.

3. Choose **Delete**.

4. Choose Close to return to your document.

Glossary Files

To abandon the glossary entries you have created in a session:

1. Exit Word without saving the current glossary.

2. When you see the alert box informing you that you haven't saved the glossary, choose **No** to abandon the entries you have created.

To clear all the glossaries you created and saved in a glossary file:

1. Choose **Edit Glossary** (Alt-EO).

2. Choose **Clear All**.

3. Choose **Yes** to confirm the action.

4. Choose **Edit Glossary** (Alt-EO).

5. Choose **Save Glossary**.

6. Choose OK.

To save the current glossary entries to NORMAL.GLY:

1. Choose **Edit Glossary** (Alt-EO).

2. Choose **Save Glossary**.

3. Choose OK.

To save the entries in a new glossary file:

1. Choose **Edit Glossary** (Alt-EO).

2. Choose **Save Glossary**.

3. Type a file name for the glossary file.

4. Choose OK.

To load a glossary file other than NORMAL.GLY:

1. Choose **Edit Glossary** (Alt-EO)

2. Choose **Open Glossary**.

3. If you see the glossary file name in the **Files** list box, highlight the name. If not, use the **Directories** list box to find the file in another directory.

4. Choose **OK**.

To merge two glossary files:

1. Choose **E**dit Glossary (Alt-EO).

2. Choose **O**pen Glossary and open the first glossary file.

3. Choose **Me**rge.

4. If you see the glossary file name in the **F**iles list box, highlight the name. If not, use the **D**irectories list box to find the file in another directory.

5. Choose OK.

6. If you want to save the merged glossaries, choose **S**ave Glossary.

To print the current glossary:

1. Choose File **P**rint (Alt-FP). Alternatively, use the Shift-F9 keyboard shortcut.

2. Drop down the **P**rint list box.

3. Choose Glossary.

4. Close the Print list box.

5. Choose OK.

Series Code Names

To create a series code name and number the items in a series automatically:

1. Position the cursor where you want the automatic number to appear.

2. Type the text, such as *Table* or *Figure*, that will precede the number Word automatically supplies. Leave a space after the text.

3. Type a series code name, such as *table:* or *figure:* (don't forget the colon).

4. Press F3 to define the series code name.

5. Repeat steps 1 through 4 for each additional item (such as additional tables or figures) that you want Word to number automatically.

Supplied Glossary Entries

To enter the current time or date:

1. Place the cursor where you want the time or date to appear.

2. Type *time* or *date*.

3. Press F3.

To enter the time or date at the time of printing:

1. Place the cursor where you want the time or date to appear when your document is printed.

2. Type *timeprint* or *dateprint*.

3. Press F3.

Chapter 13

Creating Indexes and Tables of Contents

oday's businesses must cope with a phenomenal amount of paperwork. The British firm, Marks and Spencer, recently estimated that its employees crank out more than 30 million pages of paperwork each year. American firms generate enough paperwork each day to circle the globe many times over. In 1984 alone, more than 14 million file cabinets were manufactured so that an estimated 200 billion pieces of paper would have some place to go!

Much of this amazing output of paperwork involves the production of business reports and proposals. To cope with new regulations, the oil company Exxon had to submit a 500,000-page report to the Department of Energy. To deal with the documentation for a single government contract, RCA's Missile and Surface Radar facility had to publish more than 100,000 pages of technical manuals a year. Cutting down the labor involved in producing all these reports and proposals can produce a handsome payoff.

Word comes in handy for anyone faced with the job of creating a report or proposal. Previous chapters already have discussed some of the reasons for Word's usefulness. For instance, Word's outline mode greatly aids the tasks of planning, organizing, and restructuring complex documents. This chapter explains two features that will save you large amounts of time if your report or proposal must have an accurate index and table of contents. As you learn in this chapter, Word can compile an index and table of contents, insert the correct page numbers, and print both tables for you. If you make changes to your document, Word makes the necessary corrections to the tables without any intervention on your part.

In this chapter, you learn how to do the following:

- Insert codes into your text that Word will read as index entries

- Compile the index automatically after you have finished coding your document

- Code headings so that Word treats them as table of contents entries

- Compile the table of contents automatically after you have finished coding your document

- Create a table of contents from an outline of your document, without any coding

- Create additional tables you may need, such as tables of figures and tables of lists

This chapter is useful for readers whose reports and proposals will be reproduced directly from Word printouts, because the index references and tables of contents refer to the pages Word creates. If you're preparing a document to be typeset, you need to prepare the table of contents and index from the page proofs the printer gives you. In such circumstances, Word cannot help. The index must be prepared manually from the page proofs.

Users of previous versions of Word will find few changes in the way Word 5.5 handles indexes and tables of contents. However, the keyboard shortcut for formatting hidden text has changed from Alt-3 to Ctrl-H, and the dialog boxes have been improved.

Caution: If you're planning to compile an index and table of contents for a report of 100 pages or more, or for a book-length manuscript, you probably will need expanded memory to complete the job. These operations are memory-intensive. Unfortunately, if Word runs out of memory before completing the index or table of contents, the program cannot complete the job. Remember this point before spending hours coding hundreds of terms!

Creating an Index

To create an index with Word, you begin by marking in your document those terms you want included in the index. You then compile the index, using the Insert Index command. Finally, you format the index to suit your tastes or style guidelines.

Word's indexing command isn't completely automatic—you must mark manually the terms to be indexed. An automatically generated index using every word in your document would run many times the length of the document itself. A good index begins with a working idea of who the reader will be and what terms the reader is likely to consider when searching for information. No computer program yet devised can approach this level of analytical capability.

Types of Index Entries: An Overview

You can create two different kinds of index entries with Word: concordance entries and conceptual entries.

A concordance entry is a word in your document that you mark for indexing. Word prints the concordance entry in your document and prints the entry again in the index. Use concordance entries to mark words that actually appear in your text.

A conceptual entry is a word that you embed in the text (formatted as hidden text so that the word doesn't print) and mark for indexing. Word prints the conceptual entry only in the index, not in the text. Use conceptual entries when the words in your document aren't quite right for indexing. For example, if a passage you want to index contains the word *industrialization*, but you think *industry* is a better term for the index, use *industry* as a conceptual entry.

You also can use subentries in your index. A main entry is printed flush to the margin in the index, and Word alphabetizes these terms. A subentry is indented and appears beneath an entry. For example, the main entry *industry* may be followed by the subentries: *labor-management relations, marketing, technology transfer*. You can create up to five levels of subentries, although one or two is usually sufficient.

> *Tip:* Marking index entries manually is a tedious job when the same word or words occurs more than once in a manuscript because you must mark the word every time it appears. If your manuscript is long, you can mark concordance entries more easily by using a macro Microsoft supplies with the Word program. (A macro is a recorded series of Word keystrokes or commands that you can play back just by choosing the macro's name from the **Macro Run** menu or by pressing the macro's Ctrl keyboard shortcut.) This macro is called INDEX and is accessed using the Ctrl-V8 keyboard shortcut.

Note: To use Word's supplied macros, you must open the glossary called MACRO.GLY. For more information, see Chapter 21, "Creating and Using Word 5.5 Macros."

To use Index, you type the words you want indexed in a separate file. Next, you open the document to be indexed and run the macro. The macro codes the words you listed as concordance entries. This macro is easy to use; therefore, even if you have no previous experience with macros, you're wise to begin your indexing task this way.

Marking Index Entries

To mark index entries manually, you need to know that every index entry has three parts:

- Index code (.i.). You must format this code, a lowercase i surrounded by periods, as hidden text. The code tells Word that the text that follows should be treated as an index entry.

- Index entry. The index entry is the text you want indexed (normally one or two words). If you do not format the entry as hidden text, Word treats it as a concordance entry; that is, Word prints the term in the text and in the index. If you do format the entry as hidden text, Word treats it as a conceptual entry. The word doesn't appear in the text but does appear in the index.

- Index end mark (;). This code, a semicolon formatted as hidden text, tells Word where the index entry stops. If you don't insert the code, Word considers all the text to the end of the paragraph as part of the index entry.

You can mark index entries as you type or after you type. In most cases, you will mark index entries after you complete your document. Indexing is usually one of the last steps in document production. Therefore, the tutorials in this chapter are designed to be used after you have typed the text.

Before you mark index entries, choose View Preferences (Alt-VE) and make sure that you have an X in the Hidden Text check box. You need to see hidden text on-screen if you want to mark index entries correctly.

> ***Caution:*** If you fail to mark the index code and end mark as hidden text, Word will not remove these codes from your document or print the entry in the index. You must make sure that all the codes and end marks are properly formatted as hidden text.

Marking Concordance Entries

To mark a concordance entry, use the following steps:

1. Place the cursor on the first character of the word you want to index.

2. Press Ctrl-H to enter hidden text and type the index code (*.i.*).

3. Now place the cursor directly after the word.

4. Press Ctrl-H again and type the end mark (*;*).

Figure 13.1 shows two concordance entries: *.i.information;* and *.i.knowledge;*.

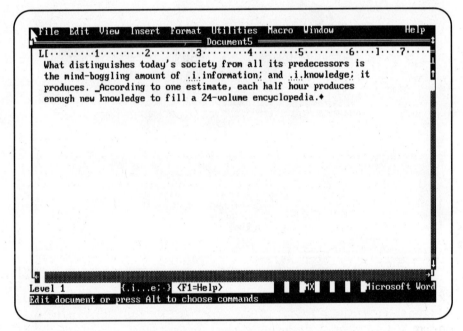

Fig. 13.1. Words coded for inclusion in an index (concordance entries).

If the entry you're marking contains punctuation (commas, quotation marks, or colons), surround the entry with quotation marks so that Word doesn't get confused. The following entry is marked correctly:

.i."Los Angeles, California";

Be sure to format the quotation marks as hidden text so that they don't print in your document.

> ***Tip:*** If you have opened the glossary called MACRO.GLY, you can use a supplied macro called index_entry to mark concordance entries. To use index_entry, select the term you want to index. Choose the **Macros Run** command and select index_entry.mac from the list. You also can use the Ctrl-VI keyboard shortcut.) For more information on using Word's supplied macros, see Chapter 21, "Creating and Using Word 5.5 Macros."

Marking Conceptual Entries

To mark a conceptual entry, follow these steps:

1. Place the cursor just before the text that discusses the concept you want to index.

2. Press Ctrl-H.

3. Type *.i.* followed by the conceptual entry and the semicolon. Everything you have just typed should be formatted as hidden text.

Figure 13.2 shows a conceptual entry (.i.Growth of knowledge;).

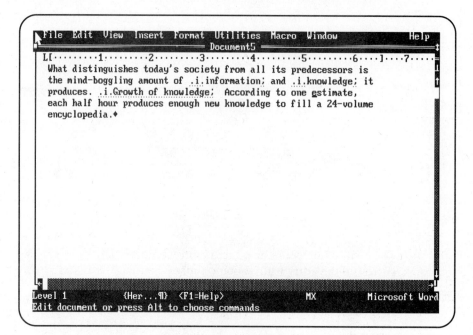

Fig. 13.2. Phrase ("Growth of knowledge") coded as a conceptual entry.

Marking Subentries

Subentries are preferred when an entry otherwise would be followed by a long list of page numbers. In such cases, subentries help the reader locate the correct information. The following example has several subentries:

Industrial ventures

aluminum cookware 60
graphite processing 32
luxury goods 59
matches 38
textiles 23

Subentries are like conceptual entries in that the whole entry is formatted as hidden text—you don't want the subentry code to appear in your document.

To create a subentry:

1. Place the cursor just before the text you want to index.

2. Press Ctrl-H.

3. Type the index code *(.i.)* followed by the main entry, a colon, the subentry, and the end code *(;)*.

   A properly formatted subentry appears as follows:

   .i.industrial ventures:textiles;

Figure 13.3 shows an example of a subentry.

Marking a Range of Pages

Often you will need to index a topic that is discussed on more than one page, such as

Industry 19-43

Use the following steps to create an entry that marks a range of pages:

1. At the beginning of the discussion of the topic, insert an entry, using the following coding scheme:

   .i.industry;

   Format the whole entry as hidden text.

2. At the end of the discussion of the topic, insert exactly the same entry.

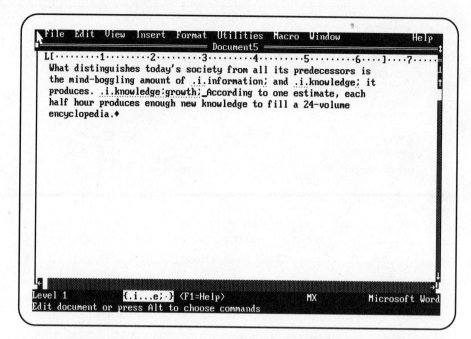

File Edit View Insert Format Utilities Macro Window   Help
══════════════════════════════ Document5 ═══════════
L[·······1·······2·······3·······4·······5·······6····]····7····

What distinguishes today's society from all its predecessors is
the mind-boggling amount of .i.information; and .i.knowledge; it
produces. .i.knowledge:growth;_According to one estimate, each
half hour produces enough new knowledge to fill a 24-volume
encyclopedia.♦

Level 1   {.i...e;·} <F1=Help>   MX   Microsoft Word
Edit document or press Alt to choose commands

Fig. 13.3. Word ("growth") coded as a subentry of the main term ("knowledge").

After Word compiles your index, the page range is indicated with a comma and a space, as in

Industry 19, 43

You must edit the entry manually so that the page range is expressed correctly, as in

Industry 19-43

Creating Cross-References

You can create an entry that directs the reader to another entry, such as

Manufacturing
See Industry

To create such an entry, use the following coding scheme:

.i.manufacturing:See Industry;

Format the whole code as hidden text. You can place the entry anywhere in your document.

Table 13.1 summarizes your index coding options.

Table 13.1
Summary of Options for Coding Index Entries

Appearance in Index	Coding in Text
Capital investment 11	.i.capital investment;
Industry 38	.i.industry;
Industry capital goods 60	.i.industry: capital goods;
Graphite 19-26	.i.graphite; .i.graphite;
Graphite 19-26 mining 20	.i.graphite: mining;

Graphite 19-26
  mining 20
    capital 22
	.i.graphite: mining: capital;

Manufacturing See Industry	.i.manufacturing: See Industry;

Compiling and Formatting the Index

After your document is in its final form and you have marked all the index entries, you need to compile the index.

To compile the index, follow these steps:

1. Choose **Insert Index** (Alt-II).

   As shown in figure 13.4, the Index dialog box appears. By default, Word creates the index with a 0.2-inch indentation. Page numbers are separated from the index entries by one default tab, which is symbolized by the ^t code in the text box called Separate Page Numbers from Entry by. Main entries are capitalized. You can change these settings. For example, to tell Word to insert a comma and a space between the entry and the page number, type a comma and a space in the Separate Page Numbers from Entry by text box.

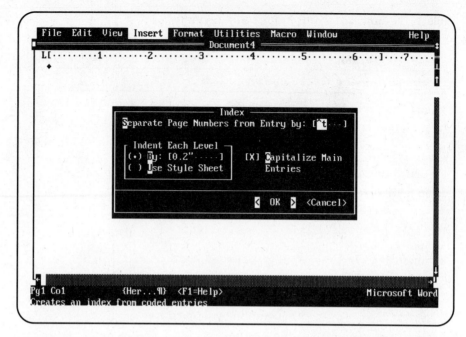

Fig. 13.4. *The Index dialog box enables you to format the appearance of your index.*

    2. Choose OK.

        Word compiles the index. For a lengthy document, the process can take several minutes. Word places the index at the end of your document, beneath a division mark. The index begins with a hidden text code (.Begin Index.) and ends with another one (.End Index.). Do not delete these codes unless you are sure that the index is complete. If you delete the codes, Word cannot erase the index and create a revised version.

If you find that terms are missing from your index or the index contains errors, insert or correct the codes in your document. Use Insert Index again to recompile the index.

After Word compiles your index to your satisfaction, you can format the index as you would any text. Because the index is in its own division at the end of your document, you need to turn page numbering on if you want the index's pages numbered. Add character emphasis, multiple-column formatting, and other formats as you prefer. For more information, see Chapter 4, "Word 5.5 Formatting Strategies: Characters and Paragraphs."

Creating a Table of Contents

The easiest way to generate a table of contents for your document is to outline the document using the techniques discussed in Chapter 10, "Organizing Your Document with Outlining." With the outline technique, you don't need to code headings and subheadings; they will appear in your table of contents automatically.

If you haven't used an outline, you still can generate a table of contents, but you have to code the headings and subheadings manually. The procedure closely resembles the one you used to mark index entries.

Creating a Table of Contents with an Outline

If you outlined your document, you can generate a table of contents quickly from the outline headings.

To create a table of contents from an outline, do the following:

1. Choose **View Preferences** (Alt-VE) and remove the X from the Hidden Text check box.

   The pagination will be inaccurate if hidden text is visible.

2. Choose **View Outline** (Alt-VO) or press Shift-F2 to switch to the outline view of your document.

3. Hold down the Shift and Alt keys and then press a number key corresponding to the lowest level of headings you want to include in the table of contents.

   For example, to create a table of contents that includes only first-level headings, press Shift-Alt-1. To create a table of contents that includes first-, second-, and third-level headings, press Shift-Alt-3.

4. Choose **Insert Table of Contents** (Alt-IC).

   As shown in figure 13.5, you see the Table of Contents dialog box. By default, Word compiles the outline from codes, indents each level by 0.4-inch, shows page numbers, and separates the page numbers from the entry by a default tab. You can change the formatting settings.

5. Choose **Outline**.

6. Choose OK.

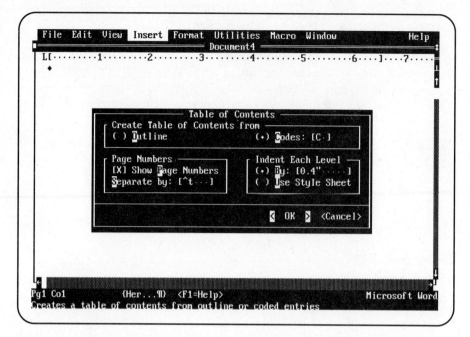

Fig. 13.5. *The Table of Contents dialog box enables you to format your table of contents.*

Word compiles the table of contents and places it at the end of your document (see fig. 13.6). Like the indexes Word compiles, the table of contents begins and ends with hidden text codes. Do not delete these codes. They will not print. Word needs the codes to locate the table if you decide to revise it.

You can format the table of contents by adding character emphases, indentations, blank lines, and other formats to suit your tastes and style guidelines.

Coding Table of Contents Entries

Marking headings for inclusion in a table of contents is much like creating concordance entries for an index. You must distinguish between three parts of a completely marked table of contents entry:

- **Table of contents code** (.c.). You must format this code, a lower-case *c* surrounded by periods, as hidden text. The code tells Word the text that follows this code is a table of contents entry.

- **The heading**. Because you want the heading to print in your document, do not format the heading as hidden text.

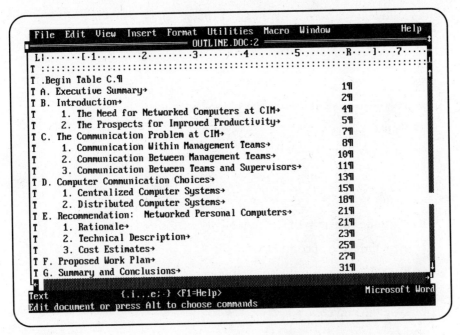

File   Edit   View   Insert   Format   Utilities   Macro   Window   Help
═══════════════════════ OUTLINE.DOC:2 ═══════════════════════
L¦·······[·1········2·········3·········4·········5·········R···]····7·····

T .Begin Table C.¶
T A. Executive Summary→   1¶
T B. Introduction→   2¶
T   1. The Need for Networked Computers at CIM→   4¶
T   2. The Prospects for Improved Productivity→   5¶
T C. The Communication Problem at CIM→   7¶
T   1. Communication Within Management Teams→   8¶
T   2. Communication Between Management Teams→   10¶
T   3. Communication Between Teams and Supervisors→   11¶
T D. Computer Communication Choices→   13¶
T   1. Centralized Computer Systems→   15¶
T   2. Distributed Computer Systems→   18¶
T E. Recommendation: Networked Personal Computers→   21¶
T   1. Rationale→   21¶
T   2. Technical Description→   23¶
T   3. Cost Estimates→   25¶
T F. Proposed Work Plan→   27¶
T G. Summary and Conclusions→   31¶

Text   {.i...e;·} <F1=Help>   Microsoft Word
Edit document or press Alt to choose commands

Fig. 13.6. The compiled table of contents appears at the end of your document.

- **End Mark** (;). This code, a semicolon formatted as hidden text, tells Word where the table of contents entry stops.

Before you begin marking entries, choose View Preferences (Alt-VE) and make sure that you see an X in the Hidden Text check box. You must display hidden text on-screen to mark table of contents entries accurately. However, you must turn hidden text off before generating your table of contents. If the hidden text is still displayed, the page numbers may be inaccurate because Word will take hidden text into account when computing the page breaks.

Marking Major Headings

When Word generates the table of contents, the program formats major headings (or first-level headings) flush to the left margin. These headings are chapter titles in a book or report or major section headings in an article or a proposal.

You can mark table of contents entries as you type or after you finish typing.

Use the following steps to mark major headings as you type them:

1. Place the cursor where you want the heading to appear and press Ctrl-H.

2. Type the table of contents code *(.c.)*.

3. Press Ctrl-H again to toggle hidden text off.

4. Type the heading.

5. Press Ctrl-H to toggle hidden text on again.

6. Type the end code *(;)*.

To code major headings after you type the headings, do the following:

1. Place the cursor at the beginning of the heading and press Ctrl-H.

2. Type the table of contents code *(.c.)*.

3. Place the cursor on the space following the heading and press Ctrl-H.

4. Type the end code *(;)*.

Coding Headings at Lower Levels

To code headings at second and other subordinate levels, use the codes listed in table 13.2. Use second-level codes for subject headings within chapters, third-level codes for sections within the second-level units, and so on.

Table 13.2
Table of Contents Codes

Level	*Code*
First	.c.
Second	.c.:
Third	.c.::
Fourth	.c.:::
Fifth	.c.::::

The following example shows a second-level table of contents entry:

.c.: Analysis of data ;

Compiling the Table of Contents from Codes

To compile the table of contents after you code your headings:

1. Choose **View Preferences** (Alt-VE) and remove the X from the Hidden Text check box.

2. Choose **Insert Table of Contents** (Alt-IC).

    You see the Table of Contents dialog box (see fig. 13.5). By default, Word indents each level by 0.4-inch, shows page numbers, and separates the page numbers from the entry by a default tab. You can change the formatting settings.

3. Choose **Codes**, if it is not selected already.

4. Choose OK.

Including the Table of Contents in Your Document

When you print your document, the table of contents appears at the end. Because Word places the table of contents in its own section, without page numbering, you can physically place the table of contents printout at the beginning of the document.

If you are assembling a document in which the front matter is paginated with lowercase Roman numerals, move the table of contents to the front of the document on-screen. Add a title page and other front matter to the section containing the table of contents. See Chapter 5, "Word 5.5 Formatting Strategies: Page Formatting," for information on printing Roman numeral page numbers. Don't forget to format the body text section so that page numbering begins with page 1 in Arabic numbers.

Recompiling the Table of Contents

If you make changes to your document after compiling the table of contents, these changes may affect the pagination. If so, you should recompile the table of contents to make sure that the page references are accurate. Fortunately, recompiling a table of contents is easy to do.

To recompile the table of contents after making changes, follow these steps:

1. Choose Insert Table of Contents (Alt-IC).

2. Choose Outline or Codes and alter the default formats.

3. Choose OK.

   Word detects the previous table of contents and displays an alert box with the message, `Replace existing table?`

4. Choose Yes.

   Word replaces the existing table of contents with the new, more accurate one.

   If you choose No, Word compiles the new table of contents but appends it to the existing one.

Chapter Summary

In this chapter, you learned how to use Word to automate two tedious tasks: indexing your document and compiling a table of contents. You learned how to mark conceptual and concordance entries manually and how to use Insert Index to compile the index automatically.

You also learned how to compile a table of contents quickly and easily from an outline. As this chapter explains, many good reasons exist for outlining your document; one of these reasons is to make generating a table of contents easier. If you don't outline your document, you can generate a table of contents from manually coded document headings. However, if your document is lengthy and has many headings, it's easier to outline the existing document rather than code all the headings.

Word can generate other tables besides the ones discussed here. You can create up to 24 separate tables for a single document. As you learn in the next chapter, you can put this capability to work to generate a table of authorities for legal documents.

Quick Review

Generating the Index

To generate the index:

1. Choose **Insert Index** (Alt-II).

2. Choose OK.

Generating the Table of Contents

To create a table of contents from an outline:

1. Choose **View Preferences** (Alt-VE) and remove the X from the Hidden Text check box.

2. Choose **View Outline** (Alt-VO) or press Shift-F2 to switch to the outline view of your document.

3. Hold down the Shift and Alt keys and then press a number key corresponding to the lowest level of headings you want to include in the table of contents.

4. Choose **Insert Table of Contents** (Alt-IC).

5. Choose **Outline**.

6. Choose OK.

To create a table of contents from manually marked headings:

1. Choose **View Preferences** (Alt-VE) and remove the X from the Hidden Text check box.

2. Choose **Insert Table of Contents** (Alt-IC).

3. Choose **Codes**, if it is not selected already.

4. Choose OK.

To recompile the table of contents after making changes:

1. Choose **Insert Table of Contents** (Alt-IC).

2. Choose **Outline** or **Codes** and alter the default formats.

3. Choose OK.

4. Choose **Yes** to replace the existing table of contents.

Index Entries

To mark a concordance entry:

1. Place the cursor on the first character of the word you want to index.

2. Press Ctrl-H.

3. Type the index code *(.i.)*.

4. Place the cursor directly after the word.

5. Press Ctrl-H again and type the end mark *(;)*.

To mark a conceptual entry:

1. Place the cursor just before the text that discusses the concept you want to index.

2. Press Ctrl-H.

3. Type *.i.* followed by the conceptual entry and the semicolon. Everything you have just typed should be formatted as hidden text.

To mark a subentry:

1. Place the cursor just before the text you want to index.

2. Press Ctrl-H.

3. Type the index code *(.i.)* followed by the main entry, a colon, the subentry, and the end code *(;)*.

To create an entry that marks a range of pages:

1. At the beginning of the discussion of the topic, insert an entry using the following coding scheme:

       .i.subject;

2. At the end of the discussion of the topic, insert exactly the same entry.

To create a cross-reference entry:

1. Press Ctrl-H.

2. Type *.i.* followed by the term you want cross-referenced, a colon, the word *See*, the index entry to which you want to refer the reader, and the end mark (for example, .i.manufacturing:See Industry;).

Table of Contents Entries

To mark headings as you type them so that they are included in a table of contents:

1. Place the cursor where you want the heading to appear and press Ctrl-H.

2. Type the table of contents code *(.c., .c.:, .c.::, .c.:::, or .c.::::)*.

3. Press Ctrl-H again to toggle hidden text off.

4. Type the heading.

5. Press Ctrl-H to toggle hidden text on again.

6. Type the end code *(;)*.

To mark headings after you type the headings:

1. Place the cursor at the beginning of the heading and press Ctrl-H.

2. Type the table of contents code *(.c., .c.:, .c.::, .c.:::, or .c.::::)*.

3. Place the cursor on the space following the heading and press Ctrl-H.

4. Type the end code *(;)*.

14

The Legal and Scholarly Word

Word provides excellent tools for anyone writing in fields requiring documentation in the form of footnotes or endnotes. Word can position notes at the bottom of the page or at the end of a division. If the footnote text is too long, Word floats the text to the next page. Word numbers footnotes, and you can display a special footnote window that shows the footnotes with reference marks currently displayed in the document window. If you reorganize your manuscript, Word renumbers all the notes.

Word is adept at handling other documentation tasks, too, and these capabilities are discussed in this chapter. You can use Word's capability to generate up to 24 tables to create a table of legal authorities or tables of figures. For legal briefs and other documents, you can print line numbers.

This chapter covers the following topics:

- Creating, numbering, editing, and deleting footnotes and endnotes

- Creating a table of authorities for legal documents

- Printing line numbers in a legal document

About Footnotes and Endnotes

A note, whether a footnote or endnote, has two parts:

- Footnote Reference Mark. This mark, which is a number or a symbol such as an asterisk, appears in the text where you insert a footnote. If you choose numbers, Word inserts the correct numbers and updates these numbers if your editing makes changes necessary.

- Footnote Text. This text is positioned in the special footnote area after the end mark in your document. When you print, you choose between printing endnotes at the end of a division or footnotes at the bottom of each page.

To create, format, and print footnotes and endnotes, you use a variety of commands and dialog boxes. The following list gives you a quick overview:

- **Format Section (Alt-TS).** You choose this command to determine where the notes will print (on the same page as footnotes or at the end of the section as endnotes).

- **Insert Footnote (Alt-IN).** You choose this command to insert a numbered or nonnumbered footnote reference mark and to type the text of the footnote.

- **Edit Go To (Alt-EG).** You choose this command to move the next footnote reference mark when you're editing a document and to move from the reference mark to the footnote text.

- **View Footnote/Annotation (Alt-VF).** You choose this command to open the footnote pane, which is a special pane that displays the footnotes or annotations shown in the document pane. For more information on annotations, see Chapter 15, "Enhancing Group Productivity: Using Annotations and Redlining."

Choosing Footnotes or Endnotes

You may choose between footnotes and endnotes for each section you create. As you learn in Chapter 5, "Word 5.5 Formatting Strategies: Page Formatting," you can create more than one section in a document. If your document has only one section, the choice you make applies to the whole document.

By default, Word prints footnotes at the bottom of the page and floats excess footnote text to the bottom of the next page if the text cannot fit on one page. The program inserts a two-inch rule to separate the text of the document from the text of the notes.

You choose footnotes or endnotes in the section dialog box. By default, Word prints footnotes, but you can change the placement to endnotes.

To change footnote placement, follow these steps:

1. Place the cursor in the section that contains the footnotes you want to affect.

Because most documents have only one section, this instruction probably doesn't apply to you. However, if you created a special section for front matter (such as a table of contents), be sure to place the cursor in the section containing the footnotes you created.

2. Choose Format Section (Alt-TS).

   You see the section dialog box.

3. Choose Same Page to place the notes at the bottom of the page or choose End of Section to place the notes at the end of the section.

   If your document has only one section, choosing End of Section is the same as placing the notes at the end of your document.

4. Choose OK.

Caution: The position of notes is a section format, controlled by the Section dialog box. The footnote numbers that Word inserts are also a section format. When Word comes to a new division, the program restarts footnote numbers at 1. You have no way to change this numbering system. This point is important to remember if you're thinking about dividing your document into two or more divisions.

Inserting the Reference Mark and Typing the Note

You use Insert Footnote to insert a footnote or endnote in your document. Each time you insert a note, you choose whether you want Word to number the notes. If you don't want Word to number the notes, you can type your own footnote reference mark, such as an asterisk.

To insert a footnote, do the following:

1. Position the cursor where you want the footnote reference mark to appear.

2. Choose Insert Footnote (Alt-IN).

   The Footnote dialog box shown in figure 14.1 appears.

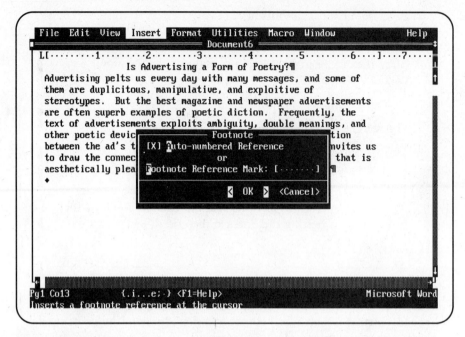

Fig. 14.1. The Footnote dialog box.

3. Type a footnote reference mark (up to 28 characters). Or, leave the X in the **Auto-numbered Reference** box if you want Word to number the note.

4. Choose OK.

   Word repeats the footnote number or the reference mark you typed in the special footnote area beyond the end mark. You can see this area in figure 14.2. After you choose OK, Word positions the cursor after the number so that you can type the note.

5. Type the text of the footnote.

   You can use character and paragraph formatting as you type the note. However, if you plan to create many footnotes, delay using this formatting until you write all your notes. This way, you can select all your notes and use the formatting commands just once.

   Be sure to leave the cursor within the text of the footnote you have just typed before going on to the next step.

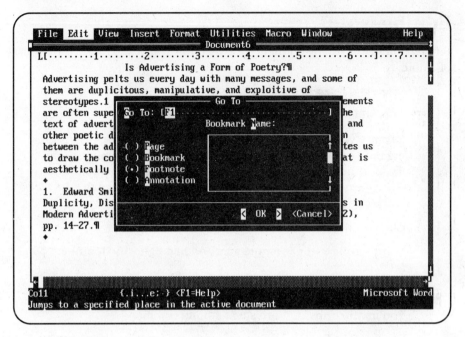

Fig. 14.2. The special footnote area.

6. Choose **Edit** **G**o To (Alt-EG).

   Because the cursor was in the footnote you just typed, the Go To dialog box proposes the footnote number you just typed as the destination, and the Footnote option is selected already.

7. Choose OK.

   The cursor moves back to your document and highlights the footnote reference mark.

8. If you would like the reference mark to appear as a superscript, press Ctrl- =.

Many Word users are annoyed because Word does not create superscripts by default. Remember, though, many style guidelines call for reference marks to be enclosed in brackets or parentheses. Programs that automatically show reference marks as superscripts and don't enable users to change this format are unusable in such situations. If you plan to use footnotes extensively, you can change the default format for all documents so that Word enters reference marks as superscripts. See Chapter 20, "Style Sheet Formatting," for more information.

Editing Notes

Editing notes after you insert them is easy. Follow these steps to revise the text of a note:

1. Select the reference mark of the note you want to edit.

2. Choose Edit Go To (Alt-EG) or use the F5 keyboard shortcut.

   Because you selected the footnote reference mark before choosing this command, Word assumes that you want to move to the footnote area. The program chooses the Footnote option. In the Go To text box, the program proposes the number of the note you highlighted.

3. Choose OK.

   Word scrolls to the footnote area and highlights the footnote you selected.

4. Edit the note.

   You may use any of Word's text-editing commands.

5. Choose Edit Go To (Alt-EG) or use the F5 keyboard shortcut.

   Again, Word assumes that you want to jump to a footnote reference mark and proposes the number of the footnote in which the cursor is positioned.

6. Choose OK.

   Word scrolls to the footnote reference mark in your document.

Searching for the Next Reference Mark

As you have learned already, the Edit Go To command performs different tasks depending on where you use the command. If you position the cursor on a footnote reference mark, the command takes the cursor to the footnote text. If the cursor is in the footnote text, Edit Go To moves the cursor back to the reference mark.

Word offers still another way to use the Edit Go To command. If the cursor is positioned in ordinary text when you use this command, Word scrolls to the next footnote reference mark in the document.

To move the cursor to the next footnote reference mark, do the following:

1. Choose **Edit G**o To (Alt-EG) or use the F5 keyboard shortcut.

2. Choose **F**ootnote.

3. Choose OK.

Remember this use of the command when you need to search for your next footnote reference mark.

To browse through your list of footnotes, press Ctrl-PgDn to move the cursor to the end mark. You then can scroll through the list.

Deleting a Note

If you need to delete a footnote, don't try to do it by deleting all the footnote text in the footnote area. It won't work, and a much easier way is available.

To delete a note, position the cursor on the reference mark and press Del. Word cuts the footnote and removes the footnote text from the footnote area. To cancel the deletion, choose **E**dit **U**ndo (Alt-EU or the Alt-Backspace keyboard shortcut) immediately.

Moving a Note

If you need to move a footnote, don't try to rearrange the remaining notes in the footnote area. This maneuver will not work. To move a note, you move the footnote reference mark, and the text of the note goes with it.

Use the following procedure to move a note:

1. Highlight the footnote reference mark.

2. Choose **E**dit **C**ut (Alt-ET) or use the Shift-Del keyboard shortcut.

3. Move the cursor to the place you want the note to reappear.

4. Choose **E**dit **P**aste (Alt-EP) or use the Shift-Ins keyboard shortcut.

   Word renumbers the footnote sequence.

Using the Footnote Pane

The footnote pane is a special window pane that displays the text of footnotes with reference marks currently displayed in the document window. (In Layout View, the footnote pane displays the current page's footnotes. To toggle the Layout View on, choose View Layout or Alt-VL.)

You can use the footnote pane while you create footnotes. After you open the pane, you don't have to use Edit Go To to move back and forth between the footnote area and the footnote reference marks; you move the cursor from one pane to the other.

The footnote window also is convenient to use while you're editing. As you scroll through your document, Word displays the notes relevant to the text you're editing. You can move to the notes to edit or format them just by switching panes.

The footnote pane resembles the panes described in Chapter 9, "Customizing Word and Using Windows." However, you use a different technique to open the footnote pane; the View Footnotes/Annotations command opens and closes the pane.

To open or close the footnote window, choose View Footnotes/Annotations (Alt-VF).

As shown in figure 14.3, when you open the footnote pane, Word splits the screen and displays the current footnotes in the bottom pane.

The footnote pane only shows the footnotes with reference marks in the document window (or, if you have chosen the Layout View, the current page). You cannot use the footnote pane to scroll through all the footnotes you have created. Don't be concerned if you don't see some of the footnotes you created; they come into view when you display their reference marks in the document pane.

After you split the screen into two panes, you easily can move the cursor from the document to the footnote pane. If you're using the mouse, click the cursor in the pane you want to activate. Alternatively, press F6 to move the cursor to the next pane.

Formatting Notes

When you create a note, Word formats the reference marks with the standard style for characters. The footnote or endnote text also is formatted in a standard style. If you choose, you can change the paragraph formatting.

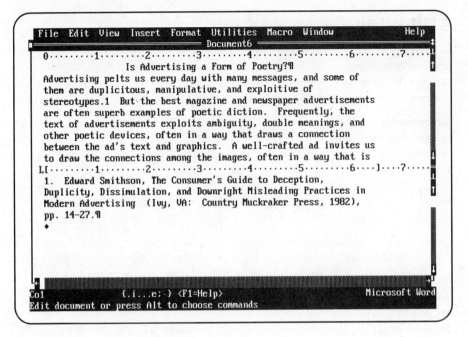

File Edit View Insert Format Utilities Macro Window   Help
```
                        Document6
 0········1·········2·········3·········4·········5·········6·········7·····
            Is Advertising a Form of Poetry?¶
 Advertising pelts us every day with many messages, and some of
 them are duplicitous, manipulative, and exploitive of
 stereotypes.1  But the best magazine and newspaper advertisements
 are often superb examples of poetic diction.  Frequently, the
 text of advertisements exploits ambiguity, double meanings, and
 other poetic devices, often in a way that draws a connection
 between the ad's text and graphics.  A well-crafted ad invites us
 to draw the connections among the images, often in a way that is
 L[········1·········2·········3·········4·········5·········6······]····7·····
 1.  Edward Smithson, The Consumer's Guide to Deception,
 Duplicity, Dissimulation, and Downright Misleading Practices in
 Modern Advertising  (Ivy, VA:  Country Muckraker Press, 1982),
 pp. 14-27.¶
 ◆
```
Co1   {.i...e;.} <F1=Help>   Microsoft Word
Edit document or press Alt to choose commands

Fig. 14.3. The footnote pane.

You can format each note as you enter it. However, an easier method is to format all the notes at one time, after you finish typing your document and inserting your notes.

Follow these steps to format all your notes at the same time:

1. Press Ctrl-Home to move the cursor to the first character in your document.

2. Choose **Edit Go** To (Alt-EG) or press the F5 keyboard shortcut.

3. Choose **Footnote**.

4. Choose OK.

   Word jumps to the first footnote reference mark.

5. Choose **Edit Go** To.

   Word jumps to the first footnote and highlights it.

6. Use any selection technique to expand the highlight until you have highlighted all the footnotes.

7. Use character and formatting commands to format all the notes at the same time.

Cross-Referencing Footnotes

In Chapter 12, "Using Glossaries and Bookmarks," you learn how to create in-text cross-references, such as "For a discussion of the company's second-quarter performance, see page 16." In this section, you learn how to cross-reference text you place in a footnote.

Revisions to the *The Chicago Manual of Style* saddle authors with a footnote referencing problem that Word's cross-referencing feature can tackle. When you type footnotes, you type the the complete citation the first time the footnote appears. In the past, you didn't type the full citation the second time. Instead, you typed a Latin abbreviation that directed the reader to go hunting for the footnote in which the citation appears in full form. Today, you must tell the reader which footnote contains the full citation (for example, "Smith, n. 46").

These cross-references can be difficult to produce in a work with dozens or even hundreds of footnotes. A word processing program may number the notes automatically, but if you move the notes around, the cross-references to the full citations are thrown out of order. Word's cross-referencing capabilities solve this problem.

To mark the footnote containing the full citation of a work, do the following:

1. In the document, *not in the footnote area*, place the cursor on the space immediately following the footnote reference mark.

2. Choose **Insert Bookmark** (Alt-IM) or use the Ctrl-Shift-F5 keyboard shortcut.

3. In the **Bookmark** Name area, type the author's last name, an underscore character, and the date of publication.

   For example: *Robertson_1987*

4. Choose OK.

Use these steps to cross-reference the full citation of a work in a footnote:

1. Insert the footnote and type the footnote text, including the text that immediately precedes the cross reference (such as *See footnote n.*).

2. Type the code name *footnote:* (don't forget the colon), followed by the bookmark name you chose for the footnote containing the document's full citation. Don't include any spaces.

   For example: *footnote:Robertson_1987*

3. Press F3.

When you print your document, Word removes the code name and bookmark name. In their place, you see the number of the footnote that contains the full citation (See footnote n. 24.)

Generating a Table of Authorities

Legal scholars, legal secretaries, and attorneys must cite authorities by appending to the end of the document a list of the statutes, cases, or other authorities cited. This list usually includes page references.

To assist legal personnel with tables of authorities, Word supplies two macros, authority_entry.mac and authority_table.mac, which you can use to mark authorities and to generate a table of authorities.

Before continuing this section, turn to Chapter 21, "Creating and Using Word 5.5 Macros," and read the section titled "Using Word's Supplied Macros."

Marking a Citation

After you have opened the glossary (MACRO.GLY) that contains Word's supplied macros, you can proceed with this section, which explains how to mark a citation the first time you type it.

To mark a citation the first time you type it, do the following:

1. Place the cursor where you plan to type the citation.

2. Choose **Macro Run** (Alt-MR).

   You see the Run Macro dialog box shown in figure 14.4.

3. Highlight *authority_entry* in the Macro **Name** list box.

4. Choose OK.

5. When you see the message `Type the new citation`, **highlight it and press Enter.**

   You type the citation in your document, but Word formats the citation as hidden text.

6. When you see the message `What is the source?`, **choose a number from the list (1=Previous Case, 2=Statute, 3=Regulation, or 4=Other). If you choose 4, Word asks you to name the category of this citation.**

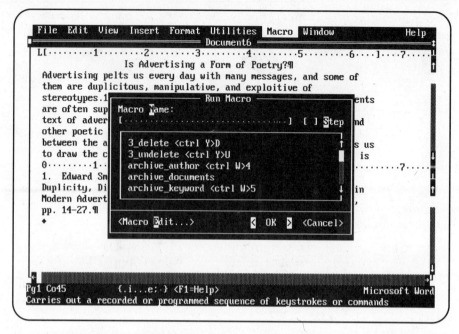

Fig. 14.4. The Run Macro dialog box.

7. **When you see the message** Move the cursor to the beginning of this citation, **press the up- and left-arrow keys to expand the highlight so that the whole citation is selected. Press Enter.**

8. Choose a name that Word can use to store this citation in a glossary.

   Word stores the citation, complete with all the formatting needed for the table of authorities, in the glossary you created.

Use these steps to mark the second and subsequent instances of the citation:

1. Place the cursor where you want the citation to appear.

2. Choose **Edit Glossary** (Alt-EO).

3. Choose the glossary entry you created for the citation in step 8 of the preceding series of steps.

4. Choose **Insert**.

Compiling the Table

After you finish typing and revising the document, follow these steps to compile the table of authorities:

1. Choose **Macro Run** (Alt-MR).

   You see the Run Macro dialog box

2. Highlight *authority_table* in the Macro **Name** list box.

3. Choose OK.

   Word creates a table of authorities and places the table at the end of your document. You can format this table as needed.

Printing Line Numbers

Legal documents frequently include line numbers in the left margin. You can print documents with line numbers for each page, each division, or the whole document.

Line numbering ignores any blank lines entered with the Paragraph dialog box's **Before** and **After** text boxes. This fact is a good reason to add blank lines with this command rather than by pressing Enter. Similarly, Word's line-numbering scheme ignores blank lines entered when you have chosen double-line spacing or other line spacing options.

To add line numbers to your document, follow these steps:

1. Place the cursor in the section of your document for which you want line numbers printed.

   If your document consists of only one section, skip this step. If your document has more than one section, and you want line numbers in all sections, press Ctrl-K5 to select your entire document.

2. Choose Format Section (Alt-TS).

3. Choose Add Line Numbers.

   After you choose this option, Word activates the From Text and Count **by** text boxes shown in figure 14.5. By default, Word places the line numbers 0.4-inch to the left of the text and prints

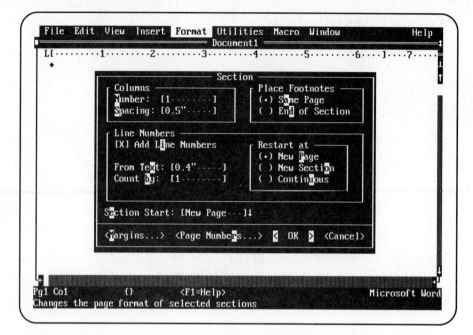

Fig. 14.5. Adding line numbers with the Section dialog box.

line numbers for each line. You can change these options. For example, to print line numbers every tenth line, type *10* in the Count **by** text box.

4. Choose OK.

Chapter Summary

This chapter showed you how easily you can access Word's referencing features to include footnotes, endnotes, tables of authorities, or line numbering in your documents. You learned how to choose between footnotes or endnotes and how to insert, format, edit, and delete a note. You learned how to use Word's supplied macros to create and compile a table of legal authorities. You also received a step-by-step explanation of printing line numbers in your document and displaying them in the status line.

The next chapter includes a discussion of annotations, a special form of the footnote that enhances collaborative writing.

Quick Review

Creating Footnotes

To insert a footnote:

1. Position the cursor where you want the footnote reference mark to appear.

2. Choose Insert Footnote (Alt-IN).

3. Type a footnote reference mark (up to 28 characters). Or, leave the X in the Auto-numbered Reference if you want Word to number the note automatically.

4. Choose OK.

5. Type the text of the footnote.

6. Choose Edit Go To (Alt-EG).

7. Choose OK.

8. If you would like the reference mark to appear as a superscript, press Ctrl-= (equal sign).

Cross-Referencing the First Citation

To mark the footnote containing the full citation of a work:

1. In the document, *not in the footnote area*, place the cursor on the space immediately following the footnote reference mark.

2. Choose Insert Bookmark (Alt-IM) or use the Ctrl-Shift-F5 keyboard shortcut.

3. In the Bookmark Name box, type the author's last name, an underscore character, and the date of publication.

4. Choose OK.

To cross-reference the full citation of a work in a footnote:

1. Insert the footnote and type the footnote text, including the text that immediately precedes the cross reference (such as *See footnote n.*).

2. Type the code name *footnote:* (don't forget the colon), followed by the bookmark name you chose for the footnote containing the document's full citation. Don't include any spaces.

3. Press F3.

Editing Footnotes

To edit a footnote:

1. Select the reference mark of the note you want to edit.

2. Choose Edit Go To (Alt-EG) or use the F5 keyboard shortcut.

3. Choose OK.

4. Edit the note.

5. Choose Edit Go To (Alt-EG) or use the F5 keyboard shortcut.

6. Choose OK.

To move the cursor to the next footnote reference mark:

1. Choose Edit Go To (Alt-EG) or use the F5 keyboard shortcut.

2. Choose Footnote.

3. Choose OK.

To delete a footnote:

1. Position the cursor on the footnote reference mark.

2. Press Del.

To move a note:

1. Highlight the footnote reference mark.

2. Choose Edit Cut (Alt-ET) or use the Shift-Del keyboard shortcut.

3. Move the cursor to the place you want the note to reappear.

4. Choose Edit Paste (Alt-EP) or use the Shift-Ins keyboard shortcut.

Footnote Pane

To open or close the footnote window:

Choose View Footnotes/Annotations (Alt-VF).

To move the cursor to the next pane:

Press F6.

Footnote Placement

To determine footnote placement:

1. Place the cursor in the section that contains the footnotes you want to affect.

2. Choose Format Section (Alt-TS).

3. Choose Same Page to place the notes at the bottom of the page or choose End of Section to place the notes at the end of the section.

4. Choose OK.

Formatting Footnotes after You Type Them

To format footnotes after you type them:

1. Press Ctrl-Home to move the cursor to the first character in your document.

2. Choose Edit Go To (Alt-EG) or press the F5 keyboard shortcut.

3. Choose Footnote.

4. Choose OK.

   Word jumps to the first footnote reference mark.

5. Choose Edit Go To.

6. Use any selection technique to expand the highlight until you have highlighted all the footnotes.

7. Use character and formatting commands to format all the notes at the same time.

Table of Authorities

To mark a citation the first time you type it:

1. Place the cursor where you plan to type the citation.

2. Choose Macro Run (Alt-MR).

   You see the Run Macro dialog box (see fig. 14.4).

3. Highlight *authority_entry* in the Macro Name list box.

4. Choose OK.

5. **When you see the message** Type the new citation and highlight it. Press Enter, **follow the steps.**

6. **When you see the message** What is the source?, **choose a number from the list.**

7. **When you see the message** Move the cursor to the beginning of this citation, **press the up- and left-arrow keys to expand the highlight so that the whole citation is selected. Press Enter.**

8. **Choose a name that Word can use to store this citation in a glossary.**

To mark the second and subsequent instances of the citation:

1. Place the cursor where you want the citation to appear.

2. Choose Edit Glossary (Alt-EO).

3. Choose the glossary entry you created for the citation.

4. Choose Insert.

Chapter 15

Enhancing Group Productivity: Using Annotations and Redlining

Much professional and business writing is collaborative—and for good reason. Two (or more) heads are better than one. When your future is riding on the success of a proposal, for instance, it makes sense to assemble a team of experts, each with his or her distinctive strengths. It is not surprising that approximately one in every five professional documents stems from collaborative efforts; in some fields, the figure is as high as three in five.

Collaborative writing poses special challenges, especially when word processing comes into the picture. Every word processing program is designed to maintain a single authoritative version of a document. The older versions disappear into the void when you save changes to disk. (Each of Word's BAK files always contains the preceding version of a file; however, if you save to disk several times during a session, as you should, the BAK file closely resembles the DOC file by the end of the session.) What this arrangement means, in principle, is that one reviewer can make major changes to a document, leaving no trace of what's been changed or omitted. But what happens if the other reviewers or the document's original author doesn't like the changes?

Word's solution to this problem is a nifty feature called *redlining*, a special editing mode that displays editing changes and enables reviewers to confirm them. The key to the redlining mode is the Utilities Revision Marks command. When you turn on the Utilities Revision Marks command, the text you insert appears in a special typeface, the text you delete is marked with strikethrough characters, and a symbol—a vertical bar—appears in the style bar.

Redlining solves the problem of how to handle editing changes in collaborative writing but leaves one question unanswered: how should collaborative writers make comments to one another in the text? You can enter a comment with some special marking phrase, such as *!!!Hey, these figures aren't correct!!!*, but doing so makes your document hard to read and edit. Worse, someone has to go through the document manually and remove the comments.

To solve this problem, Word includes an extremely useful feature called *annotations*. Annotations closely resemble footnotes (see Chapter 14), but the reference mark can include text—such as your initials—as well as a number. Each reviewer can use his or her initials to insert personalized annotations. In addition, Word can display all the annotations in the footnote window as you scroll through the document.

These two features—redlining and annotating—facilitate collaborative writing as no other currently available options can. If you frequently write in teams, you will want to read this chapter with special care. The chapter covers the following topics:

- Toggling the redlining mode on and off with Word's Utilities Revision Marks command

- Accepting or undoing a reviewer's changes using the Utilities Revision Marks command

- Creating and using annotations in collaborative writing situations

About Redlining

Think of redlining as a mode (like the Overtype mode) in which Word's characteristics change. When Word is in the redlining mode, the text you enter appears in a distinctive character emphasis of your choice, such as uppercase, boldface, or double-underlined. The text you delete does not disappear; instead, text you delete displays as strikethrough characters. If you want, you can display *revision bars*, which are lines in the margin that indicate edited passages.

After a document has been revised in Revision Marks mode, you (or other reviewers) have the option of accepting the changes or undoing them. If you accept the changes, Word removes the deleted text and removes the emphasis from the text that has been inserted. If you reject the changes, Word restores the document to its original state. You can accept some changes and reject others.

Turning On Redlining

To turn on the redlining editing mode, follow these steps:

1. Choose **Utilities Revision Marks** (Alt-UM).

   The Mark Revisions dialog box appears (see fig. 15.1).

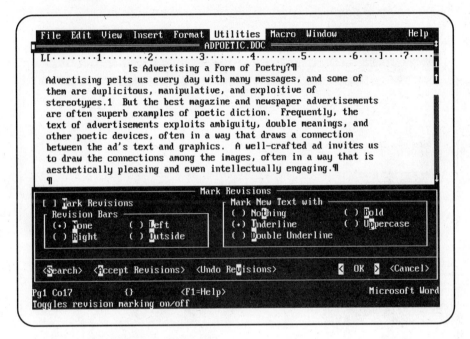

```
 File  Edit  View  Insert  Format  Utilities  Macro  Window          Help
                              ADPOETIC.DOC
 L[········1········2········3········4········5········6···]····7·····
                  Is Advertising a Form of Poetry?¶
 Advertising pelts us every day with many messages, and some of
 them are duplicitous, manipulative, and exploitive of
 stereotypes.1  But the best magazine and newspaper advertisements
 are often superb examples of poetic diction.  Frequently, the
 text of advertisements exploits ambiguity, double meanings, and
 other poetic devices, often in a way that draws a connection
 between the ad's text and graphics.  A well-crafted ad invites us
 to draw the connections among the images, often in a way that is
 aesthetically pleasing and even intellectually engaging.¶
 ¶
                             Mark Revisions
 [ ] Mark Revisions            ┌ Mark New Text with ─
 ┌ Revision Bars                 ( ) Nothing           ( ) Bold
 │ (·) None      ( ) Left        (·) Underline         ( ) Uppercase
 │ ( ) Right     ( ) Outside     ( ) Double Underline

 <Search>  <Accept Revisions>  <Undo Revisions>        ◄ OK ►  <Cancel>

 Pg1 Co17        {}              <F1=Help>               Microsoft Word
 Toggles revision marking on/off
```

Fig. 15.1. The Mark Revisions dialog box.

2. Choose **Mark Revisions** so that an X appears in the check box.

3. If you want, choose an emphasis for new text.

   By default, Word underlines new text. Choose another option if
   you want. If you work in graphics mode, you can choose double
   underlining, which distinguishes the text from ordinary underlined passages.

4. To display revision bars next to passages that have been edited,
   choose **Right** (to display the bars in the right margin), **Left** (left
   margin), or **Outside** (in two-sided documents, the margin away
   from the binding).

5. Choose OK.

You see the code RM on the status bar, informing you that Word is functioning in the Revision Marks mode.

Revising a document with redlining differs from the usual editing process. You can see all the changes you have made right on the screen. Figure 15.2 shows how a document looks when you have edited in redlining mode and you display the document in graphics mode.

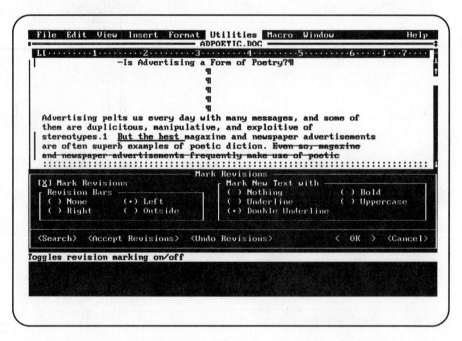

Fig. 15.2. Document edited in redlining mode and displayed in graphics mode.

Note the following aspects of figure 15.2:

• Revision bars appear in the left margin to indicate passages that have been edited.

• Deleted text is shown with strikethrough characters.

• Inserted text is shown with double underline characters.

In text modes, you see the deletions and insertions in distinctive colors, depending on the emphasis you have chosen. With Color Set 1, for example, strikethrough text appears in red, and double-underlined text appears in yellow. Even with the distinctive colors, however, conceptualizing revision marks in text mode is more difficult because you cannot see the strikethrough characters, and you easily can confuse the color with other emphases.

Accepting or Rejecting a Reviewer's Changes

Suppose that a reviewer gives you a document that has been edited in redlining mode. Rather than scroll through the document manually to look for each new change, you can instruct Word to search automatically for your reviewer's changes.

To search for changes automatically, follow this procedure:

1. Position the highlight at the beginning of the file. (Press Ctrl-Home to move to the beginning of the file with one keystroke.)

2. Choose **Utilities Revision Marks** (Alt-UM).

3. Choose the **Search** button.

   After Word finds and highlights the first unit of text that has been changed, the program continues to display the Mark Revisions dialog box.

4. To accept the highlighted revision, choose the **Accept Revisions** button. To reject the revision, choose the Undo Revisions button. To skip the highlighted revision and continue the search, choose Search.

5. Repeat steps 3 and 4 until you have accepted or rejected all revisions.

You also can accept or reject all the changes in a selection if you want, but remember that your actions will affect the entire selection—you don't get a chance to accept or reject each revision, as you do when you choose the Search button.

To accept or reject the changes in a selection, follow these steps:

1. Select the text.

   You can select any amount of text. To select the entire document, press Ctrl-Keypad 5.

2. Choose **Utilities Revision Marks** (Alt-UM).

3. Choose **Accept Revisions** or Undo Revisions.

4. Choose OK.

If you chose the wrong button, choose **Edit Undo** (Alt-EU) or use
the Alt-Backspace keyboard shortcut immediately. Word then
restores the revision marks to their state before you chose the
commands.

Creating Annotations

Annotations closely resemble footnotes, and they work much the same way.
(See Chapter 14, "The Legal and Scholarly Word," for a discussion of footnotes.)
As with footnotes, Word places annotations at the bottom of the page. A major
difference between annotations and footnotes is that annotations can be
deleted from your document after they have served their purpose. Although
annotations and footnotes are numbered, an annotation also can contain up to
28 characters, which you can use to identify yourself as the author of the
annotation.

Why create annotations? Annotations are useful in collaborative writing for
comments such as, "John, this section is really well-written. I would suggest that
you add a section on the maintenance procedures we're proposing." However,
Word's annotations aren't like the annotations you sometimes find in scholarly
manuscripts. Scholarly annotations appear in the margins of texts, and they are
intended to serve as a permanent, running commentary on the interpretation
or translation of a text. Word's annotations are temporary notes that facilitate
the revision process, particularly in collaborative writing.

An annotation has two parts:

- The *annotation reference mark* is the mark that appears in the text
  where you insert an annotation. The reference mark includes a
  number that Word supplies and text that you specify, such as your
  initials.

- The *annotation text* is the text of the annotation itself. In your
  document, this text is positioned in the special annotation area after
  the end mark in your document. If you want, Word can add the
  current date or time to the annotation text.

  Note: If you include footnotes in your document, Word includes the
  annotations in the footnote numbering sequence. But don't worry
  that annotations will ruin the footnote numbering sequence; when
  you and your colleagues have finished editing your document and
  have removed the annotations, the footnotes remain, and Word
  renumbers them properly.

Within a document, you can tell the difference between a footnote and an annotation. A footnote's reference mark contains a number or a reference mark that you type, such as an asterisk. An annotation contains a number and text, such as your initials.

To create, format, and print annotations, use the following commands:

- **Insert Annotation (Alt-IA).** Choose this command to insert an automatically numbered reference mark, the text you want to include in the reference mark, and the text of the annotation itself.

- **Edit Go To (Alt-EG).** Choose this command to move to the next annotation reference mark when you are editing a document and to move from the reference mark to the annotation text.

- **View Footnotes/Annotations (Alt-VF).** Choose this command to open the footnote pane, a special pane that displays footnotes or annotations that are displayed in the document pane. (For more information on footnotes, see Chapter 14, "The Legal and Scholarly Word.")

Inserting the Reference Mark and Typing the Note

You use the Insert Annotation command to insert an annotation in your document. Like the Insert Footnote command, Insert Annotation provides a text box in which you can type the reference mark. The dialog box also contains check boxes that you can select if you want the reference mark to include the current time and date.

To insert an annotation, follow these steps:

1. Position the cursor where you want the annotation reference mark to appear.

2. Choose **Insert Annotation (Alt-IA).**

   The Annotation dialog box appears (see fig. 15.3).

3. Type an annotation reference mark (up to 28 characters).

   For collaborative writing, use your initials as an annotation reference mark. Your initials indicate to other authors that the note contains your comments on the passage you have annotated.

4. Choose **Include Date,** if you want, to insert the current date into the annotation text.

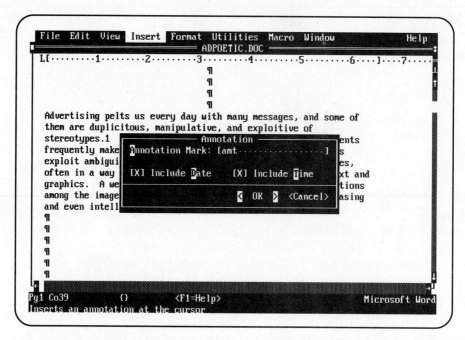

File Edit View **Insert** Format Utilities Macro Window   Help
═══════════════════════════ ADPOETIC.DOC ═══════════════════════════
L[········1·········2·········3·········4·········5·········6····]···7·····
                                    ¶
                                    ¶
                                    ¶
                                    ¶
Advertising pelts us every day with many messages, and some of
them are duplicitous, manipulative, and exploitive of
stereotypes.1 ┌─────────────── Annotation ───────────────┐ ents
frequently make│ [A]nnotation Mark: [amt···············] │ s
exploit ambigui│   │ es,
often in a way │ [X] Include [D]ate   [X] Include [T]ime │ xt and
graphics. A we│   │ tions
among the image│   ◄ OK ► <Cancel>   │ asing
and even intell└──┘
 ¶
 ¶
 ¶
 ¶
 ¶
 ¶
Pg1 Co39   {}   <F1=Help>   Microsoft Word
Inserts an annotation at the cursor

Fig. 15.3. The Annotation dialog box.

5. Choose Include **T**ime, if you want, to insert the current time into the annotation text.

6. Choose OK.

   Word echoes the annotation reference mark in the special annotation area beyond the end mark. If you choose the Include **D**ate and Include **T**ime check boxes, you see the date and the time at the beginning of the annotation text (see fig. 15.4). Word automatically positions the cursor so that you can type the note.

7. Type the text of the annotation.

   Because you remove annotations before printing the final draft of the document, you need not worry about formatting the note.

   Before going on to the next step, be sure to leave the cursor within the text of the annotation that you just typed.

8. Choose Edit **G**o To (Alt-EG).

   Because the cursor was in the annotation you just typed, the Go To dialog box proposes the annotation number you just typed as the destination, and the Annotation option already is selected.

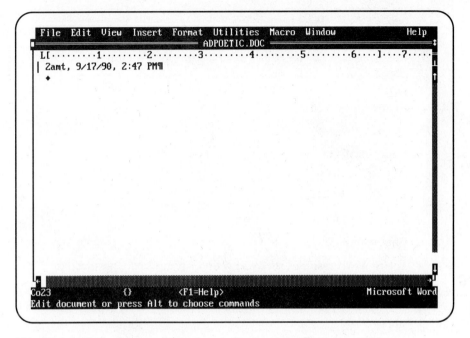

Fig. 15.4. *Initials, date, and time inserted automatically in annotation.*

9. Choose OK to return to the document (at the footnote reference mark).

   The cursor moves back to your document and highlights the annotation reference mark.

> **Tip:** To view annotations on-screen as you scroll through your document, open the footnote pane. The footnote pane displays annotations as well as footnotes. For more information on opening and using the footnote pane, see Chapter 14, "The Legal and Scholarly Word."

Editing Annotations

You revise an annotation the same way you revise a footnote: by choosing **E**dit **G**o To, which moves the cursor to the annotation area.

To edit an annotation, follow these steps:

1. Select the reference mark of the annotation you want to edit.

2. Choose **Edit Go** To (Alt-EG) or use the F5 keyboard shortcut.

Because you selected an annotation reference mark before choosing **Edit Go** To, Word assumes that you want to move to the annotation area. The program automatically chooses the Annotation option. In the **Go** To text box, Word proposes the number of the note you highlighted.

3. Choose OK.

Word scrolls to the annotation area and highlights the annotation you selected.

4. Edit the annotation.

You may use any of Word's text-editing commands.

5. Choose **Edit Go** To (Alt-EG) or use the F5 keyboard shortcut.

Again, Word assumes that you want to jump to an annotation reference mark and proposes the number of the annotation in which the cursor is positioned.

6. Choose OK.

Word scrolls to the annotation reference mark in your document.

Searching for the Next Annotation Reference Mark

As you have learned, the **Edit Go** To command performs different tasks depending on where you use it. If you position the cursor on an annotation reference mark, the command takes the cursor to the annotation text. If the cursor is in the annotation text, **Edit Go** To moves the cursor back to the reference mark.

Word offers still another way to use the **Edit Go** To command. If the cursor is positioned in ordinary text when you use **Edit Go** To, Word scrolls to the next annotation reference mark in the document.

To move the cursor to the next annotation reference mark, follow this procedure:

1. With the cursor in your document (not the annotation area), choose **Edit Go** To (Alt-EG) or use the F5 keyboard shortcut.

2. Choose **Annotation**.

3. Choose OK.

If you want to browse through your list of annotations, press Ctrl-End to move the cursor to the end mark. You then can scroll through the list.

Deleting an Annotation

If you need to delete an annotation, don't try to do so by deleting all the annotation text in the annotation area. That method will not work. Word provides an easy way to delete annotations.

To delete an annotation, simply position the cursor on the reference mark and press Del. Word cuts the annotation and removes the annotation text from the annotation area. To cancel the deletion, choose Edit Undo (Alt-EU) or use the Alt-Backspace keyboard shortcut immediately.

Moving an Annotation

If you need to move an annotation, don't try to rearrange the notes in the annotation area. Again, that method will not work. Word provides an easy way to move annotations. To move an annotation, you simply move the annotation reference mark, and the text of the note moves with it.

To move an annotation, follow these steps:

1. Highlight the annotation reference mark.

2. Choose Edit Cut (Alt-ET) or use the Shift-Del keyboard shortcut.

3. Move the cursor to the place you want the annotation to reappear.

4. Choose Edit Paste (Alt-EP) or use the Shift-Ins keyboard shortcut.

   Word automatically renumbers the annotation sequence.

Consolidating Annotations

After you have created a document, you may need to distribute the document to other individuals. The best way to do so is to circulate only one authoritative version of a document, which each reviewer can examine in sequence. Save the document with redlining turned on so that the insertions and deletions the reviewers make will be highlighted. Also, tell the reviewers to explain their changes or to make comments by using annotations.

Although this method is the easiest, deadlines often prevent reviewers from waiting their turns to examine the file. In such cases, you should give each reviewer a disk containing a copy of the file. The reviewers all can work simultaneously, and the process can move quickly. (When you distribute copies of a file in this way, be sure that each copy has its own unique file name, such as COPY1.DOC, COPY2.DOC, and so on.) But when you, the document's author, get these disks back, you're faced with a problem. Must you load each separate file, one after the other, to read each reviewer's annotations? That method would be tedious, to say the least.

To solve this problem, Word 5.5 offers macros that consolidate annotations from several copies of a file. Word 5.5 consolidates annotations in the following two ways:

- By merging the annotations from several copies of a file into a master copy. This approach works best when the reviewers haven't altered the file in any way other than inserting annotations.

- By collecting all the annotations into a separate file and listing the annotations by page number. This technique is best if the reviewers have altered their copies by inserting or deleting text.

Note: To use the macros called annot_merge, annot_collect, and annot_remove, you must open the MACRO.GLY glossary. To open it, choose **Macro Edit** (Alt-ME); then choose **Open Glossary**. Locate MACRO.GLY, and choose OK.

Merging Annotations

You probably want to merge annotations if the various copies of the document are identical except for their annotations. If the reviewers have changed the sentences on which they have made annotations, you need to collect the annotations in a separate file or print them, as described in the next section.

To merge annotations into one copy of a document, follow this procedure:

1. Choose **File Close All** (Alt-FL) to close all document windows.

2. Choose **Macro Run** (Alt-MR).

3. Highlight annot_merge.

4. When you see the Macros dialog box, type a name for the new document into which Word will place the annotations.

5. When you are prompted to type the name of the destination document, type the file name of the master copy of the document. Don't forget to specify path information if the document isn't in the default directory.

6. After the macro splits the screen, type the name of the first source document, the document from which the macro will copy annotations. Use the name of the file in which the first reviewer included comments.

   The macro compares the source document to the destination document. If the two files are identical, the merge process is automatic. If the two files are not identical, however, the macro pauses and asks for instructions on where to insert the annotations.

7. When the macro finishes merging the first source file, Word prompts you for the name of another source document. Type the name of the second source document. If you do not have another another source document, quit the macro by pressing Esc.

The annot_merge macro doesn't delete the annotations from the source documents—the macro simply copies the annotations from all source documents and consolidates them into a single authoritative version of the file.

Collecting Annotations

Word uses the annot_collect macro to collect annotations from a series of identical (or nearly identical) documents and to generate a new file containing all the annotations listed by page number. This technique does not require the copies of the document to be identical, but the process works best if all copies have the same pagination. You can "freeze" the pagination you have given the master document by turning off Word 5.5's auto-pagination feature (Background Pagination in the Utilities Customize dialog box) before you distribute copies of the file. That way, the page breaks remain the same even if reviewers insert or delete text.

To collect annotations, follow these steps:

1. Tell all reviewers to turn off the Background Pagination option in the Utilities Customize dialog box before they review their copies of the document. Turning off the Background Pagination option ensures that reviewers' comments will not affect pagination.

2. Choose File Close All (Alt-FL) to close all document windows.

3. Choose Macro Run (Alt-MR).

4. Choose annot_collect.

5. Choose OK to run the macro.

6. When you are prompted to do so, type the name of the file that will receive all the annotations. This file should be a new Word document. Choose a file name you haven't used previously.

7. When the macro asks whether you want to be prompted for the file names of the source documents, press Y and type the name of the source file—the file from which the macro copies the reviewer's annotations. If you press N, the macro displays the File Management dialog box, which you can use to retrieve the source files.

When the macro finishes compiling the annotations, it saves them to disk using the file name you have chosen. You can print this file or examine the file on-screen.

Removing All the Annotations from a Document

After you have reviewed and responded to all annotations, you can delete all of them at once by using the macro called annot_remove.

To remove all the annotations from a document, follow these steps:

1. Choose File Close All (Alt-FL) to close all document windows.

2. Choose Macro Run (Alt-MR).

3. Choose annot_remove.

4. When the macro finishes removing the annotations, it prompts you to save the document using a new file name (thus preserving the old copy with the annotations intact). Type a new file name and press Enter.

Chapter Summary

Word 5.5's Utilities Revisions Marks and Insert Annotation commands make Word the program of choice for collaborative writing. With Utilities Revisions Marks, a reviewer can insert or delete text and still enable the document's original author (or other reviewers) to accept the changes or undo them. With Insert Annotation, reviewers can enter queries or comments right into the document without disturbing the flow of text. The annotations then can be removed from the entire document with just one command. If you collaborate even occasionally, Word 5.5's features can help your team communicate effectively and produce a top-notch document.

Quick Review

Annotations

To insert an annotation:

1. Position the cursor where you want the annotation reference mark to appear.

2. Choose Insert Annotation (Alt-IA).

3. Type an annotation reference mark (up to 28 characters).

4. Choose Include **D**ate, if you want, to insert the current date into the annotation text.

5. Choose Include **T**ime, if you want, to insert the current time into the annotation text.

6. Choose OK to insert the annotation.

7. Type the text of the annotation.

8. Choose **E**dit **G**o To (Alt-EG) to return to the document (at the annotation reference mark).

   Because the cursor was in the annotation you just typed, the Go To dialog box proposes the annotation number you just typed as the destination, and the Annotation option already is selected.

9. Choose OK.

To edit the annotation:

1. Select the reference mark of the annotation you want to edit.

2. Choose **E**dit **G**o To (Alt-EG) or use the F5 keyboard shortcut.

3. Choose OK.

4. Edit the annotation.

5. Choose **E**dit **G**o To (Alt-EG) or use the F5 keyboard shortcut.

6. Choose OK to return to the document (at the annotation reference mark).

To move the cursor to the next annotation reference mark in your document:

1. With the cursor positioned within the text of your document, choose **Edit Go** To (Alt-EG) or use the F5 keyboard shortcut.

2. Choose **Annotation**.

3. Choose **OK**.

To move an annotation:

1. Highlight the annotation reference mark.

2. Choose **Edit Cut** (Alt-ET) or use the Shift-Del keyboard shortcut.

3. Move the cursor to the place you want the annotation to appear.

4. Choose **Edit Paste** (Alt-EP) or use the Shift-Ins keyboard shortcut.

To merge annotations into one copy of a document:

1. Choose **File Close All** (Alt-FL) to close all document windows.

2. Choose **Macro Run** (Alt-MR).

3. Highlight annot_merge.

   If you don't see the annot_merge macro in the list, choose **Macro Edit** and open the MACRO.GLY glossary. Repeat steps 2 and 3.

4. When you see the macro's dialog box, type a name for the new document into which Word will collect the annotations.

5. When you are prompted to type the name of the destination document, type the file name of the master copy of the document.

6. After the macro splits the screen, type the name of the first source document, the document from which the macro will copy annotations. Use the name of the file in which the first reviewer included comments.

7. When the macro finishes the first source file, Word prompts you for the name of another source document. Type the name of the second source document. If you do not have another source document, quit the macro by pressing Esc.

To collect annotations:

1. Tell all reviewers to turn off the **Background Pagination** option in the Utilities **Customize** dialog box before they review their copies of the document. Turning off the **Background Pagination** option ensures that reviewers' comments will not affect pagination.

2. Choose **File Close All** (Alt-FL) to close all document windows.

3. Choose **File New** (Alt-FN) to open a new, blank document.

4. Choose **Macro Run** (Alt-MR).

5. Choose annot_collect.

   If you don't see annot_collect, choose **Macro Edit** and open the MACRO.GLY glossary. Repeat steps 4 and 5.

6. When you are prompted to do so, type the name of the file that will receive all the annotations. This file should be a new Word document. Choose a file name you haven't used previously.

7. When the macro asks whether you want to be prompted for the file names of the source documents, press Y and type the name of the source file—the file from which the macro copies the reviewer's annotations. If you press N, the macro displays the File Management dialog box, which you can use to retrieve the source files.

To remove all the annotations from your document:

1. Choose **File Close All** (Alt-FL) to close all document windows.

2. Choose **Macro Run** (Alt-MR).

3. Highlight annot_remove.

   If you don't see annot_remove, choose **Macro Edit** and open the MACRO.GLY glossary. Repeat steps 2 and 3.

4. When the macro finishes removing the annotations, it prompts you to save the document using a new file name (thus preserving the old copy with the annotations intact). Type a new file name and press Enter.

Redlining (Revision Marks)

To turn on redlining:

1. Choose **Utilities Revision Marks** (Alt-UM).

2. Choose **Mark Revisions** so that an X appears in the check box.

3. If you want, choose an emphasis for new text.

4. To display revision bars next to passages that have been edited, choose **Right**, **Left**, or **Outside**.

5. Choose OK.

To turn off redlining:

1. Choose Utilities Revision Marks (Alt-UM).

2. Choose **Mark Revisions** so that the X is removed from the check box.

3. Choose OK.

To search for revision marks and to accept or reject them:

1. Press Ctrl-Home to position the highlight at the beginning of the file.

2. Choose Utilities Revision Marks (Alt-UM).

3. Choose the **Search** button.

4. To accept the highlighted revision, choose **Accept Revisions**. To reject the revision, choose **Undo Revisions**. To skip the highlighted revision and continue the search, choose **Search**.

5. Repeat steps 3 and 4 until you have accepted or rejected all the revisions.

To accept or reject all the changes in a selection:

1. Select the text.

2. Choose Utilities Revision Marks (Alt-UM).

3. Choose **Accept Revisions** or **Undo Revisions**.

4. Choose OK.

16

Creating Form Letters

Surely you have received a letter that begins "Dear Mr. or Ms. So-and-So, Here's great news for you and the So-and-So family! You definitely have won at least one of the following fantastic prizes: a Lincoln Continental Town Car, a six-month trip to the South Seas, $30,000 in cash, or a cheap digital wrist watch! To claim your prize, all you have to do is visit our fine new recreational center, the Happy Acres Landfill and Hazardous Waste Repository, and listen to six hours of grueling cross-examination by our sadistic sales staff!" More likely than not, your name is printed slightly out of register, betraying the ploy: everyone in your neighborhood is getting the same letter. You have received, in other words, a personalized form letter—a letter that is sent to many people but personalized by a computer so that the letter appears as if it is sent only to you.

Letters of this sort are irritating, but personalized form letters have many legitimate uses in business and the professions. Whenever you want to send the same message to many people, but with a personal touch, consider sending a personalized form letter. And when you do, remember that Word offers one of the most powerful form-letter features you will find in any word processing package.

Unfortunately, these form-letter features—collectively called Merge—also are among the most challenging Word features to use, for it can be difficult to get a form-letter application to work correctly with Word. To be fair to Microsoft, similar features in other programs are not easy to use, either. Even a novice Word user, however, can develop and use a simple form-letter application. By means of the extended tutorial in this chapter, you will learn how to create a form-letter application, one that involves a membership mailing list for a small organization. You can build on what you learn in this tutorial to take full advantage of Merge's powerful features.

You learn to do the following in this chapter:

- Design a form-letter application, specifying in advance what kinds of information you will need to include in your letter

- Create the data document, a Word file containing the information you want Word to insert into your form letters

- Create the main document, the file containing the text of your letter

- Use simple conditional statements, which insert additional text in the letter if the data meet specified criteria

- Use the Print Merge command, a special print command that generates form letters

- Cope with error messages, which you most likely will get when you try to print your first form-letter application with Word

- Print mailing labels from your mailing list data document

A tutorial on creating and printing form letters and mailing labels runs through this chapter. The application described is a mailing list to generate form letters for members of a small neighborhood organization formed out of concern for local environmental and public safety issues. This tutorial introduces several time-saving (and frustration-avoiding) techniques born out of other users' experience with this powerful feature. If you explore this tutorial, you will learn what you need to know to develop your own custom form-letter and mail-list applications.

 Users of previous versions of Word, take heart: the menu names and dialog boxes have been changed to assist the beginner, but Merge applications still work as they did in Versions 4.0 and 5.0. If you have created Merge documents, they should work just fine with Version 5.5.

Don't worry just yet about specifying your own Merge application in detail. Just make notes to yourself about the way you're planning to create your own data document and main document, and improve your plan as you grasp the Merge features this chapter introduces.

Creating the Data Document

You begin the tutorial by creating the data document, the Word file that contains the information you want Word to insert into your form letter.

Most experienced Word users probably would agree that the data document is the weakest part of Word's form-letter capabilities; it's difficult to enter data in a way that's amenable to updating or error correcting. In the tutorial that follows, you learn how to separate field entries using tabs, and how to use lines and borders to differentiate records. These steps will make it easier to fix the problems that inevitably arise the first time you run a form-letter application.

> *Tip:* You can separate the items in a data record using commas, instead of tabs, if you want. The data record lines take up less room on the screen. However, the data fields don't align, so it's hard to tell whether each data record has the same number of commas. If you accidentally type more or fewer commas in one data record, the Merge application won't work. That's why using tabs, lines, and borders is preferable: you can see at a glance whether every data record is complete and correctly typed.

Creating the Header Record

The data document begins with a header record, a special record that lists the field names you plan to use. Without the header record, Word would not know the field names you have chosen for the data you enter.

To create the header record, follow these steps:

1. Open a new, blank Word document.

2. Choose **View Preferences** (Alt-VE).

   You see the Preferences dialog box.

3. Turn on the **Tabs** and **Paragraph Marks** check boxes in the Non-Printing Characters area.

4. Choose OK to return to your document.

5. Choose Forma**t Margins** (Alt-TM).

   You see the Section Margins dialog box.

6. Type *15"* in the Width text box.

   Why 15"? Each record must be contained on one line ending with a paragraph mark. To get all the information on one line, you need to widen the "page" to make sufficient room. You could specify an even wider width if you like.

7. Choose OK to return to your document.

   You see a section mark.

8. Press Enter to create a blank line above the section mark.

9. Press the up-arrow key to place the cursor at the top of the screen.

10. Choose View **R**uler (Alt-VR) or click the Ruler icon if the Ruler is not already displayed.

11. Press Shift-Ctrl-F10 to place the cursor on the Ruler, and set flush left tabs (L) at the locations indicated in the following list. You can also set tabs with the mouse; click the tab alignment character (at the extreme left of the Ruler) until you see an L. Click tabs at the locations indicated as follows:

>   0.5"
>
>   2.0"
>
>   3.5"
>
>   5.0"
>
>   8.0"
>
>   10.0"
>
>   10.6"
>
>   11.3"

Note: If you're using the mouse, click the horizontal scroll bar to bring the rest of the page into view.

These tab settings set up a format that enables you to enter the data in neat columns.

12. Now insert vertical tabs just to the left of all the tab stops you have set.

13. Choose Forma**t B**orders (Alt-TB).

You see the Format Borders dialog box.

14. Choose **B**ox Each Paragraph.

15. Choose OK.

You see a box on-screen, which extends beyond the right side of the window (fig. 16.1). The vertical tabs intersect with the box.

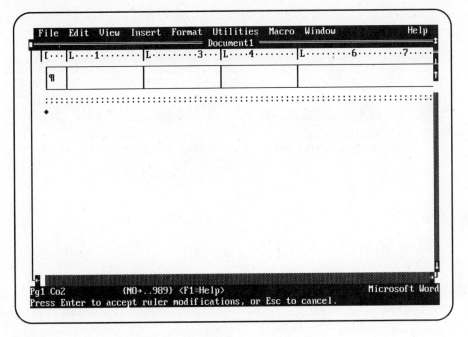

Fig. 16.1. *Box created with Format Borders.*

16. Select the paragraph mark inside the box and type the following
    field names, pressing Tab after each one (except for the last one):

> NO
>
> LASTNAME
>
> FIRSTNAME
>
> SALUTATION
>
> ADDRESS
>
> CITY
>
> STATE
>
> ZIP
>
> DUES1991

Make sure that you have spelled each of these field names correctly and that each is followed by a tab keystroke, except the last one.

Your header record should look like the one shown in figure 16.2.

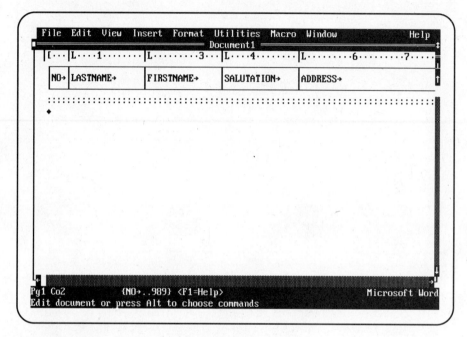

Fig. 16.2. *Header record with tab keystrokes.*

Adding Data

Now that you have created the header record, you need to add the data. Don't worry about adding the data in alphabetical order; Word will sort the list automatically.

> ***Caution:*** Do not use commas anywhere in a field entry. If you do, the form-letter application will not work unless you enclose the entry in quotation marks. To be on the safe side, get into the habit of avoiding commas entirely when you create data documents.

Add the data by following these steps:

1. Position the cursor on the paragraph mark at the end of the header record and press Enter. (Note that in figure 16.2 you cannot see the paragraph mark at the end. That's because you see only the first half of the 15 inch-wide "page.") This step copies the tab and border formats to the next paragraph (fig. 16.3).

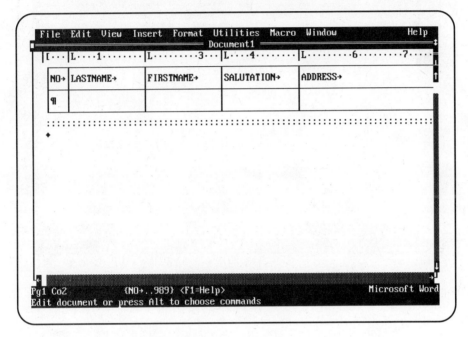

Fig. 16.3. *Tab and border formats copied to the next paragraph.*

2. Select the first blank line under the header record and add a record, as shown in figure 16.4.

   Important: Be sure to press Tab after typing each item, but don't press Tab after the last item (under DUES1991). You press Enter at the end of each line, not Tab.

   Begin by typing *1.* (don't forget the period) and press Tab. Press Tab after each item, type *Clapham* under LASTNAME, *Sara* under FIRSTNAME, and *Miss* under SALUTATION. Type *227 Carnival Drive* under ADDRESS and press Tab. Type *Happy Valley* under CITY and press Tab. Type *CA* under STATE and press Tab. Type *90123* under ZIP and press Tab. Type *yes* under DUES1991. Don't press Tab after the last data item.

Carefully check you work to make sure you pressed Tab at the end of each item you typed, but not after the last one. There should be eight tab keystrokes on the line—not more, not less.

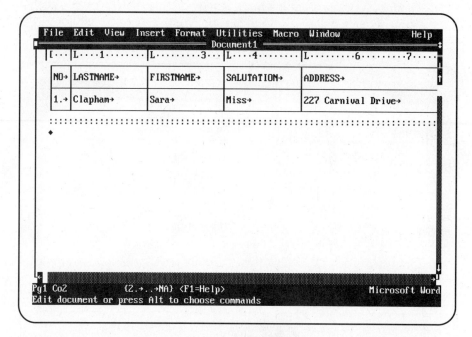

Fig. 16.4. Data document with one record entered.

3. With the cursor at the end of the first line of data, press Enter to start a new line and copy all the tab and border formats.

4. Continue typing the data, pressing Enter at the end of each line.

Caution: You're probably accustomed to typing a comma after the name of a city. But be careful to avoid doing so here. If you place an extraneous comma in your data document, you will see the message "Too many fields in record such-and-such" when you try to print your form letter application.

Type the following data:

No: 1

    LASTNAME: Clapham
    FIRSTNAME: Sara
    SALUTATION: Miss
    ADDRESS: 227 Carnival Drive
    CITY: Happy Valley
    STATE: CA
    ZIP: 90123
    DUES1991: no

No: 2

    LASTNAME: Abraham
    FIRSTNAME: Michelle
    SALUTATION: Dr.
    ADDRESS: 121 Hampstead Place
    CITY: Happy Valley
    STATE: CA
    ZIP: 90123
    DUES1991: yes

No: 3

    LASTNAME: Miller
    FIRSTNAME: Glenda
    SALUTATION: Ms.
    ADDRESS: 119 Carnival Place
    CITY: Happy Valley
    STATE: CA
    ZIP: 90123
    DUES1991: yes

No: 4

    LASTNAME: Cleveland
    FIRSTNAME: Tom
    SALUTATION: Mr.
    ADDRESS: 125 Hampstead Place
    CITY: Happy Valley
    STATE: CA
    ZIP: 90123
    DUES1991: yes

No: 5

> LASTNAME: Smith
> FIRSTNAME: Constance
> SALUTATION: Ms.
> ADDRESS: 134 Hampstead Place
> CITY: Happy Valley
> STATE: CA
> ZIP: 90123
> DUES1991: no

No: 6

> LASTNAME: Furnival
> FIRSTNAME: Alfred
> SALUTATION: Prof.
> ADDRESS: 139 Hampstead Place
> CITY: Happy Valley
> STATE: CA
> ZIP: 90123
> DUES1991: yes

No: 7

> LASTNAME: Brickston
> FIRSTNAME: Harry
> SALUTATION: Sergeant
> ADDRESS: Happy Valley Police Dept.
> CITY: Happy Valley
> STATE: CA
> ZIP: 90123
> DUES1991: yes

When you are finished, your data document should look like the one shown in figure 16.5. Note that you can see only the first half of the 15 inch-wide "page."

5. Save the document with the file name MAILLIST.DOC.

Caution: If any record has more tab keystrokes or fewer tab keystrokes than the header record, the application will not work. Check your data document carefully.

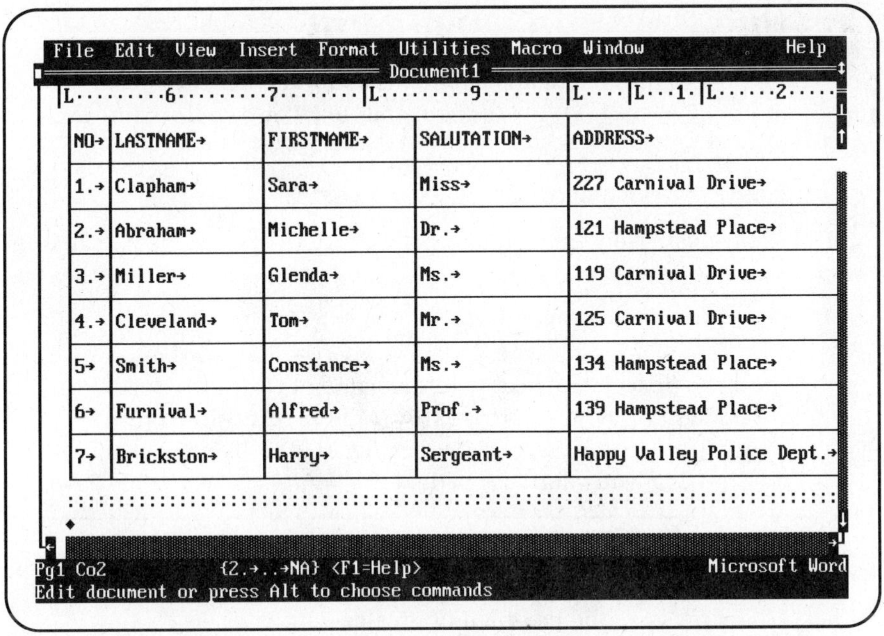

```
  File   Edit  View  Insert  Format  Utilities  Macro  Window           Help
═══════════════════════════ Document1 ═══════════════════════════════
 L·········6·······7········|L·········9········|L····|L··1·|L·····2·····
 ┌───┬──────────┬──────────┬───────────┬─────────────────────────────┐
 │NO→│LASTNAME→  │FIRSTNAME→│SALUTATION→│ADDRESS→                     │
 ├───┼──────────┼──────────┼───────────┼─────────────────────────────┤
 │1.→│Clapham→   │Sara→     │Miss→      │227 Carnival Drive→          │
 ├───┼──────────┼──────────┼───────────┼─────────────────────────────┤
 │2.→│Abraham→   │Michelle→ │Dr.→       │121 Hampstead Place→         │
 ├───┼──────────┼──────────┼───────────┼─────────────────────────────┤
 │3.→│Miller→    │Glenda→   │Ms.→       │119 Carnival Drive→          │
 ├───┼──────────┼──────────┼───────────┼─────────────────────────────┤
 │4.→│Cleveland→ │Tom→      │Mr.→       │125 Carnival Drive→          │
 ├───┼──────────┼──────────┼───────────┼─────────────────────────────┤
 │5→ │Smith→     │Constance→│Ms.→       │134 Hampstead Place→         │
 ├───┼──────────┼──────────┼───────────┼─────────────────────────────┤
 │6→ │Furnival→  │Alfred→   │Prof.→     │139 Hampstead Place→         │
 ├───┼──────────┼──────────┼───────────┼─────────────────────────────┤
 │7→ │Brickston→ │Harry→    │Sergeant→  │Happy Valley Police Dept.→   │
 └───┴──────────┴──────────┴───────────┴─────────────────────────────┘

 Pg1 Co2              {2.→..→NA} <F1=Help>                  Microsoft Word
 Edit document or press Alt to choose commands
```

Fig. 16.5. *Data document after adding data.*

> **Tip:** Many users will find that Word's data documents suit their needs. However, Word can also use the ASCII output of many popular database management programs, such as dBASE IV. As long as a database management program can print data to an ASCII file, with the data separated by commas or tabs, Word can use the data. Note, though, that you must add a header record to the ASCII file these programs create.

Using a database management program to maintain a mailing list has an advantage over Word's data documents. Unlike Word's data documents, database management programs are designed with special, useful features that enable you to enter data, maintain it so that it is correct, sort it in a variety of ways, and search for just the records that satisfy criteria you specify. What's more, these programs are designed to facilitate these tasks even if you create large numbers of records (say, one thousand or more). With Word, maintaining a large mailing list becomes a very tedious and error-prone job after you have added more than 100 or 200 names to the list.

Creating the Main Document

Now you need to create the main document. You will enter several commands surrounded by chevrons(«»). These commands tell Word where to find the data and which data to insert.

To create the main document, follow these steps:

1. Choose **File New** (Alt-FN) and press Enter to create a new, blank Word document.

2. Hold down the Ctrl key and press the left bracket key (Ctrl-[ ). This command enters the left chevron. Type the word *data* and press the Space bar. Next, type the name of your data document (*maillist.doc*). Finally, press Ctrl-] (right bracket) to enter the right chevron. This expression (see fig. 16.6) tells Word where to find the data you want inserted.

Caution: You must enter the chevrons by holding down the Ctrl key and pressing the left or right bracket key. Don't try to create the chevrons by pressing the less-than or greater-than keys.

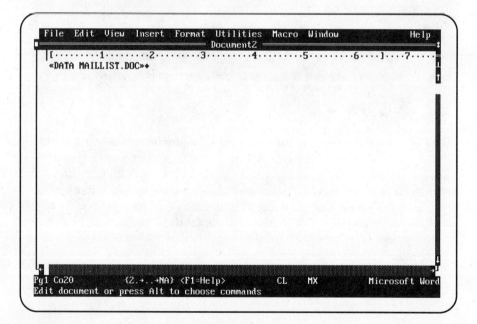

```
 File  Edit  View  Insert  Format  Utilities  Macro  Window          Help
                            Document2
[·········1·········2·········3·········4·········5·········6····]····7·····
«DATA MAILLIST.DOC»•




















Pg1 Co20        {2.→..→NA} <F1=Help>              CL    MX       Microsoft Word
Edit document or press Alt to choose commands
```

Fig. 16.6. DATA instruction in main document tells Word where to find the data document.

3. If you want to, you can press Enter one or more times after typing the DATA instruction. Word will enter blank lines, however, at the top of your document. One or two blank lines are usually necessary for letters.

4. Type a return address, and insert the dateprint glossary by typing *dateprint* and pressing F3 (see fig. 16.7).

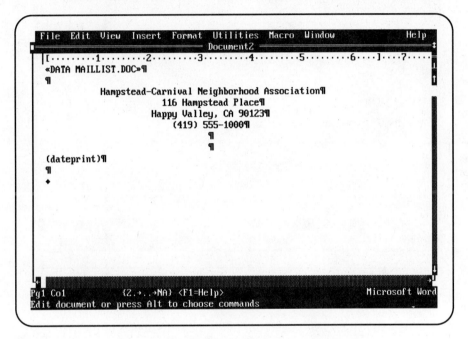

Fig. 16.7. *Return address and DATEPRINT glossary in main document.*

5. Surrounding each field with chevrons (Ctrl-[and Ctrl-]), type the field names as shown in figure 16.8. Begin by typing *«FIRSTNAME»*, and then press the Space bar so that Word will leave a space after it inserts the name. Type *«LASTNAME»* and press Enter. Continue in this way. Be sure to leave a space after the comma that separates «CITY» and «STATE», and leave a space between «STATE» and «ZIP». Similarly, leave a space between all the words in the salutation.

Note: Each field name must be surrounded by chevrons entered with Ctrl-[and Ctrl-]. Carefully check your work to make sure that each data field name is spelled correctly, just the way you spelled it in the data document's header record. Although you do not have to, you should type the field names in capital letters, which makes them easier to distinguish from ordinary text.

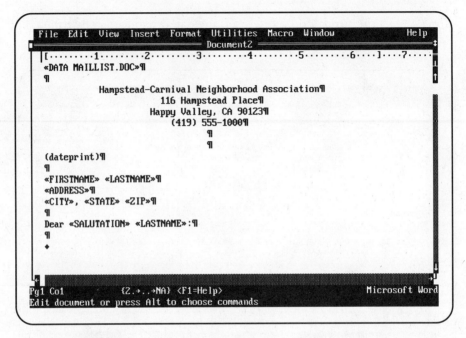

Fig. 16.8. Data fields entered in main document.

As you can see, you need not enter the field names in the order the data document lists them. You simply place them where you want the information to appear.

6. Type the text of the letter (see fig. 16.9):

The Euphoria County Planning Commission is holding a hearing (next Tuesday night) on the extension of Tacky Boulevard so that it intersects with Heavenly Drive.

The proposed extension would bring a significant increase in traffic to our neighborhood, since commuters will then have an even better shortcut to Highway 29. As you are doubtlessly aware, a commuter traveling at high speed struck and severely injured one of our neighbors, Jane Williams, as she was bicycling in our neighborhood last year. More traffic accidents, injuries, noise, and pollution are sure to follow if Tacky Boulevard is extended.

We plan to attend the hearing to voice our opposition. Won't you join us? If you need transportation or child care, give me a ring.

Sincerely,

Richard Jones
President, Hampstead-Carnival Neighborhood Association

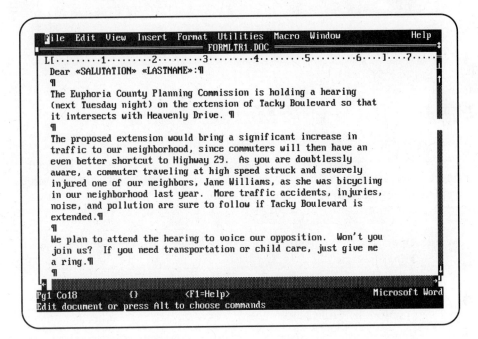

Fig. 16.9. Letter with text added.

7. Save the main document to disk. Use the file name FORMLTR1.DOC.

Caution: Before proceeding, double-check your work. The main document should begin with a DATA statement, which correctly identifies the data document. Be sure to include path information if the data document is located on a drive or in a directory other than the default directory. Be sure, too, that the DATA statement is surrounded by chevrons. (Note that you cannot enter the chevrons by typing less-than or greater-than symbols—you must use the Ctrl-[and Ctrl-] commands.) Check the field names to make sure that each is surrounded by chevrons. And make sure that you have spelled the field names exactly the way they're spelled in the data document.

Using the Print Merge Command

Now you're ready to print your form-letter application. But be prepared for error messages—it isn't easy to get a form-letter application to work correctly the first time. If you see an error message, see "Troubleshooting Form-Letter Applications," the next section of this chapter.

To print your form letters, do the following:

1. Open the main document (if it isn't already) and choose File Print Merge.

   You see the Print Merge dialog box (fig. 16.10). As you can see, you can print **All** the records (the default option) or just the **Records** you want. For now, choose **All**, if it's not already turned on.

   At the bottom of the screen are two command buttons, **Print** and **New Document**. If you choose **Print**, Word prints one letter for each data record in the data document. If you choose New Document, Word creates a new document and places each letter on its own separate page.

2. Choose **Print**.

   You see the Print dialog box.

3. Choose OK.

If you have created the data and main documents correctly, Word will format and print each letter in turn.

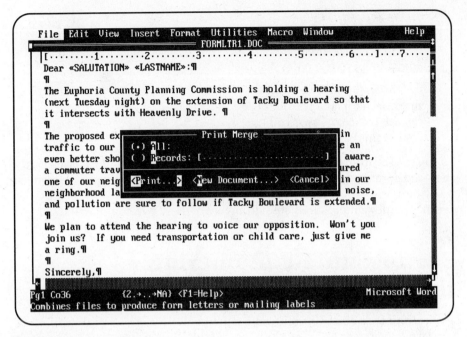

File   Edit View Insert Format Utilities Macro Window   Help
FORMLTR1.DOC
[·······1·······2·······3·······4·······5·······6···]···7····
Dear «SALUTATION» «LASTNAME»:¶
¶
The Euphoria County Planning Commission is holding a hearing
(next Tuesday night) on the extension of Tacky Boulevard so that
it intersects with Heavenly Drive. ¶
¶
The proposed ex┌──────────── Print Merge ────────────┐in
traffic to our │ (•) All: │e an
even better sho│ ( ) Records: [....................] │aware,
a commuter trav│   │ured
one of our neig│<Print...> <New Document...> <Cancel>│in our
neighborhood la└─────────────────────────────────────┘noise,
and pollution are sure to follow if Tacky Boulevard is extended.¶
¶
We plan to attend the hearing to voice our opposition. Won't you
join us? If you need transportation or child care, just give me
a ring.¶
¶
Sincerely,¶

Pg1 Co36   {2.→..→NA} <F1=Help>   Microsoft Word
Combines files to produce form letters or mailing labels

Fig. 6.10. The Print Merge dialog box.

Troubleshooting Form-Letter Applications

If you see error messages while trying to print your form-letter application, you have probably made a simple error that is easily corrected.

The following are the most common error messages users see:

- *Not a valid field name.* The field names in your data document's header record must begin with an alphabetical character (not a number). They must be 64 characters or less, and the only punctuation you can include is the underscore character. A field name must not contain spaces.

- *Too few fields in data record.* One of the records in your data document contains fewer tab keystrokes than the header record. Check your data document and fix the mistake.

- *Too many fields in data or header record.* One of the records contains more tab keystrokes than the header record. Check your data document and fix the mistake. You will see this message, too, if you attempt to use more than 256 fields.

- *Unknown field name.* Your main document contains a field name that doesn't match the ones used in the data document's header record. Make sure that you have spelled the field names correctly in your main document.

As you can see from this troubleshooting guide, every record must have exactly the same number of tab keystrokes, and the field names in the main document must be consistent with the ones in the data document. If you're having problems, they almost surely stem from one of these two common difficulties.

Sorting and Renumbering the Data Document

The sorting techniques introduced in Chapter 11 are very useful for putting your data document in order, alphabetized by last name. And you can use the **Renumber** command to number the records accurately. Sorting and numbering your data document aren't luxury operations; they're very important steps to take if you want to troubleshoot your application quickly and effectively. You will learn why in the section titled "Printing Just the Records You Specify."

The following procedure shows how to sort your data document and update the numbering:

1. Open the data document (MAILLIST.DOC).

2. Position the cursor at the upper left corner of the LASTNAME column, and press Ctrl-Shift-F8 to toggle on the column-select mode.

   You see the C S code in the status bar.

3. Select the entire column of last names (see fig. 16.11). Don't select the header record.

4. Choose Utilities Sort (Alt-UO).

   You see the Sort dialog box.

5. Choose Ascending sort order and, in the Key Type area, Alphanumeric. (These are default options, so they're probably already selected, unless you have already used this command in this operating session.)

```
 File  Edit  View  Insert  Format  Utilities  Macro  Window        Help
                          MAILLIST.DOC
 [···|L·····1········|L········3···|L····4········|L·········6········7·····

   NO→ LASTNAME→      FIRSTNAME→     SALUTATION→    ADDRESS→

   1.→ Clapham→       Sara→          Miss→          227 Carnival Drive→

   2.→ Abraham→       Michelle→      Dr.→           121 Hampstead Place→

   3.→ Miller→        Glenda→        Ms.→           119 Carnival Drive→

   4.→ Cleveland→     Tom→           Mr.→           125 Carnival Drive→

   5→  Smith→         Constance→     Ms.→           134 Hampstead Place→

   6→  Furnival→      Alfred→        Prof.→         139 Hampstead Place→

   7→  Brickston→     Harry→         Sergeant→      Happy Valley Police Dept.→



 Pg1 Co17           {2.→..→NA} <F1=Help>                    Microsoft Word
 Edit document or press Alt to choose commands
```

Fig. 16.11. Last names selected as the key for sorting of mailing list.

> *Important*: *Don't* choose the Sort Column **Only** option. If you
> do, Word will scramble the data by not moving the rest of the
> data items when it sorts this column.

6. Choose OK.

   Word sorts the mailing list. As you can see, the mailing list is now
   alphabetized by last name, but the numbers are out of order (see
   fig. 16.12). All the lines of data are automatically selected.

7. Choose Utilities **Renumber** (Alt-UR).

   You see the Renumber dialog box.

8. Choose **All** and make sure that an X is in the Restart **Sequence**
   check box. (These are the default options, so they're probably
   already selected, unless you have already used this command in
   this operating session.)

9. Choose OK.

   Word renumbers the mailing list correctly (see fig. 16.13).

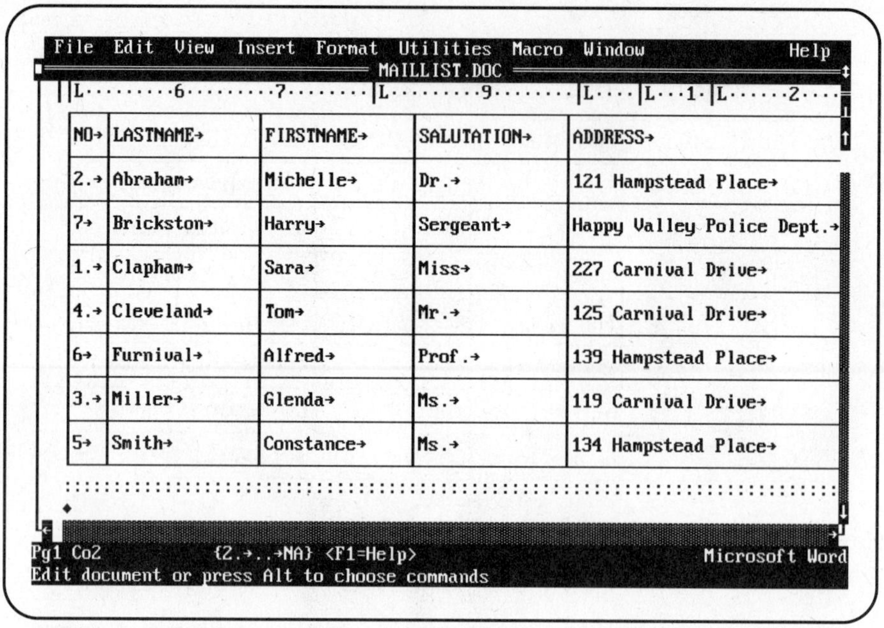

Fig. 16.12. Mailing list sorted by last name (but with numbers out of order).

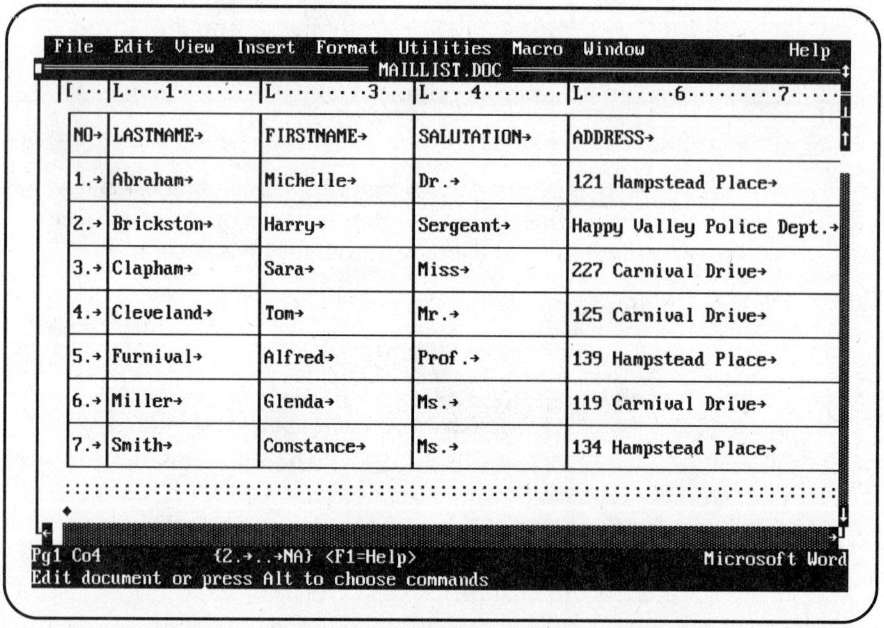

Fig. 16.13. Mailing list sorted by last name (with numbers in order).

If Word didn't number your data records correctly, you probably left the period off one or more of the numbers when you typed the data. Word won't renumber the records unless you typed a number and a period in each NO field.

Printing Just the Records You Specify

If you set up your data document with record numbers, as this chapter's tutorial suggested, it's easy to print just the records you specify. Suppose, for example, you want to send letters to the people whose addresses are listed in records 1, 4, 9, and 12, or in records 13 through 27. You can do so even if you didn't number the records, but it's much easier to keep track of what you're doing if you see the numbers on the data document screen.

To print just the data record numbers you specify, do the following:

1. Open the main document.

2. Choose **File Print Merge (Alt-FM)**.

   You see the Print Merge dialog box.

3. Choose **Records**.

4. Type the numbers of the data records you want to print.

   To print individual records, type the numbers separated by commas (*1,4,9,14*). Be sure to omit spaces. To print a series of records, use a hyphen (*9-28*). You can combine the two (*1,4,9-27,29*).

5. Choose **Print**.

   You see the Print dialog box.

6. Choose OK.

Getting Fancy: Using a Conditional Instruction

Now that you have successfully printed a simple form-letter application, try including a conditional instruction which includes additional text in a letter if a condition you specify is met. A glance at your data document reveals that you have kept track of who has paid dues and who hasn't.

In the following tutorial, you will learn how to admonish those who haven't paid their dues and praise those who have.

1. Load the main document (*FORMLTR1.DOC*) and add the following after the body of the letter (but before the closing):

   «IF DUES1991="no"»By the way, my records show that you haven't paid your dues for the year. Won't you send us a check for $5.00 today?«ENDIF»

   «IF DUES1991="yes"»Incidentally, thanks for paying your 1991 dues. Everyone in the Association appreciates your support and community spirit!«ENDIF».

   Be sure to enclose the IF expressions with chevrons, entered (as usual) with Ctrl-[and Ctrl-]. Don't forget the quotes around "yes" and "no." And don't forget the «ENDIF» expressions.

   See figure 16.14 for the correct appearance of the letter after this text has been added.

   The first part of this IF instruction says, in English, "If the DUES1991 field matches 'no,' then print `By the way, my records show that you haven't paid your dues for the year. Won't you send us a check for $5.00 today?'" An example of a letter generated by this instruction is shown in figure 16.15.

   The second part of this instruction says, in effect, "If the DUES1991 field matches 'yes,' then print `Incidentally, thanks for paying your 1991 dues. Everyone in the Association appreciates your support and community spirit!'" See figure 16.16 for an example of a letter containing this text.

   By implication, the instruction also says that if the DUES1991 field contains something other than "yes" or "no," such as "na" (not applicable), do nothing.

2. Choose **File Print Merge** to print the form letters with the conditional instructions.

Fig. 16.14. Form letter with conditional instructions.

Printing Mailing Labels

Now that you have created the form letters, you will find it helpful to print mailing labels. Word can print the labels from the mailing list you have already created. Depending on your printer's capabilities, you can print addresses on the following labels:

- Continuous-feed (tractor-feed) mailing labels. You use these labels on impact printers, such as dot-matrix printers.

- Sheet-feed labels. You use these labels with laser printers and other printers that can print one page at a time.

To set up a mailing label application, you create a new main document, complete with the DATA instruction and field names. The procedure differs for continuous-feed and sheet-feed labels.

> **Hampstead-Carnival Neighborhood Association**
> *116 Hampstead Place*
> *Happy Valley, CA 90123*
> *(419) 555-1000*
>
>
> March 24, 1991
>
> Sara Clapham
> 227 Carnival Drive
> Happy Valley, CA 90123
>
> Dear Miss Clapham:
>
> The Euphoria County Planning Commission is holding a hearing (next Tuesday night) on the extension of Tacky Boulevard so that it intersects with Heavenly Drive.
>
> The proposed extension would bring a significant increase in traffic to our neighborhood, since commuters will then have an even better shortcut to Highway 29. As you are doubtlessly aware, a commuter traveling at high speed struck and severely injured one of our neighbors, Jane Williams, as she was bicycling in our neighborhood last year. More traffic accidents, injuries, noise, and pollution are sure to follow if Tacky Boulevard is extended.
>
> We plan to attend the hearing to voice our opposition. Won't you join us? If you need transportation or child care, give me a ring.
>
> By the way, my records show that you haven't paid your dues for the year. Won't you send us a check for $5.00 today?
>
> Sincerely,
>
>
> Richard Jones
> President, Hampstead-Carnival Neighborhood Association

Fig. 16.15. Letter sent to member with unpaid dues.

Continuous-Feed Labels

To print continuous-feed labels, you create a main document with a page size corresponding to the size of the labels. To do so, you use the Format Margins (Alt-TM) command.

To print continuous-feed labels, follow these steps:

1. Open a new, blank document.

2. On the first line of the document, type a DATA instruction to tell Word where to find the data.

Hampstead-Carnival Neighborhood Association
116 Hampstead Place
Happy Valley, CA 90123
(419) 555-1000

March 24, 1991

Michelle Abraham
121 Hampstead Place
Happy Valley, CA 90123

Dear Dr. Abraham:

The Euphoria County Planning Commission is holding a hearing (next Tuesday night) on the extension of Tacky Boulevard so that it intersects with Heavenly Drive.

The proposed extension would bring a significant increase in traffic to our neighborhood, since commuters will then have an even better shortcut to Highway 29. As you are doubtlessly aware, a commuter traveling at high speed struck and severely injured one of our neighbors, Jane Williams, as she was bicycling in our neighborhood last year. More traffic accidents, injuries, noise, and pollution are sure to follow if Tacky Boulevard is extended.

We plan to attend the hearing to voice our opposition. Won't you join us? If you need transportation or child care, give me a ring.

Incidentally, thanks for paying your 1991 dues. Everyone in the Association appreciates your support and community spirit!

Sincerely,

Richard Jones
President, Hampstead-Carnival Neighborhood Association

Fig. 16.16. Letter sent to member with paid dues.

If your data document is called MAILLIST.DOC, type *«DATA MAILLIST.DOC»*. (You can omit the period and extension, if you want.) Be sure to enter the chevrons with Ctrl-[and Ctrl-].

3. *Important:* Type the first line of field names on the same line as the DATA instruction, with no space between the DATA instruction and the first field name.

If you're using MAILLIST.DOC, type the following to print the first line of the label correctly:

«DATA MAILLIST.DOC»«FIRSTNAME» «LASTNAME»

Note the space between «FIRSTNAME» and «LASTNAME»

4. Press Enter to start a new line.

5. Type the second line of field names you want printed on the mailing labels.

   With MAILLIST.DOC, you type *«ADDRESS»*

6. Press Enter to start a new line.

7. Type the third line of field names you want printed on the mailing labels.

   With MAILLIST.DOC, you type *«CITY», «STATE» «ZIP»*

   Note the punctuation and spaces.

8. Choose Format Margins (Alt-TM).

   You must set a new page size and margins to print the labels. The page size and margins you choose will affect the current document only.

9. In the **Height** text box, type the height of the labels you're using.

   Most continuous-feed labels are 1" in height.

10. In the **Top**, **Bottom**, and **Right** text boxes, type *0"*.

    Margins would interfere with the proper placement of text on the labels, which are only 1" high.

11. In the **Left** text box, type an indentation (such as *0.25"* or *0.5"*) so that Word won't start printing at the left edge of the labels.

12. Choose OK.

    Your document should look like the one in figure 16.17.

13. Choose File Print Merge (Alt-FM).

    You must print your document with the Print Merge command— the **Print** command won't work.

14. Choose **Print**.

15. Choose OK.

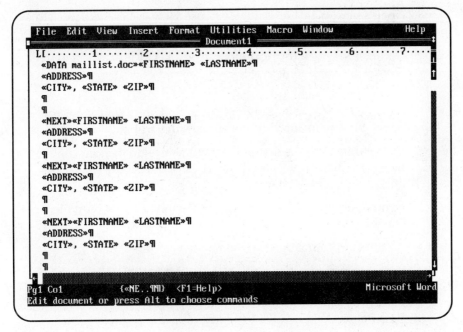

Fig. 16.17. Main document for continuous-feed mailing labels.

Sheet-Feed Labels

To print sheet-feed labels, you type a set of address label fields for each of the labels on the sheet. Most laser printer label sheets have 10 or 11 labels. Each set of address label fields must be followed by a NEXT instruction.

Sheet-feed labels are available in single-column sheets (with 10 or 11 labels per sheet) and three-column sheets (with 30 or more labels per sheet). The procedure for printing single-column sheet labels differs from the procedure for printing three-column sheets.

Printing Single-Column Sheet-Feed Labels

When you print sheet labels, you must create one set of address data fields for each label on the sheet. For most single-column sheet-feed labels, you must create a main document with 10 or 11 sets of data fields, each followed by the NEXT instruction. The NEXT instruction tells Word to print the next label without starting a new page.

To print single column sheet-feed labels, do the following:

1. Open a new, blank document. Choose **View Preferences** (Alt-VE) and make sure that an X is in the **Paragraph Marks** check box.

2. On the first line of the document, type a DATA instruction to tell Word where to find the data.

   If your data document is called MAILLIST.DOC, type «MAILLIST.DOC». (You can omit the period and extension if you want.) Be sure to enter the chevrons with Ctrl-[and Ctrl-].

3. *Important:* Type the first line of field names on the same line as the DATA instruction, with no space between the DATA instruction and the first field name.

   If you're using MAILLIST.DOC, type the following to print the first line of the label correctly:

   «DATA MAILLIST.DOC»«FIRSTNAME» «LASTNAME»

   Note the space between «FIRSTNAME» and «LASTNAME»

4. Press Enter to start a new line.

5. Type the second line of field names you want printed on the mailing labels.

   With MAILLIST.DOC, you type *«ADDRESS»*

6. Press Enter to start a new line.

7. Type the third line of field names you want printed on the mailing labels.

   With MAILLIST.DOC, you type *«CITY», «STATE» «ZIP»*

   Note the punctuation and spaces.

8. Press Enter *twice*.

   You press Enter twice so that Word skips to the next label before printing the next address. You may have to adjust the number of blank lines so that the labels print properly.

9. Type *«NEXT»*, and without pressing Enter, type the first line of field names on the same line as the NEXT instruction with no space between the DATA instruction and the first field name.

   If you're using MAILLIST.DOC, type the following to print the line correctly:

«NEXT»«FIRSTNAME» «LASTNAME»

Note the space between «FIRSTNAME» and «LASTNAME»

10. Type the rest of the field labels, and press Enter twice.

The text in your document should look *exactly* like the one in Figure 16.18. You select the text in the next step.

11. Select the second set of data fields. Be sure to include the NEXT instruction and the two trailing paragraph marks.

See figure 16.18 to see how the data fields should be selected.

12. Choose **Edit C**opy (Alt-EC) or press Ctrl-Ins.

13. Place the cursor on the last paragraph mark in the document and press Enter.

14. Choose **Edit P**aste (Alt-EP) or press Shift-Ins to paste copies of the data fields in your document.

If the sheets have 10 labels, choose this command eight times. Your document should look like the one in figure 16.19.

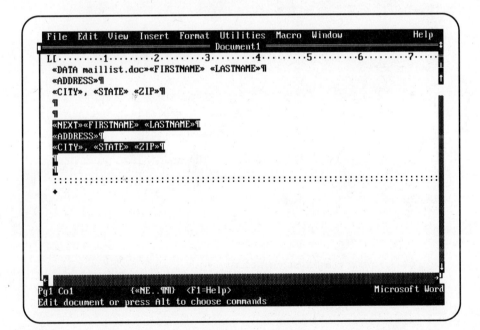

Fig. 16.18. Address data fields with NEXT instruction.

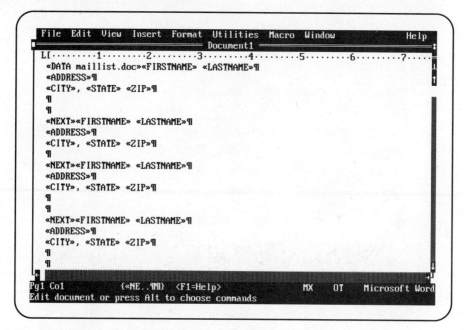

Fig. 16.19. Main document for printing single-column sheet-feed labels.

15. Make sure there are exactly two blank lines between each set of data fields.

16. Choose Format **M**argins (Alt-TM).

    You must set margins of 0" top, bottom, and right.

17. In the **T**op, **B**ottom, and **R**ight text boxes, type *0"*.

    These margins would interfere with the proper placement of text on the labels, which are only 1" high.

18. In the **L**eft text box, type an indentation (such as *0.25"* or *0.5"*) so that Word won't start printing at the left edge of the labels.

19. Choose OK.

20. Choose **F**ile Print **M**erge (Alt-FM).

    You must print your document with the Print **M**erge command— the **P**rint command won't work.

21. Choose **P**rint.

22. Choose OK.

Note: Some laser printers may have difficulty printing close to the margins (within 0.5 or 0.25 inch). You may have to add a 0.25-inch top margin and a 0.5-inch bottom margin to get the labels to print correctly.

Printing Three-Column Sheet-Feed Labels

When you print sheet labels, you must create one set of address data fields for each label on the sheet. Most three-column sheet-feed labels contain at least 30 labels. Therefore, you must create a main document with 30 or more sets of data fields, each followed by the NEXT instruction. The NEXT instruction tells Word to print the next label without starting a new page.

Besides creating one set of data fields for each label on the sheet, you must create a three-column section format to print your labels properly.

To print three-column sheet-feed labels, follow these steps:

1. Follow steps 1 through 13 in the preceding section.

2. Choose **Edit Paste** (Alt-EP) or press Shift-Ins to paste copies of the data fields in your document.

   If the sheets have 30 labels, choose this command 28 times. At this point, your document should look like the one in figure 16.19.

3. Make sure there are exactly two blank lines between each set of data fields.

4. Choose **Format Section** (Alt-TS).

5. Type *3* in the **Number** text box.

6. Type *0"* in the **Spacing** text box.

7. Choose Column in the **Section Start** drop-down list box.

8. Choose **Margins**.

9. In the Section Margins dialog box, set margins of 0" top, bottom, and right.

10. In the **Top**, **Bottom**, and **Right** text boxes, type *0"*.

    These margins would interfere with the proper placement of text on the labels, which are only 1" high. If you're using a laser printer, try setting a top margin of 0.5" and a bottom margin of 0.25".

11. In the **Left** text box, type an indentation (such as *0.25"* or *0.5"*) so that Word won't start printing at the left edge of the labels.

12. Choose OK.

13. Choose File Print **Merge** (Alt-FM).

    You must print your document with the Print Merge command— the **Print** command won't work.

14. Choose **Print**.

15. Choose OK.

Chapter Summary

This chapter explains how to create a form-letter application that requires a data document and a main document. The data document contains field names separated by tabs, and the data, with each data record occupying its own line. The main document begins with the DATA instruction that tells Word where to find the data to insert. The text of the letter is contained also in the main document, with field names inserted wherever you want Word to fill in the information automatically. You should always double-check the field names before printing your form letter with the Print **Merge** command. This chapter also discusses error messages and what to do to fix the problems, and concludes with instructions for printing mailing labels.

Merge has more capabilities than this chapter discusses. You can use comparison operators (such as greater than and less than), Boolean operators (AND, OR, NOT), and other advanced features to refine your IF...THEN expressions, and you can also use an IF...THEN...ELSE instruction. You can use the SET and ASK instructions to define variables or prompt the user for input at the time of printing. If your data document contains figures, you can write expressions that perform calculations on these figures. Most of these advanced features lie beyond the scope of this book, but you find a discussion of the SET and ASK commands in the next chapter, "Creating Forms and Illustrations."

This chapter concludes Part III, "Word 5.5's Features and Applications." The next section of the book covers what are perhaps the most exciting features of Word 5.5: its graphics and desktop publishing capabilities.

Quick Review

Data Document

To create a data document:

1. Open a new, blank document.

2. Type the header record, separating each field name with a comma or tab keystroke.

3. At the end of the line, press Enter.

4. Type the first data record, entering the data in the order established in the data record. Be sure to use exactly the same number of tabs you used in the header record.

5. Press Enter to start a new line.

6. Repeat steps 4 and 5 until you have typed all the data records. Don't press Enter at the end of the last record.

7. Save the data document.

To use data drawn from a database management program:

1. Print the data to an ASCII file, separated by commas or tabs.

2. Open the ASCII file with Word.

3. Add a header record at the beginning of the document. You must add one field name for each data field in the data records below.

4. Check to make sure each data record has exactly the same number of fields.

5. Save the document.

To sort and renumber the data document:

1. Open the data document (MAILLIST.DOC).

2. Position the cursor at the upper right corner of the column you want to use as the sort key.

3. Press Ctrl-Shift-F8 to toggle on the column-select mode.

4. Select the entire column, but don't select the header record.

5. Choose Utilities Sort (Alt-UO).

6. Choose **Ascending** sort order and, in the Key Type area, **Alpha-numeric**.

7. Choose OK.

8. Select all the lines of data (but not the header record).

9. Choose Utilities **Renumber** (Alt-UR).

10. Choose **All** and make sure that an X is in the Restart Sequence check box.

11. Choose OK.

Mailing Labels

To print continuous-fed labels:

1. Open a new, blank document.

2. On the first line of the document, type a DATA instruction to tell Word where to find the data.

3. *Important:* Type the first line of field names on the same line as the DATA instruction, with no space between the DATA instruction and the first field name.

4. Press Enter to start a new line.

5. Type the second line of field names you want printed on the mailing labels.

6. Press Enter to start a new line.

7. Type the third line of field names you want printed on the mailing labels.

8. Choose Format **Margins** (Alt-TM).

9. In the **Height** text box, type the height of the labels you're using.

10. In the Top, **Bottom**, and **Right** text boxes, type *0"*.

11. In the **Left** text box, type an indentation (such as *0.25"* or *0.5"*) so that Word won't start printing at the left edge of the labels.

12. Choose OK.

13. Choose File Print **Merge** (Alt-FM).

14. Choose Print.

15. Choose OK.

To print single-column sheet-feed labels:

1. Open a new, blank document. Choose **View Preferences** (Alt-VE) and make sure that an X is in the **Paragraph Marks** check box.

2. On the first line of the document, type a DATA instruction to tell Word where to find the data.

3. *Important:* Type the first line of field names on the same line as the DATA instruction, with no space between the DATA instruction and the first field name.

4. Press Enter to start a new line.

5. Type the second line of field names you want printed on the mailing labels.

6. Press Enter to start a new line.

7. Type the third line of field names you want printed on the mailing labels.

8. Press Enter *twice*.

9. Type «*NEXT*», and without pressing enter, type the first line of field names on the same line as the NEXT instruction with no space between the DATA instruction and the first field name.

10. Type the rest of the field labels, and press Enter twice.

11. Select the second set of data fields. Be sure to include the NEXT instruction and the two trailing paragraph marks.

12. Choose **Edit Copy** (Alt-EC) or press Ctrl-Ins.

13. Place the cursor on the last paragraph mark in the document, and press Enter.

14. Choose **Edit Paste** (Alt-EP) or press Shift-Ins to paste copies of the data fields in your document.

15. Make sure there exactly two blank lines appear between each set of data fields.

16. Choose **Format Margins** (Alt-TM).

17. In the **Top**, **Bottom**, and **Right** text boxes, type *0"*.

18. In the **Left** text box, type an indentation (such as *0.25"* or *0.5"*) so that Word won't start printing at the left edge of the labels. If you're using a laser printer, try a 0.25" top margin and a 0.5" bottom margin.

19. Choose OK.

20. Choose **File Print Merge** (Alt-FM).

21. Choose Print.

22. Choose OK.

To print three-column sheet-feed labels:

1. Follow steps 1 through 13 in the preceding set of instructions (on printing single-column sheet-feed labels).

2. Choose **Edit Paste** (Alt-EP) or press Shift-Ins to paste copies of the data fields in your document.

3. Make sure there are exactly two blank lines between each set of data fields.

4. Choose **Format Section** (Alt-TS).

5. Type *3* in the **Number** text box.

6. Type *0"* in the Spacing text box.

7. Choose Column in the Section Start drop-down list box.

8. Choose **Margins**.

9. In the **Top**, **Bottom**, and **Right** text boxes, type *0"*.

10. In the **Left** text box, type an indentation (such as *0.25"* or *0.5"*) so that Word won't start printing at the left edge of the labels.

11. Choose OK.

12. Choose **File Print Merge** (Alt-FM).

13. Choose Print.

14. Choose OK.

Main Document

To create the main document:

1. Type a DATA instruction on the first line. Press Ctrl-[to enter the left chevron. Type the word DATA followed by a space, and then type the name of the data document. (You can omit the period and DOC extension, if you want.) Press Ctrl-] to close the DATA instruction.

2. Press Enter.

3. Type the text that you want to print on every copy of the document.

4. Insert field names into the document where you want Word to insert data from the data document. To type a field name, press Ctrl-[to enter the left chevron. Type the field name exactly the way you typed it in the data document's header record. Press Ctrl-] to enter the right chevron.

5. Save the main document.

Printing

To print the Merge application:

1. Open the main document.

2. Choose **File Print Merge** (Alt-FM).

3. Choose **Print**.

4. Choose OK.

To print to a Word file:

1. Open the main document.

2. Choose **File Print Merge** (Alt-FM).

3. Choose **New Document**.

4. Type a name for the document.

5. Choose OK.

To print records you specify:

1. Open the main document.

2. Choose **File Print Merge** (Alt-FM).

3. Choose **Records**.

   In the **Records** box, type the numbers of the data records you want to print. You can type individual numbers (*1,3,9*), a series, (*9-27*), or a combination of the two (*1,3,9-27*).

4. Choose **Print**.

5. Choose OK.

Part IV

Desktop Publishing
with
Microsoft Word

Includes

Creating Forms and Illustrations

**Page Layout I: Adding Graphics and
Anchoring Paragraphs**

**Page Layout II: Multiple-Column Text
and Newsletters**

Chapter 17

Creating Forms and Illustrations

When people think of desktop publishing, they frequently think of the more glamorous and exciting applications, such as creating newsletters that win design awards or experimenting with exotic fonts. The bread and butter of desktop publishing, however, comes from much more mundane applications, such as creating and printing business forms: invoices, employee pay sheets, or quarterly report forms, to give a few examples.

Common as they are, forms represent a big expense for most organizations. A well-designed form prompts an individual to provide precisely the information an organization needs to accomplish a task. Organizations pay much money to have printers design and print custom forms to suit the way the organization does its business. If you have Word 5.5 and a reasonably good printer, however, you may be able to save your organization the expense of paying a professional to design a custom form, because Word 5.5's tools for designing forms are very good.

Word includes many useful tools for designing and filling in forms. The Format Border command makes it easy to create boxes and lines. Word's tab capabilities include a vertical tab, which you also can use to create vertical lines within boxes. You can add finishing touches with Word's Line Draw mode, which turns the cursor into a "pen" capable of drawing straight vertical and horizontal lines wherever you want.

After you have finished your form, you can set up a merge application with the SET and ASK commands so that you're automatically prompted to supply the needed information. With the addition of a few simple math expressions, you can create a form that automatically totals the figures you supply. You also can use the Line Draw mode to create simple illustrations for reports and proposals. All these tools are useful in business and professional settings, and it's well worth your time to investigate them.

523

This chapter covers the following subjects:

- Creating a good-looking form using the Paragraph Borders dialog box and vertical tabs

- Adding data entry marks to your form, which give you a way to move the cursor around your form without disturbing the text or the tab keystrokes

- Creating an automated form application with the merge ASK command, which prompts you to type the information to be printed on the form

- Understanding the many Border options

- Using the Line Draw mode to create simple illustrations with Word

Note: To make full use of the material in this chapter, your printer must be capable of printing the IBM extended character set. If you're not sure that your printer can print these characters, check your manual or call your dealer before proceeding. Sometimes it's necessary to set a switch before your printer can handle these characters.

This chapter assumes that you have some knowledge of tab formatting, math, and the File Print Merge command, so you might find it helpful to read or skim Chapter 11, "Creating Tables and Lists with Tabs, Sort, and Math," and Chapter 16, "Creating Form Letters," before proceeding.

Creating the Form

Using Word 5.5's easy-to-use vertical tabs and the Format Border command, you can create a form quickly. After you have created your form, you can print and duplicate it so that people can fill it out by hand. If you prefer to keep the form application completely automated, however, you can fill out the form using Word.

Like the preceding chapter, this chapter includes several tutorials. Although it's tedious to follow keystroke-by-keystroke tutorials, they are worthwhile when you're dealing with difficult or complicated material. Besides, the tutorials illustrate many important Word 5 techniques besides cranking out forms.

> *Caution:* Use a 12-point, fixed-space font, such as Courier for this exercise. If you use a proportionally spaced font or a font larger or smaller than 12-point type, your printer may not print the form the way it looks on the screen.

To create your first form, follow these steps:

1. If the Ruler is not displayed, choose **View Ruler** (Alt-VR) or click the Ruler icon.

2. Choose **View Preferences** (Alt-VE) and make sure there are X marks in the **Tabs** and **Paragraph Marks** in the Non-Printing Characters area.

   You need to see the tab and paragraph marks to create your form.

3. Choose **Format Margins** (Alt-TM) and choose new left and right margins of 0.75". Choose OK.

   This form requires a 7-inch line length.

4. Press Ctrl-C to center the cursor; then type the heading shown in figure 17.1.

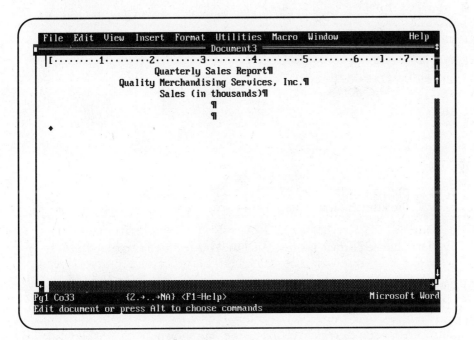

Fig. 17.1. *A heading for a business form.*

5. Press Enter after you type the heading.

6. Press Ctrl-L to align the line flush left.

7. Set the following centered tabs:

    0.5"

    1.5"

    2.5"

    3.5"

    4.5"

    5.5"

    6.5"

    For instructions on setting tabs, see Chapter 11, "Creating Tables and Lists with Tabs, Sort, and Math."

8. Set vertical tabs at the following locations:

    1.0"

    2.0"

    3.0"

    4.0"

    5.0"

    6.0"

9. Type *Model* and press Tab.

10. Continue typing the rest of the headings (*North*, *South*, and so on) shown in figure 17.2, pressing Tab after each, until you get to the last heading (Total). Don't press Enter or Tab after you type *Total*.

11. Choose Forma**t B**order (Alt-TB). You see the Paragraph Borders dialog box.

12. Choose **B**ox Each Paragraph.

13. Choose OK.

    Your screen should look like the one shown in figure 17.2.

14. With the cursor placed on the paragraph mark at the end of the line of headings, press Enter.

    Word copies all the formats you have chosen, including the vertical tabs and the border, to the next paragraph.

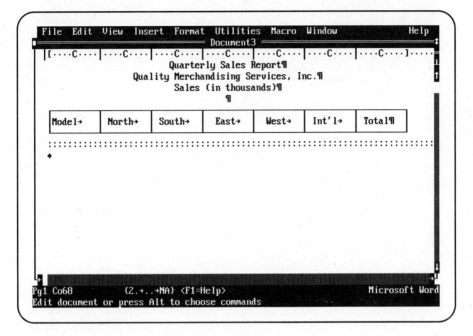

File   Edit   View   Insert   Format   Utilities   Macro   Window   Help
                                      Document3
[···C····|····C····|····C····|····C····|····C····|····C····|····C····]····|····

                            Quarterly Sales Report¶
                        Quality Merchandising Services, Inc.¶
                            Sales (in thousands)¶
                                      ¶

Model→	North→	South→	East→	West→	Int'l→	Total¶

Pg1 Co68   {2.→..→NA} <F1=Help>   Microsoft Word
Edit document or press Alt to choose commands

Fig. 17.2. Boxed headings for a business form.

15. Change the centered tabs at 1.5", 2.5", 3.5", 4.5", 5.5", and 6.5" to decimal tabs.

16. Press Enter twice to copy down the screen the format you have just created.

Your form should look like the one shown in figure 17.3.

As you can see, setting up a handsome form with Microsoft Word is easy. You can print this form and duplicate it if you want.

To create a more visually interesting form, use Format Position to position text and boxes on the screen. This command is introduced in Chapter 18, "Page Layout I: Adding Graphics and Anchoring Paragraphs."

Filling In Forms On-Screen

When people fill in forms like the one you just created, they do so on duplicates of the printouts you make. If you prefer, though, you can create a form that you or others can fill in right on the screen.

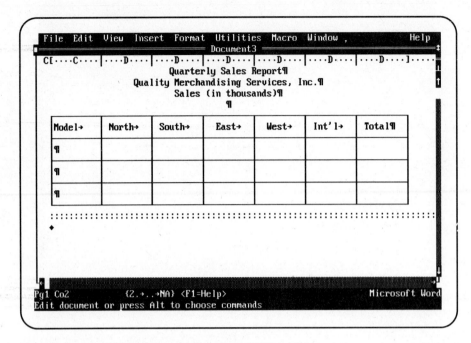

Fig. 17.3. Boxed headings copied by pressing Enter.

There are two ways to fill in forms on-screen:

- **Using Data Entry Marks.** To create a form this way, you add data entry marks to the areas where you want the user to type data. To move the cursor directly to the mark, you use the Ctrl-→ and Ctrl-← commands. You use this technique to create a filled-in form that you can save or print.

- **Using the SET and ASK Commands.** To create a form with the SET and ASK commands, you add these Merge commands to your document, and place field names where you want Word to print the information. When you choose **File Print Merge**, Word prompts you to supply the needed information. The program then prints a copy of the form, with the information inserted in the proper areas of the form. The result is a printout with all the information filled in. You can print the document to disk.

Filling In the Form Manually

In the following tutorial, you add data entry marks to the form you created earlier in this chapter. You enter the data entry marks by pressing Ctrl-], the same command you use to create a right chevron in a Merge application. You then use the Ctrl-→ and Ctrl-← commands, which move the cursor directly to the data marks.

Adding the Data Entry Marks

The form you created needs to have data entry marks added to it so that information is inserted in the appropriate place.

Follow these steps to insert the data entry marks:

1. Choose View Preferences (Alt-VE).

2. Make sure that an X is in the Hidden Text field.

3. Type model names in the first column as shown in figure 17.4. Press Enter after you type each model name.

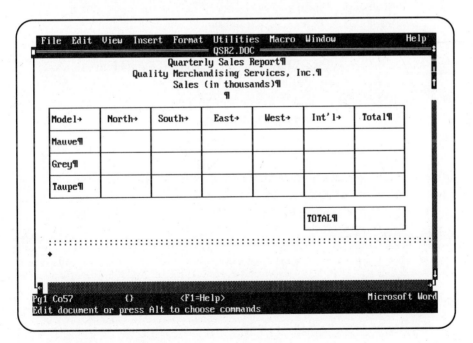

Fig. 17.4. The sales report form with model names.

4. Position the cursor after the first model name and press Tab.

5. Press Ctrl-H to format the data entry mark as hidden text.

6. Press Ctrl-] to enter the first data entry mark (a right chevron—»).

7. Press Ctrl-H to toggle hidden text off.

8. Press Tab, and continue pressing Tab until you have entered tab marks in all the boxes except the last one (under "Total").

9. Add tab marks to the next two lines. Now all the blank boxes contain tab marks, except the boxes under Total.

10. Select the data entry mark (the right chevron—») that you formatted as hidden text. It's not enough to place the cursor on the character; you must highlight it.

11. Choose Edit Copy (Alt-EC) or use the Ctrl-Ins keyboard shortcut.

12. Place the cursor on the next tab mark, and choose Edit Paste (Alt-EP) or use the Shift-Ins keyboard shortcut to paste in a copy of the hidden text data entry mark. Make sure that NumLock is off.

13. Repeat step 12 until you have added data entry marks, formatted as hidden text, before all the tab marks and before all three paragraph marks (see fig. 17.5).

   If you have followed these steps correctly, the data entry marks are formatted as hidden text, but the tab marks and paragraph marks are not.

14. Save the form and close the document.

You use a special command, Ctrl-→, to jump to the next data entry mark. This command makes it very easy to fill in the data without disturbing the headings or tab settings in the form. And after you have filled in the data, you can use Word's built-in math capabilities to obtain totals.

Adding the Data

Now that you have the data entry marks inserted, you need to know how to put them to use.

Follow these steps to add data to your form:

1. Choose File Open (Alt-FO).

2. Choose Read Only.

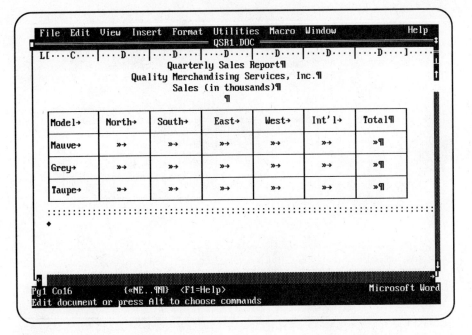

Fig. 17.5. The form showing data entry, tab, and paragraph marks.

You want to preserve your blank form for use at another time. By loading the file in read-only mode, you ensure that you cannot overwrite the blank form; you can save your work, but you must do so using a new file name.

3. Choose OK.

   Important: After the file is open, check the status bar to make sure that OT (overtype mode) is turned off. Don't type anything until overtype is turned off.

4. Press Ctrl-→ to move to the first data entry mark.

5. Type the first sales figure shown in figure 17.6.

6. Press Ctrl-→ to move to the next data entry mark.

   Don't press Tab; if you do, you will disturb the tab settings. If you press Tab accidentally, be sure to delete the extra tab keystroke symbol by pressing Del once.

7. Continue in this way until you have added data to the whole form, as shown in figure 17.6.

If you want to go back to a previous data entry mark, use the Ctrl-← command.

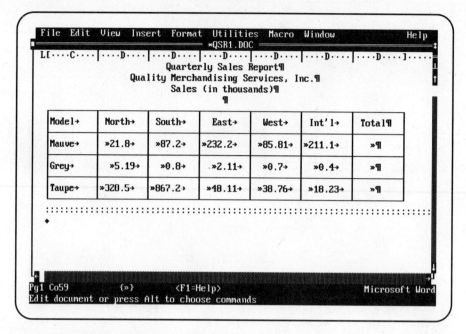

Fig. 17.6. The sales report form with data.

Obtaining Totals with Math

You can use Word 5.5's built-in math capabilities to add the values.

Follow these instructions to use math in your form:

1. Select all the numbers in the the first row of the form, except the model name (see fig. 17.7). If you select the model name, Word will ignore the name and not include it in the total because it's composed of letters, not numbers.

2. Press F2. The total appears in the scrap (see fig. 17.7).

3. Position the cursor on the paragraph mark in the Total column.

4. Press Shift-Ins. Word inserts the total at the cursor's location.

5. Continue in this way until all the rows are totaled (see fig. 17.8.)

You can total the Total column by selecting the column in the column-select mode (Shift-Ctrl-F8) and pressing F2 (see fig. 17.9).

```
   File  Edit  View  Insert  Format  Utilities  Macro  Window              Help
                              ═*QSR1.DOC ═══════════════════════════════════
 L[···C···│···D····│···D····│···D····│···D····│···D····│···D····]····
                           Quarterly Sales Report¶
                       Quality Merchandising Services, Inc.¶
                            Sales (in thousands)¶
                                   ¶
   ┌──────────┬──────────┬──────────┬──────────┬──────────┬──────────┬──────────┐
   │ Model→   │ North→   │ South→   │ East→    │ West→    │ Int'l→   │ Total¶   │
   ├──────────┼──────────┼──────────┼──────────┼──────────┼──────────┼──────────┤
   │ Mauve→   │ »21.8→   │ »87.2→   │ »232.2→  │ »85.81→  │ »211.1→  │ »¶       │
   ├──────────┼──────────┼──────────┼──────────┼──────────┼──────────┼──────────┤
   │ Grey→    │ »5.19→   │ »0.8→    │ »2.11→   │ »0.7→    │ »0.4→    │ »¶       │
   ├──────────┼──────────┼──────────┼──────────┼──────────┼──────────┼──────────┤
   │ Taupe→   │ »328.5→  │ »867.2→  │ »48.11→  │ »38.76→  │ »18.23→  │ »¶       │
   └──────────┴──────────┴──────────┴──────────┴──────────┴──────────┴──────────┘
   :::::::::::::::::::::::::::::::::::::::::::::::::::::::::::::::::::::::::::::::
   ◆

 Pg1 Co57          {638.11}   <F1=Help>                        Microsoft Word
 Calculation result is 638.11
```

Fig. 17.7. Highlighting a row of values for addition.

```
   File  Edit  View  Insert  Format  Utilities  Macro  Window              Help
                              ═*QSR1.DOC ═══════════════════════════════════
 L[···C···│···D····│···D····│···D····│···D····│···D····│···D····]····
                           Quarterly Sales Report¶
                       Quality Merchandising Services, Inc.¶
                            Sales (in thousands)¶
                                   ¶
   ┌──────────┬──────────┬──────────┬──────────┬──────────┬──────────┬──────────┐
   │ Model→   │ North→   │ South→   │ East→    │ West→    │ Int'l→   │ Total¶   │
   ├──────────┼──────────┼──────────┼──────────┼──────────┼──────────┼──────────┤
   │ Mauve→   │ »21.8→   │ »87.2→   │ »232.2→  │ »85.81→  │ »211.1→  │ »638.11¶ │
   ├──────────┼──────────┼──────────┼──────────┼──────────┼──────────┼──────────┤
   │ Grey→    │ »5.19→   │ »0.8→    │ »2.11→   │ »0.7→    │ »0.4→    │ »9.20¶   │
   ├──────────┼──────────┼──────────┼──────────┼──────────┼──────────┼──────────┤
   │ Taupe→   │ »328.5→  │ »867.2→  │ »48.11→  │ »38.76→  │ »18.23→  │ »1300.80¶│
   └──────────┴──────────┴──────────┴──────────┴──────────┴──────────┴──────────┘
   :::::::::::::::::::::::::::::::::::::::::::::::::::::::::::::::::::::::::::::::
   ◆

 Pg1 Co69          {1300.80}   <F1=Help>                        Microsoft Word
 Edit document or press Alt to choose commands
```

Fig. 17.8. The sales report form with line totals.

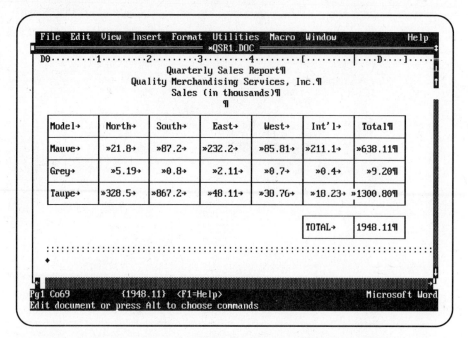

Fig. 17.9. The sales report form showing the total of the Total column.

You created the border format for the Total entry at the bottom of the form by indenting the paragraph 5.0" from the left margin, adding a box, and adding the necessary tabs (vertical at 6.0", decimal at 6.5").

You can print this form. To save the form to disk, choose the Save **As** command. If you choose Save, you see the message, `File is read-only. Save with a different file name.` In this way, you preserve the blank version of the form on disk.

Creating a Form Application with Print Merge

Using the Ctrl-→ command, you can fill in a form manually quite easily. However, you must move the cursor around the screen. An even easier way to fill in a form is to set it up so that Word automatically prompts you to supply the required information. The key is to use some of the same commands you use to create a form-letter application and to print your form using Print Merge. The goal isn't to print many copies of the form; you will print just one copy. But using these commands helps to automate what could be a tedious task.

When you add the ASK instruction to your document and print it with Print Merge, Word pauses and asks you to enter a certain type of information. After you do, Word links the information you have supplied to a field name and prints the information wherever you have inserted the field name in your document. You can use the SET instruction to perform computations on the information you have linked to field names.

In the following tutorial, you learn how to create a Print Merge version of the form document you just created.

Follow the instructions outlined in the following steps to learn how to create a Print Merge document:

1. Open the form you just created and delete all the data entry marks and tab marks.

   Your document should look like the one in figure 17.10.

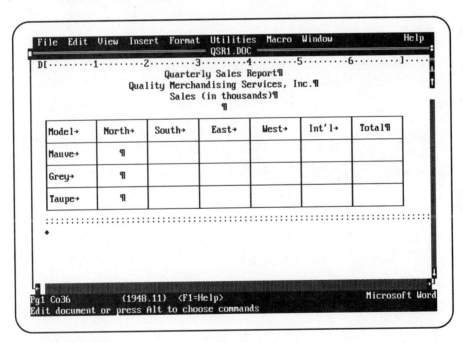

Fig. 17.10. *A blank form for a Print Merge application.*

2. Add the line

   Sales for month of «month», «year»

   below the title (see fig. 17.11). Add the chevrons by using the Ctrl-[and Ctrl-] commands.

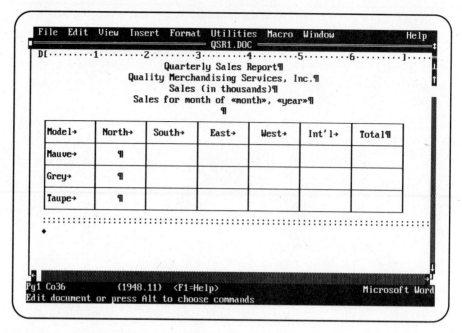

Fig. 17.11. Adding a line to the total.

3. Add field names to each cell in the form, using a unique (but brief) name for each, such as mN for mauve north (see fig. 17.12). Enter the chevrons with the Ctrl-[and Ctrl-] commands.

4. Press Ctrl-Home to move the cursor to the beginning of the document, press Enter to create a blank line, press ↑ to highlight the new line, and press Ctrl-L to cancel the centered paragraph formatting.

5. Now enter the ASK and SET commands as they are shown in figure 17.13. Enter the chevrons by using the Ctrl-[and Ctrl-] commands.

   Double-check the field names. If you enter one of them improperly, the application will not work correctly. Enter all the equal signs and question marks carefully, too. Each ASK and SET instruction must be surrounded by chevrons.

6. Select all the ASK and SET instructions, including their paragraph marks, and format them as hidden text.

File Edit View Insert Format Utilities Macro Window Help
QSR1.DOC
Quarterly Sales Report¶
Quality Merchandising Services, Inc.¶
Sales (in thousands)¶
Sales for month of «month», «year»¶
Model→ North→ South→ East→ West→ Int'l→ Total¶
Mauve→ «mN»→ «mS»→ «mE»→ «mW»→ «mI»→ «tM»¶
Grey→ «gN»→ «gS»→ «gE»→ «gW»→ «gI»→ «tG»¶
Taupe→ «tN»→ «tS»→ «tE»→ «tW»→ «tI»→ «tT»¶
TOTAL→ «total»¶
Edit document or press Alt to choose commands

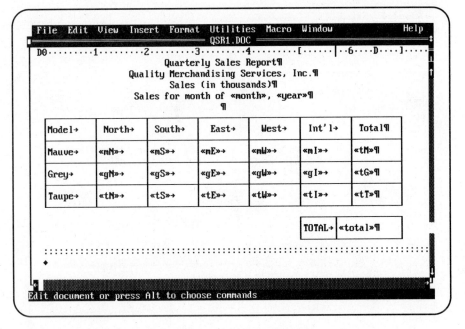

Fig. 17.12. Adding field names and chevrons to each cell.

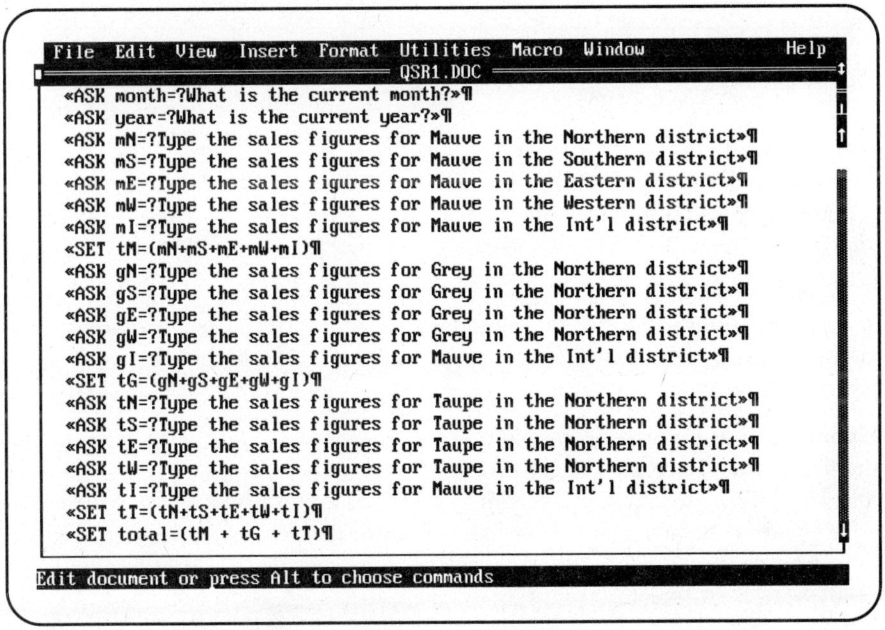

File Edit View Insert Format Utilities Macro Window Help
QSR1.DOC
«ASK month=?What is the current month?»¶
«ASK year=?What is the current year?»¶
«ASK mN=?Type the sales figures for Mauve in the Northern district»¶
«ASK mS=?Type the sales figures for Mauve in the Southern district»¶
«ASK mE=?Type the sales figures for Mauve in the Eastern district»¶
«ASK mW=?Type the sales figures for Mauve in the Western district»¶
«ASK mI=?Type the sales figures for Mauve in the Int'l district»¶
«SET tM=(mN+mS+mE+mW+mI)¶
«ASK gN=?Type the sales figures for Grey in the Northern district»¶
«ASK gS=?Type the sales figures for Grey in the Northern district»¶
«ASK gE=?Type the sales figures for Grey in the Northern district»¶
«ASK gW=?Type the sales figures for Grey in the Northern district»¶
«ASK gI=?Type the sales figures for Mauve in the Int'l district»¶
«SET tG=(gN+gS+gE+gW+gI)¶
«ASK tN=?Type the sales figures for Taupe in the Northern district»¶
«ASK tS=?Type the sales figures for Taupe in the Northern district»¶
«ASK tE=?Type the sales figures for Taupe in the Northern district»¶
«ASK tW=?Type the sales figures for Taupe in the Northern district»¶
«ASK tI=?Type the sales figures for Mauve in the Int'l district»¶
«SET tT=(tN+tS+tE+tW+tI)¶
«SET total=(tM + tG + tT)¶
Edit document or press Alt to choose commands

Fig. 17.13. The ASK and SET commands.

7. To run your application, choose the Print Merge Printer command. You will be asked to respond to prompts that appear in the command area (see fig. 17.14).

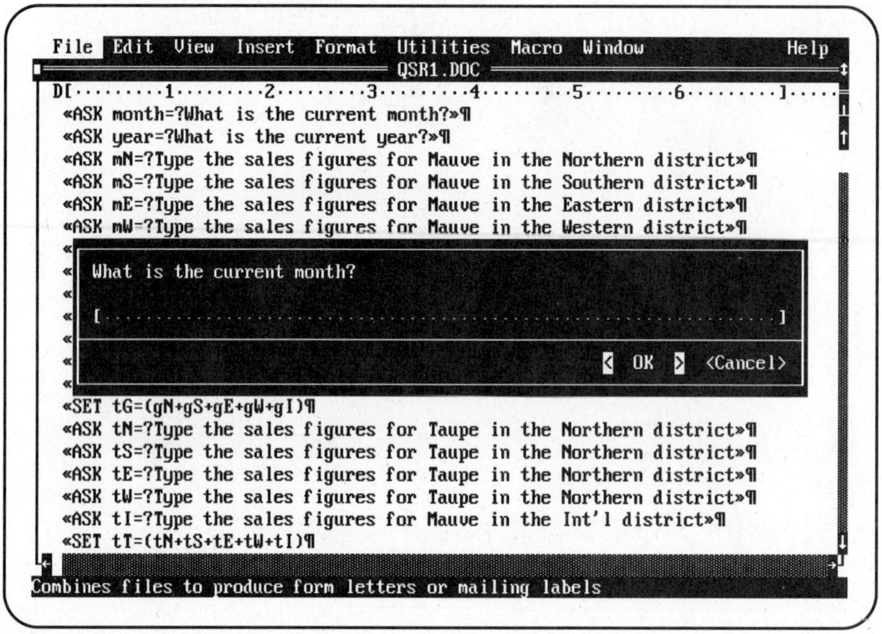

```
  File  Edit  View  Insert  Format  Utilities  Macro  Window            Help
 ════════════════════════════════ QSR1.DOC ══════════════════════════════
  D[········1·········2·········3·········4·········5·········6·········]····
  «ASK month=?What is the current month?»¶
  «ASK year=?What is the current year?»¶
  «ASK mN=?Type the sales figures for Mauve in the Northern district»¶
  «ASK mS=?Type the sales figures for Mauve in the Southern district»¶
  «ASK mE=?Type the sales figures for Mauve in the Eastern district»¶
  «ASK mW=?Type the sales figures for Mauve in the Western district»¶
  «
  «    What is the current month?
  «
  «    [·············································································]
  «
  «                                              ◄  OK  ►  <Cancel>
  «
  «SET tG=(gN+gS+gE+gW+gI)»¶
  «ASK tN=?Type the sales figures for Taupe in the Northern district»¶
  «ASK tS=?Type the sales figures for Taupe in the Northern district»¶
  «ASK tE=?Type the sales figures for Taupe in the Northern district»¶
  «ASK tW=?Type the sales figures for Taupe in the Northern district»¶
  «ASK tI=?Type the sales figures for Mauve in the Int'l district»¶
  «SET tI=(tN+tS+tE+tW+tI)»¶
 Combines files to produce form letters or mailing labels
```

Fig. 17.14. Dialog box generated by ASK command.

When you supply information to a response command menu, Word links the information you type to the field name you included in the ASK instruction. When you're asked to name the current month, for instance, Word links what you type with the field name called Month. Wherever you have inserted that field name in your form, Word prints what you have typed.

To test the application, enter simple figures (enter 10 for all the Mauve sales, 20 for all the Gray sales, and 30 for the Taupe) to check whether the application is working properly.

If your application doesn't work properly, make sure that you have spelled all the field names correctly. Make sure, too, that each field name, as well as each ASK and SET instruction, is surrounded by chevrons. Check what you see on your screen carefully against the figures in this chapter.

More About Format Border

The lines and boxes you create with the Paragraph Borders dialog box are paragraph formats (see fig. 17.15). That means the lines and borders are stored in the paragraph mark: if you delete the mark, you lose the lines and boxes. If you press Enter at the end of a paragraph, Word copies the lines and boxes to the next paragraph.

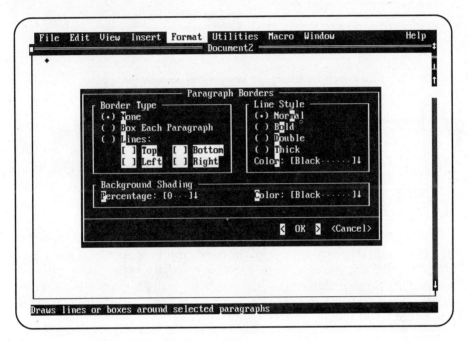

Fig. 17.15. The Paragraph Borders dialog box.

You can box a paragraph, or if you want, you can place a line above it, below it, to the right, and to the left. You can choose among several line styles (Normal Bold, Double, and Thick). If you have a color printer, you can choose a color. Figure 17.16 shows the various box and line options.

If you choose the **B**ox Each Paragraph option, Word keeps the lines together on one page. If there isn't enough room on the current page, Word moves all the lines to the next page. Don't choose the **B**ox Each Paragraph option for a paragraph that's longer than one page.

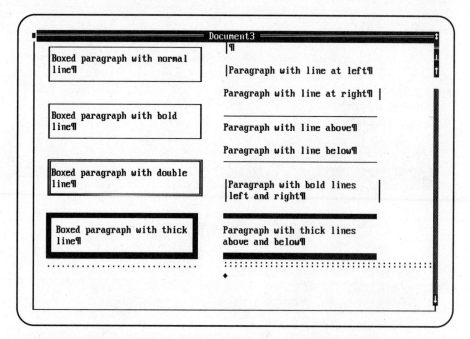

Fig. 17.16. Box and line options.

The lines and boxes you enter with the Paragraph Borders dialog box aren't affected by the text you enter or delete, unless you delete the paragraph mark in which they're stored. If you do, the line or box will disappear. If you add or delete text without deleting the paragraph mark, Word adjusts the size of the line or box as needed.

Left and right borders and lines are printed at the paragraph indent position. To indent a box from the left and right, type an indentation in the From **L**eft and From **R**ight text boxes of the Paragraph dialog box.

You can shade the bordered paragraph. If you're using a non-PostScript printer, Word uses graphics characters drawn from the standard IBM character set to shade the paragraph; the results may not be satisfactory, however. Users of PostScript printers can expect excellent results.

If you have a color printer, you can color the shading you have chosen.

To remove lines, borders, or shading, place the cursor in the paragraph containing these formats. Choose Format **B**orders (Alt-TB) again and delete the options you have chosen.

If you place boxes around two paragraphs, Word draws a common border between them if they have the same indentation. If they have different indentation or if they have different line styles, Word draws separate boxes. Word also draws separate boxes if you have added blank lines between the paragraphs using the Before or After text boxes option of the Paragraph dialog box (or the Ctrl-O keyboard shortcut). For an illustration, see figure 17.17.

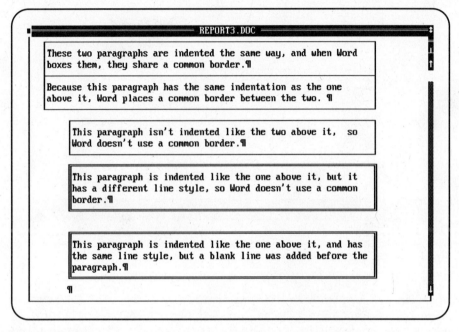

Fig. 17.17. Paragraphs with and without common borders.

Creating Illustrations with Cursor Line Draw

If your printer can print the IBM extended character set, you can create simple illustrations with Word's Line Draw mode (Utilities Line Draw). Line Draw turns the cursor into a "pen" that draws vertical and horizontal lines by using graphics characters from the extended character set. You can use Cursor Line Draw to create very simple illustrations (see fig. 17.18).

Line Draw is no substitute for a good graphics or illustration program. You can enter only horizontal or vertical lines, and it is easy to make mistakes that are difficult to fix. Worse, the line draw characters are made up of the standard IBM graphics characters, and like any character, they can be disturbed if you enter

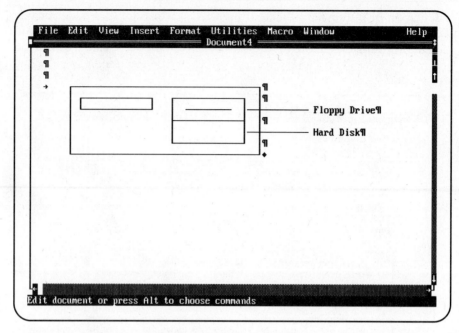

Fig. 17.18. Simple illustration created with Line Draw.

or delete text. Generally speaking, mixing text and line draw characters is challenging—and often very frustrating. (Adding simple labels or headings is less difficult, as you will see.) You should try to avoid the Line Draw mode when you're creating tables and forms.

Keep the following suggestions in mind:

- Use the Format **B**order command to add horizontal lines to tables and forms rather than using Line Draw. The lines you create with the Paragraph Borders dialog box are paragraph formats, so you can type and tab over them without disturbing them. Moreover, if you change the paragraph format, the lines change too.

- Use vertical tabs to add vertical lines rather than drawing them with Line Draw. Vertical tabs, like the lines you enter with the Format Border command, are paragraph formats, so you will not disturb them if you type or tab over them.

- Don't try drawing over existing text. If you want to use Line Draw, create the drawing in a blank part of your document. Add the text after you make the drawing.

- If you want to add text to your drawing, keep the text to a minimum, and be sure to use a fixed-width (monospace) font such as Courier or Pica. Add the text in the overtype mode (press F5) so that you don't delete the spaces Word has inserted.

To use Line Draw, do the following:

1. Position the cursor where you want to start drawing, and choose Utilities Line Draw (Alt-UL).

   Word displays the LD code in the status bar, and you see the message Draw lines with the direction keys. Press Esc to Cancel in the message bar. Be sure to draw in a blank section of your document.

2. Press the right, left, down, and up arrows to draw with the cursor. Press Home to draw a line to the left margin, and press End to draw a line to the right margin.

   As you can see, Word automatically enters spaces and paragraph marks to make room for the characters you're entering. When you join lines, the program automatically smoothes the junctions.

3. To move the pen elsewhere on the screen, exit the Line Draw mode by pressing Esc or clicking either mouse button. Reposition the cursor, and choose Utilities Line Draw again.

4. To correct mistakes, exit Line Draw by pressing Esc. Press Ins to toggle the overtype mode on. Delete the unwanted characters as you would delete ordinary text.

To change the line draw character, follow these steps:

1. Choose Utilities Customize (Alt-UU).

2. Drop down the Linedraw Character list box.

   Reminder: To drop down the list box, activate the box and press Alt-↓. Alternatively, click the arrow.

3. Choose a line draw character or type the character you want to use.

4. Choose OK.

Word doesn't save your choice in this list box. The next time you start Word, you see the single line character in this list box.

Chapter Summary

Creating and completing business forms are big nuisances for many organizations. In this chapter, you learned how to use Word 5.5 to reduce the cost and tedium of creating forms. Using Word, it is easy to design and print attractive forms. You also learned how to use Word to fill in the forms automatically.

Now that you have dealt with what is surely the most mundane of Word's desktop publishing applications, turn to the most glamorous: integrating the text you create with Word 5.5 with graphics created in other programs.

Quick Review

Borders: Lines, Boxes, and Shading

To add a box around a paragraph:

1. Place the cursor in the paragraph.

2. Choose Format Borders (Alt-TB).

3. Choose **Box** Each Paragraph.

4. If you want, choose a line style other than the default Normal (single).

5. Choose OK.

To add lines around a paragraph:

1. Place the cursor in the paragraph.

2. Choose Format Borders (Alt-TB).

3. Choose **Lines** and choose the options you want (Top, Left, Bottom, Right).

4. If you want, choose a line style other than the default Normal (single).

5. Choose OK.

To add shading to a paragraph:

1. Place the cursor in the paragraph.

2. Choose Format Borders (Alt-TB).

3. Drop down the **Percentage** list box.

4. Choose a shading option.

5. Choose OK.

To delete lines or boxes without deleting the text of the paragraph:

1. Place the cursor in the paragraph.

2. Choose Forma**t B**orders (Alt-TB).

3. Choose **None** in the Border type area.

4. Choose OK.

Forms

To add a data entry mark to a form:

1. Position the cursor where you want the data entry mark to appear.

2. Press Ctrl-].

3. Format the data entry mark as hidden text.

To move the cursor to the next data entry mark:

Press Ctrl-→

To move the cursor to the previous data entry mark:

Press Ctrl-←

To create a form that prompts the user to supply the needed information:

1. At the top of the form you created, press Ctrl-[to enter a left chevron.

2. Type *ASK* followed by a field name, such as *socsecno* or *lastname*, an equal sign, and a question mark. If you want Word to display a message on-screen when it prompts the user to supply the needed data, type the message after the question mark.

3. Press Ctrl-] to close the ASK statement.

4. Place the cursor where you want Word to print the information the user will supply.

5. Press Ctrl-[to enter a left chevron.

6. Type the same field name you used in the ASK statement.

7. Press Ctrl-] to enter a right chevron.

8. Repeat steps 1 through 7 until you have written ASK statements and entered field names for all the information you want the user to supply.

9. Format the ASK statements as hidden text.

To print a form that includes ASK statements:

1. Choose File Print Merge (Alt-FM).

2. Choose Print.

3. Choose OK.

Line Draw

To make a simple illustration with Line Draw:

1. Position the cursor where you want to start drawing and choose Utilities Line Draw (Alt-UL).

2. Press the right, left, down, and up arrows to draw with the cursor. Press Home to draw a line to the left margin, and press End to draw a line to the right margin.

3. To move the pen elsewhere on the screen, exit the Line Draw mode by pressing Esc or clicking either mouse button. Reposition the cursor, and choose Utilities Line Draw again.

4. To correct mistakes, exit Line Draw by pressing Esc, and press Ins to toggle the overtype mode on. Delete the unwanted characters as you would delete ordinary text.

To change the line draw character:

1. Choose Utilities Customize (Alt-UU).

2. Drop down the Linedraw Character list box.

3. Choose a line draw character or type the character you want to use.

4. Choose OK.

Chapter
18

Page Layout I: Adding Graphics and Anchoring Paragraphs

Desktop publishing programs, such as Aldus PageMaker or Ventura Publisher, are designed to facilitate the tasks of page layout: positioning graphics, adding lines and boxes, and inserting text into columns without disturbing the overall design. Layout artists used to do these tasks with razor knives, glue, and layout board. Desktop publishing technology provides users with an on-screen workshop for creating and revising a document design. Users manipulate the design on-screen and wait to print until the design is perfect. Professionals whose jobs require them to lay out newsletters, brochures, and camera-ready copy can benefit from a desktop publishing program's capabilities.

Most people, however, don't have such elaborate needs. Also, desktop publishing programs are for desktop publishing, not word processing. These programs provide few tools for creating and revising text. Most desktop publishers create and edit the text in a program such as Word; only later do they paste the text into the desktop publishing program for page layout purposes.

Unless you create a large number of publications requiring layout and design, you probably don't need a desktop publishing program. For users who only occasionally create a newsletter or illustrated report, Word 5.5's tools for text and graphics integration are sufficient.

Using Word, you can do the following:

- Incorporate graphics images, such as graphs generated by spreadsheet programs, into document files

- Size, move, and enclose the graphics in boxes or add lines

- Anchor any paragraph to an absolute position on the page. The paragraph can include text, graphics, or both. You can let Word

547

compute the location by choosing a location such as "centered vertically and flush-right horizontally," or you can specify measurements. After you anchor the paragraph, it stays put, even if you add or delete text above the paragraph. To make room for text, Word flows text around the graphic (if there's room) and below it. You can use this technique to control precisely where graphics, captions, and many other document design elements appear on the page.

Using these Word 5.5 features, you can produce documents that look as though they were produced in Ventura or PageMaker (see fig. 18.1). After you create a page design and anchor elements to absolute positions on the page, you can continue to add and edit text, switch to outline view, check spelling, and add footnotes. Word seamlessly integrates desktop publishing and word processing.

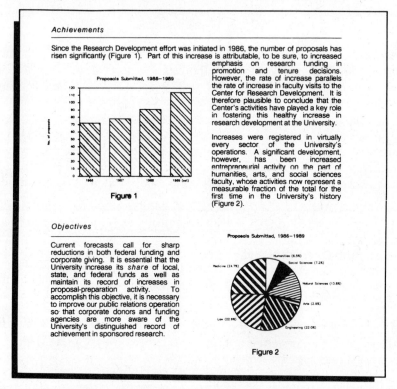

Fig. 18.1. Spreadsheet-generated graphics incorporated into a Word document.

The Format Position command, which is a command few Word users understand, is an important part of Word's page design tools. This command anchors any paragraph to a fixed position on the page, whether the paragraph contains text or graphics. For example, you can use this command to anchor a graphic flush to the left margin and centered on the page, and you also can specify a width of 3.5 inches for the paragraph. Word will flow the text around the anchored paragraph, producing effects such as those you see in figure 18.1.

This chapter explains how to use Format Position with graphics. However, you also can use this command with any other paragraph, including headings and other units of text. Therefore, even if you don't plan to use graphics in your documents, this chapter contains important information.

This chapter covers the following subjects:

- Importing graphics into Word documents from a variety of programs

- Sizing and positioning the graphic within the Word document

- Adding borders and captions to the graphic

- Capturing graphics screens from graphics programs using the program CAPTURE.COM

- Anchoring text and graphics so text flows around the absolutely positioned paragraph (which can contain text or graphics)

With the exception of new command names and dialog boxes, Word's features for inserting graphics and anchoring paragraphs haven't changed significantly since Version 5.0. If you used Word 5.0 to create documents with graphics and absolutely positioned paragraphs, you can view and edit these documents with Word 5.5.

About Graphics Files

The world of graphics files has little standardization. Many competing file formats exist, and some programs use their own unique format. Fortunately, Word can read several important graphics formats directly. For those Word cannot read, you can use the CAPTURE.COM utility on Program 1 disk. This utility captures any graphics screen image to a Word-readable file format. In short, if you can display a graphic on your computer's screen, you can print the graphic in a Word document.

You will learn more about CAPTURE.COM elsewhere in this chapter. The following overview lists the graphics files Word 5.5 can read directly:

- Hewlett-Packard Graphics Language (HPGL) format. Many programs support the HPGL standard, which initially was devised for Hewlett-Packard plotters. Word can read files printed to disk using this format. Programs capable of producing HPGL plotter files include ChartMaster, Diagram-Master, Generic CADD, Harvard Graphics, Microsoft Chart, and Versacad.

- Lotus and Symphony PIC files. Word can read Lotus and Symphony graphics files directly.

Note: Many Lotus-compatible spreadsheet programs produce files Word can read; among such programs are VP-Planner, Quattro, and SuperCalc 4.

- Windows Clipboard images. If you're running Word within Windows, here's some very good news: anything you can get into the Clipboard in bit-mapped format can be imported into Word, including the charts you create with Microsoft Excel.

- Microsoft Pageview and Windows Paint picture files.

- PC Paintbrush PCX or PCC files. Word reads the files created by this program, which Microsoft distributes with the Microsoft Mouse.

- PostScript files. You can import any graphics image generated by the PostScript printer control language, but you will not be able to view the image in Print Preview.

- Tagged Image File Format (TIFF) files. Scanners, such as the DFI Handy Scanner, produce images conforming to this format. Word can read TIFF B (monochrome) files in compressed or uncompressed form, as well as uncompressed TIFF G (gray scale) files.

Tip: Many graphics programs permit you to save files in one of the formats Word can read. For example, you can save a Harvard Graphics chart in PCX, EPS, or HPGL format, and Word can read any of these.

Importing and Sizing Graphics

When you import a graphics file, Word places the graphic into a *frame*, which the program treats as if it were a paragraph. While you're editing, you don't see the graphic on-screen. Rather, you see a paragraph with a .G. code, the graphic's file name, the graphic's dimensions, and the file format. This information is formatted as hidden text.

After you import the graphic, you can size it, add borders, add captions, move the graphic to another location in the document, and anchor the graphic to an absolute position on the page. Each of these subjects is discussed in detail in this section.

Importing the Graphic

When you import a graphic image into Word, by default the program assumes you want the image to print with the same width as the margins you're using. When you name the file, Word examines the file's format and proposes for the image a height that is proportional to the width you chose.

To import an image into a Word document do the following:

1. If you see the code LY on the status bar, choose **View Layout** (Alt-VL) to toggle the layout view off.

   You turn the layout view on later. For now, leave it off. You learn what it does in the next section.

2. Place the cursor where you want the image to appear.

3. Choose **Insert Picture** (Alt-IP).

   You see the Picture dialog box (see fig. 18.2).

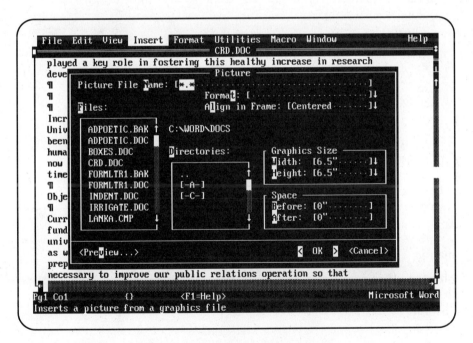

Fig. 18.2. *Importing a graphic with the Picture dialog box.*

4. Highlight the graphic's file name in the **F**iles list box.

   Because the file is probably in a directory other than Word's, choose the parent directory symbol (..) in the **D**irectories list box. Choose the directory in which you stored the graphics file. You should see the graphic's file name in the **F**iles list box.

   For now, just accept Word's defaults for the other settings in this dialog box. You learn more about them in the next section.

5. Choose Preview to import the graphic and to see how the page will look with the graphic imported into the cursor's location. Alternatively, choose OK to import the graphic without previewing it.

   After Word imports the graphic, you see a hidden-text message at the cursor's location, as shown in figure 18.3. This message specifies the file's name and location, the width and height of the image, and the file's format.

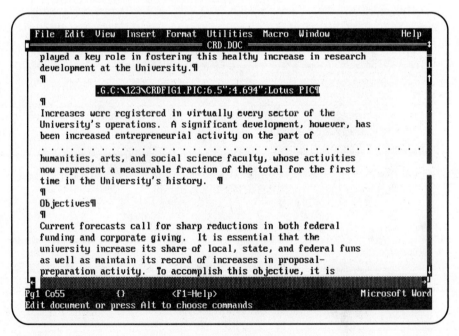

Fig. 18.3. *After you import a graphic, you see a hidden text message at the cursor's location.*

Word's Defaults for a Graphic's Size and Position

After you import a graphic, choose File Print Preview (Alt-FV), or press Ctrl-F9 to preview the graphic on-screen. As you can see from figure 18.4, the way Print Preview sizes graphics may produce moiré distortions and other problems. Remember, the preview is an on-screen graphics simulation only; your document and the graphic will print at your printer's highest resolution.

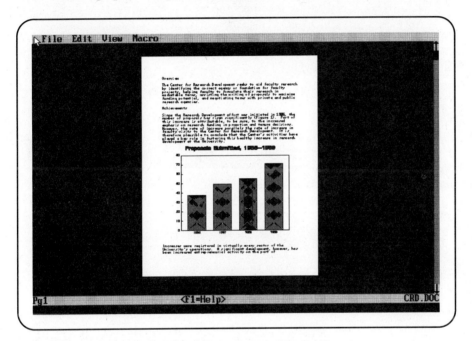

Fig. 18.4. Print Preview may produce problems with graphics.

Word uses the defaults to size and position the graphic you import. You can change these defaults by making choices in the Picture dialog box. You may do so after importing the graphic, as explained in the following section.

Word uses the following defaults for sizing and positioning imported graphics:

- **Alignment in Frame** (default: Centered). You also may align Left or Right by dropping down the **Align** in Frame list box.

- **Width** (default: 6.5 inches of space between 1-inch margins). You can specify a different width by typing a measurement in the **Width** list box.

- **Height** (default: a measurement that preserves the **aspect ratio** of the original graphic, given Word's choice for the graphic's width.) The aspect ratio is the height-to-width ratio of the original graphic. If you don't preserve the aspect ratio, you may see unattractive distortions in the graphic, particularly when you're importing a bit-mapped graphic image. However, you may type a measurement in this list box or choose a height that is the same as the width.

- **Space** (default: no space before and after). Most graphics images are surrounded by at least some white space. If you need to add more, you can add additional space in the **Before** or **After** text boxes.

Viewing the Graphic's Frame in View Layout

When you choose View Layout to toggle on the View Layout mode, you see an on-screen representation of the graphic's *frame*: the area that Word has set aside for the graphic in your document (see fig. 18.5). Dots indicate the frame's perimeter. Word keeps the frame on one page; if there isn't room, the program moves the frame to the top of the next page.

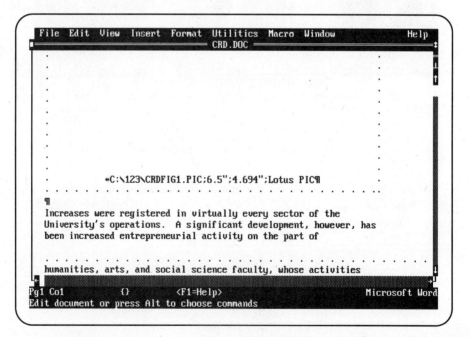

Fig. 18.5. Choosing View Layout enables you to preview the graphic's frame.

Tip: Use the Format Position command to anchor a graphic's frame so it stays put, even if you add or delete text above the frame. This command is easy to use, and after its benefits become clear to you, the command will become an important part of your Word formatting skills. For more information, see "Anchoring Paragraphs" in this chapter.

Sizing and Positioning the Graphic

Word's sizing capabilities provide a quick way to import a graphic without worrying about its size or position. if you want to control the size, you can specify the image's height and width by typing measurements or choosing options in the Picture dialog box. You can specify these measurements when you import the picture or afterward. This section explains how to size and position the graphic after you import it.

Use these steps to size or position a graphic after importing it:

1. Highlight the hidden text code Word inserted when you imported the graphic.

   The code begins with .G. If you don't see the code on-screen,
   choose **View Preferences** (Alt-VE) and choose **Hidden**.

2. Choose **Insert Picture** (Alt-IP).

   You see the Picture dialog box, showing the settings for the
   graphic you already imported.

3. To change the alignment of the graphic image in its frame,
   choose an option from the **Align in Frame** list box.

4. To change the width of the graphic, type a measurement in the
   Width list box.

   After you choose a width, Word computes a height that preserves
   the graphic's aspect ratio, and places that height in the **Height** list
   box.

5. If you want, override the computed height by typing a measurement in the **Height** list box.

6. To add space before or after the graphic, type measurements in
   the **Before** or **After** text boxes.

7. Choose OK.

Adding Borders or Shading

As you have learned, Word inserts graphics into a frame. The width and height of the frame are controlled by the choices you make in the Picture dialog box. If you want, you can add lines or borders using the Paragraph Borders dialog box.

To add lines or borders to a graphic, do the following:

1. Position the cursor within the graphic's paragraph.

   If you see the code on-screen, put the cursor within the text of the code. If you have switched off the display of hidden text, place the cursor directly before the paragraph mark.

2. Choose Format Borders (Alt-TB).

   You see the Paragraph Borders dialog box.

3. Choose a line style, if you want a style other than the default Normal (single-width line).

4. Choose Box Each Paragraph to enclose the graphic in a box. Choose Lines, and choose from Top, Bottom, Left, or Right, to add lines.

5. Choose OK.

After you add the lines or box, you see the rules on-screen. In View Layout , the box surrounds the actual space set aside for your graphic, as figure 18.6 shows. If you toggled View Layout off, Word shows the graphic paragraph with the lines or box, but, as figure 18.7 shows, the size is inaccurate.

Adding Captions

You can add captions that print within the borders you created by typing the caption's text within the graphic image's paragraph.

To add a caption, follow these steps:

1. Position the cursor on the paragraph mark that ends the information about the graphic, and press Shift-Enter to start a new line. Press Shift-Enter again.

2. Type the caption (see fig. 18.8).

3. Press Ctrl-C to center the caption. Preview the caption with Print Preview before printing (see fig. 18.9).

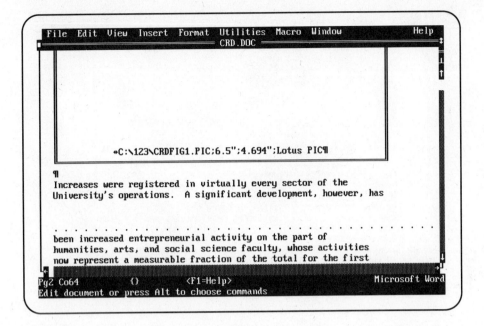

Fig. 18.6. View Layout enables you to see the boxed space you created for your graphic.

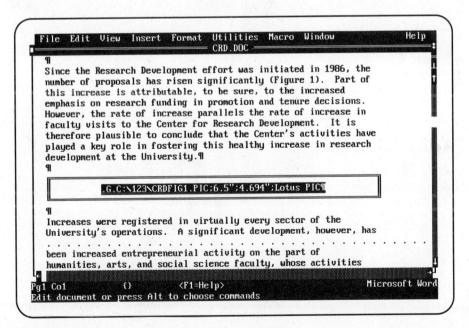

Fig. 18.7. When View Layout is off, the boxed space reserved for your graphic is sized inaccurately.

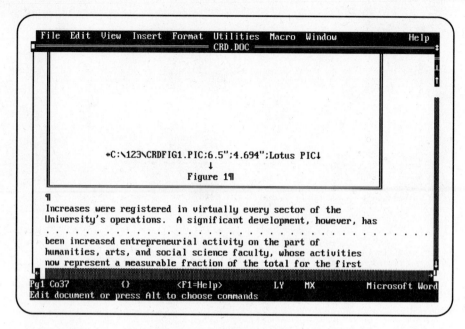

Fig. 18.8. Adding a caption for your graphic is a simple process.

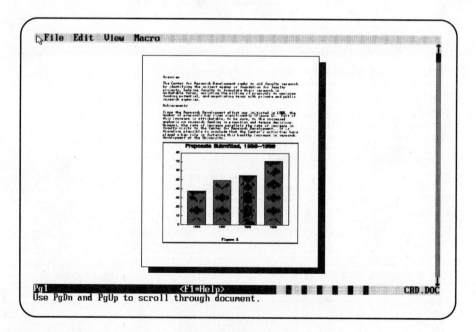

Fig. 18.9. Preview your caption by using Print Preview.

Moving the Graphic

After you import a graphic into a Word document with **Insert Picture**, you can move the image to another part of the document by moving the paragraph containing the information about the graphic. If you added lines or borders, don't forget to move the paragraph mark, too.

Changing the Graphics Resolution

When you add graphics to your document, you will want to print a draft of your document to see how the graphics fit into your page design. However, some printers take a long time to print a document containing graphics. For this reason, you may want to print a draft with a low graphics resolution to get a rough sketch of graphics placement. Printing takes less time this way. After you're satisfied with the page design, you can print the final draft with high resolution.

Use these steps to change the graphics resolution:

1. Choose **File Print** (Alt-FP).

   You see the Print dialog box.

2. Choose **Options**.

   You see the Print Options dialog box.

3. Choose **Graphics Resolution** and the list box drops down.

4. Choose the resolution you want from the list box.

   The higher the number, the higher the resolution. 300 dpi (dots per inch) is a medium-high resolution, while 70 dpi is low resolution.

5. Choose OK to confirm your choices in the Print Options dialog box menu.

Capturing Graphics with CAPTURE.COM

If Word cannot read the graphics file format created by a graphics program, you still can print the program's graphics in your Word documents. The key is to use CAPTURE.COM, a program included on the Program 1 disk. CAPTURE.COM is a terminate-and-stay-resident (TSR) program. You load it before starting your graphics program.

Use these steps to copy graphics images to a disk file with CAPTURE.COM:

1. If you're using Word, exit Word and return to DOS.

2. Make the Word program directory current.

   If Word is stored in C:\WORD, type *cd \word* and press Enter.

3. Type *capture /s* and press Enter.

   Respond to the setup questions. If you want to save a text screen as a graphics screen, choose option 0 (General IBM PC Display Adapter). If you choose one of the other options, CAPTURE will save the screens as graphics screens.

   If you already used CAPTURE.COM and chose setup options, type *capture* and press Enter.

4. Start your graphics program and display the graphic you want to copy.

5. Press Shift-PrtSc.

   To save a text screen as a graphics screen, press Esc after pressing Shift-PrtScr. You can omit Esc if you chose the General IBM PC Display Adapter option when you configured CAPTURE.COM.

6. Type a file name in the area that appears on-screen.

   Omit the period and extension; Word supplies the SCR extension for graphics screens.

7. Press Enter.

8. If you're saving a graphics screen, you see clip lines on-screen. You can use these lines to crop the graphic. Press Tab to toggle between the bottom/right and top/left lines, and press the arrow keys to move the lines. Press Keypad + to move the clipping lines in larger increments; press Keypad – to move them in smaller increments. Press Ins to move the top and bottom lines simultaneously; press Del to return to single-line control.

9. When you finish cropping the picture, press Enter.

   Word saves the graphics file to disk with the extension SCR. Saving the file can take one or two minutes.

10. Exit the graphics application.

11. Start Word and use use **Insert Picture** to insert the graphic into your document.

    Word automatically recognizes the CAPTURE.COM file format.

Caution: CAPTURE.COM is a terminate-and-stay-resident (TSR) program. After you load it, the program stays in memory, occupying approximately 20K, until you remove the program from memory or reboot your computer. Twenty kilobytes isn't much, but if you're short on memory, you should remember to remove CAPTURE.COM from memory after using the program.

To remove CAPTURE.COM from memory, type *capture /e* at the DOS prompt and press Enter.

Anchoring Paragraphs

The Format Position command is an extremely important part of Word 5.5's desktop publishing tools. Using this command, you can tell Word where you want a paragraph positioned on the page, and, after you do so, the paragraph stays in place. You can add or delete text as much as necessary without affecting the paragraph's location on the page.

Figure 18.10 shows what Format Position can do. This graph was sized with a width of 3 inches using the Insert Picture command. Next, the Format Position command was used to anchor the graphic's frame to the center of the page vertically and flush to the right margin horizontally. As you can see, Word flowed the text to the left of the graphic and wrapped it around the image, leaving a 0.167-inch margin on the three sides that contact the text. As a finishing touch, lines were added above and below the graphic.

You can use Format Position to anchor one or more paragraphs of text as well as to anchor graphics. In the next chapter, you learn how to anchor text to produce interesting effects, such as the pull-out quotes you commonly see in magazines.

Using the Format Position Command

The Format Position command acts on a selected paragraph or paragraphs. You begin by positioning the cursor within the paragraph. When you see the Position dialog box, you specify where you want the paragraph located on the page horizontally and vertically.

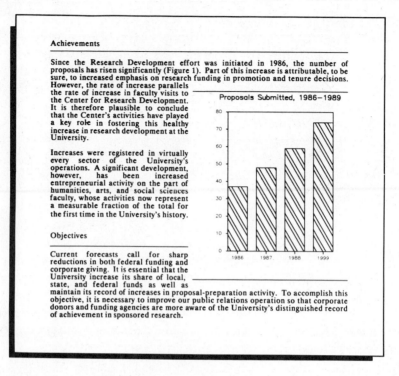

Fig. 18.10. Graph anchored with Format Position.

You can use the Format Position command to position a graphic as well as a paragraph of text. In Word, a graphic is positioned in its own paragraph (called a *frame*). Whether the paragraph contains text or a graphic, all the Position features apply.

After you use Format Position, what you see depends on whether you chose the View Layout mode. In View Layout, you see the location of the positioned paragraph on-screen, just as it will appear when printed. The paragraph's location on-screen may not correspond to its real location in the text, because Word moves the paragraph to its anchored position. For example, suppose that you open a new document and type three paragraphs. You then use the Format Position command to place Paragraph 2 at the bottom of the page. In View Layout, you see Paragraphs 1 and 3 at the top of the page, with Paragraph 2 positioned at the bottom.

With View Layout switched off, Word shows the paragraph in its actual location within the sequence of paragraphs in your document.

Note: Format Position controls *where* a paragraph prints on a page; you fix its position horizontally and vertically. But this command doesn't control on *which* page the paragraph actually prints. For example, you center a graphic on page 4. You then add a large amount of text to page 3. When you print, you discover the graphic, though still centered, has been moved to page 5. This movement happened because by using the Format Position command, you told Word, "Center this paragraph on the current page, whatever it is."

The graphic's appearance on page 5 isn't a problem because you added so much text that the graphic makes sense in its new location. Normally, the movement of a paragraph isn't a problem for this reason. However, when you use the Format Position command, remember that your paragraphs may migrate from one page to the next. If you're not happy with the paragraph's location, you can move the paragraph to the previous page or the next page using the Edit Cut command. Make sure to move the paragraph mark as well as the graphic code or text.

When you choose Format Position, you see that every paragraph is positioned using the command's default settings: flush-left relative to the current column, and inline vertically. Inline means that Word prints the paragraphs in the same sequence you see on-screen when View Layout is switched off. When you choose the Inline option, Word doesn't move the paragraph to a location other than the one in which the text actually occurs in the sequence of paragraphs in your document.

To anchor the paragraph, you choose a vertical position other than Inline. You also can choose a horizontal position. The vertical options are Top, Centered, and Bottom, and you choose these options either relative to the top and bottom margins or relative to the edge of the page. By default, Word places the text vertically measuring from the margins; you can choose the edge of the page. If the top and bottom margins are identical, it doesn't matter whether you choose to position the text vertically within the margins or within the page. However, if one of the margins is bigger, positioning the text relative to the margins will result in a placement that differs from positioning the text relative to the page's edge.

If you choose a horizontal position other than Left (the default), you choose from four additional options (Centered, Right, Inside, and Outside). By default, Word measures these placements from the sides of the current column. You also can choose to have the placements measured from the left and right margins, or from the left and right edges of the page. If you are using a single-column format (the default), positioning the text within the margins is the same as positioning the text within the column.

When you choose a multiple-column format the two positions differ. With two-column printing, the columns can be only three inches wide, so positioning the text within the column differs from positioning the text within the margins (6.5 inches, if you're using the default left and right margins). If the left and right margins are identical, positioning the paragraph within the margins doesn't differ from positioning it within the page's left and right edges. However, if one margin is bigger than the other, the margin and page options produce different results.

These options may not make much sense until you actually see them on-screen. The best way to understand Format Position is to try it and see what the command does. Use a copy of a multipage document as a guinea pig; you need plenty of text so Word can flow text around the anchored paragraph.

Tip: Unless you're using an extremely slow computer, turn on the View Layout mode when you're working with Format Position. Turning View Layout on is the only way you can see your Format Position choices on-screen while you're editing.

Caution: If you're anchoring a paragraph of text, you can control its width by typing a measurement in the Paragraph Width list box of the Position dialog box. You don't need to indent the paragraph before choosing Format Position, even if you want the paragraph to appear narrower than the column width. However, you cannot control the width of a paragraph containing a graphic in this way. If you're anchoring a paragraph containing a graphic, use Insert Picture (Alt-IP) to specify the graphic's width and height. When you use Format Position, choose Paragraph Width and select the Width of Graphic option from the list box.

To anchor a paragraph on the page, do the following:

1. Position the cursor within the paragraph or paragraphs you want to anchor.

   To anchor more than one paragraph, first select the paragraphs. To position a graphic, place the cursor within the graphic code.

2. Choose Format Position (Alt-TO).

   You see the Position dialog box shown in figure 18.11.

3. To anchor the paragraph, choose an option other than Inline in the Vertical list box.

   You can choose from Top, Centered, or Bottom. Alternatively, you can type a measurement in the list box, such as *3.0"*. If you type a measurement, Word measures from the left of whatever option you have chosen in the Relative To area (Margin or Page).

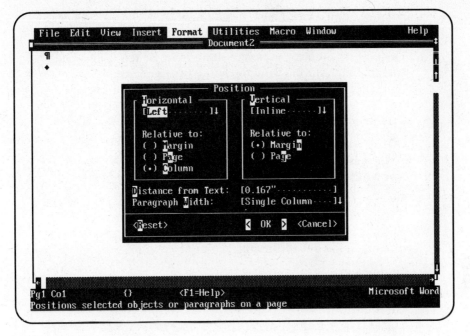

Fig. 18.11. The Position dialog box.

By default, Word positions the paragraph vertically within the current top and bottom margins.

4. If you want, choose Page in the Vertical area to position the text vertically, measured from the top and the bottom of the page.

   If you chose the Centered option and choose Page, Word will center the paragraph vertically on the page, even if the top and bottom margins differ.

5. Specify the horizontal position in the **Horizontal** list box if you want to use a horizontal placement other than flush-left.

   You can choose from Centered, Right, Inside, or Outside. The Inside and Outside options are used for two-sided printing and binding. If you choose Inside, Word always places the graphic on the side of the page that faces the binding, which is the left side for odd-numbered pages, and the right side for even-numbered pages. If you choose Outside, Word always places the graphic on the side of the page away from the binding.

6. If you want to control how Word measures horizontal placement, choose an option under Relative To in the **Horizontal** area.

   The default option is **Column**. Choose **Margin** to position the paragraph measuring from the left to the right margin, or choose **Page** to position the paragraph measuring from the left to the right edge of the page. For example, if you choose **Page** and Centered, Word will establish a center mark located at 4.25 inches for a standard, 8.5 inch page.

7. To increase or decrease the white space around the paragraph, type a measurement in the **Distance from Text** text box.

8. If you are anchoring a graphic, drop down the Paragraph **Width** list box and choose Width of Graphic. If you are anchoring text, type a width if you would like the paragraph to be narrower or wider than the default setting (Width of Column).

9. Choose OK.

An Example: Positioning Headings Outside the Left Margin

The following example shows how the Relative To: options affect the placement of the paragraph horizontally. In figure 18.12, the headings Overview and Achievements were positioned 1.0 inch from the edge of the page, while the left margin was set at 1.5 inches. Thick lines were added below the headings.

This effect is pleasing, but when the graphic is centered horizontally and vertically it's too close to the Achievements heading (see fig. 18.13).

To position the graphic more attractively, you can type a measurement. If you're using the default choice in the Relative To area (relative to **Margin**), the graphic is centered within the 9-inch space between the margins, and the center point is 4.5 inches. To move the center point down one-half inch, you can type *5.0"* in the Vertical text box. Figure 18.14 shows the results.

Note: If you have too much white space above and below the anchored paragraph, you probably added blank lines using the **Before** or **After** boxes in the Paragraph dialog box. To reduce the blank space, place the cursor in the paragraphs containing the blank lines. Choose Forma**t P**aragraph (Alt-TP) and remove them.

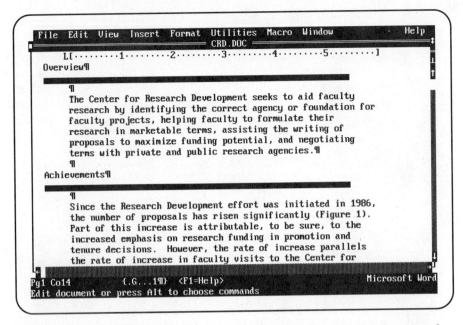

Fig. 18.12. *Leaving the left margin at 1.5 inches, Word places the headings 1 inch from the left edge of the page.*

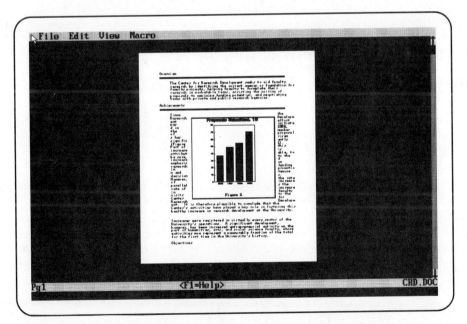

Fig. 18.13. *The graphic is centered horizontally and vertically on the page.*

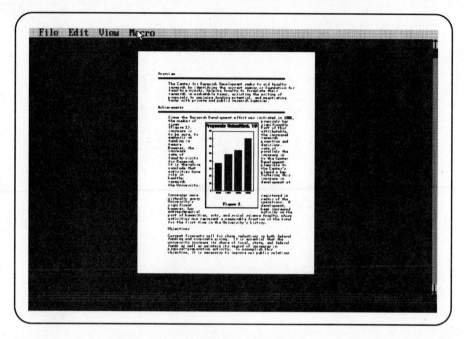

Fig. 18.14. *Moving the graphic down 0.5 inches improves the balance of the page.*

Page Layout Techniques with Format Position

Like style sheets, Format Position is among the least-understood and used Word commands: many people use the program every day and have never heard of it! Yet, this command is one of Word's most powerful, flexible, and easily used formatting tools. In this section, you learn how to use Format Position to achieve many useful effects.

Creating Pull-Out Quotes

Pull-out quotes are common in magazines, where they are used to echo an important sentence or quotation that occurs in the body text. In the following steps, you learn how to create a pull-out quote that is boxed, positioned flush-right, and placed in the bottom half of the page, as shown in figure 18.15.

To create a pull-out quote, follow these steps:

1. Place the cursor approximately where you want the pull-out quote to appear, and type the pull-out quote text.

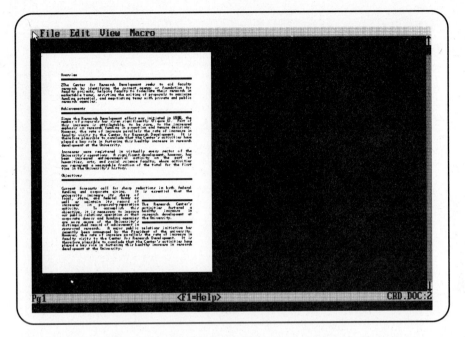

Fig. 18.15. *The pull-out quote highlights an important sentence in the text.*

2. Choose Format Position (Alt-TO).

   You see the Position dialog box.

3. Choose a horizontal alignment option in the Horizontal list box.

   In this example, the Right option was chosen.

4. Choose a vertical location in the Vertical list box.

   For this example, *6.5"* was typed.

5. So that Word will flow text to one or both sides of the pull-out quote, type a paragraph width that is less than the current column width in the Paragraph Width text box.

6. Choose OK.

7. If you want, choose Format Borders to add lines or a box to the pull-out quote text.

   For this example, thick lines were inserted above and below the pull-out quote.

8. Choose File Print Preview (Alt-FV), or use the Ctrl-F9 keyboard shortcut to see how Word will print the pull-out quote (see fig. 18.15).

Positioning the Same Graphic or Text on Every Page

In some publications, placing the same text or graphic—such as a corporate logo—on every page is desirable. You can accomplish this task by formatting a header or footer paragraph with Format Position. When you do, you can locate the header or footer paragraph outside the location where this paragraph usually prints.

Use these steps to position the same graphic or text on every page:

1. Press Ctrl-Home to move the cursor to the beginning of the document.

2. Type the text you want to appear on every page. Alternatively, choose **Insert Picture** (Alt-IP) to import a graphic.

3. Place the cursor in the paragraph you just typed or the graphics frame you just inserted. If you have more than one paragraph, select all of them.

4. If you see the code LY on the screen, choose **View Layout** (Alt-VL) to toggle the View Layout off.

    You cannot create a header or footer in View Layout.

5. Choose **Format Header/Footer.**

    You see the Header/Footer dialog box.

6. Choose **Header** or **Footer**—it doesn't matter which.

7. Choose the pages on which you want the text or graphic to print.

    Choose First Page if you want the text or graphic to appear on the first page of the document. Leave the X in Odd Pages and Even Pages to print the text or graphic on the rest of the pages.

8. Choose OK.

9. Choose **Format Position** (Alt-TO).

10. Choose a vertical and horizontal position for the text or graphic.

11. Choose OK.

12. Choose **File Print Preview** (Alt-FV) or press Ctrl-F9 to see a preview of the repeated text or graphic.

If you use this technique, you can still print normal headers or footers. Type them in separate paragraphs at the beginning of your document, and don't format these headers and footers with Format Position.

Chapter Summary

Word 5.5's new graphics features will satisfy the needs of most users whose graphics needs are limited to including graphs, charts, and other everyday illustrations in reports and proposals. Unlike a true desktop publishing program, Word doesn't display graphics and text simultaneously, except in Print Preview mode, which doesn't let you change the position of the elements you see or edit. Even so, you easily can use Word 5.5's graphics features to integrate charts, graphs, and pictures into your text. After you choose the graphic's width, Word sizes the graphic's height. With a simple command, you can control the amount of white space around the graphic and add boxes or lines to set the graphic off from the text.

To gain even more control over the position of graphics in your document, try anchoring them with the Format Position command. With this command, you can fix a graphic's location relative to the edges of the page or the margins, both horizontally and vertically. If the graphic is narrower than the text column, text flows around it automatically, producing a handsome result. You also can use Format Position to anchor paragraphs of text on the page. In this chapter, you learned how to create pull-out quotes and other text effects with this command.

In the next chapter, you will learn how you can add to the desktop publishing knowledge you have gained by creating multiple-column text. With little effort, you can produce handsomely formatted newsletters. If you combine this expertise with the formatting control provided by the Format Position command, you can produce stunning effects.

Quick Review

Anchoring a Paragraph

To anchor a paragraph on the page:

1. Position the cursor within the paragraph or paragraphs you want to anchor.

2. Choose Format Position (Alt-TO).

3. To anchor the paragraph, choose an option other than Inline in the Vertical list box.

4. If you want, choose Page in the Vertical area to position the text vertically, measured from the top and the bottom of the page.

5. Specify the horizontal position in the **Horizontal** list box if you want to use a horizontal placement other than flush-left.

6. If you want to control how Word measures horizontal placement, choose an option under Relative To in the **Horizontal** area.

7. To increase or decrease the white space around the paragraph, type a measurement in the **Distance from Text** text box.

8. If you are anchoring a graphic, drop down the Paragraph **Width** list box and choose Width of Graphic. If you are anchoring text, type a width if you want the paragraph to be narrower or wider than the default setting (Width of Column).

9. Choose OK.

Capturing a Graphics Screen

To copy graphics screen images to a disk file with CAPTURE.COM:

1. If you're using Word, exit Word and return to DOS.

2. Make the Word program directory current.

3. Type *capture* and press Enter.

4. Start your graphics program and display the graphic you want to copy.

5. Press Shift-PrtSc.

6. Type a file name in the area that appears on-screen.

7. Press Enter.

8. To crop the image, use the clipping keys. Press Tab to toggle between the bottom/right and top/left lines, and press the arrow keys to move the lines. Press Keypad + to move the clipping lines in larger increments; press Keypad – to move them in smaller increments. Press Ins to move the top and bottom lines simultaneously; press Del to return to single-line control.

9. When you're finished cropping the picture, press Enter.

10. Exit the graphics application.

11. Start Word and use use **Insert Picture** to insert the graphic into your document.

To remove CAPTURE.COM from memory:

At the DOS prompt, type *capture /e* and press Enter.

Graphics

To insert a picture at the cursor's location:

1. If you see the code LY on the status bar, choose View Layout (Alt-VL) to toggle the View Layout off.

2. Place the cursor where you want the image to appear.

3. Choose **Insert Picture** (Alt-IP).

4. Highlight the graphic's file name in the Files list box.

5. Choose Preview to import the graphic and to see how the page will look with the graphic imported into the cursor's location. Alternatively, choose OK to import the graphic without previewing it.

To size or position a graphic after importing it:

1. Highlight the hidden text code that Word inserted when you imported the graphic.

2. Choose **Insert Picture** (Alt-IP).

3. To change the alignment of the graphic image in its frame, choose an option from the **Align in Frame** list box.

4. To change the width of the graphic, type a measurement in the **Width** list box.

5. If you want, override the automatically computed height by typing a measurement in the **Height** list box.

6. To add space before or after the graphic, type measurements in the **Before** or **After** text boxes.

7. Choose OK.

To add lines or borders to a graphic:

1. Position the cursor within the graphic's paragraph.

2. Choose Format **Borders** (Alt-TB).

3. Choose a line style in the Line Style box, if you want a style other than the default **Normal** (single-width line).

4. Choose **Box** Each Paragraph to enclose the graphic in a box. Choose **Lines**, and choose from Top, Bottom, Left, or Right, to add lines.

5. Choose OK.

To add a caption:

1. Position the cursor on the paragraph mark that ends the information about the graphic, and press Shift-Enter to start a new line. Press Shift-Enter again.

2. Type the caption.

3. Press Ctrl-C to center the caption. Preview the caption with Print Preview before printing.

To change the graphics resolution:

1. Choose **File Print** (Alt-FP).

2. Choose **Options**.

3. Choose **Graphics** Resolution and drop down the list box.

4. Choose the resolution you want from the list box.

5. Choose OK to confirm your choices in the Print Options menu.

Chapter 19

Page Layout II: Multiple-Column Text and Newsletters

Among the many endearing habits of North Americans is their propensity to publish newsletters on virtually every subject known to humanity. One recent estimate is that more than 100,000 newsletters now course their way through our continent's postal systems. At that rate, a modest-sized rural county of 100,000 people may well be responsible for more than 40 newsletters—and that estimate probably is low. Considering that most newsletters traditionally have been produced on primitive equipment, one conclusion is certain: the desktop publishing revolution is sure to fuel an explosion in the number of newsletters produced.

If you're among the teeming thousands who see a newsletter in your future, you have come to the right place. Although Word 5.5 isn't a desktop publishing program in the strict sense (because it doesn't enable you to display and edit graphics simultaneously), you will find that Word 5.5 is a great program for producing a straightforward, attractive newsletter. Your newsletter can include multiple-text columns and graphics positioned just where you want them. Although you could do an even better job with a genuine desktop publishing program, producing a newsletter that will win the respect of your audience is easy with Word 5.5. In addition, Word 5.5 can do much more than a desktop publishing program can.

Best of all, with Word 5.5 you can produce a newsletter with surprisingly little effort. After all, most people do not produce newsletters because they enjoy the experience of desktop publishing. Their desktop publishing aims are modest: they want to communicate a message in a clear, professional, and attractive manner (see fig. 19.1). Word 5.5 is an outstanding choice for people with these goals.

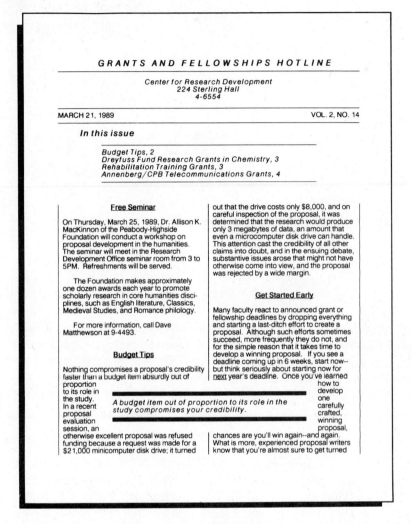

Fig. 19.1. A simple but attractive newsletter created with Microsoft Word.

In this chapter, you learn several techniques that are useful for creating brochures, newsletters, and other documents with multiple-column formatting:

- Creating *side-by-side* paragraphs. Side-by-side paragraphs are linked so that the paragraph printed on the left always is paired with the paragraph printed on the right. You see side-by-side paragraphs in price lists and other documents in which the text in one column must be linked with the text in the next column.

- Creating *newspaper columns* (also called snaking columns). Unlike side-by-side paragraphs, the paragraphs of newspaper columns have no relation to each other, except that one column begins where the preceding one left off. You see newspaper columns in many publications.

- Using layout techniques. You learn how to use the Format Position command to create attractive publication formats, such as newspaper columns separated with lines and single-column headlines above multiple-column text.

Users of previous versions of Word will find that little has changed in Word's multiple-column formatting capabilities. You need learn only how to use the new menus and dialog boxes, such as the Section dialog box. All the multiple-column formatting features work the same way they did in Version 5.0.

Side-by-Side Paragraphs

Side-by-side paragraphs are useful when you need to link the paragraphs in the left column with those in the right. For example, you can use side-by-side paragraphs for a product list in which the left column describes the product and the right column describes the product's many merits.

To create side-by-side paragraphs, you must format the left paragraph with enough right indent to leave room on the right, and you must format the right paragraph with enough left indent to leave room on the left. If you don't leave enough room, the paragraphs may overlap. Thanks to Word's layout view, seeing what you're doing when you create side-by-side paragraphs is easy; if the paragraphs overlap, you can see the problem right away and make the necessary changes.

> If all of the left paragraphs you are planning to type have just one line of text (one or two words or a short phrase), don't bother with side-by-side paragraphs. In such cases, see "The Hanging Indent Alternative," at the conclusion of this section.

In the tutorial that follows, you learn how to create a "generic" side-by-side format that you can modify as you want. You format the left paragraph with a 3.25-inch right indent, and you format the right paragraph with a 3.25-inch left indent. These choices result in a two-column side-by-side format with a 0.25-inch space between columns.

If you don't see the LY code on the status bar, choose View Layout to toggle the layout view on. If you don't see paragraph marks on-screen, choose View Preferences and choose the **Paragraph Marks** check box. In addition, you may find it easier to adjust indentations if you display the Ruler. To display the Ruler, choose View **Ruler** or click the ruler icon.

To create side-by-side paragraphs, follow these steps:

1. In a new, blank Word document, press Enter to create a blank paragraph.

2. Place the cursor in front of the paragraph mark.

    The left paragraph must be indented 3.25 inches from the right margin to provide room for the right paragraph. In addition, you must format the paragraph so that Word will place it side-by-side with the next paragraph you type. You also may want to place a blank line beneath the pairs of paragraphs. To do so, do not press Enter; you must enter blank lines in the **After** box of the Paragraph dialog box.

3. Choose Format **Paragraph** (Alt-TP).

    The Paragraph dialog box appears.

4. Type *3.25"* in the From Right text box and type *1 li* in the **After** box. Place an X in the **Side by Side** check box.

5. Choose OK.

6. Press Enter to create a paragraph.

    Word copies the formats including the indent, the side-by-side formatting, and the blank line after the paragraph.

    The right paragraph must be indented 3.25 inches from the left margin to provide room for the left paragraph.

7. Choose Format **Paragraph**. Type *3.25"* in the From Left box. Leave the other settings as they are. Type *O* in the From Right box. (When you pressed Enter, Word copied the current formats, including 1 li in the **After** box and the X in the **Side by Side** box to the new paragraph.)

8. Choose OK.

    You see the paragraph marks side-by-side on-screen if you have chosen the layout view. In figure 19.2, you see how these paragraphs would look if you had typed text. (In this example, you see only two paragraph marks on your screen.)

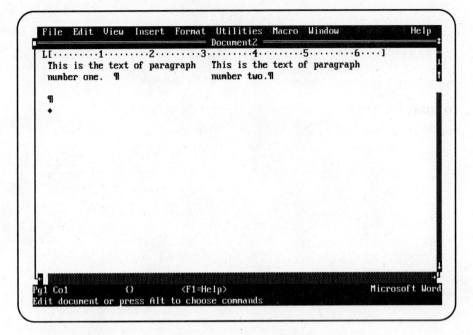

Fig. 19.2. Side-by-side paragraphs (layout view toggled on).

9. To create additional side-by-side paragraphs, highlight both paragraph marks. Next, choose **Edit Copy** (or use the Ctrl-Ins shortcut) to copy the paragraph marks to the Scrap.

10. Position the cursor beneath the pair of paragraph marks.

11. Choose **Edit Paste** (or use the Shift-Ins shortcut) to insert a copy of the pair of paragraph marks. (Be sure that NumLock is off.)

12. Repeat step 11 to enter as many pairs as you need.

13. Type the text of the paragraphs.

Moving the Cursor to the Next or Previous Column

When you have created side-by-side paragraphs and are displaying them in layout view, you can use special cursor-movement keys to move the cursor from one column to the next. (All the ordinary cursor-movement keys work as usual.) Table 9.1 lists these special keys and their functions.

Table 19.1.
Special Keys for Moving the Cursor in Layout View

To move the cursor to	Press
Beginning of previous paragraph	Ctrl-Up arrow
Beginning of next paragraph	Ctrl-Down arrow
Next column right	Alt-keypad 5-Right arrow
Next column left	Alt-keypad 5-Left arrow

Caution: When you move the cursor to the next column (to the right or left), be sure to hold down the Alt key as you press the 5 key on the keypad. If you release the Alt key before pressing 5 on the keypad, the command doesn't work.

The Hanging Indent Alternative

There is no need to bother with side-by-side formatting if you can fit all left paragraph text into one line, as shown in figure 19.3. The hanging indent format is much easier to create than side-by-side paragraphs, and you can sort the list using the Utilities Sort command.

To create a list using hanging indentations, follow these steps:

1. If you don't see the ruler, choose View **R**uler (Alt-VR) or click the ruler icon.

2. Place the cursor where you want the left column list to start.

3. Press Ctrl-T to create a hanging indentation.

   Word formats the first line flush to the left margin. The second and subsequent lines (turnover lines) are indented one default tab stop.

4. Press Ctrl-T again until the left indent mark (the left bracket) is positioned where you want the right column to start.

   To start the right column at 3.0-inches, for example, press Ctrl-T five times.

5. Set a flush left tab where you want the right column to start.

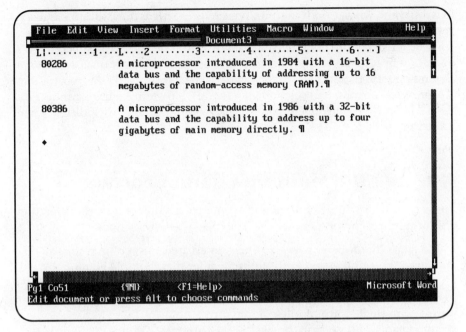

File Edit View Insert Format Utilities Macro Window   Help
                          Document3
L¦·······1···L···2·········3·········4·······5·········6···]
    80286   A microprocessor introduced in 1984 with a 16-bit
                   data bus and the capability of addressing up to 16
                   megabytes of random-access memory (RAM).¶

    80386   A microprocessor introduced in 1986 with a 32-bit
                   data bus and the capability to address up to four
     ◆   gigabytes of main memory directly. ¶

Pg1 Co51   {¶¶}   <F1=Help>   Microsoft Word
Edit document or press Alt to choose commands

Fig. 19.3. Side-by-side text created with a hanging indentation.

6. Type the word or phrase you want to appear in the left column.

7. Press Tab.

8. Type the text you want to appear in the right column.

9. Press Enter.

10. Repeat steps 6 through 9 until you have typed all the items in the list.

11. If you want to sort the list, highlight the list and choose Utilities Sort.

Creating Multiple-Column Text

To create newspaper columns with Word, you use the Format Section command to set up a section format with the number of columns you want—up to a maximum of 22. (In practice, you wouldn't want to choose more than 3 or 4 columns, so this limit will not prove constraining!) Because the multiple-column format is a section format, you can vary the number of columns you use as many times as you want within a document. In addition, you can vary the number of columns that you use on a single page.

In layout view, you see both columns on-screen exactly as they will appear when you print your document (see fig. 19.4). If you have a slow computer, however, you will find that Word operates sluggishly in layout view. You can speed Word's operation by toggling the layout view off. You work with just one column at a time (see fig. 19.5). You always can toggle layout view on to edit the two-column layout, or you can choose Print Preview (see fig. 19.6). Although you cannot edit the document in Print Preview, you see what your document will look like when printed.

Creating the Multiple-Column Format

You can format multiple-column text as you type or after you type. Formatting after you type is the best choice if you are using a slow computer.

In the steps that follow, you learn how to create a two-column format that applies to the whole document. But remember that multiple-column formatting is a section format. If you want, you can enter one or more section marks to divide your document into sections. You can format these sections as you please, with single- or multiple-column formatting. For more information on section marks and section breaks, see Chapter 5, "Word 5.5 Formatting Strategies: Page Formatting."

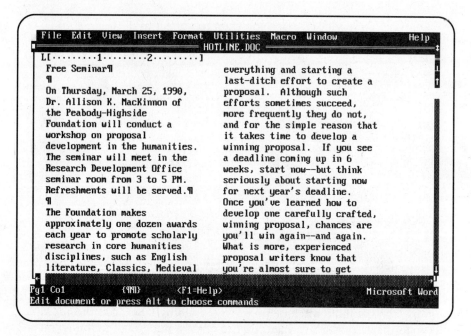

Fig. 19.4. Multiple columns (layout view toggled on).

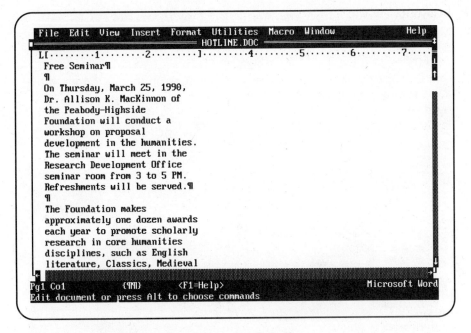

Fig. 19.5. Multiple columns (layout view toggled off).

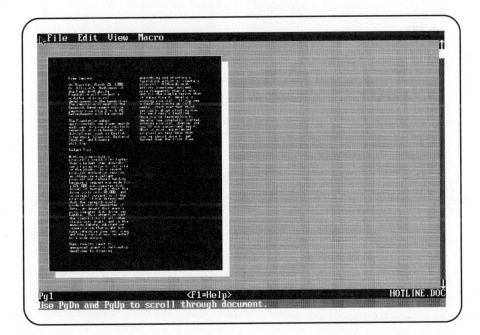

Fig. 19.6. Multiple columns (Print Preview).

When you create multiple columns, you choose the number of columns you want and the space between them (the default is 0.5-inches).

To create multiple-column text, follow these steps:

1. Place the cursor anywhere in the section you want to format with multiple columns.

2. Choose Format Section (Alt-TS).

   The Section dialog box appears (see fig. 19.7).

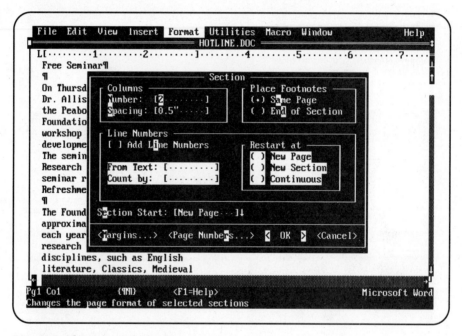

Fig. 19.7. *The Section dialog box.*

3. Type *2* in the Number box of the Columns area.

4. If you want the columns separated by a space other than 0.5-inches, type a different measurement in the Spacing box.

5. Choose OK.

6. Use File Print Preview (Alt-FV or Ctrl-F9) to see the result. Press Esc or Alt-FX to exit preview.

> If you are using layout view and do not have a mouse, remember the commands that move the cursor to the next column (Alt-keypad 5-right arrow) and preceding column (Alt-keypad 5-left arrow).

To restore single-column formatting, follow this procedure:

1. Place the cursor anywhere in the section that contains unwanted multiple columns.

2. Choose For**mat** **S**ection (Alt-TS).

    The Section dialog box appears (see fig. 19.7).

3. Type *1* in the **N**umber box of the Columns area.

4. Choose OK.

Controlling Column Breaks

After you have added multiple-column formatting, you may not like the column breaks that Word inserts automatically as it attempts to format your document. You can insert manual column breaks if you want.

To insert a manual column break in your two-column document, follow these steps:

Ctrl-Shift-Enter

1. Position the cursor where you want the column break to occur.

2. Choose **I**nsert **B**reak (Alt-IB) and choose the **C**olumn option. Choose OK. Alternatively, use the Ctrl-Shift-Enter keyboard shortcut.

Adding a Single-Column Headline

Blending single- and multiple-column formats on a page is easy. You insert a section mark and format each section as you please. In the following steps, you learn how to add a single-column headline to a document you already have formatted with multiple columns. A single-column heading spans the double-column text, creating an attractive effect that you see frequently in newspapers and magazines.

To add a single-column headline, follow this procedure:

1. Press Ctrl-Home to move the cursor to the beginning of the document.

2. Choose Format Section (Alt-TS).

 The Section dialog box appears.

3. Choose Continuous from the Section Start list box.

 If you don't choose the Continuous option, Word inserts a page break under the headline.

4. Choose OK.

5. Choose Insert Break (Alt-IB).

 The Break dialog box appears (see fig. 19.8).

6. Choose Section.

 The Continuous option already is selected.

7. Choose OK.

 A section mark appears at the top of the screen.

8. Press Ctrl-Home to place the cursor before the section mark.

9. Choose Format Section (Alt-TS).

 The Section dialog box appears again. Multiple-column formatting is in effect.

10. Type *1* in the Number box.

11. Choose OK.

 You see the section mark extending across the screen.

12. Type and center the headline (see fig. 19.9).

Adding Lines between Columns

Many newspapers and magazines use thin lines, called *rules*, to separate columns. You can create the same effect with Word. It's best to add the lines after you have finished adding all the text.

To add lines between columns, follow these steps:

1. Place the cursor in the section containing multiple-column text.

2. Choose Format Section (Alt-TS).

3. Type *0* in the Spacing box.

4. Choose OK.

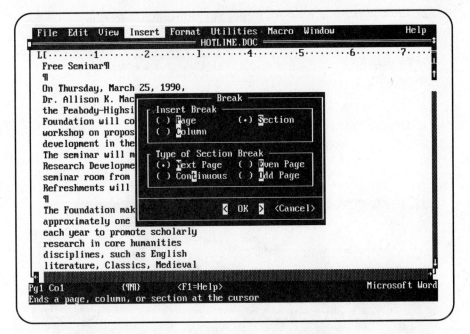

Fig. 19.8. *The Break dialog box.*

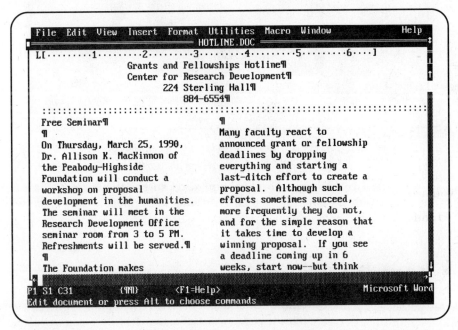

Fig. 19.9. *Layout view of multiple-column document with single-column headline.*

5. Select all the paragraphs in the multiple-column section.

6. Choose Forma**t** **B**orders (Alt-TB).

7. Choose **L**ines. When Word activates the check boxes below this option, choose Left and Right.

8. Choose OK.

9. Choose **F**ile Print Pre**v**iew (Alt-FV) or use the Ctrl-F9 keyboard shortcut to see a preview of this handsome effect (see fig. 19.10).

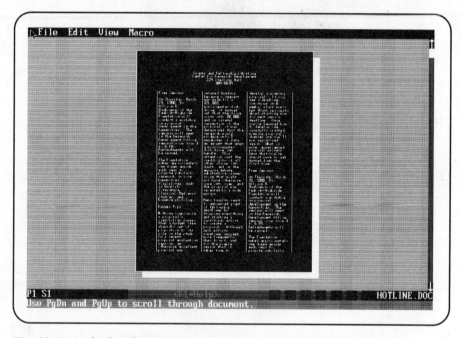

Fig. 19.10. Multiple-column document with lines between the columns.

You can separate columns with lines. You also can use the Forma**t** **B**orders command to add additional lines, such as the ones that appear in the newsletter reproduced at the beginning of this chapter (see fig. 19.1).

Chapter Summary

With Word 5.5 creating multiple-column text is easy. To pair paragraphs on the page, you can create side-by-side paragraphs, although using a hanging indent format is easier if the left paragraphs contain only one word or phrase. You also can create newspaper columns and separate the columns with lines.

With this chapter you have come to the end of Part IV, "Desktop Publishing with Microsoft Word." In the next section, you learn how to put two of Word 5.5's most powerful features—style sheets and macros—to work for you. Even if you're a beginner in personal computing, word processing, and Word, you will find that the material is comprehensible—and useful. Indeed, if you aren't putting style sheets and macros to work, you haven't come close to using Word's potential to increase your productivity at the keyboard.

Quick Review

Column Breaks

To insert a manual column break, follow these steps:

1. Position the cursor where you want the column break to occur.

2. Choose Insert Break (Alt-IB) and choose the Column option. Choose OK. Alternatively, use the Ctrl-Shift-Enter keyboard shortcut.

Cursor Movement in Layout View

To move the cursor to	Press
Beginning of previous paragraph	Ctrl-up arrow
Beginning of next paragraph	Ctrl-down arrow
Next column right	Alt-keypad 5-right arrow
Next column left	Alt-keypad 5-left arrow

Hanging Indentation

To create a list using hanging indentations, follow this procedure:

1. If you don't see the Ruler, choose View Ruler (Alt-VR) or click the Ruler icon.

2. Place the cursor where you want the list to start.

3. Press Ctrl-T to create a hanging indentation.

Word formats the first line flush to the left margin. The second and subsequent lines (turnover lines) are indented one default tab stop (0.5-inches if you haven't changed the default).

4. Press Ctrl-T again until the left indent mark (the left bracket) is positioned where you want the right column to start.

   To start the right column at 3.0-inches, for example, press Ctrl-T five times.

5. Set a flush left tab where you want the right column to start.

6. Type the word or phrase you want to appear in the left column.

7. Press Tab.

8. Type the text you want to appear in the right column.

9. Press Enter.

10. Repeat steps 6 through 9 until you have typed all the items in the list.

11. If you want to sort the list, highlight the list and choose Utilities Sort.

Headlines

To add a single-column headline in a multiple-column document, follow these steps:

1. Press Ctrl-Home to move the cursor to the beginning of the document.

2. Choose Format Section (Alt-TS).

3. Choose Continuous from the Section Start list box.

4. Choose OK.

5. Choose Insert Break (Alt-IB).

6. Choose Section.

7. Choose OK.

8. Press Ctrl-Home again to place the cursor before the section mark.

9. Choose Format Section (Alt-TS).

10. Type *1* in the Number box.

11. Choose OK.

12. Center the paragraph and then type the headline (see fig. 19.8).

Multiple-Column Text

To create multiple-column text, follow these steps:

1. Place the cursor anywhere in the section you want to format with multiple columns.

2. Choose Format Section (Alt-TS).

3. Enter a number greater than 1 in the **Number** box of the **C**olumns area.

4. If you want the columns separated by a space other than 0.5-inches, type a different measurement in the **S**pacing box.

5. Choose OK.

To add lines between columns, follow this procedure:

1. Place the cursor in the section containing multiple-column text.

2. Choose Format Section (Alt-TS).

3. Type *0* in the **S**pacing box.

4. Choose OK.

5. Select all the paragraphs in the multiple-column section.

6. Choose Format **B**orders (Alt-TB).

7. Choose **L**ines. When Word activates the check boxes below this option, choose Left and Right.

8. Choose OK.

To restore single-column formatting, follow these steps:

1. Place the cursor anywhere in the section that contains unwanted multiple columns.

2. Choose Format Section (Alt-TS).

   The Section dialog box appears (see fig. 19.6).

3. Type *1* in the **Number** box of the **C**olumns area.

4. Choose OK.

Side-by-Side Paragraphs

To create side-by-side paragraphs, follow these steps:

1. In a new, blank Word document, press Enter to create a blank paragraph.

2. Place the cursor in front of the paragraph mark.

3. Choose Format **P**aragraph (Alt-TP).

4. Type *3.25"* in the From Right text box, type *1 li* in the **A**fter box, and place an X in the **S**ide by Side check box.

5. Choose OK.

6. Press Enter to create a paragraph.

7. Choose Format **P**aragraph. Type *3.25"* in the From Left box. Type *O* in the From Right box. (When you pressed Enter, Word kept using the same formats, including 1 li in the **A**fter box and the X in the **S**ide by Side box.)

8. Choose OK.

9. To create additional side-by-side paragraphs, highlight both paragraph marks. Next, choose **E**dit **C**opy (or use the Ctrl-Ins shortcut) to copy the paragraph marks to the Scrap.

10. Position the cursor beneath the pair of paragraph marks.

11. Choose **E**dit **P**aste (or use the Shift-Ins shortcut) to insert a copy of the pair of paragraph marks. (Be sure that NumLock is off.)

12. Repeat step 11 to enter as many pairs as you need.

13. Type the text of the paragraphs.

Part V

Word 5.5's Style Sheets and Macros

Includes

Style Sheet Formatting

Creating and Using Word 5.5 Macros

20

Style Sheet Formatting

Fewer than one in five Microsoft Word users understand and use style sheets—but the proportion should be much higher because style sheet formatting is the key to high-productivity word processing with Word.

Can you use style sheet formatting? Try this quick test. Have you ever wanted to redefine Word's formatting defaults so that every document uses the font you prefer, superscripts footnotes automatically, and prints page numbers in a smaller font than the body text? Have you ever wanted to enter more than one format with a single keyboard shortcut? Have you ever spent time formatting a lengthy document, only to be told something like, "That's nice, but I need each paragraph indented 4 spaces, and please use 2 blank lines under each heading"? Chances are you can answer "yes" to one or more of these questions.

The following is a quick overview of what you can do with style sheets:

- *Change almost any of Word's default formats so that they apply to every document you create.* By making changes to Word's default style sheet (NORMAL.STY), you can change any of Word's defaults. Some of the formats you can redefine are normal character font and point size, footnote font and point size, footnote position (superscript), page number font and point size, line draw character, normal paragraph alignment, normal paragraph indentation, normal paragraph line spacing, header/footer formats, index formats, and many more. With just a few simple commands, you can change Word's defaults so that the program automatically uses the Times font, prints body text in 10-point type and headings in 14 point bold, and positions footnotes at the end of a section. (If you change these defaults, you're not stuck with them. You can override the styles, or change them again, if you want.)

- *Create your own keyboard shortcuts for formatting purposes.* You can define a Shift-Ctrl keyboard shortcut, for example, that enters all the following formats for a level 1 heading: boldface, Helvetica 14, centered, one blank line before, two blank lines after, and page breaks prevented beneath the heading. To attach all these formats to a heading using ordinary formatting techniques would require the use of several commands. By creating keyboard shortcuts, you give several commands by pressing just one key. And with Word 5.5's Ribbon, you can access the styles you create by choosing them from the Style drop-down list box at the top of the screen.

- *Instantly reformat all the text you formatted with the keyboard shortcut.* To understand the productivity gains you realize with style sheets, begin by recalling the way ordinary formatting works. With ordinary formatting (called *direct formatting*), you format each unit of text independently. To center and boldface level 1 headings in your document, for instance, you must choose these formats for each heading. Suppose you have 12 headings and you must change the format to flush-left and italic. What do you do? You must go through your document and make the changes 12 times. If you enter the format with your own keyboard shortcut, however, you make just one change, a change to the style sheet where the heading style is stored. The change instantly affects all the text to which the style has been applied.

If style sheet formatting is so great, why haven't more people used it? The answer lies in penalties previous versions of Word inflicted on the user who wanted to develop style sheet skills. The style sheet commands had names with no obvious connection to their function, and the procedures were both difficult and costly: creating a style sheet meant losing all the default keyboard shortcuts! With Word 5.5, style sheet formatting is much easier now, and every Word user should try it.

For users of previous versions of Word, here's a quick overview of the long-overdue style sheet command changes. The Gallery has been replaced by the more aptly named **Define Styles** command in the Format menu. And the odd nomenclature—"usages" and "variants"—has been replaced by the sensible terms "style type" and "style I.D." Because the Alt key is used to navigate the menus, you create Shift-Ctrl keyboard shortcuts. And here's a very welcome change: you don't lose the default Ctrl formatting shortcuts when you attach the style sheet to the document, so you no longer need to press a special key (Alt-X in the old version of Word) to access the NORMAL.STY key codes. As you learn in this chapter, creating style sheet entries and applying them is much easier with Word 5.5. You can press the keyboard shortcut you created, as always, but you also can choose the style name from Word 5.5's new Ribbon. Despite all these welcome changes, Word 5.5 can use style sheets created with previous versions of Word.

Using a series of tutorials, this chapter shows you how to make style sheets work for you.

This chapter covers the following:

- Modifying Word's default style sheet, NORMAL.STY, so that Word uses your preferences in formatting page numbers, footnote reference marks, and other styles

- Creating and defining new standard paragraph and division formats, which Word can use every time you start the program

- Creating and defining new keyboard shortcuts for special formatting jobs

- Creating style-sheet entries automatically from formats already inserted in your documents

- Creating custom style sheets for special-purpose applications

A word of encouragement for beginners: there isn't a thing in this chapter that you cannot handle, even as a novice in personal computing. This chapter presents a series of tutorials, each designed to put you in complete control of Word's style-sheet capabilities. The results place you among those who know how to obtain peak performance from this wonderful program. To get the best results from this chapter, read all the sections in order and try all the tutorials.

About Style Sheets

Every Word document has a style sheet. A style sheet is a special Word document that has the extension STY and includes style definitions. When you create a new Word document, the Open dialog box provides you with an opportunity to choose the style sheet you want to use. Thus far in this book, you have accepted the default style sheet, NORMAL.STY, when you created new documents.

The Two Paths to Style Sheet Formatting

You can get involved in style sheet formatting in two ways:

- *Modify NORMAL.STY.* Choose this approach if you want your changes to apply to all your Word documents (the only exceptions are those documents to which you have attached a custom style sheet). Most people modify NORMAL.STY because they are unhappy with one or more of Word's default formats. For example, if you have a laser printer with fonts, you probably don't want to print in Courier. By making a simple change to NORMAL.STY, all your documents will print in the font you choose (such as Times Roman or Helvetica). You also can create your own custom keyboard shortcuts and place them in NORMAL.STY, which makes these shortcuts available for all your documents.

• *Create a custom style sheet.* A custom style sheet applies only if you deliberately attach the sheet to a document. Why create a custom style sheet? Sometimes the formats you create for one kind of documents, such as letters, aren't suitable for others, such as reports. A business writer, for example, can create a series of style sheets, one for each type of document (LETTER.STY, MEMO.STY, and REPORT.STY). LETTER.STY may print letters in Helvetica, while REPORT.STY may print reports in Times Roman.

To get started in style sheet formatting, begin by making modifications to NORMAL.STY. You almost certainly have some "pet peeves" with respect to Word's default formats. For example, you probably noticed that page numbers print in your printer's default font (such as Courier) even though you choose a different font for the body of your document. To avoid this problem, you have to format the page numbers manually. You can change Word's defaults so that the page numbers always print in the font you prefer by altering one of the *automatic styles* in NORMAL.STY.

About Automatic Styles

An automatic style is a format definition that applies to your document automatically—you don't have to press a key or choose a style name from the Ribbon. When you change the definition of the automatic style, the format applies automatically to any document to which the style sheet is attached. Table 20.1 lists the Style I.D. names of Word's automatic styles. The Style I.D. is a name given to a style so that Word can keep that style separate from the others. You can redefine any of the automatic styles.

Table 20.1.
Word's Automatic Styles

Style Name	Affects
Annotation	Paragraph formats of all annotations
Annotation Ref	Annotation reference mark character format
Footnote	Paragraph formats of all footnotes/endnotes
Footnote Ref	Footnote reference mark character format
Header/Footer	Paragraph formats of all headers and footers
Heading 1	Paragraph format of heading level 1
Heading 2	Paragraph format of heading level 2
Heading 3	Paragraph format of heading level 3
Heading 4	Paragraph format of heading level 4
Heading 5	Paragraph format of heading level 5
Heading 6	Paragraph format of heading level 6
Heading 7	Paragraph format of heading level 7
Index 1	Paragraph format of index entry level 1
Index 2	Paragraph format of index entry level 2
Index 3	Paragraph format of index entry level 3
Index 4	Paragraph format of index entry level 4
Line Draw	Line draw character format
Line Number	Line number character format
Normal	Default paragraph format
Normal Section	Default section format
Page Number	Page number character format
Summary Info	Summary sheet character format
Table 1	Paragraph format of table of contents level 1
Table 2	Paragraph format of table of contents level 2
Table 3	Paragraph format of table of contents level 3
Table 4	Paragraph format of table of contents level 4

As you already know, Word divides up the world of formatting by distinguishing among character, paragraph, and section formats. Style sheet entries are the same way: Each entry has a Style Type (character, paragraph, or section). Among Word's automatic styles are character formats (such as Annotation Ref), paragraph formats (such as Heading 1), and even a section format (Normal). The following is an overview of automatic style types:

- *Automatic Character Styles.* You can modify these styles to change the way Word prints annotation reference marks, footnote reference marks, line draw characters, page number characters, and summary sheet characters.

- *Automatic Paragraph Styles.* You can modify these styles to change the way Word prints annotations, footnotes, headers and footers, headings, index entries, and table of contents entries. In addition, you can define a Normal paragraph style, which applies to every paragraph in your document (unless you override the style by choosing another format). Paragraph style definitions can include character formats as well as paragraph formats. For example, you can define the Footnote style so that footnotes are printed in single-space, 9-point Times Roman.

- *Automatic Section Styles.* Normal Section is the only automatic section style. If you change this style, you can redefine the default section formats that apply to all documents. These formats include page size, page number format, margins, header and footer location, and footnote location. (As you already have learned, however, you can change the page size and margin defaults just by checking the Use as Default check box in the Section Margins dialog box.)

Automatic styles are very convenient because you need do nothing to apply them. If you change the automatic styles in NORMAL.STY, the change applies to all your documents. Because most users will want to make such changes right away, the next section introduces style sheet formatting by showing you how to change automatic styles in Word's default style sheet.

User-Defined Styles

In addition to automatic styles, every style sheet contains *user-defined styles*—styles that you can enter by pressing a keyboard shortcut or choosing the style name from the Ribbon. You can define up to 23 character styles, 55 paragraph styles, and 21 section styles. In practice, you rarely define more than a few of each.

Like automatic styles, each user-defined style has a Style Type (character, paragraph, or section) and a Style I.D. User-defined styles have numbers for Style I.D.s, such as Character 14 or Paragraph 28.

How Do You Define Styles?

An overview of the procedure you use to define styles follows. You learn more about each step in the pages to follow.

1. You begin by opening the style sheet. The style sheet isn't a document like a normal Word document—you cannot type into the style sheet directly.

2. To create a style sheet entry, choose the **Insert New Style** command.

3. To format the style sheet entry, you make choices in the Character, Paragraph, Sections, and Margins dialog boxes. These dialog boxes are identical to the ones you use for ordinary formatting purposes.

4. You continue by creating additional entries and formatting them.

5. You save the style sheet. Until you do, your changes won't be permanent.

Modifying NORMAL.STY's Automatic Styles

As you already have learned, NORMAL.STY is Word's default style sheet. If you change one or more of the automatic styles in this style sheet, the changes you make apply to all your documents.

The tutorials that follow show you how to change several of Word's default formats. You learn how to change the base font, the footnote reference mark, the page number character format, and the formats Word applies to headings in outlines. You should try all these tutorials for two reasons: almost all Word users will benefit from making the changes these sections suggest, and, what's more, the tutorials introduce the fundamental concepts and procedures of style-sheet formatting.

Changing the Base Font

In the following tutorial, you learn how to change the *base font* of all the Word documents to which NORMAL.STY is attached. A base font is the font the program uses to print your documents, unless you specifically override the font choice.

Which base font is Word now using? That depends on your printer. Each of Word's printer driver files contains a base font definition. If the printer can print more than one font, the base font is usually a "plain Vanilla" font, such as Courier.

To change the base font, do the following:

1. Choose Format Define Styles (Alt-TD).

   You see what looks like a blank document (see fig. 20.1), which really is a style sheet. Note that the title bar shows the style sheet name, NORMAL.STY, and the message bar displays the message Select style or press Alt to choose commands. If you press Alt and display the menus, you find that many commands are missing from the menus and others are grayed. In addition, several new commands appear on some menus. You learn more about these commands in this chapter. Press Esc to close the menus.

   NORMAL.STY is blank until you modify it. You see style definitions only for those styles you deliberately have modified.

2. Choose Insert.

   You see an Insert menu with two options: New Style and Style Sheet (see fig. 20.2).

3. Choose New Style.

   You see the New Style dialog box (see fig. 20.3). Note that the Style Type field is set to Paragraph. The Style I.D. list box contains many automatic styles and user-defined styles.

4. Choose Normal in the Style I.D. list box.

5. Choose OK.

   You see the style definition for the default Normal paragraph format (see fig. 20.4), which is selected. As you can see, the default formats are Courier font, 12-point type, and flush-left alignment. The (P) indicates that the entry is a Paragraph style.

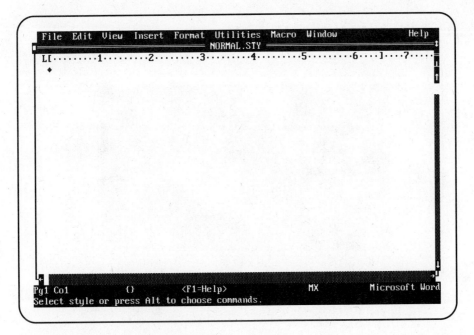

Fig. 20.1. NORMAL.STY before it has been modified.

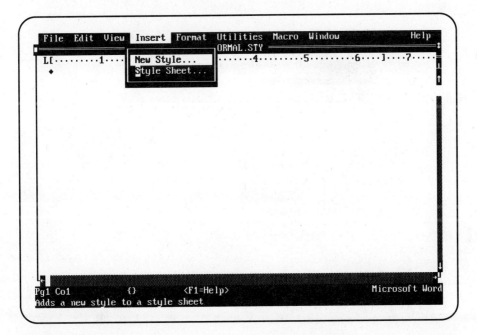

Fig. 20.2. The New Style and Style sheet options from the Insert menu.

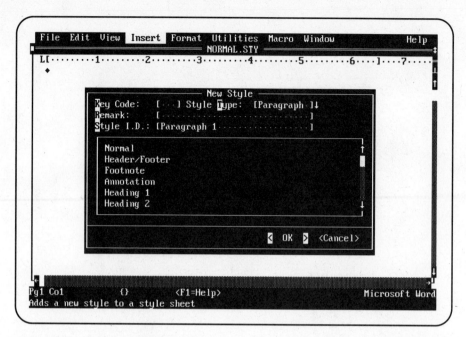

Fig. 20.3. *The New Style dialog box.*

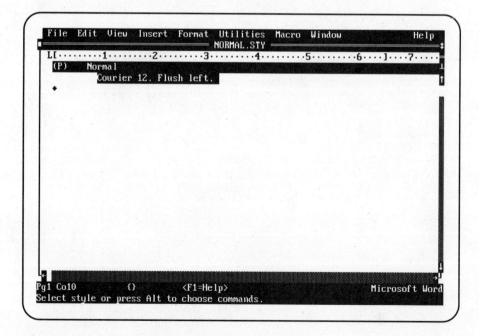

Fig. 20.4. *The default Normal paragraph format settings.*

6. Choose Format Character (Alt-TC).

   If this command is grayed, make sure the Normal style definition is selected.

   You see the Character dialog box, which looks just like the regular Character dialog box you use in ordinary formatting.

7. Drop down the Font list box and choose the new base font.

8. Choose OK.

   Word changes the font definition for the currently selected style (Normal) to Helvetica (see fig. 20.5).

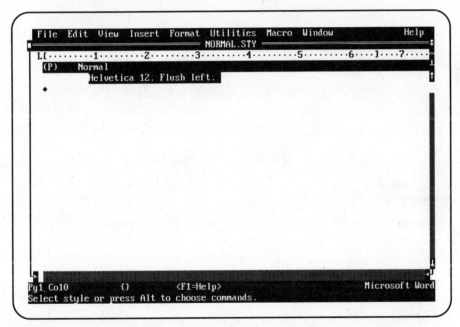

Fig. 20.5. Normal style definition with base font redefined to Helvetica.

9. Choose File Save (Alt-FS) or use the Alt-Shift-F2 keyboard shortcut.

10. Fill out the summary sheet, if you want. Title the style sheet "Modified NORMAL.STY with altered base font." Place the name of the font in the Keywords area.

11. Choose OK.

12. To return to the document, click the close box or choose File Close (Alt-FC). You see the document on-screen.

Now that you have redefined the base font, your choice applies to all the documents you create or edit with NORMAL.STY. To prove this fact to yourself, choose Format Character and look at the Font list box. You see the font you have chosen. Now open a document you created previously, one in which you did not alter the "plain Vanilla" base font. Choose Format Character and look at the Font list box again. You see the font you have chosen.

Restoring the Defaults in NORMAL.STY

What if you don't like the changes you make to NORMAL.STY? You can restore the defaults in two ways:

- Open the style sheet, select the style sheet entry you modified, and use the Format command dialog boxes to restore the old default. Choose File Save to save the style sheet.

- Open the style sheet, select the style sheet entry you modified, and press Del to erase the entire entry. Choose File Save to save the style sheet.

Changing the Footnote Reference Mark

In this tutorial, you modify NORMAL.STY again by changing the default character format for footnote reference marks.

To change the default footnote reference mark, follow these steps:

1. Choose Format Define Styles (Alt-TD).

2. Choose Insert New Style (Alt-IN).

3. Choose character in the Style Type box.

   You see a list of Character styles in the Style I.D. list box.

4. Choose Footnote Ref in the Style I.D. list box.

5. Choose OK.

   Word creates a Footnote Ref entry in the style sheet (see fig. 20.6). The (C) indicates that the entry is a character style.

6. Choose Format (Alt-T).

   As you can see, all the options are grayed except Character. When you choose a character Style Type, the only options you can choose are character formats.

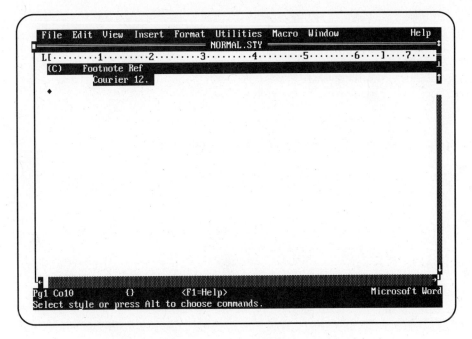

Fig. 20.6. Footnote Ref entry in NORMAL.STY (default formats).

7. Choose **Character**.

   You see the Character dialog box.

8. Choose the font, point size, and position options you want to apply to all footnote reference marks.

   Choose Helvetica 10, for example, and choose **Superscript** in the Position area.

9. Choose OK.

   You see the altered style definition in figure 20.7.

10. Choose File **Save** (Alt-FS) or use the Alt-Shift-F2 keyboard shortcut.

11. To return to the document, click the close box or choose **File Close** (Alt-FC).

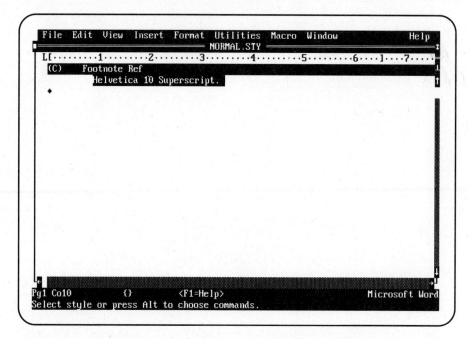

Fig. 20.7. Footnote Ref entry in NORMAL.STY (altered format).

Changing the Default Page Number Format

In this tutorial, you learn how to change the default font and point size that Word uses for page numbers. The formats you choose apply to all the page numbers Word inserts, whether you add the page numbers with the Format Page Numbers command or with the (page) symbol in headers or footers.

To change the default page number format, follow these steps:

1. Choose Format Define Styles (Alt-TD).

2. Choose Insert New Style (Alt-IN).

3. Choose Character in the Style Type box.

4. Choose Page Number in the Style I.D. list box.

5. Choose OK.

   Word creates a Page Number entry in the style sheet.

6. Choose Format Character (Alt-TC).

7. Choose the font and point size options you want to apply to all page numbers.

   For example, choose Times Roman 9.

8. Choose OK.

   Word alters the style definition.

9. Choose **File Save** (Alt-FS) or use the Alt-Shift-F2 keyboard shortcut.

10. To return to the document, click the close box or choose **File Close** (Alt-FC).

Combining Paragraph and Character Formats: Changing the Default Format for Footnotes

As you already have learned, you choose among three Style Types for each style sheet entry: Character, Paragraph, and Section. The Paragraph Style Type is particularly powerful because you can add character and tab formats as well as paragraph formats. You also can add Position and Border options to paragraph styles.

In this tutorial, you create a footnote text format that includes a character format as well as a paragraph format. When you add a character format to a paragraph style, the character format you choose applies to the whole paragraph.

To create a footnote text format, follow these steps:

1. Choose **Format Define Styles** (Alt-TD).

2. Choose **Insert New Style** (Alt-IN).

3. Choose **Paragraph** in the Style Type box.

4. Choose **Footnote** in the Style I.D. list box.

5. Choose OK.

   Word creates a Footnote entry in the style sheet.

6. Choose **Format Character** (Alt-TC).

7. Choose the font and point size options you want to apply to all footnotes or endnotes.

8. Choose OK.

9. Choose Forma**t** **P**aragraph (Alt-TP).

You see the Paragraph dialog box.

10. Choose the paragraph formats you want to apply to footnote or endnote text.

For example, choose a 1 inch left indent and add a blank line after the paragraph. If you choose a character point size other than 12, be sure to type the same point size in the Line Spacing box. (To set the line spacing to 10 points, type *10 pt*.)

11. Choose OK.

Word adds all the formats to the entry (see fig. 20.8). This entry reads, in effect, "Print the footnotes using the Helvetica font, in a 10-point font size, and with 10-point line spacing. (If you hadn't typed *10 pt* in the Line Spacing box of the Paragraph dialog box, you would see Helvetica 10/12 in the entry. 10/12 indicates that Word will print 10-point characters while continuing to use the default 12-point line spacing.) In addition, format the footnotes flush left, with a 1 inch left indent, and add one blank line after each footnote paragraph. Don't break a page or column within a footnote."

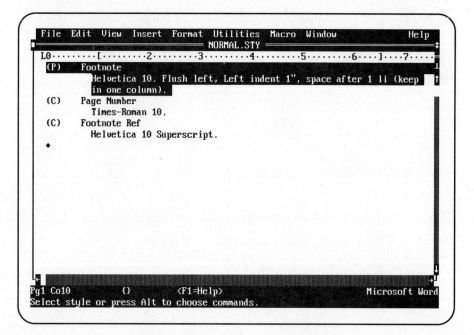

Fig. 20.8. Character and paragraph formats added to the footnote style.

12. Choose **File Save** (Alt-FS) or use the Alt-Shift-F2 keyboard shortcut.

13. To return to the document, click the close box or choose **File Close** (Alt-FC).

Changing the Default Heading Formats

As you learned in Chapter 10, you can take advantage of a powerful editing technique by defining your document's headings as outline headings. After you do so, you can reorganize a huge document quickly just by rearranging the headings on the outline. This technique is by far one of the most useful and powerful editing techniques available with any word processing program. If you are writing lengthy documents, you will want to master this technique.

The techniques you learned in Chapter 10 have only one drawback: you must format each heading individually. In this section, you learn how to change the heading formats so that each heading contains exactly the formats you want. These formats are automatic styles, so the changes you make apply automatically. All you do is define a heading as a style in the outline view, and presto! Word applies the formats you have chosen, and you see the formats when you switch back to document view.

Defining the heading styles is definitely worth your while. One very common formatting flaw is the widowed heading, a heading left alone at the bottom of the page, with no text beneath it. When you define heading styles, you can choose the Keep with Next Paragraph option in the Paragraph dialog box, which prevents Word from inserting a page break beneath the heading. You also can choose the character, blank line, and alignment options you want.

Before trying this tutorial, decide how you want to format the chapter titles, headings, and subheadings in your document. The following is an example of the way chapter titles, headings, and subheadings can be defined:

- *Chapter Title* (level 1). Character formats: bold, italic, 18-point Times Roman. Paragraph formats: flush-left, page break before, 5 blank lines after.

- *A-Level Heading* (level 2). Character formats: uppercase, bold, 14-point Times Roman. Paragraph formats: flush-left, 4 blank lines before, 2 blank lines after.

- *B-Level Heading* (level 3). Character formats: small capital letters, 12-point Times Roman. Paragraph formats: flush-left, 2 blank lines before, 2 blank lines after.

You rarely should have to (or want to) define more than two or three levels of subheadings, but Word gives you plenty of leeway.

To redefine the default heading level formats do the following:

1. Choose Format Define Styles (Alt-TD).

2. Choose Insert New Style (Alt-IN).

3. If you want to enter heading level styles using the keyboard shortcut technique, type *H1* in the Key Code box.

   Usually, you have no reason to define key codes for automatic styles. After all, Word enters automatic styles automatically! That's true for heading styles, but only if you create the headings in outline view and define them as levels in an outline. If you create a key code for each heading style, you can press the keyboard shortcut in document view and enter the heading format. (To apply a style with the keyboard, you press Shift-Ctrl and then the key code you entered. For example, to apply this style, you press Shift-Ctrl-H1. Word enters a level 1 heading in the document, and when you switch to outline view, you can see this heading as a level 1 heading in your outline.) If you really don't like the idea of creating key codes, however, you still can choose the Heading styles from the Ribbon while in document view, which has the same effect.

4. Choose Heading 1 in the Style I.D. box.

5. Choose OK.

6. Use the Character and Paragraph dialog boxes to choose the styles you want to apply to this heading level.

7. Repeat steps 2 through 4 for each heading level you want to define.

   For level 2, choose Heading 2 in the Style I.D. box and type *H2* in the Key Code box. For level 3, choose Heading 3 and type *H3*, and so on.

8. Choose File Save (Alt-FS) or use the Alt-Shift-F2 keyboard shortcut.

9. To return to the document, click the close box or choose File Close (Alt-FC).

Adding User-Defined Styles to NORMAL.STY

Thus far, you have redefined some of the automatic styles in NORMAL.STY. In this section, you learn how to create user-defined styles and add them to NORMAL.STY.

Creating a Body Text Style

In this tutorial, you learn how to create a very useful style: a style for body text paragraphs. In most reports or essays, for example, you type double-spaced, indented paragraphs, and right margin justification. After you change formats to type a table or quotation, however, you must enter all these formats all over again to resume typing the body text. Therefore, you need a style that enters all these formats again with just one command.

To define a style for body text, do the following:

1. Choose Format Define Styles (Alt-TD).

2. Choose Insert New Style (Alt-IN). You see the New Style dialog box (see figure 20.3).

3. In the Key Code box, type *BT*.

4. In the Remarks box, type *Body text style*.

5. In the Style I.D. box, scroll down the list and choose one of the user-defined Paragraph I.D.s, such as Paragraph 1.

6. Choose OK.

7. Use the Character and Paragraph dialog boxes to choose the styles you want for body text paragraphs.

   You see the style definition in the window in figure 20.9. This format, suitable for double-spaced business reports, includes 12 point Times Roman with double line spacing (24 points), right-margin justification, and an automatic first-line indent of 0.5 inches. Note that the entry includes the key code BT you have chosen for this user-defined entry. As you learn later in this section, you can enter this style at any time by pressing Shift-Ctrl-BT.

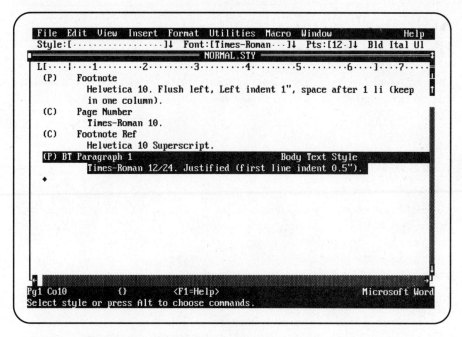

Fig. 20.9. *Style for body text paragraphs.*

8. Choose **File Save** (Alt-FS) or use the Alt-Shift-F2 keyboard shortcut.

9. To return to the document, click the close box or choose **File Close** (Alt-FC).

About Key Codes

As you just learned, you can assign a key code to the user-defined styles you create. The following gives some additional information about key codes:

- Key codes are optional. If you don't add a key code, you still can apply the style by choosing its name from the Ribbon or from the Apply Styles dialog box.

- You can define one- or two-letter key codes. The codes must be unique. If you define a style with the one-letter code K, you cannot define any two-letter codes that start with K. If you are going to define two-letter codes, therefore, make all your codes two-letter codes.

- The code must start with a letter or number, but the second character can be any printable character.

- To apply the style, press Shift-Ctrl and then the key code you have created.

- Try to create mnemonic codes—that is, codes using letters that remind you of the code's function. Create codes T2, T3, and T4, for example, for table styles that align 2, 3, or 4 columns.

Creating a Style for Tables

When you create a paragraph style, you can add character formats that apply to all the text in the paragraph. You also can add tabs, as this tutorial illustrates. In this tutorial, you create a user-defined table style that automatically enters a single-spaced format with three tab stops: a flush-left tab stop at 0.2 inches for typing the item name, and two decimal tab stops (at 3.5 inches and 4.5 inches) for typing figures in two columns.

To define a style for a two-column table, do the following:

1. Choose Format Define Styles (Alt-TD).

2. Choose Insert New Style (Alt-IN).

3. In the Key Code box, type *T2*.

4. In the Remarks box, type *Two-column table*.

5. In the Style I.D. box, scroll down the list and choose one of the user-defined Paragraph I.D.s, such as Paragraph 2.

   Word displays the Style I.D. of an unused paragraph style.

6. Choose OK.

7. Choose Format Character and use the Character dialog box to choose a font and point size for the text in your table.

8. If you don't see the Ruler, choose View Ruler or click the ruler icon.

9. Set a flush-left tab at 0.2 inches and decimal tabs at 3.5 inches and 4.5 inches.

   You see the table style you have defined on-screen (see fig. 20.10).

10. Choose File Save (Alt-FS) or use the Alt-Shift-F2 keyboard short-cut.

11. To return to the document, click the close box or choose File Close (Alt-FC).

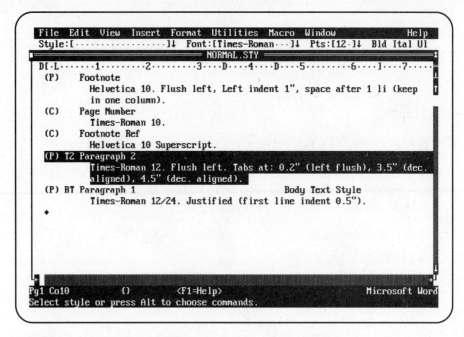

Fig. 20.10. *User-defined style for tables.*

Recording Styles from Examples

Now you have learned how to change automatic styles and how to create your own user-defined styles. Along the way, you have learned important concepts about how Word stores and defines styles.

Chances are you're thinking about storing additional user-defined styles in your NORMAL.STY style sheet. Before you go to all the trouble to create the styles manually using the techniques already introduced, however, ask yourself whether one of your Word documents contains text already formatted that way. If the answer is "yes," you can make use of a nifty feature that "reads" your formatting choices and stores them in a style sheet entry. This technique is called *creating a style by example*.

To record a style, do the following:

1. Open the document that contains the text with the format you want to record.

Note: If you want to record a paragraph style that includes character formatting, make sure the character format applies to all the characters in the first paragraph you selected, including the paragraph mark.

2. Select the text (see fig. 20.11).

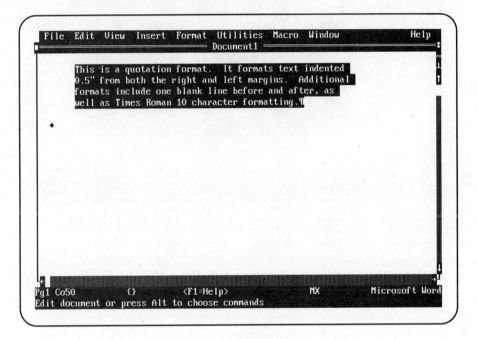

File   Edit   View   Insert   Format   Utilities   Macro   Window   Help
                                    Document1

This is a quotation format. It formats text indented
0.5" from both the right and left margins. Additional
formats include one blank line before and after, as
well as Times Roman 10 character formatting.¶

Pg1 Co50   {}   <F1=Help>   MX   Microsoft Word
Edit document or press Alt to choose commands

Fig. 20.11. Formatted text selected for creating a style by example.

3. Choose Forma**t** **R**ecord Style (Alt-TR).

   You see the Record Style dialog box (see fig. 20.12). The box lists the character and paragraph formats Word encountered in the selected text.

4. In the **K**ey Code box, type the keyboard shortcut you want to use for the recorded style.

5. In the Style **T**ype area, choose the style type (Character, Paragraph, or Section).

   If you choose Character, Word stores the format of the first character in the selection. If you choose Paragraph, Word stores the format of the first paragraph in the selection and also stores

Fig. 20.12. The Record Style dialog box.

the character format shared by all the characters in the first paragraph, including the paragraph mark. If you choose Section, Word stores the section formats in the first section within the selection.

6. In the **Remark** area, type a brief description of the style.

7. Choose OK.

8. To see the style in the style sheet, choose Forma**t** **D**efine Styles (Alt-TD).

   Word has added the recorded style to NORMAL.STY (see fig. 20.13).

9. Choose **F**ile **S**ave (Alt-FS) to save the style sheet.

10. Choose **F**ile **C**lose (Alt-FC) or click the close box to close the style sheet and return to your document.

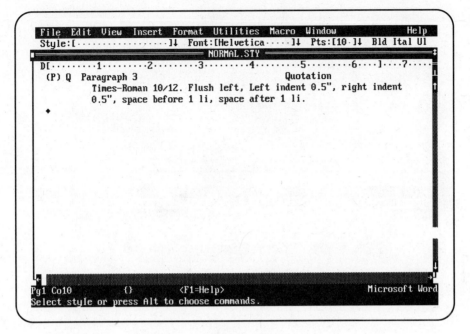

Fig. 20.13. *Recorded style added to NORMAL.STY.*

Applying User-Defined Styles

When you create automatic styles, Word applies them to any document to which the style sheet is attached. When you create user-defined styles, however, Word doesn't apply them unless you choose them deliberately. You can choose user-defined styles in three ways: you can press the keyboard shortcut you created, you can choose the style name from the Ribbon, or you can choose the style using the Format Apply Style command.

To apply a style using the keyboard shortcut, follow these steps:

1. Select the text to which you want the format to apply, or place the cursor where you want to start typing in the format.

2. Hold down the Shift and Ctrl keys and press the key code you created.

To apply a style using the Ribbon, follow these steps:

1. If you don't see the Ribbon, choose View Ribbon (Alt-VB).

2. Select the text to which you want the format to apply, or place the cursor where you want to start typing in the format.

3. Press Ctrl-S to activate the Ribbon.

4. Type the name of the style you want to apply, or choose the name of the style from the drop-down list box (see fig. 20.14).

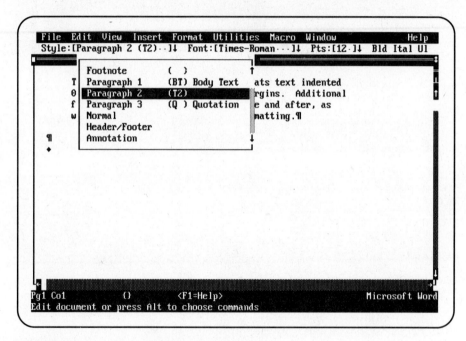

Fig. 20.14. Choosing a style from the Ribbon.

Ctrl-S To apply a style using the Apply Style dialog box, follow these steps:

1. Select the text to which you want the format to apply, or place the cursor where you want to start typing in the format.

2. Choose Format Apply Style (Alt-TY), or press Ctrl-S twice.

   You see the Apply Style dialog box in figure 20.15.

3. To choose the style, select the name in the Style I.D. list box or type the key code in the Key Code box.

4. Choose OK.

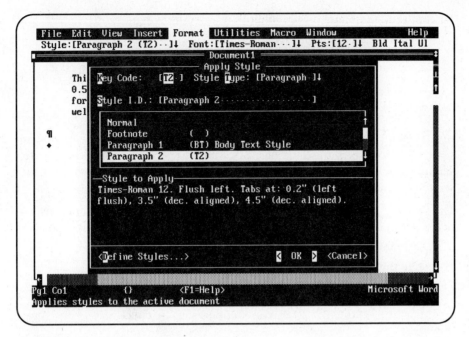

Fig. 20.15. The Apply Style dialog box.

Tip : Good typists probably will want to apply styles using the keyboard shortcuts. If you have a mouse, it's equally convenient to choose the style name from the Ribbon (you can make use of this technique even if you don't have a mouse). Both of these techniques are fast. The only good reason to use the Apply Style dialog box is to view the style definition in the Style to Apply area. By reading this definition, you can make sure that you're applying the right style and that the style really contains the formats you want.

Which Style Have You Applied?

After you have applied user-defined styles to text throughout your document, you may want to find out which style you have applied to a given unit of text. You can find out two ways: by viewing the style name on the Ribbon, or by displaying the Style Bar.

To view the style name on the Ribbon, do the following:

1. If you don't see the Ribbon on-screen, choose **View Ribbon** (Alt-VR).

2. Place the cursor in the text whose style name you want to check.

3. Look at the Style box on the Ribbon.

    The style box always shows the current style.

In previous versions of Word, the only way you could view style names on-screen was to display the Style Bar, a two-column strip running down the left side of the screen (left of the selection bar). In Version 5.5, however, you can see the current style name in the Style box on the Ribbon.

The style bar still may come in handy if you want to see the key codes instead of the style name. When you turn on the display of the Style Bar, you see the key codes you created next to the text to which you applied the style.

To toggle the Style Bar on, do the following:

1. Choose **View Preferences** (Alt-VE).

2. Choose Style Bar so that an X appears in the check box.

3. Choose OK.

    Word moves your text over two columns to make room for the Style Bar (see fig. 20.16).

Modifying Styles You Already Have Created

After you have created a style, you probably will want to modify one or more of them. You can change the key code, remark, or Style I.D. of any style you have created. You also can change the formatting you have attached to a style definition.

To change the key code, remark, or Style I.D, do the following:

1. Choose **Format Define Styles** (Alt-TD).

    You see the NORMAL.STY style sheet.

2. Select the style you want to modify.

3. Choose **Edit Rename Style** (Alt-EN).

    You see the Rename Style dialog box (see fig. 20.17).

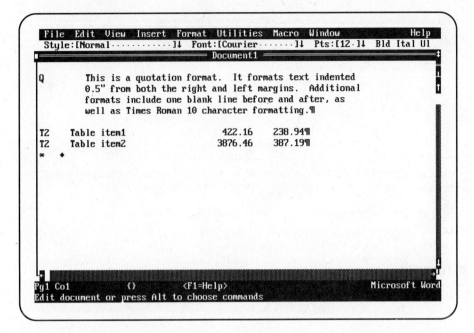

Fig. 20.16. *Style bar along left column of screen.*

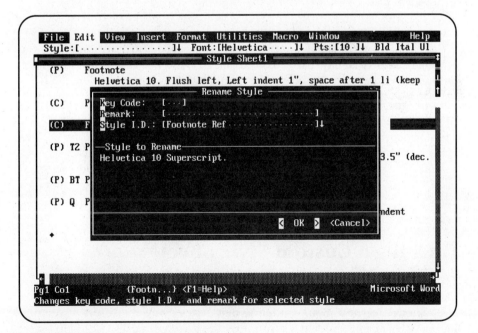

Fig. 20.17. *The Rename Style dialog box.*

4. To change the key code, type the new key code in the **Key Code** box.

5. To change the remark, type the new remark in the **Remark** box.

6. To change the Style I.D., type the new Style I.D. in the **Style I.D.** box or choose the Style I.D. from the list.

7. Choose OK.

8. Choose File **S**ave (Alt-FS) or press Alt-Shift-F2 to save your changes.

To change the formatting you have attached to a style definition, follow these steps:

1. Choose Format **D**efine Styles (Alt-TD).

    You see the NORMAL.STY style sheet.

2. Select the style you want to modify.

3. Use the Forma**t** command to choose the formats you want.

4. Choose File **S**ave (Alt-FS) or press Alt-Shift-F2 to save your changes.

Custom Style Sheets

All the techniques you have learned thus far have modified NORMAL.STY, Word's default style sheet—and with good reason. You have modified the automatic styles that have proven unsatisfactory, and you also have added user-defined styles that you expect to use in many of the documents you create.

Should you create a custom style sheet? Do you frequently create different types of documents, with each type of document having distinct formats? For example, many people prefer to type letters using a sans serif font such as Helvetica, even though they create reports using a serif font such as Times Roman or New Century Schoolbook. If you create different types of documents, each with distinct formats, you may want to create one custom style sheet for each.

Creating a Custom Style Sheet

To create a new, custom style sheet, you use the **N**ew command to open a new, blank custom style sheet, and then you add styles using the techniques you already have learned. You can define new styles using the **I**nsert Style command, or you can record styles from existing documents.

To create a custom style sheet, do the following:

1. Choose **File New** (Alt-FN).

2. Choose **Style Sheet** in the Type area.

3. Choose **OK**.

   You see a new, blank style sheet, which Word names Style Sheet1. Now that you have created the style sheet, you add styles.

To add styles to the custom style sheet, you can use a variety of techniques. You should begin, however, by asking yourself whether any of the styles you have created or modified in NORMAL.STY could play a role in your new style sheet. If they can, you can copy the styles directly from NORMAL.STY without repeating all the work you did to create them.

Copying Styles from NORMAL.STY

Chances are you already have modified many of the automatic styles in NORMAL.STY. When you begin a custom style sheet, you start out with the old, ugly defaults all over again. Do you need to duplicate your work? No, because you can open NORMAL.STY and copy the styles you already have modified or created. You can copy one or more selected styles, or if you want, you can merge NORMAL.STY into the custom style sheet you're creating.

Copying One or More Selected Styles

To copy styles from NORMAL.STY to your new, custom style sheet:

1. With your new, blank custom style sheet on-screen, choose **File Open** (Alt-F0) or choose the Alt-Ctrl-F2 keyboard shortcut.

2. Choose **Style Sheets** in the Show **Files** field.

3. Choose NORMAL.STY in the Files list box.

4. Choose **OK**.

   Word opens NORMAL.STY and places the style sheet in its own window on-screen.

5. Select the style or styles you want to copy.

   You can select more than one style using any of the extended selection techniques you have learned.

6. Choose **Edit Copy** (Alt-EC) or use the Ctrl-Ins keyboard shortcut.

7. Close NORMAL.STY by clicking the close box or choosing **File Close** (Alt-FC).

   You see your custom style sheet again.

8. Choose **Edit Paste** (Alt-EP) or choose the Shift-Ins keyboard shortcut.

Word pastes the selected entries into your new style sheet. When the entries are in your new style sheet, you can modify them.

Merging Style Sheets

If you want to add all the styles from NORMAL.STY, try this even quicker way.

To insert an entire style sheet at the cursor's location in a custom style sheet follow these steps:

1. Choose **Insert Style Sheet** (Alt-IS).

   You see the Style Sheet dialog box.

2. Choose the name of the style sheet you want to insert from the **Files** list box.

3. Choose OK to insert all the styles from the style sheet you named.

Inserting Additional Styles in the Custom Style Sheet

In your custom style sheet, you can create styles the same way you created them in NORMAL.STY. Use the Insert New Style command to create new user-defined styles (or modify automatic styles). You also can record styles from an existing document. You cannot record styles from a document, however, until you attach your custom style sheet to the document. You learn how to attach your custom style sheet to a document in the next section.

Attaching a Style Sheet to a Document

Word uses NORMAL.STY automatically; you need do nothing to attach NORMAL.STY. If you want to use a custom style sheet, however, you must deliberately attach the style sheet to the document you're working on.

You can attach a custom style sheet to a document at two times: when you create the document (using the New dialog box) and after you have created the document (using the Attach Style Sheet dialog box).

To attach a custom style sheet when you create the document, do the following:

1. Choose **File New** (Alt-FN).

   You see the New dialog box.

2. Choose **Use Style Sheet**.

   The Use Style Sheet list box lists the names of the style sheets in the document directory (see fig. 20.18).

3. Choose the style sheet you want to use.

4. Choose OK.

   Word creates the document and attaches the style sheet yoy have chosen.

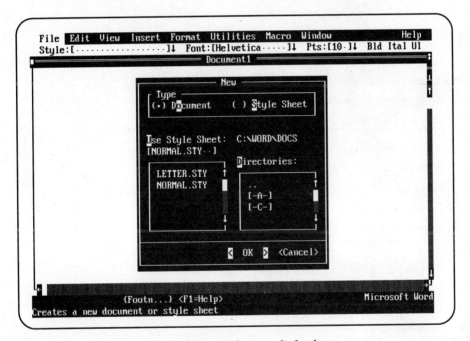

Fig. 20.18. *Attaching a style sheet using the New dialog box.*

To attach a custom style sheet to a document you already have created, do the following:

1. Open the document and display it on-screen.

2. Choose **Format Attach Style Sheet** (Alt-TA).

   You see the Attach Style Sheet dialog box (see fig. 20.19).

3. Highlight the style sheet you want to use.

4. Choose OK.

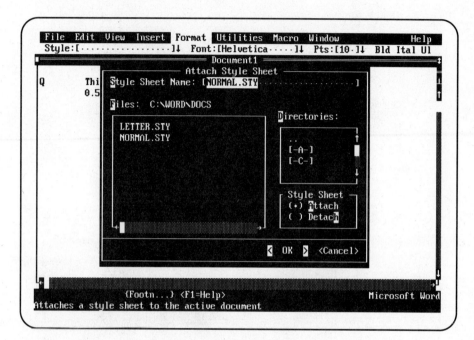

Fig. 20.19. The Attach Style Sheet dialog box.

Combining Style Sheet and Direct Formatting

Style sheet formatting is indirect formatting—you don't format a unit of text directly. Instead, you create a style definition, and you store the definition in a style sheet. If the style is automatic, the style is applied without your doing anything. If the style is a user-defined style, you apply the style to text by pressing the style's keyboard shortcut, by choosing its name from the Ribbon, or by choosing its name or key code from the Apply Style dialog box.

Ordinary formatting, in contrast to style sheet formatting, is direct formatting. You format a unit of text directly by choosing the formats you want, and the formats apply only to the selected text.

You may want to combine style sheet and direct formatting in your document at times, because re-creating all the default formats in every style sheet is a tedious job. When you combine direct and style sheet formatting, however, you must understand that direct formatting takes precedence over style sheet formatting.

When you format text using a style, you create a link between the text you have formatted and the style definition. If you change the style definition later, the text's format also changes and breaks the link between the text and the style definition. If you change the style definition, the change doesn't apply to the text you have formatted using direct techniques.

The following example shows how direct formatting takes precedence over style sheet formatting and breaks the link. Suppose that you change the default base font so that all your text is entered in New Century Schoolbook. However, you type a table and apply Helvetica using direct formatting techniques. Later, you decide to use Times Roman as your base font, and you change the base font definition in NORMAL.STY. This change, however, does not affect the table you formatted directly with Helvetica. By using direct formatting on this table, you broke the link between the text and the style definition.

Why does Word allow direct formatting to take precedence over style sheet formatting? Most often, the direct formatting you combine with style sheet formatting is intended to handle special, one-of-a-kind situations, such as the table formatted in Helvetica. In such cases, you really do want to break the link between the style definition and the text you formatted directly. You overrode the style sheet formatting to make the table look right. You wouldn't want Word to make further changes to this text without telling you.

Although direct formatting takes precedence over style sheet formatting, the link between the text and the style isn't always broken. If you apply some character emphasis directly to a paragraph that's formatted with a style, Word doesn't break the link. Similarly, if you apply some paragraph formatting to a section that's formatted with a style, Word doesn't break the link. Word breaks the link only if you apply a direct format that has the same Style Type as the style you used previously. A direct character format overrides a Character style, a direct paragraph format overrides a Paragraph style, and a direct section format overrides a Section style.

Chapter Summary

Style sheet formatting has three important advantages over direct formatting techniques. First, with style sheet formatting, you can change almost any of Word's default formats so that they apply automatically to every document you create. Second, you can create your own keyboard shortcuts that enter two or more formats simultaneously. And third, even if the text is located here and there throughout a huge document, text formatted with styles can be reformatted instantly, just by making a change to the style definition. These advantages can help you work more productively with Word.

Most Word users will satisfy their style-sheet formatting needs just by making a few, simple modifications to NORMAL.STY, Word's default style sheet. You can easily modify Word's automatic styles—the styles the program applies automatically to formats such as page numbers—footnote reference marks, and footnote text. Changing the base font that Word uses by default for every document you create also is a simple procedure.

If you want, you can add user-defined style sheet entries to NORMAL.STY. After you have created these entries, you can apply them to your document by pressing the keyboard shortcut you created or by choosing the style name from the Style box on the Ribbon.

Some Word users may want to create custom style sheets. Word doesn't use custom style sheets unless you deliberately attach the style sheet to a document. You probably will decide to create custom style sheets if you frequently create more than one kind of document, such as letters and reports.

Quick Review

Applying Styles

To apply a style using the keyboard shortcut:

1. Select the text to which you want the format to apply, or place the cursor where you want to start typing in the format.

2. Hold down the Shift and Ctrl keys and press the key code you created.

To apply a style using the Ribbon:

1. If you don't see the Ribbon, choose View Ribbon (Alt-VB).

2. Select the text to which you want the format to apply, or place the cursor where you want to start typing in the format.

3. Press Ctrl-S to activate the Ribbon.

4. Type the name of the style you want to apply, or choose the name of the style from the drop-down list box.

To apply a style using the Apply Style dialog box:

1. Select the text to which you want the format to apply, or place the cursor where you want to start typing in the format.

2. Choose Format Apply Style (Alt-TY).

3. To choose the style, select the name in the **Style I.D.** list box or type the key code in the **Key Code** box.

4. Choose OK.

Attaching a Style Sheet to a Document

To attach a custom style sheet when you create the document:

1. Choose **File New** (Alt-FN).

2. Choose **Use Style Sheet**.

3. Choose the style sheet you want to use.

4. Choose OK.

To attach a custom style sheet to a document you already have created:

1. Open the document and display it on-screen.

2. Choose Format **Attach Style Sheet** (Alt-TA).

3. Choose the style sheet you want to use.

4. Choose OK.

Automatic Styles

To change an automatic style in NORMAL.STY:

1. Choose Format **Define Styles** (Alt-TD).

2. Choose **Insert New Style** (Alt-IN).

3. Choose Character, Paragraph, or Section in the Style Type box.

4. Choose the name of an automatic style in the **Style I.D.** list box.

5. Choose OK.

6. Use the Format dialog boxes to change the format as you want.

7. Choose **File Save** (Alt-FS) or use the Alt-Shift-F2 keyboard shortcut.

Copying Styles from One Style Sheet to Another

To copy styles:

1. Open the style sheet to which you want to copy the styles.

2. Choose **File Open** (Alt-FO).

3. Choose Style Sheets in the Show Files field.

4. Choose the name of the style sheet from which you want to copy the styles.

5. Choose OK.

6. Select the style or styles you want to copy.

7. Choose **Edit Copy** (Alt-EC) or use the Ctrl-Ins keyboard shortcut.

8. Close the style sheet by clicking the close box or choosing **File Close** (Alt-FC).

9. Choose **Edit Paste** (Alt-EP) or use the Shift-Ins keyboard shortcut.

Custom Style Sheets

To create a custom style sheet:

1. Choose **File New** (Alt-FN).

2. Choose Style Sheet in the Type field.

3. Choose OK.

Merging Style Sheets

To insert an entire style sheet at the cursor's location in a custom style sheet:

1. Choose **Insert Style Sheet** (Alt-IS).

2. Choose the name of the style sheet you want to insert from the **Files** list box.

3. Choose OK to insert all the styles from the style sheet you named.

Modifying Styles

To change the key code, remark, or Style I.D:

1. Choose Format Define Styles (Alt-TD).

2. Select the style you want to modify.

3. Choose Edit Rename Style (Alt-EN).

4. To change the key code, type the new key code in the Key Code box.

5. To change the remark, type the new remark in the Remark box.

6. To change the Style I.D., type the new Style I.D. in the Style I.D. box or choose the Style I.D. from the list.

7. Choose OK.

8. Choose File Save (Alt-FS) or press Alt-Shift-F2 to save your changes.

To change the formatting you have attached to a style definition:

1. Choose Format Define Styles (Alt-TD).

    You see the NORMAL.STY style sheet.

2. Select the style you want to modify.

3. Use the Format command to choose the formats you want.

4. Choose File Save (Alt-FS) or press Alt-Shift-F2 to save your changes.

Style by Example

To record a style:

1. Open the document that contains the text with the format you want to record.

2. Select the text.

3. Choose Format Record Style (Alt-TR).

4. In the Key Code box, type the keyboard shortcut you want to use.

5. In the Style Type area, choose the style type (Character, Paragraph, or Section).

6. In the **Remark** area, type a brief description of the style.

7. Choose OK.

8. To see the style in the style sheet, choose Forma**t** **D**efine Styles (Alt-TD).

9. Choose **F**ile **S**ave (Alt-FS) to save the style sheet.

10. Choose **F**ile **C**lose (Alt-FC) or click the close box to close the style sheet and return to your document.

User-Defined Styles

To create a user-defined style:

1. Choose Forma**t** **D**efine Styles (Alt-TD).

2. Choose **I**nsert **N**ew Style (Alt-IN).

3. In the **Key Code** box, type the key code with which you want to apply the style (optional).

4. In the **Remarks** box, type a short description of the style.

5. In the Style **T**ype box, choose from Character, Paragraph, or Section.

6. In the Style I.D. box, scroll down the list and choose one of the numbered I.D.s.

7. Choose OK.

8. Use the Forma**t** command's dialog boxes to choose the styles you want.

9. Choose **F**ile **S**ave (Alt-FS) or use the Alt-Shift-F2 keyboard shortcut.

10. To return to the document, click the close box or choose **F**ile **C**lose (Alt-FC).

Viewing Style Names

To view the style name on the Ribbon:

1. If you don't see the Ribbon on-screen, choose **V**iew **R**ibbon (Alt-VR).

2. Place the cursor in the text whose style name you want to check.

3. Look at the Style box on the Ribbon.

To toggle the Style Bar on:

1. Choose **View** Pr**e**ferences (Alt-VE).

2. Choose Style **Bar** so that an X appears in the check box.

3. Choose OK.

Chapter 21

Creating and Using
Word 5.5 Macros

A *macro* is a stored list of keystrokes that you set in motion with just one keystroke. With Word, you can create macros in two ways: you can *record* a macro by keying in an operation while Word records your keystrokes, and you can *write* a macro by typing symbols that stand for the keystrokes. (Word's macros are *keyboard* macros; you cannot store mouse movements in a Word macro.)

By using the recording technique, anyone can create, save, and use macros. Writing macros is more difficult, but the payoff is worth it. You can use special commands that instruct the macro to repeat until a condition is satisfied, prompt the user for input, or change action if a problem is encountered.

Why record or write macros? You can use Word without doing so. But carefully examine your day-to-day Word habits. If you find yourself repeating a complex key sequence, it's a good candidate for a macro. Why press many keys over and over again, when you could press just one key to accomplish the same task?

For example, Microsoft Word users who have used WordStar may miss WordStar's Ctrl-T command, which deletes the word to the right of the cursor. With Word, you must press Alt-F6 twice and then press Del to accomplish the same function. It's easy to record a macro that accomplishes this old WordStar command. You choose Macro Record, name the macro, and indicate the key you want to press to retrieve the macro (Ctrl-W). After choosing OK, you press the keys you want stored: Alt-F6, Alt-F6, and Del. You then choose Macro Stop Recorder. Subsequently, you can press Ctrl-W to activate the macro.

Macros are for every Word user, and you don't have to invest much time learning how to use them. In this chapter, you learn how to record simple macros, and you can go further and learn how to write more complex ones.

The following topics are covered:

- Using Word 5.5's supplied macros, the ones Microsoft wrote for you

- Turning on the record macro mode, which "captures" your keystrokes so that you can play them back at your command

- Expanding the macros you have recorded so that they pause for user input and display messages on the screen

- Editing macros to fix mistakes

- Testing macros, using the step mode, and other helpful testing features

- Creating a menu-based shell for Word that starts automatically every time you load the program and presents you with a choice of documents to load

You should be aware of one more point before you get started: Word stores macros as glossary entries, and you start macros by retrieving them from glossaries. Before using macros, therefore, you need to understand how to copy text to glossaries, how to load and save glossary files, and how to edit and delete glossary entries. If you haven't read Chapter 12, "Using Glossaries and Bookmarks," do so now.

Word's macro features haven't changed significantly from Version 5.0. But Word's keyboard has changed almost completely. Your Word 5.0 macros will not run with the new keyboard. A program called MACROCNV.EXE can convert *simple* Word 5.0 macros so that they will run on Word 5.5, but the changes to the keyboard are so extensive that this program is not likely to work well, as Microsoft itself concedes. Your best bet is to re-record or rewrite your macros. Watch out, too, for function key changes. For example, you now press Ctrl-F3, not Shift-F3, to toggle the Record Macro mode on and off.

Using the Supplied Macros

The easiest way to get started with Word's macros is to use one of the prewritten macros that comes with the program. Table 21.1 presents a selective list of the macros included with Word 5.5 at this writing.

Table 21.1
Word 5.5's Supplied Macros

Macro name	Key	Description
3_delete	Ctrl-WD	Deletes text to glossaries (You can recover up to three deletions.)
3_undelete	Ctrl-WU	Recovers deletions from glossaries
annot_collect	Ctrl-W1	Compiles a formatted list of all the annotations included in a document (For information on annotations, see Chapter 15, "Enhancing Group Productivity: Using Annotations and Redlining.")
annot_merge	Ctrl-W2	Merges annotations from several different versions of a document into a single, authoritative version of the file
annot_remove	Ctrl-W3	Removes all the annotations from a document
archive_author	Ctrl-W4	Copies documents written by a single author to a subdirectory, in which this author's documents are stored—a useful file management macro for a computer used by more than one person
archive_keyword	Ctrl-W5	Copies documents containing specified keywords to a series of subdirectories—a useful file management macro when you need to organize many documents by subject
authority_entry	Ctrl-W6	Formats a legal citation for inclusion in a table of authorities (For information on tables of authorities, see Chapter 14, "The Legal and Scholarly Word.")
authority_table	Ctrl-W7	Compiles a table of authorities from legal citations formatted with authority_entry
bulleted_list	Ctrl-W8	Formats a paragraph so that you create a bulleted list with each item preceded by a hyphen; the text is formatted in 12-point Helvetica

continues

Table 21.1—*continued*

Macro name	Key	Description
clean_screen	Ctrl-WC	Redraws the Word screen, a necessary step after using some terminate-and-stay-resident (TSR) programs.
clear_Scrap	Ctrl-WL	Clears the scrap by copying a space to the scrap
copy_file	Ctrl-V0	Copies a document *and* all the graphics files you inserted into it
dca_open	Ctrl-WY	Opens a document saved with the DCA-RTF format
dca_save	Ctrl-WZ	Saves a document to the DCA-RTF format
envelope	Ctrl-EN	Prints an address on an envelope (requires a printer with an envelope feeder)
filename	Ctrl-V7	Inserts the document's current file name at the cursor's location
freeze_style	Ctrl-W0	Converts all style formatting to direct formatting
indent_first	Ctrl-W1	Sets up an automatic first line indentation for paragraphs
index	Ctrl-V8	Draws from a file the words you want indexed and adds hidden text index codes to the matching words in a Word document
index_entry	Ctrl-VI	Formats a concordance entry for indexing (For more information on indexing, see Chapter 13, "Creating Indexes and Tables of Contents.")
mailing_label	Ctrl-VM	Automates the printing of mailing labels in one, two, or three columns—requires editing to work with your data document
manyprint	Ctrl-W9	Links documents for printing in a continuous chain with continuous pagination

Macro name	Key	Description
next_page	Ctrl-VN	Moves cursor to the beginning of the next page (document must be paginated)
prev_page	Ctrl-VP	Moves cursor to the beginning of the preceding page (document must be paginated)
print_letter	Ctrl-VL	Prints a letter with a page one format different from second and subsequent pages—useful when using a letterhead that requires a special page one format
reduce_left	Ctrl-YP	Decreases the left indent of a paragraph one default tab stop
repl_w_gloss	Ctrl-VG	Replaces the search string you specify with the text of a glossary entry you specify
repl_w_scrap	Ctrl-VR	Replaces the search string you specify with the text currently stored in the scrap
save_selection	Ctrl-VS	Saves the selected text to a file you specify
set_function_keys5	Ctrl-WK	Changes function key assignments to those of Word 5.0
set_function_keys55	Ctrl-YL	Restores Word 5.5 function keys
sidebyside	Ctrl-VV	Formats text as side-by-side paragraphs (For information on side-by-side paragraphs, see Chapter 19, "Page Layout II: Multiple-Column Text and Newsletters.")
strike_through	Ctrl-YS	Formats the selection with strikethrough characters
table	Ctrl-V4	Creates a tab format with the first tab positioned at a location you specify, then tabs to specified intervals across the screen
tabs	Ctrl-V1	Sets tabs from left to right and allows you to specify the type of tab

continues

Table 21.1—*continued*

Macro name	Key	Description
tabs2	Ctrl-V2	Prompts you for the number of columns you want in a table, the kind of tabs you want, and (if you select decimal tabs) the number of decimal places you need; and sets up a tab format for tables
tabs3	Ctrl-V3	Just like tabs2, except that this macro adds lines and boxes to the table
test_character	Ctrl-Y1	Provides a useful test of your printer's capabilities. Prints all the characters in a font you specify, including the extended characters.
text_copy	Ctrl-V6	Moves text from one location to another in a document
toc_entry	Ctrl-V5	Formats table of contents entries (For more information on tables of contents, see Chapter 13, "Creating Indexes and Tables of Contents.")

Opening MACRO.GLY

To use the macros that Microsoft supplies with Word, you must merge the MACRO.GLY file into the current glossary.

To open the MACRO.GLY glossary file:

1. Open a new, blank document that you can use to experiment with Word's supplied macros. (Don't experiment with a valuable file.)

2. Choose Macro Edit (Alt-ME).

   You see the Edit Macro dialog box in figure 21.1.

3. Choose Open Glossary.

   You see the Open Glossary dialog box in figure 21.2. Note that Word proposes to search for *.GLY files; macros are stored in glossary files, which have the extension GLY.

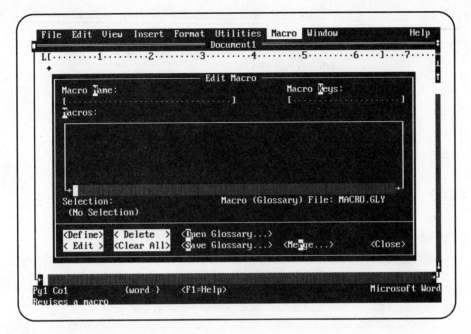

Fig. 21.1. The Edit Macro dialog box.

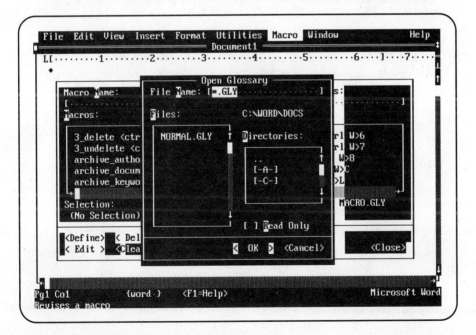

Fig. 21.2. The Open Glossary dialog box.

If, as suggested in this book, you have chosen your document directory as the default directory in the File Options dialog box, open Word's directory by choosing the parent directory symbol (..) from the **Directories** list box.

4. Choose MACRO.GLY in the **Files** list.

5. Choose OK.

Word opens the glossary titled MACRO.GLY, and you see the macros listed in the Edit Macro dialog box.

6. Choose Close.

Now that you have opened MACRO.GLY, Word's supplied macros are available. You can run them two ways: you can choose the macro's name from the Run Macro dialog box, or you can press the macro's keyboard shortcut.

To run a supplied macro by choosing its name from the Run Macro dialog box:

1. Choose **Macro Run** (Alt-MR).

You see the Run Macro dialog box in figure 21.3.

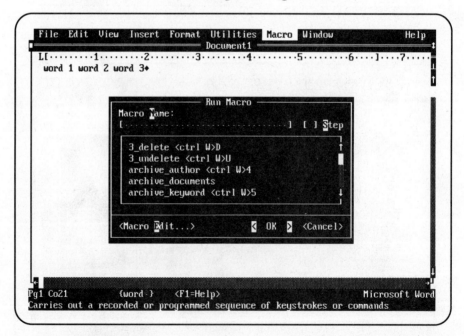

Fig. 21.3. The Run Macro dialog box.

2. In the Macro **Name** list box, highlight the name of the macro you want to run.

   Try running tabs2, sidebyside, or memo_header.

3. Choose OK.

Word runs the macro. Depending on which macro you have chosen, you may see dialog boxes asking you to supply further information.

To run the macro using the keyboard shortcut, just hold down the Ctrl key and press the key code. To run tabs2, for instance, hold down the Ctrl key and press *V2*.

Clearing Word's Supplied Macros

You have opened MACRO.GLY, which contains many macros. You may find some of them useful; however, you should clear this glossary before continuing this chapter. Word supplies so many macros that your own creations may seem lost amid the many macro names.

To clear MACRO.GLY and restore the default glossary (NORMAL.GLY) do the following:

1. Choose **Macro Edit** (Alt-ME).

   You see the Edit Macro dialog box.

2. Choose **Open Glossary**.

3. Choose NORMAL.GLY in the **Files** list box.

   If you see a dialog box asking you whether you want to save changes to the current glossary. Choose **No**.

4. Choose OK.

   Word restores the default NORMAL.GLY glossary, which at this point doesn't contain any macros. You see no macro names in the **Macros** list box of the Edit Macro menu.

5. Choose Close.

Recording Macros

Now that you have practiced with one or two of Word 5.5's supplied macros, you see how convenient they are for performing complicated operations. You surely will think of many steps that you make repeatedly and that you would like to automate with macros. Although you cannot include mouse actions in a Word macro, you can automate anything you can type at the keyboard, and that includes commands as well as text.

You can create macros in two different ways: by recording them or writing them. Of the two methods, recording macros is easier. You use Word's record macro mode, which you can toggle on and off with Ctrl-F3. After you turn on the record macro mode, Word records all your keystrokes. When you turn off the mode, Word prompts you to name the recording, and then Word copies the new macro to the glossary. You can insert the recording from the glossary whenever you want, and Word plays back the macro you made.

About Macro Names and Macro Keys

Before you record macros, you should understand how to name macros and how to assign keyboard shortcuts to them.

A macro name must be one "word," one continuous string of characters without any spaces up to 30 characters in length. However, you may use hyphens, underscore characters, and periods to separate text. As you can see in table 21.1, Microsoft names its macros by using underscore characters to separate words. Try to choose a name that vividly describes the macro's function.

You cannot use some keys when you assign a keyboard shortcut to a macro. These keys are Alt (used for menus), Ctrl-Shift (used for styles), Ctrl-A (used for overriding key conflicts), and all the punctuation marks you type when you press the Shift key and a number key.

When you assign a keyboard shortcut to a macro, be very careful to avoid duplicating existing keyboard shortcuts. The keyboard shortcuts you assign to macros cancel existing keyboard shortcuts. For instance, if you assign a macro to Alt-F6, you will not be able to select a word using the existing Alt-F6 keyboard shortcut. Instead, Word will run the new macro you have assigned to Alt-F6.

The best way to avoid keyboard conflicts is to use one of the Ctrl key combinations that Microsoft hasn't already assigned to a keyboard shortcut (such as Ctrl-E and Ctrl-G), preferably in combination with a second key. Choose one of these unassigned keys to be your "macro key," and assign keyboard shortcuts using the following form:

Ctrl-E1   Macro 1

Ctrl-E2   Macro 2

Ctrl-E3   Macro 3, and so forth

You can also use a letter key for the second key that reminds you of the macro's function.

> Ctrl-ED Delete to end of line
>
> Ctrl-EW Delete word right
>
> Ctrl-ES Split screen to display two windows

Using this keyboard assignment technique, you can assign 10 numbered macros and 26 letter key macros for a total of 36 macros, which is more than sufficient. If not, you can create another 36 macros by using Ctrl-G.

A Macro To Delete the Word to the Right of the Cursor

In the following tutorial, you learn how to create the macro mentioned at the beginning of this chapter, the one that deletes the word to the right of the cursor like the WordStar Ctrl-T command.

1. Open a new, blank Word document.

2. Type a sentence or two in the document so that you have some text with which to experiment. Place the cursor in the middle of a sentence, within a word.

3. Choose **M**acro Re**c**ord (Alt-MC, or press the Ctrl-F3 keyboard shortcut).   **Ctrl-F3**

   You see the Record Macro dialog box in figure 21.4.

4. In the **M**acro Name box, type a name for your macro.

   Name the macro *delete_word_right*.

5. In the Macro **K**eys box, press the keys you want to use to start the macro.

   Press *Ctrl-EW*.

6. Choose OK.

   You see the code M R on the status bar, and on the message bar, you see the message Mouse inactive. Press Ctrl-F3 to stop recording the macro. You cannot use the mouse while you're recording a macro; all the actions you want recorded must be keyed using the keyboard.

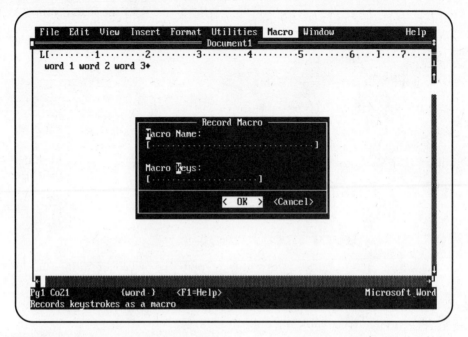

Fig. 21.4. *The Record Macro dialog box.*

7. Press the following keys (omit the commas):

   Alt-F6, Alt-F6, Shift-Del

8. Choose **Macro Stop Recorder** (Alt-MC) or Ctrl-F3 to stop recording the macro.

Testing the Macro

Testing your macro isn't just a prudent step that you could omit if strapped for time; it's a necessity. Macros are very powerful, and if you're not careful when you record one, you could create a macro that wipes out valuable text or even whole files. You can interrupt a running macro at any time just by pressing Esc, but it's better to test the macro by using Word's macro step mode before inflicting it on valuable text. The step mode actually runs your macro step-by-step. You press Enter to move on to the next step. If something goes wrong, you can press Esc before any serious damage is done.

To test a macro:

1. Choose **Macro Run** (Alt-MR).

   You see the Run Macro dialog box.

2. In the Macro **Name** list box, highlight the name of the macro you want to test.

3. Choose **Step** so that you see an X in the check box.

4. Choose OK.

   You see the message S T on the status bar, which informs you that Word is running the macro in the step mode.

5. Press any key other than Esc to move to the next step in the macro.

   If something is going wrong, press Esc to stop running the macro.

6. Repeat step 5 until the macro is finished running.

   You still see the code S T on the status bar.

7. Choose **Macro Run** (Alt-MR) and remove the X from the Step check box.

What do you do if your macro didn't work? Try to understand what went wrong, and re-record the macro. When you type the same macro name and key code in the Record Macro, Word will ask you to confirm the replacement of the existing macro. You should choose **Yes**, because it doesn't work. Try recording the key sequence again, with changes, and repeat the test.

Using a Recorded Macro

After you have recorded and tested a macro, and you are satisfied that it's running properly, you can retrieve it in three ways:

- Type the glossary's name (such as *Delete_Word_Right*), and press F3

- Choose **Macro Run** (Alt-MR), and select the macro from the **Macros** list box.

- Press the Ctrl-key code to start the macro.

You can see an obvious advantage to assigning a macro to a Ctrl key code. The first two techniques require more keystrokes to enter the macro than would be required to delete the word by using ordinary techniques.

Macro Recording Pointers

As you will discover quickly when you try to record your own macros, it isn't easy to record one that proves useful in all situations. To create a really useful macro, you need to do some advanced planning.

Ask yourself these questions before you record a macro:

- What keys must I press to carry out the action successfully? Run through the key sequence two or three times before you try recording. Use a test document as a guinea pig.

- Where should the cursor be placed when the macro starts running? Should I include cursor-movement commands in the macro to make sure the cursor is in the correct location?

- If your macro changes one of Word's operating modes, do you want to change it back when the macro quits running? For example, you can write macros that turn on the extend-selection mode. If you don't press Esc at the end of the macro, the mode stays on when the macro quits.

- Does the macro perform any operations that could lose data? What if another window is open, and it contains unsaved text? In general, avoid creating a macro that deletes large amounts of text or closes files without saving their contents.

Understanding How Glossary Files Work with Macros

As you have already learned, Word stores macros in glossaries, along with normal glossary entries. Note the following two points carefully:

- If you want your macros to be available in every Word session, save them to Word's default glossary file, NORMAL.GLY.

- If you save your macros to a file other than NORMAL.GLY, you have to load the glossary file by using the Open Glossary command in the Edit Macro dialog box.

You can move glossaries from one glossary file to another, and you can also edit a glossary file to remove unwanted macros. If you move glossaries from MACRO.GLY to NORMAL.GLY, the macros you leave will be available in every editing session, because NORMAL.GLY is the default glossary.

To move glossaries from MACRO.GLY to NORMAL.GLY:

1. Choose Macro Edit (Alt-ME).

   You see the Edit Macro dialog box, and you see NORMAL.GLY in the Macro (Glossary) File area. If you don't see this, choose Open Glossary and open NORMAL.GLY.

2. Choose **Merge**.

You see the Merge Glossary dialog box in figure 21.5.

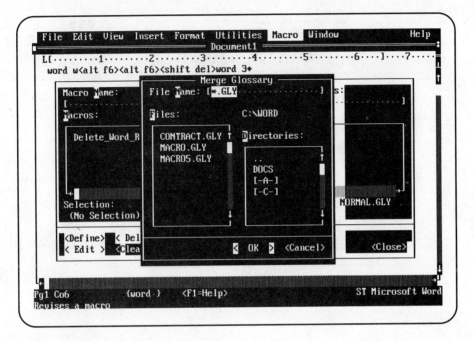

Fig. 21.5. *The Merge Glossary dialog box.*

3. If you don't see MACRO.GLY on the list, use the **D**irectories list box to locate the file.

If Word is in your document directory (such as C:\WORD\DOCS), you probably need to select the parent directory symbol (..) to move up the tree to Word's directory.

4. Highlight MACRO.GLY.

5. Choose OK.

Word copies all the MACRO.GLY macros into NORMAL.GLY. You see all these macros in the Edit Macro dialog box's **Macros** list box in figure 21.6.

6. Highlight one of the macros you don't want to keep, and choose **D**elete.

7. Repeat step 6 until you have deleted all the unwanted macros.

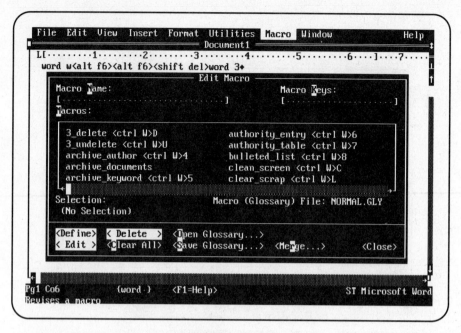

Fig. 21.6. MACRO.GLY macros merged into NORMAL.GLY.

8. Choose Save Glossary.

   You see the Save Glossary dialog box in figure 21.7.

9. Choose OK.

Writing Macros

Of the two techniques for creating macros, writing macros is by far the more powerful, but it is also more challenging.

When you record macros, you are limited to the sequence of keystrokes you enter directly at the keyboard. When you write macros, however, you can include special macro instructions, which greatly increases your options. Using these special macro instructions, you can force a macro to pause while the user does something, such as selecting text (PAUSE). You can ask the user to type a response, which becomes the contents of a variable (ASK). You can set up conditional instructions that cause the macro to branch this way or that depending on whether a test condition is met (IF...ENDIF). You can create a set of instructions that continue until a condition is fulfilled (WHILE...ENDWHILE). You can create instructions that repeat a certain number of times (REPEAT...ENDREPEAT). And you can perform complex calculations and

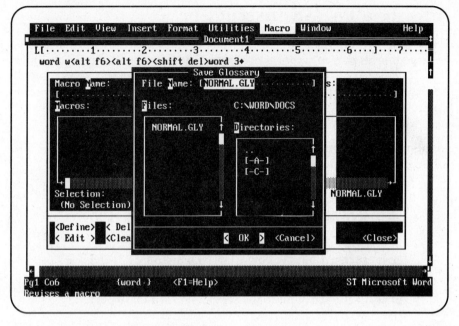

Fig. 21.7. *The Save Glossary dialog box.*

logical comparisons on the data stored in the macro's variables. In short, you can write macros with a sophisticated, but simple and elegant, programming language.

To write a macro, you must type the key names and commands using an exact nomenclature and in the correct order. These niceties are collectively known as *syntax*, and you have to get it right before the macro will work. To create macros that work correctly, you need much information and practice. This book cannot provide all the reference information you need, but the following tutorials can get you started.

Adding a Confirmation Message to a Macro You Have Recorded

Writing macros isn't easy. But try this trick to reduce the amount of information you must learn to introduce some powerful features into recorded macros. Begin the macro by recording it, and let Word worry about writing down all the steps with the correct keynames and syntax. Edit the macro, adding an instruction here or there. You're cheating somewhat, but no one will ever know the difference.

Adding a PAUSE Instruction

The PAUSE instruction is one of the most useful features of written macros because it gives you an opportunity to present a message to the user. In this tutorial, you learn how to add an ASK instruction to a macro you have recorded. This approach is very simple because you need to know very little about the syntax of Word's macro programming language or even about the correct key names to use.

In this tutorial, you record a macro that deletes the text to the end of the line. You then add a confirmation message.

1. Choose **Macro Record**, and when the Record Macro dialog box appears, name the macro *Del_To_End_of_Line*, and assign the key code Ctrl-EY.

2. In Macro Record mode (M R on the status bar), press the following keys *exactly* (omit the commas): F8, F8, End, Shift-Del, Esc.

   These keys select a word, extend the selection to the end of the line, cut the selection to the scrap, and turn off the extend-selection mode.

3. Press Ctrl-F3 to stop recording the macro.

4. Choose **Macro Edit** (Alt-ME).

   You see the Edit Macro dialog box.

5. Highlight the macro you just created.

6. Choose **Edit**.

   Word places the macro in your document (see figure 21.8). As you can see, when you recorded the macro, Word recorded the keystrokes automatically using the correct nomenclature and syntax: the key names are surrounded by angle brackets, and they're listed in the exact sequence you pressed them.

7. Place the cursor between the ⟨end⟩ and ⟨shift del⟩ key names. Make sure that O T is off.

8. Pressing Ctrl-[and Ctrl-] to enter the chevrons, type the following *exactly*:

   «PAUSE Press Enter to confirm the deletion or Esc to cancel»

   Your screen should look like the one in figure 21.9.

Fig. 21.8. *Editing a macro you recorded.*

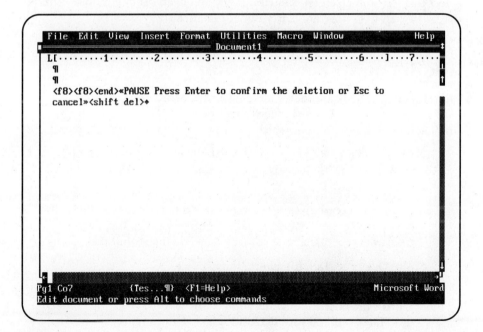

Fig. 21.9. *A macro PAUSE instruction.*

9. Select the entire macro.

10. Choose **Macro Edit** (Alt-ME).

    You see the Macro Edit dialog box.

11. Choose the name of this macro again (Del_To_End_of_Line).

12. Choose **Define**.

    You see an alert box with the message, `Do you want to replace the existing macro?`

13. Choose OK.

Try running the macro. After the macro performs the selection, you see the message, `Press Enter to confirm the deletion or Esc to cancel` **on the** message bar. If you press Esc, you see a dialog box informing you that the macro was interrupted. Press Esc again to cancel the macro.

If the macro doesn't work correctly, make sure that you have entered both chevrons and that you entered them with the Ctrl-[and Ctrl-] commands (the same ones you use with Merge).

The PAUSE instruction is useful in macros not only because it gives the user a chance to confirm an operation. While PAUSE has halted a macro, the user can select text, scroll the screen, switch modes, and even use the mouse (but not the keyboard) to choose and carry out commands.

Adding an ASK Instruction

An ASK instruction is another way to use the record-and-edit trick you just learned. Begin by recording a macro that opens and names a file at the same time. Add an ASK instruction, which prompts the user to supply a name.

1. Choose **Macro Record**, and when the Record Macro dialog box appears, name the macro *New_Named_File*, and assign the key code Shift-Ctrl-T.

2. In Macro Record mode (M R on the status bar), press the following keys *exactly* (omit the commas). When you get to the word *filename*, type the actual characters "filename" (omit the quotes).

   Alt-FO, Home, Del, filename, Enter, Enter

   These keys choose the Open dialog box, delete the asterisk in Word's proposed file name, replace the asterisk with the characters "filename," choose OK, and then confirm the creation of a file named FILENAME.DOC.

   FILENAME.DOC isn't such as great name for a file, but read on.

3. Press Ctrl-F3 to stop recording the macro.

4. Choose **Macro Edit** (Alt-ME).

   You see the Edit Macro dialog box.

5. Highlight the macro you just created.

6. Choose **E**dit.

   Word places the macro in your document (see figure 21.10).
   When you recorded the macro, Word recorded the keystrokes
   automatically using the correct nomenclature and syntax: the key
   names are surrounded by brackets, and they're listed in the exact
   sequence you pressed them.

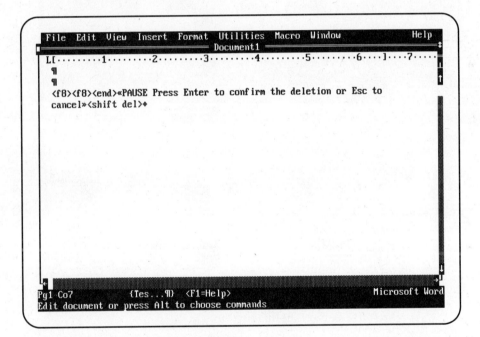

Fig. 21.10. Editing a macro you recorded.

7. Carefully place chevrons around the word `filename`. Enter the
   chevrons with Ctrl-[and Ctrl-].

   The macro will not work if you enter the chevrons as normal text;
   you must use Ctrl-[and Ctrl-].

8. Place the cursor at the beginning of the macro.

9. Pressing Ctrl-[and Ctrl-] to enter the chevrons, type the following *exactly*:

«ASK filename=?Please type the name of the file you want to create.»

Your screen should look like the one in Figure 21.11.

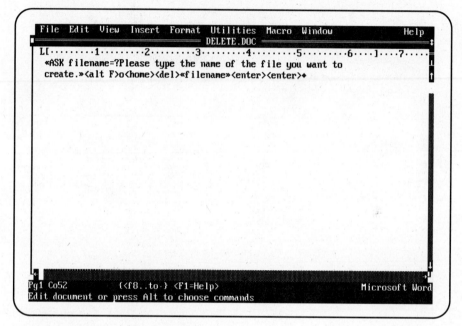

```
 File  Edit  View  Insert  Format  Utilities  Macro  Window        Help
                          DELETE.DOC
 L[·········1········2·········3·········4·········5·········6····]···7·····
 «ASK filename=?Please type the name of the file you want to
 create.»<alt F>o<home><del>«filename»<enter><enter>♦




















Pg1 Co52           {<f8..to·} <F1=Help>                Microsoft Word
Edit document or press Alt to choose commands
```

Fig. 21.11. *A macro ASK instruction.*

10. Select the entire macro.

11. Choose **Macro Edit** (Alt-ME).

    You see the Macro Edit dialog box.

12. Choose the name of this macro again (New_Named_File).

13. Choose **Define**.

    You see an alert box with the message, Do you want to replace the existing macro?

14. Choose OK.

When you run this macro, you get a neat-looking alert box asking you to supply the file name (see figure 21.12).

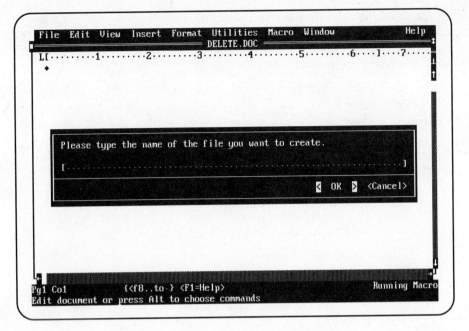

Fig. 21.12. *Delete box presented by New_Named_File macro.*

Studying an Advanced Example: An AUTOEXEC Menu System

One of the best ways to learn programming techniques is to study a working program, understand how it works, and modify it to suit your needs. This section contains an advanced Word macro that uses many of the language's features. Even if you don't understand everything in the macro, you can still type it into a Word document, define it as a macro, and experiment with it. And as you do, your understanding of Word's macros will grow by leaps and bounds.

This macro solves a problem you will encounter if you use more than one directory to store you documents. As you have already learned, it's convenient to store your Word documents in a special document directory, such as C:\WORD\DOCS, and to make this directory the default directory for all your Word sessions. But you may have more than one document directory, if more than one person uses the computer. For instance, Rob stores his documents in C:\WORD\ROBDOCS, and Susan stores her documents in C:\WORD\SUEDOCS.

This macro presents an on-screen menu at the beginning of every Word session, and asks you to identify the directory you want to use as your default document directory for the current session. The macro displays the Open dialog box, from which the user can open a file or create a new one.

Before creating this macro, create directories called C:\WORD\SUEDOCS and C:\WORD\ROBDOCS. You can substitute your own directory names after you learn how this macro works, and you can also delete these subdirectories later.

Typing the Macro

1. Open a new Word document and type this macro. Be sure to use the Ctrl-[and Ctrl-] commands to enter the chevrons, and type angle brackets (< <)around the keynames.

   ```
   «SET response="false"»
   «WHILE response="false"»
      «ASK directory=?Type S to choose \SUEDOCS or type R to
      choose \ROBDOCS as the default directory»
   «IF directory = "S"»
      «SET response = "true"»
   «ENDIF»
   «IF directory = "R"»
      «SET rcsponse = "true"»
   «ENDIF»
   «ENDWHILE»
   «SET echo = "off"»
   «IF directory="S"»
      <menu>fo<alt O>C:\WORD\SUEDOCS
      <alt a>
      «IF field= "yes"»<space>«ENDIF»
      <enter>
   «ENDIF»
   «IF directory="R"»
      <menu>fo<alt O>C:\WORD\ROBDOCS
      <alt a>
      «IF field= "yes"»<space>«ENDIF»
      <enter>
   «ENDIF»
   «PAUSE  Select a file or name a new file in the File Name box»
      <enter>
   ```

2. Select the entire macro.

3. Choose **Macro Edit** (Alt-ME).

   You see the Macro Edit dialog box.

4. In the Macro **Name** box, type *autoexec*.

5. Choose **Define**.

6. Choose OK.

Test the macro by running it in the step mode. If it doesn't work, and it probably will not, check carefully that you have entered all the chevrons with the Ctrl-[and Ctrl-] commands and that you surrounded keynames with the angle brackets.

A Line-by-Line Explanation of the Macro

Unless you have some computer programming background, much of this macro probably means little to you. Even so, the concepts are easy to understand. Reading this section will give you a better understanding of Word's powerful macro programming language. Armed with the reference information in Word's manual (see Chapter 22 of the Word documentation), you will have the ability to write your own macros.

Here are two points to remember. First, Word "reads" the macro sequentially, from the first line down, unless it's specifically instructed otherwise. As you will see, a loop (WHILE...ENDWHILE) as well as a branch (IF...ENDIF) interrupts the sequential flow. Second, this macro creates a couple of variables, *response* and *directory*, that store values temporarily while the macro is running. These variables play an important role.

The first line is as follows:

«SET response="false"»

This SET instruction creates a variable called "response," and gives it the value "false." The value stays set to "false" until another SET instruction changes it. You will see why in a moment.

«WHILE response="false"»
    «ASK directory=?Type S to choose \SUEDOCS or type R to choose
    \ROBDOCS as the default directory»

    [...]

«ENDWHILE»

This instruction means, "While the value of the variable response is set to 'false,' keep asking the user to type 'S' or 'R,' and don't give up until 'response' is set to something other than 'false'."

Without creating the response variable and the WHILE...ENDWHILE instruction, Word would be satisfied with any response the user would make to the ASK instruction, which is embedded within the WHILE...ENDWHILE loop. ASK merely creates a variable and accepts any keyboard input as the variable's contents. To Word, the text that comes after the question mark is just text to be displayed on the screen. The text doesn't limit the range of responses the ASK instruction accepts as legal input. The user could thus type *x* or *Zanzibar* in response to this prompt, and ASK would dutifully accept it and define the document variable to contain whatever the user has typed.

«ASK directory=?Type S to choose \SUEDOCS or type R to choose \ROBDOCS as the default directory»

You have seen this command before. It presents an alert box, which asks you to type *s* or *r* before proceeding.

Also included within the WHILE...ENDWHILE loop are the following IF statements. Note that each IF statement must end with an ENDIF, just as WHILE ended with an ENDWHILE:

```
«IF directory = "S"»
   «SET response = "true"»
«ENDIF»
«IF directory = "R"»
   «SET response = "true"»
«ENDIF»
```

These statements set the "response" variable to "true" if the user types *s* or *r*. They are conditional statements; they execute only if the test condition (such as, "Does directory contain 'S'?") is met. Remember, the WHILE loop keeps executing as long as "response" is set to "false." That means, in practice, that the dialog box stays on-screen until the user types *s* or *r*. When "response" is set to "false," the dialog box closes.

This statement tells Word not to display the drop-down menus and dialog boxes while the macro is running:

```
«SET echo = "off"»
```

Here's what happens if the variable "directory" is set to "S," if the user types *s* in response to the dialog box.

```
«IF directory="S"»
   <menu>fo<alt O>C:\WORD\SUEDOCS
   <alt a>
   «IF field= "yes"»<space>«ENDIF»
   <enter>
«ENDIF»
```

This statement boils down to choosing the **File Open** command, choosing the File Options dialog box, typing the directory name in the Default **P**ath box, and making sure that no X is in the **A**lways Use as Default check box.

Now take a closer look at the second line of this statement:

<menu>fo<alt O>C:\WORD\SUEDOCS

This line begins with the <menu> command, which is the same as pressing Alt to toggle the menu's boldfaced characters on. The next two characters, "fo," choose the **File Open** command. When the Open dialog box appears, Alt-0 (the letter, not the number) chooses the **Options** command button. And when the File Options dialog box appears, the text C:\WORD\SUEDOCS replaces the selection in the Default **Path** box.

The third, fourth, and fifth lines of the IF statement contain some important techniques:

<alt a>
«IF field= "yes"»<space>«ENDIF»
<enter>

Alt a selects the **Always Use as Default** check box of the File Options dialog box, which is still open. The next expression («IF field = "yes"...) checks to see whether an X is in this check box. If there is an X, the rest of this statement removes it. If there isn't an X, Word doesn't execute the rest of the statement, so the check box remains blank. Why? Because you don't want the current directory choices (such as C:\WORD\SUEDOCS) to become a new, permanent default.

The last statement, <enter>, chooses OK in the File Options dialog box, and leaves the Open dialog box on-screen. Now the user can load files.

The following IF statement has exactly the same structure as the preceding one. It tells Word what to do if the user types *r*.

«IF directory="R"»

  <menu>fo<alt O>C:\WORD\ROBDOCS
  <alt a>
  «IF field= "yes"»<space>«ENDIF»
  <enter>
«ENDIF»

The last two lines of the macro present a message on the message bar telling the user what to do while the Open dialog box is displayed, and the final statement, <enter>, chooses OK in the Open dialog box after the user presses Enter.

  «PAUSE Select a file or name a new file in the File Name box»
  <enter>

This macro is short and very useful—no more changing directories every time you sit down to use a computer that someone else uses too. It's fun to program in Word's macro language; you can write a short and simple program like this one, yet the program does impressive tasks. Try modifying this macro so that it opens the directories on your disk.

Starting a Macro When You Start Word

In the preceding section, you learned how to create an *autoexec macro*: a macro that executes automatically when you open the glossary in which it is stored. If you place the autoexec macro in NORMAL.GLY, it will execute automatically when you start Word. You can also start a macro when you start Word by typing a special command on the DOS command line:

> WORD/M MACRONAME

To start Word and launch a custom macro named "TYPELETTER," you would type *word /m typeletter*.

Word starts and the "TYPELETTER" macro starts executing.

Modifying the Supplied Macros

Most programmers learn by emulating well-written programs. Because Word supplies so many macros in MACRO.GLY, you have a treasure trove from which you can choose. To display the text of a written macro so that you can study it, edit it, or modify it do the following:

1. Open a new, blank Word document.

2. Choose **Macro Edit** (Alt-ME).

3. Highlight the name of one of Word's supplied macros.

   If you don't see the supplied macros, choose **O**pen Glossary and open MACRO.GLY.

4. Choose **Edit**.

   You see the text of the macro.

5. Edit or modify the macro.

6. Select the macro.

7. Choose **Macro Edit** (Alt-ME).

8. Select the macro's name, or type a new name for the macro in the Macro **Name** box.

9. Choose **Define**.

Chapter Summary

Anyone can create and use Word 5.5 macros to automate complicated, repetitive tasks. To record macros, you use the record macro mode to record your keystrokes. You can create more sophisticated macros by recording macros, and then modifying them with one or two written instructions. For fancier programs, you can learn to use more of Word's powerful macro instructions.

Quick Review

Glossary Files

To open a glossary file:

1. Choose **Macro Edit** (Alt-ME).

2. Choose **Open Glossary**

3. Highlight the glossary name in the **Files** list box.

4. Choose OK.

To merge a glossary file into the current glossary:

1. Choose **Macro Edit** (Alt-ME).

2. Choose **Merge**.

3. Highlight the glossary name in the **Files** list box.

4. Choose OK.

To delete macros from a glossary file:

1. Choose **Macro Edit** (Alt-ME).

2. Highlight the name of the glossary you want to delete.

3. Choose **Delete**.

To clear all the macros from a glossary file:

1. Choose **Macro Edit** (Alt-ME).

2. Choose **Clear All** .

3. Choose OK.

To save a glossary file:

1. Choose **Macro Edit** (Alt-ME).

2. Choose **Save Glossary**.

Recording a Macro

To record a macro:

1. Choose **Macro Record** (Alt-MC, or press the Ctrl-F3 keyboard shortcut).

2. In the Macro Name box, type a name for your macro.

3. In the Macro **Keys** box, actually press the keys you want to use to start the macro.

4. Choose OK.

5. Press the keys you want recorded.

6. Choose **Macro Stop Recorder** (Alt-MC) or Ctrl-F3 to stop recording the macro.

Running a Macro

To run a macro, use one of the following techniques:

- Type the glossary's name (such as *delete_word_right*) and press F3.

- Choose **Macro Run** (Alt-MR) and select the macro from the Macros list box.

- Press the macro's Ctrl-key code to start the macro.

- Start Word by Typing *word* /m followed by the macro's name.

Supplied Macros

To open MACRO.GLY:

1. Choose **Macro Edit** (Alt-ME).

2. Choose **Open Glossary**.

3. Highlight MACRO.GLY in the **Files** list. If you don't see MACRO.GLY, use the **Directories** list box to look for the file and highlight it.

4. Choose OK.

5. Choose Close.

To run one of Word's supplied macros:

Choose **Macro Run** (Alt-MR), and highlight the name of the macro you want to run. Choose OK. Alternatively, press the macro's keyboard shortcut. You can also type the macro's name and press F3.

To clear MACRO.GLY and restore the default glossary (NORMAL.STY):

1. Choose **Macro Edit** (Alt-ME).

2. Choose **Open Glossary**.

3. Choose NORMAL.GLY in the **Files** list box.

4. Choose OK.

5. Choose Close.

Testing a Macro

To test a macro:

1. Choose **Macro Run** (Alt-MR).

2. In the Macro **Name** list box, highlight the name of the macro you want to test.

3. Choose **Step** so that you see an X in the check box.

4. Choose OK.

5. Press any key besides Esc to move to the next step in the macro.

6. Repeat step 5 until the macro is finished running.

7. Choose **Macro Run** (Alt-MR) and remove the X from the Step check box.

Writing a Macro

To write a macro:

1. Write the macro in a new, blank Word document.

2. Select the macro.

3. Choose Macro Edit (Alt-ME).

4. In the Macro Name box, type a name for the macro.

5. In the Macro Keys box, press the keys you want to use to activate the macro.

6. Choose **Define**.

7. Choose Close.

Installing Word 5.5

You can use Word 5.5 on virtually any IBM-compatible computer system, even a very basic one. To get maximum performance from Word, however, you may want to choose certain advanced components. This Appendix briefly surveys ways to optimize your system for Word and covers the installation procedure you use when you run SETUP, Word's installation utility.

Note: If you already have installed Word and the program is running well on your system, you can skip most of this Appendix. However, be sure to read the section titled "Creating a Document Directory."

Word 5.5 and Your Computer System

An IBM-format computer system for word processing with Word must include, at the minimum, two disk drives, 384K of RAM, a monochrome video adapter and monitor, and a printer. To get the most from Word 5.5, however, you should consider upgrading your system to include a hard disk, at least 640K of RAM (using an expanded memory board), a graphics adapter, a color monitor, and a laser printer.

Disk Drives

At the minimum, you need an IBM-compatible computer with two 360K disk drives. Although Word 5.5 will run on such a system, you will discover that it isn't much fun. Word goes to disk frequently, and you often will find yourself waiting while Word looks for information it needs. With 360K drives, moreover, you frequently must swap disks in and out of the computer. The program performs much better with two 720K drives, a configuration common among laptop computers. Word 5.5 is at its best on hard disk systems, however, which is the minimum configuration assumed in this book. If you don't have a hard disk, consider adding a hard disk to your system.

Like its predecessors, Word 5.5 doesn't maintain your whole file in memory. Word 5.5 goes to disk frequently to store and retrieve sections of your file and to obtain program information from a variety of files. On floppy drive systems, all this disk activity adds up to frequent interruptions of your work and mediocre performance—so much so, in fact, that a hard disk is assumed in this book to be a minimal system configuration. As the Word manual explains, it is possible to install Word on a two-floppy system. But after using Word on such a system, you will surely agree that you need a hard disk to get your money's worth out of Word.

System Speed and Memory

Word runs at a tolerable pace, even on 4.77-MHz systems equipped with the 8088 microprocessor chip. However, performance improves significantly on 80286 and 80386 systems.

As Word has grown over the years, the program has consumed more and more free memory space. With Word 5.5, the program has become large enough to reduce free memory space to the bare minimum, even on systems with 640K. The program will run on computers equipped with only 384K, but not very well. Word needs large amounts of free memory to perform operations such as search and replace (see table A.1 for a list of such operations). On a 384K system, you may not be able to use these commands for any but the most trivial sorting or searching operations.

Even with 640K, Word 5.5 may not be able to complete lengthy replace, sort, or indexing operations. If memory is insufficient to complete an operation, you see the Insufficient Memory message. You can save your work, clear Word, reload your document, and try again; but even so, you may not have enough memory to carry out the command. Even if Word can complete the operation, you probably will see the SAVE indicator on the status line after using one of the commands listed in table A.1. At this point, you must save your document. Sometimes you must clear Word's memory completely by using **File Close All** in order to make the SAVE indicator disappear. In such cases, you must reload your file to continue working. These interruptions are frustrating and detrimental to concentration.

Fortunately, Word 5.5 can use expanded memory conforming to the LIM (Lotus-Intel-Microsoft) expanded memory specification 3.2 or above. You can

Table A.1

Operations Requiring Free Memory

Complex macros

Complex math operations

Extended editing sessions

Utilities Sort

Insert Index

Insert Table of Contents

Pagination operations (auto or manual)

Edit Replace

Edit Search

add expanded memory to your system by installing an optional memory board. Your computer already may be equipped with expanded memory on the main circuit board, so consult your computer's documentation for details. If you plan to create lengthy documents, use Word for all-day writing and editing sessions, or compile indexes from lengthy documents, consider adding expanded memory to your system. Add expanded memory, also, if you want to get maximum performance from Word. The more memory you have, the faster Word runs.

If you are running Word 5.5 under OS/2 on an 80286 or 80386 machine, Word uses all the available memory beyond the 640K barrier.

Caution: When you run Word 5.5 under MS-DOS on 640K systems, avoid loading memory-resident programs such as SideKick. You need all the free memory space you can get to run Word 5.5 efficiently. Most memory-resident programs include a command that removes the program from memory. Use this command before starting Word.

Mouse

Word 5.5 fully supports the Microsoft mouse, a hand-held input device that is used to move the cursor, highlight text for editing purposes, and give commands. As you slide the mouse around on the tabletop next to the keyboard, a pointer on-screen parallels its moves.

Many word processing programs claim to be compatible with the mouse, but on closer inspection, the mouse capability these programs provide turns out to be little more than an afterthought, added on to the program to increase its marketability. With such programs, you quickly find that controlling the cursor with the mouse is difficult, and editing operations take far longer with the mouse than they do with the keyboard. Word virtually is alone among IBM-format word processing programs in having been designed around the mouse from the beginning. With Word, the mouse provides precision cursor control, super fast text highlighting, and convenient command capabilities. Using a mouse with Word is truly a pleasure, and most people who try the mouse feel handicapped when they must use a computer that lacks a mouse. In this way, Word 5.5 provides much of the convenience and feel of Apple's Macintosh computers, which—like Word—were designed around the use of the mouse.

Still, you can use Word 5.5 without a mouse without suffering any penalty. Almost every command can be given using the mouse or the keyboard. If you are an expert typist and prefer not to take your hands away from the keyboard, you can omit the mouse from your system. In this respect, Word is unlike most Macintosh software (and even the Macintosh version of Word), which frequently fails to provide keyboard alternatives to mouse commands. Word 5.5's keyboard commands are exceptionally well-conceived, and as you learn in this book, you can reconfigure the keyboard to your heart's content.

Video Adapters and Display Monitors

Laptops aside, most IBM-compatible computers can be equipped with a variety of video adapters (a circuit board that controls the screen display) and display monitors. You generally can choose from monochrome (green, yellow, or white text and black background) or color adapters and monitors. Adapters and monitors also differ in their resolution, or their ability to display fine-detailed images on-screen. Resolution usually is expressed by the number of distinct dots the adapter and monitor can display, measured horizontally and vertically. The IBM Color Graphics Adapter, a low-resolution adapter, can display 640 dots horizontally but only 200 dots vertically. Some adapters and monitors can display only the characters built into IBM-compatible computers, while others can display graphics. Word 5.5 is designed to work with all these video displays and monitors, and you can use the program even with very basic display systems (such as the Color Graphics Adapter or IBM Monochrome Adapter).

If you want to use a mouse or display graphic images, Word 5.5 is at its best with a high-resolution graphics display adapter and monitor, such as the Hercules Graphics Card, Hercules Graphics Card Plus, the Enhanced Graphics Adapter (EGA), or the Video Graphics Array (VGA) adapter. New Word 5.5 features make a good case for adding one of these color monitors and video display adapters to your system. You can "paint" the screen with your own choices for character emphases, point sizes, and other screen features.

If you are a professional writer, editor, or publisher, consider adding a Genius full-page display and monitor to your system. In graphics mode, Word can display 66 lines with a resolution of 1,024 by 768 lines, an exceptionally high resolution.

Printers

Like all word processing programs, Word 5.5 is at its best when used with a supported printer. A supported printer is one for which the program includes a printer driver, which is a special file that contains information about the printer. This information enables the program to "translate" its printing and formatting commands so that the printer can respond to them. For this reason, you don't have to worry about all those complicated control codes you see in your printer's manual. Just hook up and prepare your printer as the manual suggests and install Word, using the SETUP program. Word translates your formatting commands so that your printer prints your work properly.

If Your Printer Is Not Supported by Word 5.5

Microsoft Word is famous for supporting many printers, and more than 100 printer drivers come with Word 5.5. Even if your printer isn't on the list of supported printers, however, you still may be able to use your printer with Word. Many printers are compatible with a better-known brand's command set. Dot-matrix printers, for example, frequently respond to EPSON commands, and laser printers frequently respond to Hewlett-Packard commands. Check your printer's manual to find out whether your printer responds to another brand's commands. If it does, try using your printer with the better-known brand's printer driver. For more information on installing printer drivers, see "Using SETUP," later in this Appendix.

Word and Laser Printers

Today's laser printers are increasingly affordable, and if you want to get maximum performance from Word 5.5, you should consider adding one to your system. Laser printers fall into the following two categories:

- *Hewlett-Packard LaserJet Printers and Compatibles.* These printers construct text by drawing characters from complete character sets, one for each type style (font) and size. These printers usually come with one built-in font (Courier), a typewriter-style font that is not spaced proportionally. To use additional fonts, you must purchase font cartridges. Alternatively, you can purchase additional memory for the computer, and use downloadable fonts. Downloadable fonts are provided on disk. For most printers in this category, Word 5.5 downloads fonts automatically when you print your document. Many fonts are available in both cartridge and disk form from the printer manufacturers, as well as from third-party suppliers.

- *Apple LaserWriter Printers and Compatibles (PostScript printers).* These printers construct text by using a mathematical formula written with an advanced printer control language called PostScript. These printers usually come with 10 or more such formulas built into the printer's memory. You do not need to purchase a cartridge, and you do not need to download the fonts built into the printer. If you want, you can choose among approximately 200 downloadable fonts available on disk. You can set up Word to download fonts automatically.

Hewlett-Packard printers and compatibles are significantly cheaper than Apple LaserWriters and compatibles, and they have an advantage with Word 5.5. As you learn in this book, you can integrate text and graphics with Word 5.5. If you are using a PostScript printer, however, you cannot see the graphic image on-screen in the Print Preview mode. (The reason is that PostScript printers construct graphic images from mathematical representations, the same way they construct text. Hewlett-Packard LaserJet printers and compatibles, in contrast, print bit-mapped graphic images, which are made up of tiny dots. Your computer's screen can display the dots, but it cannot construct an image from a formula. You therefore can see the image in Print Preview.) Choose a PostScript-compatible printer only if you are interested in pursuing professional layout and document design.

If your budget is limited, note that Word 5.5 fully supports the Hewlett-Packard DeskJet, which is priced at the level of a good impact printer. The DeskJet is a sophisticated ink jet printer that produces output virtually indistinguishable from that produced by the same company's LaserJet, but at substantially slower speeds (two pages per minute). You can use font cartridges and downloadable fonts to supplement the printer's built-in Courier font. The ink used in a DeskJet is water-soluble, however, and smears if you get it wet.

Most laser printers cannot print on the perimeter of the page. In previous versions of Word, the margin settings you chose in the Format Division Margins command menu did not take these unprintable regions into account, so you had to adjust your margins to get them to print correctly. The printer drivers supplied with Word 5.5, however, automatically compensate for these regions.

Another welcome feature of Word 5.5 is its support for downloadable fonts. If you are using a printer driver that supports downloadable fonts, Word 5.5 automatically downloads the fonts you need when you print your document. Among the drivers that support automatic downloading are the ones for the Hewlett-Packard DeskJet and the Apple LaserWriter.

If you are using downloadable fonts, note that you may have to send in a coupon to receive the Supplemental Printers Disk, which gives you full support for these fonts. The coupon for this disk comes with your Word package. Microsoft does not charge for the disk.

Using SETUP

The only way to install Word 5.5 is to use the SETUP program. You cannot install Word 5.5 without SETUP because many of the files on the Word disks are in compressed form. SETUP decompresses these files. In addition, SETUP modifies several files so that they will work with your system. You cannot perform these tasks without SETUP.

Preparing To Use SETUP

Before you run SETUP, you need to gather some information. You need to know your printer's make and model, as well as the output port to which your printer is connected (such as LPT1: or COM1:). You also need to know the make and model of the video adapter you are using.

Running SETUP

To run SETUP, follow these steps:

1. Place the Setup disk in Drive A.

2. Type *setup* and press Enter.

   SETUP takes time to load—don't think your computer has crashed! After SETUP loads, you are asked many questions about your computer system. Just answer the questions and insert disks as you are instructed. If you have enough space on your hard disk, be sure to install the Thesaurus and Spelling.

3. When you are asked whether you want to change Word's default settings, choose the option that continues SETUP without altering the defaults. The lessons in this book assume that you're using the defaults.

When SETUP finishes, you see the DOS prompt. But you're not quite finished installing Word. Be sure to create a subdirectory for your Word documents, as explained in the next section.

Caution: SETUP creates, or makes modifications to, two files on your hard disk, called AUTOEXEC.BAT and CONFIG.SYS. If you erase or change these files, Word may not run. If Word does not run, use SETUP again. Incidentally, be careful when you use the installation software provided with some programs. Sometimes these installation utilities wipe out existing AUTOEXEC.BAT and CONFIG.SYS files without asking your permission, and then write their own. (SETUP does not erase these files; if these files exist, SETUP just modifies them.) If one of these utilities wipes out the files SETUP created, Word may not run. Before installing a new program, make copies of these files so that you can restore the files if the installation utility wipes them out.

Creating a Document Directory

When you run SETUP, the program adds a PATH instruction to your AUTOEXEC.BAT file that enables you to start Word from any directory on your hard disk. You should realize, however, that Word stores your documents in the directory from which you started the program. If you start Word from your disk's root directory (C:\), for example, your documents are saved to the root directory (unless you specifically override this default when you choose the File Save As command). Saving documents to the root directory is not a good idea because doing so slows down your disk's performance and makes understanding your disk's directory structure when you use the DIR command more difficult.

Before you use Word, you should create a subdirectory to store your documents. With your documents safely stored in a subdirectory, you have little chance to confuse them with Word files, which you might delete accidentally while erasing unwanted documents. Moreover, you can start Word from this document directory, and Word automatically makes this directory the default directory for your documents.

To create a document directory for your Word documents, do the following:

1. Obtain the DOS prompt on drive C.

   You see C> on the screen.

2. Type *mkdir c:\word\docs* and press Enter.

   If you chose a different name for your Word directory when you ran SETUP, type the name you used. Suppose that you named your Word directory MSWORD. You then type *mkdir c:\msword\docs* to create your document directory.

3. Type *chdir \word\docs* and use the DIR command to make sure that you created the document directory properly.

4. Type *chdir c:* to return to your disk's root directory.

After you create the document directory, you should start Word from this directory. However, making this directory current using the DOS directory commands is a hassle. You would have to type *chdir c:\word\docs* every time you wanted to use Word. To avoid this typing, create a batch file to start Word and place the file in your root directory.

To create a batch file to start Word, follow these steps:

1. Type *chdir c:* to make sure that the root directory is current.

2. Type *copy con word.bat* and press Enter.

3. Type *chdir c:\word\docs* and press Enter.

4. Type *word* and press Enter.

5. Hold down the Ctrl key and press Z. You then press Enter.

DOS creates a file called WORD.BAT. To start Word from the root directory, you just type Word and press Enter. The batch file changes to Word's document directory and starts the program.

Now that you have installed Word and created your document directory, you're ready to start learning Word. Chapter 1 gets you started in the right way.

Index

assigning keyboard shortcuts to macros, 646-647
Attach Style Sheet dialog box, 627-628
attaching custom style sheets to documents, 626-628
automatic page breaks, 104-105
automatic styles, 598-599
    character styles, 600
    paragraph styles, 600
    section styles, 600
    Style I.D., 598-599
Autosave feature, 45-46

B

background
    pagination, 305
    printing, 250-251
backing up documents with File Management, 287-289
Backspace key, 23, 112
Bad command or file name error message, 18
BAK files, 272
base font, 602-606
blank lines before paragraphs, 161-162
block move, 75-77
    with keyboard, 75-76
    with mouse, 76-77
body text
    adding to outlines, 338-339
    styles, 613-614
boilerplate text
    importing bookmarks, 416-418
    updating bookmarks, 418
bookmarks, 407-408
    boilerplate text, 415-418
    cross-references, 412-415
    jumping to, 410

    marking text, 408-409
    moving, 411
    reassigning names, 412
    removing, 412
    updating, 418
borders, 539-541
    graphics, 556-557
boxed headings, 526-528
Break dialog box, 104
built-in glossaries, 65-66

C

Caps Lock key, 23
captions (graphics), 556, 558
capturing graphics (CAPTURE.COM program), 559-561
case, 148-149
case-sensitive searches, 117
centering text, 57-59
Character dialog box, 25-27, 138-140
character formatting, 135-136
    after you type, 139
    as you type, 64, 138
    automatic character styles, 600
    case, 148-149
    copying formats, 167-168
    default settings, 130-131
    displaying formats on screen, 136-138
    emphases, 144-145
    errors, 151-152
    fonts, 145
    repeating formats, 167
    replacing formats, 170-171
    Ribbon, 142-143
        choosing fonts, 143-144
        choosing point size, 143
    searching for formats, 168-170
    vs. paragraph formatting, 63-64

D

U

Computer Books From Que Mean PC Performance!

Spreadsheets

1-2-3 Database Techniques	$29.95
1-2-3 Graphics Techniques	$24.95
1-2-3 Macro Library, 3rd Edition	$39.95
1-2-3 Release 2.2 Business Applications	$39.95
1-2-3 Release 2.2 PC Tutor	$39.95
1-2-3 Release 2.2 QueCards	$19.95
1-2-3 Release 2.2 Quick Reference	$ 8.95
1-2-3 Release 2.2 QuickStart, 2nd Edition	$19.95
1-2-3 Release 2.2 Workbook and Disk	$29.95
1-2-3 Release 3 Business Applications	$39.95
1-2-3 Release 3 Workbook and Disk	$29.95
1-2-3 Release 3.1 Quick Reference	$ 8.95
1-2-3 Release 3.1 QuickStart, 2nd Edition	$19.95
1-2-3 Tips, Tricks, and Traps, 3rd Edition	$24.95
Excel Business Applications: IBM Version	$39.95
Excel Quick Reference	$ 8.95
Excel QuickStart	$19.95
Excel Tips, Tricks, and Traps	$22.95
Using 1-2-3/G	$29.95
Using 1-2-3, Special Edition	$27.95
Using 1-2-3 Release 2.2, Special Edition	$27.95
Using 1-2-3 Release 3.1, 2nd Edition	$29.95
Using Excel: IBM Version	$29.95
Using Lotus Spreadsheet for DeskMate	$22.95
Using Quattro Pro	$24.95
Using SuperCalc5, 2nd Edition	$29.95

Databases

dBASE III Plus Handbook, 2nd Edition	$24.95
dBASE III Plus Tips, Tricks, and Traps	$24.95
dBASE III Plus Workbook and Disk	$29.95
dBASE IV Applications Library, 2nd Edition	$39.95
dBASE IV Programming Techniques	$24.95
dBASE IV Quick Reference	$ 8.95
dBASE IV QuickStart	$19.95
dBASE IV Tips, Tricks,and Traps, 2nd Edition	$24.95
dBASE IV Workbook and Disk	$29.95
Using Clipper	$24.95
Using DataEase	$24.95
Using dBASE IV	$27.95
Using Paradox 3	$24.95
Using R:BASE	$29.95
Using Reflex, 2nd Edition	$24.95
Using SQL	$29.95

Business Applications

Allways Quick Reference	$ 8.95
Introduction to Business Software	$14.95
Introduction to Personal Computers	$19.95
Lotus Add-in Toolkit Guide	$29.95
Norton Utilities Quick Reference	$ 8.95
PC Tools Quick Reference, 2nd Edition	$ 8.95
Q&A Quick Reference	$ 8.95
Que's Computer User's Dictionary	$ 9.95
Que's Wizard Book	$ 9.95
Quicken Quick Reference	$ 8.95
SmartWare Tips, Tricks, and Traps 2nd Edition	$24.95
Using Computers in Business	$22.95
Using DacEasy, 2nd Edition	$24.95
Using Enable/OA	$29.95
Using Harvard Project Manager	$24.95
Using Managing Your Money, 2nd Edition	$19.95

Using Microsoft Works: IBM Version	$22.95
Using Norton Utilities	$24.95
Using PC Tools Deluxe	$24.95
Using Peachtree	$27.95
Using PFS: First Choice	$22.95
Using PROCOMM PLUS	$19.95
Using Q&A, 2nd Edition	$23.95
Using Quicken: IBM Version, 2nd Edition	$19.95
Using Smart	$22.95
Using SmartWare II	$29.95
Using Symphony, Special Edition	$29.95
Using Time Line	$24.95
Using TimeSlips	$24.95

CAD

AutoCAD Quick Reference	$ 8.95
AutoCAD Sourcebook 1991	$27.95
Using AutoCAD, 3rd Edition	$29.95
Using Generic CADD	$24.95

Word Processing

Microsoft Word 5 Quick Reference	$ 8.95
Using DisplayWrite 4, 2nd Edition	$24.95
Using LetterPerfect	$22.95
Using Microsoft Word 5.5: IBM Version, 2nd Edition	$24.95
Using MultiMate	$24.95
Using Professional Write	$22.95
Using Word for Windows	$24.95
Using WordPerfect 5	$27.95
Using WordPerfect 5.1, Special Edition	$27.95
Using WordStar, 3rd Edition	$27.95
WordPerfect PC Tutor	$39.95
WordPerfect Power Pack	$39.95
WordPerfect Quick Reference	$ 8.95
WordPerfect QuickStart	$19.95
WordPerfect 5 Workbook and Disk	$29.95
WordPerfect 5.1 Quick Reference	$ 8.95
WordPerfect 5.1 QuickStart	$19.95
WordPerfect 5.1 Tips, Tricks, and Traps	$24.95
WordPerfect 5.1 Workbook and Disk	$29.95

Hardware/Systems

DOS Tips, Tricks, and Traps	$24.95
DOS Workbook and Disk, 2nd Edition	$29.95
Fastback Quick Reference	$ 8.95
Hard Disk Quick Reference	$ 8.95
MS-DOS PC Tutor	$39.95
MS-DOS Power Pack	$39.95
MS-DOS Quick Reference	$ 8.95
MS-DOS QuickStart, 2nd Edition	$19.95
MS-DOS User's Guide, Special Edition	$29.95
Networking Personal Computers, 3rd Edition	$24.95
The Printer Bible	$29.95
Que's PC Buyer's Guide	$12.95
Understanding UNIX: A Conceptual Guide, 2nd Edition	$21.95
Upgrading and Repairing PCs	$29.95
Using DOS	$22.95
Using Microsoft Windows 3, 2nd Edition	$24.95
Using Novell NetWare	$29.95
Using OS/2	$29.95
Using PC DOS, 3rd Edition	$24.95
Using Prodigy	$19.9

Using UNIX	$29.95
Using Your Hard Disk	$29.95
Windows 3 Quick Reference	$ 8.95

Desktop Publishing/Graphics

CorelDRAW Quick Reference	$ 8.95
Harvard Graphics Quick Reference	$ 8.95
Using Animator	$24.95
Using DrawPerfect	$24.95
Using Harvard Graphics, 2nd Edition	$24.95
Using Freelance Plus	$24.95
Using PageMaker: IBM Version, 2nd Edition	$24.95
Using PFS: First Publisher, 2nd Edition	$24.95
Using Ventura Publisher, 2nd Edition	$24.95

Macintosh/Apple II

AppleWorks QuickStart	$19.95
The Big Mac Book, 2nd Edition	$29.95
Excel QuickStart	$19.95
The Little Mac Book	$ 9.95
Que's Macintosh Multimedia Handbook	$24.95
Using AppleWorks, 3rd Edition	$24.95
Using Excel: Macintosh Version	$24.95
Using FileMaker	$24.95
Using MacDraw	$24.95
Using MacroMind Director	$29.95
Using MacWrite	$24.95
Using Microsoft Word 4: Macintosh Version	$24.95
Using Microsoft Works: Macintosh Version, 2nd Edition	$24.95
Using PageMaker: Macintosh Version, 2nd Edition	$24.95

Programming/Technical

Assembly Language Quick Reference	$ 8.95
C Programmer's Toolkit	$39.95
C Quick Reference	$ 8.95
DOS and BIOS Functions Quick Reference	$ 8.95
DOS Programmer's Reference, 2nd Edition	$29.95
Network Programming in C	$49.95
Oracle Programmer's Guide	$29.95
QuickBASIC Advanced Techniques	$24.95
Quick C Programmer's Guide	$29.95
Turbo Pascal Advanced Techniques	$24.95
Turbo Pascal Quick Reference	$ 8.95
UNIX Programmer's Quick Reference	$ 8.95
UNIX Programmer's Reference	$29.95
UNIX Shell Commands Quick Reference	$ 8.95
Using Assembly Language, 2nd Edition	$29.95
Using BASIC	$24.95
Using C	$29.95
Using QuickBASIC 4	$24.95
Using Turbo Pascal	$29.95

For More Information, Call Toll Free!

1-800-428-5331

All prices and titles subject to change without notice. Non-U.S. prices may be higher. Printed in the U.S.A.

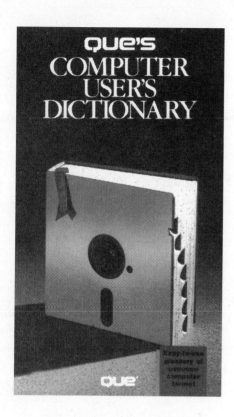

Next window pane	F6
Previous window pane	Shift-F6
Maximize window	Ctrl-F10
Move window	Ctrl-F7
Size window	Ctrl-F8
Restore window to previous size	Ctrl-F5
Close window	Ctrl-F4

Outlines

Outline view (toggle)	Shift-F2
Outline edit mode (toggle)	Shift-F5
Turn text into heading	Ctrl-9
Turn heading into text	Ctrl-X
Lower heading one level	Ctrl-0 (zero) or Alt-Shift-Right arrow
Raise heading one level	Ctrl-9 or Alt-Shift-Left arrow
Collapse all subheadings and body text	Keypad - – (minus) or Ctrl-8
Expand heading	Keypad + (plus) or Ctrl-9
Expand body text	Shift-Keypad + or Shift-Ctrl-7
Expand all subheadings below heading	Keypad* (asterisk)
Expand headings to a level you specify	Alt-Shift-number

Command Shortcuts

Edit Copy	Ctrl-Ins
Edit Cut	Shift-Del
Edit Go To	F5
Edit Paste	Shift-Ins
Edit Repeat	F4
Edit Undo	Alt-Backspace
File Exit Word	Alt-F4
File Open	Ctrl-F1 or Alt-Ctrl-F2 or Ctrl-F12
File Print Preview	Ctrl-F9

File Print	Shift-F9 or Ctrl-Shift-F12 or Alt-Shift-Ctrl-F2
File Save	Alt-Shift-F2
File Save As	Alt-F2
Format Character	Ctrl-F2
Insert Bookmark	Ctrl-Shift-F5
Insert File	F9
Macro Record	Ctrl-F3
Utilities Calculate	F2
Utilities Spelling	F7
Utilities Thesaurus	Shift-F7
View Outline	Shift-F2
Window Close	Ctrl-F4
Window Maximize	Ctrl-F10
Window Move	Ctrl-F7
Window Restore	Ctrl-F5
Window Size	Ctrl-F8

Function Keys

F1	Help
F2	Utilities Calculate
F3	Insert named glossary
F4	Repeat last command
F5	Edit Go To
F6	Next window pane
F7	Utilities Spelling
F8	Extend selection
F9	Insert File and update link
F10	Activate menus
F11	Next data field
F12	File Save As
Shift-F2	View Outline (toggle)
Shift-F3	Toggle uppercase/lowercase
Shift-F4	Repeat last search
Shift-F5	Outline edit mode (toggle)

Shift-F6	Previous window pane	Alt-F3	Copy selection to Scrap
Shift-F7	Utilities Thesaurus	Alt-F4	File Exit Word
Shift-F8	Reduce selection	Alt-F5	Overtype on/off
Shift-F9	File Print	Alt-F6	Select word
Shift-F10	Select entire document	Alt-F7	Line break display on/off
Shift-F11	Previous data field	Alt-F8	Select sentence
Shift-F12	File Save	Alt-F9	Toggle text/graphics mode
Ctrl-F1	File Open	Alt-F10	Select paragraph
Ctrl-F2	Format Character (choose point size)	Alt-Shift-F1	Previous data field
Ctrl-F3	Macro Record on/off	Alt-Shift-F2	File Save
Ctrl-F4	Window Close	Alt-Shift-Ctrl-F2	File Print
Ctrl-F5	Window Restore	Alt-Ctrl-F2	File Open
Ctrl-F6	Next window pane	Ctrl-Shift-F2	Choose point size
Ctrl-F7	Window Move	Ctrl-Shift-F5	Insert Bookmark
Ctrl-F8	Window Size	Ctrl-Shift-F6	Previous window
Ctrl-F9	File Print Preview	Ctrl-Shift-F8	Column-selection mode
Ctrl-F10	Window Maximize	Ctrl-Shift-F10	Place cursor on Ruler
Ctrl-F12	File Open	Ctrl-Shift-F12	File Print
Alt-F1	Next data field		
Alt-F2	File Save As		

que®

CORPORATION

LEADING COMPUTER KNOWLEDGE